Concepts of Personality

Concepts
of Personality

edited by

Joseph M. Wepman *and*
Ralph W. Heine

ALDINE PUBLISHING COMPANY / CHICAGO

Copyright © 1963 by Aldine Publishing Company

First published 1963 by
ALDINE PUBLISHING COMPANY
64 East Van Burean Street
Chicago 5, Illinois

Library of Congress Catalog Card Number 63-12476

Designed by Joan Stoliar
Printed in the United States of America

Contributors

Norman M. Bradburn, Ph.D., is Assistant Professor of Behavioral Sciences at the Graduate School of Business of the University of Chicago and Senior Study Director of the National Opinion Research Center.

John M. Butler, Ph.D., is Professor of Psychology in the Department of Psychology and the Committee on Human Development at the University of Chicago.

Raymond B. Cattell, Ph.D., is Research Professor and Director of the Laboratory of Personality and Group Research at the University of Illinois.

Rudolph Driekurs, M.D., is Professor of Psychiatry at the Chicago Medical School, Visiting Professor of Education at the University of Oregon, and Director of the Alfred Adler Institute, Chicago, Illinois.

Charles W. Eriksen, Ph.D., is Professor of Psychology at the University of Illinois.

Donald W. Fiske, Ph.D., is Professor of Psychology at the University of Chicago.

Sol L. Garfield, Ph.D., is Principal Research Scientist at the Missouri Institute of Psychiatry and Research Professor of Psychology at Washington University.

Benson E. Ginsburg, Ph.D., is Harper Professor of Biology at the University of Chicago.

PATRICKE JOHNS HEINE, Ph.D., is engaged in sociological research and writing in Chicago.

RALPH W. HEINE, Ph.D., is Associate Professor of Psychology in the Departments of Psychiatry and Psychology and Chief Clinical Psychologist in the Department of Psychiatry at the University of Chicago.

HEINZ KOHUT, M.D., is a member of the staff of the Chicago Institute for Psychoanalysis and is Professorial Lecturer in the Department of Psychiatry at the University of Chicago.

JACOB S. KOUNIN, Ph.D., is Professor of Educational Psychology at Wayne State University.

ROBERT A. LeVINE, Ph.D., is Assistant Professor of Anthropology in the Committee on Human Development of the University of Chicago.

ROBERT W. LUNDIN, Ph.D., is Associate Professor of Psychology at Hamilton College.

SALVATORE R. MADDI, Ph.D., is Assistant Professor in the Department of Psychology of the University of Chicago.

LAURA N. RICE, Ph.D., is Assistant Professor of Psychology in the Department of Psychology of the University of Chicago.

LEE SECHREST, Ph. D., is Assistant Professor in the Department of Psychology of Northwestern University.

PHILIP F. D. SEITZ, M.D., is a member of the staff of the Chicago Institute for Psychoanalysis.

JOHN M. SHLIEN, Ph.D., is Associate Professor of Psychology in the Department of Psychology and the Committee on Human Development of the University of Chicago.

JANET TAYLOR SPENCE, Ph. D., is Research Psychologist at the Veterans Administration Hospital in Iowa City, Iowa.

JOSEPH M. WEPMAN, Ph.D., is Professor of Psychology and Surgery and Chairman of the Interdepartmental Committee on Clinical and Counseling Psychology of the University of Chicago.

Preface

Under the aegis of the University of Chicago, the Department of Psychology and the Committee on Human Development, in close collaboration with the Department of Education, recently established an Interdepartmental Committee on Clinical and Counseling Psychology. The Committee has constantly sought to augment the traditional course offerings in psychology by bringing to the University outstanding lecturers and exponents of new concepts as well as modern interpreters of classical viewpoints in the broad subject realm of psychology. One such colloquium was designed to explore the basic processes on which much of clinical and counseling psychology rests—the area of personality and personality theory. The present book is in part the product of this series of lectures.

Probably nowhere in psychology has a greater diversity of thought, of philosophy and of method been expressed and been revised under the impact of new evidence. Whole schools have been started and flourished, waned and flowered again, around such theories as those expounded by Freud, Adler, Lewin, Watson, Allport, Murray, Kelly and Rogers. Exponents of each school in its modern dress are represented here. Underlying many of the theories presented are some of the basic processes in personality development and expression, such as learning and perception as well as genetics and the effects of early experience. The book presents these fundamentals as the necessary foundation for the study of man.

Contemporary psychology also takes full cognizance of the emergence and behavior of the individual deriving from his membership in various social groups. To encompass this area, the book includes a section on social process and personality, including the cultural, anthropological and sociological climate in which the individual behaves.

Finally, the book recognizes the extensive role of research in personality by presenting viewpoints on assessment—vital to an objective evaluation of the individual.

From this inclusive design has come the present work. Its many contributors represent a cross-section of what is accepted in psychology today, what needs to be questioned, and what may be expected as psychology recognizes its broad relations throughout our society.

The editors are indebted to a number of assistants, reviewers, typists and indexers, who contributed to the final product. Credit is especially due to Robert Lipgar for his painstaking collection of the original lectures—not a spoken word was missed; to Linda Rothstein for her punctilious reading, indexing and grammatical revisions; to Mary Riege for her untiring transcription and attention to the detail of preparing the copy. We gratefully acknowledge the support of the Department of Psychology, then chaired by Professor Howard Hunt; of the Committee on Human Development, headed by Professor Robert Hess; and of the Interdepartmental Committee on Clinical and Counseling Psychology, for their assistance in selecting and bringing to the campus the speakers whose lectures, revised and augmented, are included in the book.

Similar acknowledgment is given to the many members of our staffs who so patiently read each chapter with the critical eye needed to complete the compilation as it is here presented. Finally, to the various authors who worked so diligently to fit their thoughts and ideas into the structure of the book, goes our thanks for their diligence, their erudition, and their patience with the editors.

Joseph M. Wepman
Ralph W. Heine

Contents

III. Social Process and Personality

IV. Methods of Personality Assessment

Introduction

The psychologist who pursues an interest in personality is constantly faced by a dilemma. He seeks to investigate what is to him the most intriguing and interesting subject—the multifaceted operations of man in his natural environment. The predicament lies in the discrepancy between the complexity and richness of man's subjective experience, and the pallid analog of these experiences the psychologist is able to study effectively with the research procedures available to him. If he holds to the premises of strict objectivity through controlled observations he finds himself driven to the periphery of the very problem he seeks to understand, to a place where the reliability of measurement and the validity and predictability of his instruments can often be specified but only at the cost of abandoning the goal of useful generality or of application to the individual in his ordinary life circumstances. Despite this formidable problem, the subject matter—man —is so intriguing, so necessary to understand, and the potential rewards so great, that psychology has never lacked for serious, creative students. It appears that this will continue, as the present volume indicates.

While striving for a recognition as a hard objective science in the model of the physical sciences, psychology has continued to support intuitive, empathic approaches to the understanding of human behavior. In developing and sustaining a variety of approaches to the understanding of man, it has borrowed, when it needed to, from the methods of other sciences but has always recognized that the explanations of man's complex behavior cannot ever be completely reduced to the terms of biology, chemistry and physics.

As this multifaceted volume shows, the study of personality has not lacked for investigators whose methods of choice fall at every point on the continuum from the most objective to the most subjective. We conjecture that this wide diversity of opinion, of explanation and study is in itself an expression of the diversity of 'personality' among the authors. The variety of statements and objectives reflected in the book strongly suggest that almost any constellation of aptitudes and interests can be matched with an established field of research or application in the study of personality. Whether one is inclined toward mathematics, social philosophy or neurophysiology as a content area, or toward research, teaching or public service as a career, there is room for him to become an expert in personality.

It is no doubt this very fact that psychology as a science has a complexity of convergent and divergent patterns and many underlying themes in theory and application which makes contemporary personality theory less elegant or aesthetic in structure than that of many of the older scientific disciplines. One thing can be said about it, as the book so amply and aptly demonstrates; personality theory is living, dynamic, and in a constant state of flux. It has reached no level of final solution. It grows and changes. It is alive, and the psychologist must ever be aware of the changes occurring in it. The present volume is in fact intended for that purpose.

It is hoped by the editors that there will always be vigorous disputation over theoretical issues. Nevertheless, while similar debates exist within the physical sciences, they have at least arrived at a position of some agreement on the definition of data acceptable for resolving conflicting viewpoints. This is certainly not the case in personality theory. Proponents of one theoretical position may adhere to a set of propositions and methods of data collection which are literally not comprehensible to other equally esteemed theorists. One seeks substantial communality without finding it in the literature, as the interpretations by the proponents of the many viewpoints included herein show. It is to be hoped that as multiple theories continue to be advanced, if no single theory can be accepted, that each school might offer a systematic program for testing empirically the postulates it holds, and at the same time promote a kind of ecumenical movement with respect to method. In this way, the relative heuristic values of competing theoretical positions could be measured against such familiar criteria as parsimony, relevance, power or logical consistency. Yet today, as the reader of the book will see, such is not the case. In fact, many of the theoretical positions taken are constructed in such a way as to make them virtually unsusceptible to confirmation by generally accepted empirical techniques and methods. ·

Cattell's chapter on multivariate analysis, for example, suggests a means for making, as the clinician does, complex assessments in the domain of personality theory—yet his voice is essentially unheard, or at least not responded to, by the very people he wishes to assist. It is almost as though everyone wants to admonish and instruct, but no one wants to listen . . . no one really wants to subject his own propositions to the light of systematic investigation proposed by others. In part, however, esteemed critics of theories not their own are not blameless. For example, Cattell has much of worth to communicate to other psychologists but attempts to make his contribution in a language not easily comprehended by more than a small fraction of potential beneficiaries. Similarly, other theorists and methodologists speak in a language so private that their message is often lost on the uninitiated. While this is decried by the editors, they believe that in time, in a field such as this, simplicity of statement will evolve naturally. To the present-day student of personality theory, and his successors, falls the great challenge of reconciling these many and diverse viewpoints, for each in its own way has something valid to say about man.

Psychologists who are distressed by the confusing welter of ideas, beliefs, and propositions in the field of contemporary personality theory are prone to defend the science by pointing to its youth as an empirical discipline. It is argued that like other sciences it must necessarily go through a series of developmental stages before it can reach maturity and take its proper place in the adult scientific world.

While this may be a comforting analogy, it may be acceptable only for that reason. The dilemma posed in our first paragraphs may reflect that the subjective-objective puzzle inherent in studying man's personality prevents understanding ever being completely achieved by the methods devised in and for other sciences, or by psychological methods now available. This in no way depreciates the values that have accrued to man by the knowledge and practices which have followed from the theories thus far advanced. None can deny the significant insights into individual and social behavior that have followed from the teachings of Freud, Adler, Jung, Mead, Sullivan, Allport and others. Whether or not these views incorporate reflections of the authors' personal images of man takes nothing from their value. The 'truth' of their theories in terms of verifiable propositions may by most scientific standards be untestable, yet the conceptions of man entertained by disciplined, gifted and articulate men cannot fail to produce many far-reaching and useful observations. Who else but man, it might be asked, is in a position to construe human behavior?

Each of the chapters in this book has many implications beyond those conveyed by its specific contents. By stepping back a bit, it is possible to gain some perspective on the total fabric of which each contributor is a part. In the paragraphs which follow, the editors attempt in some instances to identify threads tying together chapters widely different in content, and in others to underline particular problems in theory and application demonstrated by various chapters.

Personality theory has drawn upon the resources of many basic areas, both in and out of the main stream of psychology. However, one of the chronic sources of irritation among students of personality is the seeming unwillingness of the major learning theorists to provide them with information in the form that can readily be adapted to human behavior theory. No contemporary personality theorist has ever really doubted the central importance of learning in the development of man. Thus the reluctance of the learning theorists to address themselves to complex 'real life' phenomena has seemed to be at the very least, an evidence of poor 'colleagueship.'

Spence elucidates the motives of learning specialists in this regard —their wish to isolate relationships between certain stimulus and response variables under conditions of experimental control. In so doing she delineates a major division in psychology along methodological lines. Learning theorists, in general, have adopted a univariate experimental approach, modeled after the physical sciences. They seek to discover lawful but abstract relationships between stimulus and response and attempt, therefore, to minimize the variance contributed by the subject—whether animal or human. In contrast, other investigators using multivariate techniques of data collection and analysis, attempt to take characteristics of the subject into account along with environmental factors. Cattell's and Garfield's chapters reflect this orientation. Contemporary learning theory has nevertheless been reconciled within the study of personality in at least one way, described in a later chapter by LeVine and certainly these two chapters clearly supplement each other.

Whenever psychologists develop a methodology which permits experimental controls without at the same time removing the findings some distance from the experiences of everyday life, there is reason for rejoicing. Ericksen's chapter describes a line of investigation which promises to be a firm bridge between the psychology of the laboratory and psychology in schools, clinics and other applied centers. Study of the perceptual process provides one of the major sources of experimental data which have a direct link with personality theory. The role of perception in personality formation and as a determinant of behavior cannot be overestimated. Ericksen's report on contemporary approaches to the study of perception includes a critical review of the utility of the experimental method for studying psychodynamics.

Although the nature-vs-nurture controversy has become less prominent in psychological literature, Ginsburg points out how very alive this topic should be. While geneticists have aroused greater interest among professional breeders of animals than among students of man's behavior, this may not be to man's best interest. Certainly the new research and discoveries in genetics should be cause for a re-evaluation of psychology's opinion in the matter. While the geneticist demonstrates the essential inequality of man, psychology out of its environmental bias, tends to give at least lip service to man's equality. Ginsburg argues for a look at the data from the laboratory—significant aspects of personality, like other features of man may be genetically determined. In particular, he raises the startling question of whether there might not be genetically determined anlage for symbolic representation of events the organism has not experienced. If this speculation could be reliably demonstrated, its effect on contemporary (and future) personality theory would be profound.

From one standpoint, the field of personality can be viewed as a systematic study of the manner in which the human organism transforms energy mobilized by its 'basic' drives. Indeed, the question of how (if not why) the motive power generated from man's biochemical processing of energy from sources external to himself is translated into complex behavior has always held a prominent position in any theoretical discussion. Thus, while the Butler-Rice chapter does not fall easily into any of the major categories into which the book is divided, it nevertheless concerns itself with issues which are directly or indirectly pertinent to all. Asserting as Hegel did, that social and scientific development invariably proceeds as an unending dialectic—thesis, antithesis, synthesis—may be ascribing the quality of natural law to a commonly observed mode of thought. However, the concept appears to have application in personality theory, where with respect to primary motivation, there has been persistent and sharply drawn division between the reductionists (the "nothing buts") who see human motivation as originating in the spur of physiologic tensions asociated with hunger, thirst, and sexual deprivation, and the humanists (the "something mores") who regard man because of his unique capacity to bind time with language, as being pulled by his aspirations. In the chapter by Butler and Rice, the authors present a synthesis of these two viewpoints which should provide at least a small patch of ground on which the antagonists in theory construction can both stand comfortably, and together contemplate the future more calmly.

The book turns from these general considerations related to personality and personality theory to an exposition of some of the more important theoretical contributors themselves.

Psychoanalysis has probably been the single most significant intellectual force in the twentieth century, reshaping as it has thought in such widely separated fields as medicine and art history. Curiously, however, it has probably had less effect on academic psychology than on other related social sciences. It was primarily through the introduction of training in clinical psychology to graduate schools that psychoanalytic theory gained a prominent place in the curriculum.

As a comprehensive theory having its origins in and applications to clinical work, the reasons for its adoption by clinical psychology are patent. As a theory based on inherited contents deriving from instinctual drives, it conflicted with the dominant behavioristic-environmental position of American psychology. Moreover, since academic psychology was wedded to logical positivism, and most Freudian concepts could not be defined operationally, they were regarded by the experimentally minded psychologist as having no meaning.

Kohut and Seitz offer a modern psychoanalytic viewpoint which unlike many other interpretations stresses its value as a theory rather than as a heuristic device for comprehending behavior of psychiatric patients.

Lewin's version of field theory was enthusiastically embraced when it first appeared, for it seemed to students in the 30's that at long last there was at hand a means of analyzing behavior in metrical terms without sacrificing the plasticity and adaptiveness of the human which were so apparent.

It was, moreover, a theory which took the intrinsic structure and function of the individual into account without eliminating the powerful influences of the surround. A whole generation of graduate students began recasting psychology in terms of barriers, goals, valences and vectors before they realized that the means of measurement of field forces lay in reviewing behavior sequences already concluded. There was no way, as it turned out, that values could be reliably assigned to forces in advance—an achievement which would have converted the mathematics of psychology from those of probability statistics to vector analysis.

Kounin's chapter reveals clearly the qualities of Lewin's thought which excited students, and recounts among other features his brilliant analyses in field-theoretical terms of commonplace behaviors. These analyses which were sometimes contrary to "common sense" and yet confirmed in careful experiments, have been a continuing inspiration to social psychologists in particular.

Although often criticized as being "merely descriptive," the theoretical writings of Allport and Murray are representative of the highest achievement of American psychology in the area of personality. As Maddi demonstrates, they set themselves the formidable task of integrating virtually *all* that is known or confidently suspected to be true about human behavior without losing sight of their objective— the explication of the intact, fully functioning complex human, in his familiar environment.

An unfortunately large segment of American psychology has retreated from the task of collating and integrating the data of the field as it applies to human behavior, and of risking broad speculations about its meaning. While both Allport and Murray are empirical scientists in every sense of the word, they have not permitted themselves the easy rationalization that facts produced in sufficient amounts will spontaneously and meaningfully pattern themselves.

Perhaps the domain of psychology is now too wide and too complex to permit the kind of scholarly, insightful explanation and speculation which characterizes the writings of Allport and Murray. If indeed, they are among the last proponents of comprehensive theory building and scholarly commentary which characterized the second half of the 19th century and the early 20th century, it marks a change in the profession in which more will be lost than will be gained.

Psychology in the mid-west is noted for its 'dust-bowl' empiricism and complete lack of sympathy with scholarly speculation or with introspection as a source of usable data about human behavior. Thus it is testimony to the unpredictability of human behavior from professional environmental factors alone that George Kelly—than whom none is more mid-western—should reveal a stubborn interest in the philosophic underpinnings of psychology, and in a geographical area infested with laboratory animals, retain a resolute interest in humans, and, moreover, in construing what accounts for their behaving as they do in 'real life.'

He is one of the few contemporary psychologists, as Sechrest shows, who has addressed himself specifically to the problem of determinism—most psychologists blandly accept a deterministic position without rigorously examining its implications. His ingenious solutions —the individual's behavior is determined within his construct system but he can change the framework within which and in terms of which he evaluates, predicts, and thus directs his behavior—emphasized the teleologic factors in comprehending behavior and rejects the notion that humans are victims of their biographies.

Kelly has been at various times identified with phenomenological, Adlerian, Sullivanian and Rogerian theory, but he has never acknowledged more than a partial congruence with other positions.

In view of the influence of the viewpoints of such psychologists as George Kelly and Carl Rogers, it is not completely explicable why Adlerian individual psychology has failed to 'catch on' in America, whereas Freudian psychoanalysis has. The Adlerian position, in comparison with that of Freud's, is buoyantly optimistic in tone, holistic in outlook, and pragmatic in principles of treatment. That is to say, it was congruent with many major facets of American thought and belief, whereas Freud's views were largely strange, and to many, unpalatable.

In one important respect, however, as Dreikurs points out, Adler was out of step with his times in rejecting 'prime causes.' He postulated no immutable instincts, no biological substrata, no inherited mental contents to which motivations could ultimately be reduced. Freud, at least, could be thought of as advancing a 'drive theory.' Instead, the meaning of human behavior for the Adlerian could only be determined from its consequences within a given social circumstance and the same behavior, therefore, could have different meanings at different times. Although in this respect individual psychology seems to resemble phenomenological views, it rejects self-awareness as a significant avenue to understanding and insists that only the objective observer can deduce the intentions of an individual, and the personal constructs (fictions) around which the individual's "Life Style" is built.

Some of the most significant applications in the realm of science had their origins in the willingness of a student to start with a set of premises contrary to the postulates of existing systems and often even to accepted common sense and to follow them to their logical conclusions. Sometimes such experiments existed for decades as curiosities until it was discovered that they fit some newly developed aspect of science or technology. Behaviorism had no such long wait before it was pulled on-stage and warmly embraced by a large segment of academic psychology. Nevertheless, the theory contained some propositions that at the time of its inception were viewed by many psychologists as contrary to common sense and this remains true of behavior theory even today. Many of its premises were at odds with those advanced by reigning theorists early in this century, and even today many eminent psychological theorists find nothing palatable in its contemporary version. It was, however, a theoretical approach to the study of behavior, which fitted very closely the rigorous operationism of the logical positivists. Due to this parallel of thought and method, it gained wide and early acceptance.

The theory was launched at a time when denial of consciousness in man was heretical in the extreme, and its corollary of environmentalism was scarcely less so. As the old adage has it, man first lost his soul, then his will, and now was being deprived of his mind.

While the mind-body problem as such is not as hotly debated today, there is far from general acceptance of the physiological-deficit-drive theory with which behaviorism has always been closely identified. There is an almost downright resistance to the belief that the exquisitely complicated thoughts, fantasies, planning ability, and problem solving, which comprise mental life as we subjectively know it, can have had its origins and development within the limits of a simple conditioning paradigm.

As Lundin shows, if there is some withering away of radical naive behaviorism, it is perhaps because the movement has served its purpose. Its insistence on rigorous operational definition and verification of hypotheses by methods which permit replication and its rejection of armchair psychology with its introspective bias has helped effect psychology's separation from philosophy. Perhaps more than any other single factor, the widespread adherence to behaviorism has contributed to the establishment of psychology as a respectable and respected empirical science.

American psychology has been loosely characterized by many observers as outwardly oriented, buoyant in spirit, pragmatic, preoccupied with the measurement and cataloging of overt behaviors and dedicated to the belief in change both temporary and enduring through environmental influences. One's personality, according to this view, is mainly a collecting, sorting, storage and dispensing center for the social, educational and interpersonal experiences. If the processing of influences is carried out efficiently, it is a 'good' personality; if inefficient, a 'poor' personality. If the input (environmental influence) is of poor quality, then clearly the output will be no better for the personality does not create or repair but merely puts together packages of behavior from the stock available for delivery on order from the environment.

Westen European psychology, on the other hand, is generally described as dour and pessimistic in tone, preoccupied with inner experience, devoted to identifying and elucidating fixed structures in personality and underplaying environmental influences in favor of constitutional factors. Thus, speaking very broadly, the European *has* his character as a given, and is charged with the responsibility of intensive self-study so as to make the most of it. The American, in contrast, develops a set of characteristics which, if subsequently displeasing to him, he can change or augment by subjecting himself to appropriate influences . . . additional education, psychotherapy, a new wife, a move to another climate, a different job, etc.

To the extent that this dichotomous arrangement of views toward personality is valid, phenomenology must be viewed as more "European" in its flavor than domestic. According to the phenomenologist, it is the person who perceives and shapes the world in a manner consistent with his inner self, rather than his being a predictable product and a faithful reflection of the influences impinging on him if these were fully known. It should perhaps be noted that phenomenology, described in Shlien's chapter, has less to do with experimental phenomenology which deals with perceiving, remembering and thinking, than with phenomenological methods for reaching understanding of human personality. Thus it is closely allied both in method and philosophic outlook to Existentialism. Whereas in America, psychology is almost universally defined as the 'science of behavior,' the phenomenologists would define the field as the 'science of experience.'

Some phenomenologists will agree that one cannot have a science of behavior based on studies of unique individuals and that the point of investigating the phenomenal world of individuals is to develop more sophisticated hypotheses which are then tested in the usual way. Perhaps the answer lies in the observation of Kluckhohn that a man is in some respects like all other men, in other respects like some other men, and in still other respects, like no other man. The science of behavior may be limited to the first two categories but only through intensive exploration of individuals will the full range of likeness be comprehended.

With the exposition of several major theorists at hand, the book turns to a relatively new emphasis in personality theory—the relationship between the environment and man, between life space and its occupier.

It is generally conceded, in fact is scarcely debatable, that for a society to endure it must provide avenues for the satisfaction of all basic human needs. It has, however, been sharply debated whether or not there is any consistent relationship between the particular arrangements for need satisfaction in any society, or its modal beliefs and values, and the personality characteristics of its members. The question is a most important one scientifically, and is coming to have considerable practical significance in view of the increasing level of necessary interaction between members of widely differing cultures.

No one contests the fact that people in various societies achieve similar goals in very different ways. Indeed the customs of strangers have always provided a source of amusement for the unsophisticated and a stimulus to the curiosity of all. The serious question that must be answered however, is how profoundly or unchangeably does one's rearing in a given society condition the view one has of himself, or his behavior toward others, and toward the physical world. A related question concerns the variations in cultures within large societal groups and whether the diversity within a society is equal to, greater than or less than the variation between societies. The effect of culture upon the individual within it and of one culture upon another presents to its students a medley of methodological problems not frequently encountered in behavioral research. For example, a crucial test of the effects of rearing in a given society or culture on personality can be seen in the mass transplantation of populations from one environment to another, significantly different in almost every outward aspect. If acculturation consisted essentially of changing these outward aspects only, such as clothing, social etiquette and vocational skills, undoubtedly the effect could be reliably measured, and if easily achieved would suggest that cultural influences on personality are weak. However, when acculturation requires a total revision of thought and language expressing thought which underly the change in both mores and custom, then significant personality changes are involved and assessment of the effect of such changes upon the individual becomes a major problem.

Although acculturation has been studied intensively both within cultures (e.g., adjustment of Southern Negroes to Northern urban living) and between cultures (e.g., adjustment of Japanese-born immigrants to American society and culture), definitive answers to questions raised have not been forthcoming. Adequate controls have been difficult to maintain and given sets of variables have been difficult to isolate while holding 'all other factors' constant. The cultural anthropologist and social psychologist have had to accept less demanding, less rigorous standards for their studies than have some other behavioral scientists. In Bradburn's essay, the author describes recent methodological developments in social environmental research in some detail against the background of a brief history of earlier methods. The conceptual approaches to the difficult but highly vital problems of how and to what degree culture determines adult personality is the major thesis explored, and the relationship between methods and concepts in this too frequently underplayed aspect of personality development and change is succinctly but clearly treated.

Academic disciplines go through a predictable course in their development, and anthropology is no exception. From its historic beginnings in the diaries of discerning travelers, the letters and memoirs of missionaries and reports of colonial bureaucrats, anthropology, like other sciences, slowly divested itself of dilettantism by devising techniques for studying primitive cultures which led to the collection of rigorous, detailed, and comprehensive data. However, the aim for a considerable time remained that of, so to speak, assembling, classifying, and eventually cross-indexing, specimens of languages, kinship systems, political structures, art forms, economic systems, beliefs, values, technologies etc.

The anthropologist typically visited one or at most a small number of cultures in a geographically circumscribed area in order to establish himself as area specialist. He might further address himself to becoming very highly knowledgeable about some particular aspects of the cultures he chose to become identified with. This specialized focus could in turn lead him to expand his interest in a segmented way, to a wide range of cultures. Eventually he might have a relatively reduced interest in maintaining an intimate knowledge of *his* primitive societies, in favor of investigating relatively abstract problems, cross-culturally.

It is at this point that the traditional methodology of anthropology, that is highly refined techniques for studying one culture, could no longer meet his needs. His situation would be somewhat analogous to that of the skilled clinical psychologist being confronted with the need to investigate a particular aspect of personality discursively instead of intensively, in a single individual.

To examine a single problem cross-culturally, if he were not to approach it impressionistically, would require a conceptual scheme and a method for controlling factors which interacted with the one he wished to investigate. Thus, many contemporary anthropologists, like other scientists in related fields (psychology, for one), are deeply involved in methodological as well as substantive research. LeVine illustrates one line of development, the application of methods and concepts deriving from behavioristic psychology, in response to this need.

One man's profession may be another's error variance. Sociology's mission is to account for man's behavior in terms of the experiences impinging upon him by reason of his multiple and overlapping memberships in social groups. That portion of man's behavior, or perhaps more properly, that segment of society which behaves contrary to the sum of social forces being exerted upon it, reflects an 'error' in the sociologist's predictive formulae.

For example, in analyzing delinquent behavior of juveniles, the sociologist may do an ecological study to determine the probability of a youth becoming known to the police by reason of the neighborhood in which he lives. He may then add to his predictive accuracy by determining for each area the relationship between incidence of delinquency and such social factors as family status, religious affiliation, race, nationality, intactness of family, informal and formal social group memberships, availability of social services, sub-cultural values, etc. Each of these factors is likely to contribute some increment to the accuracy of prediction and taken altogether, they enable the sociologist to anticipate with considerable confidence the rate of delinquency in a given area, and with fairly high probability the fate of any individual.

However, the most exhaustive analysis of social factors will not lead to a fully accurate prediction of the careers of individuals. All of the social factors may load on the side of a particular career line, and a given individual may perversely adopt another. In fact, as moviegoers and readers of novels know, two members of the same family may in a dramatic fashion choose virtually opposite life styles and goals. At this point the sociologist must turn the problem over to the psychologist (whose record in such predictive studies indicates he will not be of much help), or give some attention to the forces distinctly "inside" the individual which influence his career.

A unique contribution to the sociology of personality theory, the concept of role-analysis as it is used in intensive studies of family interaction, pushes the analysis back to the social microcosm, to the actual life-space of the individual, but still leaves only partially answered the question of why an individual seeks or accepts some roles, declines or avoids others, and shows varying degrees of adequacy or performance in those thrust upon him.

It has been observed elsewhere in these notes that Americans think of personality in terms of change and susceptibility to external influence while Europeans are more prone to be characterologists who look for that which is inner and immutable. In this sense, role-theory is understandably popular in America and is exemplified in an extreme form by such personality theorists as H. S. Sullivan who defines personality as "the relatively enduring pattern of recurrent interpersonal situations which characterize a human life." A prominent and fully acknowledged influence in Sullivan's thinking is that of G. H. Mead, a sociologist.

As Heine's essay clearly shows, there has long been significant interaction between sociology and psychology precisely around the question of how 'personality' should be conceptualized. The major contemporary influence appears to be that of sociologists on psychologists rather than the reverse, although earlier the functionalists in sociology and anthropology must have drawn considerable nourishment from behaviorism.

Personality theory encompasses such broad parameters that most of its literature is discursive. With the advances in technology of assessment, however, more effort toward reducing the posulates of personality theory to data susceptible to statistical analyses has become commonplace. Cattell very appropriately and correctly points out that experienced as people in general and psychologists in particular are, in making intuitive factorial analyses, they cannot do as well as the psychometrician who has exhaustively analyzed a domain and devised carefully refined instruments which systematically cover every facet of it. Why then, asks Cattell, do clinicians not respond more directly to his oft-repeated appeal that they take greater advantage of the methods he espouses?

The answer seems to lie in the multi-faceted role of the psychologist in the modern world. On the one hand, as a clinician responsible for a relationship between himself and a single other person he expresses a legitimate doubt as to the utility in a clinical setting of the multi-variate analyst's product. Perhaps unwittingly he resists in his own way the intrusion of 'automation' into his vocational sphere. He rejects not the method but the probabilistic nature of the product in contrast to the uniqueness of his patient, and to his need to reach categorical decisions. However, as a researcher, where such factored instruments might be most appropriate, he may find his bias as a clinician compromising his judgment. As a researcher, he is well advised to use factored instruments, in the circumstances Professor Cattell outlines.

It is to this problem—the wider and more appropriate use of multivariate analyses—that Cattell directs his attention. That the method is complex is granted, but certainly it is no more complex than the subject matter it is designed to measure. This chapter attempts what many sophisticated psychologists believe to be impossible by any simpler means—to shed some controlled illumination on a very complex problem—the identification of and interrelationship between parameters of personality.

The lucidity of Fiske's chapter makes it possible to detect what is not in it as well as what is. Psychometrics is distinctly homegrown in its contemporary development, although it must necessarily acknowledge its English ancestry, and in the spirit of a behavior-oriented psychology, psychometricians have never seriously doubted that they could devise a yardstick to take the measure of man. Measurement however, requires that the subject perform in such a way that a given behavior can be reliably distinguished from other behaviors and that the behavior is quantifiable. In personality measurement, this means that a given act cannot simultaneously have two contradictory meanings, that personality must be viewed as susceptible to analysis into relatively discrete components, and that these elements in personality exist in greater or lesser amounts.

Satisfying these requirements has meant that psychometric researchers have implicitly adopted a version of faculty psychology. Explicitly, however, psychometrists seem to have adopted no comprehensive theory of personality at all—this, therefore, is what is necessarily missing from this chapter, through no fault of the author. Psychometrists have drawn out of several theories, such domains, constructs or concepts as could be defined in terms of items or scales which would yield a score. If an inventory describing a particular concept, or group of related concepts passed muster in terms of reliability and validity (insofar as this could be assessed) the instrument was put to work. Thus the personality theory of psychometricians is in one sense represented by the sum total of scores on instruments cataloged in the Buros handbook.

Present day psychometrists, however, are showing very clear signs of dissatisfaction with their early aspirations of completely covering the domain of personality with a proliferation of separate tests, and are showing far greater willingness to collaborate with personality theorists.

The author of this chapter must certainly be counted among those psychometricians most alert to both the need for and the difficulties involved in closer collaboration between the measurement specialist and the theory builder.

A distinguished psychiatrist once made the wry comment that if one does not understand a patient the best thing to do is to make an immediate diagnosis. He went on to explain that much of psychiatric language is not denotative but is nevertheless instrumental in precipitating constructive action. If one diagnoses a patient, then some treatment program follows; since there are almost no highly specific treatments associated with particular nosological categories, any diagnosis will suffice as a stimulus for a therapist and the patient to begin transacting.

It may be some such sequence of events as that described above which accounts for clinical psychologists being able to say with much truth that their psychodiagnostic assessments are almost invariably found to be useful to their colleagues, even though formal evaluations of the clinician's instruments seem to attest to their relative invalidity. There is, in a word, a great deal more to the clinician than his battery of tests, but without his tests, he would be appreciably less effective.

The pragmatic proof of the value of the clinician-with-his-tests, lies in the evaluation of what happens during and following his intervention into the life of a client. The validity of an instrument cannot, in the final analysis, be tested apart from such considerations as when it is used, by whom it is used, and for what purpose it is used—and how, and to whom the results are reported. Under one set of conditions the clinician's tools can be highly valid. Under another, quite useless.

Some readers will surely say this is a specious, misleading argument which altogether begs the question, The issue, they will say, is not whether the clinician is a socially useful person who knowingly with altruistic motives employs a bag of tricks to enhance his effectiveness. It is not the question of the clinician's adequacy in helping to initiate constructive action in behalf of clients which is under discussion. The *real* question, they will insist, is whether the *methods* used by clinicians generate *dependable knowledge* about human behavior. The test of the method lies in whether an examination made at point A in time, will permit one to predict behavior at points B, C or D. The clinician will reply, "Well, if that's all you want, I can select an individual of school age with an IQ of 50 and guarantee that he will be having great difficulty in his school subjects at any time in the future you care to choose."

The critical reader will indicate that this would be no real test, but he would like to see the clinician predict which of 100 college freshmen, with IQ's ranging from 125 to 150, will and which will not graduate. The clinician will agree to do this but only if all sources of variance other than those contributed by personality factors are controlled. In this imaginary dialog, the critical reader will object that this is impossible and the clinician will point out that he does not assess social environmental factors with his tests—only those related to personality.

This interchange, however, defines the dilemma. The clinician working near the borders of the range of human capacities whether in the domain of intellectual functioning or personality functioning can predict quite accurately because the variance contributed by personality factors is very great. As he moves toward the middle range, the variance contributed by personality factors alone is less and less in relation to the total variance, and is therefore less able to predict what an individual's behavior will be. This incapacity seems scarcely to be an adequate basis for indicting either the clinician or his instruments. As Garfield will point out at greater length, the debates between clinicians and their professional colleagues have not always generated as much light as they have heat, but both will be around for a long time, and the talks will continue.

As a concluding remark, it should be noted that from the modest handful of scholars who first met in 1892, the American Psychological Association has grown to a membership of nearly 20,000. Of this number, it is often said, too few are now devoted researchers and never have so many practitioners attempted to apply so little in the way of firmly established knowledge. Nevertheless, it may also be argued that empirical research has proliferated at a rate which greatly exceeds the capacity of existing theoretical structures to assimilate the flood of facts and put them into some comprehensible arrangement.

In a succinct and telling critique of the contemporary status of behavior theory, Roby * (1959) makes the following observations:

"For some years, the growth of behavior theory has been marked by an increasing concern with details and by the burgeoning popularity of the 'miniature system.' Fundamental reappraisal of the major systems of psychological thought has given way to improvement and exploitation of selected features of these systems. To borrow a phrase of Whitehead's, modern behavior theory is becoming a series of footnotes to the original theoretical systems, and footnotes in ever smaller type.

Several historical factors may be responsible for this narrowing of theoretical scope. First there has been a tendency for the dominant schools of thought to adopt a "with us or 'against us" attitude which does not encourage searching examination from within. Since the accepted pursuit of a theorist within an established framework is exegesis, any attack on core concepts must come from other schools. Such external criticism may still be superficial simply because the critic does not have a sympathetic understanding of the concepts he is assailing. A rather different influence in the fractionation of theory has been the very rapid advance in the technical facilities available for laboratory and field experimentation. Gadgets, both physical and conceptual, have accelerated the discovery of behavioral phenomena which were in no way envisaged by previous theory. Such findings clamor for some measure of theoretical benediction and the resulting formulations are inevitably circumscribed."

It is beyond the scope of these few introductory remarks even to attempt to identify all of the factors which have contributed to the conditions which Roby delineates. One salient influence, however, must have been and continues to be the availability of almost unlimited funds to finance the generation of empirical data. Psychology, perhaps prematurely, has found itself widely admired in a society which believes devoutly in the benefits of scientific research, but holds contemplation in low esteem. In a situation in which turning out empirical data is highly regarded, and thinking about the broader implications of the data is scarcely rewarded at all, it is not surprising that facts are being stockpiled at an unprecedented rate, while theory building languishes.

In the chapters which follow, neither the contributors nor the

* Roby, T. B. An opinion on the construction of behavior theory. *The American Psychologist*, Vol. 14, No. 3, pps. 129-134.

editors purport to go beyond the contemporary status of the science. Rather, the selection of essays is designed to comprise a reasonably adequate sampling of modern view of classical theories, of basic structures underlying personality, and of significant new areas and of methods of analysis of personality data.

Thus the student using this volume will properly conclude that present day psychology is a sprawling, multi-faceted field seriously in need of integration. Psychology is a wide-open frontier science which resists, yet sadly needs, the genius of a new generation of comprehensive theorists. The editors are willing to predict that the comprehensive theories yet to be developed will most prominently move in the direction of trying to make man less self-conscious about consciousness. As Rapoport * (1962) comments,

> "As detailed knowledge of the physicobiological basis of our mental apparatus increases, the questions concerning the nature of mind will become less charged with affect and anxiety. Perhaps in due time our title as beings endowed with a mind will come to mean considerably less to us than it does today; just as occupying the center of creation has come to mean considerably less to men as they have acquired appreciation of the vastness and grandeur of the cosmos."

If Rapoport is correct, psychology will at least escape what Feigl † (1959) has called a major embarrassment. It seems almost certain that in a relatively short time, psychologists devoted to the study of personality will devise a conceptual scheme which both views man's behavior as a lawful phenomenon in nature, and yet provides for the full range of his capacities which are undeniably unique among the animals walking the earth.

J. M. W.
R. W. H.

---

* Rapoport, A. An essay on mind, in *Theories of the Mind,* Jordon Scher (Ed.) Free Press of Glencoe, N.Y. 1962 (pps. 271-304).

† Feigl, H. Philosophical embarrassments of psychology. *The American Psychologist,* Vol. 14, No. 3, pps. 115-128.

I

Basic Processes

1

Learning Theory and Personality

Janet Taylor Spence

In the present chapter we will be concerned with what one kind of psychological theory may have to contribute to another. The two types of theories, of learning and of personality, provide many contrasts that will be profitable to consider if attempts to integrate them are to be understood in proper perspective.

One obvious difference between learning theories and theories of personality may be found in the particular empirical phenomena on which each is based. Personality theorists have focused their attention on complex patterns of human behavior that occur in real life, particularly those with social and motivational overtones.[1] Of fundamental concern are the persistent reaction patterns that characterize a given individual and, typically, differentiate him from other individuals, i.e., define his uniqueness.

In contrast, learning theorists have traditionally been concerned with relatively simple, controlled situations within the laboratory, often using animals as subjects. While not completely ignoring the individual differences among their subjects and never denying their importance, learning theorists, in common with other experimentalists, have none-

---

[1] The orientation of the present chapter is to consider overt behavior and the ways in which one group of psychologists attempt to explain or predict it. Certain kinds of behavioral patterns are typically said to constitute or reflect a person's "personality," as opposed, let us say, to behavior reflecting his manual dexterity. Used in this manner, "personality" is a convenient label to identify an interrelated group of empirical phenomena and will be so used in the present chapter.

3

theless been primarily interested in determining the functional relations between their experimental stimulus variables and behavior, or, to express the matter more concretely, in systematic differences among groups of subjects tested under various stimulus conditions. The specific experimental arrangements that have occupied the attention of these theorists are, of course, those in which behavior change takes place with practice, i.e., learning and extinction.

With few exceptions, learning theories have not been concerned merely with the variables contributing to the hypothetical learning process but with all of the other variables relevant to the behavior being measured (e.g., motivational variables). Thus, they might more accurately be described as *behavior* theories about situations in which learning takes place. Even here, however, learning theorists have tended to be limited in the empirical phenomena with which they have been concerned. As an example, consider that class of variables designated as positive rewards. Many objects or events can serve as positive rewards, even for the white rat. Learning theorists typically have not been at all interested in cataloguing and investigating all of these specific examples. Rather they have chosen to introduce only a few of them into their experimental situations, selecting them primarily on the basis of convenience. This procedure reflects the intent of the theorist to provide general and fairly abstract laws, i.e., laws that will apply to the whole range of specific variables that could or would fall into a given class, should anyone be interested in enumerating them. Here, then, is another difference in emphasis between the learning and the personality theorist; while both may seek to develop general laws, the latter is forced, by the very nature of his interests, to pay attention to specifics, e.g., the variety of events that may serve to reward and motivate man's behavior.

All in all, the empirical events that learning theorists have attempted to explain have little resemblance to those phenomena that we commonly refer to as reflecting "personality." What bearing, then, do contemporary learning theories have on personality? In the strictest sense, little or none. While learning theories are in such a form that testable predictions may be logically derived from them, none of these predictions are directly related to the type of behavioral events that are the immediate concern of the personality theorist.

Nonetheless, there has been an increasing number of attempts, particularly within the last decade, to apply empirical principles or theoretical constructs from the learning laboratory to the kinds of problems to which students of personality have addressed themselves. That such applications should be attempted should not be too surprising. Personality theorists have, after all, devoted much of their effort toward identifying the kinds of life experiences that lead to subsequent patterns of behavior ("personality") and the conditions that lead to change in these patterns, as in the therapeutic process. In short, many theorists are committed to the position that personality is to some degree—perhaps even to a large degree—learned and that personality change, i.e., relearning or extinction, is possible. Whether or not the empirical laws and theoretical notions that have to date been developed by the experimentalist are relevant to these latter types of phenomena is, of course, another question. In the absence of equally well developed learning theories that were specifically devised to account for complex, real life phenomena, the temptation to try them out is strong.

The many psychologists who have attempted to blend an amalgam of learning theory and personality have often drawn upon a common set of theoretical constructs, particularly those of the Hull-Spence system. Nonetheless, their contributions have been diverse. They differ, first of all, in the specific empirical phenomena that they consider, some limiting themselves to fairly circumscribed problem areas and others being more comprehensive. More important, each psychologist chooses for himself the particular empirical learning principles and, out of a given theory, the particular constructs that he believes to be applicable. These must then be combined with additional empirical or theoretical assumptions about the nature of the events to-be-explained. In part these assumptions consist of statements, which are often unverified guesses, as to the empirical variables that influence behavior (e.g., the childhood experiences that determine certain adult characteristics). But they also involve decisions as to the technical manner in which learning principles are to be used to derive these presumed empirical relationships and as to whether additional explanatory principles are also required to permit this derivation. Nothing in any contemporary learning theory dictates or demands what assumptions these should be.

The further one gets from simple laboratory situations, the greater the number of assumptions that must be made. Since our scientific knowledge about complexly determined patterns of behavior is less exact than about simple ones, comprehensiveness in these theoretical accounts is thus gained at the expense of empirical confirmation, i.e., they become more and more a series of untested and occasionally, untestable speculations.

Rarely are these additional assumptions completely novel. As in most scientific endeavors, they are heavily influenced by existing knowledge, provided in this instance by such sources as clinical observation, the results of formal investigations of personality phenomena, and the speculations of personality theorists (e.g., Freudian psychoanalysts). Thus, it is possible to have quite contradictory "learning theories of personality," even among those who subscribe to the same conceptual system. At the same time, one may find essential agreement at many points between a given learning theory approach and long established personality theories which include no explicit statements about learning.

This state of affairs creates a dilemma for anyone who is charged with discussing learning theory approaches to personality. Summarizations of the views of even the major contributors to this general enterprise are almost impossible to accomplish within realistic limitations of time or space. The task becomes even more formidable if attempts are first made to explain the empirical learning principles and theoretical constructs employed in various analyses of personality phenomena. In resolving this dilemma, one can, at one extreme, make a series of abstract statements that are applicable to all of the various approaches but never get down to the specifics of any one in particular. At the other extreme, it is possible to concentrate on reviewing one particular set of views and to ignore the rest. Although leaning toward the former, the present chapter represents a kind of compromise solution. For reasons that will shortly be made apparent, certain methodological and empirical orientations that the various learning theory approaches have in common will be considered on an abstract level in subsequent sections. This discussion will be followed by illustrations of several different kinds of attempts to bring learning principles and personality phenomena together.

THE METHODOLOGICAL ORIENTATION OF LEARNING THEORY APPROACHES TO PERSONALITY

In searching for communalities among the various integrations of learning theory and personality, one is struck by the similarity of the views about the nature of science and the scientific method that they reflect. The methodological position these contributions represent is most commonly identified philosophically with the positivist tradition and, within psychology, with methodological behaviorism. The pre-dilection of those psychologists identified as behaviorists for focusing their attention on certain kinds of empirical laws has led to an alternate label for the contributions of this group: stimulus-response or S-R psychology.

While the methodological views accepted by S-R behaviorists have been extensively treated by philosophers of science (e.g., Bergmann, 1957; Feigl, 1945; Hempel, 1949) and, as these views affect their own scientific discipline, by psychologists (e.g., Pratt, 1939; K. W. Spence, 1948), restatement of certain basic tenets seems to be in order. Although many psychologists, particularly experimentalists, adhere to the behaviorist position, its acceptance is far from universal, especially perhaps among those concerned with personality. Examination of the methodological orientation of the S-R behaviorist may thus serve as an introduction to the contributions of those who find value in the principles of learning in understanding personality and to distinguish them in several basic respects from certain other types of approaches.[2]

Psychology as a Scientific Discipline

One of the fundamental commitments of the behaviorist is that science, of which psychology is conceived to be a part, is a public endeavor. Its basic data are provided by observations of objects and events that may be made by all with the requisite sensory capacities and technical skills; its basic task is to establish interrelationships among these publicly observable data, i.e., to formulate empirical laws and theories which permit their integration. These laws and theories, of course, are what constitute for science the "explanation" of the events to which they refer, and which permit prediction. One of the most crucial—and technically complex—aspects of this endeavor concerns the rules governing the language of science. In broad and oversimplified terms, these rules are aimed toward achieving un-ambiguous communication among scientists. Not only must there be a high degree of actual or potential interobserver agreement about

[2] On the basis of differing conceptions of the nature of the hypothetical learning construct, a distinction is sometimes made between cognitive learning theories, such as Tolman's, and association or S-R types of theories, such as Hull's or Guthrie's. To avoid misunderstanding, it should be understood that the reference above to "S-R" behaviorists is here intended only to designate the interest of a given individual or group in formulating empirical laws holding between stimuli and responses and not to a particular brand of learning theory. Used in this general sense, the term thus includes even cognitive theorists like Tolman.

the description of any given empirical datum, but proposed laws interrelating classes of events must be stated in such a form that their implications are clear and susceptible to empirical test.

Restriction of the raw data of science to publicly observable events implies that there are other classes of data, including those falling into the realm of private experience, that are excluded from scientific consideration. In like manner, insistence that all postulated explanations of these events be capable of empirical confirmation or disconfirmation implies that scientific knowledge is but one of many forms that man's knowledge of himself and his universe may take. There is nothing implicit or explicit in the methodological tradition of behaviorism that denies the existence or the importance of non-scientific knowledge about man, e.g., denial that man has a rich inner life or that knowledge about it is not a legitimate concern of the non-scientist. The behaviorist is, however, committed to the assumption that scientific knowledge of the behavior of living organisms is possible, i.e., is at least in part lawful, and merely asks that, like other scientists, he be allowed to restrict his activities to this single pursuit.

These brief statements concerning the conception of the nature of science and of scientific methodology accepted by behaviorists contain no rules that will guarantee that one's hunches or hypotheses will be confirmed when subjected to empirical test and no prohibitions that state, for example, that one cannot introspect, empathize or be stimulated by the speculative insights of the poet or philosopher in arriving at these hypotheses. Although the context of discovery, as Meehl (1954) has put it, is poorly understood, it is probable that such sources are often used. If one is interested in the source of ideas that lead to the formulation of useful hypotheses or that scientists actually utilize, one must investigate these matters empirically rather than seeking answers from metatheoretical analyses.

Nor are there any prescriptions that will allow one to decide, a priori, the most useful starting point in any scientific enterprise, e.g., with molecular descriptions of behavior or molar ones, with simple phenomena or complex ones. Implicit in these latter statements, however, is a commitment to a set of standards by which any given scientific contribution may be judged. Many psychologists, particularly those whose empirical interests are in complex, real life phenomena, assess the importance of psychological theories and research in terms of their immediate practical significance, the degree to which they contribute to the solution of the pressing problems of everyday life. The reasons for adopting these standards are varied and may include a conviction that what is important to understand about man involves an emergent set of principles that can be discovered only by direct investigation of the phenomena themselves.

A quite different standard of evaluation is more likely to be adopted by behaviorists. As Spence (1957) has expressed it, *scientific significance is judged by the extent to which an activity leads to the discovery of empirical laws or to the formulation of comprehensive theories that serve to integrate them.* The preference of many behaviorists for investigating simple rather than complex phenomena rests on the belief that scientific progress will be more rapid in these areas. Assuming that many of the variables and laws governing simple forms of behavior will, in combination with additional factors, also be operative in more complex forms of behavior, understanding the latter may well be achieved more rapidly and more effectively if investigation proceeds from the simple to the complex.

The conviction that there is some continuity in the laws and variables governing situations of varying degrees of complexity, is, of course, what underlies learning theory approaches to personality. In passing, it might be noted that those who attempt to apply the principles of learning discovered in the laboratory to real life are often caught in a cross-fire of criticism. On the one hand, personality theorists who are unsympathetic to S-R behaviorism and its products are likely to regard any efforts to find continuity between the phenomena of the laboratory and the "important" aspects of real life as a useless attempt at best, and at worst, as an affront to the true nature of man. On the other hand, there are experimental psychologists, perhaps made uneasy by speculations too far in advance of empirical data, who also doubt the usefulness of these attempts, at least at the moment.

The Empirical Data of Psychology

The empirical data among which psychologists attempt to establish interrelationships may be grouped into three major classes:

1) Response variables: the overt behavior of living organisms.

2) Stimulus variables: events in the social or physical environment of the organism that are contemporaneous with the behavior being observed or that have occurred in the past.

3) O-variables: anatomical and physiological properties of the organism.

Before proceeding further it should perhaps be emphasized that among the kinds of events labeled as "responses" is verbal behavior, including verbalizations elicited by instructions to an individual to introspect and report his feelings and thought processes. In principle, such verbal behavior is, of course, just as publicly observable as non-verbal behavior. Behaviorists, however, deny that introspective reports have any unique methodological status: that one is able to assume that they, or any hypothetical state of the organism defined in terms of them, are necessarily isomorphic to the private world of the individual or that, in principle, they yield a kind of information about the individual that is unobtainable by other means. Whether or not a given psychologist or group of psychologists believes that verbal reports will prove to be more *useful* than non-verbal behavior in understanding a particular type of phenomena is, like so many matters that divide psychologists, an empirical issue, having to do, if you will, with the tactics rather than the strategy of acquiring scientific knowledge.

The Empirical Laws of Psychology

Scientific laws basically consist of statements concerning the inter-relationships holding between independently measured sets of empirical events. Interrelationships can, of course, be investigated within or among any of the three classes of variables described above.[3] However, the interests of most psychologists, as well as the relative lack of physiological knowledge about complex phenomena, have led to primary emphasis on the discovery of two major classes of laws: those involving the relations between stimulus and response variables (S-R laws) and between independent sets of response variables (R-R laws). Examples of the former run all the way from the effects of magnitude of reward on the running speed of the white rat in a straight alley to such phenomena as the effects of certain childhood experiences on adult

---

[3] In the discussion that follows, only the types of empirical variables that enter into various kinds of laws will be discussed. It should be understood, however, that the process of formulating such empirical laws may be bolstered by theory. That is, a series of abstract constructs may be defined in terms of or inferred from one set of empirical variables, rules laid down concerning the manner in which these constructs are interrelated, and finally, from this theoretical network, predictions derived about another set of empirical variables (typically measures of behavior).

personality patterns and the relations between various psychotherapeutic procedures and therapeutic outcome.

The R-R type of correlational law, it will be recognized, forms the basis of diagnostic testing, as well as providing the empirical data for the theories of the field theorist and phenomenologist. Since these latter theorists often call attention to the unimportance of the objective stimulus situation in their thinking, some comment might be appropriate on the role of the external environment in R-R laws, particularly in comparison to its role in S-R laws. Behavior, of course, never occurs in an environmental vacuum, and rarely, if ever, are predictions made about the relations between sets of behavioral observations without consideration of the context in which the behavior takes place. To take a frivolous example, one would be likely to make different inferences or predictions about the characteristics of an individual who claimed that a lion was devouring him if a lion was or was not visible. Implicitly or explicitly, the proposed correlation between two sets of behavioral observations is assumed to hold only if the responses have occurred in certain types of situations, e.g., responses to the Rorschach as related to behavior toward members of the opposite sex.

Specification of the appropriate boundary environment conditions under which a proposed correlation may legitimately be tested is often based on a known or assumed S-R law, i.e., the objective stimulus conditions that will elicit the behavior under consideration. For example, in a classic study growing out of the field theory of Kurt Lewin (Barker, Dembo & Lewin, 1941) the amount of frustration exhibited by children in the experimental situation was related to constructiveness of play. It was tacitly assumed that the experimenters' manipulations of the external environment (introducing a barrier) would produce the kind of behavior from which they inferred frustration. In contrast, the S-R psychologists is actively interested in acquiring more formal and extensive knowledge about S-R relationships (which an R-R theorist may merely take for granted) by systematically varying the properties of the objective environment so that, for example, the conditions producing frustration can be better understood.

Individual Differences and S-R Laws

The concern of the learning theorist has almost exclusively been in establishing S-R laws. As is universally recognized, organisms observed under the same external stimulus conditions, even in the relatively simple, well-controlled environment of the laboratory, rarely respond in exactly the same manner. Putting the matter differently, the state of the organism at the time a response is made is determined by more factors than those in the immediate stimulus situation. This fact has frequently led to the criticism that since S-R laws are forced to make the same prediction about the behavior of every individual observed in a given situation, they do not permit the degree of precision in predicting the behavior of individuals that the clinical psychologist or personality theorist seeks. To the extent that the specific environmental conditions in a given S-R law refer only to those immediately antecedent to the behavior being measured, there is some justice to this claim. However, it is possible to expand or modify this simple type of S-R law to take individual differences into account. Referring once again to the three classes of empirical events with which psychologists deal, one may classify individuals according to some physiological index, thus predicting that behavior is a function of both the present stimulus conditions and the individual's physiological properties $[R=f(S,O)]$. A more commonly used method for classifying individuals is to measure or observe their behavior, e.g., responses to a diagnostic test, behavior in a social group, verbalizations in an interview or therapy session, etc. Expanding S-R laws to include individual differences defined in this manner, one arrives at $R_1 = f(S,R_2)$, the subscripts indicating that the individual difference variable is measured independently of the behavior being predicted.

Finally, one can differentiate among individuals in terms of past experiences and postulate that these interact with properties of the current situation to determine behavior $[R = f(S_{past}, S_{present})]$. When prior environmental events that may have a fairly permanent and profound effect on later behavior are being considered, ethical considerations, of course, prohibit us from experimenting with human subjects. One could not, for example, deliberately specify the conditions under which children are to be reared so that their effects on adult personality could be ascertained. Instead, one selects for study individuals who have already been subjected in their life experience to the kinds of events in which we are interested. However, experiments in which the histories of the subjects are systematically manipulated are frequently conducted with animals as subjects.

The context in which these investigations dealing with past experiences have just been discussed has some misleading implications. In most of these studies, historical variables were not included merely as one of several possible methods of accounting for individual differences in behavior in the experimental situation. Rather, the investigators were actively interested in these variables and their later effects on behavior or, to put the matter conversely, they were concerned with discovering the experiential factors that were responsible for the development, in the sense of acquisition, of certain response patterns. While R-R laws yield valuable information and are almost indispensable for diagnostic purposes, historical S-R laws of this type appear to be necessary if we are ever to be able to understand such matters as how individuals come to be as they are, what long range effects certain child rearing practices have, or how the most effective psychotherapy is to be conducted.

TWO ILLUSTRATIONS

As has previously been indicated, a number of psychologists have attempted to provide fairly comprehensive accounts of real life situations and behavior by the use of learning theory (e.g., Bandura, 1961; Dollard & Miller, 1950; Mednick, 1958; Mowrer, 1950; Whiting & Child, 1953). In these accounts, learning principles are brought out of the laboratory and, in a speculative leap, applied to complex, naturalistic phenomena. One of the most ambitious and influential contributions of this type may be found in the work of John Dollard and Neal Miller of Yale University. To give the flavor of their approach, certain of their views will be discussed below.

At the opposite extreme are attempts to introduce personality variables into a learning theory and to test their hypothesized properties by studying performance on conventional laboratory tasks (e.g., Eysenck, 1957; Mandler & Sarason, 1952; Spence, 1958). As an example of this kind of endeavor, some of the work centered about the Manifest Anxiety Scale (MAS) in which the present writer has been involved will be reviewed.

Dollard and Miller on Conflict and Displacement

In their well-known book, *Personality and Psychotherapy,* Dollard and Miller (1950) brought together three hitherto separate traditions: Freudian psychoanalysis, Hullian learning theory, and social anthropology. The integration was accomplished by restating and amplifying many of the descriptive concepts of psychoanalytic theory in the language of learning. By these means, Dollard and Miller hoped to provide a more explicit account of the acquisition or development of personality characteristics, as well as a set of theoretical propositions that are more susceptible to empirical investigation than the stimulating but often untestable hypotheses of psychoanalysis. To these principles were added data accumulated by social anthropology and related disciplines so that a particularistic account could be given of the actual social conditions that contribute to the development and maintenance of specific personality patterns in various cultures. Although also concerned with normal personality, Dollard and Miller, like the psychoanalysts, have paid particular attention to neurotic processes and the social-familial context in which they are likely to appear.

Underlying neurotic behavior, Dollard and Miller state, is an intense, unconscious emotional conflict. Typically the origins of adult conflict are to be found in childhood and are related to the manner in which the individual's parents or parent surrogates met his needs and to the way in which he was trained to fulfill the expectations of his culture. Particularly crucial areas of training are those concerned with feeding, cleanliness, sex and aggression. In each of these situations, there is ample opportunity for making contrary demands on the child or for instilling intense fear, guilt or resentment. These emotional reactions may interfere with later expression of these various needs in a manner that is both gratifying to the individual and acceptable to society, or may lay the groundwork for distorted, ambivalent attitudes of the individual toward himself and others. In part because of the child's lack of intellectual development, in part because of repression, intense early conflicts and their later derivatives are likely to remain unconscious. The neurotic is thus unable or unwilling to understand the emotional bases of his behavior and hence unable to capitalize on the problem-solving ability of which he is intellectually capable to find a resolution of his difficulties.

As may easily be recognized, none of the statements contained in this brief overview is particularly novel and most of them are widely accepted, especially among culturally oriented Freudians. The unique contribution of Dollard and Miller, as has been previously emphasized, is their attempt to refine and add detail to these kinds of general propositions. As an illustration of their approach, we will consider here Dollard and Miller's treatment of approach-avoidance conflict and its extension to certain types of displacement phenomena. Not only does approach-avoidance conflict run through their thinking about human personality as a leitmotif, but their treatment of the topic provides an excellent demonstration of the interplay between rigorous experimentation in the laboratory and speculative applications of these experimental findings to events in real life.

In his role as experimentalist, Miller, along with his co-workers, has conducted an extensive series of studies of approach-avoidance conflict in spatial situations. The typical experimental arrangement employed in these investigations has been to train hungry animal subjects (usually rats) to run down a straight alley to get a food pellet; the subjects are then given several shocks at the place where the food is located. Thus, the cues (stimuli) of the alley, in conjunction with the subject's hunger, elicit approach responses towards the goal area. But, through the process of classical conditioning, the same external cues are also assumed to have gained the capacity to elicit emotional responses (fear) similar to those elicited earlier by the noxious shock. Since learned or conditioned fear responses have also been shown to have drive properties (Miller, 1951; Miller, 1959), the fear will motivate avoidance responses.

In arriving at predictions about the behavior of subjects in this type of conflict situation, Miller has made a number of assumptions. First, both approach and avoidance tendencies become stronger as the subject nears the place where both reward and punishment have been experienced (gradients of strength of approach and of avoidance tendencies). The absolute height of each of these gradients is in part dependent on the strength of the associated drives (hunger or fear). Second, it is assumed that the slope of the avoidance gradient is steeper than the slope of the approach gradient. This assumption is the most novel of Miller's hypotheses and is particularly crucial to his analysis of conflict behavior. Finally, it is assumed that when competing response tendencies are elicited, the strongest of them is most likely to occur in overt behavior. Thus, if approach and avoidance tendencies are of relatively equal strength (i.e., their gradients overlap), a complex pattern of behavior is predicted. As illustrated in Fig. 1, the subject will vacillate, hesitate and change direction in the vicinity of the intersection of the gradients, moving toward the goal location when at a distance from it and running back should momentum carry the subject so far that fear becomes dominant. Although alternative interpretations of the data are possible (Maher, 1962), many of the implications of this conflict model have received experimental support. An excellent summary of the relevant literature has been provided by Miller (1959).

Since conflict along purely spatial dimensions is probably quite infrequent in naturalistic settings, the potential importance of the spatial conflict model for human behavior lies in Dollard and Miller's contention that these assumptions are applicable to other and more complex dimensions as well. Among these are regular sequences of events, often culturally determined, that may quite reliably be predicted to lead to some end result. A young man, for instance, may wish to marry and establish a family but be fearful or guilty about the commitments attendant upon marriage. He may be able to attend mixed social events and take girls out casually (approach tendencies are stronger), but as he comes to be emotionally involved with one person and closer to engagement and marriage, his fear or guilt mounts more rapidly than his desire to marry. If his fear becomes sufficiently strong (if the gradients of approach and avoidance intersect), he may then attempt to disentangle himself from this threatening relationship.

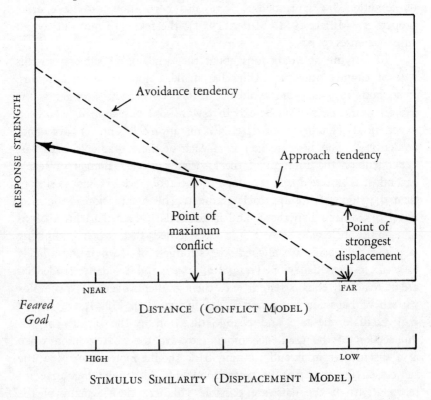

The assumptions outlined above concerning the gradients of approach and avoidance are based in part on the principle of stimulus generalization: response tendencies acquired in one stimulus situation will tend to be evoked in similar situations, the strength of these generalized tendencies being related to the degree of similarity to the original training conditions. Returning again to the laboratory studies of spatial conflict, in a homogeneous alley the subject receives cues that become increasingly similar to those near the feared goal area as he moves down the alley toward it; thus both approach and avoidance tendencies increase in strength with nearness to the goal.

The role of stimulus generation in determining conflict behavior can, of course, be studied more directly. For example, subjects may be given approach-avoidance training in one situation and their behavior then observed under conditions of varying degrees of similarity to the training conditions. Thus it should be possible to extend the assumptions made about the spatial model of conflict to the dimension of stimulus similarity, as is illustrated in Fig. 1. Precisely this type of extension has been made by Miller and his coworkers under the heading of *displacement* (Miller, 1948; Miller, 1959).

In order to understand the usage of the term displacement in this context, it is necessary to point out its meaning in psychoanalytic theory, in which the concept of displacement refers to several types of redirection of behavior: substitution of one kind of impulse gratification for another, modification of the expression of an impulse, or redirection of its expression towards a different object. The various forms of displacement may be due to the unavailability of the appropriate object but frequently represent an attempt to resolve a conflict: acting in a manner that gives some satisfaction without arousing the degree of guilt or anxiety that an unmodified mode of expression would evoke.

By extending his spatial conflict model to the dimension of stimulus similarity, Miller (1948, 1959) was able to suggest more precisely the conditions under which displacement, as a method of conflict resolution, will occur and the substitute objects that will elicit displaced responses. Giving an illustration from real life rather than discussing the evidence gathered in the laboratory, an adolescent may be resentful of his father's attempts to dominate him but too fearful to express his feelings and to demand more independence. These hostile attitudes may generalize to other authority figures, such as his school teachers, but he will tend to express resentment only toward those who are sufficiently dissimilar to his father (e.g., his older brother) to reverse the balance between the strengths of fear and resentment.

Dollard and Miller have also suggested that by appealing to the

principle of *response* generalization, their model is able to account for
another type of displacement phenomenon: the modification of the
form of a response. For example, although our rebellious adolescent
may be too fearful to challenge his father directly, he may feel safe in
indulging in subtle forms of disparagement. Few of the implications
of these hypotheses, however, have yet been tested in the laboratory.

Two of Miller's students, Murray and Berkun (1955), have
recently combined the assumptions concerning conflict and displacement
into a more general theory and have tested some of the implications
of this joint model. In an experiment that had the novel feature of
permitting subjects some freedom of response, these investigators first
gave hungry rats the usual approach-avoidance training in a straight
alley. In test trials in which shock was never administered, subjects
were placed in the training alley but could escape (displace) into a
similar, adjacent alley through one of a series of windows and, in
turn, from this alley into a third alley of an even lower degree of
similarity. According to the joint theory, gradients of approach and
avoidance (conflict) are expected in each alley, because of stimulus generalization, their absolute heights becoming lower as the
similarity of the displacement alley to the training situation decreases.
The heights of the avoidance gradients, however, should fall off
relatively more rapidly, with the implication that the intersection of
the approach and avoidance gradients occurs closer and closer to the
goal end of the alley as similarity decreases. Thus, Murray and Berkun
reasoned, their subjects should proceed toward the goal in the training
alley but displace into the adjacent alley as the strength of the approach
and avoidance tendencies neared equality, proceed forward in the similar alley and then again displace to the third alley. They also assumed
that experience in the displacement alleys would be "therapeutic" in
the sense that with continued trials, the conditioned fear elicited by the
cues of the similar alleys would gradually extinguish, the extinction
taking place in these alleys generalizing back to the training conditions.
Thus, on successive trials, subjects were expected to continue further
down each alley before displacing and eventually to make goal responses
in the training alley. All of these predictions were confirmed. Several
subsequent studies (Berkun, 1957; Taylor & Maher, 1959) have
demonstrated more directly the Murray-Berkun inference that intervening experience in similar alleys hastens the reappearance of goal
responses in the training situation.

Murray (1954) has also demonstrated the applicability of the joint conflict-displacement model to human behavior by analyzing the verbalizations of a patient in psychotherapy. Because the nature of the behavior being considered and the setting in which it occurred should make this type of investigation of particular interest to those concerned with personality, the study will be discussed in some detail. The patient, an unmarried 24 year old male, had as a major problem strong dependency needs which aroused resentment he was too fearful to express. Murray reasoned that if the patient's attempts to talk about his hostile feelings in therapy elicited anxiety reactions, such verbalizations would be abandoned and emotionally safer topics substituted as defensive maneuvers. Since the therapist felt that some progress had been made in the seventeen sessions (largly supportive in nature) in which the patient participated, Murray predicted that not only would there be a negative relationship between the number of hostile and defense statements within individual therapeutic hours, but that over the course of these sessions, the expression of hostility should systematically increase, due in part to anxiety reduction, and defense decrease. Although the varied content of the patient's verbalizations did not make this type of reciprocal relationship statistically necessary, these predictions, derived from conflict theory, were confirmed.

Consideration of the case history of the patient suggested that his ambivalence centered about his mother but, on a generalization continuum, was also elicited by his aunt and to a still lesser degree by other people and situations in general. During the initial sessions, the patient expressed increasing amounts of hostility toward his mother, but after reaching a peak, shifted in subsequent sessions to talking about his resentment of his aunt, again to an increasing degree. He then shifted the focus of his hostility, once more, to other people and situations. This sequence of events, of course, strongly suggests that the patient was displacing his hostility when his expression of it toward a particular individual became strong enough to elicit intense anxiety. Although an unexpected event (the illness of his aunt) interrupted the progress of therapy, there was some evidence to support Murray's further expectation that as the patient's anxieties were reduced, he would reverse this sequence of events, finally coming to verbalize once more his negative attitudes toward his mother. Additional confirmation of the joint conflict-displacement model has been provided by similar but less extensive analyses of the verbalizations of two other patients (Murray, 1954; Murray & Berkun, 1955).

Before leaving these studies, several additional comments should be made about them. These investigations were less concerned with testing a theory about psychotherapy, even in a limited sense, than with testing a theory about conflict and displacement behavior, as that behavior is observed in a therapeutic setting. Thus it was necessary to select for analysis only those cases that met the boundary conditions of the theory (e.g., clearly exhibited an approach-avoidance conflict). Since the theory is stated in abstract terms, it was further necessary to specify for each patient individually such details as the exact nature of his conflict, the particular persons or events at various points on a generalization gradient, the types of defenses used to avoid painful topics, etc. The abstractness of a theory, of course, is precisely what permits it to be applied to a variety of individuals or situations, each of which, when considered in its entirety, has some degree of uniqueness. Accuracy of prediction about a particular situation or individual is thus achieved by combining specific data about that situation or individual with the general propositions of a theory.

Other studies bearing on the applicability of Miller's conflict and displacement notions to human behavior can also be cited. Among them are investigations conducted by Sears, Whiting and their students who, like Dollard and Miller, have also been concerned with employing S-R learning principles to analyze complex behavioral phenomena. Hollenberg and Sperry (1951), for example, tested preschool children in a play situation in which the subjects were supplied with a furnished doll house and dolls representing various members of a family and were told to invent a story about them. Two measures of home experience, based on data obtained from interviews with the child's mother, were obtained for each subject: degree of frustration (as reflected by such indices as the number and kinds of restrictive rules placed on the child and the degree of responsiveness to his needs and requests) and severity of punishment for aggressive behavior. The investigators' major concern was in the frequency and intensity of aggressive responses exhibited by their subjects as a function of home experience.

In reaching their predictions they assumed that children who have experienced a high degree of general frustration at home or have been severely punished for aggressive responses are more highly motivated to act in an aggressive fashion than less frustrated or less severely punished children. This assumption, based on a suggestion by Whiting, is in part related to the frustration-aggression hypothesis (Dollard, Doob, Miller, Mowrer & Sears, 1939). They further assumed, by appealing to Miller's displacement model, that overt expression of aggression is less likely to be inhibited in a fantasy situation in which such behavior is unpunished than under conditions more like the home situation. Combining these assumptions, they anticipated that children who experienced a high degree of frustration at home or were severely punished for aggression would exhibit more aggressive behavior during the doll play sessions than children rated low on these measures. These predictions were confirmed. The same hypotheses, however, suggest that if the children had been observed at home or in circumstances more similar to it than doll play, the differences between high and low frustration or punishment groups obtained by Hollenberg and Sperry might be less or even reversed. Sears (1951) has reported data that provides some confirmation of this expectation, children rated low on the severity of punishment variable exhibiting more aggression when observed in a nursery school setting than those rated high.

Manifest Anxiety, Drive and Learning

The studies centered around the Manifest Anxiety Scale (MAS) grew out of a series of investigations instituted at the State University of Iowa that were concerned with the role of aversive motivational or drive factors in learning situations, primarily classical defense conditioning, within the framework of Hull-Spence behavior theory. Drive level (Hull's D) has been manipulated or defined in many of these studies by such traditional methods as varying the intensity of the noxious unconditioned stimulus in the eyelid conditioning situation. Attempts have also been made to identify individual differences in emotional responsiveness and hence drive level, including such physiological measures as GSR, heart rate, and muscle action potentials recorded in the experimental situation (Runquist and Ross, 1959; Spence, 1958). The first of these attempts involved selecting subjects prior to the experimental session on the basis of their scores on the MAS, a personality test constructed especially for these studies (Taylor, 1951).

The assumption that an individual's general tendency to exhibit overt or manifest anxiety symptoms would be related to his drive level in the conditioning situation was suggested by experimental investigations of acquired fear or anxiety (Miller, 1951; Mowrer, 1950). The overt manifestations of emotionality exhibited by the animal subjects of these investigations, we noted, have many similarities to the somatic symptoms characteristic of anxiety states in humans, as defined by clinicians. Since, as will be recalled from our earlier discussion, experimentally produced, stimulus defined anxiety had been shown to have drive properties, it seemed reasonable to assume that level of response inferred anxiety in humans might also be related to drive level. A personality test was therefore constructed consisting of items (currently 50 in number) drawn from the Minnesota Multiphasic Personality Inventory (MMPI) that were judged by clinicians to be indicative of manifest anxiety.

While our purpose was to employ the MAS as a measure of drive and to evaluate its usefulness in these terms (thus taking what was later to be called by Cronbach and Meehl (1955) the construct validity approach) it is possible to inquire about the concurrent validity of the scale as an anxiety measure. Briefly, the MAS has been found in a number of studies to have statistically significant relationships with clinical judgments of anxiety and with other anxiety tests (Taylor, 1956; Taylor, 1959). Such findings suggest that our experimental results with the MAS might also be found with groups selected by other anxiety measures.

Returning to consideration of the MAS as an indicator of drive, the empirical expectations derived from our theory are as follows: in simple non-competitive learning situations in which a stimulus elicits a single or highly dominant response tendency, such as in classical conditioning or paired-associates learning in which intralist similarity is low, high anxiety (high drive) groups will perform at a level superior to low anxiety (low drive) groups. In tasks in which the stimuli elicit many response tendencies and the correct response is relatively weak, high anxiety subjects should exhibit inferior performance, at least in the initial stages of learning.

The theoretical derivations of these predictions and a review of the relevant MAS literature may be found elsewhere (Farber, 1954; Taylor, 1956; Sarason, 1960; Spence, 1958). Briefly, substantial confirmation of these hypotheses has been found, for high anxiety groups tend to be superior in performance on tasks with little intra-task competition and inferior on tasks with high competition. It should be noted, however, that except for eyelid conditioning in which the predicted superiority of high anxiety groups has almost invariably been found (Spence, 1962), performance differences between high and low anxiety groups have not always appeared. Nevertheless, on the occasions on which they have been found, the differences have typically been in the predicted direction. This inconsistency in findings may in part be due to the fact that only a minor part of the performance differences among subjects is attributable to variations in MAS scores, other characteristics such as differences in learning ability among the subjects playing a more important role. In addition, our theory is undoubtedly incomplete in the variables it specifies, both with respect to task variables and to properties other than drive level which may differentiate groups with extremely high scores on the MAS from those with extremely low scores.

Several alternative explanations of the empirical data obtained with the MAS have been offered. Eysenck (1957), for example, has suggested that the performance differences in classical conditioning between high and low MAS groups are related neither to differences in drive level nor, in a direct sense, to anxiety as a personality variable. In reaching this conclusion, Eysenck points to his proposal that there are two independent dimensions of personality: neuroticism and introversion-extraversion. Introverts and extraverts, he has further hypothesized, are differentially susceptible to work decrement or reactive inhibition (Hull's I_R), extraverts generating I_R more rapidly with work and dissipating I_R more slowly with rest than introverts. Thus, Eysenck predicts, extraverts should show a poorer performance in classical conditioning than introverts. Although neurotics may have a higher drive level than non-neurotics, Eysenck believes that this source of drive does not contribute to performance in the conditioning situation. Hence, there should be no relationship between degree of neuroticism and conditioning measures.

Although the MAS is highly correlated with Eysenck's test of neuroticism, it also has some degree of relationship to his introversion-extraversion measures (Spence & Spence, 1962). Thus, according to Eysenck, the relationship between MAS scores and conditioning comes about only because of incidental introversion-extraversion differences between MAS groups and is related to I_R and not to drive. Inspection of the empirical data (Spence & Spence, 1963) shows, however, that correlations between performance and introversion-extraversion measures do not tend to be greater in magnitude than those obtained with the MAS, thus lending little support to Eysenck's interpretation. (Attempts to test his hypotheses concerning introversion-extraversion, rather than anxiety, with other types of tasks are another matter which need not concern us here.) What is most instructive to note, perhaps, is

that even among individuals who draw constructs from the same behavior theory and consider only a relatively simple situation like classical conditioning, contradictory theories about personality variables may
still arise.

Another example of an alternative interpretation of the MAS
data within the framework of Hullian behavior theory may be seen
in what might be called the "response interference hypothesis," suggested by Child (1954). This hypothesis emphasizes not only general
drive or D with its "energizing" (multiplicative) properties, but
another aspect of the Hullian motivational complex: drive stimulus or
S_D with its capacity to elicit responses both learned and unlearned,
covert and overt. Among the responses assumed to be elicited by the
S_D associated with anxiety reactions are those that may be described as
task irrelevant: heightened autonomic reactions, covert verbalizations
reflecting self-depreciation, anger, etc. Child hypothesized that high
anxiety subjects are not only higher in drive level than the low anxious
but also exhibit irrelevant response tendencies in greater number or
with more intensity. The direction of performance differences between
high and low anxiety groups is therefore largely dependent on the
degree to which irrelevant response tendencies interfere with performance on a particular task.

Since classical conditioning, involving involuntary or semi-volun-
tary responses, is relatively invulnerable to disruption from irrelevant
response tendencies, superior performance would be predicted for
high anxiety groups, Child agreed, because of their higher drive
level. Tasks involving close attention and voluntary effort, such as
verbal rote learning, are more likely to be susceptible to interference
from irrelevant responses. Thus, Child suggested, high anxiety groups
might be expected to exhibit performance inferiority on tasks of this
general type.

The data available at the time that Child put forward his hypotheses made the latter suggestion not unreasonable. It was given further
plausibility by the investigations of Mandler and Sarason (1952), who
employed a "test anxiety" questionnaire, a scale that is moderately
correlated with the MAS. Also utilizing a response interference
hypothesis, they reported that the performance of subjects scoring
high on their questionnaire tended to be poorer than low scoring
subjects in their experimental situations, particularly under stressful
conditions. Subsequent studies of the MAS, however, failed to reveal
the uniform inferiority of high anxiety groups on all verbal learning

tasks, as Child had predicted. Rather, in line with our drive interpretation, high anxiety subjects tended to be superior in performance on lists or items with minimal competition and to be inferior only on tasks or items with a high degree of intratask competition. The studies obtaining this type of result, it is important to note, were conducted under emotionally neutral conditions.

The drive interpretation does not hold up, however, when groups are compared in situations into which some element of psychological stress has been introduced. Inspection of the literature suggests that in order to account for the data, a more complicated theoretical analysis that incorporates several of the notions outlined above is required. The present writer (1959) has proposed that manipulating the degree of psychological stress in an experimental situation has several major effects, in addition to raising drive level. The first might be described as changes in task-attending behavior. In tasks requiring some degree of voluntary effort, subjects must be cooperative in the sense of attending to the appropriate stimuli and making an attempt to perform the required response. Mildly stressful conditions, such as the use of ego-involving instructions which emphasize the importance of doing well or state that performance reflects a valued characteristic, such as intelligence, may often lead to more persistent effort and attention and hence to better performance. However, emphasis upon doing well may also arouse anxiety (fear of failure) and negative evaluations of performance (failure reports) intensify it. As anxiety, with its D and S_D components, increases in intensity, so does the intensity of the task-irrelevant responses. In situations in which the task is of such a nature that the response to be acquired or performed (e.g., as in verbal rote learning) can be adversely affected by them, these irrelevant responses will lead to performance decrement. Thus, as externally manipulated psychological stress increases, performance might first be expected to rise due to increased effort (task-attending behavior) and then to decrease as anxiety and its associated irrelevant responses are aroused.

Adding the MAS variable to these hypotheses, high anxiety subjects might be described (as Child had suggested) as having a lower threshold for anxiety arousal than the low anxious, tending to react even to mild ego-involving instructions with fear of failure. Thus, while the performance of low anxiety groups would be expected to rise and then decline as stress increases, the period of initial rise in high anxiety groups would be attenuated, if it appears at all.

Should the task be one in which intratask competition is low, high anxiety groups would initially (i.e., under affectively neutral conditions) tend to be superior in performance to low anxiety groups. In both groups, performance decrement would appear less rapidly as stress is increased, due to the opposing effects of increased drive and extratask responses. In situations with a high degree of intratask competition, the reverse would be found, high anxious being initially inferior and both groups showing more performance decrement under stress. A review of the literature concerning the performance under various stress conditions of anxiety groups selected by both the MAS and the Mandler-Sarason questionnaire may be found in Taylor (1959) and I. G. Sarason (1960).

To a certain extent, the series of hypotheses outlined above are *post hoc,* having been developed to fit the empirical data that have been obtained in studies investigating the performance of anxiety groups under stress conditions. Out of a number of alternative explanations that could undoubtedly be devised, these hypotheses were chosen not merely as a device for encompassing these particular findings but also because they are related to a broader system of theoretical notions and permit the integration of a larger set of empirical data than the results of stress studies alone. For example, our notions concerning the inter-action of drive level and intratask competition in verbal learning, which in turn were drawn from Hull-Spence learning theory, are included in the total set of hypotheses. These hypotheses, considered alone, can be extended beyond investigations of the performance of subjects selected by means of the MAS or similar instruments. Mednick (1958), for example, has recently suggested that this kind of interaction between drive level and task complexity may account for some of the anomalies in the behavior of schizophrenics. The same hypotheses have also been used to predict the results of studies that defined drive level by such stimulus manipulations as time pressure (e.g., Castaneda & Lipsitt, 1959).

Similarly, the suggestions concerning task-attending behavior and the interfering role of task-irrelevant responses can be extended into other areas of investigation. As an example, the work of McClelland, Atkinson and their colleagues with the achievement motive might be cited (McClelland, Atkinson, Clark & Lowell, 1953). These investigators have reported that subjects scoring high on their measure of need achievement exhibit better performance on a variety of tasks than low scoring subjects, due to their high level of "motivation," which is said to include not only "energizing" properties but the kinds of properties here called task-attending behavior. If one were to assume that "drive," as defined in the MAS studies, were equivalent to their "motivation," the results of many of the MAS studies could be viewed as contradictory to those obtained in the need achievement studies. The distinction between task-attending behavior and drive not only avoids the apparent inconsistency but reconciles the two sets of data.

SUMMARY AND PROSPECTS

The immediate empirical interests of many psychologists, particularly experimentalists, are primarily concerned with discovering the manner in which environmental variables determine behavior in certain general types of experimental arrangements. Their interests may thus be described as being situationally oriented. If the empirical S-R laws developed about these situations are ever to allow for accurate prediction of the behavior of individuals, it will be necessary, as we indicated earlier, to introduce into these laws variables that take account of the differences among subjects as they come to the experimental situation.

Conversely, psychologists interested in personality phenomena have concentrated their attention on the properties of individuals, with lesser concern for situational variables. But, as the examples given above have demonstrated, the behavior of any given individual depends in part upon the environmental context in which it occurs. Children who have been severely punished for aggression by their parents may exhibit more or less aggressive behavior than other children, depending on where they are; anxiety may facilitate certain kinds of behavior or interfere with it, depending upon environmental factors.

The increasing number of attempts to bring personality variables into the laboratory and to apply laboratory principles to human behavior as it occurs in naturalistic settings suggests a growing awareness that the activities of S-R experimentalists and of those interested in personality are complementary. If learning theories have often been at the center of these attempts to bridge the gap between the two areas, it is perhaps because of the shared interests of both learning and personality theorists in the role of motivational factors, innate and acquired, in determining behavior, as well as in the learning process itself.

As the review of some of the MAS literature suggested, our knowledge of even simple learning situations is far from complete, particularly with respect to individual different variables. Obviously, then, applications of principles derived from these simple situations to such personality phenomena as those suggested by Dollard and Miller are bound to be gross over-simplifications that will require refinement and modification. Investigations stemming from the various kinds of attempts to bring personality and learning theory together have yielded encouraging results to date. Future research, based on the data these studies have provided, should help to point the way to more sophisticated theories.

REFERENCES

BANDURA, A. Psychotherapy as a learning process. *Psychol. Bull.*, 1961, *58*, 143-159.

BARKER, R. G., DEMBO, T., & LEWIN, K. Frustration and regression. An experiment with young children. *Univer. Iowa Stud. Child Welf.*, 1941, *18*, No. 386.

BERGMANN, G. *Philosophy of science.* Madison: Univer. Wisconsin Press, 1957.

BERKUN, M. M. Factors in the recovery from approach-avoidance conflict. *J. exp. Psychol.*, 1957, *54*, 65-73.

CASTANEDA, A., & LIPSITT, L. P. Relation of stress and differential position habits to performance in motor learning. *J. exp. Psychol.*, 1959, *57*, 25-30.

CHILD, I. L. Personality. *Annu. Rev. Psychol.*, 1954, *5*, 149-170.

CRONBACH, L. J., & MEEHL, P. E. Construct validity in psychological tests. *Psychol. Bull.*, 1955, *52*, 281-302.

DOLLARD, J., DOOB, L. W., MILLER, N. E., MOWRER, O. H., & SEARS, R. R. *Frustration and aggression.* New Haven: Yale Univer. Press, 1939.

DOLLARD, J., & MILLER, N. E. *Personality and psychotherapy.* New York: McGraw-Hill, 1950.

EYSENCK, H. J. *The dynamics of anxiety and hysteria.* London: Routledge & Kegan Paul, 1957.

FARBER, I. E. Anxiety as a drive state. In Jones, M. R. (Ed.) *Nebraska symposium on motivation.* Lincoln: Univer. Nebraska Press, 1954.

FEIGL, H. Operationism and scientific method. *Psychol. Rev.*, 1945, *52*, 243-246.

HEMPEL, C. G. The logical analysis of psychology. In Feigl, H., & Sellers, W. *Readings in philosophical analysis.* New York: Appleton-Century-Crofts, 1949.

HOLLENBERG, ELEANOR, & SPERRY, MARGARET. Some antecedents of aggression and effects of frustration in doll play. *Personality*, 1951, *1*, 32-43.

MAHER, B. A. Approach-avoidance conflict: An appraisal. Unpublished manuscript, Harvard Univer., 1962.

MANDLER, G., & SARASON, S. B. A study of anxiety and learning. *J. abnorm. soc. Psychol.* 1952, *74*, 166-173.

MCCLELLAND, D, C., ATKINSON, J. W., CLARK, R. A., & LOWELL, E. L. *The achievement motive.* New York: Appleton-Century-Crofts, 1953.

MEDNICK, S A. A learning theory approach to schizophrenia. *Psychol. Bull.*, 1958, *55*, 316-327.

MEEHL, P. E. *Clinical vs. statistical prediction.* Minneapolis: Univer. Minnesota Press, 1954.

MILLER, N. E. Theory and experiment relating psychoanalytic displacement to stimulus-response generalization. *J. abnorm. soc. Psychol.*, 1948, *43*, 155-176.

MILLER, N E. Learnable drives and rewards. In Stevens, S. S. (Ed.) *Handbook of experimental psychology.* New York: Wiley, 1951.

MILLER, N. E. Liberalization of basic S-R concepts: Extension to conflict behavior, motivation and social learning. In Koch, S. (Ed.) *Psychology: A study of a science,* Study 1, Vol. 2. New York: McGraw-Hill, 1959.

MOWRER, O. H. *Learning theory and personality dynamics.* New York: Ronald, 1950.

MURRAY, E. J. A case study in a behavioral analysis of psychotherapy. *J. abnorm. soc. Psychol.*, 1954, *49*, 305-310.

MURRAY, E. J., & BERKUN, M. M. Displacement as a function of conflict. *J. abnorm. soc. Psychol.*, 1955, *51*, 47-56.

PRATT, C. C. *The logic of modern psychology.* New York: Macmillan, 1939.

RUNQUIST, W. N., & ROSS, L. E. The relation between physiological measures of emotionality and performance in eyelid conditioning. *J. exp. Psychol.*, 1959, *57*, 329-332.

SARASON, I. G. Empirical findings and theoretical problems in the use of anxiety scales. *Psychol. Bull.*, 1960, *57*, 403-415.

SEARS, R R. A theoretical framework for personality and social behavior. *Amer. Psychol.*, 1951, *6*, 476-483.

SPENCE, JANET T., & SPENCE, K. W. Conditioning as related to extraversion, dogmatism, and manifest anxiety. *J. abnorm. soc. Psychol.*, 1963, in press.

SPENCE, K W. The postulates and methods of behaviorism. *Psychol. Rev.*, 1948, *55*, 67-78.

SPENCE, K. W. The empirical basis and theoretical structure of psychology. *Philos. Sci.*, 1957, *24*, 97-108.

SPENCE, K. W. A theory of emotionally based drive (D) and its relation to performance in simple learning situations. *Amer. J. Psychol.*, 1958, *13*, 131-141.

SPENCE, K. W. Anxiety (drive) level and performance in eyelid conditioning. Office of Naval Research: Tech. Report #7, Contr. N-onr-1509(04), 1962.

TAYLOR, JANET A. The relationship of anxiety to the conditioned eyelid response. *J. exp. Psychol.*, 1951, *41*, 81-92.

TAYLOR, JANET A. A personality scale of manifest anxiety. *J. abnorm. soc. Psychol.*, 1953, *48*, 285-290.

TAYLOR, JANET A. Drive theory and manifest anxiety. *Psychol. Bull.*, 1956, *53*, 303-320.

TAYLOR, JANET A. Manifest anxiety, response interference and repression. Paper read at symposium on Experimental Foundations of Clinical Psychology, Univer. Virginia Med. Sch., April, 1959.

TAYLOR, JANET A., & MAHER, B. A. Escape and displacement experience as variables in the recovery from approach-avoidance conflict. *J. comp. physiol. Psychol.*, 1959, *52*, 586-590.

WHITING, J. W. M., & CHILD, I. L. *Child training and personality: a cross-cultural study.* New Haven: Yale Univer. Press, 1953.

2

Perception and Personality

Charles W. Eriksen

It has been nearly fifteen years since the "new look" at perception burst upon the psychological scene. There is some question about how new it was, but nonetheless it was remarkably effective in generating enthusiasm among psychologists and it sparked innumerable dissertations and investigatory experiments. In essence, it directed experimentalists to look at perception not from the traditional structuralist or Gestalt points of view but as a function of personality and personality dynamics.

The impetus for research into the interaction of perception and personality was probably derived more from a Zeitgeist than from any theory or set of theories in the scientific sense. One could view this interest as arising from functionalism in its extension to perceptual behavior or from the influence on psychological thought of personality theories developed out of clinical practice. However, such general attributions lack rigor and in no sense denote the specific theories and empirical studies which comprise a well-defined scientific development.

Long before Bruner and Goodman (1947) and Bruner and Postman (1947a; 1947b) introduced the "new look," scattered research papers offered evidence that motivational factors influenced perception. Ansbacher (1937) had already suggested that a person's values will influence perception of apparent size and Stephens (1931, 1936), in what can still be regarded as very well conceived experiments, demonstrated that personal interest could produce perceptual distortions of the brightness of lights and the size of angles.

Clearly the psychological climate in the thirties was not favorable to the development of a theoretical framework within which perceptual and personality variables could be reconciled. Further evidence that the "new look" was a product of the spirit of the times rather than a culmination of uninterrupted scientific endeavor lies in the fact that Stephens' early work went unnoticed in the fanfare which greeted the studies of Bruner and his associates.

Why did the work of Stephens and other early investigators go almost unremarked, while much more recent research in the same area captured the interest of a large segment of the psychologists interested in personality and in clinical psychology? Certainly among the factors producing the favorable climate in the late forties were the rapid growth in clinical psychology that had taken place during World War II and immediately thereafter, and the widespread acceptance and knowledge of projective devices.

It was a period of optimistic belief that methods for exploring the full range of personality variables were at last in hand, and moreover, it was a time when academic psychology—which had responded coldly to the psychoanalytic method and to Freudian psychology—was becoming increasingly receptive to the notion that motivations, although outside the awareness of the actor, could nevertheless significantly affect behavior. Clinical psychologists enjoyed a high level of confidence in the capacity of instruments such as the Rorschach and the Thematic Apperception Test (TAT) to explore the most obscure and subtle aspects of personality and it even seemed possible that psychology might contribute to a major breakthrough in the field of mental health.

Research in the field of perception and personality fell into two major subdivisions which corresponded with differences in projective techniques. One was the search for individual differences in perceptual behavior and the other was the investigation of the effects of motivational states or needs upon the perception of objects. Both of these problems have their parallels in the projective tests.

The Rorschach is mainly a perceptual test of personality, in that the manner in which an individual structures the ink-blots and the use he makes of form, color and shading are supposed to reveal significant information about his personality structure. The TAT, on the other hand, is primarily a measure of needs as revealed in the interpretation or perception of ambiguous material. The test assumes that the individual, in interpreting the somewhat ambiguous pictures, projects or distorts his interpretation in keeping with his own needs and adjustment mechanisms, an assumption that is also involved in the interpretation of content in the Rorschach test. Thus in many ways need-in-perception experimentation was stimulated by the clinician's desire to demonstrate experimentally what he felt he already knew as truth.

INDIVIDUAL DIFFERENCES AS REVEALED
IN PERCEPTUAL BEHAVIOR

The presence of individual differences in perceptual behavior was recognized early in psychology. Psychologists interested in the fields of perception and sensory processes have characteristically taken consider- able pains to devise experimental situations that are sufficiently simple and controlled to minimize these individual differences, in the interest of studying more accurately the phenomena with which they are pri- marily concerned. However, except for isolated experiments, little attempt was made to relate these individual differences in perception systematically to other aspects of behavior or personality. Thurstone's (1944) extensive factor analysis of perceptual tasks was predominantly oriented toward isolating or detecting general factors of perception but was not particularly concerned with personality correlates of these perceptual factors. There were no personality tests included in the bat- tery that would have made such relationships detectable. Rorschach's (1942) work on the development of his ink-blot test represents perhaps the most extensive and direct attempt of early investigators to relate systematically personality traits and perception, although much work in his area had also been done by German typologists.

Early in the modern revival of interest in experimentation on need in perception, Klein (Klein, Schlesinger & Meister, 1951) drew atten- tion to the presence of perceptual styles and perceptual modes of han- dling threatening or emotional material. In subsequent work, Klein (1958) and his associates have gone on to show the presence of a personality dimension labeled "leveling" (versus "sharpening") which is revealed not only in perceptual recognition behavior but in perceptual judgmental tasks as well.

The excellent work of Witkin and associates (1954) on the per- ception of verticality has revealed some of the potentials in perceptual approaches to personality dimensions or traits. They have shown that a common dimension underlies an ability to orient toward verticality in the absence of normal visual cues and in the perception of Gott- schaldt imbedded figures, and have related these abilities to various manifestations of personality in non-perceptual situations. However, Elliott's (1961) work has suggested that the relationships between some of these personality measures and perceptual behavior may not be quite as high as originally reported, and he further suggested that an intellective type of factor may underlie performance on some of these tasks.

There has been a tendency, often implicit, to view individual differences revealed in perceptual behavior as somehow reflecting more basic or fundamental dimensions or styles of personality than are found in the more common personality factors. However, there is little logical or empirical justification for such a position. In virtually all experimental situations individual differences constitute the largest single source of variance, typically about ninety per cent. It is not surprising that these individual differences are frequently found to have common sources of variance with extra-experimental behavior. In general, the less rigorous and complete the control on an experimental task, the greater the probability that measures of performance can be shown to correlate with more general personality traits.

To deny that traits found in perceptual behavior have any more fundamental status than traits revealed in nonperceptual behavior is not to deny the importance of the work in this area. From this work has come improved methods of measuring personality as well as greater understanding of the structure and pervasiveness of personality traits.

NEED AND PERCEPTION

For many reasons the major research emphasis in the field of perception and personality has centered around the effects of needs or motivational variables upon perception. Here again there have been two distinct approaches. One line of investigation involves study of the effects of various need states upon the degree of distortion of color, size, or other dimensions of perceptual stimuli. The other has been concerned with the recognition thresholds for neutral and various need-related objects or stimuli.

In the former approach, the work has been much more diversified and on the whole less systematic than in the latter. The work of McClelland and his associates is an exception. Beginning with the early experimental work of McClelland and Atkinson (1948), showing the effect of experimentally manipulated hunger on the perception of ambiguous stimuli, these investigators have systematically developed this approach to the present stage where sensitive measures of needs such as achievement and affiliation can be reliably and validly scored from certain TAT cards.

The extensive work on the reflection of need states in the perceptual interpretation of ambiguous stimuli has been well summarized and presented elsewhere (Atkinson, 1958) and will not be dealt with further in this chapter, other than to point out that in addition to potentially effective measures of human motivational variables, this research has also suggested promising leads toward the understanding of defense mechanisms. The work of Clark and Sensibar (1955) has illustrated the interplay of guilt and inhibiting factors in need expression and work on sleep deprivation. Murray (1959) has shown that with increasing periods of need, the expression of goal objects in perceptual interpretations of TAT cards does not become greater but is actually inhibited. Similar findings have been found in the case of food deprivation (Lazarus, Yousem & Arenberg, 1953) suggesting the same type of inhibitory mechanism that may exist in more extreme forms in certain of the neuroses.

PERCEPTUAL VIGILANCE AND
PERCEPTUAL DEFENSE

While research on the projective expression of needs has been active and fruitful, its development is in a certain sense parallel to that of the need and perception field. Historically, its antecedents go beyond the "new look" to perceptual behavior; it is more directly a development of work with projective measures of personality. Major interest in the need and perception problem has centered around the concepts of perceptual vigilance and perceptual defense. Around these concepts a major controversy has developed, and a new research enthusiasm—"unconscious discrimination"—grew from the debate.

The concepts of perceptual vigilance and defense were introduced in a series of three articles by Bruner and Postman (1947a, 1947b) and Postman, Bruner and McGinnies (1948).[1] These terms were used to describe and perhaps explain [2] various observed differences in the

---

[1] A third principle, that of value resonance, was also advanced by these experimenters, but little further was made of it, either by themselves or in the research of others.

[2] Postman has subsequently denied that vigilance and defense were meant as explanatory principles, but as Brown (1961) points out, it is difficult to appreciate Postman's distinction when reading his original papers.

tachistoscopic duration necessary for the recognition of threatening or emotional stimuli as opposed to neutral stimuli. In the first of these articles, Bruner and Postman invoked the concept of vigilance as an explanation for their finding that stimuli associated with experimentally produced anxiety had lower recognition thresholds than neutral stimuli. They suggested the principle of perceptual vigilance, whereby stimuli important to the organism were enhanced in perception and recognized sooner. The concept of perceptual defense appeared in their subsequent two articles, where the tachistoscopic durations necessary for recognition of emotional words or words representing low values (as assessed by the Allport-Vernon Study of Values) were found to have higher recognition thresholds than neutral words or words from high value areas.

In the second of these studies Bruner and Postman administered a word association test to their subjects and then subsequently studied the tachistoscopic durations necessary for the recognition of words with long, medium and short association times. They found that for some subjects words with long association times, indicating emotional disturbance, required much longer durations for recognition than words with medium or short association times. They termed this heightened recognition threshold "perceptual defense" and likened it to the process of repression, whereby anxiety-provoking stimuli were defended against in perception or prevented from attaining conscious awareness in order to minimize anxiety. They also found, however, that in certain subjects long association time words had lower thresholds for recognition. They invoked their principle of "perceptual vigilance" to account for this lowering of thresholds for affect-laden words, pointing out that in some subjects there was a range of emotionality beyond which defense did not operate but was replaced by sensitization.

In the Bruner, Postman and McGinnies study the duration thesholds for the recognition of words representing the value areas in the Allport-Vernon Study were compared with individual subjects' scores on this test. They found a correspondence between a subject's score on the respective value areas and his recognition of words denoting these values. Subjects who had a high score in the theoretical value area, for example, had lower duration thresholds for words from this value area and had higher thresholds for words from value areas on which they scored quite low. The concepts of vigilance and defense were again invoked to describe or explain these results, with vigilance assumed for low thresholds for the high value areas and perceptual defense for the higher thresholds for low value areas.

One might question at this point why two separate concepts were needed to describe the results. Could not a concept of differing degrees of vigilance be sufficient? For example, with respect to words from different value areas one might say that for high value areas a person has a high degree of perceptual vigilance that becomes correspondingly less as his interest in an area decreases. If the only evidence was the difference in recognition scores there would be some justification for the parsimony of a single concept.

However, Bruner et al felt the concept of defense was necessary to account for two factors in the data. First, they found that for some emotion-laden words thresholds were lowered, while for other words and for other subjects they were elevated. Second, in addition to the recognition thresholds the subjects' prerecognition guesses in response to words with high thresholds suggested a defensive flavor. The authors likened it to the concept of repression, where there seemed to be an active inhibitory process operating rather than mere differential sensitization.

This implication of an active inhibition of recognition in perception and its analogy to the clinical concept of repression became much clearer in the study by McGinnies (1949). Here the perceptual duration thresholds for recognition of a group of neutral words and a group of taboo words such as *whore, bitch, belly, Kotex*, etc. was studied. In addition to obtaining the recognition thresholds, McGinnies concurrently measured the subject's GSR during the prerecognition and the recognition trials. Not only did he find that the taboo words tended to require higher durations for recognition but also subjects gave greater GSRs on the prerecognition trials to the taboo words than they did for the neutral words. The higher recognition thresholds for the taboo words were considered a manifestation of perceptual defense and the greater GSR accompanying the prerecognition guesses to the taboo stimuli was considered to be not only an indication of the active nature of the inhibition occurring in perception but also to suggest an unconscious detection or manifestation of anxiety elicited by these emotional words.

There were, however, much more prosaic interpretations available for McGinnies' results, as Howes and Solomon (1950) were quick to point out. They had two main criticisms. The first concerned the question of intentional response suppression on the part of the subject. This is a rather telling criticism, if we view the experiment from the point of view of the subject. Consider the typical undergraduate brought into the experimental situation by a professor. The subject is exposed to fragmentary perceptions through tachistoscopic exposure. Let us assume that the word "house" is projected and the subject sees what looks like a medium-length word with an "h" at the beginning and what looks like an "s" toward the end. Let us say that he tries to think of some word that will fit these partial cues and comes up with "house." The next word exposed is "whore." He may pick up a fragmentary perception of something resembling a "w" and maybe an "h" and he guesses "whom." On the next occurrence of this stimulus word he actually says to himself, "My God, that looked like 'whore,' but it couldn't be. The professor wouldn't show a word like that." And so he waits for a longer duration before hazarding a guess, or overtly he says "whom" again. Of course one would expect a very sizeable GSR to accompany this rather startling subjective experience. On the subsequent exposure he may be even more certain the word is "whore" but he is not going to risk saying "whore" and being incorrect. After all, what would the experimenter think of somebody who would say a word like that when it really wasn't the word that was being shown? This possibility of deliberate response suppression is sufficient to account not only for the longer durations required for recognition of the taboo words but also for the greater GSRs accompanying the prerecognition response to these words.

The second criticism that Howes and Solomon leveled at McGinnies' experiment concerned the fact that the taboo and neutral words used differed markedly in familiarity or frequency of past occurrence in the subjects' experience. Howes and Solomon showed that the frequency with which the taboo words occurred in the Thorndike-Lorge (1944) word counts was appreciably lower than that for the neutral words. They advanced the hypothesis that differential recognition thresholds for words were a function of the frequency with which these words had been experienced in the past.

This criticism, it is to be noted, was not only of McGinnies' experiment but also of the previous work done on visual duration thresholds for the recognition of words. The phenomena of perceptual vigilance and of defense, it would seem, could both be explained as a function of the differential frequency with which the stimuli had been experienced in the subjects' past history. Stimuli of high frequency of prior occurrence would have low visual duration thresholds while infrequent or rare stimuli would be expected to have high thresholds. Solomon and Howes then went on in further studies (Solomon & Howes, 1951; Howes & Solomon, 1951) to demonstrate that duration thresholds for the recognition of words could be predicted by the Thorndike-Lorge tables of word frequency. The assumption was made in using these tables that they provided an adequate approximation to the frequency with which the subjects had been exposed to various written words during their past history.

In essence the frequency theory of Solomon and Howes considers perception as a response and therefore susceptible to learning as are other responses. The assumption is made that the more frequently a response is practiced the greater its habit-strength or the lower its evocation threshold. Thus, because we have perceived the word "house" much more frequently than we have perceived the word "beatific," we will, in a tachistoscopic situation, perceive the word "house" at a shorter level of exposure or in the presence of much more impoverished cues than would be required for the perception of "beatific." This, then, is the mechanism by which differential recognition thresholds are assumed to occur.

As we shall see later in this chapter, this interpretation of perception as a response following a single law of learning—namely, that of frequency—is at the very best a gross oversimplification of perceptual behavior and of the evidence in the field of perception. We might here, however, take note of two points with respect to the role of frequency in perceptual recognition. First, the role of frequency as assessed by the Thorndike-Lorge word count tables in determining perceptual recognition of words has been greatly over-emphasized, and second, the Thorndike-Lorge word counts have some serious inadequacies as estimates of the frequency with which college students have had past experiences with different words.

With respect to the first point, we might begin by looking at the original papers of Howes and Solomon (1950, 1951) in which the evidence for a relation between recognition threshold and Thorndike-Lorge frequency was presented. These authors reported correlations of the order of —.7 between the logarithm to the base 10 of frequency in the Thorndike-Lorge magazine and general semantic counts and the duration of tachistoscopic exposure necessary for word recognition. Fortunately, the authors not only report the correlation coefficients but also present the scatter diagrams. Careful examination of the latter reveals that practically all of the relationship is due to a difference between words having 0 or very low frequencies in the Thorndike-Lorge counts and words having high frequencies. If one considers words in the frequency range of 10 to 3,000 occurrences per million in the Thorndike-Lorge count and examines only this part of the scatter diagram, it is seen that there is virtually no relationship between Thorndike-Lorge frequency and recognition threshold.

The use of the Thorndike-Lorge word counts as a measure or indication of word familiarity and as a means of controlling or matching words on familiarity for experiments on word recognition is in itself an extremely questionable procedure. The Thorndike-Lorge counts are based upon the frequency of occurrence of words in childrens' books or popular adult magazines and are designed for the use of teachers as a guide to what words it is important to teach a child at different age levels. Perhaps the Lorge magazine count is more appropriate, but again it is considerably out-of-date and it is really questionable how representative it is for the population of college freshmen and sophomores upon whom most of the perceptual recognition experiments are carried out.

The Thorndike-Lorge tables are particularly inappropriate as a control for the frequency of "dirty" or taboo words. Unfortunately, most of the experimenters who have attempted to study differential recognition thresholds for taboo and neutral words, have, in view of the Solomon and Howes criticisms, taken the precaution of matching the taboo and neutral words according to the Thorndike-Lorge frequencies of occurrence. If this procedure were merely ineffective one could overlook it as a form of superstitious behavior, but actually the use of this supposed control seriously biases the experiment in the direction of negative results. If the familiarity of taboo words is seriously underestimated by the Thorndike-Lorge tables, then matching a neutral word and a taboo word according to these frequencies almost insures that the taboo word has a much greater degree of familiarity to the subject than the corresponding neutral word. This in itself would almost preclude obtaining a positive perceptual defense finding in such studies.

That the Thorndike-Lorge tables do grossly underestimate the frequency or familiarity of taboo words is suggested in a pilot study carried out in our laboratory some time ago. A large sample of words covering the entire frequency range from the Thorndike-Lorge semantic count were selected and a multiple choice vocabulary test devised for them. A selection of so-called taboo words was also obtained; many of them were so infrequent that they were not listed in the Thorndike-Lorge tables, but others varied in frequencies to as high as or higher than 30 in a million. These also were included for definition in the multiple choice vocabulary test. The assumption was made that familiarity or frequency of past experience with a word should correlate rather well with the number of people who could correctly define the meaning of the word. This was our finding for the neutral words. The correlation between Thorndike-Lorge frequencies and the number of correct definitions in a sample of over a hundred undergraduates was .57. However, when the correlation between the Thorndike-Lorge frequencies and the number of subjects correctly defining the meaning was examined for the taboo words, the correlation was found to be .03[3].

By way of summary we may note that the empirical relationship between frequency of past occurrence and recognition threshold has been amply demonstrated, although the magnitude of this relationship has undoubtedly been considerably overestimated. To attempt to explain all the relationships obtained between needs or motives and recognition thresholds for corresponding need-related stimuli as being primarily or solely due to differential frequencies of prior occurrence is essentially equivalent to saying that frequency of occurrence is the only principle of learning.

As was pointed out above, the frequency argument is based upon the assumption that perception is a response and that it is modified by learning via frequency of prior occurrences. This is, of course, to deny or leave no place for the differential history of positive and negative reinforcement associated with different percepts. If perception is to be considered as a learned response then we should expect it also to be modifiable by the other factors that determine other forms of learning. When we permit the occurrence of differential reinforcement to affect the learning of this perceptual response, then we have again opened the door to the possible phenomena of perceptual vigilance and perceptual defense. In other words, we are now in a position where we might attribute perceptual vigilance to the effects of positive reinforcement upon perceptual responses and perceptual defense to anxiety-

[3] The lack of correlation for the taboo words is not solely due to the reduced frequency range. If the correlation of the neutral words in the frequency range of 0-30 is computed, the relationship actually increases to .67.

provoking or negative reinforcement. As will be seen below, such a conception fits more closely with the data, although its application will have to be somewhat modified.

PERCEPTUAL DEFENSE AND PSYCHOLOGICAL DEFENSE MECHANISMS

As has been seen above, perceptual defense as applied by Bruner, Postman and McGinnies implies a definite relationship to the more general area of personality dynamics and defensive mechanisms as clinically conceived. In borrowing from these concepts it is unfortunate these experimenters did not draw more extensively upon the knowledge and ideas from personality and clinical theory, for if they had more systematically and thoroughly related their concept of perceptual defense to the clinical conception of defense, a large number of needless experiments and controversies could have been avoided.

Eriksen (1951a, 1951b, 1954b) was the first systematically to relate perceptual defense phenomena to clinical conceptions of defense mechanisms. He pointed out that the clinical concept of repression is more sophisticated than to asume that all people or even a majority of people automatically repress any sexual or aggressive ideation, or that all anxiety-arousing thoughts or feelings are repressed. Instead, repression is a defense mechanism used sometimes by some people to handle anxiety-arousing thoughts or feelings whose anxiety-provoking nature are a function of the individual's own unique past experiences. Thus one would not expect a great deal of communality among people in terms of the kind of stimuli that should lead to repression. Furthermore, theories of personality dynamics also recognize that there are other types of defensive mechanisms. Repression is not the only way individuals defend against ego-threatening stimulation.

Intellectualization, reaction formation and projection are defensive mechanisms that one might expect actually to lead to a sensitization for a stimulus related to the conflict. In the instance of reaction formation, the person manifesting this defense seems to be particularly alert to finding and stamping out the evil that he denies in himself. Similarly, in the case of projection, those manifesting this defense are considered to be hyper-alert to detecting the presence of the defended-against impulse in others. Intellectualization frequently leads to a considerable preoccupation with the subject matter of the unacceptable impulse.

These differences in defensive mechanisms would be expected to have different perceptual concomitants. In a case of repression or denial one might expect a tendency for the subject to manifest avoidance or higher duration thresholds for stimuli related to the sources of conflict. On the other hand, those manifesting defenses of intellectualization, reaction formation or projection might be expected to show a lower duration threshold for anxiety-related stimuli.

It is clinically naive to assume that even among subjects who characteristically employ avoidance or repressive defenses that *any* source of anxiety will be defended against. Defensive mechanisms are learned techniques and it is to be expected that in the learning process the subject also learns the types of situations or stimuli against which they are apt to be effective or rewarding. These mechanisms would be expected to be maximally effective against the subject's own subjective train of thought or memories and associations. They would be valueless against the perception of a charging tiger. Thus the choice of anxiety stimuli and the context in which they are presented must be so selected as to permit the defense to be effective and not in conflict with the subject's need to behave in a reasonable manner. It must be remembered that defenses are subtle devices, not to be revealed or studied by sledgehammer methods.

In view of these considerations, an experimental attempt to show that repression manifests itself at the perceptual level by higher thresholds for the recognition of threat-related stimuli (perceptual defense) must meet certain requirements. First, independent operations must exist to show that the stimuli for which perceptual defense is expected are indeed anxiety-arousing for the individual subjects in the experiment. Second, it is necessary, again through independent criteria, to show that the subject has or uses avoidance defenses.

The Postman, Bruner and McGinnies (1948) and McGinnies (1949) experiments do not meet either of these criteria. In the first of these studies, the application of the term "perceptual defense" to account for the higher recognition thresholds for words representing values areas of low interest to the subjects would seem to have little or no relation to the clinical conception of repression. Even if the subjects had been shown to respond to ego-threat with characteristic avoidance defenses, there seems little justification for assuming that a value in which a subject has low interest is ego-threatening or anxiety-arousing to this subject. It seems more likely that the results of this experiment are due to differences in familiarity with the words of different value areas which in turn might be expected to correspond with the subject's interests, as well as differences in availability of these value words as responses to the fragmentary cues the subject received during tachistoscopic exposures.

In the McGinnies study there was again no attempt to take into account individual differences in the use of defense mechanisms and also there was no independent means for assuring that the taboo stimuli employed were indeed anxiety-arousing for all or even a majority of the subjects used. There is little justification for assuming that words like "belly" and "Kotex" would generate enough anxiety in the average college subject to lead to repression or repressive-like defensive measures. The results of this study are most likely attributable (as Howes and Solomon suggest), to the subject's deliberate response suppression arising from the possible embarrassment in incorrectly verbalizing a taboo word.

The Bruner and Postman (1947) study was the only one of the experiments introducing the concept of perceptual defense that nearly satisfies the first requirement. Here the perceptual stimuli were selected for individual subjects on the basis of association times to the words on a word association test. Since word association techniques have long been recognized in clinical usage as an effective technique for determining psychic sore spots or areas of conflict, there is some justification for assuming that the perceptual stimuli in this experiment were indeed anxiety-arousing or emotion-producing for the individual subjects. However, no provision was made in this study for possible individual differences in the way the emotion or threat was handled by the subjects. The importance of these individual differences in response to anxiety is revealed in the findings of these experimenters that for some subjects recognition thresholds were high for words with long association times whereas for other subjects long association-time words showed a lower recognition threshold relative to words with medium association times.

The failure of these early studies to test adequately the concept of perceptual defense in relation to the concept of repression is to a degree understandable. The clinical concept of repression has never been too clear nor has the general theory of psychological defenses. However, as we shall see below, work on perceptual defense has done much to sharpen the clinical concept of defensive mechanisms and has yielded valuable material in terms of understanding their functioning. The importance of satisfying the two requirements in an experimental design on perceptual defense would now seem self-evident, although there are still experimenters who report studies supposedly disproving the phenomena which do not meet either or both of these requirements. As Brown (1961) has perceptively pointed out, failure to satisfy both of these requirements in a design renders an experiment incapable of testing the perceptual defense hypothesis.

Although not yet generally recognized, one of the most important contributions of need-in-perception research has been the development of an effective experimental technique for studying personality dynamics and psychological defenses. Our understanding of psychopathology and neurosis has progressed little beyond the rather crude formulations of Freud. A large factor in our lack of progress in this area has been the difficulty of devising experimental methods whereby defensive mechanisms could be studied and analyzed in the laboratory. Nearly all of the experimental efforts in this area have centered around the single mechanism of repression using various learning and memory techniques. The methods that are effective are for the most part quite cumbersome. Thus, if the perceptual recognition task could be shown to be an effective and valid method of demonstrating defensive mechanisms under laboratory situations, we would be in a position to identify the presence of these defenses in laboratory subjects, explore how they operate and investigate their antecedent conditions.

Fortunately, there is an impressive array of experimental evidence that defensive mechanisms as clinically conceived do reveal their presence in perceptual recognition behavior. In a series of experiments, Eriksen and his associates have shown quite clearly the relationship between defense mechanisms as clinically conceived and perceptual recognition behavior. Not only have these experiments revealed that defenses can be studied through perceptual recognition but also some major steps have been taken in tracing out personality characteristics associated with different types of defensive reaction and the separation of different defensive effects on perceptual recognition.

In the first of these studies, Eriksen (1951a) used psychiatric patients who were selected on the basis of having problems in specified need areas and in whom avoidance defense mechanisms might be expected to be operating. The amount of emotional disturbance in the three need areas of aggression, homosexuality and dependence was assessed by a modified word association technique, and disturbance scores on this test were then related to the subjects' perceptual recognition threshold for pictures depicting neutral and need-related scenes. Patients with high disturbance indicators on a need area were found

to require longer exposure intervals for recognition of the corresponding need-related pictures than for neutral pictures.

In another study, Eriksen (1951b) found that emotional stimuli
did not necessarily lead to higher perceptual recognition thresholds.
Subjects who were found to show extensive overt aggressive behavior
and to express freely aggressive content in stories about TAT pictures
were found to have lower recognition thresholds for pictures depicting
aggressive content than for neutral pictures. This individual difference
response to emotional stimuli was further substantiated in an experiment
by Lazarus, Eriksen and Fonda (1951). Here psychiatric out-patients
were employed as subjects and were classified on the basis of their
therapeutic interviews and other clinical tests as either sensitizers or
repressors, depending upon whether they characteristically responded
to anxiety in terms of intellectualization or rumination about the
threat or whether they tended to avoid and deny thoughts and ideas
related to the conflict sources. These investigators found that the
patients classified as sensitizers tended to give freely aggressive and
sexual endings to a sentence completion test whereas those characterized
as repressors tended to block or to distort into innocuous forms sentence
completion stems that would normally suggest either aggressive or
sexual completions. Further, when perfromance on the sentence completion test was compared with auditory perception of hostile and
sexual sentences heard against a noise background, the sensitizers were
superior to the repressors in recognition of the emotional content.

A more clear-cut demonstration of the relation between repression
as conceived in memory and perceptual recognition behavior is found
in an experiment (Eriksen, 1952) where performance on a somewhat
traditional memory repression study was subsequently compared with
behavior on a perceptual recognition task. A group of freshman pre-
medical students who might be assumed to be strongly motivated to
perceive themselves as intelligent were threatened by manipulated
failure on a pseudointelligence test. Their subsequent recall for items
on which they had been successful relative to items upon which they
had failed was determined and compared with a control group. On
the basis of this comparison it was apparent that the experimental
manipulation of failure had been successful. Subjects were then selected
who showed an extreme preponderance of recall of either successful
items or failed items. These two groups of subjects were then administered a word association test and in a subsequent session their

recognition thresholds for long, medium and short association time words were determined. It was found that subjects who were predominantly success recallers on the memory study showed higher recognition thresholds for long association time words whereas subjects who predominantly recalled their failures showed no significant relationship between recognition thresholds and association time.

There have been numerous studies by other investigators which have also revealed individual differences in perceptual recognition of anxiety-related material. Postman and Solomon (1950) reported that some of their subjects showed a significantly lower threshold for anagram solutions on which they had failed while other subjects showed significantly higher recognition thresholds for the failed solutions. Similarly Spence (1957a, 1957b) found individual differences in terms of either facilitation or impairment of recognition of words when the emotionality or threat of the words had been experimentally manipulated, again by means of failure or success on an anagrams test supposedly measuring intelligence. (In all of these experiments it is to be noted that the question of stimulus frequency is well-controlled by the experimental manipulation of the emotionality of the stimulus.)

Evidence that the individual differences in perception of anxiety-relevant stimuli are reliable has been presented by Stein (1953) and by Singer (1956). Stein demonstrated that a subject's recognition behavior for one set of anxiety and neutral stimuli significantly and appreciably predicted his behavior on subsequent sets of stimuli. Subjects who were found to require longer exposures for the perception of aggressive stimuli on a first stimulus set were found, by and large, to show this same pattern on subsequent, different sets of hostile and neutral stimuli. Similarly, subjects who showed facilitation for aggressive material tended to continue to show this facilitation on subsequent tests.

Singer selected neutral and emotional words on the basis of associative reaction times. For half of the selected words, thresholds were measured in the first session, and for the remainder in a session two weeks later. He reports a significant positive correlation between subjects' performance on the first half and the second half, even when scores were adjusted for differences in perceptual acuity.

While these studies did not make use of an outside criterion of the subjects' preferred mechanism of defense nor look for personality correlates that might predict these individual differences, nonetheless the patterns of the findings certainly are commensurate with those of the sensitizers and repressors of Lazarus, Eriksen and Fonda and the completed-incompleted task recallers of Eriksen.

Confirmation of the relation of these individual differences in perceptual recognition to clinical conceptions of defense are found in the studies of other investigators. Carpenter, Weiner, and Carpenter (1956), in a study similar to that of Lazarus, Eriksen, and Fonda, selected groups of repressors and sensitizers using the sentence completion test. Subsequent recognition thresholds were determined for words of neutral, sexual and aggressive content, and it was found that subjects with a tendency to repress sexual completions as determined by the sentence completion test had significantly higher thresholds for sexual words than did those subjects who showed a sensitization pattern on the sentence completion test. Similar results were obtained for aggressive stimuli. Kleinman (1957) used subjects with a hysterical hearing loss and compared auditory recognition thresholds for neutral and emotional stimuli. The hysteric patients showed higher recognition thresholds for emotional stimuli whereas a control group composed of patients with partial organic deafness showed no difference between the two classes of stimuli.

Blum (1955) and Nelson (1955) made use of the Blackie pictures not only to detect areas of anxiety but also to determine the type of defensive mechanism employed by the subject in this conflict area. They were successful in relating perceptual recognition behavior to the clinically assessed areas of conflict and defense.

Eriksen and his associates have been successful in relating the sensitizer-repressor variable to a hysteria-psychasthenia dimension as measured by the corresponding scales in the MMPI. In current clinical conceptions of neurosis the mechanism of denial or repression is predominantly associated with the hysteric while intellectualizing, rationalizing defenses are supposedly characteristic of the obsessive-compulsive or psychasthenic neurotic. In one study, Eriksen (1954) found a correlation between a composite of the hysteria-psychasthenia scales and recall of completed-incompleted tasks where the tasks had been administered under ego-threatening conditions. In this experiment, those scoring high on the hysteria pole tended predominantly to favor successful tasks in their recall while those scoring at the psychasthenia end of the dimension favored incompleted or failed tasks over successful ones.

A further link in the chain of evidence connecting the repressor-

sensitizer dimension with the hysteria-psychasthenia and clinical conceptions of defenses was provided in a study by Eriksen and Davids
(1956). Here it was shown that scores on the hysteria-psychasthenia
dimension were significantly and appreciably related to clinical assessments of extroversion and the use of repression. Eriksen and Brown
(1957) then extended the linkage back to perceptual recognition
behavior in an experiment in which they found that subjects high on
the psychasthenia scale of the MMPI tended to have lower perceptual
recognition thresholds for words representing experimentally failed
tasks whereas the low psychasthenia subjects (hysterics) had higher
recognition thresholds for these items.

The relation of the hysteria-psychasthenia scales to differential
response to ego threat has been well-substantiated by other investigators.
Mathews and Wertheimer (1958) found essentially the same relationships between the hysteria and psychasthenia scales and perceptual
recognition of threatening words as did Eriksen and Brown. Carlson
(1954) found that subjects high on the hysteria pole tended to recall
fewer disturbing words in a learning experiment, and Truax (1957)
reports that the repressors forget more in response to implied failure
on a learning task.

A number of other investigators have made deductions based
upon the differences in defensive reaction of the repressors and sensitizers and extended these to other aspects of behavior. Altrocchi,
Parsons and Dickoff (1960) have shown that repressors and sensitizers
differ in self-ideal discrepancy. They found that sensitizers have more
hostile and submissive self-concepts than repressors and therefore a
greater discrepancy between self and ideal self. Repressors, on the
other hand, tended to have positive evaluations of the self. Gordon
has found meaningful differences in the interpersonal predictions of
repressors and sensitizers (1957) and in the stability of the assumed
similarity response set (1959). In this latter study, Gordon found
that repressors tend to assume similarity between self and partner
more frequently than do sensitizers when predicting responses to a
personal inventory. Altrocchi (1961) has confirmed and further extended these findings showing again the usefulness of the distinction
between the repressor and the sensitizer.

In sum, these studies and others have succeeded in demonstrating
first of all a consistency in defensive reaction within individuals that
extends across learning, perceptual and interpersonal situations. It is
to be noted, however, that "repressor-sensitizer" is a dimension and

not a dichotomy. The marked consistency in defense reaction that pervades these various aspects of behavior would be expected to occur only in extreme groups such as have been typically used in the above experiments. One would anticipate that the majority of people would be inbetween on this continuum and would show greater diversity in their responses to ego threat.

The relationship of the hysteria-psychasthenia or repressor-sensitizer dimension to Eysenck's introversion-extroversion has been noted by Eriksen (1954a) and Altrocchi (1961). The similarities of the sensitizers to Eysenck's (1947) findings concerning neurotic introverts are quite apparent, as are the relations of the experimentally determined characteristics of the repressors to Eysenck's, neurotic extroverts. A further suggestion of the interrelationships of these dimensions is reported in an experiment by Brown (1961), where perceptual recognition differences comparable to those between sensitizers and repressors were related to the neuroticism and extroversion scales of the Maudsley Personality Inventory. Also, Inglis (1961) has speculated in an interesting way upon these possible interrelations.

EXPLANATIONS OF THE PERCEPTUAL DEFENSE
PHENOMENA

The evidence surveyed in the preceding section comprises a convincing testimonial as to the genuineness of the perceptual defense phenomena. It demonstrates that when experiments employ adequate precautions to insure that perceptual stimuli are indeed anxiety-arousing for the individual subjects and take into account the individual differences in defenses, defensive mechanisms, as clinically conceived, do reveal themselves in the perceptual recognition of stimuli. But if we accept the genuineness of the perceptual defense phenomena then we are faced with a need to explain the mechanism or the means by which it operates.

Before examining some of the proposed explanations of perceptual defense we should note that because of the large amount of evidence relating perceptual defense phenomena to clinical defenses, any explanation of perceptual defense should also be an explanation of defensive mechanisms in general. The evidence is impressive enough by now to indicate that perceptual defense is one manifestation of the more general ego defensive processes. Many of the explanations that have been advanced for perceptual defense have neglected this consideration.

The frequency explanation that we discussed above attempts to explain the phenomena as arising from differing degrees of familiarity or frequency of past experience with the stimulus. Many of the defects of the frequency explanation have been noted, but we are now in a position to point out that the most serious weakness of this explanation lies in its failure to take into account the large number of studies summarized in the preceding section. It is exceedingly difficult to see how a frequency explanation could be extended to cover the results of experiments such as those of Eriksen and Brown (1956), Postman and Solomon (1950) and Spence (1957a; 1957b), where anxiety was experimentally attached to the stimuli. Here the stimuli were of approximately equal familiarity to the subject and of equal recency of past experience. Nevertheless, in these studies differences were found in recognition of the stimuli depending upon whether or not they had been associated with success or failure.

It is further difficult to see how the frequency explanation could handle the consistent individual differences that have been found in perceptual defense behavior. Why, for example, would one expect repressors or subjects scoring high on the hysteria scale of the MMPI to have had low familiarity or low frequency of past experience with essentially the same stimuli for which the sensitizers or high psychasthenia subjects show a high degree of familiarity? Perhaps it is a manifestation of perceptual selectivity in those who have advocated a frequency explanation for the phenomena, since they have managed successfully to ignore the experimental evidence where care was taken to insure the emotional nature of the stimuli for the individual subjects and independent criteria were used to predict whether or not the subject would show defense or sensitization.

One of the more popular explanations for perceptual defense has assumed a subception-like process. Drawing from clinical ideas concerning the properties of the unconscious, the assumption has been made that the human subject is capable of unconsciously perceiving or discriminating among stimuli that are of too low an intensity or too short a time duration to yield conscious discriminations. In other words, the unconscious mind detects the presence of an anxiety-laden stimulus and sets into operation defensive processes designed to prevent the conscious recognition of the stimulus. Such explanations are advocated by McGinnies (1949) and most explicitly by Blum (1955). The Lazarus and McCleary (1951) subception experiment seemed to provide an experimental basis for such an assumption of unconscious autonomic discrimination.

A critical survey of the experimental evidence, however, does not support the existence of unconscious discriminations sensitive enough to account for perceptual defense effects. There is insufficient space available in the present chapter to review this evidence, but Eriksen (1960) has provided a summary of the experimental evidence for unconscious discrimination and concludes from this survey that at present there is no convincing evidence that the human organism can make discriminations by any response system that are more accurate than those that can be elicited by verbal (conscious) report.

Bruner (1951) and Postman (1951 and 1953) have both advanced a general theory of perception that may be termed "hypothesis theory." Both authors are concerned with the general theory of perception rather than with a specific explanation of perceptual defense phenomena. However, Postman has specifically attempted to explain perceptual defense (higher recognition thresholds for emotional stimuli) in terms of his more general theory. He considers perceptual defense to be attributable to the "dominance of strong alternative hypotheses" which interfere and delay the recognition of emotional stimuli. He also takes into account the individual differences corresponding to repressors and sensitizers that have been considered above. While the "defenders" have strong dominant positive—i.e., nonemotional—hypotheses, which require a large amount of appropriate information before they are rejected, the "nondefenders" are considered to have stronger negative—i.e., emotional—hypotheses than the defenders.

An excellent evaluation of hypothesis theory in relation to perceptual defense phenomena may be found in Brown (1961), but its major weaknesses are that it deals with the phenomena at too general a level and fails to take into account the relationship of perceptual defense to the more general problem of clinically observed defensive mechanisms. Much of the theory involves post facto explanation and little work has been done by either Bruner or Postman to obtain independent estimates of the subject's availability of hypotheses in order to predict perceptual performance. It also is somewhat strained as a theory in accounting for the differences between sensitizers and repressors in perceptual defense.

An adequate explanation of how perceptual defense operates must have something to say about clinical defensive mechanisms in general. An explanation that relates both the perceptual and the clinical conceptions of repression and defense has been advanced by Eriksen and Brown (1956) and Eriksen and Kuethe (1956). They made use of Dollard and Miller's (1950) behavior theory analysis of defensive mechanisms and extended it specifically to the perceptual recognition experiment and to word association test performance. The essence of the Eriksen and Brown explanation for perceptual defense lies in denying that the phenomena exists in perception but rather that it is a manifestation of response variables and response effects. To understand this argument fully it is necessary to digress a bit and examine the general concept of perception.

It is not a novel idea to point out that perception differs from the responses from which it is inferred. In perceptual experiments, the results may be the reflection of the perceptual process as well as of the response variables that the subject used in indicating his perception. Psychophysicists have shown awareness of this distinction for many years in that they do not use truly random series of stimulus presentations in threshold investigations. A long sequence of positives or a long sequence of negatives can occur with true random sequences, but subjects have distorted conceptions of randomness. Having had three positives in a row the subject is more apt to say "no" or to fail to report the signal on the fourth successive occurrence because he feels it could not have occurred as many successive times as this would imply. This is an example of a response variable influencing characteristics imputed to perception.

While the theoretical distinction between perception and response has been recognized for some time, Eriksen and Wechsler (1955) and Eriksen and Hake (1951) revived interest in this distinction by showing operational ways in which response effects could be separated from so-called perceptual phenomena. A more systematic treatment of the distinction between perception and response has been offered by Garner, Hake and Eriksen (1956). For them, perception is a concept or contruct of what intervenes between stimulation and response and the concept becomes clearer and more exact as we are increasingly successful in eliminating stimulus and response variables from it. They further point out how, through the use of converging operations, response variables can be ruled out or eliminated from the general concept of perception.

Eriksen and Brown have pointed out that the typical perceptual recognition experiment has more in common with a task of guessing than with a perceptual task. The question is, what does the subject perceive in a brief exposure of a word? If the subject is asked to describe exactly what he perceives we do not receive responses in terms of whole words such as, "That looked like the word 'small,' " or, "I guess you showed the word 'house.' " Instead, the subject gives descriptions such as, "Well, I had the impression of maybe a word, a short word, and it looked like it had a tall letter at the end," or "It is a word that begins with 's' and has an 'o' somewhere in the middle of it." But in the typical recognition experiment the subject is not asked to describe exactly what he perceives; he is either implicitly or explicitly asked to respond in terms of whole English words or of whole units, depending upon the stimulus material employed. If the subject's perception is most adequately described under conditions where he is given the freedom of the English language to describe what he perceives, then the usual recognition experiment is essentially asking the subject to guess what word might fit the vague perceptual cues he has perceived. In other words, the subject associates or tries to find a word that fits the fragmentary letters and impression of word length that corresponds to his actual perception.

If we now consider thoughts and associations as responses, following the treatment of Dollard and Miller, we are in a position to account for perceptual defense effects in terms of nothing more mysterious than the empirically established effects of punishment on the probability of occurrence of responses. We may assume that different words have different habit strength as responses to different cues. If, for example, the word "hook" is anxiety-arousing or leads to self-devaluating thoughts in the subject due to previous experiences he has had, then "hook" would be expected to have less habit strength to the fragmentary perception described by the subject, as "the impression of a short word that looks like it has an 'o' in it and ends in a 'k.' " "Look" or "took" might be expected to have greater habit strengths to this particular cue. Thus, if this cue is obtained in perception at a brief duration of exposure, "look" or "took" would have a higher probability of being elicited as a response than would the anxiety-associated work, "hook." But as the durations of exposure lengthen, the subject's cues or perception changes and he gains more knowledge about the actual stimulus. Eventually the duration is long enough so that the actual perception is "hook," in which case to this cue "hook" has the greatest habit strength and occurs as the recognition response. The operation of such a process over a number of words will statistically yield higher recognition thresholds for anxiety-evoking words relative to neutral words.

The subject does not necessarily have to feel subjectively that he is searching for a word to fit the partial cues he actually perceives. The association of a response to these cues may be as immediate and automatic as the association "white" is to the stimulus word "black." This associative connection in response to cues underlies not only the perceptual recognition but also the word association test and may well account for the correspondence between perceptual recognition thresholds and association times.

That word association connections are modifiable by punishment was established by Eriksen and Kuethe (1956). They were successful in changing a subject's preferred associative responses to stimulus words by electric shock punishment; and introspective reports of the subjects, verified by reaction time data, indicated that the new associations became automatic after a few trials.

It is to be noted that the above conception of repression is consistent with the clinical concept of the process. The original defining operation for the detection of repression came from the psychoanalytic free association procedure. Here the analyst detects or suspects the operation of a repressive mechanism when the patient's associations show peculiar gaps, blockages, or deviate from what the analyst considers to be a reasonable associative chain. A person has considerable latitude in the type of associative connections or trains of thought he subjectively experiences. There is room for considerable idiosyncrasy without it becoming too conspicuous to one's fellows. By learning to change directions of association the person effectively can prevent the occurrence of covertly stimulated anxiety, and it is only under the controlled condition of the clinician's couch that these peculiarities in associations become evident.

The above account of perceptual defense removes the phenomenon from the field of perception and places it back with response variables and relates it, then, to behavior theory. It differs from the frequency theory of Howes and Solomon primarily in that they do not explicitly distinguish between perception and the responses from which it is inferred. One could advocate an explanation of perceptual defense that applied the effects of reinforcement to perceptual learning rather than to response variables. Our preference for locating the source of action in responses rather than in terms of learned percepts is primarily on the basis of the lack of convincing evidence showing the effects of learning on perception per se. Goldiamond and Hawkins (1958), in an ingenious experiment, were able to show that the frequency effects of Solomon and Howes upon perceptual recognition could be obtained in the absence of any perceptual stimulus. Also, Pierce (1962), in an experiment that successfully eliminated the possibility of differential response bias, was unable to find any effect of frequency or familiarity upon perception. Similar results have been obtained by Goldstein (1962).

With but few exceptions the research literature on need and perceptual recognition lends itself to an interpretation in terms of the response theory advanced above. As pointed out by Garner, Hake and Eriksen (1956), most of the experiments in this area have not contained the necessary coverging operations to attribute the obtained effects to the perceptual process. There have, however, been several studies that appear to contain the necessary converging operations to localize perceptual sensitization and defense effects in the perceptual process. Blum (1955) compared the frequency with which the names of different Blackie pictures, assumed to be anxiety-provoking, were given as responses to tachistoscopic exposures where the anxiety pictures, unknown to the subject, were not exposed. The response frequencies obtained were then compared with the frequencies obtained where the anxiety pictures were actually presented. The first measure of response frequency provided a control for differential response strengths. Blum assumed that if unconscious perception occurred, then the exposures with the pictures present would lead to unconscious perception of the conflict which in turn would trip off more anxiety and activate defensive mechanisms leading to an even less frequent usage of the anxiety responses. Although he obtained positive results, investigators in other laboratories (Raskin, 1954; Smock, 1956) have been unable to replicate this aspect of his experiment.

A similar method of correcting for differential response strengths for anxiety material has been employed by Mathews and Wertheimer (1958) and by Goldstein (1962). In both of these studies there was a significant perceptual defense effect even after statistical correction had been made for response bias. However, Goldstein and his associates, in a further series of careful studies, have pursued the problem of separating response variance from perceptual variance in recognition tasks. The results of these studies (Goldstein, 1962; Goldstein, Himmelfarb & Feder, 1962; Goldstein & Himmelfarb, 1962) have suggested that statistical correction for response bias effects are not adequate. While they have consistently been able to obtain the perceptual defense effect in their studies, they have nonethelss built up an impressive amount of evidence through careful experimentation that shows this effect to be attributable to response bias, which in turn is probably due to conditioned avoidance response to the anxiety-provoking stimuli.

A SUMMING-UP

It would appear that fifteen years of experimentation on the effects of need upon perception has resulted in a conclusion that needs do not affect the perceptual process but only response occurrence. Nevertheless, the tremendously important contributions that this research has made to psychology must not be overlooked. Research in this area has played an important role in sharpening our concept of perception by leading to the experimental isolation of response variables from this concept. This distinction has not only been important in the need and perception area but has influenced traditional work on perceptual problems as well.

A most significant contribution has been made to the field of personality by furthering our knowledge of ego-defensive mechanisms and providing a means by which they may be detected and measured in the laboratory. It has provided us with the beginnings of a behavior theory account of repression, and in so doing has made available more precise concepts and language for dealing with psychopathology. In giving rise to the concepts of sensitizers and repressors, it has indicated an important dimension of ego defensiveness. The important work of Gordon and Altrocchi and associates, as well as that of Ullman and Lim (1962), have indicated the fruitfulness of this dimension in understanding a wide variety of defensive behavior. The relationship of this dimension to Eysenck's introvert-extrovert dimension has already been noted and there are a number of indications (Eriksen & Davids, 1955; Greenbaum, 1956; Osler & Lewinsohn, 1954) that this same dimension is related to the Taylor Manifest Anxiety Scale and to the leveler and sharpener dimension of Klein and his associates (Holzman and Gardner, 1959). The nature of these interrelationships will require a large research effort to confirm and consolidate. An important attempt at integration in this area has been made by Inglis (1961), but the data are yet too scattered and too many links in the chain are missing to achieve more than suggestive consolidations.

Perhaps the major contribution of the need and perception experimentation will come from its provision of a means of detecting and measuring ego defenses. Our concepts of psychodynamics and defensive processes are primitive and inadequate largely due to the lack of experimentation in this area. This, in turn, has resulted from the inadequacy and the lack of techniques for conveniently studying defenses in laboratory settings. While experimentalists in the clinical and personality area have been slow to seize upon this new methodology for studying defensive processes, the work of Shannon (1962) and Ullman and Lim (1962), who have used the perceptual recognition technique in working out a new classification of defensive mechanisms, should do much to stimulate research employing this methodology.

REFERENCES

ALTROCCHI, J. Interpersonal perceptions of repressors and sensitizers in component analysis of assumed dissimilarity scores. *J. abnorm. soc. Psychol.*, 1961, *62*, 528-434.

ALTROCCHI, J., PARSONS, O. A., & DICKOFF, H. Changes in self-ideal discrepancy in repressors and sensitizers. *J. abnorm. soc. Psychol.*, 1960, *61*, 67-72.

ANSBACHER, H. Perception of number as affected by the monetary value of the objects. *Arch. Psychol.*, 1937, No. 215, N. Y.

ATKINSON, J. W. (Ed.) *Motives in fantasy, action, and society.* New York: D. Van Nostrand,. 1958.

BLUM, G. S. 1955. Perceptual defense revisited. *J. abnorm. soc. Psychol.*, 1955, *51*, 24-29.

BROWN, W. P. Conceptions of perceptual defense. *Brit. J. Psychol.*, Monogr. Suppl., 1961.

BRUNER, J. S. Personality dynamics and the process of perceiving. In R. R. Blake & G. V. Ramsey (Ed.) *Perception: an approach to personality,* New York: Ronald Press, 1951.

BRUNER, J. S., & GOODMAN, C. C. Value and need as organizing factors in perception. *J. abnorm. soc. Psychol.*, 1947, *42*, 33-44.

BRUNER, J. S., & POSTMAN, L. Emotional selectivity in perception and reaction. *J. Pers.*, 1947, *16*, 69-77. (a)

BRUNER, J. S., & POSTMAN, L. Tension and tension-release as organizing factors in perception. *J. Pers.*, 1947, *15*, 300-308. (b)

CARLSON, V. R. Individual differences in recall of word association test words. *J. Pers.*, 1954, *23*, 77-87.

CARPENTER, B., WIENER, M., & CARPENTER, J. *J. abnorm. soc. Psychol.*, 1956, *52*, 380-383.

CLARK, R. A., & SENSIBAR, MINDA R. The relationship between symbolic and manifest projections of sexuality with some incidental correlates. *J. abnorm. soc. Psychol.*, 1955, *50*, 327-334.

DOLLARD, J., & MILLER, N. E. *Personality and psychotherapy*. New York: McGraw-Hill, 1950.

ELLIOTT, R. Interrelationships among measures of field dependence, ability, and personality traits. *J. abnorm. soc. Psychol.*, 1961, *63*, 27-36.

ERIKSEN, C. W. Perceptual defense as a function of unacceptable needs. *J. abnorm. soc. Psychol.*, 1951, *46*, 557-564. (a)

ERIKSEN, C. W. Some implications for TAT interpretation arising from need and perception experiments. *J. Pers.*, 1951, *19*, 283-288. (b)

ERIKSEN, C. W. Defense against ego-threat in memory and perception. *J. abnorm. soc. Psychol.*, 1952, *47*, 430-435.

ERIKSEN, C. W. Psychological defenses and ego strength in the recall of completed and incompleted tasks. *J. abnorm. soc. Psychol.*, 1954, *49*, 45-50. (a)

ERIKSEN, C. W. The case of perceptual defense. *Psychol. Rev.*, 1954, *61*, 175-182. (b)

ERIKSEN, C. W. Discrimination and learning without awareness: A methodological survey and evaluation. *Psychol. Rev.*, 1960, *67*, 279-300.

ERIKSEN, C. W., & BROWN, C. T. An experimental and theoretical analysis of perceptual defense. *J. abnorm. soc. Psychol.*, 1956, *52*, 224-230.

ERIKSEN, C. W., & DAVIDS, A. The meaning and clinical validity of the Taylor Manifest Anxiety Scale in the hysteria-psychasthenia scales from the MMPI. *J. abnorm. soc. Psychol.*, 1955, *50*, 135-137.

ERIKSEN, C. W., & HAKE, H. W. Anchor effects in absolute judgments. *J. exp. Psychol.*, 1957, *53*, 132-138.

ERIKSEN, C. W., & KUETHE, J. L. Avoidance conditioning of verbal behavior without awareness: A paradigm of repression. *J. abnorm. soc. Psychol.*, 1956, *53*, 203-209.

ERIKSEN, C. W., & WECHSLER, H. Some effects of experimentally induced anxiety upon discrimination behavior. *J. abnorm. soc. Psychol.*, 1955, *51*, 458-463.

EYSENCK, H. J. *Dimensions of personality*. London: Routledge and Kegan Paul, 1947.

GARNER, W. R., HAKE, H. W., & ERIKSEN, C. W. Operationism and the concept of perception. *Psychol. Rev.*, 1956, *63*, 149-159.

GOLDIAMOND, I., and HAWKINS, W. F. Vexierversuch: The log relationship between word frequency and recognition obtained in the absence of stimulus words. *J. exp. Psychol.*, 1958, *56*, 457-463.

Goldstein, M. J. A test of response probability theory of perceptual defense. *J. exp. Psychol.*, 1962, *63*, 23-28.

Goldstein, M. J., & Himmelfarb, S. The effects of providing knowledge of results upon the perceptual defense effect. *J. abnorm. soc. Psychol.*, 1962, *64*, 143-147.

Goldstein, M. J., Himmelfarb, S., & Feder, W. A further study of the relationship between response bias and perceptual defense. *J. abnorm. soc. Psychol.*, 1962, *64*, 56-62.

Gordon, J. R. Interpersonal perdictions of repressors and sensitizers. *J. Person.*, 1957, *25*, 686-698. (a)

Gordon, J. R. The stability of the assumed similarity response set in repressors and sensitizers. *J. Person.*, 1957, 27, 362-373. (b)

Greenbaum, M. Manifest anxiety in the tachistoscopic recognition of facial photographs. *Percept. mot. Skills*, 1956, *6*, 245-248.

Holzman, T. S., & Gardner, R. W. Leveling and repression. *J. abnorm. soc. Psychol.*, 1959, *59*, 151-155.

Howes, D., & Solomon, R. L. A note on McGinnies' emotionality and perceptual defense. *Psychol. Rev.*, 1950, *57*, 229-234.

Howes, D., & Solomon, R. L. Visual duration threshold as a function of word probability *J. exp. Psychol.*, 1951, *41*, 401-410.

Inglis, J. Abnormalities of motivation and "ego functions." In H. J. Eysenck (Ed.), *Handbook of abnormal psychology.* New York: Basic Books, 1961.

Klein, G. S. Cognitive control and motivation. In Gardner Lindzey (Ed.), *Assessment of Motives,* New York: Rinehart, 1958.

Klein, G. S., Schlesinger, H. J., & Meister, D. E. The effect of personal values on perception: An experimental critique. *Psychol. Rev.*, 1951, *58*, 96-112.

Kleinman, M. L. Psychogenic deafness and perceptual defense. *J. abnorm. soc. Psychol.*, 1957, *54*, 335-338.

Lazarus, R. S., Eriksen, C. W., & Fonda, C. P. Personality dynamics in auditory perceptual recognition. *J. Person.*, 1951, *19*, 471-482.

Lazarus, R. S., & McCleary, R. A. Autonomic discrimination without awarenesss: A study of subception. *Psychol. Rev.*, 1951, *58*, 113-122.

Lazarus, R. S., Yousem, H., & Arenberg, D. Hunger and perception. *J. Person.*, 1953, *21*, 312-328.

Mathews, A., & Wertheimer, M. A 'pure' measure of perceptual defense uncontaminated by response suppression. *J. abnorm. soc. Psychol.*, 1958, *57*, 373-376.

McClelland, D. C., & Atkinson, J. W. The projective expression of needs. I. The effect of different intensities of the hunger drive on perception. *J. Psychol.*, 1958, *25*, 205-222.

McGinnies, E. Emotionality and perceptual defense. *Psychol. Rev.*, 1949, *56*, 244-251.

MURRAY, E. J. Conflict and repression during sleep deprivation. *J. abnorm. soc. Psychol.*, 1959, *59*, 95-101.

NELSON, S. E. Psychosexual conflicts and defenses in visual perception. *J. abnorm. soc. Psychol.*, 1955, *51*, 427-433.

OSLER, S. F., & LEWINSOHN, T. M. The relation between manifest anxiety in perceptual defense. *Amer. Psychologist*, 1954, *9*, 446. (Abstract)

PIERCE, J. R. Some parameters of tachistoscopic thresholds. *J. exp. Psychol.*, in press.

POSTMAN, L. Towards a general theory of cognition. In J. H. Rohrer & M. Sherif (Ed.), *Social psychology at the crossroads*, New York: Harper & Bros., 1951.

POSTMAN, L. On the problem of perceptual defense. *Psychol. Rev.*, 1953, *60*, 298-306.

POSTMAN, L., BRUNER, P. S., & McGINNIES, E. Personal values as selective factors in perception. *J. abnorm. soc. Psychol.*, 1948, *43*, 142-154.

POSTMAN, L., & SOLOMON, R. L. Perceptual sensitivity to completed and incompleted tasks. *J. Pers.*, 1950, *18*, 347-357.

RASKIN, A. 1954. A learning theory paradigm for perceptual-vigilance and perceptual-defense phenomena. Unpublished doctoral dissertation, Univer. of Illinois.

RORSCHACH, H. *Psychodiagnostics*. Berne: Hans Huber, 1942.

SHANNON, D. T. Clinical patterns of defense as revealed in visual recognition thresholds. *J. abnorm. soc. Psychol.*, 1962, *64*, 370-377.

SINGER, B. R. An experimental inquiry into the concept of perceptual defense. *Brit. J. Psychol.*, 1956, *47*, 298-311.

SMOCK, C. D. Replication and comments: "An experimental reunion of psychoanalytic theory with perceptual vigilance and defense." *J. aborm. soc. Psychol.*, 1956, *53*, 68-73.

SOLOMON, R. L., & HOWES, D. Word frequency, personal values, and visual duration thresholds. *Psychol. Rev.*, 1951, *58*, 256-270.

SPENCE, D. P. A new look in vigilance and defense. *J. abnorm. soc. Psychol.*, 1957, *54*, 103-108. (a)

SPENCE, D. P. Success failure and recognition threshold. *J. Person.*, 1957, *25*, 712-720. (b)

STEIN, K. B. Perceptual defense and perceptual sensitization under neutral and involved conditions. *J. Pers.*, 1953, *21*, 467-478.

STEPHENS, J. M. The influence of different stimuli upon preceding bonds: an examination of the law of effect. Teachers College contribution to education, 1931, *493*.

STEPHENS, J. M. The perception of small differences as affected by self interest. *Amer. J. Psychol.*, 1936, *58*, 480-484.

THORNDIKE, E. L., & LORGE, I. *The teachers word book of 30,000 words*. New York: Columbia Univer. Press, 1944.

THURSTONE, L. L. *A factorial study of perception.* Chicago: Univer. of Chicago Press, 1944.

TRUAX, C. B. Repression response to implied failure as a function of the hysteria psychasthenia index. *J. abnorm. soc. Psychol.,* 1957, *55,* 183-193.

ULLMAN, L. P., & LIM, D. T. Case history material as a source of the identification of patterns of response to emotional stimuli in a study of humor. *J. consult. Psychol.,* 1962, *26,* 221-225.

WITKIN, H. A., LEWIS, H. B., HERTZMAN, M., MACHOVER, K., MEISSNER, P. B., & WAPNER, S. *Personality through perception.* New York: Harper & Bros., 1954.

3

Genetics and Personality

Benson E. Ginsburg [1]

When a geneticist writes about genetic determinants of personality or behavior, there is an automatic conversion factor in the mind of the reader that translates any title whatsoever to "Nature versus Nurture," or "Heredity versus Environment." In this unequal contest, the environment always wins. Modern anthropology and psychology, with their emphases on cultural and experiential differences as prime causal agents of behavior, as well as the odor of burning flesh that attaches to the Hitler racism of the '30's and '40's, and indeed to that of our own race problems, combine to make any genetic-deterministic view not only unpopular, but threatening, and to erect emotional blocks against it. It is certainly far pleasanter to think of ourselves as infinitely plastic. Then, with proper cultural and other environmental advantages, there is no limit to our potential.

On the very briefest reflection, it becomes intuitively apparent that this view is sheer nonsense. One must immediately put boundaries around the plasticity. The first one is the boundary of the species. We are human. We do not ordinarily think of our potential as transcending the human. Even Greek and Roman mythology, where the dividing line between gods and men was not absolute, accomplished the jump from the human to the supra-human by largely genetic means.

[1] The author's data reported herein were obtained from studies aided by a grant from the Dr. Wallace C. and Clara A. Abbott Memorial Fund of the University of Chicago and by Grant #MY-3361 from the National Institutes of Mental Health.

Granted that genetically man is human, with all that this implies, the plasticity under discussion here must be restricted further. Few can aspire to true virtuosity, and fewer still to genius, whatever our environmental advantages. A Bach is a rarity, as is a Darwin, a Galton, an Einstein or a Fermi, let alone an all-around genius like Leonardo da Vinci. If we examine the begats of the Bachs, a disproportionately high number of musical virtuosi are to be found. Darwin and Galton are in another genetic compartment that contains more than its share of eminence. They were cousins. By contrast, comparable geniuses can be found in families that produced them only as single unique individuals. For a geneticist, this conforms to expectation, since genes segregate, and complex genetic combinations have little chance of staying together in the absence of inbreeding or other assortative mating that would tend to keep them that way. Evidence dealing with the genetic basis for musical ability, mathematical ability, and other familial traits affecting human abilities indicate that they generally show up quite early and somewhat independently of any environmental push in the direction of the ability. Some musical geniuses have displayed their talents against overwhelming odds. Mathematical ability, or memory of the kind that a chess virtuoso has, is not necessarily correlated with other qualities, and the people who possess either of these are not necessarily very good at anything else. This does not apply to an Einstein or a Mozart. Such people have a high order of "intelligence" in addition to particular traits of the kind we have been noting (Galton, 1892; Scheinfeld, 1950).

If we continue to belabor the obvious and examine the other side of the coin, it is well known that apes which have been reared like children in human homes from early infancy have behaviorally remained apes (Hayes & Hayes, 1952). Aggressive terriers fostered on placid beagle mothers and raised among beagles retained the personality of terriers. Whites residing for generations in Africa do not become blacks through non-genetic means, nor does the reverse occur. How much plasticity, then, does man actually have?

The common view is that he has a great deal, There is support in the biological literature for the idea that the potential for complex behavior has developed along two separate lines in animals: one of these lines maximizes heredity, while the other maximizes environment. The first is best illustrated through the social insects, where behavior is built in genetically. The second is best illustrated by the vertebrates, where there appears to be a gradual increase in the flexibility of behavior with a concomitant dependence on experience, with the apex of flexibility represented by man.

Communication is quite different in these two lines of evolution. The well-known studies of von Frisch (1950) on the language of bees demonstrate that the bees do not have to learn their language as we have to learn ours. They also build geometrical chambers in their hives without an architect's plan. Termites build air-conditioned nests. Each individual contributes an infinitesimal amount, like the slaves who built the great pyramids of Egypt; yet the whole develops according to a plan. The termites' nest plan is built into the termites. Professor Alfred Emerson (1958) has demonstrated that one can classify the termites taxonomically according to the nest they build. He considers these nests to be fossilized bits of behavior, the master plan for each species being a part of the genetic endowment of that species.

Vertebrates too have their genetically built-in automatisms, which are, perhaps, more extensive than most of us realize. A frog with the higher centers of the brain removed, leaps very well. Fish, amphibians, reptiles, and birds are noted for their stereotyped courtship patterns, in which a particular structure complex, moved in a certain way by the female will elicit a stereotyped response in an inexperienced male. This response then elicits a further response in the female, while this in turn produces the next movement in the male, and so on until the courtship is carried to its conclusion (Tinbergen, 1951). In the parlance of some biologists, these particular events have been called "releasers" and with but little extrapolation, they can be applied to the understanding of human behavior. The concept of genetically determined releaser mechanisms will be discussed later in this chapter, in the context of the theories of certain schools of dynamic psychology. The effect of early traumatic experiences in humans and in sub-human vertebrates is another field that is pertinent in relation to the argument about the plasticity of behavior and the degree to which it may be biologically determined.

Recent investigations have demonstrated that much of vertebrate behavior that we have hitherto regarded as plastic is not really so. People have been watching domestic sheep and goats for a long time, and yet very little was known scientifically about their behavior until some recent studies made at the Cornell Behavior Farm (Blauvelt, 1956; Collias, 1956). Time and motion studies were made of the behavior of sheep and goats, beginning with birth. When these films are examined, and when experiments are then performed to test the validity of the observations, it becomes apparent that what seems at first like purposeful, intelligent learning behavior consists of a series of automatisms with varying degrees of flexibility—some not very flexible at all.

A superficial observation of the maternal behavior of goats makes it appear that the mother pays attention to her individual young, recognizing it, licking it, massaging it, and inducing it to get up on its wobbly legs and nurse. Later attempts at nursing are better than the early attempts, further adding to the impression of learning. If mother and young lose each other, especially during the first few hours, the neonate will bleat, the mother will appear to recognize the voice of her offspring, and will come to it. The young will appear to recognize the mother and will nurse. As the kid grows, the mother protects the territory around it, again verifying the impression of individual identification of the young by the mother and vice versa. When the same behavior is analyzed through the use of time and motion studies and further tested by experiments, these impressions are reduced to anthropomorphisms that have little correspondence to the way in which the behavior actually occurs.

The studies cited have shown that under the influence of placental hormones the mother goat has a definitive response to the neonatal bleat for a period of about 4½ hours. After this time, if one were to separate her from her kid, and it were to bleat, she would not perform the purposeful-appearing orientation. The neonate bleats as it is passing from the mother's body during birth. The mother orients to its head under the influence of placental hormones and begins to lick. The licking massages the young and stimulates it to stand. There is an automatic reflex flicking of the tail, which causes the mother to orient to it. Because of their size relation this orientation positions the kid so that it can nurse. If it does not begin the nursing in short order, it bleats. When it bleats, the mother quite mechanically turns around, orienting automatically to the head and starting the behavior cycle over again—that is, the tail flicks, the mother orients to the tail, again positioning the young, so that it may nurse. If contact with the teat is not made, the young goat bleats, the mother orients to the head, etc. The mother never picks up in the middle, nor does the kid, nor do they engage in anything but this series of automatisms that result in putting the kid on its feet and starting it nursing. The reason that the mother appears to recognize the individual bleat of her own kid is that this is the one which is usually in closest proximity to her, and also that it is unlikely that any adjacent kids will have been born during the few hours when the hormone levels of a particular mother make her peculiarly responsive to the neonate bleat.

We have recently been studying dogs and their wild relatives. They too are full of built-in automatisms. A wild wolf mother put at some distance from her young will feed it by regurgitating solid food beginning with the third week. Such mothers will supplement their normal ration by gobbling up extra food, carrying it to where their young are, and regurgitating it as a warm chopped-up meal for their young to eat. This is only an occasional occurrence in the domestic dog, where the genetic capacity for this behavior seems to have lost its importance and has not been maintained under the selection pressure that applies in the wild.

The social structure and organization among vertebrate animals is extremely important in relation to territoriality, access to mates, and many other aspects of group living. Animals that interact in this way have a highly stereotyped form of communication, having to do with social dominance, with courtship, and with territoriality. In these wild forms, there is usually a tremendously elaborate warning communication that is not intended to culminate in vicious attack, but to reduce fighting through rituals that are built into the behavior. Our research includes studies of delayed socialization in adult timber wolves (Ginsburg, Woolpy, Kleiman and Edwards, 1962). In carrying out these studies, we take advantage of the fact that the communication system of the wild *Canid* is stereotyped.

One can very reliably separate real or ambivalent threats from mere bluff and guide oneself accordingly (Schenkel, 1948). Needless to say, this is of great importance if the research calls for the investigator to enter the animal's cage. With the domestic dog, no such dependable series of signals can be elicited. Some retain the behavior of the wild animal, but others do not. These traits seem to have dropped out under domestication, so that short of knowing the individual dog, one cannot tell whether or not a dominance posture, for example, corresponds to the meaning it would have in the wolf.

Extreme aggressiveness is another trait that appears genetically determined—although it is certainly susceptible to conditioning as well. When the writer first came to the University of Chicago, he worked with guinea pigs in the colony of Professor Sewall Wright. Most of these could be picked up and handled with impunity, but every once in a while he would put his hand in a cage and come out with a guinea pig attached to it. Conditioning? We thought not, because all animals were handled in the same manner, and whenever we checked the pedigrees of the animals that bit us, we found they belonged to one family. When those guinea pigs related to this family were finally eliminated from the colony, no further incidents of this sort occurred. Similar traits have been found in rabbits, mice, dogs, and other mammals, on a comparable genetic basis (Ginsburg, 1958).

The Jackson Laboratory has maintained families of wire-haired fox terriers so aggressive that it is difficult to rear four or more in a litter. If the litter is kept together after weaning, and one puppy goes down in a fight, the others immediately gang up on him. Usually, one puppy can hold off two attackers, but is unable to hold off three or more, and is eventually mutilated or killed when facing these odds. In studies made there (Fisher, 1955) such terriers were isolated from the mother and littermates very early in life and reared on bottles. After the weaning period, they were put together in the usual litter groups. The innate genetic aggressiveness, which was there as a potential, never developed under these conditions. Four, five terriers, or even larger litters could be reared together quite successfully. The genetic trait, then is not invariably expressed in behavior, but is there potentially. The environment brings it out in terriers who have the genetic potential for it, but will not induce it where the genetic potential does not exist.

Jumping from dogs to mice, and moving to the realm of early experience, an event in the writer's own research further points up some of these genetic-environmental interactions. One of our studies of animal behavior involved an attempt to control genetic variability by working with highly inbred strains—where every animal is essentially an identical twin of every other. We were rating the aggressiveness of three strains of mice, using tests that had been accepted by other investigators, and were pleased to achieve very clear-cut results, thus demonstrating that when the genetic make-up of the animal was controlled, the results were absolutely predictable. There was no doubt in the least as to which was the most aggressive strain, which the least aggressive, etc. (Ginsburg and Allee, 1942). However, another geneticist working with exactly the same stocks in a similar situation obtained results that did not agree with ours (Scott, 1942) in spite of the genetic controls. The solution to the problem was finally traced experimentally to slight differences in the manner in which the animals were handled at an early age, although the aggressiveness was not tested until much later, after sexual maturity. With two of the three strains, these differences in early handling made no difference to the later results. With the third, however, it made all the difference between its being most aggressive or least aggressive after sexual maturity. It should be stated, parenthetically, that only males are used in these aggressiveness experiments. The effect of early experience is, therefore, dependent on the genotype of the individual.

In the face of such findings as these one must be cautious indeed, in the selection and handling of laboratory animals. One mouse is *not* like another, nor all rats like standard parts flowing off a punch press. In a biological sense all men are *not* created equal yet in an uncomfortably large proportion of behavioral research, this simple fact is overlooked.

The convention in much behavior research is to take the organism for granted, whether the experiment calls for modifying its early experience, changing its hormone level, plying it with chemical agents, or training it in various types of apparatus. The standard assumptions and standard experimental designs permit one to take a group of experimental animals (including humans) and a "matched" group of controls, and to conclude that if the majority in the experimental group are consistently enough affected by the experimental procedures to give statistically "significant" differences from the controls, one has discovered a generalizable psychological fact. This is simply not true, except in a very restricted sense. A biologist must conjecture about the many exceptions to the rule, and seriously question the assumption that the biological category "rat" or "mouse" or "dog" or "human" is indeed a unitary biological entity. Perhaps the minority in either the experimental or control group which did not effectively "vote" in these statistical samples was, biologically speaking, in a different category from the majority.

In the aforementioned mouse experiment, we found that each genetic combination or mouse strain had a different potential for interacting with environmental variables, as measured by later aggressive behavior in males. Genetically then, differences in early handling did not affect the later behavior of two inbred strains, but did affect a third strain very profoundly. It is interesting that since then this third strain has been found in all of our experiments to be extremely labile behaviorally (Ginsburg, 1958). One suspicion is that perhaps the strain is not as genetically pure as we supposed. However, this has been repeatedly checked by selecting from the extremes of the distribution on any given test. Such selection experiments have been carried out for up to seven generations and have failed to demonstrate any genetic differences, thereby confirming the hypothesis that we are dealing with a genetically uniform strain that is unusually susceptible to environmental influences.

These experiments have since been extended to other inbred mouse strains and to other behaviors. Our findings are that the same experimental variables, namely, manipulation of the young mice early in life, either by pinching their tails or by removing them from the home cage for a short period and putting them individually into small dishes for several minutes before returning them, demonstrated that some strains showed an increase in aggressiveness as a result of handling, others showed a decrease, and still others were unaffected (Ginsburg, 1960).

What, then, is the effect of early manipulation in the "mouse"? It clearly depends upon the genetic constitution of the particular mouse.

These "handling" experiments have been interpreted by other research groups as involving stress, and their effects have been attributed to early stimulation of the adrenal cortex and early release of adrenal cortical hormones (Levine, Alpert, and Lewis, 1958). In our laboratory we have been working with more spectacular stresses. One of these has been fatal, sound-induced seizures, which also occur in mice on a genetic basis. Under suitable experimental conditions, a number of different strains will show similar susceptibility to seizures when stressed by a mixed noise of appropriate intensity (Ginsburg, 1958). This is a developmental phenomenon. Some of our susceptible strains show it very early, that is during the third week of life, at about the time that they begin to hear. These strains usually recover from this susceptibility early—within a week or ten days. Other strains show susceptibility to seizures later, and recover only with the onset of sexual maturity. Still others continue to be susceptible throughout their lifetimes, and some, as you may suspect, only with the onset of mouse senility. In those strains in which we have studied the seizures most thoroughly, it appears that however similar the phenotype—that is, the seizure susceptibility which we measure—may appear, the rule is that response to palliative measures used to control the seizures is specific to the genotype rather than the phenotype. Where a difference in the genetic basis for this phenotypic seizure susceptibility exists, "treatment" must be geared to the genotype (Ginsburg, 1954). Stated more simply, there are several genetic deficiencies that predispose to seizures. The measures that can be used to prevent seizures for one of these genetic deficiencies will usually not work for another. One hardly needs to be reminded that almost without exception, medical treatment of genetically determined disorders in humans is related to the phenotype.

There are, then, a variety of genetically controlled "reasons" for seizure susceptibility. Each of these involves different mechanisms or different aspects of related mechanisms, so that an agent affecting the seizures in one pedigree may or may not do so in another. These differential effects of treatment by a given drug—for example, in similar phenotypes that differ genotypically—are valuable jumping-off points for physiological genetic investigations. The seizures themselves are only one aspect of reaction to stress. Of several so-called seizure-susceptible strains, for example, only two genetically related ones have their seizures alleviated by injected mono-sodium glutamate. Other susceptible strains that we have tested do not respond similarly to this agent (Ginsburg, 1954).

In a collaborative study with a psychologist, S. Ross, we have found that our seizure-susceptible animals are also susceptible to what might be interpreted as the very mild stress of encountering learning tasks on the borderline of their ability. These animals were tested along with other strains in a series of maze-learning experiments, and showed deficits in their ability to perform certain mazes. On the basis of the error and time scores, the stress seemed to be associated only with those mazes which required their maximum ability for mastering. Mazes easily mastered by other strains were usually also easily mastered by stress-prone mice. Those that were too difficult for other strains were invariably too difficult for these mice also, but a few of intermediate difficulty separated some of our seizure-susceptible strains sharply from other strains. The administration of mono-sodium glutamate aided the learning only of those animals belonging to strains where this same chemical agent also reduced seizures. Further, it helped them only on those mazes, the difficulty of which was near the limits of their capacity. We can interpret these data as suggesting that the same mechanism is involved both in the maze and in the seizure situation. Thus, those particular genotypes that were helped by mono-sodium glutamate in the more severe stress of the audiogenic seizures were also helped in the situation of milder stress imposed by being pushed to the boundaries of their ability in their efforts to master a learning situation. Control strains that were not helped by mono-sodium gluta-mate in the seizure situation were not helped by it in the learning situation.

It has been stated that the two strains affected by glutamate were genetically related. It should also be mentioned that they are not affected in the same way. The major difference is that, whereas one strain shows an effect proportional to dosage until a maximum is reached, the second strain is improved by glutamate only on initial administrations. As they continue to be treated, the effect drops off. If the comparison is extended to another stress-susceptible strain, which is not affected by glutamate, one can, nevertheless (in similar behavioral situations involving stress) find along pedigree lines mice unaffected by this agent, mice consistently affected by this agent, and mice that, though affected, maintain equilibrium and quickly escape from the effect.

One is, of course, interested not only in the description of these situations and in their genetic analysis, but in the use of these kinds of information to analyze the intermediaries between the presence of genes that predispose to each of the conditions referred to and the behaviors described. It is clear that no general answers about mouse behavior can presently be provided. Only information about this or that pedigree within our colony is available. Even information about seizure-susceptible mice or manipulatively labile mice is lacking since these too occur in various genotypes. The mouse strains can be parsed accord-ing to genotype or even within a given phenotype as a first step on the road to analysis of mechanism. When the various mechanisms that occur in the mouse on a genetic basis for each of the phenotypes under study is understood, we will, within the limits of the research, at least, be able to make some general statements about mouse behavior. It is further hoped that we will be able to identify the normal mechanisms by comparison with the number and variety of abnormal ones, each of which should identify a particular physiological departure from normal. When all of these data are eventually collated we will, hopefully, have an understanding of these aspects of mouse behavior and will no longer obscure in statistical analyses that very genetic variability that may be crucial to the understanding of the phenomena that is being investigated.

There is another aspect of genetic methodology that needs men-tion. Science is filled with analogic and correlational approaches to problems. The more complicated the field, the more of these one finds, and the less sure one is of their validity. In studying behavior this is spectacularly true, but the genetic method gives us a way of separating causal mechanisms from some false trails. What is done is to follow not only the occurrence of a trait, but the segregation of the genes that predispose to that trait. If a presumed causal mechanism can be separated from the genes that are involved in the determination of the potential for the trait, then the correlation is considered to be specious, and it is dropped as a false trail. This is the methodology of our laboratory. The attempt is made to reduce these problems to problems of gene action.

Since much has been made of the effects of early experience on later behavior, it is desirable to point out that the plasticity which appears to be so marked is often more apparent than real. Most early experience work involves manipulation of timing, quality, and intensity of experience, and the conclusions refer to a spectrum of results in which the central tendencies are summarized. When the biological substrata are also controlled through genetic selection, the results are both variable and predictable. They are variable in that the existence of a critical period which may affect later behavior is a function of the genotype; in that the precise stage in the life history of the organism when the critical period occurs, is also a function of the genotype; and in that the direction of the effect on later behavior is, again, a function of the genotype.

We have even been able to trace these effects to the intrauterine period by demonstrating differential effects of ova transplants on later behavior, between highly inbred strains of mice (Ginsburg & Hovda, 1947). The characteristics of the intrauterine environment are, in turn, determined by the genes of the mother. There is also a responding genotype, namely, that of the implant. These studies were made with later stress. In stress studies with other animals, investigators are beginning to find the very interesting evidence that, depending on the genotype, some animals will react with cardio-vascular systems, others primarily with disturbances of appetite and digestion, etc.

Our laboratory is currently interested in genetic wildness and in its response to various manipulations, including the use of tranquilizing drugs. Here again, it is found as predicted on the basis of the work already described that some individuals and some types of wild animals will respond quite differently to the same drugs from others similarly reared and conditioned (Ginsburg et al, 1962). As a matter of fact, using interactions between animals and people as the test situation, these responses are so diverse as to constitute polar opposites. For example, some of the animals do become more placid and are more easily approached and handled. Others, however, are "tranquilized" in the sense that they lose their fear of the experimenter and are, therefore, much more dangerous. Such individual differences within or between species occur on a genetic basis.

A question arises as to whether applications from these animal studies to the behavior of humans are justified. While direct comparisons cannot be made, the analogies are obvious. It is, moreover, hardly necessary to point out that we have a vertebrate-mammalian-primate ancestry, and that our own nervous systems although overlaid with layers of new developments that are uniquely human, incorporate more primitive systems as well. One hypothesis, which has been advanced independently by several investigators, is that major evolutionary breakthroughs such as the development of the double circulation of blood through the heart, depend upon a great deal of genetic variability in systems so affected. This is necessary so that selection can act on such variability and, teleologically speaking, select the best "model." When, as a result of these processes, a major evolutionary breakthrough occurs, and a significant change in structure and physiology results in a new plateau in evolution, the variability that has led to this innovation must then be buffered. Where variability was previously advantageous, departures from the new norms now become disadvantageous. Genes with such buffering effects that limit further variability then become favored in the population. Applying these notions to man, it has been contended that the human nervous system, as one of the most recent breakthroughs in evolution, is not yet at the stage where it is adequately buffered, hence, the high proportion of mental illness (Allen, 1957). We have already mentioned "releasers" involved in the behavior of many lower vertebrates. Evolution has, according to this notion, resulted in the production of special structures and movements that are capable of eliciting appropriate responses resulting in a chain of adaptive behaviors. Releasers can be analyzed and compared, and there is even a phylogeny of releasers.

The adaptive value of such mechanisms is evident. It permits the appropriate individuals to recognize each other as mates. It permits parents to signal to young. It permits territories to be claimed and defended without actual fights, and various other "socially integrating messages" to be transmitted to the appropriate group. It has been found that highly abstract models of structures and movements that serve as releasers retain the meaning of the original releasers in terms of their ability to induce appropriate behavior in a responding organism. What is interesting is that a phylogeny of such releasers amounts to a phylogeny of symbolic behavior and indicates an innate capacity in vertebrates to derive meaning from abstract symbols. What this meaning is, is not known on an ideational level, but it does have its analogical counterpart in human behavior if we accept the Jungian or Freudian viewpoints. Freud found that through the technique of free association alone, the meaning of a mental event could not always be revealed. In analyzing reports of dreams and fantasies, certain elements recurred in subject after subject. Although their meaning was obscure, the context in which they appeared and related cues provided some insight. These elements could be classified and their referents have been frequently interpreted as being sexual. They are referred to as symbols, and the level at which they are said to have meaning in the Freudian scheme seems to me to be analogous with the meaning of symbols abstracted from releasers.

Jungian theory makes even more extensive use than the Freudians of the notion of inherited mental contents called "archetypes" which are reflections of a "collective unconscious." These archetypes, although not inherited in concrete form, are said to account for the spontaneous appearance in fantasy, folk-tales, myths, rituals of certain figures—the "Sage," the "Great Mother," and the "Devil"—in widely separated societies. Jung also refers to the recurrence of certain symbols in the art of widely separated cultures.

Psychoanalysis is largely based on the proposition that a mental event can have a meaning of which the individual is not consciously aware. He can sometimes become conscious of its meaning through the use of psychoanalytic procedures. In the case of the symbols referred to they must at some level have meaning for us, since the manner in which they are used makes their meaning evident to the trained observer. Yet they do not have meaning at either the conscious or even some of the unconscious levels, as psychoanalysts use these terms. Taken together these findings suggest a continuity between human and sub-human forms at a level at which we are usually reluctant to see any comparison. The building blocks of symbolic behavior are there in lower forms, and the level at which they may have meaning in these forms is analogous to, if not identical with, a level which is thought to exist only in our own psyche. We have of course added a remarkable plasticity and at least two new levels of meaningfulness to our own ability to abstract and symbolize from a relatively lowly point on the phylogenetic tree (Ginsburg, 1949).

It would be well to end on a note that is less speculative and more conventionally genetic. Recent studies of chromosomes and chromosomal aberrations have involved new techniques that enable studies to be done that could not be done before. This has resulted in a tremendous upsurge of knowledge. One of the fruits of the new techniques is the discovery that mongolism is almost invariably associated with the occurrence of an extra chromosome (Lejeune, Gautier, & Turpin, 1959). Several cases of schizophrenia and concomittant mental retardation originating in infancy have been associated with a trisomic X (Money & Hirsch, 1963). As we begin to learn more about the biological correlates of behavioral and mental anomalies, the hope for a new kind of understanding, and therefore of treatment, becomes bright. Much work, for example, has been done on human sex anomalies (Money, Hampson & Hampson, 1955). It is now possible to determine the genetic sex of an individual. This is not always consistent for all tissues within the individual's body. Even where it is, genetic sex and hormonal sex are not always identical, nor is the genetic sex always identical with the sex in which the person has been reared. This has made it possible to do a profound and searching series of "nature-nurture" type studies on human sex anomalies, including behavioral ones, and to re-think these problems on a very different basis than was possible only a few years ago.

The approach of our own laboratory is that of collecting behavioral phenotypes and parsing each phenotype into several genotypes. Thus, in many instances, we can have several genetic ways of getting at each anomaly in order to compare and contrast the underlying mechanisms. We are striving for an understanding of the physiological basis of behavior and are approaching the problem at all levels, from the molecular to the social group. Even if we are magnificently successful, we will only be successful on one side of the problem. We have every reason to pursue our deterministic causal research philosophy. Given the appropriate skills and time, the problem of the genetic determination of behavioral potentials can be cracked, and we will achieve a quite complete explanation in mechanistic terms. Let me point out that this represents only the physical part of the psychophysical parallelism. The "psycho" part overlaps it, as has been pointed out by another geneticist, Professor Sewall Wright (1953), by 100 per cent, and one can only be in the pure psychological realm by introspection. This involves one individual, because you can extrapolate only from your own consciousness to other consciousnesses. The deterministic approach, which I think will yield the usual kind of casual-physiologi-cal-biochemical-morphological explanation, will not apply to the psycho-logical meaning of introspective events, but will only parallel these. The writer holds with his teacher, Professor Wright, that only one of these is really knowable in the usual scientific sense. The other is knowable only in the way in which you can know yourself.

REFERENCES

ALLEN, G. Genetic aspects of mental disorder. In conference of the Milbank Memorial Fund on *The nature and transmission of the genetic and cultural characteristics of human populations.* New York: Milbank Memorial Fund, 1957.

BLAUVELT, H. Neonate-mother relationship in goat and man. In B. Schaffner (Ed.), *Group processes.* New York: Josiah Macy, Jr. Foundation, 1956.

COLLIAS, N. E. The analysis of socialization in sheep and goats. *Ecology,* 1956, Vol. 37, 228-238.

EMERSON, A. The evolution of behavior among social insects. In Roe and Simpson (Eds.), *Behavior and evolution.* New Haven, Conn.: Yale Univer. Press. 1958.

FISHER, A. E. Unpublished doctoral dissertation, Pennsylvania State University, 1955.

GALTON, F. *Hereditary genius.* New York: Horizon Press, 1952.

GINSBURG, B. E. Genetics and social behavior—a theoretical synthesis. In *Lectures on genetics, cancer, growth and social behavior.* Roscoe B. Jackson Memorial Labora-tory twentieth anniversary commemoration lectures, 1949.

GINSBURG, B. E. Genetics and the physiology of the nervous system. In D. Hooker & C. C. Hare (Eds.), *Proceedings of the Association for Research in Nervous and Mental Disease.* Vol. 33: *Genetics and the inheritance of integrated neurological and psychi-atric patterns.* Baltimore: Williams and Wilkins Co., 1954.

GINSBURG, B. E. Genetics as a tool in the study of behavior. *Perspectives in Biology and Medicine,* 1958, Vol. 1, 397-424.

GINSBURG, B. E. Genetic control of the ontogeny of stress behavior. Paper presented at the Amer. Psychol. Assn. symposium entitled *Evocation mechanisms of genetic potentialities in behavior,* Chicago, Sept. 7, 1960.

GINSBURG, B. E., & ALLEE, W. C. Some effects of conditioning on social dominance and subordination in inbred strains of mice. *Physiol. Zool.,* 1942, Vol. 15, 485-506.

GINSBURG, B. E., & HOVDA, R. B. On the physiology of gene-controlled audiogenic seizures in mice. *Anat. Rec.,* 1947, Vol. 99, 65-66 (Abstract).

GINSBURG, B. E., WOOLPY, J. KLEIMAN, D., & EDWARDS, C. Comparative studies of *Canid* behavior, III. Socialization to humans on various schedules of experience and of tranquilizing drugs. *Amer. Zool.,* 1962, Vol. 2, 144 (Abstract).

HAYES, K. J., & HAYES, C. Imitation in a home raised chimpanzee. *J. comp. physiol. Psychol.,* 1952, Vol. 45, 450-459.

LEJEUNE, J., GAUTIER, M., & TURPIN, R. Les chromosomes humaines en culture de tissus. *C. Rend. Acad. Sci.,* 1959, Vol. 248, 602-603.

LEVINE, S., ALPERT, M., & LEWIS, G. W. Differential maturation of an adrenal response to cold stress in rats manipulated in infancy. *J. comp. physiol. Psychol.,* 1958, Vol. 51, 774-777.

MONEY, J., HAMPSON, J. G., & HAMPSON, J. L. An examination of some basic sexual concepts: the evidence of human hermaphroditism. *Bull. Johns Hopkins Hosp.,* 1955, Vol. 97, 301-319.

MONEY, J., & HIRSCH, S. R. Chromosome anomalies, mental deficiency, and schizophrenia. *Arch. gen. Psychiat.,* 1963, Vol. 8, 242-251.

SCHEINFELD, A. You and heredity. Philadelphia & New York: Lippincott, 1950.

SCHENKEL, R. Ausdrucks-studien an wolfen. *Behaviour,* 1948, Vol. 1, 81-130.

SCOTT, J. P. Genetic differences in the social behavior of inbred strains of mice. *J. Hered.,* 1942, Vol. 33, 11-15.

TINBERGEN, N. *The study of instinct.* London: Oxford Univer. Press, 1951.

VON FRISCH, K. *Bees: their vision, chemical senses and language.* Ithaca, N.Y.: Cornell Univer. Press, 1950.

WRIGHT, S. Gene and organism. *Am. Nat.,* 1953, Vol. 87, 5-18.

4

Adience, Self-Actualization, and Drive Theory

John M. Butler and Laura N. Rice

INTRODUCTION

For more than thirty years it has been a dominant belief in American psychology that human motivation originates in drives, and that behavior is primarily or secondarily based on drive-reduction. This view has been as pervasive in clinical psychology and psychiatry, through the influence of psychoanalysis, as it has been among learning theorists and comparative psychologists. Nevertheless a dissident minority has consistently opposed drive theory because it seemed to them inadequate to explain the complexities of human motivation and behavior as subjectively experienced and to represent a premature attempt at closure. It was to be expected that many humanists would resist any position expressly excluding a teleological element in construing human conduct, but many psychologists in their roles as scientists have also dissented from the prevailing motivational concepts.

While it has been admittedly difficult fully to comprehend human behavior within the confines of drive-reduction theory, there has been little such pessimistic dissatisfaction with respect to lower animal forms. Thus it has been unsettling to many to have to acknowledge that, over the last decade, both experimental and careful observational evidence has clearly indicated the existence of what has appeared to be non-driven behavior in rats and other laboratory animals. Studies of learning under conditions of satiation, of exploratory and "play" behavior, of alternation behavior and of "exteroceptive motivation" have all seemed to converge to invalidate the drive-reduction concept both in its specific and in its generalized forms.

Why are such findings disturbing? Most simply, because psychologists, like all scientists, value dependable propositions as a foundation for their research and theory-building. It is tolerable if a hungry rat loiters in its pursuit of a pellet of food because it has not yet learned the shortest path, but if the deprived rat's behavior suggests that some casual "interest" in its environment takes precedence over a psychologic need for nourishment, some basic securities are threatened.

Do such findings invalidate the drive-reduction concept? We believe they do not but, at the same time, we believe they require a reformulation of the concept of drive reduction. Before pursuing our argument, it may be useful to delineate briefly the bases of the discontent of those who opposed drive-reduction as a central explanatory concept and to examine as well the arguments of those who have supported the concept. At issue is the utility of basic propositions regarding the behavior of organisms on which most research and all theory rests. Those who have opposed drive-reduction as a basic construct have done so because they are convinced that behavior, as they have observed it, and particularly human behavior, cannot be elucidated in terms of the construct except by way of the introduction of additional complex, uneconomical and even untestable propositions. Those who have supported the drive-reduction hypothesis assert that their critics are teleologists who are, in effect, supporting an *elan vital* principle which places them outside modern science.

SELF-ACTUALIZATION

The concept of self-actualization has been discussed by many personality theorists, among them Goldstein (1939), Maslow (1950, 1959), and Rogers (1951). These theorists have emphasized that the evidence for the existence of self-actualizing processes comes from clinical experience. Maslow (1950) in particular has delineated characteristics of the self-actualizing person and stresses what he calls self-expression or growth motivation in self-actualizing people, as opposed to deficiency motivation which he identifies with the primary drives of drive theory. He states that self-actualizing people do not strive in the usual sense but rather develop in contrast with others who attempt to compensate for their lack of basic need gratification. The self-actualizing person does not lack basic need gratification, yet he is motivated. For self-actualizing people, Maslow suggests, motivation is character growth, character expression, maturation and development. The distinctive characteristic of the self-actualizing person is that he is autonomous; his development is not based on deficiency motivation nor can it be derived from the primary drives which represent deficiency motivation.

Among psychotherapists, the Rogerians (Rogers, 1951) rely most firmly upon growth motivation. Anyone who has observed or heard a competent Rogerian therapist during a therapeutic hour would undoubtedly react negatively to his behavior unless he shared with the therapist the idea that the client has inherent capacities for self realization. The Rogerian therapist is not a resource for the client, as this concept is usually understood, for he does not give information to the client; he does not provide any new frame of reference from his own store of concepts; he does not impose regimes; and he attempts neither to reassure nor to support the client. He does not manipulate anxiety, acting so as to reduce it when it is too high or increase it when it is too low. Instead he relies in the main upon displaying prizing behavior and communicating his understanding of the client as he presents himself "here and now." It is difficult to imagine a more complete reliance upon the self-restorative capacities of the client than that shown by the Rogerians.

The issue with respect to self-actualizing tendencies, we think, has to do not with their existence but with their origin. Maslow, Goldstein, Rogers, and others (Butler & Rice, 1960) think that self-actualizing motives are inherent, basic and primitive, whereas drive theorists tend to think that self-actualizing motives are based on higher-order reinforcement stemming ultimately from the primary drives and from learnable drives such as fear. The issue as it has been discussed for twenty years or more (much more if psychoanalytic theory is classified as a drive theory) centers about, first, whether self-actualizing motives are primary or derived, and second, whether, if they are primary, they can be conceived in terms of drive reduction.

Those who hold that self-actualizing tendencies are inherent and primal hold also that self-actualizing motives cannot be discussed profitably in terms of drive reduction. On the other hand drive theorists, such as Dollard and Miller (1951), who believe motivation depends ultimately on the reduction of primary drives would, no doubt, hold that self-actualizing motivations are derived drives. As virtually everyone now accepts, the notion of drive-reduction—when viewed as involving a deficit external to the nervous system acting as a persistent stimulus that energizes the organism to make responses, one of which is finally reinforced—is not adequate even to account for behavior based on the hunger drive. As Miller (1961) has pointed out, the neural centers and humoral factors must enter into the concept of drive in a way not included in the "orthodox" concept. For example, the research of Sheffield, Wulf and Backer (1951) has shown that drive arousal itself may be reinforcing. Thus, even within the framework of drive theory, it has become apparent that the older formulation was considerably oversimplified.

Even though the drive concept at present includes the effects of central neural activity and humoral and biochemical factors, which complicate and attenuate the earlier conceptions of drive, we believe nevertheless that drive-reduction, the keystone of the old concept, is still central when reformulated. We believe also that the drive concept applies more to such phenomena as exploratory behavior, manipulative behavior and preference for complexity than to those drives usually designated as primary or as learnable. We believe, in short, that there is a drive—we shall call it *stimulus hunger* [1] or *adient motivation*— which is a primary drive, perhaps even the most pervasive primary drive. We believe that this drive is the primal base for self-actualizing behavior and may be characterized fairly as a developmental drive in the sense that it results in development. In discussing this drive we shall rely primarily upon studies of prolonged and temporary sensory deprivation rather than upon studies of exploratory or adient behavior. The latter category of studies seems to raise questions; the former to answer them.

Our discussion of the relevant literature will touch only some of the more significant studies, since the mass of literature is large and much of it has been ably reviewed in the volumes by Berlyne (1960) and by Fiske and Maddi (1961).

RADICAL SENSORY DEPRIVATION

Stimulation is so pervasive for every organism that the very concept of a completely unstimulated organism is meaningless. It has long been noticed that dramatic changes take place in human beings imprisoned

---

[1] Freud (1949) mentions the concept of hunger for stimulation in an essay on sexual aberrations but did not consider it as very important (p. 29). Fenichel (1945) also holds that hunger for stimulation is a derivative of the need to abolish or reduce stimuli (p. 59).

for years of solitary confinement in the dark and it is well-known that children raised without parents in dull institutional surroundings suffer some form of developmental arrest. Biochemical and neuro-physiological studies have indicated for half a century that the very development of the nervous system is crucially dependent upon metabolic processes which themselves are dependent upon stimulation. Since development is by definition cumulative, early stimulation or lack of it is necessarily an important factor in development.

The most radical sensory deprivation which can be inflicted upon an organism is that accomplished by deafferentiation. It has been found for rats (Hess, 1958) that visual deafferentiation before birth results in degeneration and developmental arrest, and this occurs more quickly than in rabbits, cats and primates (Riesen, 1961, Ch. 2). Apparently the higher the species the more rapid the degeneration and the developmental arrest. Such irreversible deafferentiation results in pallor of the optic disk and reduction in RNA and in the ganglion cell layers.

When deafferentiation is accomplished functionally by withholding visual stimulation, experimental results (Rasch, Swift, Riesen & Chow, 1961) indicate partial but slow reversibility of the effects of the deprivation. Their results also indicate that vision is adequate even after severe visual deprivation until RNA and cellular density fall below 50 per cent. Thus it seems that extreme conditions of neural arrest or atrophy must occur before actual behavioral incapacity becomes evident.

A fact that seems to be of the utmost significance is that motor neurons become hypersensitive (Riesen, 1961) in the absence of stimulation and that locomotor sequences may then be initiated by minimal excitation. With stimulus control absent or minimal during early development, intrinsic behavior patterns appear that are minimally responsive to environmental events.

Withholding patterned visual stimulation produces deficiencies in sensory-motor associations necessary for coordinated behavior dependent upon vision. Discriminations requiring pattern vision and movement, interocular transfer and initial learning are retarded; the retardation increases as one goes up the phylogenetic scale. Since withholding visual stimulation requires restricted environments, some of the retardation noticed may be due to interference in learning stemming from high levels of activation occasioned by new stimulation (Melzack, 1962).

Riesen (1961, Ch. 2) considers that the maximum need for stimulation is early and that critical exposure effects result from patterns of stimulation. He has suggested, however, that there is a continuing requirement for stimulation that defies treatment in terms of a critical period hypothesis. He notes, for instance, that man and the higher primates develop a fear of unusual stimulus patterns. This type of behavioral effect depends upon previous exposure to specific stimulus patterns. At four or five months of age fear of new stimulus patterns can be observed in chimpanzees, but in animals kept in pattern-free light to seven months, the fear does not appear until ten months of age. As Riesen notes, the older infant chimpanzee is able to avoid more energetically once the critical stage in the sequence of stimulation has been reached.

While later work may show that functional stimulus deprivation is reversible even when severe, early experience is more critical than later experience in relation to development since it is less subject to response-competition and to increments in capacity as simple as greater muscular strength. Also, for example, the development of intrinsic neck and eye movements in the absence of visual stimulation competes with the responses that must have external stimulation in order to develop. Thus the organism is handicapped in developing responses requiring muscle and eye movement integration once the intrinsically developed movements have become established (Riesen, 1961b).

The experimental results alluded to above and many others attest to the fact that withholding stimulation early in the life of the organism results in sensory, perceptual, and motivational anomalies that are only with difficulty reversed or corrected and that result in adult organisms unable to adapt efficiently to variable environments. The ability to deal with and to integrate a varied sensory influx is definitely lowered when stimulation is markedly reduced early in the life of the organism. This is due to the deterioration of innate mechanisms in the absence of stimulation or because stimulation is required for the development of the necessary mechanisms.

On the other hand it has been shown that unusual early stimulation of organisms produces measurable effects on later behavior. For example, rats handled early in infancy are more resistant to the effects of food and water deprivation than non-handled rats (Levine & Otis, 1958), and Harlow (1958, 1959) has shown that for young monkeys appropriate cutaneous stimulation early in life seems to enhance the animals' resistance to stress situations.

What the studies on both stimulus deprivation (impoverished experience) and unusual amounts of stimulation seem to indicate is that in a relative way the *amount* of stimulation may be more important for younger organisms and the *complexity* of stimulation more important for older organisms. The studies suggest that physical development, ability to learn, resistance to stress and motivation are all drastically affected by early experience.

TEMPORARY SENSORY DEPRIVATION

The preceding discussion indicates that the effects of temporary sensory deprivation should be considered in relation to the total experience (or lack of it) of the organism up to the time of the deprivation.[2] At this time little is known about the effects of temporary deprivation under varying antecedent conditions of severe and prolonged deprivation. One of the best studies of relatively short-term deprivation is that of Fox (1959). His experiments were so well controlled that our consideration of temporary sensory deprivation will be restricted to his reports. His study consisted of four experiments:

Experiment I. Monkeys were placed in darkened cages for periods up to eight hours. After varying periods of light deprivation, constant response rates were obtained when the response was bar-pressing for .5 seconds of light stimulation while the monkeys were still in the dark. Rates of response increased with increase of time in darkness during the pre-test period of light deprivation.

Experiment II. During the period in which bar-pressing brought sensory reward, various amounts of free ambient light were introduced. The introduction of ambient light decreased response rates for all of the various periods of light deprivation.

Experiment III. Injected amphetamine, an adrenergic drug, increased rates of bar-pressing for light in both normal and light-deprived monkeys. The drug's action seemed to indicate an increased requirement of the animal for stimulation, even though it is known that amphetamine activates (as judged by EEG patterns) and thus might be a substitute for stimulation.

Experiment IV. Electrodes were implanted in the diffuse projecting nuclei of six animals. Deep EEG recordings taken in the dark during response-free periods throughout the test cycle showed increasing proportions of high voltage slow activity immediately preceding the appearance of bundles of responses. During and after pressing the bar to receive light reward an activated type of EEG was seen.

[2] After this chapter was written, our attention was called to a report by Lockard (*Science*, Feb. 2, 1961, Vol. 135) which indicates that albino rats kept in darkness for twelve days strongly prefer darkness to 1.0 milleamps light, while rats kept in 100 milleamps light for twelve days prefer 1.0 milleamps light for substantial periods. His results are consistent with Fox's hypothesis of a chronic activation level.

Fox interpreted his data to indicate a need for sensory reward or input after varying degrees of light deprivation. He viewed the bar-pressing response for light as determined by the reduction in activation of non-specific areas of the brain stem. Lowered neural activity then triggered responses that were instrumental in restoring optimal sensory input. He accounted for an increased need for light under amphetamine by postulating an intrinsic or chronic activation level, representing all previous sensory input and especially that occurring early in the history of the organism. The chronic activation level, he proposed, changes slowly over time and is relatively permanent. Thus the organism's immediate need for stimulation is a function of the match (or lack of it) between the chronic activation level and the acute activation level induced by transient stimulation. The amphetamine raised the chronic level of activation, thus increasing the discrepancy between the chronic and acute levels. The need for experience might, therefore, be regarded in much the same way as the need for water or the need for food. As Fox (1959, p. 81) put it, "In the case of behaviorally maintained sensory input, the diffuse activating systems have been assigned the function of mirroring the level of acute activation. On the other hand, the cortex, for example, may be found to store and provide information concerning the chronic activation level."

Fox's experiments show clearly that visual deprivation leads to the performance of responses that change the environment so as to increase visual stimulation. Each experiment taken alone can lead to the conclusion that "increasing stimulation" is rewarding. Considered together, his experiments lead instead to the conclusion that increasing the match between acute and intrinsic activation levels is rewarding rather than merely increasing stimulation. Closely controlled experiments such as Fox's indicate that the organism actually transacts with the environment in such a manner as to obtain an optimal inner state, such a state being in this case an (hypothetically) optimal relationship between acute and chronic activation levels.[3]

[3] A study by Wendt, Lindsley, Adey and Fox (*Science,* Jan. 25, 1963, Vol. 139) indicates that monkeys reared in darkness for 16 of their 17 months of life, except for daily one-hour periods of explosure to unpatterned light, show apparently insatiable responding at very high rates when allowed to press a lever to obtain unpatterned light. They conclude that the effects of short-term experimental sensory deprivation cannot be isolated from the total sensory history of the animal. Although their results are open to alternative interpretations, the results do suggest that there is an absolute need for stimulation as well as a need for stimulation based on a discrepancy between chronic and acute levels of activation.

ADIENT BEHAVIOR AND MOTIVATION

Holt, in his treatise, *Animal Drive and the Learning Process,* proposed in 1930 that there was an innate approach tendency (adience) to mild stimulation that was omnipresent in the waking state, and that most avoidance tendencies (abience) were learned. In terms of Fox's results and formulation, adience might be viewed as a tendency to behave in ways resulting in closer matches of acute and chronic activation. Later, Carmichael, Coriona, and Schlesberg (Carmichael, 1946, Ch. 2) showed that in the fetal cat moderate stimulation with a bristle resulted in adient movement toward the stimulus source. It was as though the animal were trying to increase the stimulation or to get more of the same sort of stimulation. Contrarily, vigorous stimulation resulted not in avoidance or withdrawal but in mass action.

From extensively discussed and well-known studies mentioned by Berlyne (1960) and by Fiske and Maddi (1961) it is known that:

1. The more complex a stimulus, the more adient behavior it elicits in the sense that it is behaviorally preferred over less complex stimuli.

2. Exploratory behavior is highly persistent and stimulus novelty can be used as a positive reinforcer for instrumental and discrimination learning.

3. Visual deprivation increases the strength of adient tendencies.

4. Animals under high levels of thirst or hunger drives will, nevertheless, exhibit adient behavior.

From studies of child development it is known that very young children will attempt to track auditory and visual stimuli and, as their musculature develops, they will progressively orient in a more total fashion to novel stimuli or to change in the environment. First they orient; then, when able, they move toward the stimulus object: they touch it, grasp it, place it in their mouths, against the eyes, ears, nose, rub it over the body surfaces, etc. In short, they "monkey" with it. But it is significant that all possible sensory modalities are used and that many different parts of the body come in contact with the stimuli.

Adient behavior is currently interpreted as a "wish for new experience," or in terms of motives different from the "physiological drives." But current studies are quite complex and depend upon notions such as novelty and complexity, concepts that are not well-defined. In our opinion, the work on curiosity, exteroceptive motivation, exploratory behavior, spontaneous alternation, etc., can be interpreted in accordance with the work of Fox. On the assumption that the chronic level of activation is usually greater than the acute level of activation, orienting behavior and manipulative behavior (including manual, tactile, oral, olfactory and visual exploration of stimulus complexes) increase activation and produce a closer match between chronic and acute activation levels.

The work on prolonged and temporary sensory deprivation (and on exploratory behavior) when considered in relation to Fox's hypothesis of chronic activation, has many implications. For example, a complex object will have many possibilities for crossing sensory modalities with their separate potentialities for transmitting information and will thereby evoke further response-produced stimuli which in turn contribute to the acute or immediately produced activation level. Hence complex objects can present diverse sources of acute activation and can lead to a close match between the two types of activation level when the level of acute activation is below the level of chronic activation.

In terms of Fox's conception we infer the following:

1. A match between the two levels of activation corresponds to a lack of interest. It is known that adaptation occurs when a stimulus is continuously presented; this adaptation may be interpreted as a loss in the power to produce acute activation. A stimulus source may initially produce a match between the acute and chronic activation levels, but soon thereafter the stimulus may lose its capacity for producing acute activation. It is expected, therefore, that an organism will be induced to scan its environment and orient to other stimuli.

2. When the chronic activation level is higher than the acute level, adient behavior toward an activating stimulus will follow. At the point at which the two types of activation are matched, orienting to other stimuli or making new movements even in a familiar environment will cease, for these would tend to increase the acute activation level. However, if it is granted that the capacity of a stimulus to activate decreases over time, a discrepancy between the acute and chronic activation levels develops and orientation to other stimuli begins again.

3. When the acute level is higher than the chronic level, the stimuli producing the acute level will be avoided, will assume an aversive character. In other words, the positive valence and negative valence of stimuli correspond to a state of the organism in relation to stimuli; they are not intrinsic characteristics of the stimuli themselves.

Many of the ambiguities in the concept of stimulation are removed by identifying the term with the degree of discrepancy between the semi-permanent, chronic and constantly shifting acute activation levels. For example, the precise meaning of the words "strong" and "weak" stimuli has always been somewhat vague and ill-defined. A clicker sounded when a child is awake will arouse its curiosity and stimulate orienting and manipulative behavior. In the present context, the elicitation of such behavior implies that the chronic activation level is above the acute level when the clicking begins. In the waking state the sound will begin to raise the acute activation to a level closer to the chronic level, thus eliciting orienting and adient behavior. When the child is falling asleep, the chronic level may be low, and the clicker will often produce a startle reaction with resultant prolonged wakefulness and sometimes crying. In such a case it seems likely that the auditory stimulus rapidly increases the acute activation level above that of the intrinsic level. From this point of view, a strong stimulus may be conceived as one that raises the acute level of activation above the chronic level. When the rise in acute activation is abrupt, a startle reaction may occur, sometimes followed by avoidant behavior. When the rise is relatively slow, only avoidant behavior may ensue. Since the acute activation level can be expected to subside rather slowly when it has greatly exceeded the chronic level, our hypothetical child will first be startled into wakefulness, and matching of the activation levels can in this case be occasioned by a fall in the acute level of activation. Thus the stimulus can lose its aversive quality.

It is well known that the startle response itself adapts quickly. This can be understood if it is conceived that the chronic activation level varies during the diurnal period and, in particular, during the waking state. Fox (1959) has assumed that this is the case. If a sudden rising and falling of stimulus intensity occurs when the chronic level of activation is at a high point in the cycle, it can be expected that the startle response will disappear with relative rapidity. If the same stimulus occurs when the chronic activation level is at a low point in the daily cycle, it is to be expected that the startle response will disappear more slowly because of the greater differential between activation levels.

Given an organism that is startled but does not show a fear reaction or is restrained from fleeing, one can predict that as the acute activation level drops following the startle situation and becomes less than the chronic activation level, adient behavior will ensue. Although this question has not been approached experimentally to our knowledge, it seems to be a commonly observed fact. For instance, when a novel object is thrown into a group of pigeons in a loft, they will fly from the floor to perches, but will then—especially the young and sexually immature birds—approach the object, peck it, etc., in a display of curiosity typical of pigeons. The reaction is especially noticeable shortly after pigeons have been fed and watered or after they have bathed.

Again, it is a common observation that the young of a species engage in more exploratory behavior than adults, but the young organism has had a relatively short history of transaction with the environment. Thus immediate experience may be expected to have more effect upon the acute activation level than at a later date. Moreover, the chronic level is, we conjecture, more labile early in life. When both levels of activation are rising, and the acute level, whether rising faster or slower than the chronic, is below the chronic level, adient behavior can be expected to occur.

We think of the concept of chronic activation level as extremely fruitful, although for Fox it was simply a concept used to account for experimental results. Acute activation, on the other hand, has empirical status in terms of peripheral stimulation and in terms of the injection of adrenergic sensitizing agents such as amphetamine, with their known effects on EEG activity. Furthermore, the effects of agents such as amphetamine run parallel to behavior. Supporting evidence for chronic or intrinsic activation in the waking state comes from the observation that direct stimulation of the brain (particularly the cingulate, orbital and lateral frontal regions) awakens the animal without initiating behavior or after-discharge that might result in indirect peripheral sources of activation (Magoun, 1958). Furthermore, since adrenergic substances produce activation running parallel to behavior whereas cholinergic substances do not, it seems reasonable to assume that cholinergic substances may be associated with cortically initiated activation whereas adrenergic substances may be associated with peripheral activation of the ascending reticular system. Moreover, Sharpless and Jaspers (1956) have proposed that the more caudally directed part of the reticular activating system functions mainly in the maintenance of long period wakefulness, while the rest is sensitive to slight changes in the quality of stimuli. In view of these lines of experimental evidence, it seems plausible, to conjecture that wakefulness may be sustained in part by impulses from the cortex that affect chiefly the caudally situated portion of the ascending reticular activation system.

This would be particularly true in the absence of stimulus change or in the presence of low levels of stimulation. Rinaldi and Himwich (1946, 1955) indicate that this is associated with cholinergic activation mechanisms. It seems, then, that the wakefulness of the organism may be in part intrinsic or autonomous, and wakefulness in the face of relative non-stimulation can be sustained to a certain extent by the cortex.

It should be emphasized that the neurophysiological speculation outlined in this chapter is intended to show that Fox's hypothesis of chronic activation level is consistent with results from studies unrelated to his. The effect which he calls chronic activation level could, as we have seen, be mediated by the cortex. It is possible, however, that it could reside entirely within the ascending reticular activation system. In any event, his hypothesis of a chronic activation level dependent upon experience and varying diurnally seems to be consistent with current neurophysiological knowledge.

Riesen (1961b) indicates in another illuminating way that stimulation can be motivating. Among a number of cats one cat was reared in total darkness for nine months. On being transferred to an environment of people who played with him, this cat developed normal accuracy for striking swinging balls, jumping over hurdles, and performing visual responses with one-minute delays. In contrast, cage-confined cats with the same upbringing could not show such coordination or delay a visual response for sixty seconds like the apartment-housed, family-surrounded cat. Thus, later perceptual learning requires, as Riesen says, "exceptionally favorable conditions, especially motivational, if the developmental arrest is to be overcome." What might these motivational conditions be in the case of the cat transferred to the apartment?

First, being raised for nine months in total darkness, the cat's chronic activation level would necessarily have been low. But in the apartment there were many and varied sources of stimulation including many different kinds of movement (proprioceptive stimulation). Although we do not know this, since Riesen's statement does not specify, it is to be expected that when moved to the enriched environment, the acute activation level often became higher than the chronic with resultant avoidant behavior. But the apartment had many retreats where overstimulation could be nullified. As time went on (a few weeks, Riesen reports), the cat could see what he was doing and was very playful (adient behavior). In other words, the enriched environment of the family-raised cat may well have elevated the chronic activation level with the result that not only did the visual-motor coordination of the animal increase but its commerce with the environment increased. It is true that the cage-confined compeers of this cat were in an enriched environment compared to total darkness, but it was relatively static and the behavioral possibilities were very limited. One would expect the chronic activation level in these creatures to be somewhat elevated, but the crucial factor of movement-directed commerce even with the total visual environment was lacking. Hence, one would expect the acute and chronic levels of activation in these animals to approach a match, with a resultant picture of quiescent and unmotivated animals. In the apartment, however, the environment included people. The selected animal was protected, fed, petted, lifted, and subjected to long sequences of patterned stimuli. These sequences motivated the cat possibly by changing activation levels and the relationships between them, and made of him a "self-actualizing" animal which realized in behavior various potentialities apparently not actualized in the cage-confined cats.

The behavior of this cat lends support to Riesen's contention that there are periods during which sensory stimulation and association learning experiences (in which movement-produced stimulation is itself essential) are critical in the realization of growth and of behavioral potential. Should the critical stimulation be missing at the optimum period, later stimulation may counteract the early deprivation with behavioral capacities making their appearance more slowly or being lower in their behavioral adequacy. And one of the essential ingredients, it would appear, is the motivating effect of elevating chronic activation levels.

TYPES OF DRIVE

The research on early radical visual deprivation, isolation, and later mild deprivation, indicates that stimulation is a critical necessity if the mammalian organism is to be truly adaptive to varied environments. This research also indicates that an optimally stimulated organism is in touch with its environment in an exquisitely delicate way. Its interaction with its environment is, in effect, motivating, since it is the activation mechanisms (in accordance with which activation levels rise, subside, and match in ways that render stimuli attractive, unattractive, aversive or uninteresting) that govern the organism's transactions with its surround. The need for stimulation has many of the characteristics of the food and thirst drives. However, the difference may be more significant than the similarity. Weak stimuli, those unable to elevate the acute activation level above the chronic activation level, lose their power to maintain the acute activation level rather quickly, due to adaptation. Hence in an impoverished environment, the animals will quickly become quiescent. But new stimuli or a change in stimulation will raise the level of activation and general approach behavior when the acute activation level is below the chronic level. However, more food and more water will have a less pronounced effect when given at a satiation point, although it is well known that animals will eat more and drink more when *new* food is introduced at the satiation point. A new female presented to a male rat that has just abandoned sexual behavior will elicit additional behavior even though the female is not in oestrus (Grunt & Young, 1952). However, the limit of responsivity of the physiologically satiated organism is reached much more quickly than are the limits of organisms confronted with environmental stimulus variation. New situation after new situation generates approach behavior until the organism becomes so fatigued as to require sleep, whereas the satiation point for food can seldom be even doubled by the introduction of varied foods.

A critical difference in these two circumstances seems to be that drives such as hunger and thirst are necessary primarily for maintenance of the organism, while stimulus hunger, or the need for variation or manipulative drives or exteroceptive motivation, are essential to maximum functional efficiency of the organism in its environment. Thus in one sense they may be characterized as developmental drives—not instinctual push for development as such, but drives resulting in development. As studies of radical sensory deprivation show, the development of animals whose maintenance drives are satisfied but who are sensorily deprived develop autochthonous patterns of behavior which match the organism poorly to a complex and demanding environment. The inadequate match is a consequence of perceptual-motor deficiencies that are reversible only with time and difficulty, if at all. Varied and shifting environments produce orienting, approach and manipulative behavior which on the one hand is related to the match of activation levels, and on the other to the actual development of neuro-muscular structures. The eventual result is a Darwinian organism optimally adaptive and optimally developed biologically.

In our view, exploratory drives, manipulation drives, effectance motivation, mastery drives, exteroceptive motivation and the like, are, to the extent that they are distinctive drives or motives, secondary to and derived from stimulus hunger—from the need to match intrinsic and acute levels of activation. These drives all function in behavior to effect changes in the environment which makes it more complex or shifting and therefore productive of differing channels of stimulation. These in turn tend to elevate and sustain the acute activation level. Thus these drives are purely mechanical, although they function so as to develop the organism in a biological sense and to make it more adaptable. The maintenance drives, on the other hand, have the unique and in many respects limited function of replenishing the organism. They also may function in development, but to the extent that they do, they seem to function in the same way as stimulus hunger—that is, by way of raising the acute activation level. The maintenance drives, in contrast to stimulus hunger, at a certain point raise the acute level of activation above the chronic level. In this way they may function like the emergency or pain drives and thus at this point the behavior may be regarded as avoidant and the internal stimulus as aversive. Stimulus hunger, on the other hand, depends on the elevation of chronic over acute activation; hence we may think of the maintenance drives when strong as a sub-class of the emergency or pain drives. The expressions "mild" and "strong" here refer to ratios between chronic and acute activation levels, not to absolute "strength."

Emergency and pain drives are similar in that they involve levels of acute activation higher than the chronic. The drives may be differentiated on the basis of rate of onset with emergency drives typified by rapid rises in acute activation level and pain drives by slow rise in onset. Thus electric shock may produce the effect of startle or surprise initially, but when continued at length or when damaging to end-organs, may take the character of pain.

Anxiety, from this point of view, may be thought of as internally self-produced stimuli rising relatively slowly in intensity until the acute activation level is somewhat above the chronic level. It may remain above the chronic level for relatively long periods of time.

In our view, then, there are three main classes of drives. Maintenance drives serve to replenish and supply the organism. They may produce acute activation levels below the chronic level (low strength) and may rise until the acute level is above the chronic level (high strength). Emergency and pain drives, of which anxiety may be a sub-class, are characterized by acute levels of activation above the chronic level. Developmental drives are characterized by chronic levels of activation that are above the acute level. The three classes of drives in the order named lead to consummatory responses, avoidant responses, and approach responses. When considered in relation to the type of stimulation involved, as for example, in electric shock, a weak shock producing acute levels of activation below the chronic level may induce approach, manipulative and exploratory behavior. When the hunger drive is weak but rising, exploratory and search behavior may be confounded (or both present). But when the acute level of activation surpasses the chronic level, stimuli assume an aversive quality and avoidance behavior ensues when the situation allows, and when the organism has acquired a repertory of avoidant responses. When stimuli from the external evironment are mild, the acute level of activation tends to be below the chronic level; approach behavior ensues, and an effort will be made to produce a new or changed environment. If this is unsuccessful, the chronic level will change and the animal becomes, descriptively speaking, bored and finally apathetic. Apparently, the environmental stimuli become aversive. However, what actually happens is that the chronic level at first becomes progressively higher than the acute level and the properties of the stimuli are quite different than is the case when the acute activation level is abruptly and markedly raised above the chronic level.

Speaking of human experience, the pain of "boredom," i.e., a marked discrepancy between chronic and acute levels of activation with the chronic level higher, is quite distinguishable from the pain of strong stimulation in which acute activation is greater than chronic activation. Finally, "optimal level of stimulation" here refers to balance between chronic and acute activation levels; the "complexity" of an object refers to the possibilities of its providing from varied sources acute activation, and the "novelty" of an object refers to its capacity to provide acute activation. Since the chronic level is assumed to vary diurnally as well as over relatively long periods of time, the complexity and novelty of unchanging stimuli, as reflected in behavior of the organism, will covary with chronic activation levels as well as with acute activation levels.

ADIENT MOTIVATION AND PERSONALITY DEVELOPMENT

It is tempting to give further consideration to hypotheses growing out of the concept of developmental drives which could be easily tested in experiments with animals. For example, it can be inferred that mildly hungry animals will eat more in a complex, mildly novel environment than in a bland or boring environment. However, it is our purpose here to consider developmental drives in relation to human development and psychotherapy. With regard to human development, it can be hypothesized that stimulus hunger is on the average stronger than the maintenance and pain drives, at least in a well-ordered society. A society functions so as to provide food, drink, shelter, sexual partners, biological health, etc. In other words, these drives are generally mild because they are well-satisfied, and possibly because in a complex society they have, relatively speaking, low value. This being the case, one might suspect—and indeed it is a matter of common observation— that in the young human being, adient behavior is prominently displayed. On the other hand, property, especially the personal property of the household, leads to exploratory behavior which is punished or, when not punished, is frustrated. In an unpublished study (Butler, 1948) which was conducted in student housing units, adient behavior was found to be overwhelmingly the behavior that was punished because it involved destroying valued family property, or was embarrassing to parents because it was "unmannerly," or because it was dangerous to the child. Parents who did not believe in punishment most often frustrated the child by suppressing the adient behavior. Those parents who used "distraction" techniques found that the varieties of distraction did not equal the varieties of the environment; they were, in their own frustration, prone to "blow up" and resort to sudden and (to the child) inconsistent and unpredictable behavior. Punishment for childish aggression and sexual behavior occurred relatively less frequently, because these were sophisticated parents. It seemed clear that adient behavior provided the most frequent occasion for both punishment and frustration and that, in fact, the greater part of punishment and correction was oriented around it.

On the other hand, these well-educated and sophisticated young parents encouraged, most often by the use of carrot-and-stick techniques, those varieties of adient behavior relating to achievement and competence. These children were generally encouraged to be pleased with themselves when exhibiting competence and displeased with themselves when not. Observing these children and their parents, it was tempting to predict that as adults their competence motivation would be based on both adient and avoidant tendencies or anxiety. Yet one could see how a relatively primitive sense of competence could develop in the younger children, especially those less than one year old. To them, the great majority of the responses of the parents were to the behavior of the child, whether adient or based on fear, and demonstrated how the child could come to feel in some primitive way that he caused everything to happen, good as well as bad. The more loving parents were especially enchanted by their babies' adient behavior. They responded positively to most of it while responding much more negatively to a much larger share of the adient behavior of their older and more active siblings. We believe that the childish sense of omnipotence is largely based on this responsiveness of parents to children, whether positive or negative. Mothers and fathers who responded to their younger children, crooning over them, petting them, rocking them, and providing them with new toys or varied ways of playing with old toys, seemed to produce adient behavior in their offspring which in turn elicited more playful, affectionate behavior in the parents. In such recurrent circumstances, one could see how the child might at some point arrive at a primitive generalization which may be phrased, "I cause almost everything, and that which I cause is good or pleasing."

The younger children of parents who responded negatively to adient behavior more frequently showed signs of discomfort, such as crying and other less adient responses. These children, who seemed more often than not to get negative responses regardless of what they did, might generalize in the following way: "I cause everything and most of what happens is bad or displeasing." The circular effects of the response tendencies were clearly noticeable. The children initiated the responses and in general received the kind of responses they initiated. Probably this was not initially true of the children receiving negative responses, but by the time they were observed by the investigator there was a well established circularity. The children receiving positive responses showed much more adient behavior and less crying; the children receiving negative responses revealed less adient behavior and cried more often.

In terms of activation level, the children receiving positive responses were getting optimal levels of stimulation, since their chronic activation level was often matched by their acute level as a consequence of new stimuli constantly being brought in. The other children initiated responses which more often and more quickly resulted in the acute level of activation being elevated above the chronic. The behavior repertory of these very young children was limited to crying and thrashing around, and the ensuing parental responses often tended again to raise acute activation levels above chronic levels. Such a situation understandably can lead in the extreme to a child being afraid to behave except in response to specific cues, to a child with a high need for structure. More accurately, in such a child impulses to behave in an experimental exploratory fashion would arouse anxiety, thus tending to inhibit adient behavior.

If one effect of anxiety is to inhibit behavior, and the tendency of parents is to react to children rather than to initiate responses, adient behavior may well be inhibited. The child that is frequently punished or punished too severely may experience recurrent cycles of anxiety in which the chronic level is below the acute level of activation. This may be followed or accompanied by boredom in which the chronic level is well above the acute level. The very tendency to respond is inhibited in this instance, since the impulse to respond becomes the conditioned signal for anxiety.

In the course of development, the effect of stimulation begins to have less effect upon the chronic level because the immediate transitory stimulation comes to be a lesser and lesser portion of individual experience. At the same time more of the environment is familiar and has less capacity to elevate the acute activation level. Consequently, the individual seeks a wider territory and new experiences which involve higher output of effort, and more adient behavior in the sense of more exploratory behavior occurs.

However, there is a concurrent implication associated with the development of conceptualizing ability. As the ability to conceptualize increases, the individual generalizes from his separate experiences and symbolizes for himself past transactions with his environment. Probably the most important part of the environment is the response environment and in particular the responses of other people. If adient behavior has been encouraged by parents and peers, the individual is likely to conceptualize himself and others as interesting, capable, worthwhile, competent, lovable, friendly, likable, etc. He therefore concludes (and projects) symbolically that most of his spontaneous reactions are regarded favorably and he is likely to conceive of himself as an attractive and potent individual in a receptive world.

This outcome is due not to the unique quality of stimulus hunger but to the fact that on the average the maintenance and emergency drives have not been as strongly evoked as stimulus hunger. Children generally are fed, clothed, provided with liquid, protected from noxious stimulations, etc. Thus reasonably well-cared-for children can be expected to produce more behavior engaging the attention of parents on the basis of adient motivation than behavior consonant with maintenance or emergency motivations. They are also likely to be persistent and courageous, for while any environment has its share of punishment and aversive stimulation, for these lucky children punishment and frustration will be intermittent with the balance on the side of reward. It is this intermittent reinforcement that makes him courageous and persistent.

ADIENT MOTIVATION AND THINKING PROCESSES

The individual whose adient behavior is rewarded more often than not, who is sufficiently stimulated, will develop conceptual systems and cognitive structures that lead to varied environments and transactions with the environment that are rewarding. Thus his chronic level of activation continuously rises and he continuously interacts with his environment in a way that makes this environment interesting to him. As a consequence, his concepts of self and other are constantly enlarged in a way that confirms his expectations and is consistent with his earlier development.

The growth of conceptualizing ability has many consequences, one of the more important of which might be characterized by what we call autonomy. Autonomy here refers to the capability of having differentiated conceptual experience. The individual may, as he develops conceptually, reward or punish himself in such a manner as to change in important ways without displaying overt behavior and without having subsequent consequential transactions with his environment. Thinking, as has often been pointed out, may in many instances be vicarious behavior. The individual whose adient behavior has been rewarded more often than punished will not be rendered anxious and thus inhibited by many of his impulses and thoughts. Keeping in mind that thinking processes may be substantially initiated in the cortex and recognizing that there are pathways linking the cortex with the reticular activating systems, one result of thinking is that of keeping the individual alert and wakeful. Not many lower organisms keep themselves awake and alert for long periods when not under strong maintenance drives, but human beings notoriously keep vigils and remain awake by means of thinking, talking, reading or looking.

Another consequence of thinking, we surmise, is that thinking processes as vicarious behavior act much like stimuli in raising the acute activation level. The elaboration of thinking processes then affects both the chronic and acute activation levels, thus paralleling the affect of transactions with a changing environment. In this view, a train of thought may have the effect of a train of stimuli; it is rewarding in that acute activation levels are raised toward the chronic level. There may be other kinds of rewards in thinking for the sophisticated organism but this primitive reward is also present. In other words, the more information contained in a train of reflective thought, the more novel or more original or more complex it is, the more rewarding it is—and, it might be added, the better remembered.

The individual whose adient behavior has been rewarded more often than not in the course of his development will, it is believed, be one who is self-rewarded through thinking, who is autonomous and unpredictable because he develops new and richly meaningful cognitive structures on an intrinsic as well as on a transactional basis. Such a person is one who may have a wealth of experience and who is spontaneously self-interesting while apparently doing nothing but keeping awake. He will be self-absorbed, not in the sense of a primitive self-occupation but in the sense of having as lively a concern with objects of thought with which he has transactions as he does when he has adient transactions with his environment. In this sense he is objective. The creation of new cognitive structures creates novelty in the familiar environment. To the extent that the individual can thus renew his environment he is able to overcome the effect of familiarity, and in the process of renewal his environment again becomes interesting.

One of the noticeable characteristics of self-actualization is the production of interesting cognitive structures which lead to renewal of the environment, make the environment interesting, and open up new possibilities in "familiar" situations. The transactions of the self-actualizing person with his environment are subtle and lead to subtle elaborations of cognitive structures. These differentiating processes make the individual self-interesting and the environment fascinating. One consequence of the elaborated conceptual life and of the renewal of the environment is that one would expect the individual to have an elevated chronic activation level because he is self-stimulating even when behaviorally quiescent.

It is possible that a highly self-actualizing person would be extremely resistant to the effects of sensory deprivation reported in the literature, because of his ability to be self-stimulating and to create new experience for himself. It is also to be expected, other things being equal, that he would be biologically healthy, because of the beneficial tonic effects of self actualization, and that he would be resistant to the onset of symptoms associated with senility.

SELF-ACTUALIZING PROCESSES AND PSYCHOTHERAPY

For Freud the problem of psychotherapy was the problem of anxiety. There is a deep truth in this statement. The client in psychotherapy is anxious and he almost never comes to psychotherapy with self-actualization as a goal. He wishes to find more efficient symptoms, symptoms that keep the acute below the chronic activation level or change the effects of stimuli and thought patterns that disadvantageously affect the relation between the activations.

But as the client continues, the goal in psychotherapy changes. As he comes to accept the notion that there are few grounds for anxiety arising out of the psychotherapeutic relationship itself, he often, paradoxically, becomes more rather than less anxious. When the external sources of anxiety have been removed, the rise in interpersonal anxiety often seen in therapy is, in the biological context of our discussion, self-actualizing because the anxiety is now recognized as originating in the self. The client is confronted not with a need to neutralize an external threat but with a need to come to terms with self-generated fears and anxiety. The process by which this crucial change may take place can be spelled out in terms of the formulations thus far proposed in this chapter.

It has been suggested that the self-actualizing person is one with a well-developed need for a high acute activation level who nevertheless has become relatively independent of his environment. On the one hand, he can provide his own acute activation through thinking new thoughts and is, therefore, not firmly bound to any set of external stimuli. On the other hand, he is able to derive a maximum of new experience from an environment that is in the least favorable. He can allow novel experiences access to consciousness, since he is not made anxious by adient behavior.

The neurotic can be seen as a person who cannot risk internal encounters with novel thoughts and impulses, but must constrict self-experience. It is not simply that his approach to particular thoughts becomes the signal for anxiety; the danger has become more generalized. Just as a child who is frequently punished for adient behavior may come to generalize danger as being attached to the act of approaching any new stimulus, so may he come to fear novelty within himself.

Whether he is an hysteric who has put whole areas of thought out of bounds or an obsessive who ruminates, using thinking to ensure that nothing new will get in, or an impulsive person who escapes thoughts by seeking intense external stimulation, the basic similarity would be that thinking as a source of new experience is only partially open to him. He is continually threatened with boredom, but he has placed such extreme external and internal restrictions on himself that few avenues of stimulation remain.

Although symptoms of whatever description may function so as to reduce anxiety or tension, they also act so as to constrict thinking processes and experience. To the extent that the individual is neurotic he is faced with the alternative between anxiety and ennui.

The task of psychotherapy is to facilitate self-experiencing, to help the individual to enrich his experience of himself in such a way that self-experiencing does not automatically arouse anxiety. When this end can be achieved, the person has resources with which to create new and satisfying conceptual structures. These resources are, in particular, conceptualizing ability and stimulus hunger. When the client comes into the psychotherapeutic situation, consistent prizing and understanding communicative behavior will ordinarily result in the reduction of anxiety having interpersonal origins. Clients very frequently begin self-explorations that are satisfying new experiences until they generate intrapersonal anxiety, at which point there is often reversion to strategies and symptoms that have the effect of constricting experience. Anxiety reduction reinforces these strategies and symptoms while at the same time increasing stimulus hunger. The individual is thus in a conflict situation in which he is reducing one drive at the expense of increasing another. The therapist, on the other hand, is constantly behaving in such a manner as to create a safe psychological climate (reducing anxiety), so the equilibria reached by the client are labile: the relative balance between anxiety motivation and stimulus hunger (adient motivation) is continually being changed with adient motivation becoming relatively stronger. The client is thus, as it were, working on the edges of self-created anxiety. He is adiently motivated to create new experience, new cognitive structures, and avoidantly motivated by the anxiety associated with any impulse to seek new experience. It is the constant prizing permissiveness and understanding of the therapist, serving to create a safe interpersonal climate, that tips the scales in favor of adient motivation. The degree to which the therapist is not perceived as exhibiting prizing understanding is the degree to which avoidant motivations prevail over adient motivations. Some therapist communications—e.g., deep interpretations—obscure the perception of the therapist as exhibiting prizing and understanding. Thus, while a given interpretation might be highly stimulating it might also be a cue for anxiety in which the acute activation level becomes higher than the chronic activation, with consequent activation of defense strategies. The interpersonal effect of a highly stimulating deep interpretation might be cues leading to inhibiting and channelizing effects. Such interventions leave the client with little control over the kind and quantity of internal arousal.

The discussion of stimulus hunger and adient motivation indicates that, in addition to affecting the balance of conflict discussed above, the therapist can contribute to the enrichment of experience and capitalize on adient motivation by employing stimulating styles of communication. From listening to tape recordings of therapy hours, it becomes apparent that there are, quite independent of the message conveyed, great stylistic differences, in choice of words, vividness of imagery, voice quality, etc., among both therapists and clients. Given n paraphrases of the same message, one may possess a greater range of connotations than the others, thus providing a basis for an increased range of thinking or experiencing in a respondent.

Some of those who come for therapy are able to experience freely and express themselves vividly. There are many more who seem to have learned to avoid new experiences within themselves or in the external environment and whose constricted and stereotyped communication mirrors their limitations within. While the therapist himself may be a freely-thinking person capable of generating new experience, his level of expression will tend to be controlled or at least limited by the expressive level of the client. The "difficult" client will be the one who tends to dampen the responsiveness of the therapist, thus indirectly creating a more impoverished experience for himself. On the other hand, the client who has a stimulating communicative style will be stimulating to his therapist, enabling the therapist to be sensitive and empathic to a high degree and to communicate in a stimulating style. The client thereby indirectly stimulates himself.

It seems probable that the communicative style of the client reflects the limitations on his capacity for experiencing, and is therefore little subject to his voluntary control. On the other hand, we postulate that the therapist can learn relatively easily to become stylistically independent of the client's influence. The closer he approximates the self-

actualizing person, the more he should be capable of a wide range of
styles, adaptable to new situations. He can learn to avoid abstract,
inexpressive language that only serves to constrain and package the
client's experience. He can learn to maximize satisfaction by making
responses with greater connotative range and more far-reaching rever-
berations within the receiver. We further assume that the client who
is optimally stimulated becomes increasingly open to and motivated
for new experience, and hence increasingly expressive. He becomes
more able to seek out and generate new experience for himself, thus
profiting maximally from therapy.

Although there is no present proof that our assumptions are
correct, there is evidence bearing on the assumptions. Rice, Wagstaff
and Butler (1961) and Wagstaff, Rice and Butler (1960) have studied
therapist and client behavior analyzed in terms of classification systems
emphasizing such stylistic aspects of verbal behavior as voice quality,
choice and combination of words, and concreteness and vividness of
imagery. They studied client and therapist interview behavior for
twenty-four client-therapist pairs and analyzed the behavior by use
of a technique similar to factor analysis. Three client types and three
therapist types emerged from the analysis, which differentiated clearly
among different degrees of expressiveness. It was found that the more
expressive clients tended to have more favorable therapy outcomes, as
judged by therapist ratings and changes in test scores. It was further
found that the clients with more expressive therapists tended to have
more favorable outcomes. There was substantial correspondence between therapist expressiveness and client expressiveness across therapeutic hours. Clearly, then, there is a close relationship between client
expressiveness and that of the therapist during the hour and a significant
relationship between the expressiveness of both and the outcome of
therapy, but the study leaves largely unanswered the question of the
direction of influence.

A more molecular analysis of these same interviews indicates that
the expressive level of each participant was being shifted by that of
the other, with the client changing more slowly than the therapist. The
second interview in each of the client-therapist pairs mentioned above
was analyzed by thirds. That is, it was possible to characterize each third
of each interview according to the degree to which it resembled the
maximally expressive client type and the maximally expressive therapist
type that had been identified by factor analysis. The twenty-four clients
were then ranked on expressiveness on each third of the interview, as

were the twenty-four therapists. It was found that when there was a discrepancy in favor of the therapist on the first third, the client's expressiveness went up on the second third while the therapist's tended to go down toward the client's. When the discrepancy was in favor of the client, the therapist's expressiveness went up and that of the client went down on the second third. In each case the change for the therapists was more clear-cut than the change for the clients. Similar though less pronounced changes were found from the second to the third section of the interview.

Another line of evidence has come from an unpublished study by Rice on the training of therapists aimed at increasing expressiveness. A group of therapists in training were given special instruction in certain styles of participation for about nine weeks while another group at the same level of experience were given the usual training experience. Two taped interviews from each of two clients were collected from each therapist, experimental and control, immediately before the training period. At the close of the period two more interviews from each of these same clients were collected. Samples were taken from each of the interviews and analyzed by means of the client and therapist classification systems discussed above, The findings indicate clearly that it is possible to train therapists to vary their styles of participation in a predetermined way without introducing artificialities and distortions into the therapy relationship. The experimental therapists were significantly different from the controls both in final level and in amount of change. The effect of this therapist change on the behavior of the clients was then studied. Here, as expected, the results were less clear cut. The client's in-therapy behavior had shifted, but to a slighter degree.

These three studies taken together support the view that the level of expressiveness in therapy sessions is related to favorableness of therapy outcome, and that each member of the therapeutic dyad is influencing the expressive aspects of the participation of the other. They suggest further that the therapist's style changes more quickly and is more subject to his own control, although this point needs further investigation.

SUMMARY

On the basis of experimental evidence it can be hypothesized that adient motivation is a pervasive drive which usually, particularly in humans, is stronger than maintenance or emergency drives. In human beings the drive of stimulus hunger is considered largely to originate in and to be satisfied by on-going thought processes. The human being, living in a culture which sustains and protects, lives to a very large degree in a conceptual, symbolic environment that is motivating. That is to say, the individual is to a large extent his own environment. Therefore, the human is autonomous: reward, punishment, behavioral and personal change, occur on a basis that cannot wholly be traced to stimulus and response relationships except perhaps in some ultimate and programmatic sense. In the psychotherapeutic situation, highly expressive modes of therapist communication will be activating and rewarding to a client by way of enriching his experience if care is taken not to produce anxiety. Since experience is per se rewarding within broad limits, a primary and immediate aim of psychotherapy should be to enrich the experience of the client. When the enrichment of experience initiated in psychotherapy becomes continuously self-initiated, it can legitimately be said that the client has become self-actualizing.

REFERENCES

ADEY, W. R., SEGUNDO, J. P., & LIVINGSTON, R. B. Corticofugal influences upon intrinsic brain stem conduction in cat and monkey. *J. Neuro-psychiat.*, 1957, *20*, 1-16.

BERLYNE, D. E. *Conflict, arousal, and curiosity.* New York: McGraw-Hill, 1960.

BONVALLET, M., DELL, P., ET HIEBEL, G. Tonus sympathetique et activite electrique corticale. *EEG clin. Neurophysiol.*, 1954, *6*, 11-144.

BRADLEY, P. B., & ELKES, J. The effect of some drugs on the electrical activity of the brain. *Brain*, 1957, *80*, 77-117.

BUTLER, J. M. Parent-child relationships. Unpublished study, 1948.

BUTLER, J. M. The interaction of client and therapist. *J. abnorm. soc. Psychol.*, 1952, *47*, 366-378.

BUTLER, J. M. The goals of counseling. Vol. II, No. 20. *Counseling Center Discussion Papers,* Univer. of Chicago Library, 1956.

BUTLER, J. M. Client-centered counseling and psychotherapy. In D. Brower & L. E. Abt (Eds.), *Progress in clinical psychology.* Vol. III. New York: Grune & Stratton, 1958.

BUTLER, J. M., & FLAPAN, M. The evaluative attitudes of the client-centered counselor. Vol. VII, No. 8. *Counseling Center Discussion Papers.* Univer. of Chicago Library, 1961.

BUTLER, J. M., & RICE, LAURA N. Self-actualization, new experience, and psychotherapy. Vol. VI, No. 12. *Counseling Center Discussion Papers,* Univer. of Chicago Library, 1960.

BUTLER, J. M., RICE, LAURA N., & WAGSTAFF, ALICE K. On the naturalistic definition of variables: an analogue of clinical analysis. In Lester Dubarsky & Hans Strupp (Eds.), *Research in Psychotherapy.* Washington, D. C.: Amer. Psychol. Assn, 1962.

BUTLER, R A. The effect of deprivation of visual incentives on visual exploration motivation in monkeys. *J. comp. physiol. Psychol.* 1957, *50,* 177-179.

CARMICHAEL, L. *Manual of Child Psychology.* New York: Wiley, 1946.

CASSIRER, E. *Language and Myth.* New York: Harper & Bros., 1946.

CARTWRIGHT, E. S., KIRTNER, W. L., & FOX, SOPHIE. An operator-display analysis of psychotherapy. Vol. II, No 17. *Counseling Center Discussion Papers.* Univer. of Chicago Library, 1956.

DELL, P. Tonus sympathetique, adrenative, et controle reticulaire de la matricite spinale. *EEG clin. Neurophysiol.,* 1954, *6,* 599-618.

DEMBER, W. N. Alternation Behavior. In D. W. Fiske & S. R. Maddi (Eds.), *Functions of Varied Experience.* Homewood, Ill.: Dorsey Press, 1961, Pp. 227-253.

DOLLARD, J., & MILLER, N. E. *Personality and psychotherapy,* New York: McGraw-Hill, 1951.

FENICHEL, O. *The psychoanalytic theory of neurosis.* New York: Norton, 1945.

FISKE, D. W., & MADDI, S. R. *Functions of varied experience.* Homewood, Ill.: The Dorsey Press, 1961.

FOX, S. S. *Sensory deprivation and maintained sensory input in monkeys.* Unpublished doctoral disseration, Univer. of Michigan, 1959.

FRENCH, J. D., AMERONGEN, F. K., & MAGOUN, H. W. Projections from the cortex to cephalic brain stem (reticular formation) in monkeys. *J. Neurophysiol.,* 1955, *18,* 74-95.

FREUD, S. The sexual aberration. In S. Freud, *Three essays on the theory of sexuality.* London: Imago Publishing, 1949.

GENDLIN, E., JENNEY, R., & SHLIEN, J. M. Counselor ratings of process and outcome in client-centered therapy. Vol. III, No. 15. *Counseling Center Discussion Papers.* Univer. of Chicago Library, 1957.

GOLDSTEIN, K. *The organism.* New York: Amer. Book Co., 1939.

GRUNT, J. A., & YOUNG, W. C. Psychological modification of fatigue following orgasm. *J. Compar. physiol Psychol,* 1952, *53,* 267-293.

HARLOW, H. F. Mice, monkeys, men, and motives. *Psychol. Rev.,* 1953, *60,* 23-32.

HARLOW, H. F. The nature of love. *Amer. Psychologist,* 1958, *12,* 673-685.

HARLOW, H. F. Basic social capacity of primates. In J. N. Spuhler (Ed.), *The evaluation of man's capacity for culture*. Detroit: Wayne Univer. Press, 1959.

HARLOW, H. F., & WOOLSEY, C. N. (Eds.) *Biological and biochemical bases of behavior*. Madison: Univer. of Wisconsin Press, 1958.

HARLOW, H. F. & ZIMMERMAN, R. R. Affectional responses in the infant monkey. *Science*, 1959, *130*, 421-432.

HEBB, D. O. Drives and the CNS (conceptual nervous system). *Psychol. Rev.*, 1955, *62*, 243-254.

HEBB, D. O. The motivating effects of exteroceptive stimulation. *Amer. Psychologist*, 1958, 109-113.

HOLT, E. B. *Animal drive and the learning process*. New York: Henry Holt & Co., 1931.

JASPER, H. H. Reticulo-cortical systems and theories of the integrative action of the nervous system. In H. F. Harlow & C. N. Woolsey (Eds.), *Biological and biochemical bases of behavior*. Madison: Univer. of Wisconsin Press, 1958.

JASPER, H. H., AJIMONE-MASSON, C., & STOLL, C. Corticofugal projections to the brain stem. *Arch. Neurol. Psychiat.*, Chicago, 1952, *67*, 155-166.

JONES, A., WILKINSON, H. J., & BRADEN, I. Information Deprivation as a Motivational Variable. *J. Exp. Psychol.*, 1961, 126-137.

KLEITMAN, N. *Sleep and wakefulness*. Chicago: Univer of Chicago Press, 1939.

LANGER, SUZANNE. *Philosophy in a new key*. Boston: Harvard Univer. Press, 1942.

LEUBA, C. Toward some integration of learning theories: the concept of optimal stimulation. *Psychol. Rep.*, 1955, *1*, 27-33.

LEVINE, S., & OTIS, L. S. The effects of handling before and after weaning on the resistance of albino rats to later deprivation. *Canad. J. Psychol.*, 1958, *12*, 103-108.

LINDSLEY, D. B. Attention, consciousness, sleep and wakefulness. In J. Field, H. W. Magaum, & V. E. Hall (Eds.) *Handbook of Physiology*. Vol. III. Washington, D. C.: Amer. Psychol. Soc., 1960, Pp. 1553-1593.

MAGOUN, H. W. *The waking brain*. Springfield, Ill.: C. C. Thomas, 1958.

MALMO, R. B. Activation: a neurophsychological dimension. *Psychol. Rev.*, 1959, *66*, 367-386.

MASLOW, A. H. Higher and lower needs. *J. Psychol.*, 1943, *25*, 433-436.

MASLOW, A. H. The expressive component of behavior. *Psychol. Rev.*, 1949, *56*, 260-272.

MASLOW, A. H. Self actualizing people: a study of psychological health. In W. Wolff (Ed.) *Personality symposium*. No. 1. New York: Grune & Stratton, 1950.

MASLOW, A. H. *Motivation and personality*. New York: Harper & Bros., 1954.

MELZACK, R. Effects of early perceptual restriction on simple visual discrimination. *Science*, 1962, *137*, 978-979.

MILLER, N. E. Learnable drives and rewards. In S. S. Stevens (Ed.), *Handbook of Experimental Psychology*. New York: Wiley, 1951.

MILLER, N E. Central stimulation and new approaches to motivation and reward. *Amer. Psychologist*, 1958, *13*, 100-108.

MILLER, N. E. Analytic studies of drive and reward. *Amer. Psychologist*, 1961, *16*, 739-754.

MORRIS, C. W. *Signs, language and behavior*. New York: Prentice-Hall, 1946.

RASCH, E., SWIFT, H., RIESEN, A. H., & CHOW, K. L. Altered structure and composition of retinal cells in dark-reared animals. *Exp. Cells Res.*, 1961, *25*, 348.

RICE, LAURA N., WAGSTAFF, ALICE K., & BUTLER, J. M. Some relationships between therapist style of participation and measures of case outcome. Vol. VII, No. 5. *Counseling Center Discussion Papers*. Univer. of Chicago Library, 1961.

RIESEN, A. H. Plasticity of behavior: psychological aspects. In H. F. Harlow and C. N. Woolsey (Eds.) *Biological and biochemical bases of behavior*. Madison: Univer. of Wisconsin Press, 1958.

RIESEN, A. H. Excessive arousal affects of stimulation after early sensory deprivation. In P. Soloman et al. (Eds.), *Sensory deprivation*. Cambridge: Harvard Univer. Press, 1961. (a)

RIESEN, A. H. Is the critical period hypothesis uesful? Critical stimulation and optimum period. Vol. VII, No. 11. *Counseling Center Discussion Papers*. Univer. of Chicago Library, 1961. (b)

RIESEN, A. H. Stimulation as a requirement for growth and function in behavioral development. In D. W. Fiske & S. R. Maddi (Eds.) *Functions of varied experience*. Homewood, Ill.: The Dorsey Press, 1961. (c)

RINALDI, F., & HIMWICH, H. E. Cholinergic mechanisms involved in function of mesodiencephalic activating system. *Arch. Neurol. Psychiat.*, Chicago, 1946, *9*, 219-229.

RINALDI, F., & HIMWICH, H. E. Alerting reactions and the actions or atropine and cholinergic drugs. *Arch. Neurol. Psychiat.*, Chicago, 1955, *73*, 382-395.

ROGERS, C. R. *Client-centered therapy*. Boston: Houghton Mifflin, 1951.

ROGERS, C. R. The necessary and sufficient conditions of psychotherapeutic personality change. *J. consult. Psychol.*, 1957, *21*, 95-103.

ROTHBALLER, A. B. Studies on the adrenaline-sensitive component of the reticular activating system. *EEG clin. Neurophysiol.*, 1956, *8*, 603-621.

SHARPLESS, S., & JASPER, H. H. Habituation of the arousal reaction. *Brain*, 1956, *79*, 655-680.

SHEFFIELD, F. E., WULF, J. J., & BACKER, R. Reward value of copulation without sex drive reduction. *J. comp. physiol. Psychol.*, 1951, *44*, 3-8.

STANDAL, S. The need for positive reward. Unpublished doctoral dissertation, Univer. of Chicago, 1953.

THOMPSON, W. R., & SCHAEFER, T., JR. Early environmental stimulation. In D. W. Fiske & S. R. Maddi (Eds.), *Functions of varied experience.* Homewood, Ill.: Dorsey Press, 1961.

VOGT, M. The concentration of sympathin in different parts of the central nervous system under normal conditions and after administration of drugs. *J. Physiol.,* 1954, *123,* 451-481.

WAGSTAFF, ALICE K. Successive set analysis of verbal styles in psychotherapy. Unpublished doctoral dissertation, Univer. of Chicago, 1959.

WAGSTAFF, ALICE K., RICE, LAURA N., & BUTLER, J. M. Factors of client verbal participation in therapy. Vol. VI, No. 9. *Counseling Center Discussion Papers.* Univer. of Chicago Library, 1960.

WHITE, R. W. Motivation reconsidered: The concept of competence. *Psychol. Rev.,* 1959, *66,* 297-333.

WIKLER, A. Pharmacologic dissociation of behavior and EEG "sleep patterns" in dogs. *Proc. soc. exper. Biol. & Med.,* 1952, *79,* 261-265.

II

Theories of Personality

5

Concepts and Theories of Psychoanalysis

Heinz Kohut and Philip F. D. Seitz

RELATION OF METHOD AND THEORY

Psychoanalysis began with the famous case of Miss Anna O., who insisted that her doctor, the Viennese internist Josef Breuer, listen to what she had to say. Freud discerned the potential fruitfulness of this novel approach to treatment and he based his own method on Anna O.'s invention—"chimney sweeping," as she had called her talks with Doctor Breuer.

Psychoanalysis began, therefore, in a therapeutic setting. It was characterized from the beginning by a specific method of observing human behavior (i.e., the physician listens to the verbal expression of the patient's flow of thought, and attempts to comprehend empathically what the patient wishes to communicate about his psychic state) and by a specific mode of theory formation (i.e., the physician attempts to bring order into the data which he has obtained about the inner life of his patient.) The science of psychoanalysis has developed far beyond the limitations of the therapeutic situation; yet the fact that its principal method of observation was discovered in a therapeutic relationship, and that its predominant usefulness lies still in its therapeutic application, accounts for some of the specific assets as well as for some of the characteristic difficulties of the psychoanalytic method and theory. There can be no doubt, however, that, in spite of the confining influence of its intimate relationship with the goals of therapy, psychoanalysis has

113

become vastly more than a theory of psychopathology; the continuum that it postulates between health and disease has made it a general theory of personality.

Psychoanalysis is a science based predominantly upon a method of clinical observation. It interprets empirical data, and thus its starting point is always observation of behavior and observation of people: of things people say, things people say they feel, and things people say they do not feel. The person to be observed, the patient, is asked to follow the basic rule of psychoanalysis: i.e., he is to disclose everything that occurs to him, and he must try not to suppress anything that is embarrassing to him, or leave out anything that he believes to be irrelevant. The analyst does more, however, than simply listen to everything the patient says; his observations are made from the standpoint of certain theoretic concepts with which he orients his mind toward the observed. Psychoanalysis is not a method of "pure" observation—if such a thing actually exists in science—but observation and theory are closely interwoven: observation forming the basis of theories, and theories influencing the direction and focus of observation.

As an example of the relationship between method and theory in psychoanalysis, let us consider the investigation of the psychological significance of nursing activities. "Pure" observation tells us little about the psychology of the infant; all we can see is that the baby nurses and that it then goes to sleep. Although this sequence of events has been watched by countless generations, no scientific psychologic understanding was acquired. Psychological comprehension of the significance of the infant's oral strivings was greatly enhanced, however, by the ever increasing understanding of certain states in adult life, which while not directly applicable to earlier phases, has nevertheless given us valuable leads. Equipped with the knowledge derived from our observations of the intense reactions to object loss in the depressions of adults; of the intensity of oral wishes in additions; or—in even more direct connection—of the exquisite sensitivity to rejection of those who have suffered intense early oral frustrations, we re-examine the nursing scene and can begin to make certain hypotheses. We are now able to grasp the intensity of the infant's oral strivings; we see the relative defenselessness of the infantile psyche when it is frustrated (its lack of buffering structure); we can comprehend dimly the special status of the object which the baby does not yet experience as separate from himself; and we appreciate the importance of the fact that the baby has no recognition that there is a choice of objects or that they are replaceable. While it is true that some of these hypotheses may not seem to stand on very firm ground when contemplated in isolation, they must support each other by their internal consistency and cohesion when we form our tentative constructions of early psychological states, and they must be checked against the empirical data obtained from the direct observation of children and from the childhood memories of adults. They are, therefore, open to correction or rejection as the evidence demands.

Neither the most ingenious and empathic interpretations of adult psychological states, however, nor the most "pure" observation of children is sufficient in psychoanalysis. As we observe adult behavior, we discern the remnants of childhood experiences; and as we observe childhood behavior, we recognize the seeds for adult functions and experiences. The interplay between present and past, between direct observation and interpretation, is among the most characteristic features of psychoanalysis as a method and as a theory.

In actual (clinical) practice, however, the theoretic knowledge of the experienced psychoanalyst has become so fully integrated into his total observational attitude that he is usually no longer aware of a dichotomy between theory and observation; and, although the psychoanalytic method of observation includes a background of theoretic concepts, the analyst's attitude, in his practice, is characterized by an open-endedness of expectation. To be able to listen with suspended judgment and to resist the urge to come to quick conclusions; to accept the possibility of the emergence of an unforeseen message in a communication which may seem clearly intelligible to everyone else: that is the essence of the psychoanalyst's attitude. His attention is directed not only toward the content and form of the patient's communications or to the slow emergence of his conflict patterns, but also is open to the recognition of his own reactions to the patient. Yet neither his attention to the patient's associations nor his attention to his own reactions is focused sharply at first; premature attempts to arrange the data of observation into impeccably logical dynamic patterns interfere with analytic observation. The scrutiny of an isolated section of psychological material (e.g., the interpretation of a single dream) is not a characteristic sample of the work of the psychoanalyst; the psychoanalytically oriented, dynamic psychiatrist, however, is often expected to deduce a dynamic formulation of psychopathological symptoms or of specific character patterns from a limited number of data. While circumstances thus force the analyst (when he functions as a dynamic psychiatrist) to make inferences about the arrangement of psychological forces on the basis of relatively inert and isolated sources of information (through a limited number of interviews, for example), in his major field of competence the analyst's strength lies in his capacity to postpone closures and to observe the living ebb and flow of the thoughts and feelings of the analysand for prolonged periods until the closures are forced upon him.

The analyst validates his concepts, formulations, and theories by applying them to a variety of clinical experiences; he matches them, so to speak, with large numbers of clinical observations, testing again and again whether they lead to comprehension. If the theory, the formulation, or the concept is helpful in the understanding of a large number of clinical observations of similar type—better still if it can be intelligibly varied and then applied to related instances—then the analyst's impression of its validity grows; it is his premise, in other words, that the trustworthiness of a theory increases with each additional observation that it renders intelligible.

The theories of the psychoanalyst should be viewed predominantly, therefore, as attempts to bring order into the nearly endless variety of phenomena that he observes in his patients. Observation without implicit or explicit theory formation, without a hierarchy of the relative importance of the data, is unimaginable. How the analyst orders his data, on what he focuses his attention, and how he tries to understand the patient's communications, are questions that take us to those fundamental concepts upon which both the method and theory of psychoanalysis are based.

THE CONCEPT OF THE UNCONSCIOUS; THE LIMITED ROLE OF CONSCIOUSNESS

The tenet of the essential unconsciousness of mental activities is the cornerstone of psychoanalytic theory; it exerts a decisive influence upon the observational attitude of the psychoanalyst. Although a vaguely formed notion about the existence of an unconscious mind has found wide acceptance and has achieved a shallow popularity, Freud's revolutionary theoretic innovation is not usually understood.

Freud recognized that consciousness was not a necessary attribute of psychic activities; he postulated that it should be defined as the sensory organ of the mind. Consciousness, then, according to Freud, is a sense organ for the perception of psychic contents and qualities. One might say that, just as it is the function of the eye to see the objects and events in the external world, so it is the function of consciousness to perceive endopsychic processes.[1]

Freud had to overcome an ingrained prejudice about the mind in order to define consciousness as merely a sensory organ and to recognize not only that mental processes may occur outside of consciousness but that consciousness is not, at any time, an essential quality of mental activities. Attention to endopsychic activities may bring them to consciousness; they take their course, however, whether observed by the "eye of consciousness" or not. The clinical evidence for the relevance and validity of these concepts is overwhelming; experimental support has recently been provided by Charles Fisher (1954) who confirmed Poetzl's (1917) discovery that the unconscious perception of tachistoscopically projected images can be proved through the examination of dreams which occur subsequent to the tachistoscopic exposure.

The psychoanalytic discovery that the domain of consciousness is limited and that psychic processes may, in essence, run their regular course outside of awareness, led to the recognition of the motivational cohesiveness of unconscious psychic activities. This conception exerted a far-reaching influence upon the observation of mental phenomena. Through the acceptance and utilization of the concept of unconscious psychic determinism, a host of seemingly fortuitous and purposeless psychological occurrences turned into potentially meaningful data and, thus, an area which previously had been open only to the intuitive grasp of the artist became accessible to the investigation of the scientist. Freud reflected about the motive of mankind's tendency to overestimate consciousness and to deny the Unconscious;[2] he came to the conclusion

---

[1] Freud's concept of the relationship between consciousness and the contents and qualities of the mind can be clarified further by the use of an analogy: the psychic contents may be compared with objects and activities present in a landscape which lies in darkness. Consciousness may be conceived as analogous to an observer who has the use of a searchlight which can illuminate the landscape. The focusing of the searchlight (and the variable intensity of its light) would be analogous to what is called "attention cathexis"; the ensuing illumination would be analogous to the process by which psychic contents become conscious. To become aware of psychic contents by focusing attention cathexes on them is thus an active process. The analogy also permits the integration of the following relevant details: extensive activities in the landscape may by themselves enter into the focus of the searchlight and are thus noticed by the observer; and the processes that are already under observation may arouse specific expectations in the observer and may thus determine the direction toward which the observer turns the instrument of illumination.

[2] When used as nouns, denoting the various topographic areas of mental functioning, the terms Conscious, Preconscious, and Unconscious are traditionally capitalized.

that it is our inflated self-esteem which refuses to acknowledge the possibility that we might not be undisputed master in the household of our own minds. Just as Copernicus wounded man's self-esteem with his discovery that man is not the center of the universe, and as Darwin wounded our pride still further by finding that man cannot boast of having been separately or uniquely created, so Freud inflicted yet another blow to mankind's self esteem by the discovery that man's consciousness illuminates only a narrow and limited part of his own mental activities.

Having shed the prejudice of assigning to consciousness the position of all-inclusive sovereignty in psychic life, and having thus reduced it to the rank of an instrument of internal observation, we must not go too far and underrate its importance. Consciousness is not all that we would like it to be; many psychological processes take place in our minds which we may not happen to observe or which we are not capable of observing directly. Consciousness is the only light, however, that penetrates into the inner life of man; it illuminates enough of the surface of mental phenomena to permit convincing inferences about some important activities in the depths. Consciousness, as the instrument of psychological perception, is limited in its scope—yet it is all that we possess. It occupies the position of a fixed point of reference in psychoanalytic theory; it is the firm basis from which we must set out, and to which we must return, when we undertake the expanding explorations of unknown psychological territory. "Give me a firm spot on which to stand and I will move the earth," Archimedes is reported to have said in order to illustrate the potentialities inherent in the action of levers. Psychoanalysis has no hope of being able to move the psychological universe—yet what progress it is able to make will be derived or extrapolated through the careful scrutiny of information about psychic phenomena which are accessible to consciousness; and conscious experience will remain the testing ground for the validity of new theoretic constructions. The essence of psychic life is dynamic, Freud stated; the investigation of the interplay of mental forces, however, requires the perception of their psychological manifestations with the sense organ of consciousness.

INNATE PREDISPOSITION
TO ENDOPSYCHIC CONFLICT

Another important hypothesis which influences the way in which the analyst orders the data of psychological observation is Freud's assumption that man has an inherent propensity for the development of endopsychic conflict. The psyche is conceived of as a dynamic system with an innate tendency toward an organization of forces that oppose and balance each other. The central position of endopsychic conflict is a characteristic, but by no means a specific feature of psychoanalytic psychology. What distinguishes psychoanalysis from other conflict psychologies, however, is the theory of an orderly and stable arrangement of groups of opposing forces which are potentially in conflict with each other. These more or less cohesive groups of forces are often referred to as being located in areas of the mind, and the diagrammatic representations of these localities are the psychoanalytic models of the mind. The first diagram of the arrangement of psychic forces was proposed by Freud around the turn of the century, during his most creative period; it usually goes by the name of the Topographic Model of the mind. The opposing areas (or systems) of the psyche are called the Unconscious and the Preconscious; the modes of functioning of the forces active in these psychic locations are referred to as the Primary and the Secondary Process. The primary processes are characteristic for the Unconscious, the secondary processes belong to the Preconscious. The sense organ of consciousness may illuminate the otherwise unconsciously proceeding activities in the Preconscious and render them conscious.[3] The processes which take place in the Unconscious cannot, under normal circumstances, be reached directly by consciousness.

While we probably cannot experience or demonstrate the unalloyed primary process directly, we have become familiar with some of its most important qualities and characteristics, especially through the study of dreams and of certain neurotic symptoms. Its activities are infantile, pre-logical, and unrestrained. It coalesces logically incompatible thought contents (condensation), shifts the intensity of its forces upon objects to which they do not logically belong (displacement), and it is intolerant of delay in the discharge of its tensions (it works with free, unbound energies). The main activity of the mature

---

[3] The totality of the preconscious processes which have become conscious through the work (the focusing of attention) of the psychic sensory organ, consciousness, is sometimes referred to as a separate system, the Conscious.

psyche follows the laws of the secondary process; it is adult, logical, and capable of tolerating delay. Its energies do not shift freely but they remain sharply focused on well-circumscribed objects and contents (it works with concentrated, bound energies).

THE CONCEPT OF TRANSFERENCE

Only secondary processes can be observed directly. The properties of the primary process must be inferred from the study of the characteristic disturbances and distortions which the secondary process undergoes when it is under the influence of the primary process. The influence of the primary process on the secondary process (the penetration of unconscious psychic contents and forces into preconscious thoughts, feelings, or wishes) was originally designated by the term "transference" by Freud (1900). It is important to note that transference, in the original meaning of the term, referred essentially to an endopsychic, not an interpersonal process. An obsessive thought, for example, is a transference phenomenon: the content of the thought ("Have I turned off the gas in the kitchen?") conforms to the secondary process; the unrelenting insistence with which it intrudes, however, betrays the fact that it does not belong entirely to rational thinking but that it stems partly from the deeper layers of the mind, and that some of the forces which maintain it have the qualities of an untamed drive.

In current practice (derived largely from Freud's own later, metapsychologically less precise usage), the term transference refers customarily to the patient's revival of feelings and attitudes from childhood in his relationship with the analyst during psychoanalytic treatment. In the present essay, however, the term transference designates a metapsychological concept within the framework of the topographic point of view, in accordance with Freud's original definition. It should be noted that the later, clinically oriented use of the term transference (the misinterpretation of the analyst by the analysand due to the intrusion of feelings and attitudes that are associated with important figures from the analysand's childhood) is not superseded by the emphasis on the original, metapsychological definition which the present writers advocate: transference toward the analyst is simply one specific manifestation of a more general psychological mechanism.[4]

---

[4] For a more extensive discussion of the advantages which accrue to psychoanalytic theory through an adherence to Freud's original, precise, metapsychological definition of transference, see Kohut (1959, pp. 471-472.)

As a matter of fact, the discovery by Freud of transferences toward the analyst occurred relatively late, after he had recognized that dreams, slips of the tongue, and the symptoms of psychoneurosis are transference phenomena: i.e., they are amalgamations of primary and secondary processes which are formed as a result of the intrusion of unconscious contents into the Preconscious. Writing, for example, is an activity of the ego.[5] If repressed masturbatory impulses from early childhood are reactivated, they may attach themselves (by transference) to the activity of writing, which consequently arouses guilt and becomes inhibited. The symptom (a hysterical writer's cramp, for example) contains an amalgamation of primary and secondary processes (masturbation—writing) and is called, therefore, the symptom of a transference neurosis.

In dreams the transferences from the Unconscious to the Preconscious attach themselves to "day residues," i.e., to impressions of the preceding day which are, in themselves, either insignificant or of little practical importance. In Fisher's experiments, for example, the subjects tended to use the tachistoscopic pictures that had been flashed to them as day residues for their dreams. Why? Partly because the tachistoscopic images were isolated from the subjects' life experiences and thus without practical importance to them. Their very isolation (i.e., their lack of significant connections with other preconscious impressions) made them especially susceptible to influences from the Unconscious and, therefore, available for transferences. For the same reason, the psychoanalyst readily becomes a transference object: he has comparatively little significance for the patient as a source of realistic gratification. Conversely, if the analyst were to become the patient's supporter, helper, or friend, his availability as a transference object would be diminished.

The foregoing considerations are relevant to the clinical method of psychoanalysis and elucidate several features of the technical setting. The analyst is usually out of sight for the patient; he reveals little about his own personality, is generally sparing in how much he talks

[5] The term ego is not synonymous with the term Preconscious. The area of the mind (or the set of functions) to which the term ego is applied includes, in addition to the Preconscious, also a deeper layer which is inaccessible to consciousness. Foremost among the function of the unconscious layers of the ego are the unconscious defenses. It follows from the preceding statement that the term id is not synonymous with the term Unconscious: the Unconscious is composed of the id and the unconscious layer of the ego (these distinctions are discussed further in a later section of this essay, *The Structural Model of the Mind.*)

to the patient, and does not provide realistic gratifications of the patient's wishes as they become activated in the treatment (the "rule of abstinence"). The psychoanalytic setting is thus designed to facilitate, initially, what might be called the "day-residue function" of the analyst; it promotes the formation of transferences from the patient's Unconscious (usually pertaining to the patient's unresolved conflicts with the important figures of his early childhood) to the patient's preconscious images of the analyst. The analyst, in turn, as he observes the patient, keeps in mind that the patient's thoughts, feelings, and actions may be influenced via the mechanism of transference by the activities of another psychic system of which the patient himself remains unaware.

The following diagram illustrates the relationship of transferences to the psychic systems:

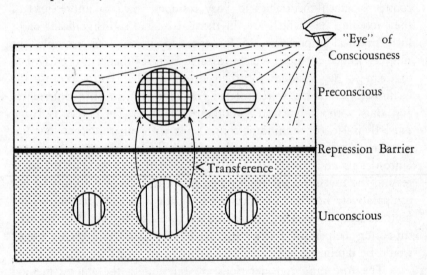

Under normal circumstances, the repression barrier effectively separates the repressed contents in the Unconscious from the Preconscious, and the activities in the Preconscious are therefore not influenced by those in the Unconscious. Under certain conditions, however, the repression barrier is weakened (for example, during sleep) and permits the intrusion of some unconscious strivings into the Preconscious, where an amalgamation with suitable preconscious contents, i.e., the formation of transferences, takes places. If these intrusions are not excessive, they are tolerated by the Preconscious; if they become too extensive, however, the Preconscious mobilizes its forces and re-establishes the original impermeable barrier. This sequence (moderate intrusions, formation of transferences, intensification of the break-through, and re-establishment of firm repression) can be observed when the unconscious components in a dream transference become intensified to the point at which the dreamer experiences anxiety, awakens, and thus interrupts the dream and re-establishes full re-pression. The mode of operation and the genesis of the barrier which wards off the repressed portion of the psyche from contact with other psychic activities will be discussed later (see *Psychic Trauma and the Repression of Infantile Drives* and the discussion of the defense mechanisms in *The Structural Model of the Mind*).

HALLUCINATORY WISH-FULFILLMENT;
THE INFANTILE SEXUAL AND AGGRESSIVE DRIVES

As set forth in the preceding section, the analyst's mind is receptive to the discovery of transferences from the first system, the Unconscious, to the second system, the Preconscious. Psychoanalytic conceptualizations and descriptions of unconscious mental processes are largely a result of extrapolations from consciously observed transference changes in the secondary process. In addition—to facilitate communication and understanding—psychoanalytic statements about the characteristics of unfamiliar, unconscious psychological processes have had to utilize descriptive terms and concepts from the familiar reference frame of consciousness. (See the preceding remarks on page 115 about the role of conscious experience in psychoanalytic theory formation).

Psychoanalysts describe the qualities of unconscious processes, therefore, in terms of characteristics associated with psychic processes which are accessible to consciousness, by indicating either how the Unconscious differs from or how it is similar to consciously experienced mental contents. Certain qualities of the primary process (for example its form, intensity, and speed) came to be conceptualized and described by pointing out how they differ from (familiar) qualities of the secondary process. The characteristic wish-fulfilling nature of un-conscious strivings, on the other hand, came to be described largely as a result of recognizing similarities with consciously observable phenomena such as wish-fulfilling day dreams. We can extrapolate, therefore (e.g., from observations of night dreams and psychoneurotic symptoms), that unconscious mental activity is similar to conscious day dreams in its striving to construct wish-fulfilling images of its desires. In contrast to our usual secondary process functioning, however, which seeks the real, external objects of its desires through attempts at mastery of the environment by realistic means, unconscious strivings are confined to the creation of hallucinatory images (as in the wish-fulfilling hallucinations of certain psychoses) or to symbolic enactments of wish-fulfillments (as in hysterical attacks).

Psychoanalytic conceptualizations regarding the nature of unconscious mental processes, mechanisms, and contents have been derived largely, therefore, from the study and description of contrasts and similarities between unconscious and preconscious mental activities. More direct observations of mental functions in small children and in psychotic patients have provided important additional data—supporting, refining, and revising the indirect reconstructions of unconscious (primary) mental processes.

The psychoanalytic concept that the dynamic processes in the id (the drives) are characterized by qualities of (infantile) sexuality and aggression was also formulated as a result of studying the contrasts and similarities between unconscious and preconscious mental activities. What the psychoanalyst understands by infantile sexuality and aggression, however, is not exactly the same as sexuality and aggression in the adult. Infantile drives have a characteristic intensity and urgency, and a pleasurable quality, that is virtually unknown to the adult, whose dominant secondary process functioning serves as a screen or buffer and usually protects him against the impact of unmodified drives. Only the height of sexual orgasm (and perhaps, under special circumstances, a paroxysm of maximal rage) can be said to be experienced with a minimum of buffering by the secondary process. The mature psyche is thus able to have intense sexual and aggressive experiences; this capacity, however, appears to be based upon the ability of the mature psyche to suspend temporarily some of its most highly developed functions. It is significant, therefore, that the experience at the height of orgasm and the experience of a paroxysm of intense rage can hardly be described through the use of language, the most important instrument of the secondary process, and that even consciousness itself appears to be altered at such times.

Freud recognized the meaningful equivalence between the processes in the Unconscious (the infantile psyche) and the sexual experiences of adults, and said that he did not want to change the term "sexuality" to characterize infantile drives and experiences because he had chosen it *"a potiori"*: i.e., he had used the term which referred to the best known of the various experiences of a similar kind. Freud found a great deal of evidence for the fact that every activity was originally sexual, with regard to the intensity of its motivation and the quality of its experience: when the baby nurses, the intensity of its pleasure is similar to sexual sensations in adults; and walking, looking, talking, writing were begun at least partially as sexual activities. Seen from the standpoint of biology, and in harmony with the tenets of the theory of evolution, we may also stress the great survival value of the intense erotic pleasure that is associated with the infantile drives and activities: the more intensely and urgently pleasurable these activities are (the baby's sucking, for example), the more the infant is motivated to perform the survival-promoting functions.

As a result of endogenous maturational tendencies (which, however, are decisively influenced by environmental circumstances) a segment of the Unconscious is transformed into the Preconscious. (As pointed out before, the terms id and ego are now used for the groups of psychic functions which constitute the polarities in this development.) The environmental circumstances which further the differentiation of the Preconscious can be described as optimal frustrations, i.e., frustrations which prevent the immediate satisfaction of the pleasure-seeking infantile drives, yet are not of such severity (i.e., not traumatic) that they obstruct development. (This topic will be pursued further in the next section.)

Every mature activity that developed from infantile drives can, however, under certain circumstances, return to its primitive form: either openly (in perversions) or covertly (in the psychoneuroses). In obsessional neurosis, for example, thinking itself, which was originally a highly pleasurable sexual and aggressive activity, may again take on the qualities and aims of infantile sexuality and aggression. In consequence of such regression, thinking becomes dangerous and is defended against by the compulsion neurotic (e.g., by the use of magical repetitions, and by other means). When the (preconscious) ego is working properly, however, a neutralization of its activities has occurred (i.e., a progression from primary to secondary process functioning), and the infantile erotic and aggressive quality of its experience disappears.

OPTIMAL FRUSTRATION AND THE
ESTABLISHMENT OF THE SECONDARY PROCESS

Although the capacity to achieve the use of mature psychic functions must be considered a part of the innate potentialities of human psychological equipment, it is only through a long series of interactions with the environment that the archaic mode of mental functioning (the primary process) becomes gradually converted into the adult form of thinking (the secondary process). Since memories constitute the basic units of the secondary process, it is profitable to examine the psychological forerunners of the memory function, and to study the circumstances which promote the development of the memory trace. To this end we turn to Freud's hypothesis about the establishment of the earliest psychological structures in the infant.

It is impossible for us to define the infant's first experience of hunger in psychological terms. We can state only that physiological processes (later to be experienced as hunger) produce a tension to which the infant responds reflexly with a series of activities. The cry, which is foremost among the infant's reflex responses, alerts the mother; the baby receives its feeding, and the physiological tension state subsides. After this sequence (hunger tension—cry—mother—feeding—satiation) has taken place, however, the infant's psyche has undergone a change; some engram of the hunger-satiation sequence has been deposited; and, when the tension reasserts itself and reaches a certain intensity, the baby's hunger-drive-wishes turn toward the engram of the previous satisfaction to achieve a repetition of the experience of satiation. It is a moot question whether we should call this first attempt to reach satisfaction a hallucination; it is obvious, at any rate, that the turning toward the engram of previous satisfaction does nothing to decrease the hunger: the tension mounts, the reflex cry occurs and real feeding leads again to satiation. The baby now has had its first opportunity to distinguish the experience of the hallucination of a previous (real) satisfaction from the experience of a (real) satisfaction in the present. Innumerable repetitions of this sequence of events lead, little by little, to a lessening of the intensity with which the psyche turns toward the engram; instead of expecting satisfaction from the engram itself, the infant learns to consider the engram as an intermediate station on the way toward satisfaction. As the excessive interest in the engram decreases, it is also experienced less vividly: it takes on a quality that is distinct from the experience of reality. A differentiation of psychic reality and external reality is thus acquired; hallucinations have become memories.

The development of the memory function from hallucinations is enhanced by experiences of optimal frustration. Overindulgence results in less incentive to learn the distinction between fantasy and reality, since feeding occurs so quickly that it coalesces with the turning toward the fantasy-image. Severe frustrations (or inconsistency of maternal response), on the other hand, create a reality that supplies hardly more gratification than the fantasy-image; thus, again, there is less opportunity (and incentive) for the firm establishment of the differentiation. By contrast, optimal frustrations involve sufficient delay in satisfaction to induce tension-increase and disappointment in the attempt to obtain wishfulfillment through fantasy; the real satisfaction occurs quickly enough, however, to prevent a despairing and disillusioned turning away from reality.

PSYCHIC TRAUMA AND THE
REPRESSION OF INFANTILE DRIVES

A certain portion of the infantile sexual and aggressive drives neither develops into adult sexuality or aggression nor becomes transformed into drive-distant preconscious secondary processes, but remains unchanged—walled off (repressed) in the Unconscious. Study of preconscious transference intrusions from the Unconscious reveals that the repressed drives have retained their original primitiveness and intensity. Having explained earlier how primary processes are converted into secondary processes under the influence of experiences of optimal frustration, we must now account for the fact that a part of the primary processes does not participate in this development.

As indicated in the preceding section, the ability of the infantile psyche to learn to distinguish reality from hallucination (and thus to transform hallucinations into memories) is hampered if the infant is either excessively indulged, or if it is exposed to frustrations of traumatic intensity. Traumatic frustrations of infantile needs ensue when the waiting period exceeds the tolerance of the infantile psyche, or when the gratifications offered by the environment are unpredictable, e.g., when feedings are dispensed inconsistently. In either case the infantile psyche turns away from reality and retains self-soothing gratification through fantasy. True overindulgence is unlikely to be encountered during the early phase of psychological development; if it does occur it may stunt development (fixation) through lack of incentive for learning to grasp reality. More important, however, is the fact that overindulgence is not maintained forever by the environment, and that a sudden switch in maternal attitude from overindulgence to frustration is experienced as traumatic by the unprepared psyche of the child.

Traumatic experiences, like experiences of optimal frustration, lay down memory traces; but in the case of traumatic frustrations the infantile drives and associated traumatic memories are walled off (primal repression) under the influence of primitive despair and anxiety. Since the psyche strives to prevent the recurrence of the former state of anxiety and despair, the repression is permanently retained, at the sacrifice of further differentiation of the repressed wishes. Traumatic frustration of drives thus produces a psychologic enclave of primary process functioning and psychic fixation upon direct wishfulfillment, for example by means of hallucinations. Unconscious contents that are sealed off from the preconscious ego are not exposed to the influence of new experiences and, therefore, are incapable of change (learning); instead, following the laws of the primary process and of the pleasure principle, endlessly repeated attempts occur to achieve immediate wishfulfillment through hallucinations or through other similar means. A symbolically wishfulfilling version of an infantile experience may be reenacted over and over again throughout a lifetime by the same recurring hysterical symptom. Since the original infantile strivings, and the context in which they arose, remain unconscious, however, the wish can neither be gratified realistically nor relinquished.

What constitutes a childhood trauma can hardly be defined objectively; it is a psychological task that the child's psyche cannot integrate into the more differentiated preconscious system either because of the intensity of the demand, or because of the immaturity of the psychological organization, or because of a transient sensitivity of the psyche at the time when the task is imposed on it, or by any combination of these factors. Trauma is thus an economic concept in psychoanalysis, referring not principally to the content of the experience but to its intensity. Trauma is overstimulation, whether from overgratifying or overfrustrating experiences; it involves not just what occurs externally but the dovetailing of external events and inner psychic organization. Although there are certain periods in childhood (most often corresponding with an as yet insecurely established new balance of psychological forces after a spurt of development) during which the psyche is especially susceptible to traumatization, we can safely say that the young child is exposed to traumata at all times.

The time factor constitutes an especially important, and frequently neglected, consideration in the economic concept of trauma. Not only is the age and the developmental stage of the child often crucial in determining the severity of a psychological task, but it may be equally decisive whether the child is expected to perform the feat of a *sudden* major transition from primary to secondary process functioning, or whether he is permitted to acquire the new functions in a fractionated way over a longer period of time.

Experiences that had not been integrated into the Preconscious during childhood are mobilized again during psychoanalytic treatment; but now, in their therapeutic reactivation, the patient has ample time for their gradual assimilation. The stepwise process, during which traumatic memories are faced again and infantile wishes are re-experienced and slowly relinquished, is called "working-through." This process has been compared with the work that the psyche performs in mourning—except that the bereaved has to give up a love object of the present while the patient learns that he must forego the hope of fulfilling unmodified infantile wishes, and that he must relinquish the objects of the past.

The interrelationship between theory and practice, and specifically the influence of the aforementioned psychoeconomic considerations on the therapeutic procedures of psychoanalysis, can be illuminated further by focusing on the method of free association. Free association is commonly described in negative terms, as a giving up of controls, a disregard of self-criticism and the like. Free association, however, involves more than relaxation; at the crucial junctures it summons the ability to tolerate the admission of unpleasant mental contents to consciousness, to be perceived and experienced. Free association, therefore, requires effort and perseverance in order to accomplish a gradual extension of the realm of the secondary process. It is not the aim of psychoanalysis, however, to achieve an ideally perfect psychological organization in which the Unconscious has become totally accessible and transformed. The defect in human psychological equipment to which Freud alluded on a number of occasions is not the existence of a repression barrier or of the defense mechanisms but their relative inadequacy. Analysis, therefore, strives to establish the dominance of the secondary process only in those segments of the psyche where the defenses have proved ineffectual. When anamnestic data from childhood or evidence obtained from dreams point toward repressed material that has been contained effectively by socially acceptable and satisfactory defensive activities, no attempt is made to stir up such dormant conflicts during an analysis. If a violently hostile attitude toward a father figure has been superseded by devotion to a life task of promoting social justice for the aged, for example, there is no indication for attempting to undermine this ego-syntonic system of values unless neurotic inhibitions (due to a threatened breakthrough of the original hostility) interfere with this segment of psychic adjustment. Any walled-off content for which the defense mechanisms are securely anchored is thus left untouched. A perfectionistic attitude about uncovering the repressed is, at best, the sign of the amateur; at worst, it may betray the fanatic who, hiding some secret from himself, must forever wrest secrets from others.

VANTAGE POINTS OF
PSYCHOANALYTIC OBSERVATION;
THE GENETIC POINT OF VIEW

The intricate system of psychoanalytic concepts and formulations (often referred to as metapsychology) becomes more easily understandable if we isolate the various interrelated lines of approach which the analyst follows in ordering the psychological data. These basic observational positions of the psychoanalyst are known as the dynamic, the economic, the topographic and structural, and the genetic points of view.

The fact that the analyst conceives of wishes, urges and drives as expressions of psychological forces, and that he sees psychological conflicts as clashes between these forces, is designated as the psychodynamic point of view. In addition, the analyst acknowledges the fact that psychological forces have a certain strength: there are lukewarm wishes, for example, and there are burning desires. The fact that the analyst pays attention to the relative strength of the psychological forces which he observes is referred to as the psychoeconomic point of view.

The recognition of a more or less stable grouping of psychological forces led to the concept of areas of the mind and to their diagrammatic rendition in the psychoanalytic models of the mind. Freud's early diagram, the topographic model, divided the psyche into two areas: the Unconscious and the Preconscious. The conceptual mode of approach to the data of observation which is based on the topographic diagram is called the topographic point of view. A growing number of observations, however, could not be fitted into the classical topographic model. It had to be revised in order to be consistent with newly gained insights about mental functioning, and it had to be expanded in order to accommodate the newly discovered areas of the psyche. The revised and expanded psychoanalytic diagram is the structural model; the mode of approach that is based on it is the structural point of view. The topographic point of view has already been discussed at length; some aspects of the structural point of view will be reviewed later.

In the following we will discuss briefly the genetic point of view. This term refers to the fact that the analyst focuses his attention on the childhood of the individual whom he studies, with the expectation that he may discover a specific set of experiences, which occurred at a specific time or during a specific period of childhood, following which a particular symptom, character trait, or behavioral tendency arose for the first time. Genetic explanations in therapeutic psychoanalysis refer, of course, most frequently to the origin of adult psychopathology and, thus, to those traumatic childhood situations in which a preceding non-pathologic arrangement of psychological forces was replaced permanently by a new, pathologic one. The potential discovery of the pathogenic experiences of childhood through the investigation of unconscious endopsychic material is a specific and characteristic objective of psychoanalysis. The modern offshoots of psychoanalysis (such as the various popular schools of dynamic psychiatry) restrict their investigations of endopsychic material to the comprehension of repetitive dynamic patterns which are then correlated with known historical data from childhood, such as the specific family constellation, the personalities of the parents, deaths of parents or siblings, etc. Their examination stops short of the ultimate goal of psychoanalysis: the therapeutic revival and recovery of the unconscious memories of traumatic experiences.

A brief clinical vignette may clarify the difference between the understanding of dynamic patterns and the penetration into genetic material.

A man described a recent job situation in which his work (which had been satisfactory previously) deteriorated after the appearance of a younger co-worker. It was found in the course of the analytic work that he had felt guilty about his jealousy towards the new worker, and that the slackening of his work had been motivated by a wish to withdraw from the competition. The same dynamic pattern could be established in relation to previous job situations. Similar conflicts had occurred in childhood with schoolmates and especially with his brothers. The pattern was repeated in his analysis. At first he did good work with a steady flow of free associations; then came a setback and resistance. His associations alluded hesitatingly one day to another patient whom he had seen in the waiting room. The same dynamic formulation as before was interpreted, and the analytic work flowed again. On a later occasion intense resistance set in, followed by the reluctant disclosure of fantasies that the other patient might be ill. Memories of illnesses in a sibling then emerged. Finally, after many phases of intense resistance, dream material made possible the reconstruction (later supported by relevant memories) that an infant brother had died during a phase of intense hostile jealousy during the patient's early childhood. The genetic elucidation of this pattern was now possible. Not only had he experienced a normal amount of hostility toward rivals prior to the fateful event (the sibling's death), but he had also gradually learned to recognize that there is a significant difference between (the psychologic reality of) angry thoughts and wishes, on the one hand, and (the external reality of) angry and hurtful actions, on the other. The death of the brother (aided by auxiliary factors, such as the parents' withdrawal from the patient during the traumatic period) had shattered the ego's barely acquired differentiation between impulse, fantasy and deed. Angry wishes and fantasies were regressively experienced as magically powerful, and the weak ego, traumatically flooded with anxiety, defended itself against the dangerous impulses by repression. Thereafter, hostile, jealous and competitive strivings were excluded from the realm of the ego, preventing their further differentiation and integration and precluding the acquisition of eventual conscious control over them.

THE STRUCTURAL MODEL OF THE MIND

As indicated before, new observational data and new insights made the classical topographic model inadequate, and necessitated (in the 1920's) the creation of a new diagram of the arrangement and inter-relationships of psychological forces, the structural model of the mind. The new model contains a series of major revisions and expansions; best known among the innovations is undoubtedly the new nomenclature, the introduction of the terms id, ego and superego, corresponding with a new division of psychic functions which conforms more accurately with the data of clinical observation than the simpler correlations of the topographic model. The very fact that Freud introduced a new terminology for the structural model bespeaks the magnitude of the conceptual changes, since Freud was usually disinclined to replace already established terms.

Later we will turn our attention to a notable expansion in the conceptual scope of the structural point of view, which permits the meaningful inclusion of a whole new range of psychological phenomena into the framework of psychoanalytic theory. First, however, we must review some of the major modifications and corrections which transformed the topographic into the structural model: the discovery of unconscious defense mechanisms, the recognition of the role of aggression, and the comprehension of the genetic and structural cohesion of the various constituents of endopsychic morality.

The investigation of new areas of psychopathology, particularly the obsessions and compulsions, led to the discovery that repression (i.e., the withdrawal of a fragile psyche, under the impact of trauma, from further participation in specific infantile wishes) was not the only mechanism by which the immature mental apparatus could maintain its organization under stress. Freud recognized that the psyche also employs other important means of keeping the dangerous archaic drives in check: chronic characterologic attitudes (the so-called reaction-formations) serve to maintain and reinforce previously established repressions; magical modes of thought and action (the mechanism of undoing) are employed to ward off threats to a weakening repression; and ideas and affects are kept apart (the mechanism of isolation) by a superstitiously fearful psyche in order to render impulses harmless which might penetrate through the repressions.

The discovery that a variety of defense mechanisms exists in the psyche contributed to the depth and the subtlety of clinical understanding; of even greater importance, however, both clinically and theoretically, was the recognition that these various defense mechanisms directed against archaic infantile wishes and impulses, were themselves not only archaic (i.e., part of the primary process) but also inaccessible to consciousness (i.e., belonging to the Unconscious). The revised conceptualization of the interrelationships of psychic forces, which takes these new discoveries into account, recognizes that the essential opposition is between an enclave of unmodified infantile strivings (the repressed id) and a system composed predominantly of mature, preconscious functions (the ego). The ego, however, applies archaic means (the unconscious defenses) to maintain the integrity of its territory of rationality. This particular structural relationship is analogous to the use of magical threats by parents, educators, and religious authorities in order to foster the creation of superstitious beliefs in children, in the service of drive control and of other rational aims.

The following diagram presents the new conceptualization of the relationship between ego, id, Preconscious, and Unconscious.

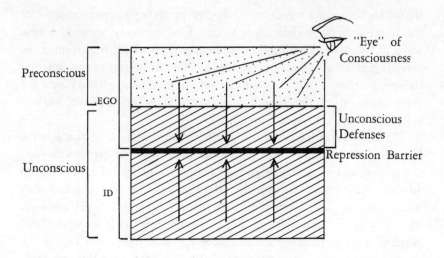

The area below the repression barrier is the id; the area above is the ego. The lined area is the Unconscious, the dotted area the Prconscious. The opposing arrows symbolize the structural conflict between repressed infantile drives and the defenses. Note that the main part of the defenses is unconscious.

Only brief mention need be made about the increasingly significant position which aggression began to occupy in psychoanalytic theory. The clinical importance of aggressive strivings had been obvious, of course, from the beginning; the Oedipus complex, for example, the foremost clinical discovery of psychoanalysis, which was presented as early as 1900, involves not only a libidinal but also an equally important aggressive component (cf. the little boy's death wishes toward his father). Unlike the later investigations of compulsion neurosis and depression, however, the early investigations of hysteria did not lead with equal clarity to the recognition that the vicissitudes of aggressive drives paralleled widely those of the libidinal drives. Like the libido, aggression is present in a repressed, unmodified, infantile form; its breakthrough is feared and defended against; it enters into transferences; and it lends itself to maturing influences and to useful integration into the higher functions of the psyche. It was on the basis of these new observations that the new dual-drive theory was incorporated into the structural model: the id was conceived of as containing not only infantile libidinal but also infantile aggressive tensions which strive for discharge and are kept repressed.

We turn now to the concept of the superego, the new conceptualization of endopsychic moral forces. The presence of endopsychic moral forces had been acknowledged from the early days of psychoanalysis, and it was recognized that they contributed decisively to the motivation for and the maintenance of repressions. The widening scope of clinical observations, however, led, step by step, to the discovery that the moral forces not only fulfill a variety of related functions but also that they constitute a cohesive genetic and functional unit which demanded their conceptualization as a distinct structure of the psyche, the superego. The study of hysteria already allowed the assumption that moral influences could be unconscious, like the drives; and this assumption became well-nigh a certainty when Freud discovered that an unconscious sense of guilt could induce people to commit crimes in order to provoke punishment. The decisive studies, however, were instigated by the discovery that, in certain depressions, the moral forces (although in a malignant state of regression) have gained a circumscribed position of tyrannical power over the rest of the personality and are in the process of subjugating and of destroying it. Freud extended and deepened his study of the various components of endopsychic morality (the censoring and punitive forces, the standards of the ego-ideal, the approving and loving powers) and ultimately came to the conclusion that the essential cohesiveness of these variegated functions resulted from the fact that they had once been united, outside the personality, in the parental authority: that the parent-authority had been the embodiment of the censor and punisher who was feared by the child, the admired ideal and prototype who could make the child feel small and inferior, the source of love and approval when the commands had been obeyed, and the reservoir of shared pride and pleasure when the child lived up to the parental example. Because Freud recognized the functional and genetic cohesion of the various aspects of the internal moral forces, he conceived of them as a distinct psychological structure. Even the name which he chose, the superego, reflected the fact that approval and disapproval, and standards and ideals are experienced as if located above the ego: a residual from the time when the child was small and looked up to the approving or disapproving admired figures.

In addition to the fact that the structural point of view introduces a number of important changes into psychoanalytic theory (e.g., revision of the theory of repression, of the theory of drives, and of the theory of endopsychic morality), it also constitutes a significant expansion of the conceptual scope of psychoanalysis: it allows the integration of the dynamic-economic-genetic understanding of a variety of non-pathological functions with those essential, classical findings and formulations of psychoanalysis which had been derived from the study of dreams and of psychopathology.

This expansion in the scope of psychoanalytic theory finds its diagrammatic expression specifically in the fact that, in the structural model of the psyche, the barrier of defenses separates only a small part of the infantile psychological depth from the areas of mature psychic functioning, while the deep, unconscious activities in the remainder of the diagram are in broad uninterrupted contact with the preconscious layers of the surface. Kohut [6] has referred to the dichotomized segment of the psyche as the area of transferences, and to the uninterrupted segment as the area of progressive neutralization.

The following diagram presents the two segments of the psyche in a schematic fashion. The actual relationships would be rendered more accurately if the barrier of defenses were made to shade into the non-dichotomized segment of the psyche. This gradual merging of the defense barrier into the neutralizing matrix of the psyche is hinted at in the diagram but is not fully carried out.

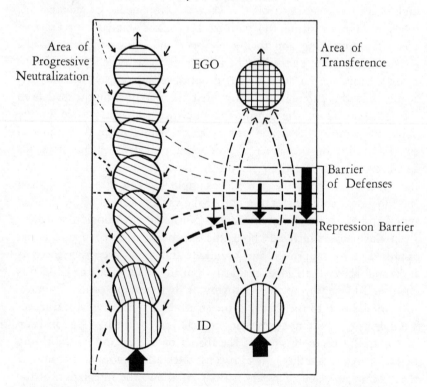

[6] Kohut, H.: Discussion of D. Beres' paper, "The Unconscious Fantasy," at the Meeting of the Chicago Psychoanalytic Society on September 26, 1961. See also *Bull. Phila. Assoc. of Psychoanal.* 11:194, 1961.

The right side of the diagram represents the area of transferences; here infantile impulses, which have met with frustration of traumatic intensity, exert their transference influence across the barrier of defenses and produce compromise formations (between primary and secondary processes) with the preconscious contents of the ego. The left side of the diagram represents the area of progressive neutralization, where the infantile impulses which have encountered optimal frustration are transformed gradually into neutralized mental activities.

Although the area of transferences constitutes only a small portion of the structural diagram, its significance remains undiminished since it is there that we find those activities and phenomena that are the result of structural conflicts and transference: dream formation; the symptoms of the transference neuroses; such psychic formations as slips of the tongue, errors, and the like, which Freud referred to as psychopathology of everyday life; and especially the transferences to the analyst in the course of psychoanalytic treatment.

As we have seen, the structural model of the mind depicts the bulk of the psychological organization as a continuum from the depths to the surface. The neutralizing psychological structure which constitutes the non-dichotomized portion of the psyche (the area of progressive neutralization) was formed by the internalization of innumerable experiences of optimal frustration. The barrier of defenses, on the other hand, which walls off an unmodified residue of infantile strivings, is the result of the internalization of frustrating experiences and prohibitions of traumatic intensity.

The differences between childhood experiences of traumatic and of optimal frustration are differences in degree. It is the difference between one mother's harsh "N-O!" and another mother's kindly "no." It is the difference between a frightening kind of prohibition, on the one hand, and an educational experience on the other. It is the difference between one father's handling a child's temper tantrum by an equally hostile counter-tantrum, and another father's picking up the child and calming him—firm but non-aggressive, and loving but not seductive. It is the difference between an uncompromising prohibition, which stresses only what the child must not have or cannot do, and the offering of acceptable substitutes for the forbidden object or activity.

Replicas of the experiences of traumatic frustration and of the experiences of optimal frustration (identifications) are established in the mind via the mechanism of introjection. The child incorporates permanently into his own psychic organization the restraining attitudes and behavior of the childhood objects who curbed his wishes, demands, needs and strivings. The child's drives are opposed originally by the prohibitions of the parents. If these prohibitions are of non-traumatic intensity, the child incorporates the parents' drive-restraining attitudes in the form of innumerable benign memory traces. In this way the matrix of the non-dichotomized portion of the psychologic structure is created, which transforms the archaic, infantile drives into aim-inhibited activities. As a result of having introjected many experiences of optimal frustration in which his infantile drives were handled by a calming, soothing, loving attitude rather than by counter-aggression on the part of his parents, the child himself later acts in the same way toward the drive demands that arise in him. Optimally frustrating experiences lead, therefore, to the formation of a drive-restraining (neutralizing) structure which, itself, is composed of neutralized memory traces and works with the aid of neutralized endopsychic forces. Crude, infantile aggressive impulses, for example, can be transformed into non-hostile purposive activities through internalized drive-restraining attitudes which, themselves, have lost their aggressive or sexual quality.

Individuals undoubtedly differ in their constitutional potentialities for the development of optimally neutralizing, drive-restraining structures. The most important source of a well-functioning psychological structure, however, is the personality of the parents, specifically their ability to respond to the child's drive demands with non-hostile firmness and non-seductive affection. Psychoanalysis also takes into account the existence of constitutional variations in the readiness of the child's psyche to be traumatized and to ward off conflictual drive demands through the establishment of repressions and of massive defenses. Even the most mature parents cannot (and need not) prevent the establishment of repressions and of other defenses, which are, after all, economical means of dealing with tensions at a time when the more subtle steps toward psychological growth cannot yet be taken. If a child is exposed chronically to immature, hostile, or seductive parental reactions toward his demands, then the resulting intense anxiety or over-stimulation leads to an impoverishment of the growing psyche, since too much of his drive-equipment is repressed and thus cannot participate in psychic development. In addition, the intensity of the unmodified infantile drives and the brittleness of the defenses are the antecedents of later psychological imbalance, and of the sudden breakthrough of repressed material which leads to neurotic illness.

The foregoing discussion has not taken up all of the major changes in psychoanalytic theory brought about by the structural point of view; and of those that were reviewed, only the high lights could be depicted. Completeness, however, is neither possible nor even desirable in a brief survey of a complex field. The aim of this presentation was, rather, to attempt to provide a better comprehension of the meaning of the theoretical formulations of psychoanalysis, a sense of the continual development and expansion of psychoanalytic theory, and an appreciation of the interrelatedness between theoretical formulation and (clinical) observation. Consideration of the structural point of view shows how earlier theoretic formulations were revised under the influence of new clinical findings; it also demonstrates with particular clarity the expansion in the scope of psychoanalytic theory, in particular its increasing ability to define and explain the most mature and highly developed psychic activities in genetic-dynamic-economic terms, and to integrate these new insights with the older formulations.

The formulations of the structural point of view exerted a considerable influence on the theoretic principles of child rearing practices. It hardly needs to be stressed that the structural point of view also modified the theory of psychoanalytic technique and the conduct of therapeutic psychoanalysis. The fact that during psychoanalysis one part of the patient's psyche observes and comprehends, while the other part permits regression and transferences (what Sterba later aptly called the "therapeutic split in the ego"), had probably been understood for a long time. The deeper comprehension, however, of the meaningful relationship of the observing part of the psyche with the analyst (i.e., of the patient's capacity to form and maintain a reliable relationship of cooperation which rests on the foundations of childhood experience yet is not transference) could only be attained through the formulations and insights of the structural point of view.

Recognition of the advances in theoretic understanding that are embodied in the structural diagram does not prevent the acknowledgment that it contains important areas that await further exploration and reformulation. What, for example, is the nature of the psychic contents of the id? Are its primitive wish-strivings attached to memories and fantasies; and, if so, is there, beneath the barrier of defenses, a further differential layering between id-contents of greater and lesser primitiveness? Are there formal distinctions between the archaic psychic processes in the unconscious part of the ego and those in the id? What are the differences between the early identifications in the deepest layers of the psyche and those that are deposited later, nearer the surface? These and other topics await detailed exploration, and there is little doubt that the structural diagram will be modified in due course as a result of further clinical research.

The development of psychoanalysis has, in fact, not ceased since the introduction of the structural model. The newer formulations seem to point toward an increasing preoccupation of analysts with the functions of the ego. Analysts (cf. H. Hartmann) now emphasize that ego functions mature in a predetermined fashion which is to some extent independent of environmental influences (primary autonomy), and also that ego functions may ultimately free themselves from the nexus of endopsychic conflicts and thus, again, become independent (secondary autonomy).

It is neither possible nor desirable to present an orderly survey of the most recently formulated theories of a developing science such as psychoanalysis. The modern theories have been mentioned primarily to prevent the possible misapprehension that psychoanalysts consider the theories of the structural point of view as the final word of wisdom. True, psychoanalysis, like any other science, does not discard well-established theories lightly; a degree of conservatism is necessary to prevent a theoretical and conceptual chaos. Yet, if we take a broad view we can safely say that while the theory of psychoanalysis influences the analyst's mode of observation and the evaluation of his data, it remains itself open to change by the impact of new experience.

REFERENCES

BRENNER, C. *An Elementary Textbook of Psychoanalysis*. New York: Inter. Univer. Press, 1961.

FISHER, C. Dreams and perception: The role of preconscious and primary modes of perception in dream formation. *J. Amer. Psychoanal. Assoc.* 2:389-445, 1954.

FREUD, S. (1900). *The Interpretation of Dreams. Standard Edition*, Vols. 4-5. London: Hogarth Press, 1963, pp. 562-63.

FREUD, S. (1917). *A General Introduction to Psycho-analysis*. New York: Perma Giants, 1949.

FREUD, S. (1926). *The Problem of Anxiety*. New York: Norton, 1936.

HARTMANN, H. & KRIS, E. The genetic approach in psychoanalysis. *The Psychoanal. Study of the Child, 1,* 11-30, 1945.

HARTMANN, H., KRIS, E. & LOEWENSTEIN, R. M. Comments on the formation of psychic structure *The Psychoanal. Study of the Child,* 2:11-38, 1946.

KOHUT, H. Introspection, empathy, and psychoanalysis—An examination of the relationship between mode of observation and theory. *J. Amer. Psychoanal. Assoc.* 7:459-483, 1959.

POETZL, O. Experimentell erregte Traumbilder in ihren Beziehungen zum indirekten Sehen. *Ztschr. F. Neurol. u. Psychiat.* 37:278-349, 1917.

WAELDER, R. *Basic Theory of Psychoanalysis.* New York: Inter. Univer. Press, 1961.

6

Field Theory in Psychology: Kurt Lewin

Jacob S. Kounin

I. INTRODUCTION

At varying times in his career Kurt Lewin's works were labeled as
dynamic theory, topological theory, vector psychology, and field theory.
He is now probably most closely associated with the designation "field
theorist," and, as Cartwright (1959) points out, this seems to have
been his final preference. Lewin (1951a) characterized field theory as
a method of analyzing causal relations and of building scientific constructs. Aspects of this "method" were such ideas as these: psychological
science should deal with the total concrete reality of human behavior
and experience; theories should evolve by a process of successive approximations without losing sight of the totality of relevant events;
an event is determined by its relations to a system of events of which
it is a part; psychological phenomena should be described and explained
with psychological concepts; one should distinguish systematic, ahistorical explanations from historical explanations; and psychological science should use "constructive," genotypical concepts in preference to
"classificatory," phenotypical concepts.

A basic Lewinian concept is that of the Life Space, which refers
to the totality of coexisting facts that influence the behavior of an
individual at a particular time. This includes the structure and state of
the person (P) and of the psychological environment (E). The rep-

resentative formula for this is: $B = F(P,E) = F(LSp)$. Both the person and the environment, then, have to be considered as *one* constellation of interdependent factors.

Lewin felt it was possible to represent the structure and dynamics of the Life Space by means of mathematical concepts. In an attempt to attain this goal he utilized three types of interrelated concepts: (1) Topological concepts to deal with relationships among regions and boundaries. These enable one to deal with such positional-structural properties as degree of differentiation, centrality-peripherality, part-whole relationships, overlappingness, and so on. (2) Hodological concepts to deal with problems of psychological distance and direction. (3) Dynamic concepts, such as tension-system, valence, force, to deal with issues that might traditionally be labeled as "motivational."

The nature of his concepts and his delineations of the task of scientific psychology were such as to operate against the separation of theories into those of learning, perception, personality, childhood and adolescence, or any other type of classification of human behavior. The content of his inquiries cut across a variety of traditional fields such as psychology, sociology, ecology, and even economics, and dealt with a variety of problems from "inside the person" variables such as needs, to group atmosphere, to the ecology of food marketing and consumption.

Traditionally, personality theory may be said to deal with "inside the person" variables, or with the P part of the Life Space. The reader should realize that this chapter, in its attempt to discuss Lewin's personality theory, is an oversimplification. It represents an artificial removal of the Person from his Environmental context and places emphasis upon merely a few Lewinian concepts that, in the writer's selective abstraction, are the most person-related in Lewin's system of thought. The reader is referred to the writings of Cartwright (1959), Deutsch (1954), and Leeper (1943) for more complete reviews of Lewin's formulations. These reviews summarize Lewin's later work in the field of social psychology and also present critiques and elaborations of his mathematizing.

Specifically, this chapter will deal with a summary of two of Lewin's germinal ideas: the concept of need and the concept of goal.

II. NEEDS

Lewin's first approximation to his later tension-system theory began with his discussions with Ach pertaining to association theory. As a result of experiments with paired nonsense syllables Lewin demonstrated that an association, per se, is not a sufficient cause for the recall of an associated symbol in response to a stimulus syllable. At this time Lewin (1936) affirmed that "Connections are never causes of events"; that "One must therefore inquire of every psychical event whence the causal energies come"; that "Rather, certain psychical energies, that is, tense psychical systems which derive, as a rule, from the pressure of will or of a need, are always the necessary occurrence—in whatever way —of the psychical event."

One may regard this as a germinal idea in Lewin's thinking. At that time, terms such as "will," "need," "motor," "energy," and "tense psychical systems" were used interchangeably without any attempt at precise formalization. This was followed by observations and inquiries into phenomena of everyday life. In one article, Lewin (1951b) dealt extensively with the mailing of letters. In much the same manner that Freud would analyze the formation of a dream symbol—following through from alternative "if so—then" hypotheses—Lewin analyzed the conditions in real life that would cause one to remember or to forget to mail a letter. Along with this line of thinking, some aspects of these ideas were formulated with sufficient clarity to be subject to experimental tests. In connection with the concept of tension-system, various experiments on the resumption and recall of interrupted activities, substitute-value, and satiation were conducted. Following the experimental confirmation of part-theories, the germinal idea was elaborated and formalized within the framework of both topological and dynamic concepts.

A. A definition of need

The construct "tension-system" refers to the state of one region relative to the state of surrounding regions in the person. If the magnitudes of tension of two or more neighboring regions are unequal, there are forces acting at the boundaries of the regions such that the state of region-A becomes equal to that of region-B. We may say, then, that tension-systems exert pressure and tend to spread. A need is defined as a tension-system inside of the person.

One notes in this definition both positional (topological) and dynamic properties. "Inside the person" is a topological relation. Food, for example, would have a position in the Environment region of the Life Space rather than in the Person region; hence, food would not qualify as a need. Needs are further assumed to be "surrounded by" the motor-perceptual part of the Person, which places the latter in a position between the inner needs and the Environment. Any need also has some position in relation to other needs, for example, a neighboring relationship. The dynamic properties of needs are those of tension-systems.

It is these dynamic properties that enable one to "explain" related psychological events. One may say that the pressure exerted by tension-systems "cause" certain events to happen. It should also be noted that tension-system is a scalar concept, in that it has magnitude but no specific direction. Rather, pressure (tendency to spread) is exerted in all directions simultaneously. One cannot, then, explain directed behavior solely on the basis of the existence of a postulated tension-system inside the person. Depending upon the position of a particular tension-system, the pressure may be exerted either upon the perceptual-motor regions of the person, or upon other needs, or upon both.

B. *The resumption and recall of unfinished activities*

The original experiments designed to test the tension-system hypothesis were those of Ovsiankina (1928) and Zeigarnik (1927). Both used the method of comparing the effects of completed and unfinished activities. The former dealt with overt behavior (doing) and the latter with covert behavior (thinking about). Both assumed that an intention to reach a certain goal corresponds to a tension-system within the person (a "quasi-need" or an "intention") and that this need would be satisfied or the tension-system would be released upon reaching the goal (completing the activity). Should the goal not be reached, the tension-system would remain. In the case of needs that have a position on the "outer layer" of the person, such as conscious intentions, "quasi-needs" or activity-needs, the unresolved tension-systems should exert a pressure on the perceptual-motor regions of the person and "cause" some behavioral manifestation. Ovsiankina's demonstration of these propositions was obtained by showing that people spontaneously resumed interrupted activities when left in a free situation. Zeigarnik's confirmation of the tension-system theory was obtained by showing that people tended to recall more interrupted activities than completed ones.

C. Some elaborations of tension-system theory

Having established experimentally that unfinished activities are both resumed and recalled more frequently than finished activities, research strategy could have gone in several directions. One strategy might have been to search for more "precision" by securing more cases to provide exact percentages of resumption or recall and to relate changes in such percentages to specific variables. Or, one could attempt to establish a variety of different derivations and to test as many of these as possible in order to clarify the conceptual properties of the concept of tension-system and to test its fruitfulness and explanatory-power. At this point in time, Lewin chose the latter. Following are examples of some of the other derivations from the tension-system concept. (A student may wish to compare the fruitfulness of these with other definitions of need such as "inner stimulus to behavior.")

Since a tension-system is defined as a difference in state between one region in the person and surrounding regions, and since tension tends to spread, one could infer that the differences between the resumption or recall of unfinished versus finished activities would decrease with the passage of time. Zeigarnik found that the Zeigarnik quotient (unfinished activities recalled over completed activities recalled) did in fact decrease in this way.

One premise of Lewin's thinking was that the Life Space should be characterized by its psychological rather than by its physical properties. Psychological rather than physical properties should also be used to characterize goals and the judgment as to whether activities toward goals should be designated as unfinished or completed. If the subject achieves his goal in relation to the task even though it is physically unfinished, one should expect no force to recall, and if the subject's goal is not obtained even though the task is physically completed, one should expect tension to persist.

Marrow (1938) devised an experiment in which the subject was told that the experimenter was interested in finding out whether the subject was able to perform a task and that he would stop the subject as soon as he knew. In this case, an unfinished task from the physical point of view would be a finished task from the psychological point of view. The Zeigarnik quotient in these cases was less than one.

In an experiment with children on the resumption of interrupted activities, Adler and Kounin (1939) found that children resumed an unfinished activity which they had begun themselves and did not return to an identical unfinished task which they were shown.

Experiments have also been performed relating the size of the Zeigarnik quotient to the intensity of needs. Zeigarnik found the quotient higher when activities were interrupted toward their end than when they were interrupted toward their beginning. She also found that subjects who were rated as "ambitious" (independently from their Zeigarnik quotients) and who were thus more prone to become highly involved in activities had higher Zeigarnik quotients than subjects who were rated as low in "ambition" and tended merely to do "what the experimenter told them to do." Marrow (1938) experimentally varied the intensity of quasi-needs by means of competition, praise and blame, and found that these experimental manipulations increased the size of the Zeigarnik quotient.

The above examples of derivations from tension-system theory all pertain to properties of the quasi-needs themselves. More complicated derivations are possible if one considers what happens to a tension-system in relation to such other conditions as: (a) the state of other tension-systems in the person, (b) the spatial (topological) relations between one tension-system and others, and (c) the fluidity of the boundaries between a tension-system and its surroundings.

D. The effects of surrounding needs

The effect of tension-systems other than those corresponding to the task involved in the experiments was studied by Zeigarnik. She argued that a general tension-system of a higher magnitude than those corresponding to the relatively weak quasi-needs created by the experiments would have the effect of making the differences between the unfinished and completed tasks relatively negligible, or of destroying the boundaries between the tension-systems, thus producing an effective state of dedifferentiation. The experimental demonstration of this would involve finding a significantly lower Zeigarnik quotient during or following strong emotional states. She found that creating emotional excitement resulted in a sizable decrease in the Zeigarnik quotient. (This tendency of stronger tension-systems to overshadow or eliminate weaker tension-systems may well account for the results of some experiments that failed to replicate Zeigarnik's findings. Some have introduced success or failure as variables rather than completion or interruption. By definition, success and failure involve the need for self-esteem, which we may assume is stronger than the need to complete an experimental activity. One should expect, then, that the use of "failure" instead of simple interruption would result in the unsatisfied need for self-esteem dominating or eliminating the need to complete an activity, with the result that the Zeigarnik quotient does not obtain.)

E. The effects of spatial relations among needs

The effects of spatial relations among need systems refer to such questions as whether or not tension-systems are subparts of a more inclusive system, whether or not they are adjacent to other systems, and other relations of dependence that influence the degree of communication between two or more regions. One condition for the occurrence of the Zeigarnik effect is that the systems corresponding to the unfinished and completed activities are structured so as to be separate within the person. Should they be subparts of one inclusive system, no appreciable difference in tension between them can remain. Zeigarnik found that when tasks are not separated but are presented as parts of a more inclusive series, the Zeigarnik quotient does not obtain. (This condition has also not been accomplished by some experiments purporting to replicate Zeigarnik's findings.)

Spatial relations among needs also have considerable bearing upon the phenomena of substitution. Experimental studies of substitution have utilized the technique of the resumption of unfinished activities. The tendency spontaneously to resume unfinished activities follows the same general laws as the tendency to recall unfinished activities. If an original activity (OA) is interrupted and is followed by a substitute activity (SA) that is completed, one can determine whether SA has substitute-value for OA by seeing whether the subject resumes OA or not. If he resumes OA we may assume that the tension-system for OA still remains and that SA had no substitute value. If he does not resume OA then we may assume that SA had substitute-value and satisfied the need coresponding to OA. The experimental studies of substitute-value have demonstrated that in order for an SA to resolve the tension corresponding to an OA the two systems must be connected and not separated.

This connectedness has been experimentally created by increasing the perceived similarity between the original and the substitute activity. Substitute-value is also increased by increasing the difficulty or valence of the substitute activity. It is to be noted here that Lewin distinguished between substitute *expression* and substitute *value*. A substitute expression is any behavior, overt or covert, that is symptomatic of the pressure exerted upon the motor-perceptual system of the person by a need. This has substitute value only if the original goal is attained.

F. *The effect of fluidity*

The degree of fluidity of the boundaries between tension-systems also plays a part in determining the degree to which one need affects another. If the boundaries surrounding tension-systems are very fluid ("permeable"), then the difference between the tension levels of the systems cannot be maintained for any appreciable period of time, nor could a specific tension-system be built up in a highly fluid state of the person. By assuming that a state of fatigue could be characterized as a state of increased fluidity of the person, Zeigarnik was able to demonstrate the above proposition. Subjects who were tired, whether during the performance of activities or during a period of recall, did not show the Zeigarnik effect.

The process of satiation has also been used to demonstrate the effect of fluidity-rigidity upon the degree to which one need affects another. Satiation is the process whereby the psychological repetition of an activity changes the valence of the activity and the corresponding state of the need. The direction of change of valence is from decreasing positive valence to increasing negative valence with increasing repetition. Karsten (1928) has demonstrated the following behavioral signs of the process of satiation: decreasing quality of performance, spontaneous introduction of variations, breaking up and dedifferentiation in the meaning of the activity, resorting to various leaving-the-field behaviors, and eventual stopping of the activity. Assuming that the female is in a more fluid state during the menstrual period than between menstrual periods, Freund (1930) related the speed of satiation to the degree of fluidity of persons. The same subjects became satiated with activities more rapidly during their menstrual periods than during their intermenstrual periods.

The process of cosatiation provides another example of how one need affects another and how this depends upon the fluidity of boundaries. Cosatiation refers to the effects of satiating activity-A upon the valence and corresponding need for activity-B. By postulating decreasing fluidity with increasing chronological age, Kounin (1941) was able to demonstrate experimentally that the younger the individual, the more one tension-system affects other needs of the person. Holding mental age constant, he showed that the younger the person, the more the satiation of one need results in the cosatiation of other needs.

The studies of substitution and cosatiation demonstrate how one need affects others in the direction of domination-elimination. Theoretically, since tension exerts pressure and tends to spread, one should also expect a need to affect other systems in the direction of activation and infiltration. Stone and Barker (1939) compared the interest and likings of premenarcheal and postmenarcheal girls of the same chronological age, socioeconomic status and educational levels. These groups differed not only with respect to an inferred strength of sexual need but also with respect to the strength of other interests, preferences, and likings. Using tension-system theory, one could explain this finding by saying that the sex-tension spreads to infiltrate and increase the effective strength of other systems (dating, romantic novels, glamorous occupations, etc.) that are connected with it.

G. The dimensions of "inner-outer" and "central-peripheral"

In his earlier writings, Lewin (1951b) expressed the explicit yet unformalized idea that all needs, even when of the same strength, are not of equal importance. At that time, he referred to some needs as "quasi-needs" in contrast to "true" or "genuine" needs, but did not elaborate any conceptual definitions around which to give dimension to this difference.

At a later time, Lewin (1951b) formally introduced the concept of the stratification of the person into various layers of needs. "Outer" layers were those adjacent to the "motoric" (sensory-perceptual-motor) sphere of the individual and closest to the environment. "Inner" layers were more distant from the motoric and the environment. In an article discussing the differences between personality types in Germany and the United States, Lewin utilized this dimension of inner-outer formally to derive a variety of other obtained differences. Among these derivations were such characteristics as: (a) the degree to which different regions are made public or kept private, (b) the degree to which events are reacted to emotionally, (c) the degree to which relatively close relationships could be maintained with other persons yet without deep friendship or danger of personal friction, (d) the degree to which actions are emphasized relative to philosophy and ideals, (e) the degree to which such persons would form homogeneous or heterogeneous social groups, and (f) the degree of similarity between members of different groups. At this time, Lewin sometimes used the concepts of centrality-peripherality interchangeably with the concepts of inner-outer. (In many ways this mixture of the dimensions of inner-outer and central-peripheral corresponds roughly to the unformalized clinical usage of "surface" needs and "deep" needs.)

At a still later date, Lewin (1951a) formally distinguished between central-peripheral systems and between this dimension and the inner-outer dimension. The degree of centrality-peripherality of a need has more to do with the degree of importance of a need—with how much a need, because of its position, affects the behavior and other needs of the individual. Even when two needs are of equal strength, the more' central need has more effect upon the person than does a peripheral need. Topologically, the most central system in a person can reach all other systems in the person in the fewest number of steps. A more peripheral cell requires more cells to be passed before reaching all other cells. As a consequence of being in a central position, then, and because, by definition, needs exert pressure and tend to spread, the more central a need the more does it affect other needs either by tending to dominate them or by activating or infiltrating them.

The meaning of central-peripheral and inner-outer may be simply illustrated by considering three concentric circles. The outer one may be labeled o, the innermost one i, and the one in between c. O would be the outer layer since it is closest to the outside or to the environment and i would be the innermost layer since it is, hodologically speaking, farthest from the environment. However, c would be central, and i and o would be equally peripheral. The reason for this is that c requires but one step to communicate with both i and o, whereas two steps are required to reach i from o or o from i. A tension-system in c, then, would exert pressure directly on both i and o; i and o would exert pressure directly on c; but neither i nor o could exert pressure directly on each other.

From the degree of centrality of a need one can logically derive such consequences as: (a) the number of other needs affected by it, (b) the degree of effect upon the person as-a-whole, (c) the variety of expressions (though not necessarily substitute-satisfactions), (d) the resistance to change and tendency to longer lastingness (since it is connected with more other needs and hence involves changing more other systems of the person as well).

From the degree to which a need has a position in the outer-inner dimension one can derive such consequences as: (a) the degree to which it is private or public, (b) the degree to which the behavioral expression has a one-to-one relationship with the content of the need as compared to a "disguised" or indirect relationship with the content of the need, (c) the degree to which it may be diagnosed, (d) the degree to which it is influenced by events emanating from outside the person.

Should a need be central and also occupy a position in an inner layer, it is possible to formulate even more complicated derivations that combine some of the above consequences or entail still others. A high level of sensitivity and emotionality, for example, would obtain for a need that is both central and occupies an inner position.

In summary, Lewin's tension-system theory provides a conceptual framework which enables one to derive ("explain") a variety of phenomena. It provides an explanatory system for behavioral effects as well as for effects inside the person that are not directly expressed in motoric action. It can account for why one need may affect another, but it also rejects the oversimplified slogan that "everything affects everything else." The degree to which a tension-system changes other systems of the person depends upon a variety of conditions such as: (a) the magnitude of the difference one defines as a change, (b) the strength of the need, (c) the tension state of surrounding needs, (d) the fluidity-rigidity of the boundaries between needs, and (e) the position of the need in the person.

Lewin did not formulate any theory of need-content. He did not provide a system of need-types. Tension-system theory is, in a sense, content-free but allows the inclusion of any content. Believing that problems of individual differences should be subsumed from more general psychological laws, he stressed more general dimensions. One could study individual differences in respect to such general dimensions of needs as strength, degree of differentiation, and degree of stratification along the dimensions of inner-outer and central-peripheral.

III. GOALS

Tension-system theory does not enable one to derive directed behavior. The direction of behavior, whether toward or away from some region, is determined by psychological forces. Force, as a concept, does have the conceptual property of direction, as well as of strength and point of application. If a region (an activity, object, or person) has positive valence, it results in a force acting upon the person in a direction *toward* the region, a positive driving force. A region with positive valence is called a goal. If a region has negative valence, it produces a force acting upon the person in a direction *away* from the region, a negative driving force.

The discussion in this section will be restricted to some issues involved in the goal-setting behavior of an individual. It will start by listing some findings of research studies, selecting some concepts applicable to these findings, abstracting some "empirical laws" pertinent to these findings, and, lastly, presenting a "theory" from which one could derive both the empirical laws and the specific findings.

A. Some empirical findings

1. In one of the earliest Lewinian experiments on the goal-setting behavior of individuals, Hoppe (1930) had subjects perform various tasks such as shooting at targets, throwing rings on hooks passing on a moving belt, and other simple motor and intellectual tasks. Some of his general findings were these: (a) Feelings of success or failure were not developed for all levels of difficulty of a task, but were reported only in a relatively limited zone of performances. Where task-goals were too easy or too difficult, subjects did not report such feelings. (b) Feelings of success or failure resulted only when a person attributed the consequence ("score") to his own self. Performances that were attributed to "luck," for example, did not result in such reported feelings. (c) Feelings of success or failure did not depend upon the score obtained but rather upon whether the score obtained was below, equal, or above the score the person said he expected to get. (d) Following experiences of success, the subjects tended to set higher scores as their goals, and following feelings of failure, they tended to set lower scores as their goals.

2. Fajans (1933) hung a goal-object out of the reach of children and measured the duration of their efforts to reach it. Whether the child reached or did not reach the object was experimentally varied by imperceptibly raising or lowering it. Following success in reaching the object, the child's persistency increased. Following failure to reach the object, the duration of effort decreased. When the child was given the object by the experimenter (but did not reach it by himself), his persistency following this was midway between what it was following success or failure.

3. Fales (1940) observed the behavior of nursery school children when they were dressing in preparation for going outdoors. She noted when they refused the help of an adult. Refusals of help occurred predominantly when help was offered for an activity the child was able to perform by himself. After children were trained to increase their skills in these performances, the amount of refusal of help for them increased.

4. Anderson (1940) studied the behavior of children ranging from three to nine years of age in one game involving throwing five rings into a pan and another involving knocking down ten-pins with three balls. Some of his findings were these: (a) The youngest children stood closest to the pan; the oldest furthest from the pan. (b) Some of the youngest children merely placed the rings in the pan or knocked the pins down with their hands. The older ones all threw the rings. (c) Many of the younger children retrieved and rethrew missed rings. The oldest rarely retrieved missed rings except after all five rings were tossed. (d) The children tended to stand closer after missing a shot and to stand farther back after getting a shot in the pan. This movement back and forth occurred after single shots in the case of the younger children but occurred only after all five rings were thrown in the case of the oldest children. (e) Most of the children tended to miss between 40-60 per cent of the shots in the free situation. (f) When the experimenter offered the children a prize ("reward") for getting all the rings in the pan, they stood closer to it than they did in the "free" situation. (g) When the experimenter offered the prize and also insisted upon their throwing from a certain distance, the children who did not retrieve single missed rings in the free situation now tended to retrieve and rethrow missed rings.

5. Jucknat (1937) classified school children into those who were consistently good, medium, or poor in their school work. When presented with mazes placed in an ascending order of difficulty, the good students selected mazes high in the order of difficulty and the medium students selected mazes in the middle range of difficulty. The poor students selected mazes that were either very difficult or very easy.

6. P. S. Sears (1940) also selected school children on the basis of whether they had consistent histories of success or failure in the school subjects of reading and arithmetic. They were experimentally presented with tests involving verbal and arithmetical functions. The success group showed a pattern of low positive *discrepancy scores;* that is, the difference between their known past score on a test and their

stated expected score on a subsequent test was small, but the expectations were slightly higher than their past performance. The failure group showed two patterns: high positive and high negative discrepancy scores; they either stated expected scores much higher or much lower than their known past performances on similar tests. The success group can be said to have set more "realistic" goals than the failure group. The success group was also more "flexible" than the failure group in that they shifted more readily from one expected score to another, corresponding to shifts in their performances and in the level of difficulty of the tasks.

7. Anderson and Brandt (1939) administered a series of cancellation tests to fifth-grade children. After a practice series, the children were informed of their own scores, the average score of the class, and were also shown a graph showing each child how his performance compared with that of the group. Following this, the children were asked to write down privately the scores they expected to make on a succeeding test. The children above the group average tended to lower their scores toward the group average and the children below the average tended to have positive discrepancy scores. Hertzman and Festinger (1940) also showed that knowledge of the aspiration scores of a group influences the score college students state they expect to make on synonym and information tests.

8. Chapman and Volkmann (1939) showed that the standards and performances of groups other than one's own influence an individual's goal-setting behavior. College students were given a test of literary knowledge and given fictitious averages of scores made by literary critics, other students, and WPA workers. These fictitious scores were all the same, but clearly affected the scores the students stated they expected to make. Their scores were lowest when the literary critics' score was used as the reference and were highest when the average score of WPA workers was used. Festinger (1942) further showed that the discrepancy scores of college students were influenced by knowledge of the average scores of high school students, undergraduate college students, and graduate students. Shifts in the direction of positive discrepancy scores obtained when high school students' performances were given and shifts in the direction of negative discrepancy scores obtained when graduate students' scores were given.

The above studies do not exhaust the researches pertaining to the goal-setting behaviors of individuals. Many other studies are cited by Lewin, Dembo, Festinger, and Sears (1944) and by Atkinson (1953).

The above studies are cited, however, to provide the reader with some empirical findings that are illustrative of the concepts and theory to follow.

B. *Some relevant concepts*

1. *Level of aspiration.* We may refer to the concept of level of aspiration whenever a goal-region can be graded along some scale of difficulty or value. The level of aspiration is that degree of difficulty of attainment of a goal toward which the person is striving. In terms of one of the studies quoted, it may refer to the distance from which a child throws the rings, the number of rings out of five he aspires to get in, the score he aspires to achieve on a test.

2. *Goal-structure.* Goal-structure is a further refinement of the simpler concept of goal. Goal-structure refers to the content and degree of differentiation of the goal-region. Thus, in Fales' study, "getting the shoes on by myself" (and hence a refusal of help) is a more differentiated goal than "getting the shoes on." In Anderson's study, "getting the rings in by means of throwing" is more differentiated than "getting the rings in" (as manifested by some of the younger children "putting" the rings in the pan). Seeing all five rings as one goal unit is a more differentiated goal than seeing each ring as a separate goal (as manifested by retrieving and rethrowing missed rings as well as by changing positions after single throws). What might "logically" be represented as a means to a goal may be psychologically represented as part of the goal-structure. Thus, "making a fire" and "roasting" may be part of the goal-structure of a wiener-roast and not simply a means to the goal of "eating a wiener."

3. *Success and failure.* These concepts are to be distinguished from simple "satisfaction" or "frustration." The requirements for success include: (a) some barrier or difficulty, (b) the method or path used in reaching the goal (goal-structure), (c) attribution to self, and (d) achieving or surpassing the level of aspiration. A success experience may be defined as a person overcoming a barrier equaling or exceeding his level of aspiration in accordance with his goal-structure, and attributing the achievement to his self. Failure means not attaining the level of aspiration or goal-structure set, and attributing the nonattainment to one's self.

C. *Some empirical relations*

The studies referred to may be taken as illustrative of the following empirical relations:

1. Failure tends to lower a person's level of aspiration (A1 and A4).

2. Failure tends to lower a person's persistency in efforts to reach a goal (A2).

3. Success tends to raise a person's level of aspiration (A1 and A4).

4. Success tends to increase a person's persistency in efforts to reach a goal (A2).

5. A person's level of aspiration tends to correspond to his zone of ability (A1, A3 and A4).

6. Chronic failure tends to produce discrepancies between a person's level of aspiration and his ability (A5 and A6).

7. Group standards, whether these groups are present or not and whether or not the person is a member of these groups, tend to influence a person's level of aspiration. The direction of influence is related to the prestige and attributed knowledgeability of the comparison group. Knowledge of these groups' performances and aspirations may also produce a discrepancy between a person's levels of aspiration and his abilities (A7 and A8).

D. *A theory of level of aspiration and persistency*

Having established certain relationships between the level of aspiration and persistency on the one hand, and such factors as ability, success, failure, reward, and group standards on the other, one may ask why these relationships obtain. A theory that would enable one to derive these varied relationships could be said to have more explanatory-power than separate empirical laws. A further advantage of a theory is that it could explain "exceptions" to empirical laws. For example, under what conditions would failure not result in lowering the level of aspiration or in reducing persistency? Or, when is there a discrepancy between ability and level of aspiration? One might abstract "types" of persons ("ambitious," "unrealistic") to account for exceptions, or one might derive them from variables in a general theoretical formulation.

The following theoretical formulation attempts to derive the phenomena pertaining to level of aspiration and persistency from the propositions of psychological forces in general. One may say that the goal-setting behavior of an individual is a resultant of the positive driving forces, negative driving forces, and restraining forces acting upon him.

1. *Positive driving forces.* The positive driving forces operating when a person sets a level of aspiration consist of the following: (a) The needs involved. When speaking of success and failure one would have to include the need for self-esteem as well as the need relating to the activity or object. One may say that the stronger and more lasting the needs, the more pressure there is to persist in efforts to reach a goal. (b) The valence of the goal. One may say that the more difficult the goal, the higher the positive valence. Thus, $1,000.00 has more positive valence than $5.00. (c) The positive valence of success. Since success involves the need for self-esteem we may say that the region "to succeed" has positive valence, and that the more difficult the task the higher the positive valence of success. (d) The expectation of success. It is assumed that when a person is in the region of setting a level of inspiration he also makes some judgment about the probability that he will reach the region of success. The expectation of success may be said to be highest for easy tasks and lowest for difficult tasks.

2. *Negative driving forces.* In setting a level of aspiration, two negative driving forces are involved: (a) The negative valence of failure. To fail may be said to have negative valence and to produce a force on the person in the direction away from that region. The negative valence of failure may be assumed to be highest for easy tasks and lowest for difficult tasks. To fail at something easy is worse than to fail at something difficult. (b) The expectation of failure. The subjective probability of failure is highest for difficult tasks and lowest for easy tasks.

3. *Restraining forces.* Barriers that have a position between a person and a goal produce restraining forces. Objectively, these are greater, the more difficult the task. The possession of an abiilty or a resource reduces the strength of these restraining forces. Thus, a person with a skill or capital has fewer restraining forces operating toward earning a large sum of money than a person without these.

Where a person sets his level of aspiration, or how much effort he exerts in his attempts to reach a goal, may be said to be a resultant of the positive, negative and restraining forces. Some of these forces are in the direction of high levels of aspiration and effort and some are in the direction of low levels.

These theoretical factors may be used to "explain" both the empirical laws and the specific events. For example, "Success experiences increase the duration of effort towards a goal" may be explained by assuming that success experiences increase the value of success-expectation; "The child stood closer after missing a shot" could be explained by assuming that failure increased the value of failure-expectation. Hypothetically, for example, one could also explain "exceptions" by means of the same general formula. Theoretically, a person with a backlog of success experiences in a particular kind of activity may well react to a failure by increasing his effort, if the failure experience increased the amount of tension of his needs but did not reduce his success-expectation appreciably.

Findings pertaining to the relationships between level of aspiration and ability may also be explained by the same general formula. One might group these factors into "motivational" factors (needs, goals, positive valence of success and negative valence of failure) and "cognitive" factors (restraining forces, and expectations of success or failure). One may further note that all the motivational factors push toward high levels of aspiration. It is at the difficult goals that needs are best satisfied and goals have most attraction. It is at the difficult levels of aspiration that success is sweetest and failure least distasteful. Should these forces alone be operating or have too much potency, one would expect a person to set unrealistically high levels of aspiration. On the other hand, the "cognitive" factors all operate toward low levels of aspiration. It is at the easy level that barriers are weakest, success-expectation greatest and failure-expectation lowest. Should these forces alone be operating, one would expect a person to set low levels of aspiration.

The law that "the level of aspiration corresponds to the zone of ability" applies where all these factors are operative and where all have significant weight or potency. One should expect "exceptions" to this law where some factors are not operating or where there are disproportionate potencies for one or more of the factors. Lack of "realism" or high discrepancy scores, then, could result from lack of knowledge (cognitive forces have low potency); repeated failures (which increase the strength of tension-systems or increase the potency of the region of failure); prizes and rewards (which increase the potency of success-expectation and reduce the potency of the activity-valence).

The effects of group standards upon an individual's level of aspiration may also be derived from their influence upon the variables in the general theory. Group standards may be said to influence both the motivational and cognitive factors. Knowledge of group performances and aspirations induces valences and provides a frame of reference for estimating difficulty and the probability of success or failure. The positive valence of a score of 20 on a test of literary knowledge is greater when this score corresponds to the performance of literary experts than when it corresponds to the score of less prestigeful unskilled workers. The probability of obtaining a score of 20 is also less when this is the standard of the more knowledgeable literary experts than when it is the standard of unskilled workers.

The concern of Lewin with social psychological problems in his later years resulted in a diminution of his contributions and those of his students to problems traditionally categorized as personality theory. Even his seemingly simple germinal concepts of needs and goals, however, can be shown to have a richness, clarity of meaning and explanatory power that contribute to our understanding of individual behavior. They hold promise of even greater fruitfulness if further explored.

REFERENCES

ADLER, D. L., & KOUNIN, J. S. Some factors operating at the moment of resumption of interrupted tasks. *J. Psychol.*, 1939, 7, 255-267.

ANDERSON, C. The development of a level of aspiration in young children. Iowa City: Ph.D. dissertation, 1940.

ANDERSON, H. H., & BRANDT, H. F. Study of motivation involving self-announced goals of fifth grade children and the concept of level of aspiration. *J. soc. Psychol.*, 1939, 10, 209-232.

ATKINSON, J. W. The achievement motive and recall of interrupted and completed tasks. *J. exp. Psychol.*, 1953, 46, 381-390.

CARTWRIGHT, D. Lewinian theory as a contemporary systematic framework. In S. Koch (Ed.), *Psychology: A Study of Science*. Vol. 2, New York: McGraw-Hill, 1959. Pp. 7-91.

CHAPMAN, D. W., & VOLKMANN, J. A social determinant of the level of aspiration. *J. abnorm. soc. Psychol.*, 1939, 34, 225-238.

DEUTSCH, M. Field theory in social psychology. In G. Lindzey (Ed.), *Handbook of Social Psychology*. Cambridge, Mass.: Addison-Wesley, 1954. Pp. 181-222.

FAJANS, S. Erfolg, Ausdauer und Aktivitat beim Saugling und Kleinkind. *Psychol. Forsch.,* 1933, *17,* 268-305.

FALES, E. Genesis of level of aspiration in children from one and one-half to three years of age. (Reported in Anderson, C., 1940.)

FESTINGER, L. Wish, expectation and group performance as factors influencing level of aspiration. *J. abnorm. soc. Psychol.,* 1942, *37,* 184-200.

FREUND, A. Psychische Sättigung in Menstruum und Intermenstruum. *Psychol. Forsch.,* 1930, *13,* 198-217.

HERTZMAN, M. & FESTINGER, L. Shifts in explicit goals in a level of aspiration experiment. *J. exp. Psychol.,* 1940, *27,* 439-452.

HOPPE, F. Erfolg und Misserfolg. *Psychol. Forsch.,* 1930, *14,* 1-62.

JUCKNAT, M. Leistung, Anspruchsniveau und Selbstbewusstein. *Psychol. Forsch.,* 1937, *22,* 89-179.

KARSTEN, A. Psychische Sättigung. *Psychol. Forsch.* 1928, *10,* 142-254.

KOUNIN, J. Experimental studies of rigidity, I & II. *Charact. & Pers.,* 1941, *9,* 251-282.

LEEPER, R. W. *Lewin's topological and vector psychology.* Eugene, Ore.: Univer. of Oregon, 1943.

LEWIN, K. *A dynamic theory of personality.* New York: McGraw-Hill, 1936.

LEWIN, K. *Resolving social conflicts.* New York: Harper, 1948.

LEWIN, K. *Field theory in social science.* New York: Harper, 1951. (a)

LEWIN, K. Intention, Will and Need. In Rapaport, D., *Organization and pathology of thought.* New York: Columbia Univer. Press, 1951, Pp. 95-151. (b)

LEWIN, K., DEMBO, T., FESTINGER, L., & SEARS, P. S. Level of aspiration. In J. McV. Hunt (Ed.), *Personality and the behavior disorders.* New York: Ronald, 1944, Pp. 333-378.

MARROW, A. J. Goal tensions and recall (I & II). *J. gen. Psychol.,* 1938, 3-35, 37-64.

OVSIANKINA, M. Die Wiederaufnahme von unterbrochenen Handlungen. *Psychol. Forsch.,* 1928, *11,* 302-389.

SEARS, P. S. Levels of aspiration in academically successful and unsuccessful children. *J. abnorm. soc. Psychol.,* 1940, *35,* 498-536.

STONE, C. P., & BARKER, R. G. The attitudes and interests of premenarcheal and post-menarcheal girls of the same chronological age. *J. genet. Psychol.,* 1939, *54,* 27-71.

ZEIGARNIK, B. Über das Behalten von erledigten und unerledigten Handlungen. *Psych. Forsch.,* 1927, *9,* 1-85.

7

Humanistic Psychology:
Allport and Murray

Salvatore R. Maddi [1]

Although the works of Gordon W. Allport and Henry A. Murray are widely known in the field of personality, this familiarity does not make presenting and comparing their viewpoints a simple, straightforward task? The complications begin with the phenomena to be explained, for people are bewilderingly multi-faceted and changeable in their manner of living. Moreover, both of these psychologists have been uncompromising in their effort to encompass the entire personality, whatever the toll in conceptual complexity and indefiniteness. They have approached theory construction inductively, with sensitivity and imagination, concentrating more on completeness than on formal elegance and precision. Throughout their long and productive careers, Allport and Murray have both felt free to follow their shifting apperceptions wherever they might lead, to a more compelling elaboration of a basic concept here, to the change of a general manner of thinking there.

For the sake of clarity in the face of formidable difficulties such as these, general orientations toward the nature of personality are here considered separately from the specific concepts and definitional statements that comprise the actual theories of these two men. There is so much material available that it has been necessary to select for

[1] I wish to express my gratitude to Barbara Scott Propst for her valuable suggestions and criticisms concerning this chapter.

presentation only what seems most central to their positions. In this, I have tried to avoid gross misinterpretation by using as a guide their most recent writings and their explicit or implicit directives. Although differences as well as similarities are considered, care has been taken not to underscore small differences that may vanish as the language of their viewpoints becomes more specific and consistent.

While the major purpose of this chapter is to present and compare the content of both the general frames of reference and the actual theories of Allport and Murray, a secondary aim is to appraise their theories from the point of view of usability. The criterion of usability is neither mysterious nor new. Consider the application of a personality theory to the observed functioning of a particular individual or group. If the theory has been developed to the point where it has adequate usability, it will permit decision as to whether the observations are relevant. If they are relevant, the theory will provide guide lines for their description according to a specified set of data terms. Then it will be possible to generate a precise explanation of the description by a deductive process that is explicit and unambiguous. The explanation will provide the basis for deduction of equally precise predictions concerning functioning that has not yet been observed. In this entire process, it will be possible for competent and conscientious psychologists to reach substantial agreement, regardless of their preference or dislike for the theory.

A brief consideration of the viewpoint adopted in this chapter concerning the nature of theory will suggest some of the characteristics determining usability. A theory is a convention consisting of a number of concepts that are interrelated and have different levels of generality. The most concrete concepts have the primary function of referring directly to what is observable. Whatever empirical implications the very general concepts have is subsidiary to their function of referring to each other and to less general concepts, thereby providing integration. Some of the typical conditions that limit the usability of theories are: (1) imprecise or incomplete specification of the observables that are to be considered, (2) The absence of relatively general concepts, relatively concrete concepts, or statements of relationship, and (3) vagueness due to the use of figurative, inconsistent or otherwise ambiguous language in the definition of concepts and the delineation of relationships, incomplete operationalization of the concepts that refer directly to observables, and the adoption of concepts that are inherently heterogeneous (cf., Fiske, Ch. 16).

In considering usability, this chapter will not, thereby, be appraising the empirical validity of the theories. The crucial evidence about empirical validity involves tests of the predictions made by a theory. If these predictions are disconfirmed often enough, then the theory is brought into serious doubt, regardless of its usability and the apparent adequacy of its post-hoc explanations. The assessment of empirical validity, though a basic method of evaluation, is premature until the theory is sufficiently well developed so that the kinds of facts that are actually relevant, and the precise manner in which the theory addresses itself to these, can be unequivocally discerned. Usability, in that it is a mark of sufficient development, is a prior concern to that of empirical validity. Before adequate usability has been attained, empirical observations are probably most effectively utilized for theory construction rather than test.

Considering usability also says nothing about the criterion of stimulus value. According to this criterion, a theory is worthwhile to the degree that it provokes others to thought and investigation. An individual might find the theory congenial and be motivated to enhance and support it; he might simply associate freely to it and be caught up in the novel ideas thus generated; he might react against it and be driven to demonstrate its inadequacies. It does not make much difference which of these courses is taken as long as careful thought and research are undertaken that might not otherwise have occurred. This criterion is not considered here because it is assumed that the ample stimulus value of the viewpoints of Allport and Murray has long been apparent.

Legitimate and important as stimulus value is, a theory probably will not make a lasting, specific contribution to understanding in an empirical discipline like psychology unless it achieves adequate usability and proves to have considerable empirical validity. It is fruitless, however, to be condemnatory because psychology has not gone far in producing such theories. These criteria simply define a goal to be worked toward.

Theories typically do not start out being usable. The cognitive operations underlying the creation of ideas are simply more indirect, idiosyncratic, and metaphorical than those that facilitate communicative clarity and precise formulation. The employment of usability as an evaluative criterion is premature when a theory is still in its early stages of inception. But the theories of Allport and Murray had their beginnings more than 20 years ago, and hence consideration of their usability seems appropriate, and even timely, insofar as it may provide suggestions relevant to their further development.

GENERAL ORIENTATIONS TOWARD THE NATURE OF PERSONALITY

Hall and Lindzey (1957, p. 4) observe that personality theorists have been rebels in their time, and to judge from the dissatisfaction of Allport and Murray with the orthodoxies of the last few decades, they are not exceptions to this generalization. Faithful rendition of the bases for the considerable impact these two psychologists have had requires attention not only to their positively and consistently affirmed assumptions about the nature of man, but also to their enriching critical remarks, so often leveled against radical behaviorism and classical Freudianism.

Man is proactive

Perhaps the most basic ~~of the convictions~~ shared by ~~the two theorists~~ is that man has internal processes and structures that have a causal influence upon perception, though, feeling and action. Some of these internal characteristics, such as the instincts (~~Murray, 1956, pp. 23-24~~), are endogenous, while others, such as individual styles of life (Allport, 1961, ~~pp. 266-267; Murray, 1959, pp. 32-33~~), are learned. ~~Both theorists~~ feels that it is impossible to provide an adequate explanation of a person's functioning in any given situation by consideration of the external features of the stimulus situation alone. Hence, any approach that focuses exclusively, or even predominantly, upon external factors is a target for criticism. These approaches, "associationism of all types, including environmentalism, behaviorism, stimulus-response . . . psychology" (Allport, 1955, p. 8), are pejoratively labeled "Lockean" by Allport and "peripheralistic" by Murray (1938, pp. 5-11). Among the assumed errors made by adherents to these views are a disregard of extensive observational, logical, and introspective evidence for proaction (Allport, 1961, pp. 24-28; Murray, 1959, p. 15) and a treatment of personality as no more than a logically superfluous concept (Allport, 1961, p. 27). The theorists could very well point to the extensive literature on individual and group differences in functioning under objectively similar stimulus conditions to bolster their view.

Although they both have steadfastly given primary causal importance to internal characteristics, they have not overlooked the role of external factors. Neither sees much value in the behavioristic type of situational analysis, however, because it tends to oversimplify the subtlety and complexity of human interaction with the environment and restricts the range of stimulus meaning considered. They feels more satisfied with cultural and sociological variables, such as peer group and role pressures.

Of the two, Murray has given more place in his thinking to external determinants. Recent elaborations of their positions still show this difference, although both seem to be giving more weight than formerly to external factors. Murray (1959, p. 45) writes that under the long influence of such colleagues as Kluckhohn, he has ". . . come to think that no theoretical system constructed on the psychological level will be adequate until it has been embraced by and intermeshed with a cultural-sociological system." He has not abandoned primary emphasis upon proactive, individual personality factors, nor has he embraced the extreme interactional position exemplified by Sullivan (Murray, 1959, pp. 30-31), but external determinants are given considerable importance. In contrast, Allport's (1961, pp. 165-195) endorsement of such determinants is still tentative and qualified. He takes pains to delimit the province of strong external instigation of functioning to those situations that are highly structured (Allport, 1961, pp. 178-179).

The theorists also differ in their perception of the typical nature of the interaction between proactive and external forces. Murray (1959, pp. 45-56) emphasizes the almost continual conflict produced by the antagonism between the two sets of forces, while Allport (1961, p. 186) believes that external factors usually function to set rather wide limits on the range of behavioral possibilities available to the person, still leaving considerable latitude for proactive tendencies to be expressed without severe conflict.

Man possesses psychological organization

In man's proactive functioning, both theorists finds regularity and order to be typical, and attribute this to the unified, organized nature of personality. Allport (1961, pp. 376-391) finds that the individual's behavior shows complex integration) and Murray (1938, p. 4) feels that "personality is a temporal whole and to understand a part of it one must have a sense, though vague, of the totality." Murray argues by analogy that the unending transaction of biochemical processes in the brain, the obvious bodily locus of personality, makes it unlikely that any but a holistic view is tenable. Both theorists recognize two aspects of psychological organization. The first is unity at any given moment, seen in the convergence of many personality characteristics in the determination of functioning (Allport, 1961, p. 377; Murray, 1938, p. 86). The second is unity over a longer period of time. In discussing this, both theorists maintain that at the beginning of life the infant responds as a whole (Allport, 1961, p. 377; Murray, 1938, pp. 38-39). As he becomes older, the primitive unity gives way to a more sophisticated psychological integration of the various components of personality, differentiated from the earlier whole by learning (Allport, 1961, p. 377; Murray, 1938, pp. 38-39, 395-396). As the process of differentiation leads to greater complexity, integration is maintained through the development of more general, embracing characteristics (Allport, 1961, p. 377). Important in the organizational aspect of this psychological growth is the time-binding quality of cognitive processes (Murray, 1938, p. 49).

From the theorists' view of psychological organization, associationistic positions and limited experimental approaches seem particularly inadequate. Murray (1959, p. 34) puts this criticism thus:

> I was slow to perceive that current psychological theories of behavior were almost wholly concerned with actions of relatively short duration, reflexes and consecutive instrumental acts which reach their terminus within one experimental session, rather than with long-range enterprises which take weeks, months, or years of effort to complete. . . . The behavior of animals can be explained largely by reference to attractive or repellent presentations in their immediate environment and/or to momentarily urgent and rather quickly reducible states of tension; whereas a great deal of man's behavior cannot be explained except by reference to persistent "self-stimulation" in accordance with a plan of action, which often involves the subject's commitment to a distal goal or set of goals, as well as to a more or less flexible (or rigid) temporal order (schedule) or subsidiary, or stage, goals.

Allport agrees and also expresses his (1961, pp. 258-259) opposition to most existing analytical approaches to personality (e.g., McClelland, 1951), because he feels they tend to slice personality in fictitious ways in their attempt to achieve simplification and understanding. Both theorists recommend methods of study that involve as much as possible of the individual's functioning at one moment in time and over the course of time, and that attempt to represent the

END interrelated nature of aspects of functioning, however difficult this may be.

For all their objection to narrow, particularistic approaches, both theorists recognize the importance of avoiding the seductive pitfall of holistic approaches, namely, that they encourage "those lazy white elephants of the mind—huge, catchall, global concepts signifying nothing" (Murray, 1959, p. 19). Murray (1959, p. 51) hurls a challenge at exponents of this extreme that is fully as biting as that leveled at the opposite extremists:

> The terms "personality-as-a-whole" and "personality system" have been very popular in recent years; but no writer, so far as I know, has explicitly defined the components of a "whole" personality or of a "system of personality." When definitions of the units of a system are lacking, the term stands for no more than an article of faith, and is misleading to boot, in so far as it suggests a condition of affairs that may not actually exist.

Begin A similar note is struck by Allport (1955, pp. 36-41), when he considers it unwise to adopt an unelaborated, undetailed form of the concept of self because doing so would perpetuate the aura of mystery and the supernatural attending an unfathomable soul.

As indicated by some of the previous quotations and other statements (Allport, 1961, p. 380; Murray, 1959, pp. 19-21), both theorists *HE HAS* have attempted to avoid holistic vagueness by focusing primarily upon the organizational characteristics of personality involving purposiveness. But little organization is produced by the easily satisfied, and therefore relatively transitory, viscerogenic drives. Organization is primarily a function of those endogenous and learned purposes, such as life-goals (Allport, 1955, p. 49), dispositions to create (Murray, 1959, pp. 38-45), and competence motivation (White, 1959), that are non-specific as to the particulars of goal-states and hence relatively insatiable and continuing. Secondary in importance for unity are the less clearly purposive, more expressive, styles of functioning (Allport, 1961, pp. 460-494).

Man is psychologically complex

By emphasizing organization, the theorists do *Allport* not mean to imply that man's functioning is simple. It is staggeringly complex if one focuses upon the many different elements that develop through the process of differentiation. ~~Indeed,~~ In order to find great organization, it is necessary to observe the abstract or general features of functioning that can be grouped together into classes on the basis of equivalence of purpose or meaning. Considerable inference is involved in such observation.

~~The theorists are aware that~~ the level of abstraction one chooses in analyzing behavior will determine how complex that behavior appears. The important matter for ~~them~~ him is to find the level of abstraction that does least violence to the vital qualities of human living. It is known that a quite concrete, relatively uninterpretive analysis stressing the physical characteristics of behavior would lead to a view of that behavior as very complex due to its great variability among and within individuals (Fiske, 1961). However useful such an approach is for some purposes, Allport ~~and Murray~~ would find it employing too low a level of abstraction to do justice to the pyschological meaning of functioning.

~~They~~ He would also be dissatisfied with the opposite extreme, exemplified by theories that rely rather exclusively upon concepts involving a very high level of abstraction and interpretation. Such theories typically make only a few discriminations, thus missing some of the important differences between aspects of functioning. This is the primary difficulty that leads Allport (1961, ~~p. 208~~) to make the critical statement that Freud's "general picture of motivation makes personality almost a wholly reactive product of two archaic forces. . . . Of course we gladly grant that adult motives often reflect sex and aggression . . . yet we cannot believe that Freud does justice to the diversity, uniqueness, and contemporaneity of most adult motivation." Similarly, Murray (1959, pp. 37-38) finds that his chief objection to Freud's system "is the commonplace that . . . the libido has digested all the needs contributing to self-preservation, self-regard, and self-advancement, together with a host of others, and rebaptized them in the name of Sex."

Allport ~~and Murray~~ favors the utilization of a moderate level of observational abstraction, along with the higher level that permits an understanding of organization, because ~~they are~~ he is convinced that people have many different, changing, and sometimes incompatible intentions, values, and styles that can be expressed in different ways depending upon the environmental context. ~~They believe~~ He believes that an adequate theory of personality should permit explanation of these complexities. This view leads the theorists to be critical of oversimplified explanations (Allport, 1961, pp. 208-211; Murray, 1954, pp. 442-445; Murray, 1959, pp. 37-

,to Allport

38, 43). Oversimplification has occurred when the personality constructs used (1) focus too exclusively upon the concrete physical
characteristics of responses, predicting that a high level of consistency
will be found; (2) are so abstract and few in number that psychologically useful distinctions are blurred; (3) are too rudimentary, having
been developed to account for animal behavior, to yield adequate explanations at the human level with its great range of behavioral potential and time-binding features; and (4) are not employed within a
system permitting an understanding of changes in patterns of functioning over time.

Man's functioning is rational

With the exception of some recent developments within ego-
psychology, Freudian theory has emphasized the view that man's behavior originates in and is determined largely by unconscious, inex-
orable, selfish, primitive impulses. It is true that Freud conceived of
the ego as a realistic and therefore rational agent, but it was given a
reactive role in determining functioning. According to this extreme
view, whatever rationality man seems to express in thought processes
involving planning, decision-making and achieving intellectual understanding, is in large measure a defensive use of cognition in order to
conceal the underlying irrational impulses that are the basic determinants of functioning.

For Allport (1961, pp. 145-154), this view of man is almost
wholly wrong. He believes that the adult's functioning is characteristically rational, being governed by such conscious characteristics of
personality as long-range goals, plans of action and philosophies of life.
The extreme Freudian position that Allport is reacting against would
not dispute that such phenomena exist, but they would not be considered independent, primary determinants of functioning. They would
more likely be considered justifications after the fact of the compelling
action of the id. In contrast, Allport believes that only children, who
have not developed much personality, and the mentallly ill, in whom
the maturation of rational processes has been arrested, come close to
fitting the image of extreme Freudianism.)

END

Murray's (1938, pp. 46-47, 49-54) position, though less opposed
to the classical Freudian view, is similar to that of Allport in that it
invests man with a large measure of rationality. Rational and irrational
processes are considered to exist together in the personalities of all men.

The action of irrational, unconscious processes is seen in such things as odd inconsistencies, compulsions, and ego-alien acts. But a large proportion of functioning proceeds according to the influence of plans, intentions and values that are conscious and rational. To be sure, some men are more rational than others, and the least rational are among those likely to be considered mentally ill, but in Murray there is not the sharp distinction between health and illness, adulthood and childhood, that is found in Allport.

It is largely the rationality ~~they~~ attribute to man that leads ~~these theorists~~ to take subjective experience and self-report to be data of cardinal importance for an understanding of functioning (Allport, 1953, ~~pp. 108-110; Murray, 1959, pp. 9-11~~). If people are rational, they will know themselves, and be able to give adequate accounts and predictions of their own behavior. One result of Allport's more extreme view is that he believes projective techniques to be quite useless for normal adults. One can obtain the same information by the much more simple method of asking the person, provided he has resolved to be frank. Murray (1938, p. 114, pp. 530-531) is more convinced that projective techniques are important, as they tap the areas of unconsciousness and irrationality that exist in all of us. But the data of projection are not sufficient, requiring supplementation by direct self-report.

Allport's position is so extreme ~~that it seems unlikely to be strongly~~ supported by empirical findings. Take as an example research on achievement need and achievement value (McClelland, 1958, p. 37). The need score is based on the content analysis of TAT stories, while the value score involves the individual's answers to a set of questions about achievement. There is only a very low positive correlation between the projective measure and the more direct measure of value or attitude (deCharms, Morrison, Reitman, & McClelland, 1955), indicating that the two tap largely different aspects of functioning. As the need score is not related to direct self-ratings of achievement drive, it seems likely that it reflects at least partly unconscious strivings. If Allport's position were tenable, then the need score would be superfluous in understanding the functioning of normal people. For that matter, if Freud's position were adequate, then the achievement value score would not be particularly useful. But each of these scores is related to other, different aspects of functioning (McClelland, 1958, pp. 39-40). The need score correlates with aspects of memory and performance, and the value score, though not related to these, correlates with suggestibility in an ambiguous situation. Each of the scores seems to be tapping a different, though meaningful, aspect of personality, and, as the scores may reflect different degrees of consciousness, Murray's position seems supported more than that of Allport or Freud. Arguments of the type presented here are of limited relevance, however, not only because the empirical facts are incomplete at this stage of research, but also because the variables involved would often be considered artificial representations of personality by Allport.

Man is psychologically unique

Allport is more extreme on the question of uniqueness, than is Murray. For Allport (1955, p. 22), man is so unique as a species that an approach to understanding his functioning which utilizes lower animals is virtually useless. Although Murray (1954, p. 435) has criticized the "audacious assumption of species equivalence" made by learning theorists, he is less extreme concerning the uniqueness of man, as shown by his willingness to draw certain conclusions about the human on the basis of cross-species comparisons (Murray, 1959, pp. 14-19).

The disparity in emphasis between the theorists is still apparent when the focus shifts to the difference between individual members of the human species. For Allport (1955, p. 19), "each person is an idiom unto himself, an apparent violation of the syntax of the species." In explicating this position, Allport (1955, p. 22) focuses upon the apparently limitless range of potential behavior available to man by virtue of a big brain and a relative absence of instincts, and ventures the opinion (Allport, 1955, p. 23) "that all of the animals of the world are psychologically less distinct from one another than one man is from other men." All this is strong medicine that could kill the patient—psychology—already in a fever over the struggle for general laws that psychologists believe would make its scientific status indisputable. To anyone engaged in this struggle, Allport's position must seem cruel heresy, and hence, further consideration of it is in order.

Allport (1937, p. 4) argues that the major task of psychology is to understand and predict the individual case, rather than the contrived average case. Now if nomothetic concepts and laws, derived from and applicable to the data of aggregates, were completely adequate for predicting each individual case, there would seem to be little purpose in Allport's championing of the inviolacy of individuality.

In practice, however, perfect prediction and understanding using general laws is never achieved. Indeed, there is often a sizable minority of cases to which the general law does not seem to apply. This is not surprising to Allport (1961, pp. 332-356), who believes that nomothetic concepts are merely convenient fictions that are only useful insofar as they may resemble the true personality of some people. If a moderate degree of understanding and predictive accuracy is sufficient to satisfy the investigator, then Allport is not seriously opposed to the nomothetic approach. But the paramount goal of psychology requires a greater approximation to the truth.

In the attempt to achieve this goal, it will be necessary, according to Allport, to develop laws that are derived from and applicable to the data of each individual case alone. At first he called such laws idiographic (Allport, 1937, pp. 3-23), and seemed to conceptualize them in such an extreme fashion that virtually no generalization across persons would be possible (Allport, 1942, p. 57). A concept developed to explain some behavior of one man would, strictly speaking, not be applicable to anyone else. More recently he (Allport 1961, pp. 257-361; 1962) has substituted the term morphogenic for idiographic, and seems to be formulating a position that is less extreme, permitting the use of concepts that are not in principle restricted in applicability to only one person. The emphasis is still overwhelmingly on concepts and laws that reflect the individuality of the person studied, but it is at least considered possible that those concepts and laws would turn out to apply to some other people as well. Allport makes a strong plea for freedom from the restricting nomothetic mold of the other sciences, which he believes have not been confronted with uniqueness on a grand scale, and has recently (Allport, 1962) offered a number of suggestions for concrete morphogenic methods of study.

Allport is posing an alternative to the traditional view of science that he believes will lead to the highest level of prediction and control. Although the morphogenic approach should certainly be tried in research, it raises a keen sense of futility when couched as a replacement for an approach encouraging generalization across persons. Must knowledge of individuals remain as unrelated, odd bits of information? How can significant systematization of knowledge be achieved? It should be established with certainty that nomothetic methods have been adequately tested before they are discarded on the grounds that they typically leave many individual cases unexplained.

Whether or not other sciences have been faced with overwhelming uniqueness, they certainly do recognize the necessity for deduction, from the general law and the characteristics of the situation involved, of explanations and predictions that apply to the specific case. For this to be done well, the general law must provide exhaustive specification of the conditions under which it does and does not apply, and the investigator must have sufficient knowledge of the concrete prediction situation in order to determine whether or not he should use the law. Furthermore, complex phenomena may well call for the application of more than one law, and hence, the relationships between laws must be clearly specified. Only if all this information is available will it be possible to evaluate the explanatory adequacy of nomothetic methods, and even then, particular general laws may turn out to be incorrectly formulated without this constituting a demonstration of the inadequacy of the methods they represent. The degree of theoretical and methodological care and precision/involved in the adequate application of nomothetic methods is not often recognized as important or attempted in psychology, and hence, as McClelland (1951, pp. 89-94) suggests, the development of really useful general laws may be stifled, and individuality may loom overly large as an explanatory problem.

In practice, Murray's (1954, pp. 441-442; 1956, p. 10) position on the uniqueness of each member of the human species is more moderate. Although he recognizes important differences between people, he also considers areas of substantial similarity. General concepts and laws are quite useful in that they provide adequate understanding of those features of personality concerning which most men are similar. For complete understanding of each individual, however, additional information of a more specific variety is needed. Like Allport, Murray (1938) has emphasized the clinical method of observational study in all its detail. He has also utilized many different testing situations and instruments for each individual. In this detailed, rich approach to the study of human beings, Murray seems to be groping not only for general laws, but also for the knowledgeability with which to apply them well to the individual case.

Man is future-oriented

According to both theorists, any approach that attempts to explain adult functioning as reflecting little more than sophisticated forms of early fixations, habits, and instincts misses the overwhelming importance of man's orientation toward future states of being. They take the psychological growth, or progressively greater differentiation and integration, that seems to continue throughout life, to be genuine, natural, and crucial to an understanding of man. Important to this position is a view of personality as an open system that is continually transacting with environmental contexts (Allport, 1960~~d~~; ~~Murray, 1959, p. 16~~).

For Allport, such phenomena as evolving philosophies of life, long-range goals, and a sense of personal integrity are not to be confused with the childhood tendencies toward response-repetition instilled by authoritative figures through manipulation of extrinsic rewards and punishments, or with the outcomes of early psychosexual conflicts. In a work with the revealing title of *Becoming,* Allport (1955) ~~chides~~ behavioristic and Freudian psychologists for not taking personally-valued and intended development seriously: he has concluded that they are busy tracing the individual back into the past, while he is continually straining toward the future (Allport, 1953, pp. ~~108-110~~). Allport's (1955, p. ~~28-33~~) position is so extreme that he finds normal deevlopment after the first year or so to be significantly different from the earliest beginnings.

Murray (1938, pp. 282-396) has given more weight to enduring early learnings, making his position, once again, more moderate than that of his colleague. In fact, one of Murray's (1938, pp. 360-385) contributions is an elaboration of the psychosexual stages of development and the complexes deriving from each of them. But Allport's criticism is echoed in Murray's (1959, p. 13) belief that Freud's theory was incomplete, even though it had the virtue of beginning at the beginning, because it "never reached the consummation of the allegory, the heroic adult and his tragic end."

In explaining present behavior on the basis of the rigidifying effects of early experience, behavioristic and extreme Freudian approaches have both assumed that the major principle governing man's functioning is the homeostatic tendency to return to, or maintain, a rather steady, low level of organismic tension. People tend to repeat behavior that has been followed by tension-reduction as long as this association continues to some minimal degree. This is an argument on adaptational grounds favoring the persistence of early learnings because they were, and remain, successful in reducing tension.

Allport, ~~and Murray agree that~~ this conceptualization is not adequate as a basis for explaining future-oriented, complexly-organized behavior, which seems to precipitate, rather than reduce, high levels of tension, and is not primarily a repetition of past responses. To support this criticism, the theorists could have recourse to the rapidly accumulating research evidence that lower organisms and man often engage in such seemingly arousing activities as exploration of new or changed portions of their stimulus surround, and avoidance of monotonous surrounds through various forms of response variation (Fiske & Maddi, 1961). In his criticism, Allport (1961, p. 250) has pointed out that even Cannon, who invented the concept of homeostasis, could not have meant it to be used as the only principle governing functioning and yet have said "with essential needs answered through homeostasis, the priceless unessentials could be freely sought." For Allport (1955, pp. 65-68), there must be another principle that applies to the many aspects of functioning that are not simply attempts to survive. Although agreeing that the simple conception of homeostasis adopted by many psychologists is inadequate, Murray (Murray & Kluckhohn, 1956, pp. 36-37) favors an elaboration and extension of that conception rather than the addition of a new one.

General orientation toward theorizing

Allport and Murray are displeased that certain disparaging attitudes toward theorizing hold considerable sway in psychology, and they see these attitudes as stemming in part from the influence of the doctrines of logical positivism and operationism.

The first unfortunate attitude is a distrust of theorizing as a sound, useful means of gaining understanding. One reflection of this distrust (e.g., Skinner, 1950) is the belief that theory tends to divert one from the pursuit of truth. The most direct and veridical way to build a science is through the continuing accumulation of empirical facts—these facts to be arrived at through simple methodological manipulations and extensions. Exponents of this view entertain the hope that facts will automatically fall into place at some future time when there are enough of them, thus providing us with the neat empirical generalizations that will make all behavior perfectly understandable. Another form of distrust of theorizing is the claim that theoretical constructs are logically superfluous, usually because they seem to be unnecessary, descriptive terms inserted between the stimulus and response variables of single experiments (e.g., Bolles, 1958).

The difficulty with the first point of view lies in the perverse opaqueness of uninterpreted facts. They have thus far shown little inclination to fall into place and yield their inherent measure of understanding. They must be made understandable and orderly by the interpretations of the scientist, who can then use his interpretations as a powerful tool for creating new facts that may or may not justify his theorizing. The second point of view overlooks the fact that a basic advantage of the theoretical construct is its generality. This generality permits the results of many experiments to be joined together, and suggests new experiments. It is short-sighted to argue that such concepts are unnecessary because particular experiments can be made intelligible without them.

The neglect of the synthetic, imaginative processes of thought represented in these two anti-theoretical views is anathema to Allport and Murray. A major procedural disadvantage of the views is a proliferation of isolated experiments and lines of evidence. Without active theorizing, there can be little comprehensive unification of facts toward the goal of understanding the way a man lives his life. Embracing an anti-theoretical position seems not only wasteful of the investigator's capabilities, but it may even constitute an advocacy of the impossible, and in that sense be dangerously misleading. When an avowedly anti-theoretical scientist discovers a fact, that fact owes its existence in large measure to the intuitive, preformal theorizing that preceded his research. Some scientists of this conviction might even admit that their hunches play a role in their choice of methodological manipulations, but instead of considering these intuitions as valuable foundations for theory, they are disregarded, presumably because they are either considered private, and therefore beyond the realm of science, or else quite incidental to the discovered fact. But if some level of theorizing is an unavoidable part of the process of finding facts, then overlooking this increases the risk of missing the vital facts of functioning because the implicitly held theoretical frame of reference is not considered carefully as to its logical adequacy and reasonableness. Murray (1959, p. 29) speaks for both himself and Allport when he puts it this way:

> It happens that one of my inductions from experience is that many of those who spend most time asserting their immaculate empiricism are somewhat below average in their awareness of the distorting operation of their own preferences and ambitions and, therefore, are more liable than others to sally forth with reductively incongruent versions of reality.

The doctrines of logical positivism and operationism are best considered tools for theorizing rather than substitutes for theory. In-

deed, their instrumental use in psychology has produced a valuable
rise in standards of objectivity and precision in finding facts and
formulating theory. But this usage, carried to an extreme, embodies
the second attitude prevalent in psychology that Allport and Murray
find objectionable. For them, to require a great deal of rigor in thought
and experiment at this preliminary stage of our understanding of
personality will be to stunt the vigorous, rich development of the field.

One specific effect of a premature emphasis on rigor is a focus
upon those aspects of man's functioning that can be most easily
formulated in precise, operational fashion. Such a focus invariably
means the exclusion of subjective, internal, less readily observable
states from consideration either as data or concepts. Another specific
effect of premature concern with rigor is to favor the simplest, most
readily conceived models for the explanation of man's functioning.

For the two theorists, to exclude subjective states from study is to
do such violence to the rich, multi-faceted, mainly-internal processes
of living as to obviate comprehensive understanding. Although it is
admittedly difficult to study subjective states adequately, it is by no
means impossible; it is not only potentially rewarding but indispensable.
The theorists advocate personal introspection as a basis for study and
conceptualization of the subjective states of others. Allport (1955, p.
23) says that it is in considering ourselves that we are led to an appreciation of uniqueness, and Murray (1938, p. 47) argues that "the need
to describe and explain varieties of inner experience decided the original,
and, I predict, will establish the final orientation of psychology." In
what seems a mildly exasperated plea for clear recognition that scientific study of so-called subjective phenomena is possible, Murray (1938,
p. 126) quotes effectively from Bridgman himself concerning the
operational treatment of emotional states.

Equally dangerous to comprehensive understanding is the tendency
of premature emphasis upon scientific rigor to lead to the adoption
of very simple theoretical models. This, and the additional danger
that the ambiguous, complex subject matter of man's functioning will
provoke tenacious faith in the simple models, are aptly pinpointed in
Allport's (1955, p. 17) statement that "narrow systems, dogmatically
held, tend to trivialize the mentality of the investigator and his students." Murray (1959, p. 8) agrees when he says of premature emphasis upon rigor that "it is liable to seduce some promising psychologists away from the study of personalities—the domain that is theirs,
and only theirs, to explore, survey, and map—away from the human-

istically important riddles which we should be creeping up on gradually and craftily."

It is not even the existence of oversimplified approaches that is most objectionable to Allport, but rather the tenacious, dogmatic propagandizing of them. Allport (1955, p. 17) calls for an air of intellectual ferment when he says that "censure should be reserved for those who would close all doors but one. The surest way to lose truth is to pretend that one already wholly possesses it." Murray (1951, p. 436) advocates to anyone attempting to understand a phenomenon as complex and enigmatic as personality that he take seriously and immerse himself in the painful, tedious, difficult processes of collection and classification of a great variety of human behavior before making many theoretical pronouncements. Psychologists should resist the temptation to adopt oversimple solutions in the face of cognitive and professional pressure toward certainty before more adequate comprehensive solutions become possible. To this end, Allport (1961, p. 457) and Murray (1954, p. 436) suggest careful consideration of the point of view of an old authority, Aristotle, who said "it is the part of an educated man to seek exactness in each class of subjects only so far as the nature of the subject admits." And personality is at present a horrendously complicated subject.

Both theorists agree that the full and adequate understanding of man's functioning is a serious matter of the utmost importance, and hence is worth the undivided attention of psychologists. In discussing some of the reasons for his shift from physiology to psychology, Murray (1959, p. 11) says that "influential in some degree (was) the impression . . . that human personality, because of its present sorry state, had become *the* problem of our time—a hive of conflicts, lonely, half-hollow, half-faithless, half-lost, half-neurotic, half-delinquent, not equal to the problems that confronted it, not very far from proving itself an evolutionary failure." But psychologists are failing to recognize and meet their share of responsibility to contribute to man the scientific rather than mystical knowledge of himself that would help him to lead a more effective life, and indeed, to preserve himself. Allport (1955, p. 100) points an accusing finger in this fashion:

> Up to now the "behavioral sciences," including psychology, have not provided us with a picture of man capable of creating or living in a democracy. . . . They have delivered into our hands a psychology of an "empty organism," pushed by drives and molded by environmental circumstance. . . . But the theory of democracy requires also

that man possess a measure of rationality, a portion of freedom, a generic conscience, propriate ideals, and unique value. We cannot defend the ballot box or liberal education, nor advocate free discussion and democratic institutions, unless man has the potential capacity to profit therefrom. In *The Measure of Man,* Joseph Wood Krutch points out how logically the ideals of totalitarian dictatorships follow from the premises of "today's thinking" in mental and social science. He fears that democracy is being silently sabotaged by the very scientists who have benefited most from its faith in freedom of inquiry.

Murray (1962) strikes an only somewhat less condemnatory note in his vision of the future, in which psychology is found wanting for not having contributed to man the knowledge of himself that would have circumvented nuclear holocaust, but then is recognized as having been too much in its adolescence, too much concerned with scientific respectability and the readily studied fringe details of human behavior, to be held accountable for neglecting its responsibility to mankind.

Concluding remarks

There are some basic agreements between the two theorists in their beliefs concerning the nature of personality. For them, man's functioning shows (1) the determining influence of internal, self-initiating characteristics more than of external forces, (2) both momentary and long-term organization, (3) complexity in the sense of change and the possession of many distinguishable elements, (4) the rationality of conscious intent, choice, and planning in greater magnitude than the irrationality of unconscious, irresistible impulses, (5) a large degree of species and individual uniqueness, and (6) the future-orientation of continuing purpose and a tendency toward psychological growth. Murray has a more moderate position on some of these points than does Allport. Leaving the differences in emphasis aside, however, it is clear that their overall view is a humanistic one that accords man a measure of dignity and excellence consistent with his high evolutionary status and accomplishments.

Their humanistic orientation is eloquently expressed by statements such as the following:

It is generally assumed by the uninformed and innocent that all psychologists must have at least one "orienting attitude" in common: a stout affection for human beings coupled with a consuming interest in their emotions and evaluations, their imaginations and beliefs, their purposes and plans, their endeavors, failures, and achievements. But this assumption, it appears, is not correct. A psychologist who has been constantly prodded and goaded by these propulsions, as I have been, belongs to a once small and feeble, though now expanding and more capable minority (Murray, 1959, p. 9).

Some theories of becoming are based largely upon the behavior of sick and anxious people or upon the antics of captive and desperate rats. Fewer theories have derived from the study of healthy human beings, those who strive not so much to preserve life as to make it worth living. Thus we find today many studies of criminals, few of law-abiders; many of fear, few of courage; more on hostility than on affiliation; much on the blindness in man, little on his vision; much on his past, little on his outreaching into the future (Allport, 1955, p. 18).

These words, though expressing bitterness and dissatisfaction toward some psychologists, have none of the pessimism and cynicism toward man in general seen in such approaches as classical Freudianism, which generalizes from psychopathology to all of man's functioning, and extreme behaviorism, which finds equivalences between rat and human. It is of considerable importance that Allport and Murray developed their heroic view of man from considering normal and exceptional people.

Returning to the statement made by Hall and Lindzey (1957) with which this section was begun, it seems that Allport and Murray have been rebels in one sense only. They have promulgated a view of man that was at first, and to some extent still is, outside the main stream of psychological orthodoxy in this country. The particulars of their view, however, are very old, and are held at this time by many people, intellectuals and thoughtful men, artists and scientists, outside of psychology proper.

Because they are created by personalities, theories of personality will show the influence of the beliefs, values, and motives of their creators. Hence, this section has been meant to serve not only as a presentation of Allport's and Murray's views of man, but also as an introduction or background to their formal theories. In their theorizing, there is ample evidence of a humanistic view and of tolerance for ambiguity with a concomitant interest in that which is not easily formulated.

THE THEORIES

Definition of personality

or His unique adjustments to His environment

BEGIN

END

Allport has modified his definition of personality very little over the years. For him (Allport, 1961, p. 28), "personality is the dynamic organization within the individual of those psychophysical systems that determine his characteristic behavior and thought." It is more difficult to point to any single definition for Murray, although he (Murray & Kluckhohn, 1956, p. 30) has recently considered personality to be

> the hypothetical structure of the mind, the consistent establishments and processes of which are manifested over and over again (together with some unique or novel elements) in the internal and external proceedings which constitute a person's life. Thus, personality is not a series of biographical facts but something more general and enduring that is inferred from the facts.

Both definitions distinguish between the internal characteristics that form the personality and the aspects of functioning, or data, that are determined by the characteristics.

Data language

Theories always make some specification of the observables or data to which they are properly applied. Especially because complex phenomena such as man's functioning can be described in many different ways, it is important to compare the data language, or protocol statements (Mandler & Kessen, 1959), that the two theories employ.

BEGIN

Allport's definition of personality indicates that the facts he wishes to explain are the characteristic thoughts and behaviors of the individual. The terms *behavior* and *thought* "are a blanket to designate anything whatsoever an individual may do" (Allport, 1961, p. 29), and the term *characteristic* is merely a redundancy to emphasize individuality. Allport's theory specifies virtually no data language beyond this. It is not very conducive to the consistent usage of a theory to say that it pertains to everything the individual may do, without detailing

END

the types of things that are to be recognized.

Murray has gone a little further toward a definition of the data units to which his theory applies. These units, as can be seen from his definition of personality, are called *proceedings*. A proceeding can very roughly be identified by the initiation and completion of "a dynamically significant pattern of behavior" (Murray, 1951, p. 269) that involves real or imagined interaction between the subject and an animate or inanimate aspect of his environment. Real or *external proceedings* might include a conversation concerning the Berlin crisis or the construction of a sailboat model, while imagined or *internal proceedings* might include the solitary attempt to solve a mathematics problem or daydreaming of a seduction. The most important proceedings are those involving interpersonal behavior. It is typical for a number of proceedings to overlap during any particular unit of time, or *period*. Murray (1951, p. 272) also feels it necessary to recognize the meaningful sequence of proceedings, and so he writes, "a directionally organized intermittent succession of proceedings, may be called a *serial*. Thus, a serial (such as a friendship, a marriage, a career in business) is a relatively long functional unit which can be formulated only roughly."

Allport is apparently content to consider any of the great many possible data terms that can be conjured up by anyone. Murray is more selective, attempting to focus upon terms that seem to him more vital to living than those, for example, that would be based exclusively on the concrete physical characteristics of actual movements. Although one gets a general sense of the temporal, purposive quality of behavior that he finds important, it must be said that the definitional statements associated with such terms as proceeding and serial are not sufficiently precise and delimiting to give the psychologist much guidance in identifying them. What precisely is the hallmark of a dynamically-significant pattern of behavior? Are there temporal sequences of functioning that can be definitely discarded as not significant? How long or short can a proceeding be? The questions are many, as Murray has not progressed far in his admittedly difficult but certainly worthwhile task.

At the moment, both theories rely heavily upon the heterogeneous, sometimes vague, meanings and distinctions concerning functioning that are learned by virtue of membership in our culture. This lack of complete, explicit data specification will make for inconsistency in application of the theories, and renders precise prediction virtually impossible. Although neither theorist has provided sufficient data specification, one can get a further sense of the kinds of data that are likely to be im-

portant from consideration of the actual concepts and propositions of
the theories.

The relatively concrete concepts of personality

Personality theories, as any others, are constituted of various concepts that are clarified and interrelated by the statements in which they
appear. Attention will first be given to the simpler, more concrete concepts and their interrelationships.

Begin

Allport's (1961, p. 373) basic concept, the *personal disposition,*
is defined as

End

> a generalized neuropsychic structure (peculiar to the individual), with
> the capacity to render many stimuli functionally equivalent, and to
> initiate and guide consistent (equivalent) forms of adaptive and stylistic
> behavior.

The concept that has equivalent importance in Murray's theory (1938,
pp. 123-124) is the *need,* considered to be

> a construct (a convenient fiction or hypothetical concept) which stands
> for a force . . . in the brain region, a force which organizes perception,
> apperception, intellection, conation, and action in such a way as to
> transform in a certain direction an existing, unsatisfying situation. A
> need is sometimes provoked directly by internal processes of a certain
> kind . . . but, more frequently (when in a state of readiness) by the
> occurrence of one of a few commonly effective press.

Begin   *In order to gain*   *His concept of personal disposition or need*

~~In~~ gaining greater understanding of these ~~two concepts~~, it will be
useful ~~to compare them for their attributed~~ uniqueness, neurophysio-
logical substrate, effects upon functioning, and susceptibility to arousal. *to examine the meaning of*

Uniqueness. For Allport, each personal disposition is unique to the
individual studied, while for Murray, more than one person can possess a particular need. Allport (1961, p. 349) includes in his theory the
less important concept of *common trait* to account for the similarities
stemming from the possession of a common human nature and a
common culture. But the common trait, though an admissable and useful
concept, is an abstraction arrived at by generalizing across people, and
hence will necessarily miss the actual dispositions of each individual
to some degree. The real personality emerges only when personal
dispositions are assessed, and this requires intensive study of an individual's past, present, and anticipated future functioning, through

the use of such techniques as the case history and content analysis of personal documents (Allport, 1961, pp. 367-369; 1962).) Murray *END* agrees upon the usefulness of such methods of diagnosis, but will readily generalize across people in the assessment of needs. It is this difference, probably more than any other, that has permitted Murray to compile lists of typical needs that can guide the diagnostic efforts of the *Begin* investigator. In contrast, Allport (Allport & Odbert, 1936) has been unwilling to narrow the number of dispositions any further than the combinations that would be possible using the 18,000 or so common trait names in the English language.

Neurophysiological substrate. The personal disposition is a neuro-psychic structure, and the need stands for a force in the brain region. Both theorists presume that their respective concepts refer to entities that are real not only psychologically but physiologically as well. Murray's statement of the hypothetical quality of the need is best interpreted as careful recognition that the inference a theorist always makes in specifying a concept defines the risk he takes of misinterpreting the actual state of affairs. Both men (Allport, 1961, p. 28; Murray, 1938, *HE* p. 45) believe that the brain is the only possible locus of personality, because only the brain is neuroanatomically and neurophysiologically *END* suited to play the necessary integrative role.) Even though Murray (1938, pp. 45-54), with his concept of *regnancy,* has gone a bit further than Allport in attempting to conceptualize relevant brain processes, it must be concluded that the neurophysiological emphasis of both theorists, though worthwhile as a potential source of integration of knowledge from disparate fields of psychology, is at present little more than a signpost indicating an important direction for study.

Begin *Effects upon functioning.* The major effect of both dispositions and needs upon functioning is to produce perceptions, interpretations, feelings, and actions that are equivalent in terms of meaning or *END* purpose.) In discussing the influence of a personal disposition, Allport (1961, p. 322) develops the following example. While Russians, college professors, liberals, peace organizations, and anti-segregationists may seem different to many observers, to a person with the disposition, *fear of communism,* all these stimulus configurations may be equivalent in their perceived communist properties. Such a disposition would also engender response sequences that are equivalent in their function of reducing the perceived threat of communism. The individual might advocate war with the Russians, be suspicious of teachers, vote for extreme right wing persons and policies, join the Ku Klux

Klan, and so forth. Stimulus and response equivalences are diagnosed on the basis of perceived meanings and related coping behavior, rather than on any necessarily obvious similarities. Yet one suspects, from the very example itself, that the stimuli that can be perceived equivalently by a person with a particular disposition are not unlimited. They probably share some core of denotative or connotative meaning in the general culture to which such an individual's perceptual processes have become particularly sensitive. He overlooks all other possible meanings of the stimuli and responds consistently with his selective perception. An explication of such matters would certainly make the personal disposition concept more concrete and usable.

To Murray, the diagnosis of particular needs requires observation of equivalences of meaning in the individual's (1) initiating or reacting inner state, (2) perception of the external situation, (3) imagined goal or aim, (4) directionality of concommitant movements and words, and (5) produced effect, if any (Murray, 1954, pp. 456-463). Although the description is somewhat different from that used by Allport, the emphasis upon classing certain perceptual, cognitive, affective, and actional characteristics together on the basis of their function or meaning is largely the same. Unlike Allport, however, Murray (1954, p. 459) emphasizes the importance of detailed description of the objective as well as the subjective features of a stimulus situation. Any discrepancy or correspondence between the first of these, called the *alpha situation,* and the second, called the *beta situation,* is an important clue to an identification of the existing needs, and even to such matters as their intensity and selectivity.

Both the disposition and the need concepts include properties identified with attitudes and habits, but are not as narrow in purpose or specific in action as these. Although there are attitudinal features in many dispositions and needs, these concepts are not tied so closely to a specific set of objects as is the attitude. Although there are habitual modes of behaving included in many dispositions and needs, these concepts do not imply the rigid response repetition of the habit.

There seems to be a difference between the two concepts in the degree to which they are motivational. For need, the equivalences of functioning are closely tied to the effect the individual is trying to achieve, to what might be called the "why" of behavior. Disposition seems to give a larger place to the "what" and "how" of behavior. But care must be taken not to exaggerate this difference. For Allport,

the usual distinction between dynamic and structural units of personality is inapplicable. He considers all personal dispositions to be
motivational to some degree in that they cause behavior (Allport,
1961, p. 370). Those involving greater or less *intention* (Allport,
1961, pp. 222-225) have been called *dynamic* and *stylistic,* respectively.
Also, Murray (1938, pp. 96-101) includes qualities of style or form
(the "what" and "how" of functioning) in his concept of need, calling
them *actones.*

There is another slight difference in emphasis between disposition
and need. Allport's concept refers more concretely to stimulus and
response equivalences, while Murray's concept stresses directional tension more than the specifics of its expression. Looked at from this
point of view, need is probably less analogous to disposition than is
Murray's (1938, pp. 109-110) concept of *need integrate* which refers
not only to directional tension but also to the specific object-cathexes
and characteristic actones that become grafted onto it through learning
involving the repeated expression of the need. Murray (1938, p. 110)
says "that traces (images) of cathected objects in familiar settings
become integrated in the mind with the needs and emotions which
they customarily excite, as well as with images of preferred modes. . . .
The integrate may enter consciousness as a fantasy or plan of action,
or, under appropriate circumstances, it may be objectified, in which
case it can be operationally defined as a reaction pattern that is evoked
by certain conditions."

An additional point that will be considered later should be mentioned here. The need functions according to an elaboration of the
tension-reduction principle, while most dispositions do not have such
reduction as an aim. This difference, however, is not to be construed
as indicating that Allport's concept lacks motivational significance, as
motivation for him is in its most important or propriate sense more or
less synonymous with conscious intent rather than tension state (Allport, 1961, pp. 222-225).

BEGIN *Susceptibility to arousal.* Allport gives little formal role in his
theory to the arousal of personal dispositions by particular features
of the external situation. Dispositions are not aroused, rather they
exist continuously, having an on-going effect upon functioning that is
consistent in magnitude with their intensity and centrality) In contrast, END
Murray's need, while it exists as a predisposition, typically requires the
triggering action of some perceived situational pressure in order to

become an active determinant of functioning. The subjectively experienced pressure is called *beta press,* and is to be distinguished from the objective pressure, or *alpha press* (Murray, 1938, pp. 115-123).

Murray (1938, p. 123) has found an interactional unit, the *thema,* or combination of a need and press, to be basic for the psychologist. It is the thema that determines specific proceedings. Murray is unclear as to whether the press component of the thema refers to the individual's own perception of the situation or to its objective features. If the beta perceived press is intended, then the thema may be more directly analogous to the personal disposition than is the need. The thema and the alpha (objective) press, taken together, would suggest that Murray believes clarification of the objective features of the situation that are selected for perception by the individual possessing a particular need is important for precise explanation and prediction. But it may be the alpha press that is considered to form part of the thema. This seems possible because, as has been shown, the need and need integrate concepts already include certain influences upon perception, suggesting that the beta press would be superfluous as a component of the thema. If the alpha press is intended, then Murray seems to be less phenomenological and more concerned with reactivity than is Allport. Finally it may be that both alpha and beta press are to be included. If this is so, Murray must specify the different role of each in the thema.

Classifications. Allport and Murray have attempted to produce classifications or typologies for disposition and need. One classification offered by Allport (1961, p. 365) involves the pervasiveness and consistency with which personal dispositions influence functioning. Distinctions are made along these lines between cardinal, central, and secondary dispositions. The first, if they exist in a personality, will set the pattern of an individual's life; the second, possessed by virtually all people, are significant stabilizing features of functioning; and the third are of relatively transient importance. Another principle of classification is less clear, though it bears some resemblance to the one just described. It refers to the degree to which a disposition is at the core of an individual's being (Allport, 1961, p. 264). Application of this principle leads to the Lewinian distinction between the genotypical and phenotypical disposition, the latter, though it involves some consistency in functioning, being less a reflection of the essential nature of the personality than is the former. From Allport's discussion, it is not entirely clear what difference there is between genotypical and cardinal dispositions and between phenotypical and central dispositions.

Over the years, Murray has experimented with a number of apparently overlapping classifications of types and qualities of needs. One classification takes into account the degree to which the individual's aim in his activity is intrinsic or extrinsic to the form of that activity. This leads to the distinction between *activity needs* and *effect needs*. Activity needs, or tendencies to "engage in a certain kind of activity for its own sake" (Murray, 1954, p. 445), are subdivided into *process needs,* involving performance, action, for the sheer pleasure to be derived from the exercise of available functions, and *mode needs,* which are satisfied by the excellence of activity rather than its mere occurrence (Murray, 1954, p. 446). Effect needs are marked by attempts to bring about a particular desired effect or goal which is extrinsic to the activity engaged in, that activity serving an instrumental purpose (Murray & Kluckhohn, 1956, p. 15). Although Murray is one of the few to conceptualize activity for its own sake, he has given most of his attention to effect needs.

Another classificatory attempt seems to emphasize the origin of the need, and hence, the particular direction of activity that it imposes. In this attempt, *mental, viscerogenic,* and *socio-relational needs* are distinguished (Murray & Kluckhohn, 1956, pp. 13-21; Murray, 1954, pp. 445-452). The well-known viscerogenic needs stem from tissue requirements and have very specific, easily recognizable goals. The mental needs are usually overlooked; they stem from the fact that "the human mind is inherently a transforming, creating, and representing organ; its function is to make symbols for things, to combine and recombine these symbols incessantly, and to communicate the most interesting of these combinations in a variety of languages, discursive (referential, scientific) and expressive (emotive, artistic)" (Murray & Kluckhohn, 1956, p. 16). As the viscera have certain requirements, so too does the mind, and both sets of requirements stem from the nature of man. Mental needs do not have very specific goal states. Socio-relational needs arise from the inherently social nature of man (Murray, 1959, pp. 45-57) and include such specific dispositions as the *need for roleship,* the need "to become and to remain an accepted and respected, differentiated and integrated part of a congenial, functioning group, the collective purposes of which are congruent with the individual's ideals" (Murray, 1954, pp. 451-452). As described, the need for roleship seems to imply particular learning produced by the individual's experiences against the ever present background of his inherent socio-relational nature. There are probably specific forms of each of the types of inherent needs that develop through specific learning.

In one discussion of this scheme Murray (1954, pp. 445-452) includes two other types of needs that presumably cut across the mental, viscerogenic, and socio-relational, and seem to emphasize adient and abient tendencies. These are *creative needs,* which aim at the construction of new and useful thoughts and objects, and *negative needs,* which aim at the avoidance or termination of unpleasant, noxious conditions.

An early typology (Murray, 1938, pp. 152-226) distinguishes what are primarily effect needs, of a mental, viscerogenic, and socio-relational variety, on the basis of a much more fine-grained consideration of goals. This attempt includes such familiar concepts as *n* achievement, *n* affiliation, and other needs that are considered to be of a psychogenic or learned variety along with those that are presumably innate. Extensive behavioral descriptions are included in an effort to define the needs operationally.

Added to these various classifications are distinctions between certain qualities that needs may possess. Needs can be proactive or reactive, diffuse or focal, latent or overt, conscious or unconscious (Murray, 1938, pp. 111-115; Murray, 1954, pp. 447-450).

The concepts of need and personal disposition are heterogeneous in that they refer to many observationally different aspects of functioning. Hence, any classifications of types or qualities of these general entities that can be provided might increase their usability. And yet, with the few exceptions mentioned above, Allport has not attempted to delineate any of the relatively general aspects of personal dispositions that might lead to clarifying comparisons. His strong emphasis upon the uniqueness of each disposition undoubtedly inhibits any extensive attempt to classify, even though such an emphasis does not necessarily preclude limited progress along these lines. Particular features of a disposition may be similar to those of others without jeopardizing the uniqueness of that disposition in its totality. Further, as the disposition is a concept referring directly to behavior, its operational definition would seem indispensable to consistency of usage from one investigator to another. And yet none is given, most likely because the emphasis upon uniqueness seems to render such definition fruitless if not impossible before actual diagnosis is made. But human functioning is complex enough so that, without benefit of more concrete guide lines, stimulus and response equivalences can be found at many different levels, in many different ways. Each investigator is thrown completely upon his own artistry in each diagnosis of a disposition. He cannot derive much assistance from the diagnoses of other investigators, or from his own prior diagnoses. Nor can he be entirely sure that he is using the concept in the manner Allport may have intended. ⟩ *END*

Although Murray also believes in individuality, he has found it possible to attempt extensive classification and operational definition because the need is more of a nomothetic concept than is the disposition. It is probably in the total array of a person's needs, rather than in each individual need, that Murray could best pinpoint individuality. But his classificatory and definitional attempts are only of partial assistance in making the concept more concrete and usable.

Murray's writings yield a bewildering array of overlapping classifications of needs. It is difficult to come by any one authoritative typology, and Murray has not addressed himself to the relationships between the available schemes in sufficient detail to make his thinking perfectly clear. While his shifting distinctions and the resulting ambiguities probably represent the difficulty of conceptualizing human complexities, they also stem from the extreme heterogeneity of functioning subsumed by the need concept (Fiske, Ch. 16). Each need can be manifested in many internal and external ways, and Murray wishes to consider a great number of needs and types of needs. It is not surprising that the influences upon functioning attributed to any particular need would tend to overlap with the presumed manifestations of other needs. Also, reasoning from behavioral observations to a great number and variety of needs precipitates a large and heterogeneous mass of assumed organismic requirements. No wonder that finding a basis for classifying needs that will keep them reasonably distinct in theory and in practice is difficult. Given the inherent heterogeneity of his need concept, Murray may be attempting a fineness of distinction between exemplars of the concept that is too great for classificatory neatness and clarity.

Such over-refinement of a basically heterogeneous concept should make for considerable difficulty in using or applying need analysis. A look at the detailed operational descriptions for each of the psychogenic needs is not reassuring on this score. One suspects the great difficulty of making the fine distinctions in meaning that are required in order to distinguish one need from another. This difficulty is bound to be compounded in the typical research situation, where the investigator finds available only some, rather than all, of the possible manifestations of needs. It is understandable that in a major attempt to employ Murray's (1938) typology, it was necessary to reach the diagnosis of particular needs by majority vote of a group of skilled investigators after considerable debate concerning their observations.

Perhaps because of these problems, Murray (1954, pp. 463-464) has moved in the direction of substituting the *value-vector* concept for the need. The vector principle refers to the nature of the directionality shown by behavior (e.g., rejection, acquisition, construction), and the value principle refers to the ideals that are important to people (e.g., knowledge, beauty, authority). A value-vector matrix is compiled in diagnosing what each person believes is worthwhile, and the particular ways in which he moves to make those beliefs an actuality. At this early stage in its use, the value-vector system seems to involve less heterogeneity and fewer organismic assumptions than does the need system. The values and vectors listed currently are simple enough and few enough so that it should be more possible to reach agreement among investigators on their identification in functioning.

Interrelationships between the relatively concrete concepts

Consideration of the interrelationships between personal dispositions on the one hand and needs on the other suggests that both theorists favor a hierarchical organization. Thus, Allport distinguishes between cardinal, central, and secondary dispositions on the basis of their generality and consistency. With somewhat similar intent, Murray (1938, pp. 604-605) includes the concepts of *unity-thema,* a need-press combination that is pervasive because it has been formed early in life, and *prepotency* (Murray, 1954, p. 452), or the degree to which a need takes precedence over others when it is aroused. Also relevant is the idea of *subsidiation* (Murray, 1938, pp. 86-88), whereby less potent needs can become instrumental to the satisfaction of other ones.

Both Allport and Murray recognize that a single course of action may actually reflect the operation of more than one disposition or need. Thus Allport (1961, p. 377) employs the concept of *convergence* and Murray (1938, p. 86) includes *fusion* of needs. Both also recognize that dispositions or needs can be in conflict with each other, although this idea is of greater importance to Murray (1938, pp. 88-89).

In order for these statements concerning the interrelationships to be usable, it will be necessary to delineate the conditions under which the various interrelational concepts hold. When, under what specific conditions, do fusion, convergence, subsidiation occur? What makes a disposition become cardinal rather than central? It can be seen that there is much theoretical work to be done in explicating the ways in which dispositions or needs are related to each other.

The relatively general concepts of personality and their interrelationships

Each theorist utilizes concepts that are at a higher level of generality and complexity than need or personal disposition. In these very general concepts, even more than in the relatively concrete ones, we can discern the assumptions that have been made concerning the nature of man. By and large, the portions of the theories to be considered here are less clearly delineated than those in the previous section; hence it will not be profitable to attempt the detail of presentation and comparison that was possible earlier.

For Murray (1938, pp. 134-141; 1956, pp. 23-28), the *establishments* of personality are the *id, superego, ego-ideal,* and *ego.* Although these are familiar concepts, he has elaborated their meaning from the original Freudian usage. The id, though still a repository of innate dynamic tendencies alone, contains not only the self-seeking, destructive impulses, but more acceptable tendencies as well. Among the latter are "respiration, ingestion of food, defecation, expressions of affection, endeavors to master the environment, and so forth. . . . The id is evidently the breeding ground of love and worship, as well as of the novel imaginations which are eventually applauded, instituted, and cherished by society" (Murray & Kluckhohn, 1956, p. 24). He gives the status of innate tendencies to some valuable qualities that Freud would have explained as involving the impact of the defenses upon unacceptable impulses. Murray's conceptualization of the id reflects his assumption of the basically visceral, mental, social, and growth-oriented nature of man. The id can vary in strength from person to person, according presumably to the biological and physiological features of each organism. Very strong id tendencies can be inferred from intense energy or zest, needs and appetites, emotions, and imagination (Murray & Kluckhohn, 1956, p. 26).

Murray (Murray & Kluckhohn, 1956, pp. 26-28) utilizes the superego concept to refer to the internal representation of the value system of an individual's society, in terms of which he judges and disciplines himself and others. He has elaborated the concept as used by Freud in such way as to recognize the determining influences of extra-parental factors such as peer group pressures and literature. One of the major functions of the superego is to censor expressions of id impulses that are unacceptable to society, both for the individual himself and for others with whom he comes in contact. The ego-ideal is a gradually developing, envisaged ideal self which guides the ego, when that personality component becomes sufficiently differentiated and integrated, in arbitrating between emotional impulses from the id and superego imperatives (Murray & Kluckhohn, 1956, p. 28). In order to guide effectively, the ego-ideal must stay within the organism's potentialities. If the ego-ideal is entirely divorced from the superego, the individual will very likely be trying to become something unacceptable to society. Murray's discussion of these two components of personality indicates that he provides more latitude for their alteration and change in the years subsequent to childhood than was true of Freud.

Perhaps the major elaboration made by Murray on Freud's scheme is in the conceptualization of the ego. To be sure, the ego is the rational and "differentiated governing establishment of personality" (Murray, 1956, p. 26), and functions to block and temper the expression of id impulses that are unacceptable to society and the superego through the employment of defenses. But Murray also accords the ego a much more important, active role in determining the individual's functioning and precipitating psychological growth. It arranges, schedules, controls, and otherwise facilitates and promotes the expression of the socially-valued id impulses. It includes capacities or abilities that are indispensable not only to adequate survival but to excellence of living. A perusal of these abilities as possessed by a strong, effective ego will show clearly the importance of this concept for Murray (1956, pp. 24-26). The *perceptual* and *apperceptual abilities* tend toward external and internal objectivity or veridicality, and long apperceptive span or time-perspective. The *intellectual abilities* are concentration and the conjunctivity and referentiality of thought and speech. The *conative abilities* are will power, conjunctivity of action, resolution of conflicts, selectivity in the impulses expressed and the social pressures responded to, initiative and self-sufficiency, responsibility for collective action, adherence to resolutions and agreements, and absence of psychopathological symptoms.

It is through these ego functions that the *schedules* (Murray, 1956, pp. 38-39) for the orderly expression of contiguously aroused needs, and the *serial programs* (Murray, 1956, p. 37), which insure a gradual movement toward the achievement of complex goals, come about. The schedules and serial programs also contribute largely to the proactive flavor of the proceedings and serials constituting an individual's functioning. Ideally, this organizing action of the ego is rendered more effective through being interrelated with the superego's internalized standards of acceptability in the time, place, and mode of expression of dynamic tendencies.

Turning to Allport's more complex concepts of personality, we *BEGIN* find that the closest he comes to anything like the id—and it is not very close—is the belief that organismic features determined largely by biological factors, such as temperament, serve to impart certain *BASIC* limits to the possible development of personality. The superordinate *(ESD)* concept in his system is the *proprium,* which serves an organizing and integrating role and provides an impetus to psychological growth. In an attempt to avoid the misunderstandings and bitterness that have attended concepts of self in psychology, Allport (1955, pp. 41-56) initially tried to conceptualize the proprium as a set of ongoing functions without much concern for structural substance. Currently, he (Allport, 1961, pp. 110-138) is more clearly discussing function as implying structure, even though he retains emphasis upon function. The functions of the proprium are *sense of body, self-identity, self-esteem, self-extension, rational coping, self-image,* and *propriate striving.* (Allport, 1961, pp. 110-138). These are the vital portions of personality because they have in common a phenomenal warmth and sense of importance to the individual and thus permeate his life. Although the functions of the proprium are ongoing, they are by no means static. Instead, they change throughout life, predominantly in the direction of greater differentiation and integration, or growth. *END*

There are a number of similarities in general emphasis between Allport's proprium and Murray's ego. Both broad categories of personality produce or reflect organization, rationality, consistency, future-orientation, planfulness, self-expression, cognitive complexity, and adaptability. Both theorists (Allport, 1955, pp. 56-59; Murray & Kluckhohn, 1956, pp. 24-26, 33-49) believe that the various functions or abilities fuse or act in interdependence with one another. It does not seem fruitful at this time to attempt any more precise, detailed comparison of the proprium and ego, because the theorists have not yet delineated the nature and actions of these personality components with any great degree of specificity.

Murray's concept appears to be more heterogeneous than that of Allport. One is struck by the impression that the ego includes functions or abilities that are at different levels of generality and meaning. In deciding upon the abilities to be included, Murray seems to have relied primarily upon his own estimate of those which have been most useful to man. In contrast, Allport (1955, pp. 39-40) has considered only functions that are assumed to be actually experienced by individuals as important, central parts of them. Murray's less restrictive, perhaps less differentiated, criterion has permitted the juxtaposition of strange bedfellows. Seemingly basic organismic capacities such as concentration and long apperceptive span are included together with such characteristics as freedom from psychopathological symptoms, a condition which is more a judgment about the soundness of functioning than a statement about basic ability. Certainly, Allport has not escaped the inclusion of functions at different levels of generality and meaning—witness his grouping of bodily sense and propriate striving—but his adherence to the requirement of phenomenal importance makes the proprium seem more unified than Murray's ego.

It should be recognized that in making a short list of propriate functions applying to sound adults, Allport has departed from his previously extreme idiographic position. From the point of view of adding precise meaning to, and increasing the usability of his theory, this seems a worthwhile departure, all the more because the propriate functions are sufficiently devoid of specific content to permit considerable room for individuality in the particular styles of behavior that can be identified as developing out of a propriate orientation toward living.

Interrelationships between the more and less general concepts

It is at this point, when one turns to a consideration of the relationship between very general concepts and the relatively concrete ones that refer more directly to regularities of functioning, that both theorists leave unfortunate ambiguities. In Murray's position, there is no definite superordinate establishment that is to subsume the numerous needs that develop through learning and the accrual of experience. These needs are certainly not innate, and therefore not part of the id. They are probably not considered components of the superego or ego-ideal because these are constituted primarily of values, taboos, and standards for evaluation. But the ego-ideal, at least, has motivational properties, i.e., aspirations, and leads to the formation of serial programs (Murray & Kluckhohn, 1956, pp. 26-28). To complicate things further, the recent value-vector version of the need makes clear what was already less explicitly included in such earlier concepts as the need integrate, namely, that needs include values. If the ego contains only generic abilities, then even though it develops largely through interaction with the environment it would not seem to subsume the more specific need concept. But his most extensive description of the ego does not permit one to be certain that Murray (Murray & Kluckhohn, 1956, pp. 24-26) definitely means to exclude the specific, learned, habitual styles of coping from the company of the more general, pervasive abilities. Perhaps he does not wish to keep the two kinds of unit separate. This would explain his tentative suggestion (Murray & Kluckhohn, 1956, p. 31) that general systems of learned needs may constitute the ego.

Needless to say, it would be useful to have further clarification of the relationship between learned needs, on the one hand, and the id, super-ego, ego, and ego-ideal, on the other. A reasonable lead, which does not seem inconsistent with Murray's general intent, would be to consider learned needs (value-vectors), need-integrates, and perhaps thema to be personality units that are formed out of the interaction between the establishments (reasonably well formed before adulthood is reached, and representing the general influence of society, innate needs, and developing generic capacities) and the specific environmental encounters that occur during living. The learned needs would then exist as a more changeable, less central, though more immediately expressed layer of personality. In such a scheme, it would be more possible to give the various sub-characteristics of the establishments a clear causal role in the development of learned needs.

In his most recent discussion (Allport, 1961, pp. 110-138), but not in his earlier statement (Allport, 1955, pp. 41-56), Allport also leaves one uncertain as to whether it is only general, pervasive functions, or functions plus specific classes of personal dispositions, that are to comprise the proprium. If the proprium is meant to be a collection of interdependent and important personal dispositions, then the propriate functions could not logically play a causal role in the formation of these dispositions. A possibly useful lead, similar to that suggested above, would be to consider that the propriate functions are not themselves combinations of dispositions, but rather the major forces precipitating and combining with the individual's life experiences to form the simpler units. For example, propriate striving would refer to the propensity in an individual for phenomenally important intentioning, because of which it would be possible to develop cardinal and central dispositions having dynamic properties.

Allport may be moving in this direction in his attempt to conceptualize components of personality that seem to be sets of personal dispositions which reflect the qualities of propriate functioning. Examples of this type of unit are his characteristics of maturity (Allport, 1961, pp. 275-307) such as specific, enduring extensions of the self, techniques for warm relating to others (such as tolerance), stable emotional security or self-acceptance, habits of realistic perception, skills and problem-centeredness, established self-objectification in the form of insight and humor, and a unifying philosophy of life including particular value orientations, differentiated religious sentiment, and a generic, personalized conscience. *ENO*

If one were to focus upon the high level of abilities consistent with Murray's (Murray & Kluckhohn, 1956, pp. 24-26) idea of the strong ego, and consider the specific learned methods or styles by which these abilities are expressed by individuals, one would arrive at characteristics similar in many respects to Allport's criteria of maturity. Others of Allport's characteristics come closer to the aspects of personality subsumed by Murray under the concepts of ego-ideal and superego. In these, Allport, even more than Murray, presents a view of conscience and aspirations that departs from the original Freudian view in being personal, highly-differentiated, and the product of considerable assimilated adult experience, rather than a simple carry-over of the relatively unchanged cultural values and taboos that were implanted at a psychologically tender age.

Development of personality

A brief consideration of personality development will provide yet another vantage point from which to observe the interrelationship of concepts, and the influence of assumptions about the nature of man. For Allport (1961, pp. 57-307), the infant has little personality, his undifferentiated, opportunistic behavior being determined by ongoing biochemical processes and environmental pressures. Initially, the infant can only express discomfort in relatively reflexive ways when strong viscerogenic needs exist, and functions according to the principle

of tension reduction alone. During this early period, the infant is extremely dependent upon others, particularly his mother, for succorance
and affection. If these are readily obtained, then the pre-conditions for
the development of a gradually more differentiated and personally-
integrated life-style or personality are met.

With enough security, the kernels of selfhood begin to develop
near the end of the first year of life. The first signs of consciousness
take the form of recognizable experience of the body (bodily sense).
The second and third years see the beginnings of self-identity and then
self-esteem. From four to six, the child develops some self-extension
and self-image, and from six to twelve, the rational coping qualities of
the proprium become apparent. In adolescence, propriate striving is in
increasing evidence. Although these various propriate functions begin
their development at different ages, they are all interdependent, and
become unified even further with the gradual development of the
knowing function.

As the proprium expands and grows in strength, an ever widening
system of personal dispositions is formed. All the while, opportunistic
functioning concerned with reducing tension caused by survival needs
recedes in importance, being replaced by propriate functioning and
striving, which involves increases in or maintenance of tension.
Propriate functioning is a reflection of the tendency toward psychological growth that is part of the nature of man. Development continues
on into adulthood, which is normally marked by the emergence of the
signs of maturity mentioned earlier.

But if the infant's early dependency is not warmly met, he may
react with signs of insecurity, initially including aggression and de-
mandingness, and later including jealousy and egoism. Vigorous development of propriate functioning will be jeopardized, the individual
remaining relatively undifferentiated and deficient in consciously controlled living. Tension reduction will remain an important aim. Such
an individual would be considered mentally ill.

Murray's (1938, pp. 282-396; 1956, pp. 41-49) view of development is an elaboration and extension of that associated with the psychoanalytic tradition. Initially, the infant does possess some personality in
the form of acceptable and unacceptable id impulses. With more experience and socialization he begins to develop an ego, and then a superego
and ego-ideal. Early life is divided into five stages of development that
are referred to as claustral (intra-uterine), oral, anal, urethral, and
phallic. Each stage is characterized by highly enjoyable conditions

inevitably brought to an end by socializing forces from the external environment. If the external forces over- or under-frustrate the child, a fixation will occur. This arresting of psychological growth, if it is severe or occurs frequently, will leave its mark on the developing personality in the form of a *complex* (Murray, 1938, pp. 361-393). An apparently related concept is the *unity-thema* (Murray, 1938, pp. 604-605), a combination of need-press units functioning as a relatively unconscious, dynamic component of personality which, though formed in early life, continues to exert considerable influence upon later functioning.

But if the complexes formed are not too many or too strong, personality will continue to show considerable change on into adulthood. The individual will gradually accrue a strong ego which adds flexibility, consciousness, and effectiveness to functioning, a personalized, sophisticated superego, a realistic ego-ideal, and many interrelated, learned needs. All this will occur because of the growth potential, reflected in the constructive id impulses and the innate ego potential, and because of the necessity of reducing conflicts produced by the unsocialized id impulses in interaction with the external world. The general aim of functioning will not be to maintain a low level of tension, but rather to experience the pleasurable process of tension reduction. As the individual grows in experience, he will learn to permit and encourage the build-up of tension so that the ensuing pleasure at its dissipation can be increased.

For Murray (Murray & Kluckhohn, 1956, pp. 45-48), human personality is to a large degree a compromise between the individual's own impulses and the demands and interests of other people. Normality is a state of optimal compromise, where needs can be expressed in socialized fashion, and consciousness is present. Mental illness is associated with either under- or over-socialization.

The similarities between the two preceding accounts include great emphasis upon an active, influential consciousness, the assumption (however vaguely formulated) of an inherent growth tendency, a view of development as continuing into adulthood with related emphasis upon the complex differentiations and integrations of maturity, and a belief that personality is largely learned.

There are also some differences. One is a disparity in emphasis upon individual uniqueness. This difference is reflected in Murray's assumption that a common portion of personality is present at birth, and in his stress on the degree to which the personality is fashioned through conflict with socializing forces, even to the point of using the degree of socialization as an index of psychological health. These ideas imply that men are fairly similar to one another. Allport, who is more extreme concerning uniqueness, finds no inherited personality components common to all, and limits the role of social forces to that of providing or failing to provide the necessary background conditions for adequate personality development. Not only does his conceptualization of health and illness have little to do with socialization, but one suspects that a fair degree of social autonomy would be necessary in Allport's view of maturity. Another difference is that development is somewhat more continuous for Murray than for Allport, the latter stressing the radical difference in existence precipitated by the appearance of the proprium. Finally, Allport has detailed development during adulthood to a greater degree than has Murray, although both believe that such development is important.

Despite the great importance they give to learning, neither theorist has provided a satisfactory account of the processes and mechanisms involved. Murray simply assumes learning, and appears to subscribe to general principles of reinforcement. He also believes that learned needs are developed in some way out of unlearned ones (Murray, 1938, pp. 76-77, 80). But this is not to say that learned needs are considered so transitory that they will extinguish rapidly unless occasionally revitalized by direct association with unlearned needs. Murray goes no further.

Allport (1961, p. 229), who also believes that learned dispositions are quite independent of the dispositions that may have led to their formation, has introduced the descriptive term of *functional autonomy* to refer "to any acquired system of motivation in which the tensions involved are not of the same kind as the antecedent tensions from which the acquired system developed." In attempting to add clarification, Allport has distinguished perseverative and propriate functional autonomy, the former being less central, more the stuff of habits, than is the latter. The possible mechanisms suggested whereby the perseverative type may come about seem to function either through some physiological reverberatory mechanism that becomes fairly stable, or by the appetitive influence of novelty associated with the learning situation (Allport, 1961, pp. 244-249). Propriate functional autonomy comes about because the presumed energy potential possessed by the human is in excess of that contributed by survival needs, and hence there is an ongoing tendency to utilize this excess by increasing competence and pressing toward a unification of life (Allport, 1961, pp. 249-253). Allport's thinking remains somewhat vague concerning specific mechanisms whereby functional autonomy takes place, and thus provides a number of bases for controversy. He has not circumvented the repeated criticism that functional autonomy is more of an assertion than an explanation, although he does suggest that an extremely critical reception indicates an already closed mind when he says that his concept "is merely a way of stating that men's motives change and grow in the course of life, because it is the nature of man that they should do so. Only theorists wedded to a reactive, homeostatic, quasi-closed model of man find difficulty in agreeing" (Allport, 1961, pp. 252-253).

Concluding remarks

Neither theory under discussion has yet achieved adequate usability as described in the introduction of this chapter. For the most part, the major reasons for this lack have been indicated at the points of their greatest relevance. In conclusion, the more and less general concepts included in each theory need to be further delineated and unified. A particularly important aspect of this need is for complete operational definition of the less general concepts. Among other things, this would require more explication of the concrete observables to which the theories are meant to pertain. Although Murray has attempted some operational definition and data specification, he has hardly carried his attempt far enough, and Allport has done even less along these lines. Still another great obstacle to usability is the frequent lack of specification of the relationships between the more and less general concepts and within each of these classes. When some statement concerning relationship is made, it is too likely, especially in Murray's writings, to be couched in very figurative language. This difficulty is particularly apparent in the portions of his theory that come most directly from the psychoanalytic tradition.

Shortcomings such as these lead even friendly critics to see the theories, at this stage in their delevolpment, as relegated to post-hoc explanation and to general stimulus value for other psychologists. Significantly, there has been a paucity of research designed to test specific predictions generated from the theories. The research that has been relevant to the viewpoints of Allport and Murray has sprung as much from the humanistic frame of reference exemplified by their theorizing as from the actual theories themselves.[1]

There is, however, one frequent criticism that does not seem warranted. It is sometimes said that these viewpoints are not theories at all, but simply elaborate descriptions of the observed facts. Presumably, there is no reference here to shortcomings in usability, except insofar as these contribute to the general frustration of the would-be user, disposing him to adopt a critical orientation. More likely it is the common sense content of many of the concepts that is objectionable. What seems to be overlooked is that the major characteristic of the theoretical concept is generality. For example, if one advanced the concept of courage, and embedded it in a theoretical apparatus that would permit the deduction of particular behaviors in particular contexts, the fact that the behavior might be taken by even an unskilled observer to indicate courage would not make the concept less theoretical. Although the two theories are not yet at adequate usability, they are genuine theoretical endeavors. It is often the person who has come to identify personality theory with the Freudian approach, strong in its reductionistic orientation, who is unconvinced of the theoretical status of a concept unless it leads to explanations of functioning that contradict his own experience.

Begin There is danger that in focusing upon limitations and all that remains to be done, the value of what has already been accomplished will be lost from view. Both theorists have fought hard and persistently for a recognition of the humanistic qualities of man's personality at a time when it was most unfashionable to do so in psychology. If some of the critical remarks made by Allport and Murray seem directed toward outmoded positions, it is largely because of the present accelerating trend toward emphasizing humanistic qualities. This trend must be attributed in no small measure to their influence. The ongoing fight has taken a good deal of time and energy. The careful, rich observation of man's complex, organized, conscious, and changing characteristics, and the continual attempt to describe and generalize what was seen in a meaningful manner, guided throughout by the painful self-consideration called introspection, also has taken a great deal of time. And yet, without these two struggles, psychology would not be even as far as it *is today End.*

[1] The reader unfamiliar with the research of Allport and Murray should read, as a minimum, the relevant portions of Hall and Lindzey (1957), which will serve as a frame of reference, and a number of the original reports listed at the end of this chapter.

is in attempting to conceptualize the valuable as well as the trying qualities of man. It is now possible, and certainly important, for psychologists to marshal their energies toward increasing the usability of theories such as those of Allport and Murray so that humanistic convictions can be put to empirical test. This phase of formalization and test can be accomplished, and whatever the eventual outcome, mankind and psychology stand to benefit by an increment in lasting understanding.

REFERENCES

ALLPORT, G. W. *Personality: A psychological interpretation.* New York: Holt, 1937.

ALLPORT, G. W. *The use of personal documents in psychological research.* New York: Social Science Research Council, 1942.

ALLPORT, G. W. The trend in motivational theory. *Amer. J. Ortho-psychiat.*, 1953, 23, 107-119.

ALLPORT, G. W. *Becoming: Basic considerations for a psychology of personality.* New Haven: Yale Univer. Press, 1955.

ALLPORT, G. W. Open system and personality theory. *J. abnorm. soc. Psychol.*, 1960, 61, 301-310. (a)

ALLPORT, G. W. *Personality and social encounter.* Boston: Beacon, 1960. (b)

ALLPORT, G. W. *Pattern and growth in personality.* New York: Holt, Rinehart, and Winston, 1961.

ALLPORT, G. W. The general and the unique in psychological science. *J. Pers.*, 1962, 30, 405-422.

ALLPORT, G. W. and ALLPORT, F. H. *A-S reaction study.* Boston: Houghton, 1928.

ALLPORT, G. W., and CANTRIL, H. Judging personality from voice. *J. soc. Psychol.*, 1934, 5, 37-55.

ALLPORT, G. W., & ODBERT, H. S., Trait-names: A psycho-lexical study. *Psychol. Monogr.*, 1936, 47, No. 211, 1-171.

ALLPORT, G. W. and VERNON, P. E. *Studies in expressive movement.* New York: Macmillan, 1933.

ALLPORT, G. W., VERNON, P. E., and LINDZEY, G. *A study of values* (2nd Ed.) Boston: Houghton-Mifflin, 1951.

BOLLES, R. C. The usefulness of the drive concept. In M. R. Jones (Ed.), *Nebraska symposium on motivation.* Lincoln: Univer. of Nebraska, 1958.

DeCHARMS, R., MORRISON, H. W., REITMAN, W., & McCLELLAND, D. C., Behavioral correlates of directly and indirectly measured achievement motivation. In D. C. McClelland (Ed.), *Studies in motivation.* New York: Appleton-Century-Crofts, 1955.

FISKE, D. W. The inherent variability of behavior. In D. W. Fiske & S. R. Maddi, Eds. *Functions of varied experience.* Homewood, Ill.: Dorsey, 1961.

FISKE, D. W., and MADDI, S. R., Eds. *Functions of varied experience.* Homewood, Ill.: Dorsey, 1961.

HALL, C. S., & LINDZEY, G. *Theories of personality.* New York: Wiley, 1957.

McCLELLAND, D. C. *Personality.* New York: Dryden, 1951.

McCLELLAND, D. C. Methods of measuring human motivation. In J. W. Atkinson (Ed.), *Motives in fantasy, action, and society.* Princeton: Van Nostrand, 1958.

MANDLER, G., & KESSEN, W. *The language of psychology.* New York: Wiley, 1959.

MURRAY, H. A. The effect of fear upon estimates of the maliciousness of other personalities. *J. soc Psychol.,* 1933, *4,* 310-329.

MURRAY, H. A. *Explorations in personality: A clinical and experimental study of fifty men of college age.* New York: Oxford, 1938.

MURRAY, H. A. Problems in clinical research: Round table. *Amer. J. Ortho-psychiat.* 1947, *17,* 203-210.

MURRAY, H. A. Research planning: A few proposals. In S. S. Sargeant (Ed.), *Culture and Personality.* New York: Viking Fund, 1949, 195-212

MURRAY, H. A. Some basic psychological assumptions and conceptions. *Dialectica,* 1951, *5,* 266-292.

MURRAY, H. A. Toward a classification of interaction. In T. Parsons & E. A. Shils (Eds.), *Toward a general theory of action.* Cambridge: Harvard Univer. Press, 1954.

MURRAY, H. A. Preparations for the scaffold of a comprehensive system. In S. Koch (Ed.), *Psychology: A study of a science.* Vol. 3. New York: McGraw-Hill, 1959.

MURRAY, H. A. Prospect for psychology. *Science,* 1962, *136* (No. 3515), 483-488.

MURRAY, H. A. Studies of stressful interpersonal disputations. *Amer. Psychologist.,* 1963, *18,* 28-36.

MURRAY, H. A., & KLUCKHOHN, C. Outline of a conception of personality. In C. Kluckhohn, H. A. Murray, & D. M. Schneider (Eds.), *Personality in nature, society, and culture.* (2nd ed.) New York: Knopf, 1956.

MURRAY, H. A. and MORGAN, CHRISTIANA D. A clinical study of sentiments. *Genet. Psychol. Monogr.* 1945, *32,* 3-311.

Office of Strategic Services Assessment Staff. *Assessment of Men,* New York: Rinehart, 1948.

SKINNER, B. F. Are theories of learning necessary? *Psychol. Rev.,* 1950, *57,* 193-216.

WHITE, R. W. Motivation reconsidered: The concept of competence. *Psychol. Rev.,* 1959, *66,* 297-333.

8

The Psychology of Personal Constructs: George Kelly

Lee Sechrest

Any theory of personality necessarily involves some fundamental assumptions about the nature of man. Indeed, these assumptions, it might be argued, are in large part the theory. However, as often as not the assumptions that theorists make about man are left implicit, to be inferred by the consumer of the theory.

George Kelly concluded out of his long experience with other persons' theories of personality that the assumptions about man which undergird any theory should be exposed and examined carefully. When he sought to examine them, he was struck by the detachment and distance that separated each theorist from the other persons whose behavior was to be explained. The theorist-scientist seemed implicitly, if not quite explicitly, to view himself as engaged in a determined effort to reach some understanding of his universe, or his little corner of it, so that he might eventually make accurate predictions about it and even achieve control over it. If asked, most theorists were not reluctant to view their own efforts as intellectual, rational, and oriented toward cognitive clarity. Not so the subjects of their theories. These people, quite unlike the theorists themselves, were accordingly in the hands of dark forces outside their ken. They were mechanically propelled through a maze completely beyond their comprehension and worked assiduously for separately innocuous hedonic tidbits dispensed by an indifferent environment, or were led through their lives in some other mysterious manner.

Kelly thought he saw in the people around him, with whom he was working and associating, the same goals and desires as those of the scientist, namely, to be able to anticipate and ultimately to control their environments. From his point of view, it seemed that people had hypotheses, working ideas about reality, that they sought to validate their hypotheses or to invalidate them, and that they went on from their validational experiences to achieve new hypotheses. Some of the better conceived ordinary attempts to validate ideas about the world even approached the sophistication of good scientific methodology. Starting from that position, Kelly developed the notion of construing man's behavior as an attempt to anticipate and to control, of considering every man as a scientist. Kelly did not propose that every man literally *is* a scientist—that would have been foreign to his outlook—but he did suggest that we might consider every man and his behavior *as if* he were a scientist—just as we might consider every man as if he were an animal, a machine, or a self-organizing system. We may consider man in the character of scientist if it will help us as scientists to anticipate the responses of man.

One central theme in Kelly's theory is actually a philosophical rather than a theoretical position. He suggests "we assume that all our present interpretations of the universe are subject to revision and replacement" (Kelly, 1955, p. 15). He calls this position *constructive alternativism*. The meaning of constructive alternativism might be clarified if we consider the distinction between the classical philosophical positions of realism and nominalism. Realism, undoubtedly more popular and widely influential over the years, supposes that an objective reality exists independent of any of our attempts to observe it, to think about it or to impinge upon it in any way. Such a position results in an attempt to discover the nature of the universe, to find out nature. A realist may suppose that there *is* such a thing as intelligence, that it exists in actuality, and he will then set out to find out its nature and how it manifests itself. Opposed to realism is the position designated as nominalism, which eschews the objective reality of concepts, traits, ideas or the like and insists that only individual events have reality. We are free to construe events and make sense out of them in any way that is convenient for us. The nominalist would be inclined to see whether he might devise some more useful ways of looking at the world instead of demanding that reality reveal itself to him. He would be inclined to deny that there is really any such thing as intelligence, but he might accept the term as a convenient label for certain phenomena.

Kelly is by no means a pure nominalist, but he inclines quite definitely in that direction, and in some ways may be more extreme than many self-designated nominalists in his conception of reality. At any rate, he takes the point of view that the only reality in nature consists of the events with which we are faced. If for no other reason than the passage of time, it is patently impossible that events could repeat themselves. Kelly, like Heraclitus, sees time as the universal linkage and universal separator between events. The importance of events or the use we make of them depends upon the way we construe them. The task of the scientist is not to discover what nature had in mind when she presented one or the other of her faces to us, but to invent ways of construing nature that will help us to anticipate her.

Since there are only events, it follows that there are many possible ways of construing them. Each event occurs as itself, as a whole, but we may, if we choose, construe it in a limited way from a particular point of view. Consider, for example, one event: the incident of an ulcer of the duodenum. What is it? It is in fact nothing more or less than an ulcer. However, if we ask a physician to construe the event, we are likely to receive a description of a wound of particular characteristics resulting from the persistent irritation of the digestive tract by hyper-secretion of digestive acids, or something of the sort. If we ask a psychologist, we may get an account of an individual basically dependent in character exposed to a situation that demands independence of which he is incapable, thus arousing persistent tension. A sociologist may give us some ideas about a social structure that exposes each individual to possibilities of feeling inadequate. The individual who has the ulcer may view the event in various ways. He may see it as the first signal of his mortality; he may, on the other hand, view it as a validation of his conception of himself as a victim of a cruel world. He might even view his ulcer with something akin to pride. After all, are not ulcers peculiarly masculine, a distinguishing mark of the energetic, successful man? The views held by various individuals regarding any event are not necessarily right or wrong. We construe events in ways that will enable us to anticipate related events and hopefully to control them, and the way in which we construe them dictates what the technique of control shall be. The construction we place on ulcers will determine the character of our attempts to alleviate or prevent them.

Any conception we now have about the universe may, then, be

held to be tentative, as a temporarily useful or satisfying way of construing the events with which we have to deal. We must recognize the possibility of simultaneously or sequentially existing constructions different from our own but equally or more useful. Kelly is particularly frank and disarmingly direct in admitting that even his own theory is suggested only as a temporarily expedient way of dealing with events commonly construed from a psychological point of view. It is more than a little remarkable to find a personality theorist proposing that the product of his own intellectual energies is to be regarded as a short-term effort, probably ere long to be discarded or significantly modified.

This is not to say that all ways of viewing events are equally useful or meaningful to us. Each construct or construct system is devised with a particular set of events in mind and thus has a *focus of convenience*, that is, an area in which it is particularly applicable. Moreover, any construct or construct system has a *range of convenience*, that is, a range or an area over which it works reasonably well. When a system is extended beyond the range of events for which it was intended, it may lose most of its utility. For example, the system of constructs comprising scientific methodology has as its focus of convenience a vast array of problems that are particularly amenable to measurement and experimentation, and it may also easily apply to a wide variety of other phenomena that lie within its range of convenience. However, it has often been suggested that the methods of science have a limited range of convenience, with such matters as questions of ethics and morality lying well outside their scope. The picture of Darwin carefully toting up the positive and negative features of his potential wife in order to arrive at a decision about the advisability of marriage appears ludicrous to us not because of the inherent shortcoming of his method, but because the phenomena of love and marriage presumably lie outside the range of convenience of such a precise arithmetical analysis.

Kelly's philosophical and theoretical positions unquestionably stem at least in part from his own experiences. While in a manner consistent with his conception of constructive alternativism, Kelly insists that we need not be the passive victims of our own biographies, he would not deny that our environments, the events that impinge upon us, provide the raw material of which our total outlooks are constructed. One of the immediately apparent characteristics of Kelly's biography is his diversity of experience. His geographical environment has extended from the Kansas wheat fields where he was reared to most of the important and sophisticated cities of the world. His educational background has spanned civil engineering, education, philosophy and psychology; Park College (B.A.), the University of Kansas (M.A.), Edinburgh (B.Ed.) and the State University of Iowa, where he received the Ph.D. in psychology in 1931. His professional experience has included twelve years at Fort Hays Kansas State College at Hays, the United States Navy, the University of Maryland, Ohio State University and visiting appointments at universities now too numerous to recount. Kelly admits intellectual debts to an exceptional range of fine teachers, including psychologists Sir Godfrey Thomson, James Drever, Sr., Carl Seashore and L. E. Travis, sociologists W. R. Smith and W. F. Ogburn, and even the naturalist, Edwin Teale. Is it any wonder, then, that Kelly arrived at the conclusion that it is possible, or should be, to see any number of dimensions in the world of mundane experience and fact?

Of course, it is impossible to determine whether Kelly's experiences led to his theoretical position or whether his developing theoretical position led to a search for diverse experience. (Or—most likely—both?) In any case, Kelly was responsible early in his career for the development of a remarkable clinical psychology program in western Kansas, including a traveling clinic run by him and his students. Out of this early experience, Kelly began to formulate many of the later ideas that were to be incorporated into his two-volume work on personality theory and clinical psychology (Kelly, 1955). It is probably as true of Kelly as of Freud that his conceptions of personality developed out of his clinical experience, and we may wonder whether the striking differences in their views stemmed from the divergent nature of their experiences. For example, much of Kelly's early work was with college students and public school pupils, not with the representatives of extreme pathology. In part, his later emphasis on the intellective aspects of behavior and his commitment to a theory of (relatively) rational behavior may have stemmed from his experience with persons who were still capable of construing their own behavior in communicable terms. His theory is not inapplicable at other points, but a similarly trained psychologist who worked in a mental institution might have been less likely to arrive at the precise formulation of behavior suggested by Kelly.

In his clinical experiences, particularly in public schools, Kelly became disillusioned with the standard motivational statements commonly employed to account for behavior, statements which often revealed more about the person who made them than about the person they supposedly described. It was not so much that the ideas teachers had about their pupils were wrong as that they led to anticipations that did not permit any constructive approaches to the problems which existed. The same thing might be said, of course, for the conceptions the children had of the school and their teachers. Thus, Kelly came gradually to the position that it was the terms in which people chose to cast their experience that lent importance and meaning to it (Kelly, 1958).

Kelly has made the presentation of his theory in its general terms pleasingly simple by presenting it in the form of a fundamental postulate and eleven corollaries. The fundamental postulate is: "A person's processes are psychologically channelized by ways in which he anticipates events." (Kelly, 1955, p. 46). What is proposed by the postulate is, first of all, that the system with which Kelly is dealing is psychological, that it has as its focus of convenience phenomena that are amenable to a psychological approach. Thus it is not meant to account for the behavior of automobiles, the workings of the central nervous system or the stock market. Second, it is proposed that behavior is stable across time and across situations, that is, it is *channelized*. Behavior is given its consistency by attempts to anticipate events. The particular behavior in which an individual engages presumably reflects the anticipations he has for the future, and his anticipations are expressed in his constructs.

Perhaps the central theoretical term in *The Psychology of Personal Constructs* is the term *construct* itself. By constructs Kelly means the interpretations we place on events or the terms in which we choose to look for replicability among events (Kelly, 1955, p. 50). He is nowhere quite explicit as to the origin of the constructs by which people attempt to make sense out of their universe. Kelly typically writes as if they had some existence apart from the experiences with which they deal and seems to imply that they are imposed upon events. On the other hand, the term *abstract* is frequently used in its verb form to refer to the process from which constructs arise, and the verb abstract ordinarily refers to the development of ideas *out of* experience. It often seems as if Kelly prefers to consider constructs as given, as already having been established by the time he begins to deal with the person.

However, it seems necessary to suppose that constructs come from somewhere, and it is probably easiest to suppose that they are in part a reflection of the experience of the individual; that individuals who have had similar experiences will have similar construct systems. Some evidence suggests, for example, that people who have complex personal construct systems, that is, who have many constructs with which to deal with events and who can apply them in a variety of independent ways, are likely to have had relatively complex environments as children (Sechrest & Jackson, 1961). There is also reason to believe that persons who have similar systems in terms of the verbal constructs they apply to other persons come from similar environments (Sechrest, 1962a). Thus, for example, persons who tend to use such terms as "friendly," "pleasant," "nice," "agreeable" to describe others tend to be more similar to each other than to persons who do not use such terms with respect to such factors as socio-economic level, religious belief, family constellation, etc. Such findings support the conclusion that, at the very least, constructs and experiences develop together, and that constructs are determined in part by experience.

It is necessary to take special note of the absence of any motivational construct in Kelly's system. He has, in fact, taken advantage of a number of opportunities to deny the usefulness of the concept of motivation and to suggest that it is a needless residue of an outmoded philosophical position which saw the universe as comprised of essentially inert objects. Since these objects were usually far from inert, it became necessary to conceive of forces operating on them. Carried over into terms of behavior, motivations were supposed to be the forces that impelled organisms to action, and without motivation there would be no action. By the use of the term *processes* in his fundamental postulate, Kelly means that psychology necessarily deals with processes. Behavior, its subject matter, is inherently a process. People continue to behave in spite of any motivational manipulations we may attempt. A person cannot be distinguished from the processes that characterize him. Kelly proposes that we start with the behaving organism, that it is not necessary to postulate the existence of forces outside the organism that impel him to action (Kelly, 1955, 1958, 1962).

The first of the eleven corollaries in the system is the *Construction Corollary,* which states that "a person anticipates events by construing their replications." The interpretations we place on events enable us to anticipate their replications. However, since events never actually repeat themselves, our interpretations of events merely make it possible for us to see some order in the universe—an order imposed by us and not inherent in the universe.

The interpretation or construct is not necessarily verbal; in fact, a definite distinction must be made between the construct and the label used to symbolize it. The construct is revealed only by the pattern of choices which the indiivdual makes and not necessarily by the verbal label which symbolizes it. A construct may be symbolized by other than verbal means, and probably constructs commonly have visual symbols or are so poorly symbolized that they cannot be described in words. In any case, the verbal label may be a poor representation of the pattern of choices that constitutes the actual construct.

What man construes is also a process like himself. Man attunes himself to the repeated themes in his universe and looks for repetitions. However, according to Kelly we do not deal with actual repetitions of events, since they do not repeat themselves. Man may look for identity among events, but only their replicative aspects will be found. We look at the passage of time, for example, and note a period we call a day. Tomorrow is not expected to be identical with today, but in certain respects tomorrow is going to be a replica of today. The next horse we see is not going to be identical with all previous horses or with any horse we have seen, but it will have sufficient replicative aspects to justify our calling it a horse.

The *Individuality Corollary* states the rather obvious point—consistent with the term *personal constructs*—that people differ from each other in their interpretations of events. There may be some inclination to think of a personal constructs theory as phenomenological, and Kelly might not object strenuously as long as one does not say that his theory is *nothing but* phenomenology. The pre-emptive "nothing but . . ." argument is anathema to a constructive alternativist. It is certainly true that much of Kelly's theory is consonant with a phenomenological approach, for central to his theory is the proposition that an individual will behave in a manner consistent with his own perceptions of and ideas about the universe. But while we ought to base our inferences about an individual on the things we have seen him do rather than upon the things we have seen other people do, it is never literally possible to see the world from another person's point of view. Moreover, Kelly, unlike most phenomenologists, believes that it is fruitful to look for general nomothetic principles about behavior. Thus, even though no one person's construct system is like any other's, construct systems like other events have replicable aspects, and we may look for regularities based upon the various properties of the systems. However, the psychologist is himself a construing individual, and his constructions must be taken into account in arriving at an understanding of another person. "Each study of an individual becomes a problem in concept formation for the psychologist. After he has conceptualized each of his cases, he next has the task of further abstracting the individual constructs in order to produce constructs which underlie people in general" (Kelly, 1955, p. 43).

The third corollary is the *Organization Corollary,* which states the fact of relationships of a hierarchical nature between constructs within a system. Some constructs have implications for others; for example, one may imply another, or one may have another construct as its element. Thus one of the most important characteristics of a construct is its position in a hierarchical system relative to others. A construct may, of course, be quite independent of most constructs in the system, but it is likely to be superordinate to some and subordinate to others. A construct is superordinate to other constructs that are elements forming a part of its context, and it is subordinate to those of whose contexts it is an element. There appear to be two ways in which a construct may be superordinate. First, a construct may be superordinate to another because each pole of the subordinate construct forms a part of the context for the two poles of the superordinate. For example, the construct "good-bad" may be superordinate to the construct "intelligent-stupid" if things which are intelligent are good and things which are stupid are bad. There are many things, presumably, which are good, but among them are intelligent things. On the other hand, both "good-bad" and "intelligent-stupid" might be subordinate to the construct "evaluative-objective." In this case, the whole construct "good-bad" is one of the elements forming the context of the "evaluative" pole, as is "intelligent-stupid." A construct such as "chromatic-achromatic" might be subordinate to the "objective" pole. The former type of superordination may be more common, but the latter type is probably more important in its implications. Many of the philosophical constructs by which men guide their major decision processes are of a highly superordinate nature, e.g., "spiritual-material," "charitable-selfish," "scientific-nonscientific." Williams (1958) found that the most useful constructs of an individual tend to be broadly general in the sense of cutting across many other construct dimensions.

Other aspects of the organization of construct systems will be indicated later in discussing some of the dimensions of constructs and of diagnosis.

The *Dichotomy Corollary* proposes that a person's construction system is made up of a finite number of dichotomous constructs. This corollary represents a distinct departure from most current conceptions of human thought, for it indicates that all thinking is basically dichotomous. At any one point and for any one issue, if a construct is relevant, then an either-or decision must be made. If the evaluative dimension is relevant for a particular issue, then the events to which the construct is to be applied are either "good" or "bad."

It should be understood that the context in which a construct occurs determines a part of its meaning. It has already been stated that events are anticipated by construing their replications. Having chosen an aspect of two events with respect to which they are replicative of each other, it follows that another event is definitely not a replication of the first two. A person's own choice of an aspect determines both what is considered to be similar and what is considered contrasting with respect to a set of events. The minimum context for a construct, according to Kelly, is three elements. That is, we need two elements with respect to which we can construe some similarity, in contrast to a third element. A similarity between two persons cannot be construed, for example, except in contrast to one or more additional persons. It is not always necessary to point specifically to a third element; the contrast is often implicit. Nevertheless, it is presumably the case that no similarity nor any difference between two things can be imagined except as they are compared to or contrasted with at least one other thing. This conception of constructs departs from conventional logic involving constructs of the "*A, not A*" variety.

Kelly believes that the *range of convenience* of a construct limits its applicability. Given three persons to construe, it may be decided that two of the three are masculine and that the third is feminine by contrast. The construct of sex when applied to people is definitely dichotomous, "masculine-feminine," and not a double construct of "masculine-not masculine" and "feminine-not feminine." There are many events to which the construct "masculine-feminine simply does not apply." If asked whether *time* is masculine or feminine, nearly all people would reply that it is neither, that time is an event for which this construct does not make sense. Nevertheless, having decided that the construct "masculine-feminine" is relevant in a particular context, then it follows that the events for which it is relevant are *either* masculine *or* feminine.

It must be emphasized that Kelly believes dichotomous thinking to be the characteristic mode of thought and not simply an abstract model unrelated to behavior. It is often suggested that thinking is or can be dimensional rather than dichotomous, thus permitting people to think in terms of shades of gray rather than black or white. However, Kelly believes that the dimensional character of the terms we use results from the combination of constructs of quantity and quality. Thus, the dichotomous construct "black-white" and a dichotomous quantitative construct permit a four-value scale, viz., black, slightly black, slightly white and white. If Miller (1956) is correct in his conclusion that approximately seven bits of information constitute the limit of apprehension for the human brain, it is clear that not many dichotomous constructs would have to be combined to produce the most complex scale usable by most persons.

Whether thought is in fact dichotomous is difficult to prove, but Kelly does think that Lyle's (1953) research supports such a contention. Lyle found that from the standpoint of consensual agreement in the use of common terms descriptive of personality, if his subjects were accurate in the use of a particular term, *e.g.,* "cheerful," "broad-minded," they were accurate in the use of its opposite, *i.e.,* "sad" or "narrow-minded." These results suggest that in the development of the understanding and use of such terms, the construct that is acquired is actually bipolar and dichotomous and not two distinct unipolar constructs such as "cheerful-not cheerful" and "sad-not sad." Perhaps the frequent warnings by logicians of the dangers of dichotomous modes of thought evidences the naturalness of such a way of thinking. Strong and repeated prohibitions, as noted by Freud, usually betray the strength of some response tendency.

In the personal constructs theory the *Range Corollary* states that a construct is convenient only for the anticipation of a finite range of events. As indicated in the discussion of *range of convenience,* no construct is meant to apply to the whole universe of events.

The *Experience Corollary* indicates that a person's construct system varies as he successively construes the replications of events. As an individual observes the passage of events, he places some structure on them and begins to anticipate their replications. His anticipations are in fact hypotheses about the universe, and as he is subjected to the flow of events, his hypotheses are exposed to the test of experience. As anticipations are revised following feedback concerning their adequacy, the construction system undergoes progressive change. The individual reconstrues and further develops his system. Such is the nature of experience that it occurs only when an individual revises and elaborates his system in the light of events taking place over a period of time, and it does not consist of a simple, passive submission to such events. If a clinical psychologist in the tenth year of his career is still doing things in the same way he did them in his first year (whether he is still making the same mistakes or is still accurate in the same way), from Kelly's point of view we may question whether it is correct to say that he has had "experience." Experience will have occurred only in so far as what he did and what happened to him in his first year led him to do things differently and see things differently in his second year, and so on.

The *Modulation Corollary* states the conditions under which we can expect changes in construct systems; specifically, "the variation in a person's construction system is limited by the permeability of the constructs within whose range of convenience the variants lie" (Kelly, 1955, p. 77). This corollary implies that change itself is an event or a series of events for an individual, and that the person must have some way in which the changes in his construction system may be construed. If an individual has no superordinate constructs for making sense out of change, then change cannot occur—although chaos might. For example, if a person is to abandon his construct of his father as a person toward whom he must be either dominant or submissive by the construct of respect vs. contempt, some structure must be placed upon this change. The person might construe his change in the light of the construct of "maturity-immaturity" as applied to himself, or he might construe the change in terms of the construct of "my-father-as-he-used-to-be vs. my-father-today." If the person is incapable of construing change, then change cannot occur in his system.

The *Fragmentation Corollary* states, "A person may successively employ a variety of construction subsystems which are inferentially incompatible with each other" (Kelly, 1955, p. 83). Changes in a construction system take place within the larger framework of the system itself, but the changes need not involve continuity such that the constructs which existed today are derived from those which existed yesterday. In some respects, the *Fragmentation Corollary* may be seen as related to the issue of self-consistency; but Kelly suggests that consistency, if it is meaningful at all, must be a construct with an alternative, inconsistency. What constitutes consistency or inconsistency depends upon the level at which behavior is being construed. It is possible, according to this corollary, for a person to apply aspects of his construction system that are incompatible with those he used earlier, incompatible in the sense of leading to different anticipations, and this may give rise to impressions of inconsistency. On the other hand, from a long term point of view it is supposed that an individual's choices must be somehow consistent with respect to the higher order constructs he uses.

The *Commonality* and *Sociality* corollaries have to do with the relationships between persons and their construction systems. The *Commonality Corollary* states, "To the extent that one person employs a construction of experience which is similar to that employed by another, his psychological processes are similar to those of the other person" (Kelly, 1955, p. 90); the *Sociality Corollary* states, "To the extent that one person construes the construction processes of another, he may play a role in a social process involving the other person" (Kelly, 1955, p. 95). Together, these two corollaries probably have more definite implications for research than any other statements in Kelly's theory. It is not simple to determine similarity in construction systems or to assess the degree to which one person is construing the construction processes of another, but some beginnings have been made. Assuming that persons who use similar verbal construct labels have similar construct systems, Triandis (1959) found that such persons have more satisfactory relationships with each other (in terms of better communication and greater personal gratification) than with others. Sechrest (1962c) found that personal constructs (again in terms of verbal labels) that are used jointly by two or more persons have a greater consensus in their application within a group than do constructs that are unique to a given group member. If two people both employ the construct "sincere-insincere" and a third person apparently does not customarily use that construct, the first two people are likely to agree better in applying the construct to a group of mutually known persons. Although from the standpoint of the issues involved here there are some obvious confoundings, it is interesting that Shoemaker (1955) found that persons who were construed by an individual as similar were predicted by him as likely to behave in similar ways.

There is also some research relating to the abilities of persons to play roles in relation to each other as a function of the characteristics of their construct systems, but no satisfactory procedures have been worked out for determining whether or in what way one person is construing the construction system of another. In perhaps the most directly relevant research, Payne (1956) found that knowledge of another individual's personal construct system led to more accurate predictions about behavior than did descriptions by others of that person. Thus the opportunity to construe another person's construct system seemed to enable an individual to imagine what that person might do in some situations. Shoemaker (1955) found that subjects were more accurate in their predictions of the behavior of persons with whom they felt comfortable than persons with whom they felt uncomfortable, and this can be taken to suggest that the ability to construe (anticipate) another person's behavior leads to a more satisfactory relationship with that person. In some data relating to the selection of patients for particular kinds of psychotherapeutic interventions, Sechrest (1956) found that patients selected for interpretive as opposed to supportive psychotherapy were more likely to use constructs of an abstract or inferential nature. That is, patients selected for interpretive therapy were more prone to use constructs that would be termed "psychological" or "social-personality" than constructs related to such manifest characteristics as physical appearance. Perhaps they were selected for interpretive psychotherapy because the therapist felt that he could work with them in that way, because he felt that he and his patient could mutually construe each other's way of looking at things and could achieve a more satisfactory role in relation to each other.

The last corollary to be considered (though not actually the last as listed by Kelly) is the *Choice Corollary:* "A person chooses for himself that alternative in a dichotomized construct through which he anticipates the greater possibility for extension and definition of his system." This corollary is the most directly related to the prediction of overt behavior, but, as will be seen, there are serious problems in moving from an individual's construct system to his behavior in any particular situation. The Choice Corollary indicates that when an individual is faced with a choice situation, *i.e.,* must construe an event in one way or another, he will make the choice that is most likely either to broaden his understanding of the universe or better to define the system he is already using. This is called the *elaborative choice.* What the person is looking for, then, is either constricted certainty or broadened understanding ·in relation to his construction system. In many respects the *elaborative choice* is analogous to such basic motivational constructs in other theories as self-actualization, self-consistency, striving for superiority, etc. The ultimate aim of behavior in *The Psychology of Personal Constructs* is the development and consolidation of the construction (anticipation) system. Kelly wishes to avoid the traps of hedonism and states that there is a continuing movement toward the anticipation of events rather than a general tendency of behavior in the direction of maximizing pleasure. He expresses the conviction that the orientations of people are of longer term than a "series of barters for temporal satisfactions."

If the Choice Corollary provides the essential link between the construction system and observable behavior, the nature of the link has not been precisely described. One gets the impression that the predictions to be made from the Choice Corollary are not at all exact. A construct presumably establishes the dimensions within which choices or behavior may occur, but emphasis on the personal nature of constructs implies that the behavior that follows from any one person's constructs would not become evident until after a rather exhaustive study of his construction system. Moreover, as construct labels are frequently elicited, e.g., by the *Role Construct Repertory Test* (RCRT), they are primarily descriptive of the dimensions along which other persons may be seen as moving. If it is desirable to anticipate the behavior of a person, then we must know whether his own behavior lies within the range of convenience of the constructs he applies to others.

For example, suppose a psychiatric patient uses the construct "hot tempered-even tempered" to describe other persons; what may we anticipate about his own behavior? First, it would be necessary to know whether the construct was applicable to his own behavior. It is conceivable that the patient's behavior is not governed, at least directly, by that construct at all, and we might be mistaken if we anticipated that he would be particularly hot-tempered or particularly calm. His construct represents his view of the world and not necessarily his response to it. (This problem is related to the distinction between similarity and complementary projection as described by Campbell et al, 1959.) Second, we also need to know just what behavioral elements are subsumed by the two poles of the construct. The writer once had a friend who considered himself to be quite open in his expression of anger, but most of his outbursts consisted of little more than annoyed responses of, "Well, all right!" Another person might consider anything less than an outright physical attack to be a manifestation of admirable self-control. Finally, we need to be able to determine which pole of the construct will be seen as applicable at the times or in the situations which we wish to predict.

It is certain that people will sometimes make choices of an elaborative or definitive nature in spite of the fact that these choices expose them to nonhedonic, painful experiences. In human avoidance learning, for example, it is found that (unlike dogs and rats) college sophomores will become curious whether the electric shock apparatus remains potent during the periods in which they are avoiding shock, and they will occasionally deliberately take the shock, apparently in order to keep in touch with reality and make sure their anticipatory system is working (Solomon, 1959). The behavior of children that is often described as "testing of limits" seems to be of a similar nature.

A dichotomy is posed by the separate notions of extending and defining the system. It seems that these are alternative possibilities, and there is not an exact way of specifying whether extension or definition will occur at any given time. However, in his discussion of constriction versus dilation Kelly implies that extension should probably occur when the person is most confident, when he has been generally successful in his anticipations. Definitive choices would be more likely in instances in which the construction system seemed to be in need of repair. A young man is more likely to consider asking the new girl in town for a date when he has been relatively successful in his experiences with the old ones, and he is more likely to ask her when the proposed date is for a relatively familiar function. Thus he may prefer a girl he knows well if he is about to attend his first formal, country club ball.

There is probably in the Choice Corollary an implicit assumption of some alternating extension and consolidation of the construction system. When the person feels secure and capable of anticipating events correctly, he will make choices that offer possibilities of extending his system, even at the risk of being wrong; but then a period of consolidation will follow in which he will make choices that reduce exposure to error but are confirmative. This, of course, is something of the way in which science proceeds.

Several steps are involved in the progression from construction to overt behavior. Kelly describes one possible sequence in terms of the *Circumspection-Preemption-Control (C-P-C) Cycle.* The circumspection stage involves the multi-dimensional survey of the events, simultaneously or sequentially, with constructs that are applied independently of each other. Circumspection will occur in terms of the constructs that are available for interpreting the phenomena with which the individual is faced and will establish the dimensions within which responses are possible. The second stage of the cycle, preemption, is the decision as to which of all the possible constructs is critically relevant. Control (or choice) refers to the ultimate response made in the light of the preemptive interpretation.

For example, a young man who has just been drafted into the army may circumspectively survey his situation, employing a wide variety of constructs. However, if he is to be an effective soldier, the situation must be pre-empted in terms of the construct "soldier-civilian," and the young man must decide that he is a soldier and nothing but a soldier. If he continues to think of himself as a soldier and also as the sole surviving son of a loving mother and as a fellow who loves blueberry pie and as the exclusive sweetheart of a remarkable young lady, he is unlikely to be able to make the choices that will contribute to effective soldiering. The pre-emption may be only temporary, it may be almost immediately superseded, but it provides the basis for setting the course of action.

It is not a simple matter to specify the research data that would be critical to support the choice corollary, but there is some research indicating that behavior is related to the constructions that are employed in interpreting events. For example, the writer is exploring (Sechrest, 1962b) the relationship between constructs of particular content and the behavior that might be expected to be related to those constructs. With respect to the use of the construct "friendly-unfriendly" or similar constructs on a verbal level, it is possible to identify which persons use that construct on the RCRT and which do not. What differences could be expected in their reputations for friendliness among their peers? Considering reputational ratings on the construct "pleasant-unpleasant," one could predict that persons who employ the construct "friendly-unfriendly" would be different from those who do not. However, there is nothing in Kelly's theory that would enable us to specify the direction in which the difference should exist, unless it might be expected that persons who use the construct would constitute the extremes of both the pleasant and unpleasant groups. Actually, the persons who used the construct "friendly-unfriendly" proved to have reputations toward the unpleasant end of the dimension when compared with persons who did not use the construct. On the other hand, considering scores on an anxiety measure, persons who use "anxious-not anxious" and related constructs such as "nervous-calm," "stable-easily upset" and the like, scored higher on the anxiety measure. Thus there is some indication that the constructs "friendly-unfriendly" and "anxious-not anxious" are particularly relevant for the behavior of persons who use them.

In another investigation it has been found that persons who employ a construct dimension are likely to be rated by their peers at one extreme or the other on that dimension (Sechrest, 1962c). However, it is unpredictable whether they will be rated toward the favorable or unfavorable end of any evaluative dimension. Such a finding at least supports the hypothesis that constructs set the patterns within which behavior will occur.

On the basis of his anticipatory system, the individual makes predictions about the future. In effect, he lays bets as to what he expects, how he thinks things will turn out, and presumably he then observes the evidence. Some of his bets may be large and important, and their loss can represent a serious threat to the bettor. Others are trivial and of little significance. When a prediction is correct, little change in the construction system will occur, but if the prediction is wrong, then changes will be relatively extensive (Poch, 1952). However, the outcomes of his predictions must also be construed by the person, and it is difficult at best to predict how an individual may behave following the "invalidation" of a prediction.

For example, an individual in making a prediction may assume that the people with whom he is associating are intelligent—and it turns out that their behavior is not what he anticipated. There are now several possibilities. He may assume that his associates are not intelligent after all; he will view them as unintelligent. Or he may decide that he is wrong about the behavior to be expected of intelligent people, and he may revise his system for construing the elements subsumed by intelligence. Or he may decide that the construct "intelligence" is inapplicable in the situation in which he made his observations; he should not have expected intelligent behavior in a strictly social situation. Or he may just abandon the notion of intelligence and regard it as a meaningless construct that leads to no useful, correct predictions. While it is not easy to predict what the reaction of an individual may be following an "invalidating" experience, it is assumed that the construction system is elaborated, either in the direction of extension or definition, as a result of the predictions which an individual makes and their outcomes.

Characteristics of personal constructs

Kelly has a number of constructs about constructs, i.e., he has ways of construing the constructs which he observes people to be using. Reference has already been made to the "permeable-impermeable distinction," i.e., whether new experiences may be accounted for in terms of a given construct. A *permeable* construct is one that will admit new elements to its context; an *impermeable* construct is one that has exhausted its context. It is not clear from the use which Kelly makes of this distinction whether an impermeable construct is one that will admit no new elements to its purview, or whether it is only one that is exhaustive at one or the other of the two poles. For example, a religious person may maintain the construct "miraculous-natural" to account for events with which he must deal, but he may have decided that there are no more miracles, that the last miraculous occurrences were in 1446. The miraculous pole of the construct is impermeable, but the natural pole continues to be applicable. (Some sports fans use a similar construct when they think of the "great ballplayers vs. modern day mediocrities." The former are nearly all deceased, while the latter continue to appear year after year.) On the other hand, another individual may use the construct "miraculous-natural" in a totally impermeable way and insist that current and future events are neither miraculous nor natural. While there may once have been events that could be described as miraculous or natural, the whole thing no longer makes sense. The permeability of one's constructs limits the ability to deal with new experience to the extent that impermeable constructs have not been replaced.

The *pre-emptive* construct is one that "pre-empts" its elements for membership in its own realm exclusively. Kelly sometimes refers to pre-emptive construing as "nothing but . . ." kind of thinking. For example, political labels are often used pre-emptively. If a given person is identified as a Communist, then he is typically thought of as nothing but a Communist. Even less extreme labels may be used in very nearly the same fashion. Once a politician has been categorized as "liberal" or "conservative," it is difficult for him to induce people to think of him in other ways, e.g., as an expert on foreign affairs, a champion of constitutional government, a devotee of the arts. One rather amusing example of pre-emptive construction occurred when the writer was working in a psychiatric hospital in which it became necessary to decontaminate one of the units of an infection of lice. There was one elderly gentleman in the unit, a very dignified man full of pride and a sense of propriety, who stoutly resisted the "delousing" procedure. He was almost literally dragged away shouting, "But you can't delouse a Yale man." He was a Yale man and nothing but a Yale man in that situation.

A *constellatory* construct is one that fixes the realm membership of its elements, i.e., once an event is appropriately structured by one construct, its other characteristics are fixed. Many stereotypes, for example, are of a constellatory nature. "This girl is a blonde, therefore she is dumb," "if it is a pencil, it must be more or less round and elongated." For many students, the construct "difficult" is constellatory to the construct "has to do with mathematics." On the other hand, a *propositional* construct is one that leaves open to construction in all other ways the elements subsumed by it. The construct pole "blonde" is being used propositionally to the extent that one does not suppose that any other characteristics necessarily follow. While it is easy to presume that pre-emptive and constellatory constructs are bad and propositional constructs are desirable, such is not necessarily the case. At times pre-emption is clearly necessary, and at times constellatory constructs are most useful. Propositionality only represents a contrast to pre-emptive and constellatory construction.

There are many other characteristics that constructs may have or ways in which they may be categorized; space does not permit their detailed description. Such obvious characteristics of constructs as their breadth (comprehensive vs. incidental constructs), their centrality for the person (core vs. peripheral constructs) and their preciseness (tight vs. loose constructs) are accounted for.

Common personality constructs as represented in Kelly's system

The Psychology of Personal Constructs certainly has an apparent emphasis on psychological processes at a high level of cognitive awareness, and Kelly makes no special provision for a construct of the unconscious. However, it is incorrect to suppose that "irrational" processes or processes that go on outside the individual's awareness are excluded in Kelly's system. Instead of a single construct by means of which to account for such processes, e.g., repression, Kelly actually has several theoretical constructs that are relevant to unconscious mental processes. To begin with, Kelly suggests that *level of cognitive awareness* is a dimension running through the construct system. A high-level construct is one that is effectively symbolized in socially communicable terms, with alternatives that are both readily accessible, within the range of convenience of the person's major constructions, etc.

Other constructs may be at a low level of awareness for one or more of several reasons. First, some constructs are *preverbal,* i.e., they have no consistent word symbol. They may have been formed prior to the development of language, but they may also have been formed under conditions not conducive to appropriate verbal description. Constructs may be at a low level of awareness because one of the poles is *submerged* and thus is unavailable for use. For example, the implicit pole of the construct "good people" ordinarily is "bad people," but if that pole is submerged, the person using the construct may not be aware of the implicit distinctions he is making and may not readily comprehend all his responses to the people he meets. *Suspension* refers to the omission of some element from a construct's context as a result of revision of the system. If an element is suspended, and if there is no other readily available structure for dealing with it, it may be at a low level of awareness in the system. Whole parts of a construction system may be suspended as a result of revision of superordinate constructions. If an individual were to conclude that the construct "good-evil" had absolutely no further relevance to his behavior and were to revise his system so as to exclude it, then elements (behavior) that had once been dealt with by that construct might be less well remembered than before.

Some events might lie outside the *range of convenience* of our construct system, and we might for that reason be unaware of them. The writer once knew a small girl who had been reared in an isolated but peculiarly protected environment and was utterly oblivious to threats in interpersonal situations. She apparently had no constructs within whose range of convenience threats from other persons might fall. Most persons have no convenient structure for their own digestive systems (probably fortunately), and digestive processes may be said to be "unconscious." Kelly proposes, then, to deal with the issues raised by unconcious processes by invoking a variety of constructs from within his system.

Anxiety is a commonly used personality construct that has a special meaning in Personal Constructs theory. Whether Kelly means to use such common terms as anxiety only as defined within his system or whether he means to say that what other people take to be anxiety— e.g., apprehensions concerning the future, anticipations of punishment, etc.—really amounts to or stems from his own definition is not clear. He does deny specifically that his definition of anxiety abrogates other definitions. Kelly defines anxiety as "the awareness that the events with which one is confronted lie outside the range of convenience of his construct system" (Kelly, 1955, p. 495). In other words, anxiety is the *awareness* of lack of structure for events. Kelly points out that it is not the fact that one's system is not working that is anxiety producing; one does not feel anxious merely because his anticipations are incorrect. Anxiety is produced only when it is recognized that one's system is inapplicable.

The question why the failure of structure should be "anxiety-producing" is rather difficult. Persons who work within a different conceptual system often do not understand ·just why it is that loss of structure should necessarily involve any question of affect. First, anxiety and loss of structure are related by definition in the same way that anxiety may be defined in some other system as the threat of an instinctual impulse breaking into consciousness. Second, however, loss of structure limits severely the basic process of anticipation, which is fundamental to human behavior according to Kelly. Thus anything that threatens the anticipatory system will be a source of dread to the individual. We may take it as assumed that anxiety is for Kelly, as for other theorists, a predominantly undesirable experience.

Hostility and *aggression* are treated by Kelly in a way which represents a considerable and deliberate departure from their usual usage in personality theory, where they seem to be regarded largely as synonymous. Kelly defines aggression as "the active elaboration of one's perceptual field." Defined in such a way, aggression has absolutely no implications of hostility or of undesirability of any kind. It is simply the attempt of the individual to take into account a greater portion of his universe. To the extent, then, that a student is attempting to broaden his horizons, to get a grasp on phenomena he has never considered before, he is behaving aggressively. The nonaggressive individual is one who is content with the limits of his vision. Hostility, on the other hand, is "the continued effort to extort validational evidence in favor of a type of social prediction which has already been recognized as a failure." The mythological representation of hostility lies in the legend of Procrustes, who had a bed to fit every traveler—after he had either stretched or shortened the travelers who were the wrong size. Similarly, a parent who insists that her offspring is "only a baby" in the face of obvious evidence of maturity is displaying hostility. Not all hostility need involve inflicted pain or a desire to inflict pain upon one's victim; all that is necessary is an insistence that one's victim is something he isn't. To be sure, many, perhaps most attempts to inflict pain on other persons are extortional in nature. A husband who beats his wife is probably attempting to validate a prediction he has made which is simply not working, e.g., his prediction that his wife will obey him no matter what happens.

One further personality construct that should be mentioned is *guilt,* which Kelly defines as "the awareness of dislodgment of the self from one's core role structure." It is probably true that most experience categorized as guilt by other theorists would be considered guilt by Kelly, but he would also include some experiences that would appear not at all like guilt to others. Guilt arises when the individual becomes aware that he is alienated from the roles by which he maintains his most important relationships to other persons. For many scientists, "objectivity" is a fundamental aspect of their role, e.g., it is basic to their categorization of themselves as scientists; if in some way it becomes evident to a scientist that his behavior is nonobjective, then he may be expected to experience guilt. Guilt is the common consequent to dislodgment from the roles of "loving spouse," "careful parent," "competent employee," etc.; it may ensue if the individual regards himself as dislodged from *any* role by which he maintains himself in relation to other persons. It seems, for example, that some persons may even attempt to maintain themselves by reference to the role of "an evil person." If it happens that they are dislodged momentarily from that role, e.g., by unaccountably performing some charitable deed, then they may experience guilt as Kelly defines it. Their "atonement" may well take the common form of stricter adherence to role demands, but it will result in somewhat different forms of overt response.

Many persons ask where are "the feelings" in Personal Constructs theory, and insist that Kelly does not take sufficient account of what they call "affect." In the course of a generally favorable review of Kelly's book, Bruner (1956) says he thinks that when a young man is out on a date with a girl, he is scarcely thinking at all about the elaboration of his system; there are passions of some sort involved.

It will certainly be agreed that Kelly's system does not place any particular emphasis on the affective aspects of experience. Indeed, in his book there are no index references at all to the three terms "affect,'" "emotion," and "feeling." However, in Personal Constructs theory there is no need to account for affect in any special way. Affect is where it has always been, in the individual. There are, or may be, constructs, patterns of choice by an individual that are "affective" in nature or have some internal feeling states as elements, but which are not different from any other constructs. When we construe some events as amusing or not amusing, we laugh or we do not laugh accordingly. When we construe people as "pleasing" or "distressing," "stimulating" or "dull," affect may be regarded as given, manifest in the elements that form the context for the construct.

Relationship to other personality theories

Nowhere in his two volumes does Kelly define the term personality, but he has discussed the concept in general terms in a later article (Kelly, 1961b) in which he states that personality is "our abstraction of the activity of a person and our subsequent generalization of this abstraction to all matters of his relationship to other persons, known and unknown, as well as to anything else that may seem particularly valuable" (pp. 220-221). In considering personality it is necessary to note that it involves abstraction by psychologists of processes they observe. It is not simply an object to be discovered by them. Moreover, Kelly states that personality cannot ignore the person's relationship to others, and by its nature personality is value laden. It is possible to give a definition of personality within Kelly's theoretical system, or at least to translate certain common ideas about personality into his terms. One common conception of personality is that it represents those consistencies in the individual's behavior that make him different and discriminable from other persons. From this manifest behavior view, within Kelly's system personality consists of the characteristic choices made by the individual as he attempts to anticipate his future. His personality, the view we have of it, depends upon the constructions we place on his characteristic choices. If, on the other hand, we wish to view personality as some essence underlying the more obvious manifestations of an individual's behavior, then in Kelly's system personality is probably synonymous with the constructions an individual places upon the events with which he has to deal. An individual's personality is his construct system (Kelly, 1961a, p. 229).

It is evident that Kelly's theory can be construed variously, that one can apply one's own particular constructs to *The Psychology of Personal Constructs.* The one thing Kelly would suggest is that constructs not be applied in a pre-emptive manner, insisting that his system is "nothing but" something-or-other. It should not be insisted that Personal Constructs Theory is nothing but neophenomenology or nothing but ego psychology. Kelly has stated that his theory may be construed as phenomenological—although he disagrees with that construction (Kelly, 1955, p. 517)—but it may also be construed as rational, interpersonal, experimental and in many other ways.

Like most cognitive and phenomenological theories, Kelly's tends to be ahistorical in its approach to understanding behavior. Its principal emphasis is placed upon current perceptions in the prediction of behavior. On the other hand, Kelly is quite cognizant of the importance most persons attach to historical experience in understanding behavior and in justifying it. While many, perhaps most persons, are more or less passive "victims of their own biographies," Kelly does not suppose that victimization by one's experience is necessary. Unlike, for example, psychoanalysis, Personal Construct theory places no special emphasis upon the early experiences of the individual. It is clearly antithetical to constructive alternativism to suppose that the individual's course in life is inexorably set at any one point in time, and here Kelly's theoretical ideas resemble those of many other cognitive theorists. Albert Ellis, for example, in his exposition of "rational therapy," suggests that it is not what has happened or will happen to us that is important, but the statements (interpretations) we make to ourselves about events (Ellis, 1962). With such a proposition Kelly would agree completely.

There is in Kelly a good deal less emphasis on the importance of the self and the self concept than in most phenomenological theories. He does not make the self concept the central construct in his theory, and he recognizes the possibility of behavior determined without awareness. Kelly suggests that in many instances the individual may behave in ways that even to himself seem irrational. He also suggests that his position differs from that of the self-concept theorists in that they are inclined to study the placement an individual makes of himself upon dimensions determined externally, that is, by the experimenter or the assessor of personality, while he, on the other hand, prefers to study the placement the individual makes of himself with respect to the constructs that he himself emits and has found useful.

The Psychology of Personal Constructs is an intellectual model, or rather, it is based upon an intellectual model of behavior. Kelly does not think of his theory as only intellectual, but says simply that he has taken intellectual behavior, the rational processes that people engage in, as a model in building his theory. This may have the result of giving his theory as a focus of convenience certain particular phenomena of personality rather than others. His theory may lose some utility when it is extended into areas of behavior that are usually considered to be irrational.

Inasmuch as Kelly views behavior in its anticipatory aspects, there are obvious similarities to the theories of Adler as presented by Dreikurs (Ch. 00). From the standpoint of Adlerian theory, behavior is determined by the expectations and intentions of the person. It has, then, teleological aspects. Kelly agrees that, at least for those persons who are comfortable with teleological terms, the constructs the individual places upon the events with which he has to deal serve the purpose of enabling him to achieve control over events.

It is of more than passing interest that an analysis of the interpretations made of a clinical case by a number of exponents of leading personality theories (Farberow & Shneidman, 1961) revealed that Kelly's conclusions were most similar to those growing out of Adlerian, Sullivanian and nondirective positions (Kelly, 1961b). While it is impossible to distinguish clearly between Kelly the theorist and Kelly the clinician, the three theoretical positions to which he shows the greatest affinity have a number of things in common with Personal Constructs theory. All three probably place somewhat more emphasis on the conscious determinants of behavior than, for example, Freudian and Jungian theories. All three also place a rather substantial emphasis upon the interpersonal determinants of behavior. And, finally, at least the Adlerian and nondirective positions tend to be ahistorical in their approach to predictions of behavior.

Like Freudian and Rogerian theories, *The Psychology of Personal Constructs* grew out of its originator's experience in psychotherapeutic practice. It was by his own account not a theory which he brought to his experiences and imposed upon them. Personal Construct theory probably has as its focus of convenience the process of helping people restructure their lives. Although an examination of Volume II of Kelly's work reveals that his therapeutic techniques are not radically different from those typically used by most current psychotherapists, they are certainly varied and exemplary of considerable flexibility. Personal Constructs Theory, also like psychoanalysis and the nondirective schools, proves to be the source of a novel therapeutic attack, which Kelly labels *Fixed Role Therapy*. However, fixed role therapy is obviously not meant to constitute the whole or even the major therapeutic technique for Kellian practitioners. In spite of the prominence given to fixed role therapy by its description in Volume I, it is actually a specialized variant meant to be used only in a limited number of cases for which it is particularly applicable by reason of time and goal limitations. Fixed role therapy is not at all emphasized in Volume II, which is devoted almost exclusively to the clinical applications of the theory.

The Psychology of Personal Constructs is a theory that has within its intended range of convenience an exceptional variety of behavior of which the human organism is capable, including learning, dreams, occupational choice, sexual activity, and so on. There may be wider-ranging theories, but unquestionably most theories are less broad in scope. How well *The Psychology of Personal Constructs* lives up to its intentions remains to be seen. George Kelly would never hesitate to lay his bets and note their consequences. Owing to his convictions about constructive alternativism, however, he will probably never suffer from lost bets. He may even enjoy them for the opportunities they offer to one with almost unlimited intellectual resources to risk.

REFERENCES

BRUNER, J. S. You are your constructs. *Contemp. Psychol.*, 1956, *1*, 355-357.

CAMPBELL, D. T., MILLER, N., & LUBETSKY, J. Five varieties of projection in trait attribution. Progress report to the National Institute of Health. Research Grant: M-1544. Mimeographed, Northwestern University, 1959.

ELLIS, A. *Reason and emotion in psychotherapy.* New York: Lyle Stuart, 1962.

FARBEROW, N. L., & SHNEIDMAN, E. S. *The cry for help.* New York: McGraw-Hill, 1961.

KELLY, G. A. *The psychology of personal constructs.* New York: Norton, 1955. 2 vols.

KELLY, G. A. Man's construction of his alternatives. In G. Lindzey (Ed.). *Assessment of human motives.* New York: Rinehart & Co., 1958.

KELLY, G. A. The abstraction of human processes. *Proceedings of the XIVth International Congress of Applied Psychology.* Copenhagen: Munksgaard, 1961. (a)

KELLY, G A. A nonparametric method of factor analysis for dealing with theoretical issues. Unpublished manuscript. Mimeograph, Ohio State University, 1961. (b)

KELLY, G. A. Europe's matrix of decision. In M. R. Jones (Ed.). *Nebraska symposium on motivation,* 1962. Lincoln, Nebr.; Univ. of Nebraska Press, 1962.

LYLE, W. A comparison of emergence and value as determinants of selective perception. Unpublished doctoral dissertation, Ohio State University, 1953.

MILLER, G. A. The magical number seven, plus or minus two: some limits on our capacity for processing information. *Psychol. Rev.,* 1956, *63*, 81-97.

PAYNE, D. E. Role constructs versus part constructs and interpersonal understanding. Unpublished doctoral dissertation, Ohio State University, 1956.

POCH, SUSANNE M. A study of changes in personal constructs as related to interpersonal prediction and its outcomes. Unpublished doctoral dissertation, Ohio State University, 1952.

SECHREST, L. Patients' interpretations of their psychotherapists. Unpublished doctoral dissertation, Ohio State University, 1956.

SECHREST, L. Biographical similarity and similarity in personal construction. Unpublished manuscript, 1962. (a)

SECHREST, L. Personal constructs and observable behaviors. Unpublished manuscript, 1962. (b)

SECHREST, L. Consensus in ratings and characteristics of traits rated. Unpublished manuscript, 1962. (c)

SECHREST, L., & JACKSON, D. N. Social intelligence and accuracy of interpersonal predictions. *J. Pers.*, 1961, *29*, 167-182.

SHOEMAKER, D. J. The relation between personal constructs and interpersonal predictions. Unpublished doctoral dissertation, Ohio State University, 1955.

SOLOMON, R. L. Human avoidance learning. Colloquium address at Northwestern University, 1959.

TRIANDIS, H. C. Cognitive similarity and interpersonal communication in industry. *J. appl. Psychol.*, 1959, *43*, 321-326.

WILLIAMS, T. G. The ascribed usability of personal constructs as a function of their generality. Unpublished master's thesis, Pennsylvania State University, 1958.

9

Individual Psychology:
The Adlerian Point of View

Rudolf Dreikurs, M.D.

Any theory of personality, and any technique of psychotherapy or correction, is founded on some basic assumptions of which one may or may not be aware. Some claim that their assumptions are the only possible ones, and that those of other schools are misrepresentations. Others deny that any personality theory can be scientifically validated, since our scientific tools are not suited for the complexities of the social and behavioral sciences, including psychology. Consistent with the wide range of existing personality theories are the varieties of technical procedures; but each has to be understood on the strength of the basic assumptions on which it rests.

What are the assumptions on which Adlerians proceed? What is the model of man which Adler has designed and which Adlerians accept? First of all, man is considered to be a social being, a *zoon politicon,* as Aristotle called him. This means that all qualities we call human are means of social interaction, of dealing with others, of indicating a person's approach toward others. Therefore, we consider the problems that man encounters and that create difficulties and troubles for him to be social problems (Adler, 1938). Everybody faces three major tasks in society. First, he has to contribute in a useful way through his work. Second, he has to make friends with his fellow men and participate with them in common endeavors. Third, he has

234

to establish a satisfactory relationship with a person of the opposite sex. Each individual operates within a given setting and all his problems are related to the specific ways and means by which he meets these three problems in that setting, or, better, the problems arising within these three fields of life. He is considered well adjusted if he can meet them in a satisfactory fashion, and maladjusted if he fails to do so (4, 5, 6, 7, 9, 10, 22).

The quality which enables man to function reasonably well within his social setting has been described by Adler as "Gemeinschaftsge-fuehl," which, in literal translation, means feeling of communion, of imbeddedness in the community of man. It has also been translated as "social interest," a term which, like many other psychological terms, invites misinterpretations. Social interest, in the context of the Adlerian viewpoint, means that the person experiences belonging and knows he has a place (Adler, 1938). This is a prerequisite for his ability to function socially and to participate effectively in the give and take of social living. Without sufficient social interest his tolerance level is low. If a situation is not to his liking or beyond his capacity, he withdraws, stops cooperating and participating, and offers instead either excuses or antagonistic attitudes. Our social interest is always tested by the difficulties we encounter in our relationship with others and in facing the problems of social living.

Social Interest is an innate potentiality which each human being has to develop. Thus, it is not static but changes in relation to the degree of success he has in meeting societal demands. If he becomes discouraged, because he feels he cannot meet the demands of society or certain aspects of it, then he may partially withdraw and restrict his Social Interest to those areas in which he feels belonging. One may, in fact, draw a diagram of Social Interest for any individual. By closely inquiring about those areas of Social Interest in which he really feels belonging, and about the people to whom he feels genuinely close, one can determine the extent and intensity of his Social Interest. There are some who have a very narrow circle to which they belong, confined to only a very few friends. Some feel belonging only in relation to certain members of their family, and to nobody else in the community. Others may feel very close ties to the "whole world" but not to their own family or to members of their immediate community. Nevertheless, in each case one can draw a clear diagram of the person's Social Interest.

Most people have sufficient Social Interest to function satisfactorily in most areas of their lives, at least outwardly. Yet in areas where their

feeling of belonging is absent, they cannot function, and each of us
has such limitations. As long as one is concerned with the welfare of
others, with the common good, and with the solution of problems, he
expresses Social Interest. Only where he withdraws from the tasks at
hand, from participating and contributing, does a lack of Social Interest
become apparent. If it stops altogether, then the individual withdraws
from the reality of social living and creates in a psychotic state his own
fictitious society.

A concern with Social Interest, with a person's social orientation,
and with his social problems, is characteristic of Adlerian Psychology.
Another fundamental aspect is its holistic orientation (Adler, 1959b;
Ansbacher & Ansbacher, 1959; Way, 1950). Adler was one of the first
who developed a holistic psychology. His model of man was close to
that envisioned by Gestalt psychologists. "Gestalt" means configuration; emphasis is placed on the whole, which is more than the sum total
of its parts and cannot be explained by any partial process. Adler gave
his school of thought the name "Individual Psychology" to emphasize
that the human is indivisible, in contrast with other psychological concepts which consider the individual as composed of different parts, processes and mechanisms. The individual is not the result of all the forces
that converge on him; none of them can explain the function of the
whole. On the contrary, the individual himself determines the significance of all the influences to which he is exposed; only within the
given whole do the partial phenomena and processes derive their meaning. If the term "Holism," which was created by Smuts in 1924, had
been known to Adler when he coined the name of his school, he
probably would have called it "Holistic Psychology," which would have
led to less confusion and misunderstanding than does the term "Individual Psychology"—particularly in English translations from the
German.

The term "Holism" has become fashionable, but while many
speak about the holistic approach, only a few know what it means.
The literature is full of papers in which the holistic approach is used
interchangeably with a "total" or "global" approach, but the global
approach is not holistic. Global implies a need to explore all facets of
a person in order to understand him, to know all dimensions of his
existence and development, his heredity and environment, his national,
religious and racial background, his social and economic status, in order
to get a full picture. However, this is not holistic but reductionistic.
It reduces the person to the summation of all these factors and in-

fluences whereas the holistic approach is quite different. Since the whole is more than the sum total of its parts, it cannot be understood by an explanation and analysis of partial phenomena. They derive their meaning only within the pattern of the whole. It is like a mosaic that cannot be seen or composed merely by counting the number of stones of a certain color and describing their shapes. In a mosaic, the characteristic of each stone is in its position in the whole and the part which it plays in the total picture. The design cannot be explained by the parts because it has a pattern of its own. Take the mosaic apart, and nothing is left of the design.

This example of a mosaic is not quite apt, because one can still determine the position of the various parts and thereby come to a reconstruction of the whole design. The mosaic is not a functional whole; it is only used here to clarify the fact that the whole can explain the parts, but knowledge of the parts may not be sufficient to understand or grasp the whole. This is fundamental for the understanding of man. Presently, almost all scientific approaches in medicine and in psychology are reductionistic, searching as they do for causes and mechanisms that may better explain human behavior and functioning. It is only on rare occasions that one encounters a holistic approach, because we are all trained in mechanistic and causalistic thinking, which demand explanation of all phenomena in terms of causes which produce them. There is a relationship between causes and observable phenomena, but this relationship is one of statistical probability. Under certain influences predictable consequences can be observed, but only when dealing with large numbers of cases. In each individual case, the outcome may be quite different and cannot be predicted, except in probabilistic terms. We have become so accustomed to satisfaction with such limited predictability that we do not take sufficient account of our inability to predict the behavior or reaction of any one person. Nevertheless, we still view accurate predictability as the only basis for a scientific approach. The new scientific orientation that was developed in the field of theoretical physics has not yet come to the level of the average scientist and college-educated layman; they all continue to think in terms of the 17th-century mechanistic form of science and have not become fully aware that in 1927, the Copenhagen Agreement [1] inaugurated a new scientific era in which strict causality and determination are negated.

The question then arises whether the holistic approach can have

---

[1] *Atomic Physics and Human Knowledge* by Nils Bohr. Wiley, N. Y., 1958.

practical meaning, and whether the whole can be perceived as such. It was one of the great contributions of Adler to have developed a practical approach to the problem of perceiving man as a whole. Gestalt psychologists used the concept of configuration for gaining some theoretical understanding, having particular significance for learning, but they developed no practical approach to psychotherapy or to correction. Adler developed techniques applicable to both these fields based on holistic assumptions.

What makes the whole perceptible? It seems that the whole can only be understood teleoanalytically, that is, in terms of its direction or movement. Only in his movement toward identifiable goals can the individual person be perceived as a whole. In his behavior he reflects all his past experiences and training as they are expressed in and modified by his view of present circumstances, by his concept of the future, and by his intentions and his goals. In this perspective, behavior appears as purposive, and is directed toward a goal which the individual has set for himself. Looking at behavior teleoanalytically, one can see in each act the whole human being and his outlook on life—his immediate or his long-range goals—which give significance to all his acts. Any one act, therefore, can not be explained by any one cause or stimulation whether assumed or actual. This stimulation, which in other approaches is considered to be the main causative factor, is only possible within the holistic frame of the individual. The individual is not conditioned; he decides to what kind of conditioning he will respond. He takes from his past, from the reservoir of all of his experiences and from the multitude of stimulations to which he has been exposed, only those influences which suit him for his purpose. He has a biased apperception, for he responds only to what he wants to respond, seeing only what fits into his frame of reference. It is he who directs all his activities.

The teleological approach has been in ill repute for considerable time, and certainly was not acceptable scientifically in Adler's time. This is one of the reasons why his psychology, which is basically teleo-analytic, could not find wide acceptance until basic scientific concepts evolved that supported his postulations. He was fifty years ahead of his time. Two main historical traditions in the scientific field prevented the acceptance of teleological mechanisms as valid bases for an understanding of observable phenomena. First, the term teleology was used in theology to indicate that the individual has to fulfill the purpose God has given him. This traditional use of the term was more important in Europe than in America in creating a hostile attitude among scientists to its use in psychology. Of course, the traditional theological use of the term is quite different from the way it is used today. The goals toward which the individual strives are not presented to him by God, by Divine Providence, but by his self-determination. Nevertheless, the term was pre-empted by theology and therefore resented by scientifically oriented psychologists—and the more so since, in Adler's time, science was entirely mechanistic and causalistic.

This is the second reason for scientific rejection of teleology. There was no room for the assumption that the individual can choose his own goals, that he is not determined by what happened to him in the past, but is a determining influence himself. Now, the concept of free will can find scientific acceptance once man is recognized as a quantum, and quantum mechanics will no longer be considered valid only on the sub-atomic level, but as a fundamental law pertaining to all organic wholes, be they found in physics (in super-conductivity), in biology (as "Quantum Genetics"), or in man (as free will). Classical physics, on which all basic scientific laws were founded, had no room for quantum jumps, for spontaneous mutations, nor for man's ability to determine his own actions.

Many students of psychology find it difficult even today, almost forty years after the beginning of the new scientific era, to perceive and comprehend man's ability to decide his own actions, because their training obliges them to think in mechanistic terms. We are all raised in causal thinking, whether we are laymen or scientists, and only a few of us know as yet that causal thinking is no longer scientifically accepted as such, because what appears as causation is only a statistical probability of responses. The Cartesian principle of rigid causality as well as the LaPlacian ideal of definite predictability belongs to the past—but the majority of our contemporaries still live in this scientific past. It is curious to see that the theoretical physicists who recognize the limitation of the causal principle in their field want to withhold this freedom of choice at the human level and existential analysts want to limit the freedom of choice to man. Neither of the representatives of the two extreme levels of existence have recognized freedom from determinism as a universal principle, which Smuts first described as a basic and universal principle of Holism. As soon as wholes are recognized as indivisible entities, the creative act is the logical consequence as an expression of a whole which is not determined by its parts.

This new orientation is becoming more widely recognized. The New York Academy of Science in 1948 published one of the best short descriptions of "Teleological Mechanisms" in its pamphlet of this name, and Lawrence Frank, in his introduction, gave one of the best summaries of this new development and its consequences. He pointed out how the linear approach of the causal principle—that one force affects a passive object—has to be abandoned; even inorganic matter does not respond merely passively to forces. Field theory replaces the old scheme of linear forces operating independently of each other. Until this new orientation becomes part of our general education, the new concepts of man, as proposed by Adler, expounded by phenomenologists and carried further by onto-analysis, will either not be comprehended by the students of psychology or will be misunderstood by them and even by many who otherwise lead the field into new dimensions of thinking (Ansbacher & Ansbacher, 1956).

Were it not for these changes in scientific thinking, Adlerian Psychology would have no chance of being widely accepted. Today, however, we witness an upsurge of interest in it. I have found that students find it difficult to change their orientation in order to comprehend and apply the methods developed by Adler and his fellow workers. New studies of probabilities, of decision making, and of learning theories, will probably contribute a great deal to an increased interest in the basic principles on which Adlerians operate.

To recapitulate: to Adlerians, behavior appears as self-determined movement in a given field, and this field is of a social nature. The movement of a person is not caused by any influences to which he is or has been exposed, but by his intentions. These intentions in turn depend on his concepts, on the beliefs which he has formed and primarily on his expectations, which are in line with his plan of action. It makes little difference whether he is aware of this thoughts, plans and intentions; most of our physical and mental activity never reaches the conscious level. Whether or not a person realizes the purposes of his behavior, which he has set for himself, is of little significance. He will know and admit to himself only what he needs and wants to know; in most cases his goals are not known to him since such knowledge may interfere with his pursuits. (The psychological uncertainty principle implies that man is either an actor or an observer, but cannot be both at the same time. Introspection, knowledge of what goes on in him, would interfere with the forcefulness of his actions.)[2] Aware of his goals or not, man very effectively pursues them. While he can never

[2] R. Dreikurs, The Psychological Uncertainty Principle, *Topic Probl. of Psychother.* 1963, 4, 23-31.

be sure of his own goals, because he cannot fully know himself, the trained observer or analyst is in a position to recognize them and bring them to his attention. When a patient or client does something and is asked why he did it, he will answer that he does not know or he will give incorrect rationalizations, because he really does not know why he did it. But when the trained psychologist reveals his goals to him— and this requires a specific skill and technique—then he reacts in most cases with a "recognition reflex." It is revealed in a mixed expression of sheepish surprise at being caught and satisfaction in seeing what he did not see before (Dreikurs, 1958).

This assumption, that since all behavior is purposive, what an individual is doing is always directed toward a purpose, seems pre- posterous to some and superficial to others. The latter look for deeper, more enduring drives, remote from the immediate constellation of in- fluences selectively perceived by the actor and integrated around the achievement of his purpose. Lack of training in teleoanalytic approaches is one of the reasons why so many professionals fail to understand people, and particularly children. The holistic, socio-teleological model of man provides technical approaches that seem to be highly effective, and above all, parsimonious (Adler, 1929; Freud, 1951).

In working with people, as therapists, counselors, teachers, or in any other capacity where psychological approaches are indicated, we are primarily if not exclusively concerned with the goals toward which the individual moves. In a sense, Adlerians are reviving the American pragmatism of Pierce and James, according to which every action gets its meaning from its consequences. We can distinguish short range goals, which are the immediate goals of the present situation, and long range goals, which indicate the individual's movement through life, his "life style." In this way, we perceive the pattern of the individual and of his actions. We see the whole of the movement and can under- stand its significance, without seeking first to establish its precedences and causes.

In order to do this, we have to see the individual operating in a given social arena. Only in this field can the significance of his actions become apparent. Similar behavior under other circumstances may have a completely different meaning, psychologically as well as socially. In this sense, all actions, each behavior pattern, is signficant in its present moment. Thus, we confirm Kurt Lewin's principle of contemporariness. Everything a person does has its meaning right here and now. We do not look in the past for its meaning, nor into his subconscious, nor in any kind of depths which psychologists usually first assume in order to confirm them afterwards. We look at man in terms of those movements that comprise his real existence and try to understand the private logic that makes him decide to move in a given direction. We try to recognize intentions based on the concepts which he has about himself, about others, about life in general, and about the particular situation in which he finds himself. We have to be aware of his perceptions in order to estimate what he is going to do. The cognitive process comprising the ideas and opinions that underly his actions are usually below the level of full awareness. A level of full awareness is highly overrated as a concommitant of behavior; it is seldom reached or needed.

To understand the interpretation which a person gives to his immediate situation, we must know his general outlook on life and the basic assumptions on which he operates. These may give to each actual situation a meaning completely different than someone else would attach to it. Each personality is based on definite assumptions and concepts, integrated in one basic pattern which Adler called the "Life Style" (6, 7, 9, 10, 11). Each of us has his own Life Style, resulting from our understanding of life and what we strive for in our attempt to find a place for ourselves.

These long range goals of the Life Style have been called fictitious. They constitute an idea of security which does not exist in life, an assumption of validity which is not universal, an abstraction and overgeneralization of partially correct approaches (Ansbacher and Ansbacher, 1956; Way, 1950). They result from misunderstandings in observing the world during the formative years and childhood, when we form our personal convictions. Once such a conviction is formed, one acts "as if" it were the absolute truth and the only possible choice (Vaihinger, 1925). To the extent to which our ideas of life are correct, we can function well in given situations. If we fail or misbehave, then we are acting under the impact of mistaken ideas about ourselves and about life, and particularly about the means by which we can find a place in life. These mistakes have to be recognized if we wish to help, correct, improve and treat people who are deficient or maladjusted.

While our theoretical orientation explains psychopathology, in contrast to other orientations it also permits—perhaps for the first time —a definition of normality. Adler's model of man permits a clear distinction of what is normal and what is not. Such a differentiation is almost absent in contemporary social science. Contrary to prevalent beliefs, social science is still in a prescientific stage, despite the fact that it uses the scientific method of exploration. Nevertheless, it has not established any global laws and, therefore, finds itself in the same state in which physics was before basic physical laws were discovered. Isolated phenomena were studied empirically, but their integration into one body of knowledge was impossible because the underlying basic laws were unknown.

The lack of such global laws in the social sciences is probably due to the fact that present scientific tools are inadequate to deal with the complexities that are found in the social and behavioral sciences. Since social research concerns itself with individual communities or societies, it is not surprising that each society or group is considered qualified to determine what is normal and what is abnormal behavior. Most social scientists are inclined to assume that normality depends entirely on the judgment of society. However, it is obvious that not all human societies function in a way compatible with our own idea of correct behavior. Does this mean merely a difference between social systems, in which each one has the right to establish its own norms? Are there any social and ethical values possible outside those established in a given society? Many believe in a Divine Law which supersedes temporal laws; some look for a transcendental basis for ethical standards. The quest for absolute social value is pursued constantly, but our social theorists have found no universal answer, and meanwhile various contradictory theories and beliefs compete for ascendancy. Only when we know the basic laws that regulate the relationship between individuals and between groups can we have a reliable yardstick by which not only individual behavior but societies can be judged. Only then can the contradictory laws advanced by different societies be examined and ranked in terms of the degree to which they distort the meaning of social living, as do individuals in their neuroses, psychoses and all the other manifold forms of maladjustment.

Adler provided just such a yardstick to measure the normality of an individual and of a society with its norms and regulations. "Norm" is not merely the absence of abnormality, nor the average. We feel justified in stating that it may be normal today to be abnormal—and this certainly holds true for our children. But by what standard can a norm be established? Where does abnormality begin? It begins where the Social Interest ends. In other words, adjustment and normality imply the ability to function adequately in any conceivable situation, and this ability depends on a fully developed Social Interest. One does not have to have symptoms or to be overtly sick and deficient to be abnormal in this sense. An inability to function may not become obvious, but diminished Social Interest constitutes vulnerability, regardless whether it is tested or not. Only when it is tested does a deficiency in functioning become evident. In other words, the normal person is one with an optimally developed Social Interest, who feels belonging, is willing and able to participate and to contribute, is concerned with the needs of his situation and the welfare of those to whom he feels belonging (Adler, 1929a). Any limitation or restriction of Social Interest implies pathology and abnormality, whether small and insignificant or full blown. If the full development of Social Interest is really the prerequisite for mental and social adjustment and health, then it is obvious that we in our society are far from normal.

If this is true, then one may well assume that our society is not normal either. But how can that be measured? Adler attempted to establish a basic law of social cooperation, in speaking of the "iron clad logic of social living" (Ansbacher & Ansbacher, 1956). There is a logic, a fundamental law in social living, and any society and any individual violating it will run into trouble. On the other hand, anyone who senses and accepts this intrinsic knowledge of social living will be able to function adequately and successfully. Adler considered equality as the basic requirement for harmonious social relationships, and he believed that only among equals can social harmony exist. Wherever one individual or group sets itself up as superior to any other, the relationship is disturbed. It becomes unstable, since the one in the dominant position must constantly fear loss of status, and the subordinate individual, the one in an inferior position, will always try to free himself from this predicament. Nobody wants to be less than another.

While the concept of equality is difficult to comprehend, it is all-important for both social and political progress as well as for education, counseling and psychotherapy (Dreikurs, 1961). Psychopathology, neurosis, deficiency, and maladjustment are the result of one's doubt of one's worth, of one's status and ability (Adler, 1929). Only people who feel equal to those around them can be sure of their place. If they doubt their equality, if they feel inferior or inadequate, then they must regard their fellow men as their enemies, against whom they have to defend themselves. Out of this defensiveness comes psychopathology. It is equally disturbing for cooperation if one tries to elevate himself over others or gives up in discouragement, resigning himself to an inferior position. Even those who succeed in compensating or over-compensating for a sense of deficiency and inferiority can never find peace of mind or a feeling of security. Inevitably they must feel vulnerable for they can never be sure of remaining superior by being sufficiently ahead of others.

A sense of security is only possible if one is sure of his place, sure of his ability to cope with whatever may come, and sure of his worth and value. Anyone who believes he must energetically seek his place will never find it. He does not know that by his mere presence he already does belong and has a place. If one has to be more than he is in order to be somebody, he will never be anybody. If one does not realize that he is good enough as he is, he will never have any reason to assume that he is good enough, regardless of how much money, power, superiority, and academic distinction he may amass. It is obvious that in our society few people believe they are good enough as they are, and can therefore be sure of their esteemed place. Everyone tries to be more, to be better, to reach higher, and as a consequence, we are all neurotic, in a neurotic society which pays a premium to the over-ambitious search for prestige and striving for superiority. This search inspires a desire for self-elevation and personal glory, thereby restricting our ability for co-operation and our sense of human fellowship. Yet underneath we are all frightened people, not sure of ourselves, of our worth, or of our place. It is this doubt of oneself, expressed in a feeling of inadequacy and inferiority, which restricts our Social Interest and which is at the root of all maladjustment and psychopathology (Adler, 1929b).

In contrast to the motivation for self-elevation, which at great human expense can produce useful contributions, movement is possible on the horizontal plane, where we might desire to contribute, to share, to participate and to grow, out of a feeling of belonging, of enthusiasm, of expansion and of exploration. This motivation finds little stimulation in our society, either in our homes or our schools. According to the value system in our society, parents and teachers and fellow men instill in each one of us considerable doubt of our own strength and value. Only those who resist this constant threat to their self-confidence receive support and reassurance. The less self-confidence a person has, the less encouragement he receives and the more his low opinion of himself finds confirmation. Our methods of raising children constitute a series of discouraging experiences (Dreikurs, 1958). We raise children in the constant fear that they are not measuring up, that they are not good enough as they are. We are afraid that being satisfied with themselves would stop them from growing and developing. We think that only a drive toward self-elevation and glory can stimulate, and that only fear of losing status can prompt conformity and effort. We are living in a neurotic culture where no one is sure of his place, although everyone has one.

This paradox can be demonstrated in a simple situation. If a student enters a new class, meeting others he has never known before, he may look around and ask himself how he will fit in. He may see himself as a nonentity and the others as all-important and dangerous. Rarely does he realize that for everyone else, he, even as a newcomer, is part of the class, threatening to the others' status and position. We stand in awe of life and all the magnificence of a thunder-storm, of a snow-capped mountain, of a huge waterfall, but we do not realize that *we* are life as well. We feel: *there* is life and *here* am I. We have no realization that the same power of nature is within ourselves, at our disposal. In dealing with a deficient individual, we can trace the evolution of erroneous ideas about himself and his failure to recognize his strength, the only attribute on which he can rely to give him security (Wolfe, 1934). We can trace the development of his fictitious ideals of power, of beauty, of education, or of possessions which would guarantee him a social place (Way, 1950). They are all fictitious ideas of security, for nothing that one can get from the outside can provide it, since one can never be sure that he has enough, or that he may not lose what he has. Psychotherapy actually consists of a planned effort to extricate the individual from the faulty social values of our society and to restore the self-confidence which he has lost in his past struggles with people who actually or in his interpretation deprive him of a feeling of worth (Dreikurs, 1957). All corrective efforts attempt to counteract these impressions and their detrimental consequences for the person's ability to function.

Let us now examine the factors which contribute to the development of the personality, which form the field of experience that is perceived and interpreted by each individual in his own way. These interpretations are the basis of his attitudes and concepts, of his Life Style.

There are, first, two opposing sets of experiences, presented by heredity and environment. Our prevalent mechanistic orientation leads to the general assumption that the individual is the result of hereditary endowment and environmental influences. In this scheme of thought, the individual is just a passive background on which hereditary traits encounter environmental stimulations and inhibitions. These forces are viewed as being engaged in a furious struggle, in the course of which the hapless individual is molded (Ansbacher & Ansbacher, 1956). The relative significance which a person attributes to heredity or environment seems to depend on his political outlook. The more conservative or reactionary he is, the more importance does he place on hereditary endowment; the more liberal, the greater the influence he attributes to environmental stimulations. (The pre-Hitler German psychiatrist Lange emphasized heredity in contrast to the American Watson's and the Russian Bechterev's belief in the primacy of environmental forces.) Adler felt that such mechanistic views eliminated the most important factor, namely, the individual himself. In his study of organ inferiority he observed that two individuals born with the same physical handicap or weakness may respond in an entirely different and opposite way to the same kind of deficiency which they experience in their body—their "Inner environment," as we call it. They may either stop functioning in the area where they feel deficient ánd thereby develop a full and lasting deficiency, or they may try to overcome their deficiency and in this way develop special skills in the very area in which they had encountered a difficulty of function. Therefore, what one is born with is less important than what one does with it afterwards (Ansbacher & Ansbacher, 1956).

This asserts the child's ability to decide what to do with an obstacle he encounters, although such a decision does not take place on the conscious level, for the child may not have developed more than a rudimentary verbal capacity when such a decision is required. Adler's contention of such freedom of choice was—and still is—incomprehensible to most students of psychology. They want to know what induces one child to give up, another to compensate, and still another to over-compensate. They cannot believe there is nothing that "makes" a child do it; that it is his own conclusion, his own response, his own evaluation of the situation which is influential. It is a creative act, which in itself is a phenomenon that our deterministically oriented contemporaries find difficult to comprehend.

We have to re-evaluate our concepts about infants. Their ability to size up situations and to act in accordance with their own evaluation of them transcends any notion we have about early childhood (Dreikurs, 1958). Normal infants, born to deaf mute parents, will cry with tears running down their cheeks, with face distorted and body shaking—but without a sound. They won't waste any sound on parents who do not respond to it. Even an infant a few months old can dominate a whole family of intelligent and powerful adults, who are no match for his determination and resourcefulness. To underestimate the power and ability of children is characteristic of our time. We consider them victims while they are becoming our masters. Neither the hereditary endowment nor the pressure of the environment can make a child behave in a given way. It is the child who interprets his experiences and situations, draws his conclusions about them, and acts in accordance with his perceptions and decisions.

Research into the laws of probability may eventually contribute to an understanding of the way a child develops his personality. Although he may start off with random choices, as soon as he makes one choice, this limits the number of next choices that are possible. By choosing his responses to the stimulations to which he is exposed, he tries to discover what is effective, what gives him desired results. He develops his own ideas about what is desirable to him and how he can obtain it. In establishing such a pattern, he eventually evolves a system of opinions and movements which, around the age of four and five, are pretty firmly entrenched. At that time the child has developed definite ideas of how to cope with people around him, how to meet difficulties and how to respond to frustrations.

The child, with his own concepts about life, people and himself, is well equipped to influence his parents so that they respond to him in line with his expectations, while they are usually at a loss as to how to make the child comply with their demands. As a whole society, we fail to realize the extent to which children in a democratic setting can influence adults, their parents and teachers alike, while we cling to the outdated notion that children are the result of what their parents, particularly their mothers, do to them. A mother who is accused of rejecting a child in most cases behaves in such a way that this accusation seems justified; however, the child, who for one reason or another comes to the conclusion that he is not properly loved, behaves in such a way that she constantly has to scold him. This in turn proves to him that his assumption of not being loved was correct.

In our culture, the average parent tries to do more for his children and is more concerned with their welfare than ever before in history. Most parents would sacrifice anything for the welfare of their child. And yet, there were probably never as many children who are sure that they are not loved. How is this possible? Because children are excellent observers and poor interpreters. A child who has experienced the constant attention and concern of his parents may think that being loved means getting constant attention, service, gifts, affection and whatever else he wants. Therefore, he concludes that he is no longer loved if he does not remain the center of attention, as occurs when a brother or sister is born. He really believes that his mother does not love him any more when she spends less time with him. Or some children act on the assumption that being loved means having the right to do as they please. "If you oppose me in any way, you don't care for me. If you loved me, you would let me do what I want." Children may often voice such convictions, while others may only act in accordance with them, without being fully aware of the reason that they feel insufficiently loved. But again, once they have this conviction, they proceed to prove its correctness, and untrained parents and teachers are victimized and thereby reconfirm the child's mistaken assumptions.

Unfortunately, not only unsophisticated parents and insufficiently trained teachers accept the child's mistaken evaluation of his situation. Many a disturbed child is seen by a child psychiatrist or counselor who spends hours, weeks and months with the child, listening to what he has to say and how he feels, and then comes to the conclusion that the child *is* rejected. This he then proceeds to tell the child's mother. In our over-protectiveness of children, we fail to see how they provoke, to a large extent, the treatment they receive, particularly when they are not our own children. We blame parents, teachers and society instead of helping the victims of a whole segment of our society who have found their freedom without accepting full responsibility for what they are doing. Unfortunately, in our democratic setting, a reversal to punitive retaliation and suppression has no chance to succeed either. It can only prompt more determined defiance and rebellion on the part of the children who, as a whole generation, are at war with adults— sometimes only in certain aspects of their daily living, sometimes completely and openly.

It is obvious that Adlerians see the child in a different light than is the custom today. His behavior has to be seen in the total field of his operation, and he has to be considered as an active participant from the beginning, and not as a passive recipient of what others do to him. He injects himself very early into the transactions of his family. It is his way of dealing with them and moving in the given family situation that develops his personality. He encounters his environment with all the problems it involves and takes a stand, not only for or against certain demands, but by making his own demands. If he wants to be picked up, he knows how to achieve that. If his parents are reluctant and try to convince him he shouldn't be picked up, he may cry until the parents weaken—which they usually do even after a temporary demonstration of power and assertion. It is obvious to anyone who observes the total field that children manage their parents pretty successfully and make them submit to their demands.

What are their demands? Usually parents—and teachers as well—are utterly unaware of what the children want, for it is not what the child says he wants. The overt contest between the child's conduct and the adult's objections or requests has little to do with the "issues" involved. The child, in any conflict between him and adults, uses whatever issue is convenient to pursue one of four goals (Dreikurs, 1957). These I have described as "the four goals of disturbing behavior in children." As long as the child cooperates and conforms, his goal is participation and contribution, fulfilling the implicit requirements of the given situation. When he misbehaves, he has other goals, all of which are related to his ideas of finding a place. They are, therefore, erroneous means of social participation.

The first goal is a bid for *attention* and *service*. It is found in most young children who cannot perceive their ability to find their place through what they do; therefore, they think that their place depends on what others do for them. If the struggle to stop the child's demand for undue attention becomes more intense, then the child tries to demonstrate his *power,* which is the second goal. He will refuse to do what he is told, and insist on doing what is forbidden. Should this fight become more intense and vicious, then the child cannot conceive of any other means of proving his existence than through hurting others. Thus the third goal is *revenge.* And then there are children who want to be left alone, because they are so discouraged that any demand to do something would only demonstrate their deficiency more painfully. Flaunting a real or assumed deficiency *in order to be left alone* is the fourth goal. The child is not aware of the reasons for his actions, but if properly confronted with his intentions, he quickly recognizes the situation and responds with a "Recognition Reflex." Unfortunately, neither parents nor teachers are trained to recognize the child's goals and to counteract them. As a consequence, in most cases, they do exactly what the child expects them to do. Instead of improving the situation, most corrective efforts actually enhance the child's mistaken goals and strengthen his objectionable goal-directed behavior.

These are principles applying to the behavior of children in general. They permit a psychological understanding of children and their problems without any investigation of their individual personalities. For this reason, our theory about personality development and the dynamics of behavior provides important psychological tools for those who work with people professionally and yet are not always able to explore the individual background development of each person. However, a clear perception of a person as a distinct individual requires information about certain circumstances during his formative years. From our holistic point of view, the developing pattern of the personality is linked to certain environmental patterns which are of fundamental importance and constitute significant aspects of social experiences to which the child is exposed. Hence, we do not consider *all* isolated experiences and stimulation as having a distinct influence on personality development, nor seek to unravel the almost endless series of isolated stimulations. Rather, we look for specific patterns in which all stimulations are imbedded and through which they derive their significance.

The first of these is *the family atmosphere*. The child has no direct access to society; he encounters society through his parents, who establish the characteristic pattern of each family. Through them he experiences the social values of his time—the economic, racial, national, and social conditions that affect his particular family. These conditions pertain to all children of the family alike. The parents communicate their concepts to their children, and exemplify them in their behavior, which is not random but displays a definite, recurrent pattern of relationships. One can say, by and large, that what children have in common is due to this family atmosphere, which creates a basis for values, for patterns of human relationship and for modes of behavior. The parents, by their relationship, demonstrate not only the functions of each sex, but a pattern of interactions that is usually followed by the children.

However, it is evident that the children of any one family are far from being alike, at least in our competitive society with its emphasis on superiority and inferiority. The dissimilarity of children within the same family is understandable through an examination of the specific *family constellation* (2, 3, 4, 6, 7, 9, 10, 19). The first and second child of almost every family are fundamentally different, in character, interest and abilities. This has so far escaped the attention of most experts in psychology and psychiatry (Adler, 1928). It cannot be explained by current concepts of behavior. It defies the laws of heredity, which do not provide any rationale for the difference that is always observed between the first and second child. Nor could past stimulations or the psychosexual development of each child account for the regularity of the difference.

The Adlerian interpretation of behavior provides a more satis-factory explanation than any advanced thus far. The difference in personalities of the first and second child becomes understandable if we regard character traits as modes of behavior and behavior itself as purposive, as directed toward a specific goal. In our democratic, com-petitive society, no child wants to be inferior to another. Therefore, if children are competitive, then each will move in the direction where the other fails or encounters difficulties, and in turn will shun activities where the other excels. Experience shows that the strongest competi-tion is between the first and second child. The first born wants to stay ahead, and the second does not want to remain behind. Thus, each watches for the other's areas of failure and success and acts accordingly. If the first is excellent in school, the second—in a competitive family—may not be interested in school but in other activities where the first may show a lack of interest or ability. However, if the first encounters a teacher who discourages him and consequently falls back, then the second may move in and become a good student. In this way, the children influence each other more than the parents influence them. The parents usually have no idea of what is going on, and what they are doing is apt to fortify and intensify competition and to re-affirm their childrens' assumptions of success or failure. The sibling who is most different is the one who exerts the greatest influence on person-ality development; each tries to find a different way to have his place, as each becomes discouraged by the success of the other.

Here is a typical example: A young woman, a literary agent, came to me for therapy. She had no friends, no dates, and her life consisted mainly of work. She wanted to get married, but could neither attract men nor come close to anyone. In her formative years she was impressed with the success of her older sister as a beautiful child. As they grew older, her sister became exceedingly popular with boys. Her parents forced her to take her younger sister along when she went out, and our patient felt like the fifth wheel on a wagon. She was sure that nobody except her parents liked her, and that she just had no chance to be socially, and in particular, sexually attractive. She was neither as pretty as her sister nor could she impress others the way her sister did. In the course of treatment, her mistaken ideas about her "inability" to make friends and to attract men were corrected and she made a good adjustment, giving up her high standards and her doubts as well. (This is, of course, an over-simplified account of all her problems and their meaning, but it emphasizes the crucial role her sister played in her life.)

One day she reported that her sister had come into town and wanted to talk with me. She had lived in Europe, become involved in a scandal with a man, and had come back home. As she walked into my office it became immediately apparent that she put all her eggs into one basket—her femininity. She was not only attractive but highly seductive, in the way she walked, carried and expressed herself. When she spoke about her difficulties, it was only about her relationship with men. She always tried to conquer and wanted and received constant approval as a woman. She had been married and divorced and had had numerous affairs, which ended either with her losing interest or through a scandal. Discussing with her the reason for her limitations in seeking success only in the sexual area, she immediately pointed to her sister who, because she was "good" and did well in school, was favored by the parents. "I had no chance to compete with her except by having my own way, and a lot of boy friends." It was obvious that each of the sisters blamed the other for her discouragement; each regarded the other as a "real success" and considered her own achievements to be meaningless. I told the two girls to get together and to decide who was superior to whom. This had a dramatic effect on both girls, when they realized that each had motivated her parents to draw invidious comparisons between them. The parents had actually followed the lead of each girl, impressing the older with the goodness and scholastic success of the younger, and telling the younger to be outgoing and have friends like her sister, thereby reinforcing each one's sense of inadequacy.

In a similar way, children confirm each other's erroneous ideas about themselves. The family constellation provides each with a unique position and lets each develop his own approaches, in contrast or in line with those of others. The children who compete with each other develop in opposite directions, while those who are allied with each other become more alike. The lines of demarcation depend first of all on the sequence of birth. This gives each a special place, as the first, second, middle or youngest child. But this position does not "determine" each one's development; it merely provides him with special opportunities which he utilizes in the equilibrium he establishes with the other members of his family. Each is affected by each other member of the family, as he in turn affects them. Various other factors provide a child with special opportunities, either by being an only boy or an only girl, by being sickly or being outstanding through any other accidental circumstance.

This interaction within the family during the formative years is the basis for the personality development of each child. Whatever concepts he develops then are maintained throughout life and constitute the basis for his style of life. This is not the result of forces converging on him, of stimulations which he has received, or of incidental occurrences. These constitute merely opportunities. Under the same circumstances he could have developed differently had he responded differently to the situation which he encountered. With each adult patient we can determine his life style, his present *modus operandi,* by exploring the family constellation during his formative years. Then we can show him the movements he has chosen, how he has affected others and been affected by them, children and adults alike. Because of the transaction in which they were all involved, one cannot say that one affected the other. It was a constant relationship in which each developed with each other.

After we know the movements of the patient in his childhood and later through life, we have another highly effective diagnostic tool, which Adler provided: the early recollections (ECR—Early Childhood Recollections) (Adler, 1929b; Adler, 1959c; Mosak, 1958). It has been found that out of all the millions of experiences in our childhood, we remember only those incidents that fit in our outlook on life. If we know what a person remembers from his early childhood, then we know the concepts on the basis of which he operates and his mistaken concepts about himself and life. This projective technique is indispensable if we really want to know the basic structure of a given personality. It was tragic that the verdict of one man, namely Freud, could deprive psychiatry and psychology for almost fifty years of the use of such an important diagnostic tool, used only by Adlerians. Freud, in his *Psychopathology of Everyday Life* (Freud, 1951), declared childhood recollections to be irrelevant; to him they were merely screen memories to cover up really important but repressed traumatic events. Only in the last few years has the significance of early recollections found general recognition (Mosak, 1958). However, many use them in different ways, if they are still preoccupied with instinctual and emotional processes. We concern ourselves primarily with cognitive processes, with the private logic of each person. This becomes clearly visible in early recollections, so that we can understand how a person looks at life and help him to recognize it. This leads to a reorientation which is the final goal of psychotherapy.

All the basic mistakes we make in childhood and continue throughout life are the consequence of doubts in ourself and others and reflect an underestimation of our strength. The mistaken movements we make in life are the consequences. Therefore, an effective reorientation is only possible when we help the patient to restore his self-confidence, free him from his prejudice against himself, from the doubts with which he grew up and the unnecessary limitations which he accepts for himself. Once he can believe in himself and his strength, he can gain this inner freedom, where he no longer questions his place in society but feels able to cope with it, because he is no longer confronted with the danger of his inferiority nor with the compulsion to be superior. He is not preoccupied alone with success or failure, but rather with the task at hand (Dreikurs, 1957).

In this sense, then, Adlerian psychology represents a social rehabilitation therapy, a *behavioral therapy,* as Eysenck (1959) calls it. Psychotherapy is not a medical treatment but an educational process. The person learns to understand himself and his life. Psychotherapy implies a change of concepts, a change in the modes of finding one's place, an increase in the feeling of belonging through the diminution of self-doubt and of inferiority feelings. This is the basis for all correctional efforts: to overcome doubts about value and ability, and to develop a sufficient Social Interest to cope successfully with life and people.

REFERENCES

ADLER, A. *Study of organ inferiority and its psychical compensation.* New York: Nerv. Ment. Dis. Publ. Co., 1917.

ADLER, A. Characteristics of the first, second and third child. *Children,* 1928, *3,* 14-52.

ADLER, A. *Problems of neurosis.* London: Kegan Paul, Trench, Trubner, 1929. (a)

ADLER, A. *The science of living.* New York: Greenberg, 1929. (b)

ADLER, A. *The case of Miss R.* New York: Greenberg, 1929. (c)

ADLER, A. *The education of children.* London: Allen & Unwin, 1930.

Adler, A. *Social interest*. London: Faber & Faber, 1938.

Adler, A. *The practice and theory of Individual Psychology*. Paterson, N. J.: Littlefield, Adams, 1959. (a)

Adler, A. *Understanding human nature*. New York: Premier Books, 1959. (b)

Adler, A. *What life should mean to you*. New York: Capricorn Books, 1959. (c)

Ansbacher, H. L., & Ansbacher Rowena. *The Individual Psychology of Alfred Adler*. New York: Basic Books, 1956.

Dreikurs, R. Psychotherapy as correction of faulty social values. *J. indiv. Psychol.*, 1957, *2*, 150-158.

Dreikurs, R. *The challenge of parenthood*. New York: Duell, Sloan and Pearce, 1958.

Dreikurs, R. *Equality: The challenge of our times*. Chicago: Author, 1961.

Eysenck, H. (Ed.) *Behaviour therapy and the neuroses*. London: Pergamon, 1959.

Freud, S. *Psychopathology of everyday life*. New York: New Amer. Libr., 1951.

Mosak, H. H. Early recollections as a projective technique. *J. proj. Tech.*, 1958, *22*, 303-31.

Mosak, H. H. The getting type, a parsimonious social interpretation of the oral character. *J. indiv. Psychol.*, 1959, *15*, 193-196.

Shulman, B. H. The family constellation in personality diagnosis. *J. indiv. Psychol.*, 1962, *18*, 35-47.

Vaihinger, H. *The philosophy of "as if."* New York: Harcourt, Brace. 1925.

Way, L. *Adler's place in psychology*. London: Allen and Unwin, 1950.

Wolfe, W. B. *How to be happy though human*. London: Routledge and Kegan Paul, 1932.

Wolfe, W. B. *Nervous breakdown: Its cause and cure*. London: Routledge and Kegan Paul, 1934.

10

Personality Theory
in Behavioristic Psychology

Robert W. Lundin

As a formal system of psychology, behaviorism began with the writings of John Watson (1913). One of Watson's greatest contributions to the science of psychology was his abandonment of the notion of "mind," which he identified with spiritualism. He observed that if psychology were ever to advance toward a science of behavior, rather than remaining as mental philosophy, it must limit itself to the study of natural events which could be objectively observed. He noted further, that in all other sciences the facts of observation were objective and verifiable; they were public rather than private events.

Nevertheless, the mentalism to which Watson objected still exists today. Although its proponents continue to rely on constructs which are not susceptible to observational proof, it has become appreciably more sophisticated and subtle. Theoretical conceptions are not so simple as those reflected in the mental chemistry of Wundt and Titchener, the mental functions of the Functionalists or psychic apparatus as described by Freud. Nevertheless, from the standpoint of the behaviorist, any theory which incorporates propositions not open to verification through objective observation is "mentalistic." Any theory, no matter how elegantly and logically stated, which in the final analysis depends upon such ineffable concepts as "psychic energy" or "unconscious processes" is, in the behavioral view, prescientific.

We are also indebted to Watson for his clear statement of the appropriate aims of a scientific psychology. He believed that prediction and control are necessary goals of any science and for the student of personality this means prediction and control of human behavior. Watson was convinced that eventually, through systematic observation and experimentation, the principles underlying man's behavior could be discovered. Thus as we learn more and more about the conditions under which particular behaviors occur, that is, more about the stimulus properties of observable or controllable events on organisms with ascertainable response repertories, the greater capacity we have to predict the probability of a given response or series of responses occurring in the future.

The modern behaviorist still holds in principle to these objectives and believes we have made significant progress since Watson's time toward achieving these aims of prediction and control. Extensive experimentation and carefully controlled observations have allowed us to discover many of the laws governing man's conduct. Furthermore, a better technology with more precise instrumentation allows us to manipulate as well as control the proper variables in a scientific investigation.

Of course, the behaviorism of today is not the same as that of Watson's day. Nonetheless, some opponents of behaviorism, overlooking the progress and change which have occurred, focus their attack on behaviorism as it was forty years ago. In today's terminology, one can say he is a behaviorist if he believes psychology to be the study of observable behavior and that the methods employed are the methods of science, namely, controlled systematic observation including experimentation. Now there are many kinds of experiments, some of which are poorly conceived and others which are carefully controlled and executed. The behaviorist identifies himself with the latter in which the stimulus variables are appropriately manipulated, exact controls are executed, and the resulting behavior can be accurately observed and measured.

1. THE BEHAVIORIST'S INTEREST IN PERSONALITY

Critics of behaviorism have accused its representatives of completely ignoring the study of personality as a field of psychology, of failing to accept any responsibility for its problems and data. Rejection of the human personality as a desirable object of study may typify some psychologists who restrict their interests to problems which can be answered by running rats through mazes, putting pigeons on complicated schedules of reinforcement or studying the behavior characteristic of a monkey's avoidance of electric shock. Such observations by critics of the behaviorists are not without justification. Many experimental psychologists (typically behavioristically oriented) are not strongly motivated to reconcile their research findings with data or theory outside their narrow focus of interest. As in any other science, there are psychologists whose preoccupation with the technical aspects of data collection and analysis obscures any aspiration they may once have had to apply their findings to the better understanding of human behavior. The construction and maintenance of complicated apparatus instead of being a means to an end becomes an end in itself. Particular methods of data collection, instead of being subordinated to the theoretical issue to be explored, become the prime interest. Research problems are designed to fit the apparatus instead of the reverse. The most creative and productive experimentalists never abandon their identification with the broad aims of psychology and are quite comfortable in making direct or speculative application of their findings to problems posed by personality theorists. It is most often those behaviorists who are dedicated to the ever more minute investigation of a limited area of interest who aggressively suggest that psychology should rid itself of the term "personality" along with issues and problems raised by the study of man as he functions in his normal milieu.

Having admitted that such criticism has some basis in fact, one must quickly add that it does not apply to all behaviorists. There are many psychologists who call themselves behaviorists, and quite legitimately so, who are very much concerned with problems involved in the psychology of personality. They feel that personality is a legitimate field for the psychologist to study and that the problems of personality are a rightful concern of objective psychologists. The recent publication of such works as T. R. Sarbin's *Studies in Behavior Pathology: the experimental approach to the psychology of the abnormal* (1961), A. J. Bachrach's *Experimental foundations of clinical psychology* (1962) and R. W. Lundin's *Personality: an experimental approach* (1961) attest to the renewed interest on the part of scientifically minded psychologists in personality and its related areas.

The interest of the behaviorist in the psychology of personality has its roots in the history of behavioristic psychology. Watson (1930), despite the assertions of his critics that he was merely a "muscle twitch" psychologist, was concerned with personality and considered it a legitimate domain of study for the psychologist. He considered personality to be the sum of activities that can be discovered by actual observation of behavior over a long enough period of time to give reliable information. He thought of personality as the end product of our habit systems. The way to discover just what an individual's personality consisted of was to plot a cross section of his activity stream.

Although J. R. Kantor has preferred to be called an "interbehaviorist" his systematic approach has been in the behaviorist tradition. His monumental two volume work, *Principles of Psychology* (1924-26) devotes many chapters to what he calls the *psychological individual* or *personality,* as well as to the psychological organism or *personality in action.* Kantor has considered the conception of personality to be one of the most important unifying principles in the whole range of psychology. His view is that every action we perform represents some phase of the operation of the behaving personality. Even though we may legitimately study reactions abstracted from the full repertoire of behavior, he believes we must not lose sight of the fact that we are dealing with an entire behaving organism. Without knowing the characteristics of the organism with which we are dealing, it is impossible to predict behavior of interest to a psychologist. Kantor, then, considers personality to be an individual's particular series of reaction systems to specific stimuli. Such a conception of personality is just as useful today as it was when Kantor first presented it in 1924.

As psychological theory and research developed, behavioristically inclined psychologists have tended to direct their interest toward specific areas of behavior, particularly learning, and more often than not, the dependent variables studied were precisely measured responses of limited scope. Clark Hull, B. F. Skinner, Edwin Guthrie, and Edward C. Tolman were the giants of this era, which can scarcely be said to have run its course despite forceful entry onto the stage of proponents of the mathematical models of learining. Yet learning theorists, whatever contributions to a general theory of behavior they may have believed to be implied in their work, have had little to say that is directly applicable to personality theory or for that matter, to many other fields of psychology.

In 1950, Dollard and Miller provided a bridge between learning theory and personality theory when in their book *Personality and Psychotherapy* they undertook to apply Hull's learning theories of the day. This volume helped promote the attitude that personality theorists might well draw upon principles of learning as demonstrated in the experimental laboratory. Miller's (1944) many studies on conflict, approach and avoidance gradients in conflict and the generalization of avoidance reactions, have led the way toward a rational experimental approach to problems of personality. In 1961 the present writer attempted a similar task (Lundin, 1961), namely to develop a systematic psychology of personality based on the approach to learning first advanced by B. F. Skinner (1938).

2. THE BEHAVIORIST'S CRITIQUE OF OTHER PERSONALITY THEORISTS

Hall and Lindzey (1957) have stated that personality theories as a group tend to lack explicitness. In other words, it is often difficult to obtain a stable definition of their assumption and frequently basic and derivative propositions are not presented in a logical and systematic manner. Furthermore, there is usually much difficulty in arriving at convincing empirical demonstrations of their hypothetical constructs. If the verifiability of hypothesis is a criterion of good theory, the constructs in many personality theories fall short. The problem is *not* that the hypotheses are so far unverified. It is that they *cannot* by their very nature *be* verified. Constructs which refer to ineffable and undemonstrable events can never lead to empirical statements of fact or principle.

Difficulties with psychoanalysis: As an example of this point, let us take the psychoanalytic psychology of Freud and its variations, theories that are fascinating to read and which have great explanatory power but which are on the whole completely unsusceptible to empirical verifications. Although our criticisms are aimed directly at psychoanalysis, they can apply equally well in principle to many other personality theories including personology, phenomenology and the like.

One of Freud's greatest contributions to psychology was his application of the principle of cause and effect to human behavior. Like the behaviorist, Freud was a thoroughgoing determinist, despite his impatience with quantifiable data and with empirical proof. However, Freud may have done a disservice to scientific psychology when he postulated a mental apparatus which did not necessarily possess physical dimensions, but nonetheless was capable of geographic description. Many of Freud's followers have been induced to regard this hypothetical mental apparatus as being real, but this is, in effect the substitution of a fictional construct for objective reality. Skinner (1954) has suggested that such metaphorical devices as postulated by Freud (ego, psychic forces, cathexis, anti-cathexis, etc.) are inevitable in the early stages of any science, but if we have learned anything from the logic of modern science, there is no need to continue in the mistakes of our childhood and adolescence.

Part of the time Freud located the causes of behavior inside the organism, that is within the psychic apparatus. At other times, he referred to external causes in the environment and past history of the organism. Thus Freud had three links in his causal chain of events— the external event, the mental apparatus and the resulting symptom. Two marked disadvantages grow out of this arrangement when viewed from the standpoint of modern scientific psychology. One is the lack of importance assigned to the first link, the environment, with the consequence that significant, demonstrable forces external to the individual are converted into psychic events which are no longer public. For example, if one punishes a child for sexual misbehavior, we expect to have in our analysis an empirical external event, the punishment, which leads to a marked behavioral change on the part of the organism. But when this change gets transformed into conscious or unconscious anxiety and guilt, many of the specific features of the relation between the two original events get lost.

The other great disadvantage is that the theory of the mental apparatus itself assigns to the inner "psyche" the capacity for initiating behavior rather than limiting this function to a prior external event. Thus the "causes" of behavior become incapable of physical demonstration. Furthermore, the resulting behavior lacks any definite form of physical description. Thus, the nature of the act as a physical unit of behavior is never made clear. The original data, namely overt behavior, was stripped of any quantifiable properties, since they are transformed into memories, psychic forces, ideas or repressions. Freud never developed clearly the idea that the *behavior of the individual* represents the only tangible source of information. Terms such as intra-psychic conflict, defense mechanism or libidinal force imply some kind of relationship among entities with measurable force but in the psychoanalytic literature one is not likely to find empirical referents for these psychic phenomena. Not until psychoanalysis can abandon its fictional constructs and relate its descriptive terminology to physical events in terms of environmental change and measurable, quantifiable behavior can it become a part of scientific psychology. If this were attempted the mental apparatus would be placed in jeopardy and might have to be abandoned. This, the psychoanalytic theorists are reluctant to do (Skinner, 1954).

Difficulties with trait theories: Trait theories have also had considerable currency among psychologists interested in personality and no one questions that they have generated much research resulting in personality tests and similar measures. However in the evaluation of what approach to the study of personality is likely to be the most fruitful, we must ask ourselves whether the concept of traits is the most useful kind of construct. Unlike many psychologists, those trait theorists with a psychometric orientation have taken great pains to integrate theory with empirical evidence deriving from inventories, scales and questionnaires. However, their preoccupation with methods of data analysis, ingenious as they are, may have diverted their attention from more fundamental questions. To be optimally useful, trait measurements should be indicative of future behavior in some sphere other than psychological tests. Yet the predictive validity of tests has been far from satisfactory and this has brought into question the utility of trait theory. The behaviorist would ask whether one might not be able to predict better from single unequivocal, describable responses than from a trait configuration. At best a trait is indicative of a *variety of behaviors,* which appear to have some common descriptive characteristic whereas a single response can be more readily identified and measured. Single responses are more accurately predicted than multiple reactions which could include many behaviors learned under a variety of situations.

For example, one frequently speaks of dominance as a personality trait. A person exhibits dominance in the presence of an acquiescent person, but how does the same person behave in the presence of an equally dominant figure? Traits are at best mere descriptions applied to a general class of responding which appears to share some common characteristics. The fewer traits one defines, the more generalized one has to be and the less accurate one's predictions will become. Personality tests based on the trait approach have limitations in meeting the predictive aim of psychology. Whenever a prediction is made, it is always within a range of probability, and when the chances of being right nearly match those of being wrong, the predictive value of such an instrument is nil. The exhibition of a trait is based on many responses developed in the conditioning history of an organism and each response could have multiple causes. Thus the effectiveness of a trait description as a predictor of behavior is weakened by the multiplicity of variables involved, many of which are largely unknown to the person making the prediction. It seems more profitable to consider specific responses of an organism and then from the variables known to the investigator predict the response that will occur.

3. A REINFORCEMENT THEORY OF PERSONALITY

It is evident thus far from our discussion that the behaviorist's conception of personality grows out of his interpretation of learning. We have already referred to the application of Hull's learning theory to personality as expanded in the writings of Dollard and Miller and their colleagues. The student interested in this kind of behavioristic approach may do well to go to the original sources and in particular to Dollard and Miller's *Personality and Psychotherapy* (1950). An adequate summary of their position may be found in Hall and Lindzey's *Theories of Personality* (1957). We shall present here an alternate approach based primarily on the theoretical position of B. F. Skinner. From our point of view, this approach is preferable because it handles the problems relevant to the study of personality without need for long lists of postulates, hypothetical constructs or intervening variables. Both the positions of Hull and Skinner share at least one point in common, namely, that the conception of *reinforcement* is of paramount importance although they differ in their interpretation of the principle. The significance of the principle will be explained subsequently.

There is no reason to assume that the study of personality offers any new or unique problems for psychology. We can consider the study of personality to be a branch of the general field of learning which investigates in particular those processes significant to human adjustment. To be sure, many contemporary "learning" psychologists prefer to limit themselves to studies of lower animals and are reluctant to use human subjects or to extrapolate their findings to human behavior. Nevertheless, other behaviorists are willing to concern themselves with the problems related to early behavioral development, to motivation, to the effects of aversive stimuli on behavior and the behavioral consequences of frustration and conflict as well as problems of behavior pathology and the role of learning in psychotherapy. It is encouraging to note that today many behaviorists who follow Skinnerian principles are applying their attitudes and methodology to the study of human behavior. Some work at the subhuman level has been given as experimental and demonstrable proof of certain clinical insights. More and more these behaviorists are applying their experimenting to the level of human responding and discovering principles in their own right instead of merely relying on animal studies alone from which they can extrapolate.

It is evident, then, that all behaviorists do not think alike, even those who might concern themselves with the study of personality. Hence, when one asks specifically, "What is the behaviorist's conception of personality?" he must realize that the answer offered on these pages must be qualified as that of one behaviorist—the writer of this chapter. Because the vast majority of man's behavior is learned, the first problem in personality study is to determine under what conditions behavior is acquired. Once this is accomplished, the next problem is that of comprehending the *apparent* exceptions to the general law. At this point the behaviorist as a student of learning enters more fully into the field of personality. We realize that each individual develops under a different or unique set of stimulus conditions and consequently his resulting personality becomes uniquely his own. Personalities that we may designate as peculiar or abnormal, have had, among other things, unusual conditioning histories. People behave similarly, within the limits of their biological endowment, to the degree that they have been conditioned in the same manner. The unique kinds of behavior patterns one acquires over the long history of his psychological development is the behavior peculiar to him and constitutes *his* personality.

Operant and Respondent Behavior: A common distinction made by the behaviorist who follows the reinforcement theory as described in detail by B. F. Skinner (1938) dichotomizes behavior into two main classes of responding, *operant* and *respondent*. In the respondent class fall fairly simple reactions. At the human level the total number of respondents would be fairly small. These are called reflexes and are limited to a group of responses largely physiological in nature. They may be elicited in the organism if the appropriate stimuli are presented. The eliciting stimuli can quite spontaneously, without prior conditioning, call out a response. Illustrations of this class of stimuli might include a bright light for pupil contraction or food in the mouth for salivation. When these stimuli, also called unconditional, become paired with neutral stimuli, that is, stimuli which have had no previous function for the organism, the neutral ones may also take on the properties of the unconditioned stimulus. Conditioned stimuli operating at the level of human development may nevertheless be developed in the same manner as that demonstrated by the Russian physiologist, Ivan Pavlov, on lower animals. Laboratory experiments with dogs revealed that when meat was placed in a dog's mouth, it elicited salivation, but when the ringing of a bell or sounding of a buzzer was paired several time with the presentation of the meat, the sound alone could elicit the salivation. In a similar manner, the mere sight of attractive food (like cake in a bakery window) may elicit salivation or the sight of a painful object might elicit fear.

In all probability some of the behavior we call "emotional" develops according to this procedure and may legitimately be classed as respondent. The classical experiment of Watson and Raynor (1920) illustrates the process in a human infant. These experimenters conditioning crying (fear) in a nine month old infant, Albert, to the sight of a white rat (previously a neutral stimulus). They paired the sight of the animal with a sudden loud noise which was the unconditioned stimulus for eliciting the response. After several such presentations the sight of the rat alone or any other furry object elicited the crying response. Later, by presenting the rat alone without the loud noise, the crying gradually died out, or became extinguished. M. C. Jones (1924), a student of Watson's, tried a slightly different procedure. After a child had been conditioned to cry at the sight of a white rabbit, she presented this conditioned stimulus while the child was eating candy. This procedure hastened the extinction of the crying. In all likelihood, some of our adult fears and even severe phobias have developed in our childhood or infancy through this simple conditioning procedure. Other reactions may have developed in a similar manner. We may generate feelings of anger by showing pictures of the atrocities of our enemies or by telling of their maltreatment of our loved ones. We may give our sweetheart candy or give a good customer an elaborate Christmas gift to generate warmhearted feelings toward us.

Of greater concern, however, is that class of behavior called operant. In earlier days such behavior was typically called voluntary or "willed" in contrast to the involuntary or "unwilled" behavior, now more properly referred to as respondent. The term *operant* is used because the organism in his responding operates on the environment, that is, does something to it. We avoid the terms "voluntary" or "willed" because in actuality these terms are not accurate. These responses are under some form of stimulus control, usually from the external environment, and the problem for the psychologist is to discover what the stimuli are and under what conditions the operant response has developed.

Some years ago B. F. Skinner (1932) developed an experimental technique for the study of animal behavior which has come to be known as *operant conditioning*. This method of experimental analysis of behavior has become increasingly and widely employed in recent years, and has been frequently applied to the conditioning of human behavior particularly in the past decade. The methodology is quite simple to understand and allows for the careful quantification of behavior as well as the application of appropriate experimental controls. In his early studies, Skinner conditioned a rat to press a lever or bar mounted on the side of an experimental chamber. When the rat was placed in this box, in his wanderings about, he eventually pressed the lever downward with sufficient force to record the response on a kymograph. The animal immediately received a bit of food. Since the animal had been food deprived, Skinner noted a rather drastic change in the rat's behavior as a result of this simple operation. The rate of bar pressing increased appreciably and continued at a rapid rate interrupted only by the the time it took the animal to consume the food. Skinner designated the food as a *reinforcing* stimulus because its presentation strengthened the behavior it followed. Furthermore, when the reinforcement was subsequently withheld after several presentations, the conditioned behavior of bar pressing weakened and eventually died out, that is, became extinguished. Many experimental psychologists have found this basic method and its variations to have numerous applications; also a variety of lawful behavioral principles can be demonstrated through a variety of modifications such as introducing new stimuli, changing the reinforcement contingencies, as well as the kinds of reinforcement.

Many skeptics may inquire what such a methodology has to do with the study of personality. The first answer is, of course, that through this technique, the basic principles involved in the acquisition of behavior (personality) can be demonstrated. This behavioristic view, like the psychoanalytic, takes a developmental approach to the study of personality. Since learning is intimately involved in development, a study of the processes of behavior acquisition, modification and weakening is of ultimate importance. Thus, one can learn much concerning how the responses comprising personality are developed by studying groups of individuals who have in common certain salient well defined patterns of reinforcement in their history. One can also observe in natural circumstances a learning situation that can be replicated in the laboratory with better controls so that the results of a laboratory experiment, in many cases, can be applied to a counterpart situation in everyday life to illustrate our understanding of it. Another important consideration is that these techniques readily lend themselves to the study of human (as well as animal) behavior whether the investigator is working with normal, defective or autistic children or normal or psychotic adults.

The validity of the principle of reinforcement has been adequately demonstrated in the laboratory by using a variety of animals including rats, pigeons, or monkeys, frequently with food or liquid as reinforcers under the appropriate conditions of deprivation. In the Skinnerian interpretation of reinforcement, it is not necessary to appeal to internal or intervening variables (such as "drive reduction") to support the explanation. The operational definition is quite simple. We designate as positive reinforcers those stimuli that strengthen a response when they are presented, that is, increase the probability of occurrence of that response on future occasions. There are also negative reinforcers that will be dealt with in a subsequent section.

Those theorists who prefer to postulate inner states and needs frequently ask *why* a reinforcer is reinforcing. For our theoretical approach, the question is not a serious one for, once the function of a reinforcer has been demonstrated, that stimulus can be effectively used in controlling behavior. All one has to do to discover which stimuli reinforce and which do not is to try them out. We then see that the stimulus strengthens the behavior when it is presented and weakens it when taken away. A biological explanation may be as far as we can go in answering the question, "why?" but in the final analysis such an explanation is of little help in the practical control of behavior (Skinner, 1953).

Schedules of Reinforcement: One of the many significant contributions to the study of behavior by the Skinnerians has been the study of how reinforcement can be scheduled. It is obvious that a reinforcement does not need to be applied every time an organism makes a designated response in order to maintain that behavior at a given level or even to strengthen it further. As a matter of fact, certain intermittent schedules of reinforcement have been found to exert the most powerful controls over the organism's behavior. Reinforcements may be scheduled according to some preset time basis, once every minute for example, regardless of how many responses the organism makes in the intervening period (called Fixed Interval schedules, abbreviated FI). Or the reinforcements may be scheduled according to some ratio such as once every fifteen responses (Fixed Ratio, or FR). Likewise the intervals or ratios can be varied so the organism is reinforced on the average once every minute or once every fifteen responses (Variable Interval, VI, or Variable Ratio, VR). The many kinds of schedules may be combined or alternated in countless ways (Ferster & Skinner, 1957). Typically, each kind of schedule will generate its own characteristic pattern of responding, thus demonstrating how the behavior can be placed under the control of the particular schedule in operation. For example, in a Fixed Interval schedule the organism typically shows a degree of temporal discrimination after the schedule has been in operation for some time. His rate will be relatively slow following a reinforcement, gradually picking up speed in a positively accelerated fashion as the time for the next reinforcement approaches. The study of schedules of reinforcement is of more than theoretical importance since in human affairs our behavior is maintained by a variety of schedules, often in combination and usually quite complicated. We may be paid for our work by the hour or week (Fixed Interval) or paid for piece work or on commision (Fixed Ratio), or we attend social gatherings at irregular intervals (Variable Interval). Many gambling devices pay off on some kind of Variable Ratio and the degree of control exerted by the schedule over the behavior of the player is quite remarkable if we consider for a moment the compulsive gambler.

The study of reinforcement scheduling has not only been experimentally demonstrated with animals in a laboratory situation but with humans as well. For example, Bijou (1958) has applied a variety of schedules in the conditioning of pre-school age children. In one experiment he conditioned groups of children under regular reinforcement (every response reinforced) as well as under a variety of intermittent schedules. Instead of using a lever commonly employed as a minipulandum in animal experiments, he used an apparatus similar to a top, painted to resemble the face of a clown. A red lever which could be pressed downward represented the nose of the clown and acted as the response mechanism. Two colored lights represented the eyes and the reinforcements were presented via the mouth (Bijou, 1957). Using some of the schedules mentioned above, he found that the characteristics of responding were not only quite lawful but showed remarkable similarity to the response curves presented for a variety of lower organisms on similar schedules.

In operant conditioning laboratories at Hamilton College it has been found, for example, that the pre-school child when asked to press a telegraph key for pennies as reinforcements on a Fixed Interval schedule will show the same characteristics of responding as found in the pigeon or rat on the same schedule. Indeed, when the response curves are presented to an uninformed observer, he will be unable to identify which curves were recorded for each organism since the characteristics of the temporal discrimination are the same.

Conditioned Reinforcers: The kinds of reinforcement used with animals must be appropriate to their state of deprivation. Food becomes an appropriate reinforcer for the hungry rat and water for a thirsty one. At the level of human responding, it is not always practical to apply deprivation operations. Consequently, conditioned or secondary reinforcers are used. These constitute stimuli which have been appropriately associated with primary reinforcers sometime in the past conditioning history of the organism. They can be demonstrated to operate at both the animal and human levels. In an animal experiment, it is possible to use a light or tone to function as a conditioned reinforcer. Before this is possible, however, it is necessary for that same stimulus first to have acted as a discriminative stimulus. Thus, we must set up a discrimination operation by first reinforcing the organism with a primary reinforcer in the presence of our light or tone and withholding the reinforcement (extinguishing) when the light or tone is off. Eventually, the animal learns to respond only in the presence of the discriminative stimulus. Once such a discrimination has been developed, the conditioned stimulus can act as a reinforcer for other behavior. On future occasions when the animal makes a response which is followed by the stimulus (as a reinforcer), the rate of responding increases reflecting the reinforcing function of the conditioned stimulus. In all likelihood, much of our own human behavior is under the control of conditioned reinforcers. Because each of us has a unique conditioning history, we do not all respond alike to the same reinforcers. Some people are more strongly reinforced by money, others respond more readily to attention or approval of others. The list of conditioned reinforcers at the human level is almost endless. In human experiments, pennies or nickels serve well as reinforcers. With children, trinkets and small toys have commonly been used. However, as with primary reinforcers such as food or liquid, it is possible for the organism to approach a degree of satiation after continued reinforcement. Long and his associates (1958), in using trinkets with children, have found that after a while the behavior deteriorates and the reinforcers no longer operate. To offset this difficulty Stoddard, Sidman and Brady (1960) used as reinforcers tokens which could be exchanged at a variety store for candy, magazines, games, puzzles and the like. This operation bears a similarity to the use of merchandise stamps to influence the grocery buying behavior of housewives. Lindsley (1958) has found with psychotic patients that a variety of stimuli such as candy, cigarettes, seeing nude pictures or watching a live kitten being fed can act as reinforcing stimuli in an experimental situation (see below).

Bijou and Sturges (1959) have pointed out that in a laboratory situation with children the presence of the experimenter can act as a powerful conditioned reinforcer. When a child comes to the experimental situation with a history of social conditioning, signs of approval or expectation from the experimenter can sometimes be more significant than candy or trinkets offered as the contrived reinforcers. It may be difficult for the experimenter to isolate himself from the subject particularly if the experiment is concerned with social interaction. Skinner (1953) has pointed out that certain classes of generalized reinforcers may act powerfully at the human level in controlling behavior. These may include *attention, affection, approval,* or the *submission of others.* It is easy enough to demonstrate by simple experimental operations that for most people these act as positive reinforcers (see section on Verbal Behavior). One might ask, however, exactly how these reinforcers acquired their function in the past conditioning history of the organism since we have already pointed out that at some time in the past they had to be associated with primary reinforcers.

Let us take attention as an example. It is obvious one does not inherit a "need for attention." Rather, in the early life of the child, crying is one of the earliest responses observed. The initial situation may have been pain or discomfort from some internal or external condition such as the absence of food in the stomach, cramps in the bowels or possibly the point of a diaper pin. As a result, vigorous activity is emitted, accompanied by the vocalization. Crying brings the parent who *attends* the child, corrects the situation by feeding him, burping him or removing the pin, thus providing some kind of primary reinforcement. The adult's attentive behavior becomes the discriminative stimulus and the reinforcement is primary. The attentive behavior of the adult is the added stimulus to the occasion. Once, having acquired its stimulus function through early conditioning, attention on the part of parents or other people later operates as a conditioned reinforcer for a great variety of activities that may have no connection with the original conditioning situations.

Aversive Conditioning: Thus far, we have spoken only of positive reinforcers and how they operate in the control of behavior. Of equal importance is a variety of operations involving the use of aversive stimuli, sometimes called negative reinforcers. We refer to *escape, avoidance* and *punishment* reactions. In *escape* behavior, an aversive stimulus is presented until the organism responds and terminates that stimulus. For example, in the animal laboratory a rat may be presented with electric shock to his feet that continues until he presses the lever that terminates the shock for a given period of time. On future trials, as soon as the shock is presented, the animal quickly responds. Like conditioning with positive reinforcement, the escape behavior is strengthened by the *removal* of the stimulus rather than its presentation. In the classical *avoidance* operation, a warning signal is given which at some future time will be followed by a primary aversive stimulus such as an electric shock. The organism may learn to avoid the shock by pressing a lever, thus turning off the warning signal and preventing the onset of the shock. If he misses and fails to respond, the shock eventually occurs. In typical avoidance behavior the warning signal is not only a discriminative stimulus telling the organism that a shock will follow if he does not respond, but because of its pairing with the primary aversive stimulus of shock, it takes on the function of a *conditioned negative reinforcer.* Thus, the organism is reinforced by the removal of the conditioned negative reinforcer, the warning signal. Stable avoidance behavior can be maintained in this way. Eventually, the function of the conditioned negative reinforcer may die out, the rat fails to respond and receives the shock again, thus reconditioning occurs and the negative reinforcer resumes its function.

Sidman (1953) has demonstrated that stable avoidance behavior can also be maintained without the use of a warning signal or exteroceptive stimulus in the following manner. Rats are shocked every 20 seconds if they fail to respond by pressing a bar. If they do respond, however, the shock is forestalled for 20 seconds. So long as the response occurs, each response will forestall the shock for another 20 seconds. It is thus possible for an organism to go for hours without receiving a shock providing he responds within the designated time limit and resets the time period allowed. Brady (1958) has demonstrated that such a procedure can be appropriately applied to monkeys where similar avoidance behavior is readily established. However, the monkeys eventually develop stomach ulcers and ordinarily die. The explanation of stability of such an avoidance schedule of responding with no warning signal is given in terms of the function of the shock. Shock is a punishing stimulus which has the characteristic of depressing behavior (see below). In the process of conditioning the organism is punished for everything he does except for one thing, pressing the bar. All other behavior gets depressed except bar pressing.

The same experimental procedure demonstrated by Sidman (1953) can also apply to human responding. Ader and Tatum (1961) placed medical students on similar schedules of avoidance responding without warning signals with little or no instructions as to what to do. The response measured was pushing a button which could forestall an electric shock for a period of time. Each response would forestall the shock. Most of the subjects developed stable avoidance behavior which co-varied with the amount of time the response was able to delay the shock. Subjects developed a rapid rate of button pressing if the period between shocks was short and a slower rate if the delay period was long. However, there were both qualitative and quantitative differences among the subjects. Some of the subjects failed to acquire the avoidance response and others simply "walked out" of the experimental situation despite the fact they were being paid to serve as subjects (a real avoidance reaction).

The implications of avoidance conditioning are evident for personality development. Many of the effects of excessive avoidance conditioning in early life are seen in the behavior of the adult who chooses a vocation that avoids human contacts as much as possible. We are familiar with the reserved or "distant" individuals who become tense at the approach of strangers and by preference shun other people. For such shy individuals, other people seem to act as conditioned negative reinforcers for the person's avoidance behavior. Perhaps in extreme forms, we see evidence of excessive avoidance behavior in seclusive and schizoid personalities. We observe a detachment, social isolation and loss of social articulation. Certainly the ubiquity of pathological disorders like schizophrenia may be an indication that in society today the preponderance of stimuli are aversive.

Along with escape and avoidance, *punishment* is a common enough aversive operation. Instead of strengthening the response it follows, punishment depresses the response and decreases temporarily the probability of that response occurring again. The consequences of punishing stimuli have several implications. For one thing, such aversive stimuli generate anxiety in the form of respondent behavior that is frequently disruptive. Studies on punishment (Skinner, 1938; Estes, 1944) of animal and human subjects have led to a general conclusion regarding the low utility of punishment in eliminating behavior. For example, when two groups of rats have been conditioned with positive reinforcement and subsequently extinguished, a punishment of electric shock can be superimposed on the extinction responses of the experimental group. Both Estes and Skinner have found that the general effects of punishment are only temporary unless the shock is extremely intense. The response rate of the experimental group (shocked) eventually recovered to the same level of responding as that of the control group that was only extinguished and received no shock.

Without implausible extrapolation, such findings have profound implications for child rearing or, for that matter, in regard to the control of socially undesirable behavior in the adult. Our correctional programs which are based almost exclusively on a system of punishment have not been notably successful in suppressing criminality or other deviant behavior. Rather, to judge from recurring criminal offenses, the punishment serves only to develop a more alert and adroit criminal, not a law abiding citizen. Children are well behaved to the extent that such behavior is adequately reinforced positively, and consistent with their level of maturity; adults are law abiding to the extent that such behavior has been associated with dependable positive reinforcement.

Superstitious behavior: Studies in the animal laboratory, likewise, can give us an understanding of how another common kind of personality characteristic develops in humans, namely that of superstitious behavior. Using pigeons as subjects, Skinner (1948) and Skinner and Morse (1957) have demonstrated that superstitious behavior is the result of an accidental pairing of a response with a reinforcement. No true functional relationship (cause-effect) exists, but certain behavioral peculiarities can be conditioned and maintained through these non-response correlated reinforcements. For example, pigeons can be reinforced every fifteen seconds regardless of what they happen to be doing at the time reinforcement is presented. With this contingency in operation, the experimenter may find after an hour that some of his birds are turning around the cage in a clockwise position, others may be tossing their heads, and others making swishing movements back and forth. Applying this operation at the human level, one may discover many non-instrumental responses which are accidentally reinforced by reason of their contiguity with significant instrumental acts that are successful. Thus, a football coach may have a "lucky hat"—usually one he has worn during an unexpected victory—that he may then wear indefinitely and even though the response is only occasionally reinforced with subsequent victories.

Discriminative Responding: In our discussion of conditioned reinforcement, we have already referred to how a discrimination may be formed. An organism is reinforced in the presence of a given stimulus, and extinguished in its absence. We showed earlier how a rat can develop a light-dark discrimination. If we choose the pigeon, which has color vision, we may reinforce pecking on a green disc and fail to reward pecks on a red disc. Eventually, the pigeon will peck only on the green disc. By this simple procedure, discriminations are developed. The same process is obvious at the human level. When we go picking wild strawberries, we select the red ones because they are sweet, and ignore the green ones, because we have found them sour and unpalatable. Again the development of most of our verbal behavior follows the same kind of psychological operation. In the process of a child's early babbling he will emit the sound "da." If father is presented as a discriminative stimulus the baby will be reinforced. Eventually, we then reinforce only "dada" and finally "daddy." The child learns to make this vocal response only in the presence of his father, not his mother, or other adults.

Discrimination is the basic process of learning those behaviors that other psychological theories have frequently called "higher mental processes." Complex processes such as perceiving, thinking, problem solving, concept formation or imitation are based on an elaboration of the basic discrimination operation. For example, certain stimuli such as size of objects serve as clues for our judgment of distance. Large objects are judged to be closer, and are reinforced by being more often reachable while smaller objects are more likely to be judged far away. Interposition, the placement of one object in front of another, operates in the same way. The response of reaching is reinforced by receiving the closer object. In what we call *imitation* the discriminative stimuli become the *behavior of other individuals*. We imitate the behavior of someone looking up in the sky because in the past that response has been reinforced by a stimulating sight. Much of the behavior of so-called "helpless followers" among humans may be explained by the

assumptions that in the lives of many people the implied approval of a
political leader or the direct approval of the members of a clique may
offer one of the few sources of unambiguous positive social reinforcement available.

The juvenile delinquent follows his "gang" into delinquent acts
because he is reinforced in this behavior by their approval. Making an
effective discrimination between what is right and wrong in one's own
conduct can rarely occur without an appropriate set of reinforcing contingencies. One does what one is reinforced to do. If "society" wishes
the potential delinquent to do "right" then "right" behavior must be
more strongly specified, with positive reinforcers.

To understand thinking or conceptualizing we must take into account a by-product of the development of the discriminative capacity,
namely *generalization.* In the process of developing a discrimination,
an organism will also respond to similar stimuli, for example in the
rat if we use as our discriminative stimulus a light of a given intensity,
we find, following the formation of the discrimination, the rat will
also respond to lights of various intensities. The magnitude of the
response, measured perhaps in terms of rate, will be proportional to
their similarity to the orginal discriminative stimulus. In the process of
conceptualizing we are dealing with classes of objects as the stimuli.
Consider, for a moment the class of objects called "tree." It may include
tall and short trees, oaks, maples, elms as well as evergreens. We *generalize* within this class of objects called tree, but we *discriminate* them
from other classes of objects such as dogs, horses, or people. By conceptual behavior or the forming of concepts a class of objects brings out a
discriminative response. We develop the concept by finding the properties which these objects share. When classes of objects operate to bring
out different responses, we discriminate between them. We therefore
consider conceptualizing to be generalizing within classes of objects
as stimuli and discriminating between them.

Much of the behavior we designate as *intelligence* boils down to
this kind of discriminative responding. If we are attempting to measure
verbal intelligence, the concepts are mediated by verbal stimuli. For
example, a common type of question on a test is to ask the subject to
discriminate between antonyms and synonyms. Are "rigid" and "flexible" the same or opposite? Are "haven" and "refuge" the same or
opposite? Here again if the answer is the same, we have generalized
within a class of verbal stimuli. In the case of an "opposite" response,
we have made a discrimination between the classes. Another kind of

an item on intelligence tests makes use of analogies: *"Ocean* is to *pond* as *deep* is to—(1) shallow, (2) well, or (3) sea." One looks for that one among several possible significant differences between ocean and pond, which also applies to the analogy. For example, "deep" applies to ocean and the correct answer of "shallow" applies to pond. If one answers correctly, he has formed the right concept. Indeed, it may be that the so-called "g" factor of intelligence suggested by Spearman refers precisely to this process of conceptualizing whether it be involved in verbal or perceptual discriminations.

Verbal behavior: The understanding of verbal behavior is merely an extension of our discussion of discrimination. In the interaction of two individuals (which is a paradigm for social behavior) one person's verbal response serves as a discriminative stimulus for the other's. We have, then, a speaker-listener interaction in which the discriminative and reinforcing functions change intermittently. The speaker's verbal behavior is reinforced by the hearer in several ways. For example, if at the dinner table, one says, "Please pass the butter," reinforcement of the polite mode of address along with the appropriate combination of words comes directly from having the request satisfied. In a general conversation, the reply of another individual, if not aversive in character, will act to reinforce in a generalized way the speaker and serve to maintain the conversational behavior.

The analysis of verbal responding is a fairly complicated one and has been described at least in a theoretical fashion by Skinner in his *Verbal Behavior* (1957). For our purposes we might illustrate by citing several experiments to demonstrate how reinforcing and discriminative functions are involved in speech, how the content of conversations may be manipulated by selective verbal reinforcement and how the order of speaking among people can be brought under stimulus control.

Greenspoon (1955), in an experiment—by now a classic—used a situation that resembled an interview. Without giving specific instructions to subjects, he set out to manipulate through selective reinforcement the probability of occurrence of certain verbal responses. His subjects were merely asked to say words they could think of without putting them in sentences. Two classes of responses were defined, the first consisted of plural nouns and the second constituted all other verbal responses. If a speaker in one group emitted a plural noun, the experimenter replied with "mmm-hmm." In another group, responses other than plural nouns were followed by a negatively toned "huh-uh." The subjects showed a remarkable increase in the frequency of the plural nouns that had been reinforced by "mmm-hmm," and likewise a decrease in frequency of the responses followed by "huh-uh."

Verplanck (1955) has applied the technique of selective reinforcement to the control of the content of a conversation. In this experiment, a series of ordinary conversations between subjects and "experimenters" was carried out. The class of responding selected for reinforcement was *statements of opinion*. Statements beginning with the words "I think," "I believe," or "It seems to me" were reinforced by the listener (experimenter) with, "Yes, you're right," or "That's so." Since the experiment was carried on in a variety of places so as not to give evidence that this was anything more than a normal conversation, the experimenters made notes on margins of magazines, books, etc. in the form of "doodles" in order to record the rates of responding. Verplanck reports the opinion statements showed a significant increase during the reinforcement period. In the last part of the experimental period, the experimenter disagreed with the subject or said nothing. In some cases the subjects became disturbed or angry. Accordingly, the rate of the opinion statements markedly decreased. In interviews following the experimental session in no case did the subjects show any "awareness" of what was going on or that a contrived situation had been set up in which a particular class of responses was being reinforced.

Finally, Levin and Shapiro (1962) have demonstrated that the order of speaking can be controlled by the selective use of reinforcement. They asked subjects to carry out conversations in order to reach unanimous decisions on the possible solution of a simple problem, or more specifically, the agreement on a message to be sent to a receiver in an adjoining room. As soon as they all agreed on a solution, subjects were asked to stop talking. This was supposed to be a kind of "telepathic message" to be sent and the conversation involved agreement on what message was to be sent. Reinforcement consisted of announcement of the receipt of a "correct message" if a certain prearranged order of speaking in the conversational sequence occurred. For example, the last utterance of subjects might be in the order of A, B, C, the subjects being designated by letters. In this way a dependable order of conversation can be established. In interviews with subjects following the experiment, none noticed a connection between the conversational sequence and getting the correct answers, although several suggested a guessing game had been rigged in some way. The results are suggestive of ways in which group behavior can be controlled by proper manipulations of even subtle rewards.

Psychotic Behavior: Long term experimental studies applying operant conditioning techniques to the study of chronic psychotics have been carried out by Lindsley (1958, 1960). His procedure is to ask a patient on the ward if he would like to come with the experimenter to get some candy or cigarettes. The subject is led into the experimental room and told that he is seated in front of a machine which delivers candy, cigarettes or whatever the reinforcement happens to be. The subject's job is to pull a knob to get the candy which he can either eat or keep as he wishes. The primary purpose of the studies has been to gather data for the analysis of psychotic behavior. No attempt is made to "type" or classify psychotics, although many of them have been previously diagnosed as schizophrenics. All subjects have shared one characteristic: they are all chronic mental patients who have been institutionalized for a considerable period of time. Space does not permit an extensive report of Lindsley's findings, but some general results are of interest. For one thing, analysis of the response records of plunger pulling among the psychotics indicates an irregularity of responding. Unlike those of normal controls, the psychotic records are typified by pauses between responses, sometimes quite long. Lindsley has found that the irregularity is one of the most valid indices of the presence and indeed the progression of a psychosis. The most disturbed patients, as judged by their ward behavior, show the longest pauses and most erratic response rates. During the pauses, qualitative observations indicate that the patients are typically exhibiting their psychotic episodes. They may be pacing the floor, gesturing, talking to themselves (hallucinating) or engaging in some violent activity. Each patient typically has his own pattern of psychotic distraction; some are short, others long. The frequency of the pauses or their duration is not specifically related to any psychotic disorder (schizophrenia, manic-depressive, etc.). It is indicative, rather, of the degree of the disturbance. When inter-response times are measured and compared with normals, it is found that the normal subject seldom pauses for more than 10 seconds.

Lindsley has tried a number of possible reinforcers and found candy to be the most effective for the average psychotic, although individual cases work better (higher rates of plunger pulling) for cigarettes, seeing pictures of nude men or women flashed on a screen in front of them or watching a live kitten being fed. This animal only receives its milk if the patient does his job of pulling the plunger.

Long term studies of individual patients indicate that the rates of responding are often cyclical. For some months the rates of a single individual may be extremely low and then gradually increase, only to be followed again by weeks or months of slow responding. Although the techniques are not especially intended as therapeutic devices, they may possibly have beneficial effects in some instances. At any rate, improved behavior in the experimental situation (more regular rates of responding) is reflected in better adjustment on the ward as rated by the ward attendants. Finally, Lindsley has found that many severely disturbed and chronic psychotics who are not ordinarily accessible to psychotherapy or even diagnosis with various psychological tests will respond to the operant conditioning situation.

In a similar vein, Ellis, Barnett and Pryer (1960) have used the plunger pulling procedure with mental defectives. With adult defectives as subjects (IQ's of thirty or lower) and chocolate candies as reinforcers, these investigators have found their subjects amenable to various schedules of reinforcement, ratio as well as interval. Many of the subjects have limited behavioral repertoires, some even lacking speech. Yet most of them readily adapt to operant conditioning. Even subjects usually labeled as "untestable" who are not ordinarily included in psychological experiments can be conditioned in this fashion. These subjects are susceptible to schedule changes and their response curves resemble in many cases those found with animals as well as normal children. However, in some cases these investigators have found slower and more irregular rates among the defectives, rates similar to those reported by Lindsley with adult psychotics.

Psychotherapy: The basic function of psychotherapy is to provide a situation in which learning can take place, that is, learning of responses that are going to be more appropriate than those already existing in an individual's behavioral repertoire. The individual may come to the therapist with a set of behaviors that is ineffective or inadequate in dealing with his environment. It is possible for a therapeutic situation to provide positive reinforcement for behavior that is weak and in need of strengthening, or perhaps the situation may call for dealing with certain undesirable responses, including anxiety, that need to be extinguished, possibly even punished. The application of selective reinforcement may need to be used to provide for the development of new discriminations that are going to be more effective than those currently operating, or the most appropriate method may be counter-conditioning a substitution of new responses that are more reinforcing to the person.

Within recent years the reinforcement theorists have been working with problems of behavioral change in experimental settings to demonstrate the adequacy of these principles. Ayllon and Michael (1959) have considered the role the psychiatric nurse plays as a reinforcing agent in a hospital setting with psychotic patients. In their study of the behavior of the nurses and patients, they conclude that many of the problems the patients presented on the ward were the result of the kinds of reinforcement applied in the hospital setting. The investigators were not so concerned with the behavior that brought the patients to the hospital as with the annoying and disturbing behavior exhibited on the wards such as failure to eat, dress or bathe, hitting, pinching, or spitting at other patients, breaking windows and other aggressive behaviors. By instituting a special program of operant control to reduce the frequency of these disruptive activities, the nurses were placed in the role of a "therapist." By ignoring certain maladaptive behaviors—for example, delusional talk—they were able to extinguish them. Likewise, they were able to reinforce behavior incompatible with aggressive outbursts in a violent patient. In two cases in which patients refused to eat and had to be spoon fed but were very concerned with cleanliness and neatness, the nurses deliberately instituted a practice of spilling food on the patients' clothing whenever they sought to be spoon fed. Since this could be avoided by giving up the nurses help, the patients soon were feeding themselves. The therapeutic techniques were simple but effective and the means of control, of course, had to be specifically applicable to each individual case. Where extinction might be most effective for one patient, positive reinforcement might be for another; or for still another, the introduction of avoidance conditioning could be the most effective learning procedure.

As part of his general program discussed in the previous section, Lindsley (1960) examined the effects of psychotherapy by a student nurse on the response rate of pulling the plunger for candy reinforcements by a psychotic patient. Therapeutic one-hour sessions were conducted three times a week over several weeks. These were correlated with daily one-hour sessions of the patient in the operant conditioning situation. Results indicate that after the sixth therapeutic session, the patient's rate had climbed from zero, prior to therapy, to over 2,000 responses per hour. The response rates continued steady even on days when the nurse did not see the patient. Following the discontinuation of therapy, there was a marked downward change in rate. Apparently, the effects of the therapy were not permanent. We do have, however, in this experimental report an objective measure of the effects of a single therapist's interviews with a chronic psychotic.

Less severe behavior disorders, such as thumbsucking and stuttering in children have been investigated from an experimental therapeutic point of view. Flanagan, Goldiamond and Azrin (1958) have applied operant techniques to the control of stuttering in chronic stutterers. These investigators were able to increase the frequency of stuttering by allowing the subject to turn off a loud sound (105 db) with each non-fluency and conversely they decreased the frequency of stuttering by punishing each non-fluency with the same sound. They suggest that the control of stuttering may be more directly attacked by these measures than by treating the disorder as a by-product of anxiety.

Recently, Baer (1962) has controlled thumbsucking in children by means of the withdrawal of positive reinforcement. He has demonstrated that positive reinforcement may be withdrawn from young children by showing them a cartoon movie and then suddenly interrupting the picture and sound track. Applying this procedure to chronic thumbsuckers, a child may be shown the movies and the cartoons are suddenly terminated as soon and as long as the thumb remains in the mouth. This procedure has been shown to weaken the thumb sucking responses, while during uninterrupted cartoons, the thumb sucking promptly returns.

4. THE BEHAVIORIST ANSWERS HIS CRITICS

Like most psychological theories, behaviorism has been subjected to attack. Honest and searching criticism, of course, is healthy in the development of any intellectual discipline. Psychology today has somewhat outgrown the era of "schools" when groups of psychologists banded together in support of various systematic viewpoints and sharply opposed each other, but there is as yet, certainly, no complete agreement with respect to theory. As an antidote Skinner (1950) has suggested that we abandon theory altogether. Good psychological data, he contends, can stand on its own merits and a well executed experiment should demonstrate the functional relationships between variables. When lawful relations are discovered, there is no need for theory. The events and relations have been shown to exist and we need go no further. Although Skinner does not stand alone in this attitude, many behaviorists do not share his position. This latter group still feels the need for psychological theory at least at the present stage in our development and, in particular, in the field of personality where a rather wide range of man's behavior is involved. Be that as it may, behaviorism, despite its many variations, offers a stable position on the epistomological problems inherent in psychological research. Nevertheless, if we profess a behaviorist approach and prefer it to other systematic approaches, it becomes necessary for us to answer some of the criticism directed against it.

1. *The behaviorist has been charged with abandoning an investigation of the full range of human responding, limiting himself to the study of a few responses or simple units of activity.* The statement is, of course, partially true, if one takes it at its face value. However, the critic does not usually examine the problem of *why* the behaviorist typically takes the approach he does. One answer to the criticism is to be found in the attitude the behaviorist takes toward his science. He feels, first of all, that one must start somewhere. It is more parsimonious to begin with a simple event which can be objectively measured and understood than to take on a mass of behavior where the variables are complex, interrelated, and almost impossible to control. The behaviorist is interested in discovering the lawful relations between the environmental variables and the resulting behavior. He can do this only by starting at the level where this is possible. This does not mean that the behaviorist intends always to remain at this level since simple responses develop into larger chains of activity. But the simple behavior segment is the logical place to begin. Once one understands relationships at a simple level, he can then move up to more complex activity involving more of the behavior of the organism.

Let us take the development of a simple discrimination as an example. We begin with a particular response available to an organism and an appropriate stimulus. By reinforcing the organism when the desired response to the stimulus is made, the response is strengthened. By and by the organism whether he be a rat, a pigeon, or a human being, will respond immediately in the presence of the stimulus and will fail to respond in its absence. It is then possible to narrow or broaden the range of similar stimuli to which the organism will respond by appropriate application of reinforcement. From this simple operation that can be carried out with very simple organisms, we can move on to study more complex discriminations with organisms higher on the phylogenetic scale. Eventually we arrive at conceptualizing behavior, where an organism learns to generalize within a class of objects and discriminate between them. This is concept formation. At this level it is appropriate to explore a variety of human behaviors including verbal behavior where our organism can conceptualize responses mediated through language cues to behavior we traditionally call intelligence. The point should be clear. Once a relationship has been demonstrated in a simple way, its application can be made, not only to higher organisms, but to more complicated behavior. It is merely in keeping with good scientific methodology to work at a level where one has knowledge of all the relevant variables and can control and manipulate them as he wishes.

2. *The behaviorist has been accused of offering evidence only from animals and restricted experimentation from the animal laboratory which frequently have little or no relevance to human behavior.* Certainly from a point of view of history, part of the criticism is justified. Although Watson did some experimenting at the human level (Albert, for example) much of his attention was directed to comparative psychology. Likewise, in the vast literature of experimentation by the major schools of learning theory (Hull, Tolman, Guthrie, Skinner) subjects commonly used have been white rats, cats, pigeons and monkeys. The choice of these organisms, of course, goes back to the argument in the previous section. By using lower species as experimental subjects, it is possible to control the relevant variables—often difficult to do with humans, each of whom may have had a vastly different conditioning history. We know from our own experience with lower animals, in instances where we have used the same animals in a variety of different studies for purposes of student experimentation, that we can build into our animal subjects conditioning histories so complicated that the results of a single experiment will not come out as anticipated. If our subjects are no longer experimentally naive, the results become contaminated so that we do not know what complex variables are responsible for the results we achieved. Furthermore, animals are readily available and we can control their psychological histories and even their biological characteristics through selective breeding.

The second part of the criticism, namely, that these studies have little relevance to human responding, does not necessarily hold. Although there are obvious species differences, we have already accumulated enough evidence to demonstrate that the principles of conditioning, extinction, differentiation and discriminative behavior are similar in all species from rat to man. We may condition a child and a rat using the same schedule of reinforcement and the shapes of the conditioning response curves look remarkably similar. The only differences may be in the kinds of reinforcement applied and the range and type of responses we wish to measure. For the rat, it may be pressing a lever on the side of a cage to receive a pellet of food as reinforcement. For the child it could be pressing a telegraph key for candy or nickels. Furthermore, the experimental evidence reported in Section 3 indicates that there is a literature on the use of human subjects rapidly accumulating. The whole area of conditioning verbal behavior (Greenspoon, 1962) gives evidence of how appropriate experimental methodology can be applied to one of the most significant areas of man's behavior, namely, speech. The criticism that the behaviorist fails to use human subjects may have been more legitimate ten years ago than it is today. As a final note of application we mention the recent movement in teaching machines and programmed learning (Skinner, 1958, 1961) at all levels from teaching children how to spell and do arithmetic to industrial training. This is a direct outgrowth of the behavioristic experiments originated in the animal laboratory. A rat may be trained through a series of small steps and successive approximations using selective reinforcement to perform a complex chain of activity including pressing bars and pulling chains all in sequential order. In the child the stimuli are slightly different. Instead of lights and tones as discriminative stimuli for each link in the chain, the child is presented with a variety of verbal and numerical stimuli. For reinforcement, he receives immediate knowledge of results and being right almost all of the time seems to be adequate reinforcement to keep him going through the programmed material. In place of this we present the food pellet or the drop of water which is appropriate to the rat. The point is, had the principles of conditioning and differentiation (shaping of behavior) not been discovered and demonstrated in the animal laboratory, the movement of programmed learning would not as yet have become a reality.

   3. *The behaviorist has been accused of concerning himself only with overt behavior and neglecting the events which lie "under the skin."* There are really two different matters involved in this criticism. The first refers to the concept of the "inner man" the "self" or the "deeply rooted personality," while the other has reference to the problems of implicit behavior. Although these problems are interrelated, let us examine each one separately. When the critic claims that the behaviorist fails to deal with the internal psychic structures as postulated by many psychologists, the behaviorist must ask to what behavior he is referring. When one attempts to evaluate complicated hypothetical

constructs objectively one finds few dependable and unequivocal behavioral referents to which to tie research. What, indeed, are the "self,"
the "super-ego," "self-actualization," "the unconscious," and other
such concepts? These are largely abstract concepts which have no
dependable behavioral referents in space and time. Consequently, the
behaviorist can do nothing but ignore them, or attempt to reformulate
them in behavioral terms. The proponents of such notions will, of
course, argue that these are merely convenient constructs to use as
explanatory principles and what is observed is an indirect evidence
emanating from them. This seems only to over-complicate the issue.
Why not start with what can be observed, and then ask how such
intervening constructs can add in any way to the understanding of
human behavior? If a man behaves in an anxious or fearful manner,
is it not more productive to discover what environmental variables
contribute to the development of that behavior than to give as its cause
some agency that cannot be given objective identity?

The second aspect of the criticism involves a slightly different
problem. Here the problem is one of dealing in an objective way with
the so-called private events of man's existence, the behavior we call
implicit that is not readily available to the naked eye. Such behaviors
are involved in "thinking," "imagining" or "feeling." No one questions
that such events are a reality even though they may be private. However,
the questions to be answered are: What are they? What response
mechanisms are involved? Many psychologists will suggest that the
answers lie in the physiology of the sensory apparatus as well as in
cerebral functions. If one does not worry about objectivity, there is no
real problem. Identifying these events as neural traces or engrams in the
brain and nervous system may be satisfactory as an interim statement
provided we have reason to believe the physiologists will eventually
tell us much more than we know today. But if the data of the behaviorist
are responses the organism makes to real stimuli, then what can he do
with these presumed "unobservables"? Behaviorists have handled this
problem of private events in several ways. One way is to use the
verbal report. Skinner (1953) suggested the verbal report is a response
to a private event and may be used as a source of information about it.
A second avenue of approach is through improved instrumentation so
that the *private event may be made public*. The instruments should be
able to detect in a way similar to the organism's internal receptors and
should act as the independent means of checking the organism's verbal
report. Watson (1930) had suggested that thinking was nothing more

than sub-vocal speech but unfortunately he lacked the proper instrumentation adequately to demonstrate this fact. Early work on this possibility was done by Jacobson (1932) when he asked subjects to think of or "imagine" performing certain tasks. By means of surface electrodes attached to the skin, he observed from his recordings that appropriate muscle reactions occurred only minutely but followed the same pattern sequence of activity that would have occurred if the subject had actually performed overtly the tasks that he thought about or "imagined." Although there were no noticeable movements observable to the naked eye, it was clear that the difference between the actual performance of the act and thinking about it was merely one of magnitude. The organism was indeed responding when he thought. More recently, Hefferline and his colleagues (1959) have found by means of more sophisticated myographic techniques that it is possible to condition minute thumb twitches. The subjects were seated in a reclining chair while they listened to music. Superimposed on the music was an aversively loud 60-cycle hum. This could only be turned off by the minute thumb twitch of which the subject reported no awareness. The thumb twitches were recorded electromyographically. When the experimenter noticed that the record on his meter indicated a response (minute twitch) of a required magnitude, he turned off the noise for fifteen seconds, or when it was already off it could be postponed for another fifteen seconds by the same response. The technique illustrates a kind of escape and avoidance conditioning of which we spoke earlier. A period of extinction then followed in which the minute thumb twitch responses were ineffective in removing the noise. When interviewed later, subjects believed that they had been passive victims with respect to the onset and duration of the noise and were astonished to learn that their own minute responses were controlling the stimulus onset. It is obvious that supposedly inaccessible behavior can be studied objectively if the appropriate techniques are applied. It is clear that the subjects did not even discriminate their own behavior in a manner we might call "conscious" activity. Hefferline (1962) has suggested that there may be a continuity between this thumb twitch that evoked no awareness in subjects, yet constituted a measurable reality and was subject to the laws of conditioning and extinction, and the notion of the "unconsciously" motivated behavior advanced by the psychoanalysts. The important fact to be remembered is that the study of personality can be thoroughly behavioristic and include the objective study of events previously considered inescapably private. Hefferline suggests further that the region "under the skin" is the psychologists' new frontier. This environment needs to be coordinated with the external environment so that the proper stimulus control of the organism can be completed.

Thus rests the case for the behaviorist. His approaches to the problems of personality and psychology are in keeping with the best scientific tradition. Although many behaviorists have long neglected the study of personality, the tide is now turning so that this subject need no longer remain the exclusive domain of the psychoanalysts and phenomenologists, but may legitimately be approached via the methods of natural science.

REFERENCES

ADER, R., & TATUM, R. Free-operant avoidance conditioning in human subjects, *J. exper. anal. Behav.*, 1961, *3*, 275-276.

AYLLON, T., & MICHAEL, J. The psychiatric nurse as a behavioral engineer, *J. exper. anal. Behav.*, 1959, *2*, 323-334.

BACHRACH, A. J. (Ed.) *Experimental foundations of clinical psychology.* New York: Basic Books, 1962.

BAER, D. M. Laboratory control of thumbsucking by withdrawal and re-presentation of reinforcement, *J. exper. anal. Behav.*, 1962, *5*, 525-528.

BIJOU, S. W. Methodology for the experimental analysis of child behavior, *Psychol. Rep.*, 1957, *3*, 243-250.

BIJOU, S. W. Operant extinction after fixed-interval reinforcement with young children, *J. exper. anal. Behav.*, 1958, *1*, 35-40.

BIJOU, S. W., & STURGES, P. T. Positive reinforcers for experimental studies with children—consumables and manipulatables, *Child Develpm.*, 1959, *30*, 151-170.

BRADY, J. V. Ulcers in "executive" monkeys. *Scient. Amer.*, 1958, *199*, 95-103.

DOLLARD, J., & MILLER, N. E. *Personality and psychotherapy.* New York: McGraw-Hill. 1950.

ELLIS, N. R., BARNETT, C. D., & PRYER, M. W. Operant behavior in mental defectives: exploratory studies, *J. exper. anal. Behav.*, 1960, *3*, 63-69.

ESTES, W. K. An experimental study of punishment, *Psychol. Monogr.*, 1944, *37*, No. 263.

FERSTER, C. B., & SKINNER, B. F. *Schedules of reinforcement.* New York: Appleton-Century-Crofts, 1957.

FLANAGAN, B., GOLDIAMOND, I., & AZRIN, N. H. Operant stuttering: the control of stuttering behavior through response contingent consequences, *J. exper. anal. Behav.,* 1958, *1,* 173-177.

GREENSPOON, J. The reinforcing effects of two spoken words on the frequency of two responses, *Amer. J. Psychol.,* 1955, *68,* 409-416.

GREENSPOON, J. Verbal conditioning and clinical psychology. In A. J. Bachrach (Ed.), *Experimental foundations of clinical psychology.* New York: Basic Books, 1962.

HALL, C. S., & LINDZEY, G. *Theories of personality.* New York: John Wiley, 1957.

HEFFERLINE, R. F. Learning theory and clinical psychology—an eventual symbiosis? In A. J. Bachrach (Ed.), *Experimental foundations of clinical psychology.* New York: Basic Books, 1962.

HEFFERLINE, R. F., KEENAM, B., & HARFORD, R. A. Escape and avoidance conditioning in human subjects without their observation of the response, *Science,* 1959, *130,* 1338-1339.

JACOBSON, E. The electrophysiology of mental activities, *Amer. J. Psychol.,* 1932, *44,* 677-694.

JONES, M. C. The elimination of children's fear, *J. exper. Psychol.,* 1924, 7, 382-398.

KANTOR, J. R. *Principles of psychology.* New York: Alfred A. Knopf 1924-26. 2 vols.

LEVIN, G., & SHAPIRO, D. The operant conditioning of conversations. *J. exper. anal. Behav.,* 1962, *5,* 309-316.

LINDSLEY, O. R. Report on the third and fourth years on *An experimental analysis of psychotic behavior,* Behavior Research Laboratory, Metropolitan State Hospital, Waltham, Mass., 1958.

LINDSLEY, O. R. Characteristics of the behavior of chronic psychotics as revealed by free-operant conditioning methods, *Dis. Nerv. Syst.* (monogr. supp.) 1960, *21,* 1-13.

LONG, E. R., HAMMACK, J. T., MAY, F., & CAMPBELL, B. J. Intermittent reinforcement of operant behavior in children, *J. exper. anal. Behav.,* 1958, *1,* 315-339.

LUNDIN, R. W. *Personality: an experimental approach.* New York: Macmillan, 1961.

MILLER, N. E. Experimental studies in conflict. In J. McV. Hunt (Ed.), *Personality and the behavior disorders,* Vol. 1. New York: Ronald Press, 1944.

SARBIN, T. R. (Ed.) *Studies in behavior pathology.* New York: Holt, Rinehart and Winston, 1961.

SIDMAN, M. Avoidance conditioning with brief shock and no exteroceptive warning signal, *Science,* 1953, *118,* 157-158.

SIDMAN, M. Operant techniques. In A. J. Bachrach (Ed.), *Experimental foundations of clinical psychology.* New York: Basic Books, 1962.

SKINNER, B. F. On the rate of formation of a conditioned reflex, *J. gen. Psychol.,* 1932, 7, 274-285.

SKINNER, B. F. *The behavior of organisms: an experimental analysis.* New York: Appleton-Century, 1938.

SKINNER, B. F. "Superstition" in the pigeon, *J. exper. Psychol.*, 1948, *38*, 168-172.

SKINNER, B. F. Are theories of learning necessary? *Psychol. Rev.*, 1950, *57*, 193-216.

SKINNER, B. F. *Science and human behavior.* New York: Macmillan, 1953.

SKINNER, B. F. Critique of psychoanalytic concepts and theories, *Scient. mon.*, 1954, *79*, 300-305.

SKINNER, B. F. *Verbal behavior.* New York: Appleton-Century-Crofts, 1957.

SKINNER, B. F. Teaching machines, *Science,* 1958, *128*, 969-977.

SKINNER, B. F. Teaching machines, *Scient. Amer.*, 1961, *205*, 90-102.

SKINNER, B. F., & MORSE, W. H. A second type of superstition in the pigeon, *Amer. J. Psychol.*, 1957, *70*, 308-311.

STODDARD, L. T., SIDMAN, M., & BRADY, J. V. Conditioning and maintenance of human behavior by multiple schedules of intermittent reinforcement, Paper read at East. Psychol. Ass., New York, 1960.

VERPLANCK, W. S. The control of the content of conversation, reinforcement of statements of opinion, *J. abn. soc. Psychol.*, 1953, *51*, 668-676.

WATSON, J. B. Psychology as the behaviorist views it, *Psychol. Rev.*, 1913, *20*, 158-177.

WATSON, J. B. *Behaviorism.* New York: Norton, 1930.

WATSON, J. B., & RAYNOR, R. Conditioned emotional reactions, *J. exper. Psychol.*, 1920, *3*, 1-14.

11

Phenomenology and Personality

John M. Shlien

INTRODUCTION

What makes another approach to personality necessary, particularly one which stresses the very subjectivity which others have tried to avoid? Is it just one more reflection of the "clash of temperaments" in the history of a developing field, or does the answer really depend upon what one considers to be the raw material, and the avenues of access to it, in the study of personality?

At the heart of the need for a phenomenological psychology lies a fact which Kluver (1936) has expressed as follows:

> Whether or not behavior takes this or that direction is, generally speaking, dependent on whether or not this or that *phenomenal* property exists. The fact that something appears phenomenally as 'red,' 'larger than,' etc., cannot be deduced from the properties of the atom but only from studies of reacting organisms.

To this must be added the generally accepted observation that apparent phenomena differ in their appearances. Since we learn so many of our meanings from our culture—i.e., each other (Blake & Ramsey, 1951) the first fact of inscrutability plays a large part in causing those differing perceptions. It makes communication of meanings weak and uncertain. If the mind could not think silently; if there were outwardly audible and visible signs directly indicating specific mental activities,

we would all be rank behaviorists, and the history of psychology, to
say the least, would have hinged on a very different set of data. But
this is not the case. As things stand, we have both internal and external events *experienced* by the total organism; experienced, recorded
at some level of awareness, and in some cases, given meaning. The
phenomenologist is convinced that much goes on "inside," and that
the behavioristic concept of the "empty organism" is narrow, and
largely spurious. Most of our experience and its meanings exist in
"private worlds," not expressed on pointer readings. Nor is this to say
that phenomenology is only here on borrowed time.

Instruments have been and will be developed to probe the silent
and private world of inner experience, but men are not likely to
become transparent. Much will remain hidden; meanings will differ
from person to person; modes of experience and interpretation will
change over time for each individual. Physiological indexes of internal
states will have immense value for the study of experience, but heart
rate, brain waves, pupil size, endocrine output, or whatever comes will
only measure increase or decrease without meaning unless the identifying code is first given and then continually validated by the wise and
willing knower. As Kohler (1938, p. vii) says,

> Never, I believe, shall we be able to solve any problems of ultimate
> principle until we go back to the source of our concepts—in other words,
> until we use the phenomenological method, the qualitative analysis of
> experience.

And, the more the knower is wise and willing, the better the accuracy
of his information and verification. Thus the approach may be applied
to animals and infants, but reaches its more productive stage in the
study of language-using humans.[1]

It is not always constructive to haggle over terminology, but
neither is it fair to introduce the problem with a term which, if accepted, envelops the reader in a biased frame of reference. We have
referred to activity of the human "mind." Use of this word, to the
behaviorist, is at least a concession and, to the phenomenologist, a minor

---

[1] Zener (1958) advised psychologists to recognize limitations and capabilities
which vary both with the phenomena to be observed and the motivation, intelligence,
etc. *of the observer*. Not all are equal in this respect. A striking example of possibilities
in the upper ranges of observation by a psychologist is to be seen in a brilliant
analysis of the "psychology of secrets" by Bakan (1954). While anyone may make
a satisfactory "naive" subject for certain kinds of experiments, phenomenology can
best thrive through investment in sophisticated informants.

victory. J. B. Watson abhorred the word, and Pavlov is said to have levied fines upon students using such mentalistic terms in his laboratory. As recently as 1943, Clark Hull warned against the use of "mind" saying, "Even when fully aware of the nature of anthropomorphic subjectivism and its dangers, the most careful and experienced thinker is likely to find himself a victim of its seductions." (Hull, 1943). He suggests that this powerful effect be warded off by observing all behavior as if it were produced by a dog, rat, or robot. Gordon Allport, in a vein typical of the "personalistic" phenomenologist, objects to Hull's precaution as an affront to human dignity and an avoidance of human realities because it represents "an addiction to machines, rats, or infants which leads us to overplay those features of human behavior that are peripheral, signal-oriented, and genetic,[2] and to underplay those features that are central, future oriented, and symbolic" (Allport, 1947).

The quarrel exposed by this conflict over a mere word really revolves around these major issues: (1) Is the human being active or only reactive? (2) Is activity only external or also internal? (3) If it is internal, can "subjectivity" be reconciled with "science" (the latter in quotes because it has its fashions too)? We could brush aside the question of terminology by saying simply, "When you 'make up your mind' to read this chapter, we are talking about whatever you made up." That is true enough, but the phenomenologist characteristically uses mentalistic terms such as "mind." "Mind" is clearly returning as acceptable scientific language in the literature (Scher, 1962); and its use or non-use implies a decision about the legitimacy of inner life as proper subject matter. As Kurt Lewin (1951) says,

> Arguments about attributing "existence" to an item may seem metaphysical in nature and may therefore not be expected to be brought up in empirical sciences. Actually, opinions about existence or nonexistence are quite common in the empirical sciences and have greatly influenced scientific development in a positive and a negative way. Labeling something as "nonexisting" is equivalent to declaring it "out of bounds" for the scientist. Attributing "existence" to an item automatically makes it a duty of the scientist to consider this item as an object of research; it includes the necessity of considering its properties as "facts" which cannot be neglected in a total system of theories; finally, it implies that the terms with which one refers to the items are acceptable as scientific "concepts" (rather than as "mere words").

[2] Genetic here refers to history, not biology.

It matters, then, that we acknowledge the existence of each person's *faculty for knowing*. This is a basic assumption, expressed in an extreme and unabashed statement by a French phenomenologist, Merleau-Ponty (1945), "I am the absolute source." We do experience —we sense, perceive, think. Though silent and invisible, thought precedes and attends all of our behavior not accomplished through the reflex arc. Precedings are called determinants, attendings are called interpretations, and there is even evidence that thought should not be distinguished from behavior but may actually *constitute* behavior. A dozen years ago, when "transfer of training" experiments were popular, Beattie used a dart board with a graded target as a performance measure. As usual in such experiments, subjects practiced with one hand, rested, were retested with the other hand in various combinations of practice periods, hands, and rest periods. Longer rest periods seemed related to improved scores. We have long been given to think of this effect in terms of "spaced versus massed practice." But it also suggested "rehearsal" effects. Finally, some subjects were given imaginary practice, i.e., were instructed to simply sit at throwing distance from the target (after a base line performance had been established) and to "think about" throwing for a practice period. These "merely" rehearsing subjects often improved their performance as much as those who had "actual" practice trials (Beattie, 1949)! This reminds us that in the behavioristic strategy of focusing upon specifics of input and output, whatever was unseen was considered as undone (a strange and arrogant subjectivity on the part of the experimenter).

Tolman puts our unobserved learning back into proper behavioral perspective with his statement: "What [the organism] learns is, in short, a *performance* (and each such performance can be carried out by a number of different motor skills)." (Tolman, 1959, p. 133.) The phenomenologist is vitally interested in that internal performance, the process of experiencing. Whether or not the performance is also evident, he believes in the reality of the internal state as a mode of behavior. This mode consists of sensations, perceptions, thoughts, and feelings, all of which constitute experiencing that can only be approached through the standpoint of the experiencer.

The nature of this approach raises some fundamental questions. Is there really a field of study such as psychology, separate from the biological or electro-chemical basis of behavior? What is its subject matter, where to find it, and how to deal with it? To illustrate some of these points, here is an accurate report of a true event in a human transaction:

A 28-year-old graduate student in sociology finished his mid-year examinations. He wearily packed a bag and boarded a bus for a vacation journey to visit his family several hundred miles away. Choosing a seat next to the window, he stretched out as well as he could, hoping to sleep through the night since he felt quite exhausted. In his own words, the report continues:

After an hour or so, the bus stopped in a small town, and a few passengers got on. One of them was a blonde girl, very good looking in a fresh but sort of sleazy way. I thought that she was probably a farm girl, and I wished she'd sit by me. By God, she did. She was really comely, if you know what I mean, and she smiled a bit so I felt sure she'd be approachable. Oh boy, what luck. I didn't want to be too eager, and I was still exhausted, so we just smiled and talked for a minute. I made sure that she was comfortable, and then sort of dozed off for a little while, hoping to recuperate by the time the driver turned out the lights and meanwhile enjoying my fantasies about the prospects for the rest of the trip. The last thing I remember was smiling at her and noticing that when her skirt slipped up on her knee as she reached up to the back of the seat, she didn't pull it down. Wow! About four hours later we were pounding along the road in complete darkness when I opened my eyes. Her leg, the outside of it, was against mine, and the way it pressed and moved with the motion of the bus woke me up. This was more than I'd dreamed of. I was terribly excited, and when I stirred a little the steady pressure of her leg didn't move away. By this time, I had a terrific erection, and the more I thought about this cute little babe pressing against me, the worse it got. I was just about to reach out and touch her when we pulled into a gas station for a stop, and when the light came through the window, *she* wasn't there at all! She must have left while I was asleep. A fat man with a growth of beard and a dead cigar dropping ash on his vest was sprawled next to me, sound asleep. It was *his* leg pressing against me, and he was so fat and slovenly that even when I drew myself away, his sloppy flesh stayed against me. I was so dumbfounded—disappointed too, and the funny thing—I lost that erection almost immediately, got up and moved to another seat. What a let down.

From this event in someone's private life, we can draw several conclusions which bear an introduction to phenomenological thought.

First, there is such a thing as psychology. It operates in such a way as to influence behavior, and it cannot be accounted for simply in terms of physics or biology. Again quoting the extremist Merleau-Ponty, "The body is not a fact, it is a situation." An erection is a signal of a notable reaction to something in the environment—what? Not, in this case, the pressure of so many p.s.i., nor that in combination with body temperature of a certain degree, nor both those in combination with motion and friction of a specifiable sort. Those elements remained. The erection-behavior did not. Something interior changed when a certain group of stable physical sensations were given a different meaning as the perception of the experiencer was alerted. What had been exciting became revolting.

Second, it tells us that if we are to study that which is peculiarly psychological, the primary subject matter must be *experience*. Experience is subjective, i.e., it takes place within the opaque organism of the experiencer, and *may* not be public or even repeatable.

Third, from this it seems clear that the approach to this subject matter is to learn the secrets of individual perception, and sometimes of hidden consequent behavior. Whether the secrets are intended to be so, or are merely screened from view by the normal separatedness of people, they are private.

Thus, fourth, is implied a methodology which must be largely dependent upon our ability to obtain the hidden and private data, via some part of the family of introspective methods, or to deduce via such comparative experimental methods as "stimulus equivalence" those discriminant perceptions which lend themselves to this technique. Most of the investigations will have to rely on some form of self-report; this would seem a special weakness to some, but as William James (1950, p. 191) points out, "Introspection is what we have to rely on first and foremost and always" and as for its weakness, *"introspection is difficult and fallible; and the difficulty is simply that of all observation of whatever kind."*

Fifth, there is implied in this illustration a definition of pathology according to the phenomenologist' approach. Pathology would consist of a lack of awareness of one's own experience; of not knowing or understanding it; of being in a state of self-deception. Putting it more simply in perceptual terms, to see clearly is the greatest good—the blind spots are evil.

Sixth, we see in this example the "real life" nature of the context in which this approach can operate and from which it typically draws its data. The world and any part of it is a laboratory for the naturalistic observation. Its characteristic problems are the major attitudinal states which move men mightily—for example, pride, shame, grief, love, passion, loneliness, hatred, freedom, boredom, anxiety, despair, being and well-being, death, pain.[2]

BACKGROUND AND CHARACTERISTICS

Toward a Definition—Field and Streams

What is phenomenology, exactly? Exactly, no one can say. It is an old term, now stewing in its own liberal metaphysical juice, which has to allow such scope for change and individuality that during the first phases there could be almost as many phenomenologies as there are phenomenologists.[3] This is simply because the essential concern is *meaning,* and meanings can vary extensively. At the moment the term is a large envelope containing a confusing mixture of philosophies, psychology, science, myth, and fad. There is, as Boring (1950, p. 408) says, "room in phenomenology for acts as well as content; it is a tolerant discipline."

This tolerance is to its credit, and is also its peril. Always there is precaution against premature formulation of hypotheses, allowing for the "unprejudiced" naturalistic observation of events. MacLeod (1951) speaks of "a disciplined naivete"; Gibson (1959, p. 461) of "cultivated naivete." European phrasing is more extreme: French psychologist Merleau-Ponty says, "The whole effort is to recover naive contact with the world," while the German philosopher Eugene Fink speaks of the "shock of amazement at the fact of the world . . . a stunned amazement to which he assigned the function of converting the

[2] Pain is a particularly interesting and ephemeral quality, in spite of its pervasiveness. As such, it is a striking illustration of the need for a phenomenology. Everyone "knows" what pain is, but no one can feel another's pain (though the closer the involvement between people, the more a loved one's pain causes behavior in the observer; this comes close to being the behaviorist nightmare, "the interaction of two 'minds.'"). For all its ubiquity, and its frequent use in experiments, no one can "objectively" measure pain, or even accurately localize it or its source in many instances! The same stimulus, such as an electric shock of given intensity, by no means causes the same response in two subjects. Finally, outward behavior, ranging from stoicism to malingering, may or may not express inner experience of pain.

[3] In practice—in the practice of classifying, anyway—this lack of organized principles does not seem to hold. It is possible to group types of phenomenologies, usually in three or four categories ranging through "classical," "existential," "pure philosophical," "eidetic," "transcendental," "psychological," etc. (Spiegelberg, 1960, p. 642; Landsman, 1958).

trivial into what is worth questioning" (Spiegelberg, 1960, p. 600).
But which trivia are worth the conversion? *The Place of Value in a
World of Facts* (Kohler, 1938) demonstrates the unavoidable subjectivity which makes phenomenology liable to the same criticism it
has leveled at behaviorism. The only advantage lies in awareness of
the prejudice and the possibility of deliberately suspending or reversing
it, or "bracketing" it, to use Husserl's term. The bigger problem is to
find the correct balance of discipline and naivete, of course. The fresh
eyes of innocence and the free curiosity of the fascinated naturalist
need to be combined with the sophistication of the practiced researcher
—combined with, but not subdued by. That is part of the thrust of
reviving phenomenology.

The word to which so many lay claim derives from the Greek
phainesthai, "to appear," or "to appear so," or "as it appears." It is
instructive to note that in the original usage, the phenomenal was "that
which is known through the senses and immediate experience" rather
than deduction. This is still the case. One binding theme running
through all variants of phenomenology is the preoccupation and fasci-
nation with the facts (or the data) of immediate experience. This
characteristic of both the original and present usage is often taken to
pit "common sense" against "deduction," thus supposedly making
phenomenology a hopeless anachronism in the realm of science. Kimble
(1953) points out, for example, how "common sense" tells us that
the world is flat; science that it is round. The method of direct intui-
tion, or that which is known through the senses, then, would be basically
a source of error. But even on the level of description, it is not common
sense which fails; it is our constricted scope of vision which feeds in
limited information. If one can look at the ocean from a mountain top,
or take a picture of its surface with a wide angle lens, the application
of a straight edge will tell us via "common sense" [4] that the world has
a curved surface. If common sense could not confirm the shape of
the earth's surface in just this way, there would indeed be a conflict,
and "phenomenology" would have to disavow and separate itself from
"science."

The important point is that what we see tells us *our* truth—the
"world-for-us" rather than *the* truth—the "world-as-is," but that the
distinctions are not necessarily opposed or impossible of reconciliation.
The original Greek philosophies separated the *Phenomenal World*

---

[4] Anyone who has read Piaget's studies of intelligence will realize that it is a
mistake to identify "common sense" at only the lowest level of development.

from the *Ontal World* of permanent being and the *Ideal World* of permanent truth, with the Phenomenal World containing changeable and developing aspects, dealt with as perceptible aspects or appearances rather than their "true," ideal, fixed or substantial natures. We have inherited the idea that these worlds are all orthogonal to each other as a matter of fact, rather than as a matter of logical convenience or preference.

Phenomenology has a prejudice. It clearly holds that, psychologically speaking, man is the measure of all things, each man the measure of all his things, and that the reality to which he responds is his own. The frequent accusation of solipsism does not apply. Neither does Hume's philosophy that no matter exists independent of mind, the mind being nothing but representations. Kant is more to the liking of the phenomenologist with the notion that there are phenomena, and they are all we know, but there is more beyond.

The current general philosophy in American personality study would probably run to this effect: there is external reality, which we more or less distort, though it exists absolutely while its appearances are relative. But, to the purely phenomenological psychologist, does "real reality" matter? Is there anything in psychology to study except the perceptions of individuals? Psychologically, "real" things have only a relative existence. *Phenomena* are absolute (not permanent, but for the moment absolute); *they* control behavior since it is predicated upon *them;* when *they* change, behavior changes. (Behavior, not things, concerns the psychologist. If this makes "behaviorists" of all of us, so be it, only with the reservation that behavior is covert as well as overt.)

There is a limit to the profit one can take from philosophical speculations in this field. Neither the historical or functional connections between European philosophies and American psychologies are clear or prominent. MacLeod suggests that one might read Kuenzli's (1958) collection *The Phenomenological Problem* and conclude that phenomenology is an indigenous American product. But the German philosopher, Edmund Husserl, is generally credited as the main instigator of the movement. Whether he had a direct effect on modern personality theory as it developed in the group identified with Rogerian practices is a moot question. It may well be that we have here the spectacle of independent invention rather than cultural diffusion, and that the current preoccupation with Husserl is a retrospective tracing of geneology by a successful native development.

Rogers already displayed a phenomenological, almost ethological attitude when he published his first book on *Counseling and Psychotherapy* in 1942. Although the idea of the "internal frame of reference" was not yet featured, the remarkably phenomenological technique of "reflection," as a "natural" non-controlling environment was, and the book shows unmistakable signs of intention to comprehend the inner world of the client without disturbing the natural course of events—a "disciplined naivete," that is. At this time, Rogers had not heard of Husserl, nor had he yet read him when the second book *Client-Centered Therapy,* with its phenomenology showing loud and clear, was published in 1951.[5] Snygg and Combs, whose 1949 book, *Individual Behavior,* is an outstanding demonstration of a personality theory based on the concept of the phenomenal field, had certainly influenced Rogers, but there is no reference to Husserl in their work. (The up-dated edition of 1959, however, contains four references to Husserl.) Their work has been called, "A remarkably independent new type of phenomenological psychology" (Spiegelberg, 1960, p. 638). He adds, "Rogers' own approach also shows its phenomenological ingredients without any commitment to its philosophical ancestry." (What ancestry? It is very hard for a historian to accept the notion of independent invention.) These American developments lean heavily on Snygg's earlier article (1941), the import of which is expressed in its title, "The Need for a Phenomenological System of Psychology." Snygg, originally a behaviorist, is reported by Spiegelberg as having been influenced toward phenomenology by his contact with Kurt Lewin and Wolfgang Kohler. Certainly both of these men knew Husserl's work, but Lewin is said by Spiegelberg to have been influenced "much more prominently" by the phenomenology of Carl Stumpf than by Husserl. As for Kohler, he discusses Husserl extensively, critically, and is one of those who interprets Husserl's first principle of "logical requiredness" as having "little to do with psychology" (Kohler, 1938, p. 48). Husserl was often considered anti-psychological, and his major translator and interpreter, Farber (1943, p. 567), tries to heal this "misunderstanding" [6] which had been nourished by "Husserl's own repeated

---

[5] Personal communication.

[6] It is well worthwhile to quote his summary of Husserl's position:

"(c) There are a number of things which phenomenology conspicuously does not do or mean. (1) It does not 'tear the meaning loose from the act.' (2) It does not deny or reject the external world. (3) It does not try to answer all questions, and is not intended to be all-inclusive as a method for all purposes. (4) It is also not intended to be a substitute for other methods, and above all, for those involving factual and hypothetical elements. (5) It does not deny inductive truth, nor does it

efforts" to distinguish phenomenology from psychology. Husserl does have a demonstrable connection with the existential form of phenomenology [7] through his student Heidegger, and thus to Sartre, Camus, Rollo May, Tillich, and others prominent in this stream of the movement.

As a final note, it is worth comment that Van Kaam (1959) finds William James a source of the stream. He quotes J. Linscohten ("one of Europe's leading existential phenomenologists"), who in turn quotes the diary of Husserl for proof that "the father of European phenomenology admits the influence of the thought of the great American, James, on his own thinking" (May, 1961, p. 14). James, we may be sure, had a direct and deep influence on all of the American "self psychologies." (His writings on the subject have not been surpassed. They are the best single source available yet.)

The intent of this review is not to chauvinistically plant a flag on new territory. For one thing, it is very old territory which has been crossed by many travelers. The point is rather to free us of philosophical domination where those philosophies have little or no real connection with the psychologies bearing the same name, especially since "the very vaguest speculation has sometimes found shelter under the roof of phenomenology." (Kohler, 1938, p. 68.) Husserl's philosophy bears to clinical phenomenological psychology about the same order of relation as does Wundt's (or Titchner's) classical introspection to the modern forms of self-report. To understand phenomenology, it is more illuminating, and more in keeping with the very style of this approach, to look at its characteristics rather than to trace its history.

---

fail to distinguish between different types of 'truth.' (6) It is not a trap for metaphysical purposes. . . .

"(d) In contrast to these misunderstandings there are a number of things that phenomenology does do or mean. (1) It is the first method of knowledge because it begins with 'the things themselves' which are the final court of appeal for all knowledge. . . . (2) It views everything factual as an exemplification of essential structures and is not concerned with matters of fact as such. (3) It deals with not only 'real essences' but also with 'possible essences.' (4) Direct insight, evidence in the sense of the self-giveness of the objectivity is the ultimate test for it. (5) Despite the 'reduction' the phenomenologist still has a brain (an 'evolutionary' brain) in the same sense that he breathes. That statement is as true as it is irrelevant to the method.

[7] An embarrassment to some "respectable" phenomenologists as it is embarrassed itself by the Beatnik or Left Bank Existentialists, who also cherish immediacy of experience, self-consciously examine their own despair, etc.

Further Toward a Definition—Some Common Characteristics

Since phenomenology is not yet gathered together in a sufficiently homogeneous body to be identified, it is composed of like-minded people,[8] with similar attitudes, objectives, and methods, working rather independently in a gathering "third force," as Maslow sometimes calls it (May, 1961, p. 52). To help delineate this gathering, we turn to some characteristic interests or attitudes on which there has occasionally been some issue.

The Scientific Posture. In relation to science, there is a position which demands redefinition of what "sciencing" means. Phenomenology calls for intensive descriptive analysis—a description that often leads to an impatient demand for its supposed opposite, explanation via the "definitive" experiment. Science cannot be confined to the experimental alone, but must include exploration and discovery. This "naturalistic observation" is being reintroduced with a new power as "the foundation of all science" (Butler, 1962, p. 178). Zener reminds us that science consists of far more than confirming already observed relationships. A science not reviewing its problem area is dying, and he suggests "that twentieth-century psycho-physics has exploited the capital of phenomenological distinctions made in the nineteenth century—and [I] am apprehensive that no new comparable wealth of phenomenal distinctions relevant to more complex perceptions is presently being accumulated" (Zener, 1958, p. 364).

Science is subject to such change in fashion over time and even in locality that its objectives can always be questioned. Buytendijk quotes Cantril in this regard:

> The aim of science is often defined as the attempt to increase the accuracy of our predictions. While the accuracy of predictions is clearly a most important criterion of progress in scientific formulation, emphasis on prediction alone can easily obscure the more fundamental aim of science covered by the word *understanding* (David & von Bracken, 1957, p. 198.)

[8] One wonders who to name by way of illustration: Lewin, Rogers, G. Allport and perhaps F. Allport, Maslow, R. May, Bruner, Cantril, Patterson, Snygg, Jessor, as well as many others mentioned elsewhere in this chapter. And Freud, before "hardening of the categories" set in. Since these independent types seldom declare themselves, especially when the movement is still so ill-defined, others will appear more clearly in the future, as association does not imply guilt.

Prediction and control are often found linked together in the literature. The phenomenologist gives second place to prediction, as just indicated, and may reject control altogether. First, control is not science—it is just politics, or management. Second, if exercised in experimentation it is limiting and unfair, since it makes the task of the scientist all too easy, and too meaningless. The isolated reaction of the eye blink to the air puff is controlled, specific, but insignificant. The limited behavior of the man in a six by four cell is more predictable but less valuable to human beings because he is less human as he is more controlled.[9] Wellek says, "It is the task of psychology to teach men to understand themselves and each other better. Understanding presupposes phenomenology. It is itself a phenomenological act, an experience" (David & von Bracken, 1957, p. 293). It is this understanding (*Verstehen*) of fully human beings which constitutes the aim of this branch of science.

Understanding comes about through description, or is a concurrent process. Must description be opposed to explanation? What better explanation could there be than a complete description? If one really understands, if the description is fine enough, this reveals the mechanism, and explains *how*—but not why. "How" is the scientific question. "Why" belongs to the child or the theologian. A fine grained description of the digestive process tells us everything about the process from input (*subjectively* called "food") to output (*subjectively* called "waste"). Any explanation of "why" beyond that means "purpose of this process." That could be "because the person needs fuel," or "the food wants to be transformed into another state," or "God orders this process between person and food for the sake of either, both or neither but a third purpose to which they are incidental." Thus it is quite reasonable for MacLeod to put the question of science simply as "what is there" without regard to "why," "whence," or "wherefore" (Kuenzli, 1959, p. 156).

Reductionism. There is a strong anti-reductionistic bias characteristic of this movement. One finds objections to "reductionism" to biological drives (hunger, etc.), to simpler mechanisms, to lower forms, of things to each other. Jessor (1961) believes that the banishment of experience took place as psychologists sought safety in a "methodological objectivity" which forced a three-pronged reductionism: "(a) behavioral—the employment of arbitrary (physical) micro units of

---

[9] The "control group" as a comparison technique, or the "control" of variables to hold some steady while others vary is not the control referred to here.

stimulus and response, unlikely to enable meaningful constitution by the human organism; (b) physiological—employment of units logically remote from experiential significance for the human organism; (c) phylogenetic—the use of lower organisms for whom language is, of course, unavailable."

The general view is that man must be understood *as a totality*. To understand parts separately does not describe the totality they would form. Man has a special nature (his "being," currently called) which defies atomistic understanding in the way we have understood inanimate things and some lower forms of life. Half a piece of chalk is still a piece of chalk, only smaller; half a planarian worm is half of one worm, but still a worm in itself; half a man is not a man at all.

R. May (1961, p. 18) argues that man cannot be reduced to "drives" since "the more you formulate the forces or drives, the more you are talking about abstractions and not the existing, living human being." Opposition to simple stimulus-response reductionism has been steady since Dewey first wrote his objections to the reflex arc concept as the basis of all behavior. The phenomenologist is sure that between the physical properties of S and the R stands a whole system of potential choices in the prepared and evaluating, not passive organism, not at all likely to be moved on a simply stimulus receptor basis.[10] Responses may have multiple determinants, or single stimuli may have differential responses, or the organism may be downright selective about what stimulus it perceives, or even seeks out (Fiske & Maddi, 1961).

Also opposed is the genetic reductionism which tries to reduce not only complex forms to simple ones, but later states to earlier ones (Kuenzli, 1959, p. 153). The phenomenologist tries to take the fact as it is given, and to let it be as big as it is, rather than to cut it down to his size, or to the size of his measuring instruments.

The existence of this anti-reductionist bias as it applies to the genesis of behavior points to another closely related characteristic. So far as time orientation and determinism, the phenomenologist tends to be a historical. Their position is simply stated as, "the past is

---

[10] For the reader who is not acquainted with an actual statement of the contrasting view, the statement by Kimble (1953, p. 158) is quoted here.

"For all practical purposes, it is possible to construct a science of psychology in which the organism is considered as empty. For my own part, I can conceive of a psychology based on stimulus and response events entirely, one in which the existence of the organism is a completely unimportant fact. The scientific account will, after all, deal with behavior in the abstract."

To the "experientialist" this statement must sound incredible, but in fairness, the whole of his article should be read.

relevant only as it lives in the present." This refers only to the *psychological* past, of course. "The behavior's field at any given instant contains also the views of the individual about his past and future. . . . The psychological past and the psychological future are simultaneous parts of the psychological field existing at a given time." (Lewin, 1943, pp. 292-310.) While it is not true that "the past is a bucket of ashes," neither is man a prisoner of the past—indeed, besides heavy emphasis on present and immediate functioning without historical reconstruction, there is some inclination to see behavior as future-oriented more than past-restrained. Ideals, goals, striving, "self realization" figure prominently in the literature of this group.

Anti-Statistical? Is there an anti-statistical character to phenomenology? There has been, and may still be. Quantitative methods are not worshipped in the qualitative temple. The phenomenologist works on problems of *individual* behavior. He focuses on the unique, the atypical, but not the average, since groups do not perceive through a mass sensorium. By and large, group correlational methods will not tell the phenomenologist exactly what he wants to know either, since he wants to know *exactly.* There are statistical methods now developed for individual cases, and they are used with keen appreciation (Stephenson, 1953; Rogers & Dymond, 1954). Still, what the phenomenologist seeks is absolute certainty about individual circumstances, not probabilities about groups of non-identical units. In a symposium on "Clinical vs. Statistical Methods in Prediction," Meehl, representing statistical theory, described two six-shot revolvers, one containing five bullets and one empty chamber, the other one bullet and five empty chambers. Which would you choose to hold to your temple? Snygg, representing the clinical view, is not interested in the safety of numbers or the advantage of chance, therefore offered to choose the more heavily loaded gun with only one empty chamber, if he could know this particular gun to his clinical satisfaction and on that basis judge that the empty chamber was next to be fired. Wellek (1957, p. 291) puts his relation of qualitative to quantitative analysis this way:

> The assertion that description cannot yield any generally valid results is itself something subjective, an untenable dogma. If somebody can count correctly or incorrectly, he can also describe something rightly or wrongly. If a correct calculation is universally recognized, then a true description should be similarly accepted.

Mind-Body? In relation to the biological, phenomenology holds a somewhat tenuous position. If "the body is not a fact but a situation," it cannot be considered separate from its environment. As a biological substrate, it is the object of much thought in phenomenological work, especially among the perceptual specialties where neuro-anatomical structures are sought. But even there, the structures are pointed out by the functions—apparent phenomena. At the same time, it is well recognized that different structures "create" for the animal different environments—and thus different phenomenal worlds—as with simple or compound eyes, to mention an elementary example. Many phenomenologists are of the opinion that man does not live merely in order to survive, but rather to achieve some human value—"self realization" or some form of spiritual development. Part of the reservation in regard to biological "bedrock" stems from an emphasis on the social and cultural forces in shaping of behavior (for example, in the behavior of the person who starves to death in a "hunger strike"), but another comes from the anti-reductionistic bias applied to the reasoning about humans from lower and simpler forms of life. This will undoubtedly continue, but meanwhile, keen biological research is demonstrating that the simple forms are not so simple as often thought. Best (1963) mentions the example of the half-blinded (one-eyed) bee, flying in a circle, therefore thought to be an "autonomous" governed by asymmetric stimulation to its one remaining "photoelectric cell." Yet the bee has been shown to have a language "for communicating precise navigational information." The primitive worms which he trained in a Y maze showed signs of wanting freedom more than food at certain points, leading to the postulation of bio-phenomenological concepts such as "protoboredom," "protointerest," "protorebellion." [11]

[11] In connection with new findings in "protopsychology" and old thoughts on freedom, it is especially interesting to add Hebb's comments on the increasing autonomy of the "higher" evolutionary levels:

"I hope I do not shock biological scientists by saying that one feature of the phylogenetic development is an increasing evidence of what is known in some circles as free will; in my student days also referred to as the Harvard Law, which asserts that any well-trained experimental animal, on controlled stimulation, will do as he damn well pleases. A more scholary formulation is that the higher animal is less stimulus-bound.

Brain action is less fully controlled by afferent input, behavior therefore less fully predictable from the situation in which the animal is put. A greater role of ideational activity is recognizable in the animal's ability to "hold" a variety of stimulations for some time before acting on them and in the phenomenon of purposive behavior. There is more autonomous activity in the higher brain, and more selectivity as to which afferent activity will be integrated with the "stream of thought," the dominant, ongoing activity in control of behavior. Traditionally, we say that the subject is "interested" in this part of the environment, not interested in that; in these terms, the higher animal has a wider variety of interests and the interest of the moment plays a greater part in behavior, which means a greater unpredictability as to what stimulus will be responded to and as to the form of the response" (Hebb, quoted in Scher, 1962, p. 726).

However, until self-consciousness is demonstrated in lower forms, the clinical and social psychologist will probably maintain the concept of unique capacity for experience in the human being and may continue to consider it super-organic.

Freedom and Human Values. In the continuing debate between freedom and control, the phenomenologist is always found to be favoring some aspect of choice, will, decision, responsibility, as opposed to unadulterated determinism (Rogers & Skinner, 1956). This is not a stand based on punitive moralizing about blame, but an emphasis on the qualities of emergence, or "becoming" as well as "being." Freedom of action is considered to have more than political tones—it is a psychologically healthy condition for growth, i.e., the man most free has the widest scope of choice, therefore he (and his free culture) is in the best position to make adaptive responses to changing conditions. That conditions will change is also a conviction of the typical phenomenologist. Novelty is considered to be a feature of the environment, and evidence is rapidly accumulating to indicate that the organism will actively search for new experience (Fiske & Maddi, 1961). Man as a free and active agent is vividly described by Merleau-Ponty (1956), again expressing the extreme view:

> I am not a "living being" or even a "man" or even a "consciousness" with all the characteristics which zoology, social anatomy or inductive psychology attributes to these products of nature or history. I am the absolute source. My existence does not come from my antecedents or my physical or social entourage, but rather goes toward them and sustains them.

Lest that seem too strident or distant a view to take seriously, here is a statement of equally assertive force from Rogers' (1963) most recent comments:

> . . . man does not simply have the characteristics of a machine, he is not simply in the grip of unconscious motives, he is a person in the process of creating himself, a person who creates meaning in life, a person who embodies a dimension of subjective freedom.

Humanists tend to gather in this movement. They are interested in human beings as persons, albeit sometimes sensitive to accusations of "softness" (as if it referred to heads as well as hearts). Words such as "prizing" and "respect" commonly appear in the literature dealing with their conduct of human observations. The attitude is similar to that displayed by naturalists toward birds, deer, or other species which fascinate them. Out of this desire to let the object of study be free, methods develop as set by the problem rather than to suit available instrumentation—a slow and difficult process.

Behaviorism. The position with regard to behaviorism is somewhat in flux at the moment, with the bare possibility of areas of reconciliation or synthesis, but there has been basic tension and mutual antagonism for decades. This fundamental opposition has already been mentioned. It is common opinion that the "behavioral tide is ebbing." Jessor points to a shift in the literature on motivation as one sign (White, 1959) and to reconstruction in the philosophy of science (Feigl, 1959) as another. Not only has behavioristic learning theory and research proved to be largely ste.ile but "behaviorism and its canons of scientific procedure have failed in what must be considered the primary task of psychology—the scientific reconstruction of the person as we know him in ordinary life." (Jessor, 1961.) One of the main logical criticisms of behaviorism's "false objectivity" is that it always assumed the stimulus to have a peculiarly independent status—physical, invariant, and stable in its meaning, almost as if it had chosen itself to engage in the experiment (and *then* frozen). This notion is not the straw man invention of the phenomenologist. It has been suggested, for instance, by Davis (1953, p. 10), for physiological psychology:

> For a "stimulus (external event) to qualify under the proposed canon, it would have to be something which an experimenter could ascertain without there being any organism for it to work on.

But such a system would require that the experimenter himself were not an organism. For, as Koch (1959, pp. 768-769) points out:

> If stimuli and responses are acknowledged to depend for their identification on the perceptual sensitivities of human observers, then the demand for something tantamount to a language of pointer readings . . . must be given up. . . . If, further, the requirement is asserted that S be specified in a way which includes its inferred meaning for the organism, then *any* basis for a difference in epistemological status between an S-R language and what has been called "subjectivistic" language is eliminated.

Those who wishfully think that "behaviorism is dead" are mistaken. Phenomenology may have a chance to come alive in a climate no longer dominated by pseudo-physics in psychology, but behaviorism is now moving into significant areas of human behavior (Krasner, 1962), and even reformulating a "subjective behaviorism"(Pribham, 1963). (Of those earlier behaviorists who are being discarded, Hebb (1954, p. 101) says, "These men were narrow—they were wrong, and without them, without the simplification they achieved, modern psychology would not exist.") What is very likely to remain is the strong opposition of internal and external views of the subject. Even when the same event is under discussion, these two views remain in conflict. For example, when the "externalist" describes the *reinforcement* of the operant conditioning process (conducted by the outside observer), the "internalist" claims that the significant part of the process is the invention of the operant [12] (which emerges from within through the effort of the actor). (See Shlien & Krasner, in Strupp & Luborsky, 1962, p. 109.)

The "Essential Structure." One final characteristic formulated by most writers on phenomenological theory is that it should be the study of essences, or essential structures. This has to do with the notion that when one describes acts of meaning, there should be a definitive reference to the meant things. These meant things or their representations in awareness (ideal concepts) are thought to have cores, or centers of stratified structures, which centers are *irreducible categories*. These are the "things in themselves," not translatable into any other perception. (Tymieniecka, 1962, Ch. II.) For the most part, the stratified structure model is applied by European phenomenologists. Wellek applies this notion to studies of hypnosis. A subject is asked, during deep trance, to do something in conflict with his values. Refusal to execute the command in a post-hypnotic state is taken as evidence of a core region which cannot be overcome. (David & von Bracken, 1957, p. 290.) Piaget is interpreted as illustrative of this model in his studies of intelligence, finding higher mental adaptations (stages) not reducible to lower ones. Anthropologist Levi-Strauss is likewise interpreted as having made use of the stratification model in kinship studies (Tymieniecka, 1962, pp. 38-44). With few exceptions (Gendlin, 1962), American phenomenologists have not understood or used Husserl, and this aspect of stratification or essen-

[12] In this regard it is of interest to note that in studies of "imprinting," ducklings *must* be permitted to waddle after the decoy, from which Hess concluded that: "the strength of the imprinting appeared to be dependent not on the duration of the imprinting period but *on the effort exerted by the duckling.*" (Hess, 1958). (My italics.)

tial structures has not been followed in any deliberate way. It may be making an appearance in the factor analytic studies by Butler and others (Butler, Rice & Wagstaff, 1962; Butler, 1963) or in descriptive statements about the core of the phenomenal self (Snygg & Combs, 1949, p. 126), but is mentioned here chiefly because "essences" have figured in most theoretical descriptions of phenomenology, and may yet turn out to be a genuine part of the empirical system.

Characteristics in Method

Any system depends for its progress on methods. Phenomenology, like the rest of psychology, has been somewhat ill equipped in this regard, although some truly ingenious thinking has gone into Gestalt studies of phenomena, into studies of perceptual constancies, stimulus equivalence, the family of introspective and projective methods, empathic techniques, and some statistical methods applicable to individual percepts.

The overall problem is that of subjectivity. All methods in this approach depend more or less on the Response of the experiencer, and often on his own report (admission or assertion) of it. Quantitative analysis does not take the curse off, nor does the controlled experiment. Subjectivity has hung like an albatross around the neck of the phenomenologist, since it has been almost synonomous with "unscientific." [13]

Much has been said about the subjective-objective axis. It is based on a dualistic philosophy of separation between the knower and the known. "Subjective" is thought to mean the representing experience; "objective" refers to what is represented. But one person's experience can be the object of another's representation (or we can experience our own experience) so that experience itself is not subjective beyond rescue, nor the known object so separate from experience that it has a life of its own. It is not necessary to continue the "history of philosophy [in which] the subject and its object have been treated as absolutely discontinuous entities" (James, 1947, p. 52). It seems much more reasonable (to the phenomenologist) to assume that subjective/objective is a matter of degree, not of kind. (This holds with the understanding that he is not trying to study the physical world, or a class of things, but the psychological individual.)

A curious line of thinking led to what now appears to be a false

---

[13] Excellent references are Jessor, 1956; Bakan, 1954; Zener, 1958. What has passed for "scientific" has been concensus, stated in numbers and fortified by apparatus.

division, deeply imbedded in our ideology. Cantril and others who have developed a "transactional" point of view have shown that most of the behavior we analyze takes place in an *intersubjective* situation. So-called objective stimulus and so-called subjective response hardly deserve to be seen on two different levels since the latter defines the former. Further, the observer of the "subject" is himself a responding reactor: he is subjective about his "object" toward whom he was to be "objective" by simple virtue of the other *being* an object. What we really have, then, is a situation composed of two subjective viewers, either of whom might be called more objective *when viewing the other*. ("There is the objective—mind as it may be seen by others—and the subjective—mind as he the [cyberneticist] experiences it in himself.") (Ashby, 1962, p. 305.) Some scientific virtue was supposed to reside in distance from the observed according to a formula which seems to run: (a) distance makes the observer impersonal; (b) impersonal attitudes make the other an object; (c) thus, distance and impersonality contribute to "objectivity." Is this true?

It seems quite possible that distance could make for less objectivity, if by that we mean reliable and accurate representation of the phenomenon being observed. Too much distance could only lead to "projectivity," since the original object would be out of sight. Should the observer then better be the one in the very center of the experience? Is there some optimum distance? This leads to a rephrasing of the question, which should really be "who can be the most distant?" or "who can make the other more an object?" but simply "who is the best knower?" That person is closest to the truth. The problems then become: (1) Does he know? (2) Will he tell? (3) Has he the capacity to describe? If we are to have a science of experience, it will come mainly through the efforts of the skillful, intelligent, non-defensive and/or courageous persons who can know experience well and communicate knowledge, for verification and general comparisons, if possible. The current methods are approximations of that possibility.

Introspection. Introspection is supposed to have ended, with a whimper, when behaviorism outlawed it. That was one special, classical form. Bakan, as already noted, has revived the deliberate use of the method, by name, in a promising approximation which demonstrates the possibilities mentioned above. But also, Boring has pointed out that "introspection is still with us, doing business under various aliases, of which the *verbal report* is one." This verbal report is so ever-present and of such unavoidable significance that everyone must find some sort of accommodation to it. Spence (1944, p. 57) is willing to say that, "the phenomenological approach has its advantages, particularly in the complex field of social behavior of the human adult. It is obviously easier to gain some notion as to the relevant variables by asking the individual to verbalize them than it is to employ the procedure of trying to hypothesize them from knowledge of past history." At any rate, this shows some trust in the possibilities of communication, at least for convenience. Hilgard (1957, p. 4) goes farther:

> Some extremists believe that private experiences have no place in science; they believe that such experiences belong to the province of the artist or poet. But most psychologists hold that these private experiences are just as much a part of the real world as more observable activities, and they accept the *verbal report* of these experiences as data for science.

Skinner (1953, p. 282), who stands guard more sternly, is only willing to allow for some linguistic clues, as he writes by the light of the burning straw-man:

> The verbal report is a response to a private event, and may be used as a source of information about it. A critical analysis of the validity of this practice is of first importance. But we may avoid the dubious conclusion that, so far as science is concerned, the verbal report or some other discriminative response is the sensation.

True, the verbal report is not the sensation.[14] Neither is the pointer reading. But then, neither is Skinner's observation of behavior the behavior itself! Nor is his report of it his observation! The verbal report is not alone in its failure to *be* the experience it attempts to signify, and the *questions about its validity apply to all types of observations.* No sign is its referent—even the knowing is not the known, nor is the process of experiencing the experience, but it is as close as one can get, and quite close enough, I assert, for psychological study. Under certain conditions, I trust my thoughts, feelings, and even expressions of them, quite as much or more than I trust my (or your) observations of the direction of a pigeon's head, or a tennis ball's behavior in flight. (Remember, these things do not speak for themselves.)

---

[14] We dislike being limited to "sensation," the least of our concerns—and to the term "verbal report"—a slighting and pseudo-scientific reference to the full potency of language in communication, but for the moment, it is sufficient to accept the behaviorist's terminology.

All agree, some reluctantly, that there are private events. Most agree that there is private awareness of them. Can these events be considered as behavior? Not by the behaviorist, unless external signals are considered sufficiently representative to be accepted in the local and current framework of science, or "ways of knowing." Why such lack of trust in the verbal report? There are good reasons. One is that we have multiple thoughts for one voice, so that not all internal behaviors can be simultaneously expressed. Another is that we know, from our own experience, that the verbal report can be false. We have accidentally or deliberately made it so, and observed this. However, cannot the verbal report be true? It can, and can be more true than our outward behavior, and this we know from our experience also. It is more difficult (except in simple sensations and expression such as "ouch") to report the truth, if only because mistakes are easier to make than to avoid, but the verbal report cannot be said to have *by its nature* a low or negative correlation with the private event it represents. (It is odd that the determinists who rule out "free will" also distrust the verbal report, as if the behaver does have the capacity to falsify at will, if he is not merely stupid.)

Whatever stance one takes toward it, the verbal report is fundamental, and the latest technical advances are simply elegant extensions of it. This includes such excellent tools as the semantic differential (Osgood, 1960) and the Q-sort (Stephenson, 1953; Butler & Haigh, 1954; Shlien, 1962a). Introspection means, according to James, "looking into our minds, and reporting what we there discover," and these techniques are manipulatible data language for "reporting what we there discover."

Another problem in the verbal report, somewhat neutralized by tools such as those above which provide the semantic frame of reference, is the difficulty in overcoming the lack of precision in even the extensive vocabulary. It is partly for this reason (that we are only semi-articulate) that the poet in Hilgard's statement seems to have special access to private experience. What we lack is not so much the experience, or access, but the poet's refined and heightened imagery and his very hard work to formulate it. Our failure to have *le mot juste* ready at hand seems to put experience beyond accurate description. We only see the nature of our ordinary failure when we look at its exaggeration, in aphasia. It is next to impossible for one to describe the exact shade of feeling, meaning, color tone and intensity, etc., to another, especially in complex experience. There are, for simplification, yes/no answers, but then the phrasing of the question becomes complex. There is also the possibility of matching techniques, such as color matching, or with words, to match judge's perceptions of the speaker's meaning.

Kluver (1936) offered an experimental technique based on matching of response values (stimulus equivalence and non-equivalence), for the study of personality. It has been little used, though it would seem to hold some promise still. Interestingly enough, many of his early observations were drawn from the field of ethology, which has a clear but little recognized connection with phenomenological principles.

F. J. J. Buytendijk, whose early work with toads is cited by Kluver, has moved from animal observation into some of the most elusive human qualities, in his "Femininity and Existential Psychology," for example (David & van Bracken, 1957, pp. 197-211). Von Uexkull, one of the founders of ethological method, is often quoted in the literature of phenomenology, since his concept of "private worlds" or environments for each species and even each animal is very much to the phenomenological point (Tymieniecka, 1962, pp. 121-123). McKellar (1962, p. 636) in his chapter on introspection remarks, "To some extent, the ethologists like Tinbergen and Lorenz have reintroduced the methods of the naturalist into psychology." Principles of ethology as described by Hess (1962, p. 160) are highly compatible with those of phenomenology:

> Study of [animal] behavior must begin by obtaining as complete a knowledge as possible of the behavior of the species during the entire life cycle . . . . because *all facts on behavior must be acquired before any hypotheses are formulated* . . . . [Ethologists] have come to this conclusion because behavior is so multiform that a wealth of evidence can always be compiled in support of any theory, no matter how capriciously constructed." (My italics.)

Though the "entire life cycle" is beyond the reach of the study immediate experience, the other ideas, including the intent to study the animals in states which most closely resemble the natural habitat, without fear of the observer, fits phenomenology well.

Empathy. It was noted earlier that the Rogerian technique of "reflection" is almost ethological in its effort to preserve just such conditions as are described above. This technique was a remarkable invention, though it has been maligned by caricature and wooden application. It not only aims toward allowing free emergence of the dynamics of interaction without interference, but expresses perhaps better than any other form of interaction that much used and discussed quality, "empathy." Empathic understanding is described as one of the primary modes of knowing another and as a method in promoting personality change and development. According to Rogers,

> A second necessary condition of psychotherapy, as I see it, is the experiencing by the therapist of an accurate and empathic understanding of the client. This means that he senses and comprehends the client's immediate awareness of his own private world. It involves sensing the cognitive, perceptual, and affective components of the client's experiential field, as they exist in the client. Where the therapist is adequately sensitive, it means not only recognizing those aspects of experience which the client has already been able to verbalize, but also those unsymbolized aspects of his experience which have somehow been comprehended through subtle non-verbal clues by the delicate psychological radar of the therapist. The skillful therapist senses the client's world— no matter, how hallucinated or bizzare or deluded or chaotic—as if it were his own, but without ever losing the "as if" quality. (Shlien, 1961, p. 304.)

Van Kaam (1959, p. 70) calls this "co-experiencing":

> The understanding person shares at an emotional level the experience of the subject understood The prefix "co-" represents the awareness of the subject that the person understanding still remains another."

Rogers defines the act precisely in Koch (1959):

> *Empathy.* The state of empathy, or being empathic, is to perceive the internal frame of reference of another with accuracy, and with the emotional components and meanings which pertain thereto, as if one were the other person, but without ever losing the "as if" condition. Thus it means to sense the hurt or the pleasure of another as he senses it, and to perceive the causes thereof as he perceives them, but without ever losing the recognition that it is *as if* I were hurt or pleased, etc. If this "as if" quality is lost, then the state is one of identification."

Empathy, or co-experiencing, has not been thoroughly described or researched, but it is well known *as an experience.* It may be put in terms such as those already quoted, or in what we are given to call "mystical" (though this seems to refer more to our ignorance or sheepishness than to its quality) ways such as those described by Buber (1925):

A man belabours another, who remains quite still. Then let us assume that the striker suddenly receives in his soul the blow which he strikes; the same blow; that he receives it as the other who remains still. For the space of a moment he experiences the situation from the other side. Reality imposes itself on him. What will he do? Either he will overwhelm the voice of the soul, or his impulse will be reversed.

A man caresses a woman, who lets herself be caressed. Then let us assume that he feels the contact from two sides—with the palm of his hand still, and also with the woman's skin. The two fold nature of the gesture, as one that takes place between two persons, thrills through the depth of enjoyment in his heart and stirs it. If he does not deafen his heart he will have—not to renounce the enjoyment but—to love.

I do not in the least mean that the man who has had such an experience would from then on have this two-sided sensation in every such meeting—that would perhaps destroy his instinct. But the one extreme experience makes the other person present to him for all time. A transfusion has taken place after which a mere elaboration of subjectivity is never again possible or tolerable to him.

Not everyone will recognize or remember this quality of experience, and still fewer admit it, but some would vouch for it as an actuality (Shlien 1961, p. 316). At least we realize that we hesitate to cause pain (or else enjoy causing pain) because we believe that the pain of others resembles our own. At least, that.

If this type of description gives uneasiness, one can find more solid comfort in recent physiological studies (Greenblatt, 1959; Dimascio, *et al.*, 1955, 1957; Dittes, 1957) which suggest physiological evidence of "co-experiencing:"

> Studies of different doctor-patient dyads have shown us that the doctor is quite as reactive as the patient. [Findings] . . . suggest physiological rapport at least for *some* of the emotions experienced by the patient It is further worth noting that the *rapport phenomenon was most striking when the doctor was "actively listening" and less striking when he was distracted or "not listening"* . . . (Our italics.) (Bebout & Clayton, 1962.)

Lacy (1959) in his review, comments that "these are surprising data, and . . . may imply, as the authors [Coleman, Greenblatt & Solomon] seem to feel, a "physiological relationship" between the therapist and patient revealing a process of 'empathy.' "

To Rogers, empathy is not just *a* way of knowing but perhaps *the* primary method in comprehension of all phenomena. He speaks of empathy as a way of knowing both the other, and also oneself, via empathy turned inward. While objects (stones and trees) have no experience to share, even "objective" knowledge is related to empathy. Empathic understanding in that case is directed toward the reference group which objectifies, by consensus, one's experimentally derived information. Empathy, then, is the fundamental way of knowing, and its direction may turn inward or outward (Rogers, 1959, 1963). It is of singular importance in this methodology. There are two elements of knowing: (1) feeling, or the pathic way (from *pathetos,* able to suffer or subject to suffering) which is the process of *understanding,* and (2) seeing, (from *spectore,* to look at) which is the process of spection, intro or extro, or *perceiving.* Together, these two are ways of knowing for phenomenology, if not for all of science.

PERCEPTION AND PERSONALITY

Perception

This is often called a perceptual approach to personality.[15] Rogers (1951, p. 307), for instance, writes of the actual "reorganization of visual perception" during therapy in contrast to the loose descriptive analogy implied by such phrases as "seeing things differently." Combs and Snygg (1959, p. 20) base an absolute law of behavior on perceptual experience: *"All behavior, without exception, is completely determined by, and pertinent to, the perceptual field of the behaving organism."* Does this sound like S-R theory writ large, with "perceptual field" standing for "stimulus"? For clarification, they add, *"By the perceptual field, we mean the entire universe, including himself, as if it is experienced by the individual at the instance of action."* So, to the extent that the entire universe can be reduced to an identifiable stimulus in a given moment of experience, we are in bed with the enemy. Should we simply acquiesce to the inevitable and say "good night," or try to avoid the scandal?

No scientist, looking for lawful descriptions of behavior, wants to turn away from cause and effect. But by now, many phenomenological reservations have appeared; indeed these are precisely what and all that distinguish phenomenology and S-R theory. We come to the perceiving situation with differing needs. These are well known to affect the

[15] Basic references for the interested student are Combs & Snygg (1949); Rogers (1951, 1957, 1959); Patterson (1959); and Gendlin (1962).

perception of the stimulus. We also come with a different history of experience. We may even bring different perceptual structures, either in physiological capacity or psychological expectancy. What we react to is not someone else's stimulus, but *our* total perception of *our* phenomenal world. In elegantly contrived visual demonstrations, Ames has shown that "what is perceived is not what exists but what one believes exists" (Combs & Snygg, 1959, p. 84). "Seeing is believing," if one can see, but "believing is seeing," too. We construct our phenomenal world to fit expectations. (Reik, 1962) working with college "drop-out" students finds it the rule that they "describe mothers as being in delicate health, liable to become ill at any moment. What is important here is not what the parents are like in actuality, but that the student's conception of them produces a very real upset in his inner world.")

It might seem that all of these individual differences in perception are the result of the variations in need, structure, past experience, and aim or expectation, thus all "distortions." Many are, but we do not derive all differences from parataxic errors, like the blind men describing the elephant. It is worthwhile to note Bronowski's description of the "clock paradox" based on relativity theory, which proves that two clocks, moving with respect to one another, run at different speeds. It is demonstrated that two observers of a moving light, one moving with it and the other standing still, will have time pass *at different speeds for them*. If time did not, then the speed of light would have to vary. (Bronowski, 1963.) In the field of perception, then, it is not just cultural relativity or egocentrism which causes differences (though these factors must account for most of the variance) but also unavoidable physical relativity.

Because of these relativities, the perceptual system organizes on the basis of what are called "perceptual constancies." These constancies are assumptions to the effect that actions will take place as we have become accustomed to them in the past. Thus we tend to judge depth or distance by apparent size of a familiar object, or we catch a baseball that we did not see after it arrived at a point two feet from our glove. "Constancies" make us subject to optical illusions, but for the most part they make it possible to carry out relatively stable operations in a constantly active and changing environment (Ittleson & Cantril, 1954).

Before turning to a definition of personality, something should be said in the way of a definition of perception. Definitions are only opinions, of course. One opinion would be that all impingement of stimuli (such as light or sound, upon receptive nerve cells) is perception. A distinction made by J. J. Gibson (1963, p. 1) is important. *"Perception involves meaning; sensation does not."* (Our italics.) To clarify this a bit more, we would say: radar reflects; a phototropic cell senses; and a mind perceives. Ours is a perceptual theory of personality in that it: deals with *meanings,* and requires cognitive apparatus.

Personality

Now a definition of personality is in order. While these definitions are not sheer snares and delusions, neither are they scientific revelations. They are only a part of the system. In this system, personality must have some relation to the subjective, and to the perceptual. It reflects the very shift which has taken place in psychology as described by Bruner, Goodnow and Austin (1956, p. 106) who note that,

> The past few years have witnessed a notable increase in interest in and investigation of the cognitive processes. . . . Partly, it has resulted from a recognition of the complex processes that mediate between the classical "stimuli" and "responses" out of which stimulus-response learning theories hoped to fashion a psychology that would bypass anything smacking of the "mental." The impeccable peripheralism of such theories could not last long. As "S-R" theories came to be modified to take into account the subtle events that may occur between the input of a physical stimulus and the emission of an observable response, the old image of the "stimulus-response bond" began to dissolve, its place being taken by a mediation model. As Edward Tolman so felicitously put it some years ago, in place of a telephone switchboard connecting stimuli and responses it might be more profitable to think of a map room where stimuli were sorted out and arranged before every response occurred, and one might do well to have a closer look at these intervening "cognitive maps."

This well describes what has been developing throughout the chapter. Phenomenology could never have adopted a "switchboard" model. It could and did adopt the image of a map. That is how the "self-concept" or "self-structure" is often described—as a map to which the person refers when he is about to make a move. This map is, in fact, one of those "perceptual constancies" which helps to stabilize behavior, and it is also one of the reasons for the emphasis on self-consistency (Lecky, 1945). Personality is one's view of himself, the self-concept, by which he tends to order and interpret his internal and external experiences.

Rogers (1951, Ch. 11) developed theory of personality and behavior based on the phenomenal self, stated in a set of nineteen propositions which are abstracted in a summary by Shlien (1962a). Some of these fundamentals have already been mentioned in the earlier discussion.

1. Each person is unique. No one else can ever completely know his experience. Since each person's neurological capacities and life history combine in unique ways, the closest approach to another's experience is to see it through his own eyes, insofar as possible. Some of his experience is consciously symbolized. Some is at lower levels of awareness, where it has a lesser influence, perhaps a less controllable influence, on behavior.

2. Behavior is a consequence of perception. The organism reacts to reality as it is perceived and defined *by that organism*. The "objective evidence" of the thermometer not withstanding, he who thinks the room hot opens the window; who thinks it cold closes the same window. Who see a light red, stops; sees the same light green, goes; sees an object as delicious eats it; the same object as refuse, avoids it or sickens from it. Whatever "it" may be—by consensus, physical measurement, or philosophical proof, the way in which "it" is perceived will determine behavior toward it.

3. From this, it follows that if one wants to promote a stable change in behavior, one must change the *perception* of the one who is behaving. (Unstable changes can be forced from outside, but enduring alterations motivated by internal shifts depend on new perceptions.)

4. The perception of threat is always followed by defense. Defense may take many forms—aggression, withdrawal, submission, etc—but it is the general and categorical response to danger.

5. Perception is narrowed and rigidified by threat. (Experimentally, the phenomenon of "tunnel vision" can be evoked by threat.) Narrowed and rigidified perception blocks change in behavior. Threat, therefore, does not permanently change behavior. It only arouses defenses. Attacking the defense system is likely to complicate it, causing more of the psychological economy to be devoted to defense, still further restricting perception and inhibiting change.

6. Of the whole perceptual field, a portion becomes differentiated as the self. *This is the self-concept.* The self-concept has dimensions, and the dimensions have values. Thus the self-concept may be one of weakness or strength, for instance. Lovable—hateful, lucky—unlucky, worthy or contemptible, are other examples of dimensions which influence behavior. They influence behavior because the interpretation of the self leads to a reactive interpretation of the external object. For instance, if one feels strong, a boulder is a weapon to push into the treads of an armored tank; if weak, the same boulder is a refuge to hide behind. If one feels sick and helpless, the nurse is a creature of mercy, appealed

to for comfort. The same nurse may be seen as a temptress, to be sexually pursued, if the patient sees himself as well and sturdy. All experience is evaluated as friendly or dangerous, interesting or boring, possible or impossible, etc. depending *not* upon the nature of the experience so much as upon the *self-concept of the experiencer.*

7. As experiences occur, they are related to the self structure, and depending on it, each experience will be (a) symbolized accurately, perceived consciously, and organized into the self structure, (b) ignored, though sensed (as a sensation) because it has no significance to the self, or (c) denied or distorted when symbolized because it is threatening to the self.

"Conscious and Unconscious" Aspects

Throughout this chapter, we have been thinking primarily about ways of knowing. The statement in 7c (above) leads us to consider also remembering and forgetting, and selective attention and inattention..

The issue of the '"unconcious" tends to distinguish two clinical divisions—the psychoanalytic and the phenomenal—though not all Freudian concepts are completely foreign to phenomenology, and not all phenomenologists reject the unconscious. Those few who do not are mainly proponents of projective techniques, who rest their *interpretations* heavily upon psychoanalytic dynamics, though they rest their operational *assumptions* upon phenomenology. Thus L. K. Frank, writing (in the company of phenomenologists) about the "private world of personal meanings" (Kuenzli, 1959, p. 96), would readily agree that "we see things not as they are, but as we are." However, he expresses doubts, held by most adherents of projective techniques, that the individual either has a clear understanding of himself, or would reveal such understanding in the face of social pressure. Or, H. A. Murray puts it, "the most important things about an individual are what he cannot or will not say." This succinctly states the problem—is it a matter of cannot, or is it will not? There is no doubt that Murray values the interior experience. But the phenomenologist will more readily depend on the face value of the testimony or self report of the individual. Is this his strength or his weakness? It depends in part as to whether he can create conditions that do not force concealment but favor revelation. It also depends on whether or not he postulates an inaccessible unconscious. Patterson, for instance, "sees no need to postulate an unconcious" and finds support in studies and opinions which conclude "that a man's expressed opinions and values are more indicative when it comes to prediction than are projective techniques" (Patterson, 1959, p. 255). A similar finding is reported in a study of the "role of self-understanding in prediction of behavior" (Rogers, Kell, & McNeil, 1948).

It may be that the dimension of rational-irrational is the great divide between those, like Murray and Frank, who are generally phenomenologists, and those otherwise like minded theorists who do not adopt the unconscious. Allport, for instance, considers humans to be "characteristically rational. Irrational aspects appear in the undeveloped personality of the child, or the mentally ill" (Maddi, Ch. —). Rogers believes that man, as a healthy, fully functioning person, is "exquisitely rational"—even his defenses have a certain wisdom about them.

In the main, then, the phenomenological position is in some opposition to the concept of "the unconscious." There are knotty problems involved, which may be analyzed in terms of learning, differentiation, remembering, or forgetting, with self-consistency and Sullivan's concept of "selective inattention" brought into play—but which are beyond the scope of this chapter.

From the standpoint of the existential phenomenologist such as Sartre (1953), the unconscious is a rejected concept, representing "bad faith." As such, it is simply an avoidance of responsibility, via suppression rather than repression, "playing the game" of mental illness. The ideas of Rogers, Snygg and Combs, and others of their school can probably be expressed in this way: two elements, "span of attention" and "level of awareness" operate within an energy system in which energy levels are raised and lowered, and attention directed and focused, by emotions. A favorite example in the perceptual analogies commonly used is that of angle of vision as affected by threat. Normally, under relaxed conditions, the angle of vision is wide enough to permit peripheral perceptions at 80+ degrees to either side when the viewer looks straight ahead. Under conditions of intense emotion (of which threat is one) the phenomenon of "tunnel vision" can be induced. The view becomes narrow, as if the viewer were looking through a tube. In that event, the peripheral scene, which is no longer perceived, is not "inaccessible." It is simply out of sight until normal vision is restored.

Span of attention and level of awareness are thought to enlarge and constrict, or rise and fall, according to the energy available at a given time. If sensation is distinguished from perception according to Gibson's previously noted idea, then sensation registers at a very low level of awareness. There are many sensations which, depending on energy available, we do not immediately or perhaps ever (the process can be delayed) turn into perceptions. To the extent that sensations enter awareness at all, they vaguely influence behavior. A soldier on watch in a jungle slaps only those mosquitos actually noticed. The remainder contribute to some general impression of feeling tone of uneasiness,[16] much less significant than his fear for his life. As he is pinned down by enemy fire, the mosquitos may become ferocious, but fade as perceptions. Long after, at rest in his lawn chair, he may viciously swat and spray, vowing to kill all mosquitos, hating them for sensations caused years ago, now raised to perceptions in a different situation.

The idea of an energy level model is perhaps especially appropriate to a neurological system, but that is not its justification. Its value is in the distinct and important difference between it and the so-called "hydraulic" model as Freud's concept of the unconscious is often described (MacIntyre, 1958, p. 22). If, as Freud thought, the "sum of excitations" in the nervous system is constant (like the volume of blood in the circulatory system, for instance), then an experience, when forgotten, must go some place—some place "out of consciousness." The hydraulic model makes a "reservoir" an absolute necessity. In an energy model, where the sum of excitations is *not* constant but varies according to variation of intake and metabolic rate, forgetting and remembering are functions of a variable process. Once perceived, an experience moves in and out of consciousness *in time,* not in space. The forgotten does not move to an inaccessible location. It stays where it is, and the amount of light cast upon it grows dim, as it were.

Theoretically, given complete absence of threat, and a resultant complete freedom of energy from defensive activities, memory would be as complete as the needs of the moment dictated, limited only by

---

[16] William James (1950, p. 607) observed that "if you make a real red cross (say) on a sheet of white paper invisible to an hypnotic subject, and yet cause him to look fixedly at a dot on the paper on or near the cross, he will, on transferring his eye to a blank sheet, see a bluish-green after image of a cross. This proves that it has impressed his sensibility. He has *felt* it, but not *perceived* it." Some sensations, such as the weight of this book on your finger tips, may become perceptions if attention is so directed, or if the amount of available energy varies in such a way as to increase sensitivity. Obviously, in social situations which are often complex and fast moving, many high level sensations or low level perceptions are experienced and forgotten in the rush of events on the fluctuations of energy levels.

the levels of awareness permitted by energy available at that moment. Such conditions are seldom if ever achieved, and then only temporarily, since the press of new experience and changing social environment alters the situation, recreating "normal" levels of stress. Perhaps just to the extent that these ideal conditions are approximated, the phenomenologist is justified in taking at face value the self reports toward which his methodology points and which others so distrust.

Motivation

Unconscious or not, motivation is one remaining problem. Presumably the definition of motivation does not differ much throughout these chapters—it has to do with what the person is trying to accomplish through his behaviors. There is only one basic motive to which all behaviors are ascribed in this system. It is called "growth," or "self-enhancement," "self-realization" (Butler & Rice, 1962, Ch. —). Combs and Snygg (1959, p. 46) put it as *"that great driving, striving force in each of us by which we are continually seeking to make ourselves ever more adequate to cope with life."* Rogers (1963) adds, "Whether the stimulus arises from within or without, whether the environment is favorable or unfavorable, the behaviors of an organism can be counted on to be in the direction of maintaining, enhancing, and reproducing life. That is the very nature of the process we call life."

Conclusion

There is, by way of summary, a story about a psychologist which is somewhat legendary in the Chicago area. It is a commentary upon many elements which have been discussed: language, personal meanings, frames of reference, motives, private worlds, methods of observation, etc. And it points out that it is not always true that the human mind thinks silently. It can, but it sometimes thinks out loud, from which we can learn if we listen.

The upper class parents of a small boy were worried. Their son was quiet, sensitive, lonely, nervous, afraid of and highly excited by other children. He stammered in the presence of strangers, and was becoming more shy and withdrawn. The parents were embarrassed and did not want to expose their fears, but wanted some professional advice before the child entered school. The father solved their dilemma by calling a college friend whom he had not seen for years, and who had become in those years a well known clinical psychologist. For "old times' sake" an invitation for a weekend in their suburban home was extended, and with some curiosity, accepted. After dinner, the mother "casually" mentioned their concern about the child; the father amplified this and suggested that after lunch the next day, the boy might be observed at play for a psychological appraisal. The visitor understood now the purpose of his visit, asked appropriate questions about history and behavior, and prepared to take up his assignment. He watched, unseen, from a balcony above the garden where the boy played by himself. The boy sat pensively in the sun, listening to neighboring children shout. He frowned, rolled over on his stomach, kicked the toes of his white shoes against the grass, sat up and looked at the stains. Then he saw an earthworm. He stretched it out on the flagstone, found a sharp edged chip, and began to saw the worm in half. At this point, impressions were forming in the psychologist's mind, and he made some tentative notes to the effect: "Seems isolated and angry, perhaps over-aggressive, or sadistic, should be watched carefully when playing with other children, not have knives or pets." Then he noticed that the boy was talking to himself. He leaned forward and strained to catch the words. The boy finished the separation of the worm. His frown disappeared, and he said, "There. Now you have a friend."

REFERENCES

ALLPORT, G. W. The personalistic psychology of William Stern. *Charact. & Pers.*, 1936, *5*, 231-246.

ALLPORT, G. W. Scientific models and human morals. *Psychol. Rev.*, 1947, *54*, 182-192.

ASCH, S. E. *Social psychology*. New York: Prentice-Hall, 1953.

ASHBY, C. What is mind? Objective and subjective aspects in cybernetics. In J. Scher (Ed.), *Theories of the mind*. Glencoe, Ill.: Free Press, 1962.

BAKAN, D. A reconsideration of the problem of introspection. *Psychol. Bull.*, 1954, *51* (2), 105-118.

BEATTIE, D. M. The effect of imaginary practice on the acquisition of a motor skill. Unpublished M. A. dissertation, Univer. of Toronto, 1949.

BEBOUT, J. E., & CLAYTON, MARTHA. Toward a concept of shared experiencing in psychotherapy. *Counseling Center Discussion Papers,* Vol. 8, No. 10, 1962.

BECK, S. J., & MOLISH, B. (Eds.) *Reflexes to intelligence: a reader in clinical psychology.* Glencoe, Ill.: Free Press, 1959.

BERENDA, C. W. Is clinical psychology a science? *Amer. Psychologist,* 1957, *12,* 725-729.

BEST, J. Protopsychology. *Scientific American,* 1963, *208* (2), 54-75.

BORING, E. G. *A history of experimental psychology.* New York: Appleton-Century-Crofts, 1950.

BORING, E. G. A history of introspection. *Psychol. Bull.,* 1953, *50,* 169-189.

BLAKE, R., & RAMSEY, G. (Eds.) *Perception: an approach to personality.* New York: Ronald Press, 1951.

BRONOWSKI, J. The clock paradox. *Scientific American,* 1963, *208* (2), 134-148.

BRUNER, J. S., & GOODNOW, JACQUELINE J., & AUSTIN, G. A. *A study of thinking.* New York: Wiley, 1956.

BUBER, M. *Between Man and Man.* London: Kegan Paul, 1947.

BUTLER, J. M. *Quantitative naturalistic research.* New York: Prentice-Hall, 1962.

BUTLER, J. M., & HAIGH, G. V. Changes in the relation between self-concepts and ideal-concepts. In C. R. Rogers & Rosalind F. Dymond (Eds.), *Psychotherapy and personality change.* Chicago: Univer. of Chicago Press, 1954.

BUTLER, J. M., RICE, LAURA N., & WAGSTAFF, ALICE. On the naturalistic definition of variables: an analogue of clinical analysis. In H. Strupp & Luborsky (Eds.), *Research in psychotherapy,* Vol. II. Washington, D. C.: Amer. Psychol., Assn., 1962.

COLEMAN, R., GREENBLATT, M., & SOLOMON, H. C. Physiological evidence of rapport during psychotherapeutic interviews. *Dis. nerv. System.,* 1956, *17,* 2-8.

COMBS, A. W., & SNYGG, D. *Individual behavior: a perceptual approach to behavior.* New York: Macmillan, 1959.

DAVID, H., & VON BRACKEN, K. *Perspectives in personality theory.* New York: Basic Books, 1957.

DAVIS, R. Physiological psychology. *Psychol. Rev.,* 1953, *60,* 7-14.

DiMASCIO, A., BOYD, R. W., & GREENBLATT, M. Physiological correlates of tension and antagonism during psychotherapy. A study of "interpersonal physiology." *Pyschosom. Med..* 1957, *19,* 99-104.

DiMASCIO, A., BOYD, R. W., GREENBLATT, M., & SOLOMON, H. C. The psychiatric interview: a sociophysiological study. *Dis. nerv. System,* 1955, *16,* 2-7.

DITTES, J. E. Galvanic skin response as a measure of patient's reaction to therapist's permissiveness. *J. abnorm. soc. Psychol.,* 1957, *55,* 295-303.

FARBER, M. *The foundation of phenomenology.* Cambridge: Harvard Univer. Press, 1943.

FEIGL, H. Philosophical embarrassments of psychology. *Amer. Psychologist,* 1959, *14,* 115-128.

FISKE, D., & MADDI, S. *Functions of varied experience.* Homewood, Ill.: Dorsey Press, 1961.

FRANK, L. K. Projecive methods in the study of personality. In Kuenzli, A. (Ed.), *The phenomenological problem.* New York: Harper, 1959.

GENDLIN, E. *Experiencing and the creation of meaning.* Glencoe, Ill.: Free Press, 1962.

GIBSON, J. J. Perception as a function of stimulation. In S. Koch (Ed.), *Psychology: a study of a science,* Vol. I. New York: McGraw-Hill, 1959.

GREENBLATT, M. Discussion of papers by Saslow and Matarazzo, and Lacey. In E. A. Rubinstein & M. B. Parloff (Eds.), *Research in psychotherapy.* Washington, D. C.: Amer. Psychol. Assoc., 1959.

HEBB, D. O. The problem of consciousness and introspection. In E. Adrian (Ed.), *Brain mechanics and consciousness,* Oxford: Blackwell Scientific Publications, 1954.

HESS, E. H. Imprinting in animals. *Scientific American,* 1958, 198:81.

HESS, E. H. Ethology: an approach to the complete analysis of behavior. In *New directions in psychology.* New York: Holt, Rinehart & Winston, 1962.

HILGARD, E. R. *Introduction to psychology* (2nd ed.) New York: Harcourt, Brace, 1957.

HULL, C. *Principles of behavior.* New York: Appleton-Century, 1943.

ITTLESON, W., & CANTRIL, H. *Perception: a transactional approach.* Garden City: Doubleday, 1954.

JAMES, W. *Essays in radical empiricism: a pluralistic universe.* New York: Longmans, 1947.

JAMES, W. *Principles of psychology.* New York: Dover Press, 1950 edition.

JESSOR, R. Phenomenological personality theories and the data language of psychology. *Psychol. Rev.,* 1956, *63* (3), 173-180.

JESSOR, R. Issues in the phenomenological approach to personality. *J. individ. Psychol.,* 1961, *17,* 27-38.

KIMBLE, G. Psychology as a science. *Scientific Monthly,* 1953, *LXXVII* (3).

KLUVER, H. *Behavior mechanisms in monkeys.* Chicago: Univer. of Chicago Press, 1933.

KLUVER, H. The study of personality and the method of equivalent and non-equivalent stimuli. *Charact. & Pers.,* 1936, *5,* 91-112.

KOCH, S. (Ed.) *Psychology: a study of a science,* Vol. III. New York: McGraw-Hill, 1959.

KOHLER, W. *The place of value in a world of facts.* New York: Liveright, 1938.

KRASNER, L. The therapist as a social reinforcement machine. In H. Strupp & Luborsky (Eds.), *Research in psychotherapy,* Vol. II. Washington, D. C.: Amer. Psychol. Assoc., 1962.

KUENZLI, A. E. (Ed.) *The phenomenological problem.* New York: Harper, 1959.

LACEY, J. I. Psychophysiological approaches to the evaluation of psychotherapeutic process and outcome. In E. A. Rubinstein & M. B. Parloff (Eds.), *Research in psychotherapy.* Washington, D. C.: Amer. Psychol. Assoc., 1959.

LANDSMAN, T. Four phenomenologies. *J. individ. Psychol.,* 1958, *14,* 29-37.

LECKY, P. *Self-consistency: a theory of personality.* New York: Island Press, 1945.

LEWIN, K. *Field theory in social science: selected theoretical papers.* D. Cartwright (Ed.) New York: Harper, 1951.

MacINTYRE, A. C. *The unconscious.* London: Routledge & Kegan Paul, 1958.

MacLEOD, R. B. The place of phenomenological analysis in social psychological theory. In J. H. Rohrer & M. Sherif (Eds.), *Social psychology at the crossroads.* New York: Harper, 1951.

MAY, R. *Existential psychology.* New York: Random House, 1961.

McKELLAR, P. *The method of introspection.* In J. Scher (Ed.). *Theories of the mind.* Glencoe, Ill.: Free Press, 1962.

MERLEAU-PONTY, M. *La phenomenologie de la perception.* Paris: Gallimard, 1945.

MERLEAU-PONTY, M. What is phenomenology? *Cross Currents,* 1956, *6,* 59-70.

OSGOOD, C., SUCI, G., & TANNENBAUM, P. *The measurement of meaning.* Urbana: Univer. of Ill. Press, 1957.

PATTERSON, C. H. *Counseling and psychotherapy: theory and practice.* New York: Harper, 1959.

POLANYI, M. *Personal knowledge.* Chicago: Univer. of Chicago Press, 1958.

PRIBHAM, K. H. Interrelations of psychology and the neurological disciplines. In S. Koch (Ed.), *Psychology: a study of a science,* Vol. 4, New York: McGraw-Hill, 1962.

REIK, L. The drop-out problem. *The Nation,* 1962, *194* (20).

ROGERS, C. R. *Counseling and psychotherapy.* Boston: Houghton-Mifflin, 1942.

ROGERS, C. R. *Client-centered therapy: its current practice, implications and theory.* Boston: Houghton-Mifflin, 1951.

ROGERS, C. R. The necessary and sufficient conditions of therapeutic personality change. *J. consult. Psychol.,* 1957, *21,* 95-103.

ROGERS, C. R. *Becoming a person.* Boston: Houghton-Mifflin, 1961. (a)

ROGERS, C. R. Two divergent trends. In R. May (Ed.), *Existential psychology.* New York: London House, 1961. (b)

ROGERS, C. R. The actualizing tendency in relation to "motives" and to consciousness. Nebraska Symposium on Motivation, 1963. (To be published.)

ROGERS, C. R., & DYMOND, ROSALIND. *Psychotherapy and personality change.* Chicago: Univer. of Chicago Press, 1954.

ROGERS, C. R., KELL, B. L., & MCNEILL, H. The role of self understanding in prediction of behavior. *J. consult. Psychol.,* 1948, *12,* 174-186.

ROGERS, C. R.., & SKINNER, B. F. Some issues concerning the control of human behavior. *Science,* 1956, No. 3231, 1057-1066.

SARTRE, J. *Existential psychoanalysis.* New York: Philosophical Library, Inc., 1953.

SCHER, J. (Ed.) *Theories of the mind.* Glencoe, Ill.: Free Press, 1962.

SHLIEN, J. M. A client centered approach to schizophrenia. In A. Burton (Ed.), *Psychotherapy of the psychoses.* New York: Basic Books, 1961.

SHLIEN, J. M. The self concept in relation to behavior: theoretical and empirical research. In Stuart W. Cook (Ed.), *Research Supplement to Religious Education,* July-August, 1962. (a)

SHLIEN, J. M. Toward what level of abstraction of criteria. In H. Strupp & Luborsky (Eds.). *Research in psychotherapy,* Vol. II. Washington, D. C.: Amer. Psychol. Assoc., 1962. (b)

SKINNER, B. F. *Science and human behavior.* New York: Macmillan, 1953.

SPENCE, K. The nature of theory construction in contemporary psychology. *Psychol. Rev.,* 1944, *51,* 49-68.

SPIEGLEBERG, H. *The phenomenological movement: an historical introduction.* Hague: Martinus Nyhoff, 1960.

SNYGG, D. The need for a phenomenological system of psychology. *Psychol. Rev.,* 1941. *48,* 404-424.

SNYGG, D., & COMBS, A. W. *Individual behavior.* New York: Harper, 1949.

STEPHENSON, W. *The study of behavior.* Chicago: Univer. of Chicago Press, 1953.

TOLMAN, E. Principles of purposive behavior. In S. Koch (Ed.), *Psychology: a study of a science,* Vol. II. New York: McGraw-Hill, 1959.

TYMIENIECKA, ANNA-TERESA. *Phenomenology and science in contemporary European thought.* New York: Farrar, Straus & Cudahy, 1962.

of "really feeling understood." *J. individ. Psychol.,* 1959, *15,* 66-72.
VAN KAAM, A. L. Phenomenal analysis: exemplified by a study of the experience

WELLEK, A. The phenomenological and experimental approach to psychology and characterology. In H. P. David & H. von Bracken (Eds.), *Perspectives in personality theory*. New York: Basic Books, 1957.

WHITE, R. Motivation reconsidered: the concept of competence. *Psychol. Rev.*, 1959, *66*, 297-333.

ZENER, K. The significance of experience of the individual for the science of psychology. In *Minnesota Studies in the Philosophy of Science*, Vol. II. Minneapolis: Univer. of Minnesota Press, 1958.

III

Social Process and Personality

12

The Cultural Context
of Personality Theory

Norman M. Bradburn

It is a fundamental fact of human life that man is a social animal. The long developmental period and absence of a large set of instinctive response patterns insure that every child will spend most of its waking life in the presence of other people who, individually and collectively, exert "socialization" pressures. For most people the greater part of their adult life is spent with other people who have grown up under basically similar socialization pressures, who share the same language, who have many of the same basic ideas about the ways in which the world should be organized and who desire the same goals in life. Although each individual is unique, he also shares many attributes with others who live in his culture. It is important for the student of personality to consider the cultural context within which human personality develops and functions, lest he confuse factors specific to a particular culture with those that are more general in their influence on personality development and functioning.

Sociological and anthropological literature distinguishes between two sets of variables, culture and society. The term "culture" is usually taken to include such things as values ("conceptions of the desirable"), beliefs and knowledge about the world, laws, customs, arts and language. The term "society" refers to a set of relationships or "institutions" such as economic, political and religious organization, grouping and rankings of individuals as in social classes, and types of family and domestic arrangements. These two sets of variables constitute on the one hand a system of shared cognitions about the environment and the proper ways of behaving and, on the other, a set of rules or norms governing the ways in which economic, political, religious and domestic activities should be organized. The socialization process, if it is successful, insures that the maturing child will accept and internalize the system of beliefs and norms governing relationships among people. These beliefs and norms in turn become the basic frame of reference within which the adult experiences his world.

By specifying that individuals share a common cultural context, we imply that these individuals differ less from each other than they do from individuals coming from different cultural contexts. Obviously, then, cultural context is one of the most important antecedent variables to be dealt with in personality theory. Particular relationships found to exist in one cultural context may not necessarily hold true for other cultural contexts. Only when the hypothetical relationship has been tested in different contexts can its validity be extended beyond the context in which it was developed.

A crucial problem in utilizing cultural and societal variables in personality research is finding an adequate model for the interrelationship between personality, society and culture. The basic model employed in this chapter is that of a social system consisting of a plurality of actors interacting in patterned ways to achieve shared goals. Analytically one may focus attention on the characteristics of the actors as individual persons—that is, on the problems of personality formation, functioning, stability and change—or on the system as a whole—that is, on the nature of the desired goals, the norms governing instrumental activity, and the over-all patterning of behavior by which the goals are accomplished. While such a distinction is impossible to maintain in any rigid fashion, the first emphasis leads to a study of individual personality and the second to a study of roles and their relationships to one another.

A "role" is a set of rights and duties or a set of behavioral expectations associated with socially recognized positions such as "mother," "friend," "senator," "businessman," or "secretary." From the point of view of an individual role player, there exists a set of demands by other members of society that he perform certain tasks in accordance with approved norms. In exchange the role player has the right to demand that others do certain things for him. Taken together, these rights and duties constitute a stable interrelated system in which individuals for the most part know what to expect from other people and what other people will expect from them. Conformity to the role demands is induced by the use of positive and negative sanctions such as the giving or withholding of social approval, esteem, or, primarily in the case of occupational roles, money.

From the point of view of personality theory a distinction must be made between behavior patterns specific to certain roles that an individual plays and behavior patterns which are general across all roles the individual plays. The latter fall clearly in the realm of personality for they involve generalized patterns of behavior characteristic of the individual under many different environmental conditions. The former, however, pose some problems for personality theory because some types of behavior patterns are prescribed by the culture and allow for little variance among particular role players, while other types of behavior may be a product of a combination of the demand characteristics of the role and the individual personality of the role player. For example, a secretary who always arrives at her job at 8:30 A.M. is not necessarily a punctual person, and observing the behavior of a group of secretaries may not enable one to distinguish between those with a personality trait of punctuality and those who lack it. If one observes the way in which the secretaries perform certain aspects of their jobs, however, one may be able to distinguish between those who are willing, when problems arise, to take some responsibility for making decisions about their work and those who are unwilling to take any responsibility beyond what is stated exactly in their instructions. Such differences in style of role performance may be due to personality traits. Orne (1962) has shown that even in the most carefully controlled experiment the demand characteristics of the role of "good experimental subject" play an important part in determining a subject's responses. In personality research, therefore, it is important to consider the demands placed on an individual by the role he is playing and the interaction between such demands and the particular personality variables being studied.

TASKS OF PERSONALITY THEORY

A theory of personality should be able to account for three areas of human functioning: (1) the formation and development of personality, (2) personality functioning in the adult, and (3) personality change and consistency during the life cycle. While no contemporary theory comes close to being comprehensive, we can sketch in general terms what an adequate theory might look like. Our ideal personality theory, for example, would contain statements such as the following: given conditions A, B and C at time T_1, dispositions to respond in a manner R to a set of stimuli S will develop such that at time T_2 the appearance of a set of stimuli S will have a high probability of eliciting a response or constellation of responses R. Furthermore, given new and different conditions D, E and F at time T_3, the probability that at T_4 the response-constellation R will be produced in response to stimulus-pattern S will be reduced.

In less abstract terms, such a theory would consist of a set of statements specifying a series of antecedent conditions (A, B, C) for the development of response dispositions (personality traits, motives, defense mechanisms, etc.), a set of environmental conditions (S) in which there is a known probability of a particular set of responses (R) occurring, and the conditions (D, E, F) which contribute to change in the probability of the responses' occurring. A long and complex series of such statements at differing degrees of generality would be necessary to provide a really comprehensive personality theory.

The types of antecedent conditions considered by most personality theorists fall into two large classes, those stemming from within the person and those coming from outside. The first class consists of constitutional and physiological factors that influence the development of personality (particularly in the areas of temperament and expressive movements) and the stability of personality patterns during the course of the life cycle. The second class consists of environmental factors, particularly the behavior of other people, that provide the context within which people act and that play a crucial part in determining the development and functioning of personality. Since there is little reason to believe that constitutional and physiological factors differ widely from society to society, this chapter will be concerned only with the latter class of antecedent conditions.

To illustrate this conception of an adequate personality theory and to show the importance of cultural context, let us consider a set of statements derived from some current notions about personality (McClelland, Atkinson, Clark & Lowell, 1953; Atkinson, 1958). The statements might run something like this: if a mother teaches her son early in life to take care of himself, to make his own decisions, and to perform well the tasks he undertakes, he will develop a propensity to seek out and enjoy performing tasks in which doing well or competing with a standard of excellence is an important characteristic. In later life this disposition will manifest itself in an active seeking out of situations involving a moderate degree of risk and a high degree of personal responsibility for the outcome of the task. Persons who are high in this propensity will be characterized by (1) energetic instrumental activity in pursuit of their goals, (2) avoidance of situations in which success is certain or where the odds are so great that success would be a matter of luck rather than skill, and (3) a need, in order to function well, for accurate feed-back about the results of their activities. If such persons find themselves for prolonged periods of time in situations where they are forced to fail because of circumstances beyond their control, a decline in activity and a lapse into depression will occur with a resulting reorganization of response dispositions at a lower level of functioning. If, however, failure is due to some personal cause, the reaction will be one of renewed striving and greater effort to overcome whatever obstacles may be in the way.

We can conceptualize the above set of statements as follows: early independence training leads to the development in boys of a high Need Achievement (*n* Achievement). Men with high *n* Achievement are characterized by preference for situations involving a moderate degree of risk of failure, personal responsibility for success or failure, and knowledge of the results of one's activity. Prolonged exposure to situations in which success and failure are determined by external forces independent of individual activity will throw men with high *n* Achievement into states of depression which, if unrelieved, will result in a lowering of their *n* Achievement. Their reaction to situations in which failure is due to their own activity will be one of renewed striving and redoubled effort.

This set of statements specifies antecedent conditions (a set of behavior patterns of mothers) which give rise to a motivational disposition (*n* Achievement) which becomes an integral part of the boy's personality (set of response dispositions). The consequences of this personality variable for adult behavior are then specified by a set of conditions which elicit certain characteristic modes of activity and personal goals. Finally, some conditions are specified which tend to bring about changes in this personality variable as well as conditions that will produce an increase in characteristic modes of activity.

The validity of such hypothetical relationships depends, of course, on the empirical evidence offered for them. We shall consider only the first two parts of the set of statements, leaving aside those statements concerning change and stability in the adult about which there is as yet little evidence.

DEVELOPMENT OF PERSONALITY

First, let us consider the nature of the evidence concerning the development of one personality variable—*n* Achievement—in young boys. The first evidence relating early independence training to development of *n* Achievement comes from a study by Marian Winterbottom (1958), who investigated the child-rearing practices of mothers of boys whom she had identified by means of psychological tests as having relatively high and low *n* Achievement. She found that the mothers of boys with high *n* Achievement stressed the importance of a child's being able to take care of himself and make his own decisions at an earlier age than did the mothers of the boys with low *n* Achievement. From the significant differences between the ages at which the two groups of mothers expected their sons to perform certain activities, such as being able to go to bed by themselves and being able to entertain themselves, and to make certain decisions such as how to spend pocket money or what movies to see, Winterbottom concluded that early independence training led to the development of a high *n* Achievement.

The mothers studied by Winterbottom showed individual differences in certain expectations as to the proper behavior of their sons at different ages; that is to say, they placed different values on certain types of behavior at a given age. Despite the differences, however, these mothers shared many beliefs about proper ways to rear children, had the same basic orientation to the world, and lived in basically the same types of family units (monogamous, independent nuclear families). In short, they all belonged to a white, middle-class, American sub-culture.

Let us now rephrase our statement of the hypothetical relations: within the white middle-class American sub-culture, early independence training will lead to the development of a high *n* Achievement. Now what have we added by putting such a qualification on our hypothesized set of relationships? Why should the "cultural context" be an important limiting factor in the generality of such a statement?

There are three reasons why a personality theory aiming at generality above and beyond the context in which it was developed must take cultural context into account. First, insofar as the antecedent conditions specifying the development of certain personality characteristics are embedded in the shared beliefs of the members of the culture, it is an open question whether similar types of conditions will produce the same personality characteristics in different cultural contexts. Similar patterns of behavior might have different meanings in different cultural contexts. It would then be necessary to specify whether it is the behavior itself or the meaning that the behavior connotes that is important in determining the development of the personality characteristic in question. For example, early independence training in the context studied by Winterbottom connoted an affective concern over the quality of the child's performance, while in another cultural context the same behavior might connote a rejection of the child, an indication that the mother simply does not want to be bothered by the child. Further studies of the relationship of independence training to the development of n Achievement (Rosen & D'Andrade, 1959; McClelland, 1961) suggest that in fact it is the affective concern conveyed by early independence training rather than the training itself which produces high n Achievement.

These studies indicated that independence training, as measured by Winterbottom, really consisted of three separate dimensions—independence, mastery, and caretaking training. For instance, items asking at what age a mother expects her son "to make decisions for himself such as how he spends his pocket money" or "to try new things without asking for help" represent an independence dimension; items such as "to do well in school on his own" and "to do well in competition with other children" represent a mastery dimension; and items such as "to be able to undress and go to bed by himself" or "to be able to eat alone without help in cutting and handling food" represent the caretaking dimension. In Winterbottom's middle-class American sample these dimensions were so highly intercorrelated that they appeared to be one dimension. When the questionnaire was used in different societies, however, the dimensions were not highly correlated; only independence and mastery training turned out to be related to the development of n Achievement, and the antecedent conditions for the development of n Achievement were reconceptualized as early achievement training rather than early independence training.

Furthermore, the antecedent conditions specified in one cultural context may be effective only in conjunction with other antecedent conditions that are common in that context. For instance, the effect of the mother's actions in child-rearing are not independent of the actions of the father, whatever the relative importance of mothers and fathers as socializing agents from culture to culture. Rosen and D'Andrade (1959) have found that an authoritarian father who continually inter-

feres with his son's efforts at mastery may be inimical to the development of high *n* Achievement. To Winterbottom the fathers' behavior
did not seem to be a relevant variable, given the fact that in the
cultural context within which she was working most of the fathers had
relatively little to do with the rearing of the children. In a culture such
as that of Turkey, however, where the father plays a much more
dominant role and customarily governs his son's behavior down to
the minutest detail, variations in the mothers' behavior may have much
less effect than variations in fathers' behavior (Bradburn, 1963).

A third reason for considering the cultural context in which a
theory is developed is that the range of variation of observed behavior
in any one cultural context may be small in comparison with the range
of behavior which might be observed in other cultural contexts. When
the greater range is investigated, it may be found that the relation of
specified antecedent conditions to observed behavior may hold only
within the range observed in the original cultural context, while other
types of relationships hold when the range of variation is extended
further. To use our example again, McClelland (1961) found in
repeating Winterbottom's study in Japan, Germany and Brazil that
the correlation between age when achievement training was completed
and *n* Achievement was *positive* in Brazil, *negative* in Germany and
zero in Japan.

Further analysis of the data, however, revealed that the average age
at which the different types of behavior were expected by mothers in
these cultures was significantly different and that the range of ages over
all three cultures was greater than that within any one culture. Thus in
Brazil the average age of mothers' achievement demands was 7.70 years,
in Japan 8.27 years, and in Germany 8.52 years. From the data it
appeared that the relationship between age of achievement training
and development of *n* Achievement is curvilinear, with an optimum
average age of a little over 8 years, rather than linear as had been
found in the Winterbottom study. In a society where the average age
of achievement training is less than 8 years, there is a positive correlation between age of training and *n* Achievement scores, i.e., *later*
achievement training is associated with higher *n* Achievement; in a
society where the average age of achievement training is more than 8
years, there is a negative correlation, i.e., *earlier* achievement training is
associated with higher *n* Achievement; and in a society where the
average age is a little over 8 years, there is a zero correlation, i.e.,
achievement training either *earlier* or *later* than 8 years is associated

with lower *n* Achievement. Without the greater variability provided by the cross-cultural research, this relationship would never have been discovered and the hypothesized antecedent conditions for the development of *n* Achievement would have very limited applicability.

In our hypothetical statement we limited the set of antecedent conditions to the behavior of a boy's mother, implying that this was the only important set of antecedent conditions for the development of *n* Achievement. Even the qualifications suggested by evidence from cross-cultural studies were limited to the child-rearing practices of members of the immediate nuclear family. While there is nearly universal agreement that behavior of parents towards a child is of crucial importance for the development of personality characteristics, it seems clear that it is not the only relevant variable and that other factors, particularly the nature of other types of socializing agents in the culture, are important for the development of some or all personality characteristics.

When one considers the range of types of family arrangements existing in the different societies of the world, differing conceptions of sex roles, and the differential importance of peer groups and formal organizations (such as schools and religious groups) in the socialization process, the difficulties of isolating the important antecedent conditions for particular personality characteristics without taking into consideration many different aspects of the cultural context are apparent. The further one departs from the behaviors associated with the universal biological aspects of the process of development from infant to adult member of the culture, the more difficult the problem becomes. Even if one confines oneself to variables relating to such universal problems as infant feeding, toilet training, or the handling of aggressive impulses, the variety of contexts within which each of several types of child-rearing patterns could occur is very large. In order to know the effects of any particular type of child-rearing pattern (the completion of toilet training before the age of one, for example), one would need to know its effects in societies that differ in their type of family organization, ecological requirements, or even level of technology.

PERSONALITY FUNCTIONING IN THE ADULT

So far we have considered only those aspects of personality theory that deal with the formation and development of certain personality characteristics. Now let us look at a second aspect of personality theory, that dealing with personality functioning in the adult. In the discussion above we hypothesized that men with high n Achievement will seek out situations characterized by a moderate degree of risk, personal responsibility for success or failure, and accurate feed-back as to how well they are doing in the situation. Evidence for this hypothesis has been derived from a series of laboratory studies, carried out for the most part with American college students, suggesting that men with high n Achievement typically prefer situations characterized by moderate risk-taking, personal responsibility, and knowledge of results, while men with low n Achievement tend to avoid such situations (Atkinson, 1958). It has further been suggested (McClelland, 1955) that the type of occupational role which best approximates the kinds of activities preferred by men with high n Achievement is that of business entrepreneur. The hypothesis can thus be extended to suggest that men with high n Achievement will be found disproportionately among those in entrepreneurial positions and that within such positions men with high n Achievement will be more successful.

Without going into the evidence for these hypotheses (McClelland, 1961), let us examine the problem that such hypothesized relationships present for personality theory. The hypotheses are derived from a theoretical model of the relationship between role demands and personality characteristics of individuals. This model postulates that entrance into roles will be, at least partially, a function of the perception by an individual that the particular role is congruent with his needs and that pursuing need-fulfilling activity in that role will be rewarding (i.e., lead to successful role performance). The model then specifies a relationship between a particular role (entrepreneur) and a particular motivational variable (n Achievement), giving rise to hypotheses concerning the differential attractiveness of entrepreneurial roles to men with high and low n Achievement and the differential performance of such men in those roles.

As in the case of Winterbottom's study, the initial evidence for the hypotheses was derived from laboratory studies in a very specific cultural context, again largely that of white middle-class Americans. These young men shared not only a common set of values regarding achievement and work, but also a whole set of assumptions about the way the world is organized, assumptions provided by the institutional framework of the society in which they lived. That society is characterized by a highly differentiated occupational role structure, an economy based on a high degree of technology, a legal system based on notions of contract and the rule of law rather than of men, and a political structure in which authority is based on elected office rather than on personal charisma or hereditary right. In addition, they shared certain notions about the prestige ranking of different occupations, the importance of education and income in determining social rank and the possibilities of individual social mobility within the class structure. To what extent are the particular demands of the entrepreneurial role influenced by these other aspects of society? Will the hypothesized relationship between high n Achievement and performance in the entrepreneurial role hold in cultural contexts which do not have the characteristics of the United States? Do motivational variables have anything to do with recruitment into or successful performance of occupational roles?

While considerable research has been done to test these hypotheses in different cultural settings (McClelland, 1961), the evidence is not so clear as one would like. On the whole, data from such diverse countries as Japan, Brazil, India, and Germany support the hypothesis of the relationship between high n Achievement and preference for entrepreneurial-type jobs. The size of the relationship is small, however, and suggests that there are many other factors at work. Studies of men in entrepreneurial occupations in the United States, Italy, Poland, and Turkey generally support the notion that men in managerial or entrepreneurial roles have a higher n Achievement than do men in professional roles of comparable social status. The data, however, particularly in the case of Turkey, are somewhat equivocal and could be interpreted in a different manner. Taken altogether the available evidence suggests that some considerable relationship exists between a personality variable, n Achievement, and attraction to certain types of roles in society which holds true despite wide divergences in cultural context. While further data will be needed to confirm the hypothesis fully, these studies may be taken as an example of a systematic attempt to relate a personality variable to social behavior by taking into account the effects of differing cultural contexts upon the nature of the relationship.

The example we have been using has thrown little light so far on the problems of personality consistency and change during the life cycle. We can suggest, however, some of the questions that a consideration of the cultural context of adult functioning would raise. One of the most important questions concerns the effect of aging upon a person's social relationships. For example, does increased age lead to an increase or a decrease in social status, does it lead to the abandonment of roles in a society or to the taking on of new and socially valued roles? How does taking on new roles such as getting married, entering an occupation, taking on ceremonial roles, becoming a parent, etc., affect personality functioning, and how do the differing patternings of these roles in different societies affect personality? At present there has been little systematic attempt to study patterned role change and its effect on personality characteristics in a cross-cultural setting.

PERSONALITY AND THE SOCIAL SYSTEM

To summarize what we have been saying about the importance of the cultural context for personality theory, let us look now in somewhat more general terms at the relationship between personality and the social system. Much of the work in personality research today tends to concentrate on characteristics of the individual which are assumed to transcend the different roles he plays—that is, to investigate characteristic ways of behaving which would be common to all role performances. While such a strategy is feasible so long as one is working only within the context of one role structure, i.e., a relatively homogeneous sub-section of one society, with a relatively limited number of roles, it would not appear to lead to the kind of generality of findings towards which personality theory aims. Unless hypothesized relationships can be tested in the context of radically different role structures, including perhaps roles which do not even exist in our society, one's conclusions will necessarily be circumscribed.

On the other hand, the opposite tendency is characteristic of much of the work done in studying cultural variables. Here the emphasis is on the demands of social roles, with little or no consideration given to the personality characteristics of the role players or to the effect of personality variables on the manner in which the role is actually performed. The working assumption has often been that the force of role demands calls forth the necessary behavior on the part of the role player, and thus any effects of personality differences can be treated as minor idiosyncratic variations that are relatively unimportant for the over-all performance of the role.

The central point in considering role theory and personality theory together is that while the role structure of society places demands upon individual actors for certain generalized types of behavior, there must be, for a well-integrated system, some congruence between the predispositions of the individual actors (i.e., their personality characteristics) and the types of behavior demanded by the roles. Where there is a choice between entering and not entering the role, as in the case of occupational roles in modern society, the personality of an actor may be extremely influential in making a particular role attractive to him and in influencing his adjustment to it. In those cases where an actor is placed in a role without regard to his preferences in the matter, such as the role of the child in all societies or hereditary roles in some societies, the demands of the role may themselves mold the personality in such a way as to insure congruence between the expected behavior and the behavior which the individual finds satisfying. Such congruence is what Fromm (1948) talks about when he speaks of the individual who "wants to do what he has to do."

In Figure 1 the relationship between personality and social-system variables is presented in schematic form. Behavior is taken as the central dependent variable—that is, the basic phenomenon that we are trying to explain. In this scheme all human behavior can be conceptualized as role behavior. Role behavior is seen as a joint function of

FIGURE 1

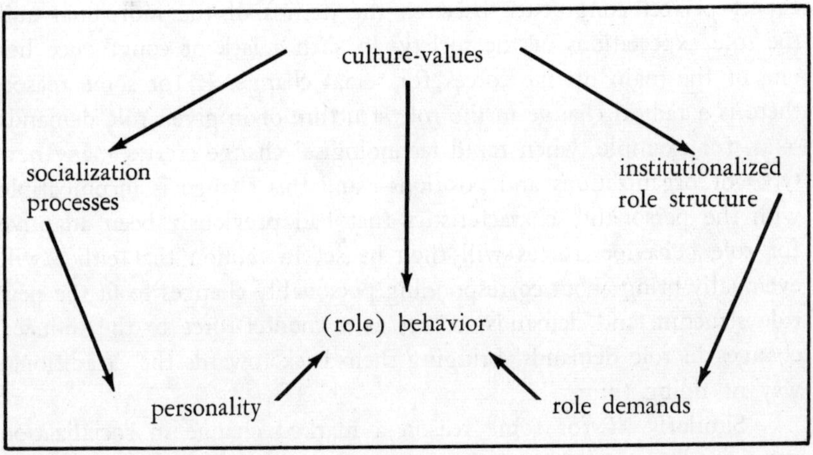

the personality characteristics of the individual, of the external role demands placed on him by the expectations of other actors in the system, and of culture-values. Personality is used here as a construct to account for the consistencies of an individual's behavior over time and is conceptualized as a set of predispositions towards particular types of activities. Personality is seen as determined largely by a set of socialization processes, primarily those that occur in the early years of life but not excluding those of the adolescent and adult years. The socialization processes themselves are determined by the culture.

Role demand is a construct employed to account for the similarity of behavior on the part of many individuals in a particular role and is conceptualized as a set of shared expectations about "the proper way of behaving" in particular roles. The fulfillment of role demands leads to positive sanctions invoked by significant others, while failure to meet the demands leads to negative sanctions. Role demands are seen as the product of an institutionalized role structure—a construct that includes the major divisions of social organization such as the economic system, the political system, the family and kinship systems and the religious system. The institutionalized role structure consists of the major ways in which the actors in a society are organized in order to accomplish the goals of the society, and is influenced by the cultural values, the state of technology, the beliefs about the nature of the universe, and so forth.

Even in the most well-integrated society, however, one would not expect perfect congruence between the desires of the individual and the role expectations of the society. In such a lack of congruence lies one of the main motive forces for social change. If for some reason there is a radical change in the role structure or in given role demands —as, for example, when rapid technological change creates many new types of organizations and positions—and this change is incompatible with the personality characteristics that had previously been adaptive for role behavior, forces will then be set in motion that either will eventually bring about corresponding personality changes to fit the new role structure and demands, or act as a counter-force to the induced changes in role demands, bringing them back towards the "traditional way of doing things."

Similarly, if for some reason a marked change in socialization practices alters the balance between certain types of personality characteristics in the society, we would expect that change to affect the role demands of society, bringing about either the creation of new roles or the modification of behavior in old roles. Here again, it is possible that the force of the traditional way of doing things might be so great as to reverse the changes in socialization practices. However, since it would take a considerable amount of time (at least one or two generations) to bring about any radical change in the distribution of personality characteristics in a society, it seems more likely that a modification of role demands would ensue rather than a return to older socialization practices. Such considerations would suggest that social changes brought about by, or at least sustained by, changes in socialization practices (and consequent changes in personality characteristics) would be more fundamental and longer lasting than those induced by external pressure to change role demands. Thus, for example, we would not expect the types of changes in role demands which the Chinese Communists have been trying to effect to result in permanent changes in behavior unless there are concomitant changes in personality patterns congruent with the new role demands. The Chinese government appears to recognize the importance of the latter changes both by its attempts at massive "thought" (i.e., personality) reform and its wholesale attack on traditional family organization and socialization practices (Lifton, 1960). The costs of such rapid and total change, in terms of personal and social disintegration, are enormous and it remains to be seen, of course, whether or not it can be successfully accomplished.

The conceptual scheme outlined here suggests that behavior is a function of three classes of variables: personality—variables specific to the individual; role demands—variables specific to the situation; and culture—a set of variables that have both general effect through their influence on personality and role demands, and direct influence in the form of beliefs about the world, technical knowledge, and values which individuals have internalized because they are members of a particular society. As yet we do not know how these classes of variables are related. Whether behavior is a simple resultant of the differing strengths of these variables or whether it is a product of more complex interaction remains to be demonstrated. For the present we must be content with recognizing the differing influences of the three classes of variables and being aware of the limitations of findings based on variations of only one type of variable.

IMPLICATIONS FOR PERSONALITY RESEARCH

What implications for personality research stem from the relationship of personality variables to cultural and social variables? As has been mentioned, the most obvious implication of considering the cultural context of personality is that the generality of findings from personality research carried out in only one cultural setting is strictly limited.

Perhaps because of its aspirations to completeness and universality, psychoanalytic theory has generated the greatest amount of, although not always the most careful, cross-cultural personality research. In the early days of this research as represented by Malinowski and Seligman (Singer, 1961), there appears to have been a genuine concern for testing the validity of psychoanalytic hypotheses. Unfortunately, the reaction of psychoanalysts to Malinowski's work was so violently hostile that anthropologists were discouraged from many further attempts to verify hypotheses derived from psychoanalytic theory. Roheim (1932, p. 7), the first psychoanalyst to undertake first-hand study of a primitive culture, set the tone in his report on his fieldwork in Australia and New Guinea:

> There are of course many degrees of understanding, but I think I may safely say that nobody can fully understand psycho-analysis who has not been analysed himself. Moreover, I may say that in order to do analytic work in field anthropology, the anthropologist ought not only to have been analysed, but must himself have practised clinical analysis at home. . . . (Malinowski) mentions that when he was in the Trobriands and Professor Seligman sent him some of Freud's books to read he set out to *test* the validity of Freud's dream-theory on the Trobrianders. Fancy! Somebody who admits that he has never analysed a dream himself—for the obvious reason that he does not know how to do it— is *testing* Freud's theory!

Ernest Jones (1925) had already laid siege by criticizing Malinowski's suggestion that in matrilineal family systems the classical Oedipus complex was replaced by a complex consisting of brother-sister attraction and nephew-uncle hatred. Jones maintained that the complex described by Malinowski was in reality a mode of defence against primitive Oedipal tendencies and that the matrilineal family system was a consequence of the mechanisms employed to cope with the Oedipal situation. While admitting the validity of Malinowski's findings "on the purely descriptive plane," Jones accused him of having insufficient knowledge of unconscious processes.

Malinowski (1927, p. 142), for his part, regretted the attitude taken by the psychoanalysts and the rift that had grown up between psychoanalysis and the empirical social sciences. He had, however, no intention of abandoning his position and showed that he could give as well as take:

> . . . The crux of the difficulty lies in the fact that to Dr. Jones and other psycho-analysts, the Oedipus complex is something absolute, the

primordial source, in his own words the *fons et origo* of everything. To me on the other hand the nuclear family complex is a functional formation dependent upon the structure and upon the culture of a society. It is necessarily determined by the manner in which sexual restrictions are moulded in a community and by the manner in which authority is apportioned. I cannot conceive of the complex as the first cause of everything, as the unique source of culture, of organization and belief.

The dispute between Malinowski and Jones is an excellent example of one of the important contributions of cross-cultural research to the development of personality theory. Within one particular culture a hypothesized antecedent condition (for example, the father's sexual relations with the mother) may be so highly correlated with another antecedent condition (the father's authority over his son) that the hypothesized consequence (the son's hostility toward his father) may result from either condition or from the combination of the two. So long as research is confined to a single culture, it is impossible to distinguish the effects of each antecedent condition. Through research in cultures in which the two conditions are separated or not highly correlated, the separate effects of each may be seen.

In this particular example, as Campbell (1961) has pointed out, the hostility of sons towards their fathers which Freud observed could be explained as a consequence of the father's role either as disciplinarian or as mother's lover. Freud chose as his explanatory variable the father's role as mother's lover; but in the Viennese society from which his patients came the two variables were confounded, making it impossible to discover which of the two variables was the real antecedent condition of the son's hostility or, indeed, whether it was a combination of the two. In the Trobriand Islands society studied by Malinowski, the two roles were distinct, the role of disciplinarian being taken by the mother's brother (the boy's uncle). The father, not concerned at all with the discipline of his son, had a warm affectionate relationship with him. On the basis of the data he collected, Malinowski suggested that in a matrilineal family system a young boy's hostility would be directed towards his uncle rather than towards his father and that the hostility of young boys towards adult males is a function not of the male's relationship to the boy's mother, that is, as a rival for her affection, but of the amount of discipline and control that the adult male exercises over a boy regardless of their biological or kinship relation. Unfortunately, there has been little attempt to extend Malinowski's work and resolve this issue by systematically studying cultures

that vary in the degree of independence between the roles of disciplinarian and mother's lover.

One need not go far afield into exotic cultures, however, to study
social and cultural variables in personality research. Recent evidence
suggests, for example, that there is a patterning of psychiatric symptoms
and types of illnesses along subcultural (i.e., social class) lines (Hollingshead & Redlich, 1958). Using data from a recent representative
national sample, Veroff, Feld & Gurin (1962) concluded that the use
of different criteria for subjective adjustment will yield opposite conclusions regarding the differential levels of subjective adjustment of
men in different social classes. Thus, using a criterion of psychosomatic
symptomatology one would conclude that men of lower socio-economic
status (as measured by years of education) are more distressed than
men of higher socio-economic status.' On the other hand, if one used
a measure of felt psychological disturbance or social inadequacy, one
would conclude the opposite, namely, that men from the higher socio
economic groups are more distressed than those in the lower socio-
economic groups. Considerations such as these suggest that hypotheses
derived from personality theories supported only by data from extremely homogeneous populations, such as college sophomores or
middle-class mothers, must be treated as extremely tentative until
confirmed by data from diverse cultural or subcultural populations.

TRADITIONS IN CROSS-CULTURAL RESEARCH

Much of the early work done by Malinowski and Margaret Mead was
concerned with simply demonstrating, by means of careful field studies,
the extensive variability of human behavior and documenting the fact
that most of the behavior that is popularly described as "just human
nature" is in fact a product of the culture in which the individual
happens to have been reared. In the beginning of her book, *Coming
of Age in Samoa,* Margaret Mead (1928, p. 4-5) says:

> The anthropologist, as he pondered his growing body of material upon
> the customs of primitive people, grew to realise the tremendous role
> played in an individual's life by the social environment in which each
> is born and reared. One by one, aspects of behaviour which we had
> been accustomed to consider invariable complements of our humanity
> were found to be merely a result of civilisation, present in the in-
> habitants of one country, absent in another country, and this without a

change of race. He learned that neither race nor common humanity can be held responsible for many of the forms which even such basic human emotions as love and fear and anger take under different social conditions. . . . With such an attitude towards human nature the anthropologist listened to the current comment upon adolescence. He heard attitudes which seemed to him dependent upon social environment—such as rebellion against authority . . . ascribed to a period of physical development. And on the basis of his knowledge of the determinism of culture, of the plasticity of human beings, he doubted. Were these difficulties due to being adolescent or to being adolescent in America?

The successful demonstration of differences in behavior patterns, however, led to further complications. The evident biological unity of mankind made attractive the notion of the "psychic unity of mankind" and led theorists to postulate or at least to suspect the existence of an underlying unity that manifested itself in different overt behavior patterns. Such thinking was, of course, extremely congenial to those influenced by psychoanalytic theory with its explanation of behavior in terms of basic instinctual and presumably universal forces. This shift in emphasis has led to several attempts to formulate a list of "univerals" in culture which transcend the apparent diversity (Kluckhohn, 1953).

Even for those who were willing to leave open the question of the universality of "human nature," the existence of diverse behavioral patterns demanded explanation: why *were* there the observed differences and, particularly, why was there such similarity of behavior within a culture in contrast to the diversity between cultures? Attempts to explain differences between cultural behavior patterns led to an emphasis on the relation of culture to the typical personality found in a particular culture.

It was assumed that while the biological needs of individuals were relatively constant in all cultures, there were different types of external reality to which the individual had to adapt in order to satisfy his needs. This external reality consisted not only of the natural environment in which members of the culture lived, but also, and perhaps more importantly, of the institutional systems of the culture. The external reality was seen as a set of forces acting on the individual members of the culture, molding their thought processes, perceptions, fantasies, ways of handling emotion—in short, shaping a considerable portion of their personalities along similar lines. The shared aspects of personality constituted the basic personality structure in a culture. As Kardiner (1939, p. 131) described it:

> Environmental conditions and some aspects of social organization included under the term primary institutions create the basic problems of adaptation for the individual. To these he must develop certain methods of accommodation, because they are fixed and unchangeable conditions. Food scarcity, sexual prohibitions, disciplines of one kind or another are conditions which the individual cannot directly control; he can only take an attitude to them and accommodate himself according to an array of patterns which have some variety. The basic constellations in the individual created by these conditions are his ego structure, subjectively considered, or his basic personality structure, objectively considered.

The basic personality structure common to members of a culture gives rise to and is expressed in "secondary institutions"—aspects of culture such as art, folklore, mythology, and religion. The study of these "secondary institutions" becomes one of the chief means for inferring the nature of the basic personality structure.

The difficulties, however, of validating conceptions of basic personality structure derived from analysis of cultural data are immense and the ultimate grounds for validity are essentially those of congruence—how well a particular interpretation "fits" the data. The goodness of "fit" depends on the particular theory being used and there is little way to decide which of two alternate interpretations derived from different theories might be correct. Thus an increasing interest developed in gathering direct psychological data on individuals that could be analyzed for common themes or profiles. Cora Du Bois' (1944) monograph *The People of Alor* was one of the first studies to test the theory of basic personality structure in this manner. To the statistical and descriptive characterizations derived from data on individuals, Du Bois gave the name "modal personality." The observed "modal personality" manifests the basic personality structure at the individual level while the "secondary institutions" do so at the cultural level.

The concept of basic personality structure appealed to students of culture because it enabled them to account for the integration of "patterns" of culture without resort to quasi-mystical concepts such as "cultural configurations" whose locus and determinants are at best obscure, and whose existence is often difficult to determine. As Linton (Kardiner, 1939, p. ix) points out:

The outstanding contribution which the *basic personality structure* approach makes to integrational studies is that it provides a logical place for cultures which are not dominated by an *idée fixe*. The various personality types which it posits as characteristic of particular societies are constellations of distinct although mutually interrelated elements. When such a personality structure is recognized as the focus for the institutions comprised within a given culture, it can be seen that such institutions need not be mutually consistent, except to the degree required for their actual functioning, as long as they are individually consistent with various aspects of the personality structure involved.

Thus the concept of basic personality structure frees the student of culture from the necessity of finding all-embracing patterns that will make all aspects of culture appear consistent and enables him to consider possibly incongruous institutions without giving up the notion of the organic nature or mutual interrelatedness of various aspects of culture.

The concepts of basic personality structure and modal personality, however, are of more importance to the understanding of particular cultures than to the development of a comprehensive personality theory. In practice they have been used primarily in the study of specific cultures or as conceptual tools to illuminate particular problems concerning the interrelations between certain personality modes and various aspects of the social system.

The increasing sophistication of anthropologists in the use of psychoanalytic theory and the influence of Kardiner have given ascendancy to psychoanalytic theory as the conceptual framework within which to investigate the modal personality. Since the bulk of the work in culture and personality has been done by anthropologists, it is not surprising that they should employ psychological hypotheses derived from personality theory for the purpose of understanding cultural processes rather than for validating any particular personality theory itself. As Singer (1961, p. 61) points out, "The problem of validating general psychological theories has been left pretty much to the psychologist, psychoanalyst, and student of individual development." Unfortunately, however, few of these people have undertaken this task.

A notable exception to this generalization is the work inspired by Whiting and Child (1953). They were specifically interested in testing general hypotheses about human behavior and were not concerned with gaining a detailed understanding of any particular culture. While they derived most of their hypotheses from psychoanalytic theory, they formulated them in terms of a general behavior theory similar to that evolved by Dollard and Miller (1950) in their restatement of Freudian theory. Specifically, Whiting and Child derived from psychoanalytic theory a set of hypotheses about the effects of specific child-rearing practices on development of personality traits (habits) that were in turn related to certain cultural variables concerning beliefs and practices in illness.[1]

METHODOLOGICAL DIFFICULTIES

In view of the importance of cross-cultural studies for the adequate testing of hypotheses, why are psychologists not more actively engaged in such studies? It is perhaps not surprising when one considers some of the difficulties involved in carrying out cross-cultural personality research. First of all, a great many practical problems are involved: the increased expense, the problem of finding researchers willing to spend the time and energy to go to another society and learn its language, the problem of the researcher's becoming accustomed to the living conditions encountered in different societies and assembling all the paraphernalia necessary to his research. Since the need is for studies of hypothesized relations not simply in *one* other society but in *many* different societies, there are the additional difficulties of coordinating research carried out by different researchers under greatly different circumstances.

But perhaps more difficult than any of these is the problem of finding adequate research instruments for use in cross-cultural settings. Many of the personality psychologist's research tools are of questionable applicability for use with other than college or middle-class subjects. Other tools require apparatus of a complexity that would preclude their use in most of the societies of the world. Beyond that, however, is the problem of the degree to which instruments "translate" into different cultural contexts—not only the problem of linguistic translation, serious enough in itself, but also the degree to which the interpretation of even non-verbal stimuli may be dependent on the cultural context. Thus, to use the Thematic Apperception Test in different cultures, how would one go about "translating" the pictures? If one were working within only one culture, he could adopt certain

[1] Later studies following those of Whiting and Child are summarized by Whiting (1961).

stimuli which were culturally standardized for that culture. But if one wishes to do systematic research in a series of societies, comparing the results of tests in each of these different societies with one another, then his "translation" problem becomes even more difficult as the comparability of stimulus situations is impaired no matter what he does. If he retains the same pictures for all societies, he runs the risk of obtaining stories about "foreign" people or situations; if he changes the pictures to get comparability of situations or "naturalness," the differences in responses he obtains may be due to differences in stimulus cues rather than differences among the individuals being tested. The popularity of the Rorschach among anthropologists who have done research on culture and personality has been due largely to the seemingly "culture-free" nature of the stimuli. (Whether or not they are in fact "culture-free" is of course an open question.) Unfortunately, however, the usefulness of such an instrument is limited, whatever virtue it may possess through ambiguity of stimuli, because, there is little consensus as to the meaning of responses in *any* culture.

While the methodological problems are immensely difficult, they are not impossible to solve. Recently, Whiting and his co-workers (B. Whiting, 1963) have been engaged in a coordinated study of socialization in six different cultures using a battery of instruments designed to be applicable in a diverse set of societies. This battery consists of such things as a standardized interview schedule concerning socialization practices, a cross-cultural projective test eliciting fantasies concerning aspiration level, and a standardized set of behavioral observations. By systematically collecting comparable data from different cultures, Whiting and his co-workers will be able to test the effects of particular socialization practices within radically different cultural contexts.

Testing individuals in different societies is not the only method of cross-culturally testing hypotheses derived from personality theory. The Whiting and Child (1953) study mentioned earlier was based on data taken from the Human Relations Area File at Yale University. This file is a compilation of ethnographic data on approximately 150 societies from all over the world, broken down and cross-indexed for a very large number of variables. Thus, in studying the effects of weaning or differing degrees of oral indulgence on the development of explanations of illness in terms of oral behavior, Whiting and Child found in the Human Relations Area File information on the age of weaning and on explanations of illness in fifty-two societies. For age of weaning, they found a range from approximately six months, among American middle-class and Marquesan parents, to around five or six years of age among the Chenchu tribe of India, with a median age of around two and one-half years (Whiting & Child, 1953, p. 70-71). (Considering how small is the amount of variation that one might find within the American middle-class group compared with this order of variation among societies around the world, it is not surprising that studies have failed to show much relationship between age of weaning and any significant personality variables in America.)

The Human Relations Area File, however, while providing with its immense amount of data on different societies of the world a vast reservoir of potential use to psychologists, is not the answer to all of the problems of cross-cultural research. First of all, the data that appear in the file are based on the published reports of a great variety of people, ranging from the work of trained ethnographers to the more casual observations of missionaries, with a resultant variation in the quality, reliability, and completeness of the data. While efforts are being made to improve the quality and comparability of data included in the file, even in the best of circumstances it will probably never contain the type of psychological data that would be necessary to test many of the hypotheses we might wish to test. In fact, most of the hypotheses so far tested using material from the file have involved rather long and tortuous deductions from socialization practices on the one hand to certain cultural customs on the other. Despite the rather remarkable success of many of these studies in predicting the occurrence of certain types of cultural patterns from hypotheses derived from psychoanalytic theory, it has been impossible to test or refine the hypotheses in the more detailed fashion necessary to make the relationships more explicit. Nevertheless, the data deposited in the file do represent a remarkable fund which psychologists have so far tapped very little and which could provide at least an initial cross-cultural test of many existing hypotheses.

Another method of testing hypotheses concerning personality variables by means of data collected systematically from many cultures has been the content analysis of certain cultural artifacts, particularly folk tales. McClelland and Friedman (1950) analyzed folk tales from a small sample of American Indian tribes for imagery reflecting n Achievement in order to test one hypothesis about the development of high n Achievement. Other studies have used content analysis of popular literature (Berlew, 1956; Cortes, 1961; Bradburn & Berlew,

1961), children's readers (McClelland, 1961; de Charms & Moeller, 1962), and expressive movements in pottery decoration (Aronson, 1956; McClelland, Lathrap & Swartz, 1961; McClelland, 1961) to test hypotheses derived from the literature on *n* Achievement. While these methods are limited by the fact that they provide estimates about personality variables based on cultural artifacts and not on tests of individuals in the society, they do offer one approach for testing a hypothesis in a large number of different cultures without involving the expense or difficulties of doing work in each of these different societies. Ultimately, however, the construction and validation of an adequate theory of human personality will require coordinated studies of individuals in different societies.

Aside from the methodological problems involved in doing cross-cultural research, there is a separate question of research strategy for developing and testing personality theories. The majority of the work in culture and personality has been directed towards the study of a "basic personality structure" or "modal" personality that is in some sense characteristic of the typical member of a culture. As was pointed out earlier, such studies have been conducted primarily to help anthropologists understand the workings of the culture rather than to test out hypotheses concerning the development or functioning of personality. Cross-cultural studies undertaken to further the development of an adequate personality theory or to test out particular hypotheses, however, will probably have to be directed towards the systematic testing of hypotheses relating specific antecedent conditions to specific consequences rather than towards ascertaining a total personality type or profile which is "modal" for a series of cultures. Such research, of course, does violence to the notion of the unity of personality and the inter-relatedness of different aspects of personality. Given the complexity of the phenomena involved, however, a strategy of testing single variables at a time and exploring the various relationships of one variable to different types of behavior in differing cultural contexts is more likely to promote the development of a comprehensive theory of personality than is a strategy which attempts to preserve a "holistic" approach to personality functioning. At present we do not even have a generally agreed-upon vocabulary which could allow us to identify personality types or syndromes and investigate their differential distribution in different societies, let alone investigate the antecedent conditions leading to their formation or the relation between such types or syndromes and particular role behavior in different cultures.

To summarize, we have examined in this chapter some of the limitations inherent in personality research utilizing only data collected on a relatively homogeneous body of subjects and have suggested that personality psychologists would do well to consider the effects of the cultural contexts in which the subjects are functioning. Specifically, we have discussed four major reasons for taking cultural and societal variables into account in formulating theoretical statements concerning antecedent conditions and consequent personality characteristics. First, so long as one is operating within a single cultural context, it is difficult to distinguish between the effects, in the socialization process, of certain behavioral patterns and the effects of the *meaning* of those patterns; systematic consideration of child-rearing patterns in different cultural contexts can aid in differentiating between the effects of the behavioral patterns themselves and the effects of other behavioral patterns that may convey a similar meaning. Secondly, a given set of antecedent conditions may be effective only in conjunction with other aspects of the cultural context. Given the interrelated nature of cultural patterns it seems in fact extremely likely that this possibility would be the rule rather than the exception. Accordingly, cross-cultural studies of personality development would appear to be extremely desirable for specifying in greater detail the nature of the relation of hypothetical antecedent conditions to consequent personality patterns. Thirdly, within a single culture significant variables may be confounded in such a way that adequate tests of hypotheses are impossible to perform. By considering different cultural contexts in which the two variables are not confounded, each variable can be studied independently and its separate effects on behavior ascertained. Finally, the range of behavioral variability that can be observed within any one cultural context is limited. Consideration of different cultural contexts greatly increases the range of variation in observed behavior, providing the investigator with a more decisive test of his hypotheses.

In short, personality theorists are in fact always dealing with cultural and societal variables whether or not they choose to spell them out. By making explicit the cultural assumptions underlying a given set of hypothesized relations, the theorist will both draw attention to the limits of the theory as formulated and open the way for further empirical investigations to refine the theory and put it in a more general form.

REFERENCES

ARONSON, E. The need for achievement as measured by graphic expression. Unpublished master's thesis. Middletown, Conn.: Wesleyan Univer., 1956.

ATKINSON, J. W. (Ed.) *Motives in fantasy, action, and society.* Princeton, N. J.: Van Nostrand, 1958.

BERLEW, D. E. The achievement motive and the growth of Greek civilization. Unpublished bachelor's thesis. Middletown, Conn.: Wesleyan Univer., 1956.

BRADBURN, N. M. Need achievement and father dominance. *J. abnorm. soc. Psychol.,* 1963 (in press).

BRADBURN, N. M., & BERLEW, D. E. Need for achievement and English industrial growth. *Econ. Develpm. cult. change,* 1960, *10,* 8-20.

CAMPBELL, D. T. The mutual methodological relevance of anthropology and psychology. In F. L. K. Hsu (Ed.), *Psychological anthropology.* Homewood, Ill.: Dorsey, 1961.

CORTES, J. B. The achievement motive in the Spanish economy between the 13th and 18th centuries. *Econ. Develpm. cult. change,* 1960, *9,* 144-163.

DE CHARMS, R., & MOELLER, G. H. Values expressed in American children's readers: 1800-1950. *J. abnorm. soc. Psychol.,* 1962, *64,* 136-142.

DOLLARD, J., & MILLER, N. E. *Personality and psychotherapy.* New York: McGraw-Hill, 1950.

DU BOIS, C. *The people of Alor.* Minneapolis: Univer. of Minnesota Press, 1944.

FROMM, E. *Man for himself.* New York: Farrar & Rinehart, 1948.

HOLLINGSHEAD, A., & REDLICH, F. *Social class and mental illness: a community study.* New York: Wiley, 1958.

JONES, E. Mother-right and the sexual ignorance of savages. *Int. J. of Psychoanal.,* 1925, *6,* 109-130.

KARDINER, A. *The individual and his society.* New York: Columbia Univer. Press, 1939.

KLUCKHOHN, C. Universal categories of culture. In A. L. Kroeber (Ed.), *Anthropology today.* Chicago: Univer. of Chicago Press, 1953. Pp. 507-523.

LIFTON, R. J. *Thought reform.* New York: Norton, 1960.

MALINOWSKI, B. *Sex and repression in savage society.* New York: Harcourt, Brace, 1927.

McClelland, D. C. Some consequences of achievement motivation. In M. R. Jones (Ed.), *Nebraska symposium on motivation, 1955*. Lincoln, Neb.: Univer. of Nebraska Press, 1955.

McClelland, D. C. *The achieving society*. Princeton, N. J.: Van Nostrand, 1961.

McClelland, D. C., Atkinson, J. W., Clark, R. A., & Lowell, E. L. *The achievement motive*. New York: Appleton-Century-Crofts, 1953.

McClelland, D. C., & Friedman, G. A. A cross-cultural study of the relationship between child-rearing practices and achievement motivation appearing in folk tales. In G. E. Swanson, T. M. Newcomb, & E. L. Hartley (Eds.), *Readings in social psychology*. New York: Holt, 1952. Pp. 243-249.

McClelland, D. C., Lathrap, D. W., & Swartz, M. An attempt at the estimation of *n* Achievement levels from archaeological materials in a non-Western tradition. Unpublished paper. Care of Lathrap, Department of Anthropology, Univer. of Illinois, 1961.

Mead, Margaret, *Coming of age in Samoa*. New York: Morrow, 1928.

Orne, M. T. On the social psychology of the psychological experiment: with particular reference to demand characteristics and their implications. *Amer. Psychol.*, 1962, *17*, 776-783.

Roheim, G. Psychoanalysis of primitive culture types. *Int. J. of Psychoanal.*, 1932, *13*, 1-224.

Rosen, B. C., & D'Andrade, R. G. The psychosocial origins of achievement motivation. *Sociometry*, 1959, *22*, 185-218.

Singer, M. A survey of culture and personality theory and research. In Bert Kaplan (Ed.), *Studying personality cross-culturally*. Evanston, Ill.: Row Peterson, 1961.

Veroff, J., Feld, S., & Gurin, G. Dimensions of subjective adjustment. *J. abnorm. soc. Psychol.*, 1962, *64*, 192-205.

Whiting, B. (Ed.) *Six cultures: studies in child-rearing practices*. New York: Wiley, 1963.

Whiting, J. W. M. Socialization process and personality. In F. L. K. Hsu (Ed.), *Psychological anthropology*. Homewood, Ill.: Dorsey, 1961.

Whiting, J. W. M., & Child, I. *Child training and personality*. New Haven, Conn.: Yale Univer. Press, 1953.

Winterbottom, Marian R. The relation of need for achievement to learning experiences in independence and mastery. In J. W. Atkinson (Ed.), *Motives in fantasy, society, and action*. Princeton, N. J.: Van Nostrand, 1958.

13

Behaviorism in Psychological Anthropology

Robert A. LeVine

INTRODUCTION: THE RELEVANCE OF BEHAVIORISM
TO ANTHROPOLOGY

The influence of psychoanalytic concepts of personality on anthropology has been widely recognized and documented. A less visible but extremely important influence in contemporary research on culture and personality is the behavioristic psychology associated with the names of Pavlov, Thorndike, Watson, and Hull, which has often been incorporated by anthropologists into their psychodynamic view of personality development and their analysis of the transmission of culture. Indeed, the most extensive cross-cultural test of psychoanalytic hypotheses, that of Whiting and Child (1953), is explicitly behavioristic in its orientation, translating Freudian concepts into the language of stimulus-response, reinforcement, and habit.

The logical connecting link between behavior theory as developed in the animal laboratory and the cross-cultural study of personality development is that both are concerned with antecedent environmental conditions that lead to modifications in the behavior of organisms. Both try to explain variations in behavior by reference to the "conditioning history" of the individual. As Hallowell (1954, p. 142) has remarked concerning some American anthropologists of the 1920's:

> Behaviorism had an appeal for the anthropologists because it, too, was opposed to the prevailing doctrine of instincts (substituting for them more specific physiological needs or drives), innate mental differences, or innate anything. . . . This extreme environmentalist doctrine fitted in very well with the idea that culture was acquired, and that individuals with different cultural backgrounds acquired different sets of habits. . . . Soon the term "conditioning," one of the verbal earmarks of the behaviorist, became almost as familiar in anthropological as in psychological literature, even though the purely technical psychological meaning of it and the theory behind it remained unexamined.

Thus the widespread anthropological assumption that culture is learned behavior makes the psychology of learning directly relevant to the study of culture, and particularly favors the acceptance of a theory in which variations in the external environment (stimuli) are held responsible for variations in what is learned. There are at least two other major compatibilities between behaviorism and common anthropological premises and interests. One is functionalism, which in one form or another is well established in anthropology. A minimal statement of the functional position is as follows: In every society there are needs that must be satisfied if the society itself is to survive. Behavior in all groups must be directed toward the satisfaction of these basic needs, regardless of what else it is directed toward; hence customs can be thought of as adaptive or maladaptive in an evolutionary sense. Similarly, Clark L. Hull, in a paper entitled "A Functional Interpretation of the Conditioned Reflex" (1929), suggested that habit acquisition was a process of individual adaptation to environment and could be viewed in evolutionary perspective. This aspect of Hullian theory was clearly seen by Bronislaw Malinowski, who was for years the major anthropological exponent of functionalism, and it made him favorable to Hull's behaviorism.

Another foundation of modern anthropology is the emphasis on observation of behavior ("participant observation") in ethnographic field methods. Field reports describe sequences of behavior, and stimulus-response theory provides a meaningful framework for the analysis of such sequences. This compatibility was also recognized by Malinowski, who is generally credited with introducing the type of intensive field work in an ongoing society that has since become standard ethnographic practice. He wrote (Malinowski, 1944, p. 23):

> The value of behaviorism is due, first and foremost, to the fact that its methods are identical as regards limitations and advantages with those of anthropological field work. In dealing with people of a different culture, it is always dangerous to use the short-circuiting of "empathy," which usually amounts to guessing as to what the other person might have thought or felt. The fundamental principle of the field worker, as well as of the behaviorist, is that ideas, emotions and conations never continue to lead a cryptic, hidden existence within the unexplorable depths of the mind, conscious or unconscious. All sound, that is, experimental, psychology can deal only with observations of overt behavior, although it may be useful to relate such observations to the shorthand of introspective interpretation.

Thus the premises that behavior is learned as well as adaptive or functional and that observation is an important method of studying behavior, are shared by behaviorism and much of modern anthropological thought. These compatibilities have served as the bases for much of the unrecognized influence of stimulus-response psychology on anthropology as well as providing some fundamental tenets for the behavioristic approach to cross-cultural personality study.

THE DEVELOPMENT OF A BEHAVIORISTIC ANTHROPOLOGY

To understand properly how anthropologists have used behavior theory in studying personality, one must bear in mind the historical circumstances under which this first happened. As mentioned by Hallowell (1954), as early as the 1920's some anthropologists like Wissler (who was originally trained as a psychologist) used the concept of "conditioning" in a non-technical sense in their formulations on the non-inherited nature of culture. It was not until about 1936, however, that a serious encounter between anthropology and behaviorism occurred. This happened at Yale University, where by that time Hull had developed much of his theoretical system unifying instrumental learning and classical Pavlovian (associative) conditioning, and where the interdisciplinary Institute of Human Relations was in operation.

At the Institute of Human Relations, O. H. Mowrer, John Dollard, Neal Miller, and others began translating psychoanalytic theory into Hullian stimulus-response theory. Finding many remarkable parallels between the two formulations, they developed a theory of personality which was based on both, involving a more molecular and yet more generally applicable analysis of the learning sequences involved in the development of adult motivations than was provided by the psychoanalytic theory of neurosis. This amounted to a theory of social learning, applicable (at least conceptually) to any society and covering situations ranging from the impact of child rearing practices to acculturation.

In the first wave of enthusiasm for the generality of Hullian behavior theory, the aim of the Yale social scientists was simply to show that its concepts could be fitted to data from a variety of sources, including those collected by ethnographers in exotic societies. Miller and Dollard (1941), enunciating the basic principles of the drive-reduction, response-reinforcement approach, went on to develop upon it a paradigm for imitative behavior and then to apply this paradigm to the diffusion or borrowing of culture traits as recorded by anthropologists. Whiting (1941) painstakingly analyzed sequences of child rearing and adult behavior among the Kwoma of New Guinea in terms of drive, cue, response, reward. Gorer (1943) formulated a set of twelve postulates based on the combined behaviorism-psychoanalysis social learning theory and then attempted to apply them in an impressionistic (and controversial) study of Japanese culture at a distance. Murdock (1945) set out "the common denominator of cultures" in terms of behavioristic learning theory, and integrated this with the societal evolution approach of Sumner and Keller. Gillin (1948) produced a textbook of anthropology based largely on behavioristic concepts with chapter headings such as "The Principles Underlying the Learning and Performance of Customs" and "The Cultural Role of Acquired Drives." Numerous other examples of published attempts by persons on the staff at Yale, or trained there, to fit behavior theory to anthropological data could be given, e.g., those of Dollard et al. (1939) and Bateson (1941, 1942).

From the viewpoint of the history of anthropology, the most interesting student at Yale during this period was Bronislaw Malinowski, then a distinguished anthropologist from England at what turned out to be the end of his career. He came to Yale in 1939 and attended a course given by Neal Miller on learning theory for non-psychologists. In an experiment on stimulus generalization, a white rat bit Malinowski's finger instead of the rod he was trained to bite. Although wounded, Malinowski was impressed. At the end of his life he was recasting his functionalist theory of culture in terms of stimulus-response psychology. This is most evident in his posthumously published work, "A Scientific Theory of Culture" (Malinowski, 1944), in which the following statements appear:

> The approval of psychoanalysis does not in any way detract from the great importance which behaviorism promises to acquire as the basic psychology of social and cultural processes (1944, p. 23).

> The way in which we anthropologists can project the experimental situation of the animal onto the beginnings of culture is by isolating the main factors which must be present if the habit is to be formed (1944, p. 134).

> The animal psychologist teaches us one important fact: a habit which is not reinforced becomes unlearned, "extinguished." It disappears. We can apply this fully to culture. No crucial system of activities can persist without being connected, directly or indirectly, with human needs and their satisfaction (1944, p. 142).

Malinowski's enthusiasm for behaviorism, especially its drive-reduction aspects, matched that of the younger social scientists who had received all their training at Yale.

After this initial enthusiasm, behavioristic anthropology entered a stage in which systematic attempts were made to test hypotheses derived from Hullian theory by means of cross-cultural surveys. The major works resulting from these efforts were Murdock's study of kinship behavior (1949) and the study of personality development by Whiting and Child (1953), the results of which are discussed below. Hypothesis-testing studies of this type were continued into the present (Whiting, 1962), and are now done at many places besides Yale.

Behaviorism has had its critics within anthropology and the field of culture and personality. Kardiner (1939, pp. 356-364) prefers psychoanalytic technique to the behavioristic approach in culture and personality because psychoanalysis uses "direct experience," i.e. the individual's reports of his reactions to stimuli, while behaviorism (he says) simply observes his overt responses and must infer what is going on inside the individual. Kluckhohn (1954, p. 957) stated that "while laws of learning and other psychological laws may be universal, they are formal and without cultural content." He went on to say that many anthropologists believe that learning theories are "the psychological counterpart of the atomistic 'trait' theory of 'historical' ethnology." Kluckhohn himself felt that the acceptance of behaviorism in American psychology reflected a "bias of contemporary American culture" for quantification and gadgetry (Kluckhohn, 1954, p. 959). The final criticism comes from within behavior theory itself, viz. the report of five social scientists (Logan, Olmstead, Rosner, Schwartz & Stevens, 1955) who examined the application of Hullian theory to social science over a three-year period at the Yale Institute of Human Relations. They are pessimistic about the utility of Hullian theory in empirical research on cultural behavior, mainly because of the difficulties of identifying crucial theoretical terms like "reinforcers" in complex sociocultural environments.

In summary, we can say that the application of behavioristic psychology to anthropological data began at Yale in the context of a mutual translation of psychoanalytic theory and Hullian theory. The initial phase of demonstrating by example how Hullian concepts could be applied to cultural data was followed by an hypothesis-testing phase, which became increasingly focused on the psychocultural effects of cross-cultural variations in child training practices. Critics have argued that behaviorism is too external for cross-cultural personality study, too atomistic in its approach, too formal and lacking in cultural content, and that its terms are too difficult to identify in complex cultural situations.

CONCEPTS OF PERSONALITY IN
BEHAVIORISTIC ANTHROPOLOGY

The approach of Hullian behaviorism to personality is that of a dynamic trait theory, concentrating on specific motivational variables rather than on personality as a global entity. This is as true of its cross-cultural applications as it is of its domestic psychological studies. Nevertheless, behaviorists operating in the field of culture and personality have used a variety of personality concepts imported from psychoanalysis and clinical psychology and have also formulated a general theory of the relation of personality to culture.

In the most purely Hullian formulation, one begins with primary (biological) drives (hunger, thirst, sex, pain, etc.), which are seen as providing a motivational basis for individual activities designed to reduce the drives. Behaviors followed by drive-reduction are reinforced and become habitual. Cultures are seen as analogous to mazes in learning experiments, i.e. they are sets of stimuli which if responded to appropriately by the individual lead to satisfaction of his needs. Since a culture is largely an interpersonal environment made up of multidimensional stimuli, it is extremely complex, and complex patterns of responses are required for adaptation to it. The stimulus-response connections, called habits at the individual level, are called customs when they are shared by members of a society as part of their adaptation to a common environment. It is recognized that many of these customs are acquired in the early years of the individual, and that his parents and other early caretakers have a formative effect on his behavior, since they control the rewards and punishments leading to drive reduction, like the experimenter in the animal laboratory.

However, this is only part of the story, for personality (or culture) is not seen as made up simply of mechanical habits. On the contrary, some of the habits acquired in early life take on drive value themselves and become secondary reinforcers in the learning of new habits, as well as potent motivating forces in the social lives of adults. Most of the motivational characteristics that we tend to think of as "personality" are acquired drives in this orthodox Hullian view. At the level of cross-cultural variations in personality, Gillin (1948, pp. 300-301) mentioned three types of acquired drives: those derived from punishment, i.e., fears and anxieties; those derived from reward, i.e., "appetites or positive cultural desires," drives for prestige or money; those derived from frustration, i.e., acquired angers or hostilities. It is apparent that in a typology of this kind there is considerable room for variation in the number and kind of acquired drives recognized by an investigator; one could speak of fears, appetites, and angers of such specific natures that each culture would have its unique, noncomparable, and endless catalogue of such drives. On the other hand, they could be defined so universally as to be devoid of cultural content. No principle in behavior theory itself dictates the level of specificity or generality at which acquired drives should be examined, and that is why behavior theorists have continually turned to other psychologies for personality-variable concepts.

The cross-cultural study by Whiting and Child (1953) remains the single most important anthropological investigation of personality in behavioristic terms, and the concept of personality contained therein is consequently worthy of attention. Whiting and Child follow Gillin and others in considering a custom as a habit shared by and characteristic of the typical member of a society. They go further, however, in creating the concept of "custom complex," defined as consisting of "a customary practice and of beliefs, values, sanctions, rules, motives, and satisfactions associated with it" (Whiting & Child, 1953, p. 27). Each of these terms is defined as a type of custom, as follows. *Practice:* "A custom whose response directly effects a change in the environment, the performer, or the relationship between the two" (1953, p. 27). *Belief:* "A custom whose response symbolizes some relationship between events" (1953, p. 28). *Value:* "A custom whose response attributes goodness or badness to some event." *Sanctions:* "The customary rewarding and punishing behavior of others following the performance of a practice (or the failure to perform it when occasion demands)" (1953, p. 29). *Rules:* They "specify the details of proper or improper performance of the practice" (1953, p. 30). *Motive:* "A custom which is responsible for acquired reward in its performer" (1953, p. 30). It should be noted that all these terms are part of the custom complex, that personality has not yet been mentioned, and that motives and values are defined as customs without reference to personality. The authors state that motives and satisfactions, being "for the most part internal and not accessible to ordinary observation," are examples of what Gillin has called "mental customs" (Whiting & Child, 1953, pp. 30-31).

Where does personality enter into this scheme, which appears to deal with behavior strictly in habit-custom terms? Whiting and Child are testing hypotheses about the relationship between one set of custom complexes, i.e., the child training customs characteristic of a number of societies, and another set of custom complexes, the responses to illness characteristic of the same societies. The hypothesized connections between these two are "personality processes," i.e., processes within the typical member of a society which are affected in early life by one custom complex and which in turn affect the other one in adulthood. The hypothetical processes are derived from psychoanalytic theory and restated in behavioristic terms. Whiting and Child regard as the subject matter of their research what they call "the personality integration of culture," i.e., the correspondence between custom complexes brought about by hypothetical personality processes in the average individual.

In their research procedure, Whiting and Child measure only "overt customs," i.e., the child training (stimulus) variables at one end and the disease-custom (response) variables at the other; they do not attempt to measure personality. For them, personality remains an unseen mediating process between observable input and output variables; one tests hypotheses about personality by finding out if alleged input-output connections based on a particular conception of personality are empirically valid. Thus, though they are careful to define every concept used directly for measurement in the investigation, they do not offer a rigorous definition of personality; there is no need to do so as they do not intend to measure it directly.

As they present their hypotheses, it becomes apparent that Whiting and Child's conception of personality processes has many elements in common with that of psychoanalytic theory, e.g., the assumption that the manifestations of personality in behavior are unconscious, non-rational, and gratifying to the individual. However, their reliance on non-behavioristic psychology goes beyond this general conception, for they are compelled to seek dimensions of personality or behavior that will dictate the selection of particular custom complexes for study. These dimensions must be found in all societies, yet exhibit considerable cross-cultural variation. To isolate such dimensions, they formulate the concept of "a system of behavior," defined as "a set of habits or customs motivated by a common drive and leading to common satisfactions" (Whiting and Child, 1953, p. 45). Five systems of behavior are identified: oral, anal, sexual, dependence, and aggression, "on the assumption that these systems would occur and be subject to socialization in all societies" (Whiting and Child, 1953, p. 45). The first three are related to primary drives and were also distinguished by Freud as universal stages in psychosexual development. Dependence and aggression they assume to be motivated by acquired drives but arising in all humans by virtue of the universal conditions of infant helplessness and childhood frustration, respectively. Within each of these systems of behavior they recognize negative fixation, in which fear or anxiety is revealed in the customary practices related to that system, and positive fixation, in which the relevant customary practices manifest an appetitional quality, positive preoccupation or desire. Thus, to put specific content in their correlational study of custom complexes, Whiting and Child had to turn to personality variables proposed by non-behavioristic personality psychology.

In the decade since the publication of the Whiting and Child study, they and their co-workers have elaborated upon the original five systems of behavior, continuing to borrow from other types of personality psychology. Referring to the concept of "system of behavior," Child (1954, p. 661) writes:

The label resembles Murray's "need" and other such terms in representing a classification of behavior by reference to drive or goal; it has the advantage, for present purposes, of referring not just to the drive itself but also to all the associated behavior organized around it. There is, of course, no absolute right or wrong about a classification of behavior into systems. A classification that is fruitful at one time for a certain purpose may at a later time or for other purposes be replaced by a different classification.

In his review of the literature on socialization, Child distinguishes the following systems of behavior: oral, excretory, sexual, aggression, dependence, achievement, affection or affiliation, reproductive, and fear (independent of fears specific to other behavior systems). In their project manual for comparative field studies of socialization, Whiting, Child, Lambert, et al (1954) have broken down some of these systems into components. For example, dependence-independence is seen as made up of eight "systems": succorance, achievement-oriented behavior, self-reliance, obedience, nurturance, responsibility, sociability, and dominance—virtually all of interpersonal behavior except aggression. Aggression is retained as a single behavior system but two separate "dispositions," "aggressive irritability" (or retaliatory aggression) and "opportunity aggression" are distinguished.

In general, the concept of behavior system, as implied in the above quotation from Child, serves to resolve for behavioristically oriented students of personality (particularly in cross-cultural studies) the problem of how to extricate an acquired drive from the habitual responses associated with it. It also provides a vehicle for the importation of trait concepts from other personality theories.

Landy (1959), carrying the notion of studying overt cultural behavior to its logical conclusion, proposes omitting the term "personality" from cross-cultural studies of learning and behavior acquisition. With behavioristic concepts of "practices" and "values" as well as various behavior systems for motivational content, he sees no need to retain the elusive notion of personality. However, this proposal is not convincing when one begins giving tests to adult individuals cross-culturally. Operationally, we may concentrate on specific behavior system variables, but eventually the problem of the structure of these variables, i.e., their intercorrelations, comes up, and we find we need a concept for handling this structure. "Personality" appears to be useful in this context. It is easy enough to shelve "personality" as such when one is measuring it only indirectly, as Whiting and Child and their co-workers have done in cross-cultural studies, but it is hard to dispense with it in the direct assessment of motives and behavior systems.

BEHAVIORISTIC CONCEPTS AND
ANTHROPOLOGICAL DATA

In this section the discussion is centered around four concepts in behavior theory that have demonstrable or potential applications in the
field of cross-cultural personality research: *drive, reinforcement, stimulus-generalization,* and *primacy effects.*

1. *Drive.* The satisfaction of primary or biological drives, i.e.,
hunger, thirst, sex (pain or pain-avoidance), elimination, sleep, and
other processes assuring individual survival, has long been recognized
by anthropologists as a functional prerequisite for social survival, and
the institutional adaptations to these needs in the technology, economy,
belief system, and group structure of nonliterate peoples have been
described by many ethnographers.

Usually, however, social scientists have contented themselves with
stating that these drives are universal, that one must be aware of them
in order to understand cultural behavior, but that they cannot be used
to account for cultural differences, since they are panculturally constant.
There has been relatively little recognition of what ethnographic investigations have established beyond doubt, viz. that the level or
strength of some primary drives varies widely from one human population to another. Holmberg (1950), in his book on the Siriono, has
given us an example of a South American tribe living under constant
food deprivation which has clearly affected the typical motivational
state of Siriono adults. Ombrédane (1954), in analyzing Thematic
Apperception Test results from several Congo tribes, claims that subjects from a tribe which has perpetual food scarcity produced a greater
proportion of responses concerning food than those from a nearby
group living in a more abundant environment. We know also, from a
wide variety of evidence (Ford and Beach, 1952), that sexual restrictiveness is extremely variable cross-culturally, and that this means fewer
opportunities for sexual outlet in some populations than in others.

This cross-cultural variation in primary drive satisfaction levels has
important implications for personality research. In the Hullian formula,
performance variables are a function of the product of habit strength
and drive strength. To account for variations in the intensity or frequency of cultural behavior patterns that are connected with primary
drives, it is necessary to assess not only how those drives were socialized
in early life (habit formation) but also the current drive state of adult

individuals. Whiting and Child (1953) tested hypotheses relating severity of socialization of sex and orality in childhood to sexual and oral preoccupations (fixations) in customary theories of disease. They did not attempt to measure the state of hunger or sexual tension of the typical adults in the societies they compared, and in this sense did not do full justice to their behavior theory framework. A Hullian approach bids us to look at the interaction of early habit-forming experience with the current drive state of the organism in order to predict behavior. A high degree of oral preoccupation might be due to weaning experiences or present hunger or a combination of the two; sexual preoccupations may reflect parental punishment or stimulation of sex in childhood but they are likely to be affected by contemporaneous sexual frustration as well. An adequate test of hypotheses derived from Hullian theory must take the habit-drive combination into account.

There have been attempts made to measure, if only indirectly, primary drive states across societies. In his cross-cultural study of the functions of alcohol, Horton (1943) devised indices of subsistence anxiety (not quite the same as hunger) and sexual anxiety and found that they correlated with alcohol usage. As mentioned above, Ford and Beach (1952) used indices of restrictiveness in several areas of sexual behavior, and Stephens (1962, pp. 80-81) has based a sex anxiety index in part on the Ford and Beach classification. Most of these studies involve very indirect approaches to the measurement of the hunger and sex drive levels, and it would seem that the better ethnographic data we now have should allow more direct measurement, particularly if advice concerning the physiology of these drives is sought from biological scientists.

With adequate cross-cultural measures of the satisfaction of some primary drives, we could test at least two kinds of personality hypotheses: (a) hypotheses relating variations in drive state to variations in cultural preoccupations as manifested in cultural fantasy (myths, folktales, dreams and jokes), recreational activity, and interpersonal behavior—while controlling for severity of socialization of the drive; (b) specific propositions derived from the frustration-aggression hypothesis, which states that drive frustration leads to aggression.

The concept of acquired drives, the difficulty of identifying them and measuring their reduction in complex social situations, and the transformation into the concept of systems of behavior, have been discussed in the last section. There will always be something arbitrary about any list of acquired drives, but we can insist on several criteria for accepting them: (a) their transcultural occurrence as behavior categories (Sears, 1961), usually because of linkages to biosocial universals of human existence; (b) their replicability in measurement; (c) their identifiability at different points in the life span of the individual; (d) ultimately, their exhibition of systematic relationships with environmental variables in cross-cultural research.

In addition to the standard primary drives, there is increasing interest in drives of social significance which may be primary in the sense of innate but that do not contribute as directly to the survival of the organism as hunger and thirst, or as directly to societal survival as sex. These come under the heading of curiosity and exploratory drives, and Berlyne (1962) has suggested that they be studied cross-culturally. This has not yet been done but it promises to throw some light on obscure areas of aesthetic, cognitive, and recreational culture patterns.

2. *Reinforcement.* The law of effect probably has greater subconscious currency in anthropology than any other principle from behavior theory. The contemporary interest in values among social anthropologists has strengthened the use of reinforcement notions, for it is widely recognized that if a behavior pattern is valued by the adults of a society, they will find a way of manipulating rewards and punishments so that their children will acquire that behavior pattern.

An ethnographic example of the relation between cultural values and reinforcement is provided by Read's (1959) study of the Ngoni of Nyasaland in Africa, who have a hierarchical and aristocratic political system. She found that parents encourage respect and obedience in their children, punishing infractions. By the time individuals are political participants they have had many reinforced trials in respect and obedience behavior which is adaptive for political functioning. Similarly, Zborowski (1955) describes how the Jews of Eastern European ghettoes, who set a high value on book-learning and scholarliness, sent three-year-old boys to strict Hebrew schools where they learned by rote and were whipped with a cat-o'-nine-tails for inattention to their books. In both of these examples the ethnographer shows how reinforced repetition in childhood shapes behavior in the direction of cultural values. This is essentially a Skinnerian view of social learning ("shaping"), uncomplicated by concepts of identification and unconscious communication.

The axiomatic nature of the law of effect in cross-cultural studies is illustrated by the study of Barry, Child and Bacon (1959) relating subsistence economy to child training practices. They show that societies with food-accumulating economies (agricultural and pastoral) stress obedience and responsibility in child training, while those with non-accumulating economies (hunting and gathering) emphasize self-reliance and achievement in their children. The investigators feel safe in making the assumption that if parents customarily put pressure toward certain behavior on their children, the children will acquire such behavior as habits; thus they have no independent measures of how obedient, responsible, self-reliant and achievement-oriented the children are in fact. It is taken for granted that over time parents in a given society have worked out effective schedules of reinforcement for producing in their children economically adaptive patterns of behavior. This assumption is plausible for economic behavior; it is not so plausible for all personality patterns.

There are dangers in assuming the general validity of the law of effect in the process of socialization. The major difficulty is that reward and punishment are not equivalent processes, i.e., while reward may reinforce a given response, punishment may not stamp it out but have a different effect altogether. In general, punishment for non-performance of a rewarded response, as in the whipping of Jewish boys for failure to pay attention to their lessons, appears to be more effective than punishment intended to eliminate a cluster of responses, particularly when these responses are highly motivated, innate or reflexive. Punishment of children in a particular drive system may condition anxiety to that drive and cause preoccupation with it, contrary to the conscious intent of the socializing agent.

The main results of the Whiting and Child (1953) study concern the differential effects of reward and punishment. They examined initial indulgence, severity of socialization, and cultural preoccupation (negative and positive) in the oral, anal, sexual, aggressive and dependent behavior systems. Simplistic Hullian theory would predict that indulgence (reward) in a behavior system would lead (by reinforcement) to preoccupation with it, while socialization severity (punishment) would lead to non-preoccupation (extinction). However, Whiting and Child found, as have numerous experimental psychologists in recent years, that punishment leads to augmentation of response. Indulgence had little effect, while socialization severity was more frequently found to be associated with cultural preoccupation, as measured by magical explanations of disease. These findings are inconsistent with a simple response-reinforcement theory. To cope with this finding, Whiting and

Child have propounded a major revision of Hullian motivation theory, and their revision is consistent with other formulations by experimental psychologists based on laboratory findings. This is the theory of conflict-produced drive strength, which states that punishment of a strong behavior tendency, whether innate or strongly conditioned, leads to an inhibitory anxiety that conflicts with the original tendency, and that the conflict produces more drive than would otherwise have been present. They show that societies in which children are severely punished for aggression are more likely to use sorcery as a disease explanation, and also more likely to displace their projected hostility farther out on a stimulus dissimilarity continuum of social and supernatural objects. Without going into their reasoning concerning the differential steepness of gradients for aggressive tendencies and inhibitory anxiety, it may be simply stated for present purposes that punishing aggressive behavior does not stamp it out; it increases its drive level and changes its form.

This line of reasoning concerning the drive-producing and displacement effects of punishment may help to account for the discrepancy between ideal values and actual behavior which many ethnographers have reported. For example, the Zuni Indians value peace and harmony in interpersonal relations, but indulge in sorcery accusations and malicious gossip to a high degree (Whiting, in press). The Gusii, an East African people (LeVine, 1959), value sexual propriety and consider themselves a most moral people with regard to sexuality (especially by comparison with surrounding groups, whom they consider promiscuous), but they have a much higher frequency of rape than most societies in the world. These apparent anomalies may be due to the fact that aggression and sexuality cannot be extinguished and that attempts to do so by parents and other socializing agents may have both positive and negative effects with respect to normative behavior. Punishing children for aggression and sexual behavior may achieve that modicum of overt behavioral conformity, i.e., marital fidelity and inhibition of violence, which is needed for group functioning, but at the cost of increasing motivation in forms of aggression and sexuality that are not normatively controlled. These latter forms may become disruptive in their own right, particularly under conditions of social change. Thus, punishment as a socialization technique can be seen as generating both conformity and deviance. This general hypothesis is consistent with Freud's view in *Civilization and Its Discontents* (1934) that the repression of sexuality required in organized social life produces neurotic disorders as a side effect or social cost. However, in the behavioristic version of this hypothesis, the mechanisms involved are more clearly specified.

The work on avoidance conditioning which has been done in experimental psychology is relevant to the analysis of these culture and personality problems. In one of the rare instances of terminological convergence to be found in the behavioral sciences, anthropologists have concerned themselves with avoidance relationships such as mother-in-law avoidance and brother-sister avoidance in various cultures and by this they have meant approximately the same thing that psychologists mean by avoidance. In these relationships the mere sight of the other person is a cue for walking away, covering one's body, or ceasing certain types of behavior. In analyzing the childhood acquisition of such avoidance patterns (as well as the acquisition of other prohibitions), ethnographers might well benefit from following the lead of the laboratory by trying to identify just what it is that the child is being taught to avoid, what responses he has made just prior to the administration of noxious or aversive stimuli, and in what situations he can perform a related response, i.e., a response in the same behavior system, without expectation of punishment. By using a finer analysis of this type rather than referring to severe sex or aggression training as general variables, we may be better able to predict the stimulus conditions that will elicit sexual and aggressive responses in adults of a society, and those that will elicit an inhibitory anxiety response.

Thus in a society in which children are punished for physical but not verbal aggression, we might be able to make better predictions about adult aggression if we distinguish the two forms in socialization and cultural behavior than if we use a global concept of aggression training. Breaking down behavior systems into response components, so as to examine what is being rewarded and what punished, can be applied to a wide variety of behavior patterns and might improve the correlations found in socialization research.

3. *Stimulus generalization.* Hull regarded stimulus generalization as a primary social science law applying to all forms of behavior. A brief and general statement of stimulus generalization is as follows: Any habitual response learned in connection with one stimulus or situational configuration will tend to be evoked by other situations or stimuli in proportion to their similarity to the former. This leads to the conceptualization of a quantitative stimulus dissimilarity continuum or scale,

with a response gradient sloping negatively toward the higher dissimilarity values.

Hull (1950, p. 226) recognized the applicability of stimulus generalization to socialization and interpersonal behavior and its congruence
with some psychoanalytic formulations:

> The law of stimulus generalization is known to apply to both the free
> motor and the symbolic social behavior of human beings, although no
> simple quantitative demonstration has come to hand. Young children
> notoriously generalize the response of calling the father "daddy" by
> applying the term to other men. They are apt to call the first rabbit
> they see a "kitty," and the first horse a "cow," and so on. Clinical
> evidence of stimulus generalization is also abundant. Both psycho-
> analysts and psychiatrists, for example, recognize that adult males in
> our society characteristically react toward a boss or other person in an
> authoritative position with types of behavior acquired in childhood and
> adolescence toward the individual's own father.

In cross-cultural research as in psychoanalytic formulations, the
typical application of stimulus generalization has involved viewing relationships in the nuclear family, which are presumably the child's first
social relationships, as constituting the set of original stimuli toward
which habitual responses are learned. It is then hypothesized that the
growing individual will generalize these responses toward social objects
outside the nuclear family in proportion to their similarity to persons
or roles in the nuclear family. The problem is to conceptualize and
make operational dimensions of stimulus similarity in the variety of
social objects existing outside the family. Murdock (1949, p. 133) has
solved this problem in his cross-cultural study of kinship and incest
taboos by concentrating on two different types of similarities and
dissimilarities:

> (1) the absence or presence of differences inherent in the very nature
> of kinship structure in consequence of the biology of heredity and of
> the universal cultural fact of family exogamy;
> (2) the absence or presence of recurrent but not universal features of
> social organization and of associated cultural rules of residence, descent,
> and marriage which have the effect of increasing or decreasing the
> degree of similarity or dissimilarity prevailing between relatives of
> particular kinship categories.

The second type Murdock conceptualizes as *social equalizers* and
social differentials. A social equalizer is an aspect of social structure or

of associated cultural behavior that creates significant similarities between relatives distinct in terms of universally inherent criteria; a social differential is an aspect of social structure or of associated cultural behavior that significantly increases the perceptible dissimilarities between such relatives. An example of a social equalizer or differential is proximity in residence, i.e., Murdock hypothesizes that if particular relatives usually live near ego's relatives he will be more likely to generalize primary kin terms to them than to other relatives who live farther away. He goes on to show, in a large sample of societies, that there are many relationships between residence and kinship terminology predictable on the assumption of stimulus generalization.

Thus, for example, if the residence pattern is such that mother's sister lives nearby, she is more likely to be distinguished from father's sister and called "mother" than if she does not customarily live nearby. Another example of a social equalizer or differential is what Murdock calls "participation," a similarity or dissimilarity in group membership. He demonstrates the effect of joint participation in descent groups on the extension of kinship terms, and subsequently shows its effect on the extension of incest taboos, in which descent group membership has a uniquely powerful place as a social equalizer and differential.

LeVine (1960) has used Murdock's stimulus generalization paradigm to propose (but not test) hypotheses concerning the extension of authority behavior learned in the family to the political system. It has often been suggested, by psychoanalysts and social scientists (as in the above quotation from Hull) that parent-child and sibling relationships give the individual a set of behavioral dispositions that are later directed toward authority figures such as political leaders and employers in the wider society. Working at the cross-cultural level, LeVine observed that the generalization from family to polity seemed more explicit and intense in stateless societies such as those found in Africa. The suggestion that this generalization was stronger in some societies than in others led to a search for social equalizers and differentials, defined in this case as aspects of social structure that promote or inhibit perception of stimulus equivalence between family and political system. The basic notion involved is that the presence of extrafamilial groups compounded of, descended from, and labeled in the same way as family groups (as in corporate descent groups) acts as a social equalizer, while the presence of extrafamilial groups based on other principles, such as age-groups, secret societies, and a centralized state, acts as a social differential. The hypotheses associated with this conception remain to be tested, but they provide a framework for testing at the cross-cultural level the notions proposed in psychological studies like *The Authoritarian Personality* (Adorno et al, 1950).

In sum, the concept of stimulus generalization is a handy tool for generating cross-cultural hypotheses concerning the impact of socialization experience upon adult interpersonal behavior.

4. *Primacy effects.* The adoption of a behavioristic point of view, especially in combination with neo-Freudian notions, leads to great emphasis on the effects of childhood experience on adult behavior. Socialization variables are seen as causes of adult behavior patterns. Implicit in this is the assumption that behavior patterns acquired early in life are more enduring than and dominant over tendencies learned in adulthood.

In cross-cultural studies of personality development like that of Whiting and Child, this consideration does not usually become explicit because the societies are assumed to have a sufficient degree of cultural stability and functional integration so that the patterns learned at different points in the life span are not violently at odds with one another. (The Whiting, Kluckhohn, and Anthony 1958 study of initiation ceremonies is an exception here.) However, this latter assumption itself raises a disturbing point: if the adult social environment reinforces the same behavior patterns that are fostered in early socialization, how do we know that the correlations between child training practices and adult behavior patterns represent an effect that is mediated by the developing personality? It is equally plausible to assert that the adult behavior patterns are reactions to the social environments in which adults find themselves, acquired in adulthood, and that the correlations with child training represent the effect of these reactions on their behavior as parents. In other words, the claim could be made that the Whiting and Child study, for example, shows a relationship between the behavior of the typical adult as patient (in magical theories and therapies of disease) and his behavior as parent (in socialization), in both cases perhaps reflecting a behavioral tendency fostered by his contemporaneous environment. Whiting and Child themselves state that an alternative hypothesis concerning the relation of aggression anxiety and severe aggression training is that adults characterized by more aggression anxiety may be more likely to punish their children for aggression. In other words, the causal sequence may be reversed, or both aspects of cultural behavior may be caused by a third variable, environmental or structural; in either case there is no need to posit an effect of child training on personality to explain the correlation. Since correlation does not prove causation, we are faced with the problem that correlations found in a sample of relatively stable cultures do not allow us to isolate the effects of early experience from pressure for adult conformity.

There are both substantive and statistical solutions to this problem but I should like to propose one that involves considerations of research design borrowed from behavioristic psychology. The laboratory psychologist would say: It is simply a problem of extinction trials. Since the behavior sequences rewarded in the training trials continue to be reinforced throughout the lifespan of the individual, it is impossible to detect what effect the initial reinforcement had, if it had any at all. What are needed are non-reinforced trials in adulthood to see how quickly the previously reinforced habits extinguish, if indeed they can be elicited at all. If they prove resistant to extinction when not being reinforced, then we can acknowledge the habit strength derived from the training trials.

Anthropologists have an analogy to extinction trials in the study of culture change. The closest approximation to an extinction trial would be a single individual forcibly removed from his native cultural setting and deposited in another place surrounded by natives of an entirely different culture. Lacking comparable evidence on a large number of such cases, we can use more remote approximations: immigrant or refugee situations, where whole groups of persons are displaced and settle in an alien cultural environment making new demands on them; and other culture change situations, where persons do not move but their sociocultural system changes significantly in less than a lifetime. In all such cases individuals have acquired behavioral dispositions in early life that are not reinforced in adulthood; there is a disjunction between socialization and adult social pressures. It is in such situations that we have the opportunity to assess the effects of child training unconfounded by cultural reinforcement.

An example will make this clearer. Ethnographers in diverse parts of Africa have noticed a similar phenomenon: Many Africans in the first generation of those attending Western schools continue to believe in witchcraft and sorcery as educated adults, despite their exposure to Western biology and their attachment to Christianity. All of the prestige and persuasiveness of Western science and the Christian church are not enough to change their beliefs in this regard. Here we have an effect of early learning to explain, for we know that they began learning about witchcraft and sorcery before their exposure to Western counter-pressures. We may attempt to explain the phenomenon in cognitive terms (e.g., the insulation of witchcraft beliefs from contradictory empirical proof) rather than in terms simply of the age of learning, but we can at least be sure we are dealing with a personal tendency that has survived some non-reinforcement in adulthood.

From an anthropological perspective, Bruner (1956) has suggested the general hypothesis that those cultural behavior patterns that are traditionally learned earlier will be more resistant to change in a culture contact situation. This formulation is congruent with the old psychological notion of the dominance of primacy over recency in the recall of memorized material, as well as with the concept of critical periods in developmental psychology. From the viewpoint of learning experiments with animals, such a hypothesis might be modified to include the effect of the aversive stimuli administered during the learning of a particular behavior pattern. Work on traumatic avoidance learning would suggest that the use of pain or punishment can make habits highly resistant to extinction. A general hypothesis could be formulated to the effect that resistance to change of a particular cultural behavior pattern in a contact situation is directly related to the earliness of its acquisition combined with the amount of aversive stimuli accompanying its acquisition. Testing such an hypothesis, providing its crucial terms could be made operational, would contribute not only to the study of cultural change *per se* but also to our knowledge of the long-range effects of socialization on personality.

CONCLUSIONS

The history of contact and influence between behavior theory and anthropological studies of culture and personality is to a large extent the history of a particular group of researchers and some of their students working at and/or trained at Yale in the 1930's. It is pertinent to ask whether this specific interdisciplinary fusion, which they found fruitful, is one that can be generally recommended in cross-cultural personality research.

From the viewpoint of anthropology, behavior theory continues to have a number of advantages. One of these is that it *is* a theory and one can derive from it testable hypotheses on a variety of subjects. There are few theoretical formulations in the behavioral sciences that approach the comprehensiveness and analytic elaboration of behavior theory, and this makes it useful to give guidance and direction to empirical re-

search. Second, anthropologists whose primary interests are in the modification of individual (though culturally patterned) behavior in socialization or culture change can find in behavior theory notions concerning
the specific mechanisms involved in change processes, and there are few
alternative sources of such ideas. Thus, the use of behavior theory as
a source of ideas to be tested empirically (often within a broader
framework such as psychoanalytic or structural-functional theories)
commends it to researchers on culture and personality. However, there
is some danger that anthropologists will naively accept as valid many
of the original Hullian notions which have been challenged by laboratory findings and theoretical work in recent years. This would not
necessarily be bad so long as the anthropologists have their own
methods of empirical validation, although it would diminish the
relevance of their work to psychological theory. The alternative is for
anthropologists to acquaint themselves with the technical literature in
which behavior theory has been revised, challenged, and combined with
cognitive formulations, and this may result in a disillusionment with
the gleaming edifice which Hullian theory appeared to be in an earlier
period.

From the viewpoint of psychological behavior theorists, cross-
cultural data may or may not be relevant. Insofar as they are searching
for primary laws operative at all levels of behavioral functioning from
the short-term behavior of experimental animals to the customary
practices of human populations, they cannot afford to ignore ethnographic evidence. In fact, cross-cultural studies are essential to establish
such primary laws. If, however, behavior theorists limit the applicability
of their formulations to a particular level, such as individual differences, or to a particuar research design, such as the controlled experiment, then cross-cultural evidence is obviously peripheral to their
interest. The psychologist involved in personality research, if he attempts to develop a comprehensive conception of the relations between
personality and socio-cultural systems, is likely to make use of behavior theory at least in those areas in which it intersects other psychological and sociological theories.

REFERENCES

BARRY, H. H.,CHILD, I. L., & BACON, M. K. Relations of child training to subsistence economy. *Amer. Anthropologist*, 1959, *61*, 51-63.

BATESON, G. The frustration-aggression hypothesis. *Psychol. Review*, 1941, *48*, 350-355.

BATESON, G. Social planning and the concept of "deutero-learning." In L. Bryson and L. Finkelstein (Eds.), *Symposimum of the Congress on Science, Philosophy and Religion*, 2:81-97. New York: Harper, 1942.

BERLYNE, D. E. New directions in motivation theory. In T. Gladwin & W. C. Sturtevant (Ed.), *Anthropology and Human Behavior*. Washington: Anthropological Society of Washington, 1962. Pp. 150-173.

BRUNER, E. Cultural transmission and cultural change. *Southwtn. J. of Anthrop.*, 1956, *12*, 191-199.

CHILD, I L. Socialization. In G. Lindzey (Ed.), *Handbook of social psychology*, Vol. II. Cambridge: Addison-Wesley, 1954. Pp. 655-692.

DOLLARD, J., DOOB, L., MILLER, N., MOWRER, O., & SEARS, R. *Frustration and aggression*. New Haven: Yale Univer. Press, 1939.

FORD, C. S., & BEACH, F. A. *Patterns of sexual behavior*. New York: Harper & Bros., 1952.

FREUD, S. *Civilization and its discontents*. London: Hogarth Press, 1934.

GILLIN, J. P. Acquired drives in culture contact. *Amer. Anthropologist*, 1942, *44*, 545-54.

GILLIN, J. P. *The ways of men*. New York: Appleton-Century, 1948.

GORER, G. Themes in Japanese culture. Transactions of the New York Academy of Sciences, Series II, 1943, *5*, 106-124.

HALLOWELL, A. I. Psychology and anthropology. In J. P. Gillin (Ed.) *Toward a science of social man*. New York: Macmillan, 1954.

HOLMBERG, A. R. Nomads of the long bow; the Siriono of Eastern Bolivia. *Smithsonian Institution, Institute of Social Anthrop.*, 1950, No. 10.

HORTON, D. The functions of alcohol in primitive societies: a cross-cultural study. *Quart. J. Stud. Alcohol*, 1943, *4*, 199-320.

HULL, C. L. A functional interpretation of the conditioned reflex. *Psychol. Review*, 1929, *36*, 498-511.

HULL, C. L. A primary social science law. *Scientific Monthly*, 1950, *71*, 221-228.

KARDINER, A. *The individual and his society*. New York: Columbia Univer. Press. 1939.

KLUCKHOHN, C. Culture and behavior. In G. Lindzey (Ed.), *Handbook of social psychology,* Vol. II. Cambridge: Addison-Wesley, 1954, Pp. 921-976.

LANDY, D. *Tropical childhood: cultural transmission and learning in a rural Puerto Rican village.* Chapel Hill: Univer. of North Carolina Press, 1959.

LEVINE, R. A. Gusii sex offenses: a study in social control. *Amer. Anthrop.,* 1959, *61,* 965-990.

LEVINE, R. A. The role of the family in authority systems: a cross-cultural application of stimulus-generalization theory. *Behavioral Sci.,* 1960, *5,* 291-296.

LOGAN, F. A., OLMSTEAD, D. L., ROSNER, B. S., SCHWARTZ, R. D., & STEVENS, C. M. *Behavior-theory and social science.* New Haven: Yale Univer. Press, 1955.

MALINOWSKI, B. *A scientific theory of culture.* Chapel Hill: Univer. of North Carolina Press, 1944.

MILLER, N., & DOLLARD, J. *Social learning and imitation.* New Haven: Yale Univer. Press, 1941.

MURDOCK, G. P. The common denominator of cultures. In R. Linton (Ed.) *The science of man in the world crisis.* New York: Columbia Univer. Press, 1945.

MURDOCK, G. P. *Social structure.* New York: Macmillan, 1949.

OMBREDANE, A. L'exploration de la mentalité des noirs congolais à moyen d'une épreuve projective: Le Congo T.A.T. *Mémoire d'Institut Royal Colonial Belge,* T. 37, 1954.

READ, M. *Children of their fathers: growing up among the Ngoni of Nyasaland.* New Haven: Yale Univer. Press, 1959.

STEPHENS, W. *The Oedipus complex: cross-cultural evidence.* New York: Free Press of Glencoe, 1962.

WHITING, J. W. M. *Becoming a Kwoma: teaching and learning in a New Guinea tribe.* New Haven: Yale Univer. Press, 1941.

WHITING, J. W. M., ANTONOVSKY, M. F., CHASDI, E. M., & AYRES, B. C. The learning of values. In E. Z. Vogt & J. M. Roberts (Eds.) *Peoples of Rimrock,* Vol. I. Manuscript.

WHITING, J. W. M., & CHILD, I. L. *Child training and personality: a cross-cultural study.* New Haven: Yale Univer. Press, 1953.

WHITING, J. W. M., CHILD, I. L., LAMBERT, W. A. et al. Field guide for a study of socialization in five societies. Mimeo, 1954.

WHITING, J. W., KLUCKHOHN, R., & ANTHONY, A. A. The function of male initiation ceremonies at puberty. In E. E. Maccoby, T. M. Newcomb, & E. L. Hartlay (Eds.), *Readings in social psychology* (3rd ed.) New York: Henry Holt & Co.

ZBOROWSKI, M. The place of book learning in traditional Jewish culture. In M. Mead & M. Wolfenstein (Eds.) *Childhood in Contemporary Cultures.* Chicago: Univer. of Chicago Press, 1955. Pp. 118-141.

14

The Problem of Personality in Sociological Theory

Patricke Johns Heine

Although there have been distinctively sociological contributions to the study of personality, it cannot be said that there is a theory of personality exclusively or even primarily sociological in origin. The resurgence of social behaviorism in the field of small group research is the practical culmination of several decades of a sociological social psychology—a social psychology whose emphasis shifted from the French "crowd psychologists" and "collective behavior" to the behavior of the person functioning in a group. While few sociologists would maintain that the latter constituted the "whole personality," their entry into the domain of individual action tended to awaken old controversies about the proper definition of person and personality. Enthusiasts of role-taking theory, in particular, are prone to identify personality with the roles a person takes. While this may often be cited as *the* sociological view of personality, it cannot properly be said to exhaust the views of sociologists on the problem.

All contemporary views of personality stem from old philosophic doctrines of the self; generally, too, the counterpart of any particular psychological theory of personality may somewhere be found in the sociological literature. Behaviorism, which denied the traditional description of mental states and the self, found its counterpart in social behaviorism and role theory. "Personalist" theory, as stated by Allport, reaffirms a very old idealist theory of the self; but even the systematic sociological theory of Talcott Parsons provides for the separate and autonomous "kingdom of personality" and both men have similar views on the ultimate limits of role theory, although that theory is peripheral to the work of the one and central to the other. Finally, the tendency to transport, in wholesale fashion, the psychological categories of character and personality in such a way as to treat society like the individual (Fromm's social character or Kardiner's basic personality structure) has also had its sociological sponsors. Modified as "modal personality structure" (Inkeles, 1961), the new statement nonetheless purports to tell us something about the central tendency of personality and to insist upon its measurability and comparability within and between societies.

Yet sociology has, in its evolution, developed its own approach to social life—an approach that stands in strong contrast to "psychologism" and the psychological perspective. Instead of seeking explanations of the social order from the standpoint of those who participate in it, sociologists turned to the analysis of the social forms and social arrangements by which men live. From this viewpoint, whether men "willed" it or not and without regard to their "consciousness," distinctive institutions, associations and social systems were seen as defining their way of life and, by extension, their ways of viewing it.

These differences of approach are often crudely summarized by identifying the psychological principle of personality as subjective and volitional, and, in turn, sociological interpretations as objective and deterministic. But recent and contemporary sociological statements are more complex and discerning, and it is now customary to emphasize that the distinctions are by no means absolute, that there remain common problems, shared interests and an array of mutual intellectual influences. This may be stated in terms of perspective whereby individuals may be viewed from the standpoint of intention and motivation (psychology) or their behavior interpreted in terms of the social functions it consciously or unconsciously fulfills (sociology), as Mannheim (1953, p. 239) did, or as a theory of action from which we build interpretations of both personality and the social system, as Parsons (1951, p. 18) has done. The "problem of personality" in either case represents a meeting ground of different perspectives and remains central to the polemic of how we define the relation between the individual and his society.

Since sociology approaches the study of behavior from the social standpoint rather than that of the individual, it has had no pressing need for a well-developed theory of personality. While tacitly acknowledged that individuals acting in concert provide the data of the discipline, only in special contexts has it been necessary to focus on the determinants of the behavior of these individuals. Theoretically, there are few points at which personality might not be meaningfully related to social process, but for purposes of sociological investigation, it is neither necessary nor relevant to attribute large significance to individual or personality "factors." Social behavior "groups" itself, and what falls outside norms or typicalities of behavior may be variously described as "error," "deviation," or "chance." Thus, the relevance of personality has usually been invoked about specific issues and specific problems, and the problem of personality can be defined in terms of how we measure its importance when, for example, we confront the "unlawful" members of a sample—"deviants" from a social norm—or the explanation of new and unforeseen turns in the course of events.

We may cite, as an example, a typical sociological problem in social stratification: the analysis of social class. Here, for the most part, the sociologist deals with objective criteria of class such as income or occupation. Suppose, however, he wishes to reveal some typical relationships between what is called "class consciousness" and objective class position; and let us further suppose that he will use as his measure of class consciousness known political identifications as these have been manifested in (a) attitude studies or (b) actual voting behavior. Now while the relationship between socio-economic class and some social attitudes, as well as voting behavior, is measurable and demonstrable, it remains a complex question precisely because of significant variation. There is not complete accord, but only a tendency toward uniformity of attitude and political preference on the part of members of particular socio-economic strata. As Kornhauser (1953) pointed out in analyzing this kind of problem, the group influences themselves are only in part those of income and occupation; part of the variation can be explained by other group identifications that cut across socio-economic class (race, sex, religion, age, etc.). Having accounted for this, there will still be found residues of variation that the psychologist may claim as lying within his own province; these are non-uniformities that probably can best be explained in terms of psychological peculiarity or personal experience. We are given, then, what Kornhauser called the "psychological bases of class division" or, as he said, "additional reasons why persons living under given 'class' conditions may develop views quite contrary to those of their fellows" (Kornhauser, 1953, p. 81).

With this careful and measured statement, few could quarrel. Rather, polemics have arisen wherever a broad and inclusive psychological determinism has been introduced to "explain" group phenomena. In this instance, a contrasting proposition might be represented by an extreme subjective theory of social class, whereby consciousness of class is made the criterion of class affiliation. Discrepancies between the two would then disappear and the procedure might be justified psychologically on the ground that it is not what people are but what they think they are that matters. Other examples would be: the proposition that all deviant social behavior indicates pathology of personality (whereas the sociologist is likely to contend that "probably most" deviant behavior is produced by clinically normal people); the proposition that prejudice is a function of personality, specifically, the "authoritarian personality," with the implication that we can ignore such factors as region, cultural influence, education or social status (all factors sociologists would regard as equally worthy of investigation); or, again, the proposition that we may assume a common character structure of a group of people on the basis of our knowledge about their cultural symbols and cultural practices (national character).

Therefore, there are important reasons why objections recurrently rise and simmer concerning emphasis on personality and the "subjective factor" in social theory. Fundamentally, what all self theories have sought to locate and explain has been some unchanging identity of person that surpassed growth and maturity, that withstood time and circumstance, that remained despite manifest external transformations. This inward emphasis implies an abstract substantial self for whose understanding historic and social circumstance may be regarded as totally irrelevant.

Attempts to grasp an inner identity that—unlike the physical person—does not change have been stated more often philosophically than psychologically. Perhaps even today many social scientists would rest content with Locke's straightforward statement that self is the person as it sees itself and person is the self seen from outside, for in a rough way this parallels their work-a-day conceptions of the division of labor between psychologists and sociologists. But the dominant modern psychologies of the self have created a world of great subjective complexity; for James, the self was many selves, and psychoanalytic theory, which contributed enormously to shattering traditional conceptions of the self, above all dramatized the complex interplay between its inner and outer expression. Old, simple definitions and distinctions are no longer plausible:

From the sociological standpoint, the interesting aspect of all "inward-turning" descriptions of self, person, or personality, is that they all tend to obscure rather than reveal the ordinary, everyday processes by which we identify others and are identified by them: name and gesture, place and role. Nor is there incontrovertible evidence that inner life is more stable or its subjective expression more determining than outward circumstance in describing the affairs of men.

To represent the factor of personality as an independent force in life not only implies ignoring all those external conditions that may, in fact, limit and shape it, but also (so it has been argued) forces us into paths of fruitless speculation concerning the nature of a self which changes and yet remains the same. Most doctrines of self, of character or of personality, which described or sought to describe something independent and immutable within the self, have stumbled over the problem of change (Frondizi, 1953). If the self changes, if there is no inner nucleus or ego that remains constant, what meaning can be attached to old theories of the self? Bergsonian philosophy called the subjective self in its endless flux the only sure reality; Freudian theory viewed the self as an uneasy and precarious balance of conflicting forces; but Behaviorism simply denied its existence and set both psychology and social psychology the task of defining the empirical person.

In a general way, those in a field of theory and research like sociology—which has been adjacent to the problems of psychology—could applaud the behaviorist critique, for indirectly it affirmed the relevance and significance of their own endeavors. The search for some kind of inner essence or core that propelled the whole human machine could hardly appear justifiable to those accustomed to reflecting upon the problems of political, economic and social life. The specific sociological contribution to the "redefinition of self and personality—in the effort to free it of the burden of old philosophic associations—is called Social Behaviorism. Identified with G. H. Mead, who approached, as he said, experience "from the standpoint of society" (instead of the psychological standpoint of individual experience), is the theory that mind, consciousness, self are to be regarded as products of the social process of communication and the shared experience that comes from taking the role of others (Mead, 1940). Mead's claim that we would be wiser and more useful if we were to turn our attention outward, to forego discussion of what man *is* and look at what he *does,* has been the theoretical spearhead for a vast body of contemporary research.

ROLE THEORY AND PERSONALITY THEORY

The sociological argument has customarily run to the effect that we need not necessarily look *within* the person for our generalizing propositions. An alternative orientation is to analyze social situations and behavior within them without at all trying to relate (consistencies of) behavior to the psychic structure of the person. It was not only the confused state of personality theory itself but its assumptions that led to this reformulation of an old problem. Behind all character and personality theory is the assumption that, in given social situations, it is the propensities one brings to the situation that count, not the specific demands of the situation or the definition of roles within it. In short, if there may be said to be a uniquely sociological approach to personality, it is to be found in an emphasis on personality as process and on a method based on the analysis of situations in terms of action and reaction among the participants. Character type or personal inclination is viewed as irrelevant to understanding behavior since what the actors bring to a given social situation matters less than the types of interaction that become established between them. Role analysis, then, represents an alternative to character or personality analysis.

Within the field of psychology itself considerable support could be mustered for this view. Character and personality theories have been a conspicuous part of the psychologist's approach to social psychology. Where the search for inner unity, pattern or coherence left off, personality theory was bogged down by the complex problems of trait analysis and trait measurement. On the assumption that individual behavior may better be defined in terms of a field of psychological forces (as in Lewinian theory), traditional trait analysis could be forsaken in favor of "situational" analysis. Professional demarcations cannot appropriately be drawn here, for important paradigms of what are now called small group studies are derived from both psychology and sociology (Riecken & Homans, 1954; Hare, Borgatta & Bales, 1955).

Role theory is not, strictly speaking, antithetical to traditional character and personality theory, but in contrast to these it tends (1) to emphasize the "ongoing social process," the act, the social situation, whereas most character and personality theories emphasize the impress of the individual self upon the act; and (2) to interpret social situations in terms of interaction with an analytically refined S-R theory as the point of departure. The actions and reactions set up between two or more people are significant, and reciprocity becomes the key point of analysis.

Role theory, from G. H. Mead onward, stands, then, in contrast to the relatively static interpretations of character and personality doctrine, in that it stresses the shifting, mutually adaptive aspects of human relationships. The self is not viewed as a relatively rigid or structured unity but as a congeries of roles, capable of extension, flexible and adaptive. Where character and personality theory lends itself to interpretations in depth, role theory is oriented to notions of extension and differentiation of experience. We learn by taking the role of the other, and the self is an image we only learn through others—it is "reflected appraisal." Thus, too, the self is enriched not through inner cultivation or virtuosity but by its capacity to reach out, to participate broadly, to be gregarious.

Needless to say, role theory has not wholly dispensed with the idea of character and personality; instead, character has been redefined in its external, active, dramatic sense. Shorn of the ideas of inwardness and autonomy, it is often equated with role performance. Roles may be consistent or discrepant (depending on the situation), harmonious or conflicting. In any case, to understand them, we need not explore the person as such but rather the various social contexts or levels on which he is functioning. While such theories may distinguish between actor as performer and actor as character, it is a distinction that is all but meaningless. Our character is our performance and vice-versa. Role theory is carried neatly and logically to these conclusions by Goffman in his *Presentation of Self in Everyday Life* (1959).

Role theory does not deny the notions of autonomy and willfulness (voluntarism) in the social process, but in a none too subtle way, these are, as prime movers, denigrated and put aside. The crucial instance here is the approach to the problem of leadership. This is a topic that Goffman avoids completely in favor of "team analysis," but that has figured prominently in small group literature. There, leadership is viewed neither as power nor as moving personal force nor as a personal trait but as a group function—a role virtually defined in terms of the criteria by which it is measured. Where we have multiple determinism (stated as reciprocity or interaction), we cannot, at the same time, emphasize the unique and the singular. The play's the thing!

Now in this interest in scene, situation, presentation, we can cer-

tainly observe some parallel limitations. The analytic refinements of
Goffman's work may occasion the protest that too great a halo of
ceremony, etiquette, and decorum is cast over all social relationships;
that in doing so we are given depictions of social roles that are too
rigid. Goffman's subtle and often illuminating essays are far removed
from the usual literature on personality and yet succeed in telling us
much about the person; but their tendency to emphasize uniformities
that coerce or elicit specific types of behavior, to rely upon strictly conventional or institutional definitions of roles, to decipher the maneuvres
of people as they act and "re-act" in definable, set situations—all of
these may appear as the very antithesis of "personality." The actors are
quick to "re-adjust" to the shifting boundaries of a social situation, or
"re-align" themselves to "save the show," or take part in a new "mas-
querade." [1] But elements of choice, spontaneity, uniqueness never make
an appearance in this description of the social process.

In the analogy to drama, on which role theory draws again and
again, it is not only the absence of a hero but the focus on prop and
setting that is notable. Against this background, there is certainly a
tendency to think exclusively of surface presentations, impressions or
appearances. What, then, it might be asked, can this theory tell us
about personal conflict? Does it not tend to deny the meaning of conflict unless it happens grossly to perturb the presentation? It is true that
Goffman refers to significant consequences "from the point of view
of individual personality" when the show is disrupted (Goffman, 1959,
p. 243), but for the most part his "presentation of self" is a self highly
sensitized to social ritual and innuendo, gregarious and expressive by
virtue of external requirement and not inner need, tension, or resolution.

The contention that role theory tends toward superficiality is, in
this sense, true. Generally it does lack depth and is to be distinguished
from other theories that view the self in stratified terms. It is a doctrine
in which all aspects of the self have been externalized, made "empirical," observable, measurable. While this has the advantage of mak-

---

[1] One may only note here some curious consequences of this type of formal role
depiction with its accompanying analysis of etiquette (what Goffman calls "rules of
politeness and decorum" that maintain the team-audience "ethos"). On the one hand,
it seemingly apotheosizes the principle of artifice in social life and, on the other, it
has a sometimes alarming tendency to over-extend its metaphors so that all social life
seems theatrical and fictional. The analysis of symbolic exchange and interactions
(though cues and signals, words and gestures are no less real because they are "symbols") seems too easily to lead to such formulations, for in a similar vein Ernest Becker
(1962, p. 497) writes of "the fictional fabric of social life" and "the social fiction of
learned meanings, goals and values."

ing it possible to conduct experiments to verify observations, it also limits the types of questions one may ask and answer.

Problem definition, method and theory are inextricably interdependent. Thus, once the integrity of the self is seen as an inconvenient fiction, so too its seemingly timeless attributes become dispensable—its unity, consistency, voluntarism and self-determinacy. The self then becomes simply a construct of "reflected appraisals" (determined but not self-determining), or it becomes the occupancy of particular roles, or, finally, no more than " a dramatic effect arising diffusely from a scene that is presented" (Goffman). Still, it is well to be wary of those theorists who claim in tough, hard-headed language that the self is but a mirage and illusion. It by no means signifies a willingness to part with the idea of the self, as might be supposed, but to support its radical re-definition.

Role theory and small group research. The relationship of role theory to the field of small groups is diffuse and general. Both, of course, share the interpretation of role in terms of group setting and group function; in both the articulation of roles is seen as a product of needs and requirements of the group; in both, the person is equated with role and function.

Contrasts between personality theory and role or situational theories become more marked if we move from the level of the abstract and analytic to specific problems as these have become defined in small group research. The problem of leadership is of particular interest because, traditionally, it has been an area of interpretation for competing personality theories and one in which the relevance of personality theory was seldom questioned. This obtained through a great variety of doctrines ranging from the heroic ("great man") to the father image to the principle of charismatic leadership. All shared a conviction of the power of the individual to cast his imprint on the course of events. Whether it is called genius, extraordinary force or charisma, this principle of leadership points to the person and his qualities vis-à-vis the group.

In role theory, of course, this becomes redefined in a very general way: leadership is a specialized function within the group. Finally, in small group studies, researchers begin with this redefinition but end with one so concrete and specific that leadership becomes a distinction measured by frequency of interaction or rating procedure or sociometric choice. Borgatta, Couch and Bales (1955) used combined indices based on interaction, sociometric choice, intelligence and leadership rating in an attempted test of the "great man theory of leadership." Consonant with traditional conceptions of leadership, they found that the ability of individuals to maintain leadership status in different sessions with different participants tends to support the idea of the leader as a generally "effective" or "influential" personality. Ordinarily, however, only a doctrine of specificity emerges from these studies: the traits of the effective leader are so closely related to the functions he performs in a group (Hare, 1962, p. 293) that we cannot generalize beyond the definition given the leadership role within the framework of any particular research (Golembiewski, 1962, pp. 131-44).

From the standpoint of old personality theory, the bifurcation of the leadership principle into dimensions called instrumental and affective (Bales) raises interesting and perplexing questions. The attempt to transfer it, as an interpretive device, from the research setting to a natural small group such as the family (Parsons & Bales, 1955) has been closely questioned (Slater, 1961). Its applicability to other groups and, in particular, to political organizations has been viewed with doubt and criticism (Verba, 1961).

In small group research, a slighting of the so-called personality factor is customarily taken for granted. Haythorn's study (1955) is exceptional in that it specifies the influence (facilitating or depressing) that individual behavior patterns or personality traits may have on group functioning. Much more common is the isolation of a specific personality factor (intelligence, extroversion-introversion, dominance, F-scale score) as this may affect simple interaction rate, sociometric choice or productivity (Hare, 1962, Ch. 6).

Recent reviews of research indicate the degree to which—if for no reasons other than methodological—the question of subjective personality factors will continue to be raised. Golembiewski, for example, has observed that the personality characteristics of S's have rarely been taken into account and controlled in these studies; but, he concludes, there is already evidence enough of "the often marked effects of personality characteristics upon group properties" (Golembiewski, 1962, p. 52). Therefore, it may be of some interest to consider the ways in which the personality principle (as we have here defined it) re-emerges in this literature after having been cast out of view.

A great variety of social-psychological theories—from G. H. Mead's distinction between the I and the Me, to Kris and Hartmann's institutionalized and non-institutionalized behavior, to Fromm's individual and social character—can be said to have preserved a lasting aspect of personality theory in leaving to the individual an essentially indefinable (because indefinite) area of freedom, spontaneity, impulse and choice. Here, too, it would seem, however strongly the new theories stress the pragmatic "process," "interaction," or "social act," they retain one conspicuous feature in common with older character and personality theories. This lies in an emphasis on creative activity, self-realization through activity, the "active agent"—albeit in the group. Its significance is as often preserved as it is disguised in the use of the concept of "participation."

Above all, there remains an assumption that isolation, privacy, solitude essentially impoverish the self, since individual realization can only be found in group participation. Probably the most interesting and patiently pursued defense of this doctrine is to be found in P. Halmos' *Solitude and Privacy* (1952). Halmos writes of the "conscientious objectors of community life who do not know the creative potentialities of a well-integrated society" (p. 105), and he at once deplores the Christian ideal of "uniqueness" and "moral autarchy" and the social changes that have increasingly tended to isolate men and deprive them of their "natural gregariousness." Again, from the conviction that it is only through role-taking and the group that social learning and social adeptness are acquired, it follows that loneliness is not good because, as one writer recently put it, "loneliness is . . . a suspension in self-acquaintance . . . cut off from one's fellows . . . a man limits his own powers, his capacity to be an active agent" (Becker, 1962, p. 498).

While participation may be relatively easy to define, this extension of its meaning is not. Abstractly, role theory simply defined the interaction process. In concrete research terms this became what the person did and to whom (and especially to how many others) he talked—i.e., the sum of his interactions. Major questions then come to center about measurement criteria: Is frequency of interaction meaningful and sufficient? Does it adequately differentiate passive and active participants? Can we measure solidarity, identification, involvement? Should we assume that any participation, any belonging, any identification implies an active interchange with others and therefore is a good and rewarding thing in itself?

Generally, small group research findings seem to confirm the relationship between participation and group cohesiveness. That is to say, participation is more equal and more intense in groups with "high cohesion" (Golembiewski, 1962, p. 165). Hence it would not seem amiss to regard participation as a good thing either from the standpoint of the perpetuation of the group or, presumably, the needs of those who comprise it. Sociologically, however, it is the "ongoing social process," not its subjective value or meaning, that is emphasized and enhanced here; and there is a tendency to impute psychological significance to participation as such which a theory of social system or organization by itself does not provide.

Thus, psychologically speaking, the notion of participation remains simplistic and undifferentiated. Interaction counts, rating procedures or sociometric choice do indeed tell us something about the group and those who constitute it, but we have to infer much, much more about a subjective need for affiliation and general affect.

Perhaps it is for this reason that attempts to obliterate subjectively active, personal or affective elements in terms like "the show must go on" or other exigencies of the "ongoing social process" often result in projecting properties formerly ascribed to the individual onto the social group. In any case, there have arisen in the literature descriptive terms painfully reminiscent of the rhetoric of old group mind theories: "emergent qualities in the social aggregate," "group emotionality," "team ethos," "group goals," "group mentality"—all are kindred references and all sufficiently suggestive of the way doctrinal tides ebb and flow. This "groupism" (as it is sometimes depreciatively called) makes us forget the fact that groups are, after all, composed of individuals who have emotions, desires and needs we cannot rightly detach and relocate somewhere in the "atmosphere." To do so is to obscure the very process the social psychologist has dedicated himself to uncover: the complex and problematic fusion of the individual and the social.

Culture-personality theories. Generally, social psychological theories have vacillated between sociological doctrines about the individual and psychological dicta about the social group. Where social behaviorism defines the social determinants of individual minds, theories of social character represent an alternative extreme of deriving generalizations about society from our knowledge about individual psychology. The attempt to define "psychologically determined" aspects of culture, and especially the direct importation of personality theory into a general statement of culture and society has—via recent neo-Freudian doctrine —acquired considerable, if much debated, prominence. This literature is now grouped as culture-personality theory.

It has often been suggested that more interdisciplinary enthusiasm than discipline has accompanied these many efforts. The description and measurement of personality is a complex and debated field in itself, and those outside this psychological specialty who have sought to incorporate its provisional findings have often done so boldly ignoring its many problems (Kaplan, 1961). Like individuals, groups of people appear different. That we might codify or summarize these differences either along the lines of individual characterization or in a measure of central tendency might appear to be a reasonable and ordinary procedure. It might even be (and has been) argued that the complicating factors are fewer, for we are really seeking only to define large differences. The central difficulty remains that, in the absence of a generally accepted theory of personality or method of its proper assessment, we are often left only with impressions and competing interpretations of them.

Where it is regarded as important either to describe or to measure personality traits within a given society or to compare personality traits in different societies, there may be sufficient justification for the sociologist's interest; but this is not his métier. Having measured and described personality we have not described society, but only one aspect of it, just as when we have described social institutions we do not in consequence know the individual psychology of those who participate in them. It is, therefore, the too facile inferences that are made in moving from individual psychology to the social order that have aroused controversy.

It may be observed that it has proved difficult to disengage the idea of a central personality tendency—by whatever name it goes—from its old associations with national character literature. As a slogan, the idea of a unitary character or characterization proved useful for national and international politics; as impartial concept, it has proved mischievous and difficult. National character discussions have usually been revived in an atmosphere of controversy, developing with and following periods of war. So specific is this association that, between wars, the concept falls into rather complete discredit, its texts dismissed, as Morris Ginsberg once observed, as mere *"livres de circonstance"* (Ginsberg, 1948, p. 131).

Impassioned interest in character, and the character analysis of other nations and other peoples, has notably given way to more sober concern for the measurement of specific problems—whether these are narrowly psychological (e.g., the administration of tests to exotic peoples) or sociological (e.g., the composition of national élites or the analysis of occupational groups) or social psychological (e.g., international survey and opinion data). It is, therefore, to awaken old ghosts when we ask what is the function and significance of a psychological characterization of society or, as one writer has put it, of what importance is it to sociological theory that societies, cultures or nations may have ethoses?

Fundamentally, what all these theories shared—however various their starting points—was the assumption that if we could view a society or culture as the epitome of a character type we could analyze its typical institutions and predict behavior, presumably just as we could predict individual behavior. Unfortunately, the predictive value of character and personality doctrines remained notably disputed, and their descriptive value was often vitiated by a clinical terminology we associate with psychopathology, not normality, in our own society.

Sociologists, among others, shared these objections, but their protests usually began at a quite different point (Bendix, 1952; Lindesmith & Strauss, 1958). In this view, the need structure of the individual gives us only the most rudimentary statement of something psycho-biological in man. Alone, it is not only inadequate to explain the elaborate institutional arrangements that arise in different societies but leads to a narrow, "reductionist" psychological view of society. It can give us neither a key to nor a characterization of a "whole society," for a society and its institutional order is more than character "writ large" (Parsons). It is, then, the psychological determinism that is disturbing and, with it, a psychological interpretation of things social and cultural that contradicts rather than amplifies the sociological perspective.

This difficulty becomes apparent once we ask what the relation is between social character and culture or society? Is it more than a statement, from a psychological standpoint, of what the sociologist commonly refers to as "norm" or social "convention" or "consensus"? For Fromm and Kardiner, social character or basic personality meant characteristics shared by most members of the same culture; for M. Mead, it meant the "culturally regular"; for Gorer, "shared motives and views of the world." In these variant terms, some stressed the psychological incorporation of things cultural; some, the psychological "causes" of culture; some, its diffuse "psychological impact."

Since culture is not simply social character nor social character the whole culture, it can only be assumed that "character" summarizes something special about a society. And, indeed, this has been its claim: to give diagnostic clues and even well-grounded prognoses by analyzing societies from the standpoint of individual character analysis in our own society. Individual traits reveal the "whole person"; common traits, the "whole society."

Pressing this claim, however, has often meant straining the logic of analogy beyond credibility. The relationship of society to the groups and individuals that comprise it is very different from the relation of a person to his own behavior. Theoretical disapprobation of these often fluid characterizations of whole societies then came to center about the concrete questions: How can we justifiably ignore the significance of class or status, regional or religious differences? Of competing power groups within a society? Of the variable distribution of values that makes the very term "common values" suspect?

To the idea of unitary social character or "whole culture" was counterposed the idea of "sub-culture" (or "sub-system")—a term that involves some ambiguity but which has the advantage that at least the researcher specifies the social group he sets out to describe. Clearly the concept of sub-culture reduces the strain involved in characterizing the "whole," but as yet an assessment of the uses to which the two ideas have been put is lacking. Once we introduce the idea of subculture we invoke with it the question of what, properly, is to be ascribed to the culture or society "as a whole." Does the definition of what is "generally shared" shift, then, with each sub-culture being analyzed? Who participates fully in his culture or society? Who may be said to represent it generally? Some of these difficulties are exemplified in Spinley's study, *The Deprived and the Privileged* (1953), an attempt to apply the concept of basic personality structure to social class. Its hypothesis, that different social classes would have typical personality structures but that a basic personality structure also existed, presented problems that were solved simply by ascribing overlap—i.e., traits found in both classes—to basic personality structure.

Whether stated as the psychological investigation of sub-culture, sub-system or group, the trend has been toward specificity. Ginsberg (1951), summarizing the reaction to national character studies after World War II, concluded that the "study of national characteristics should begin not with the nation but smaller groups within it." Duijker and Frijda's recent summary of the literature, *National Character and National Stereotypes* (1960), includes research proposals that are similarly specific and limited in scope, such as the study of national élites or of values along class or other lines.

A conviction that empirical findings may eventuate in some generalizing proposition akin to national character has been the impetus behind the concept of "modal personality structure." Once made statistical, the distributive rather than unitary aspect of personality becomes important. For Kardiner, basic personality structure was based upon individual needs which were expressed in typical social institutions. For Parsons, basic personality is the internalization of social values. Different modal personality types accompany different sub-systems (e.g., age, sex, ethnic groups) and the concept of modal personality gives recognition to this fact of diversity. Thus, too, Inkeles and Levinson (1954) assume that probably there is not a character type common to all members of a group—that there will be more than one mode, though particular types or traits may predominate at a given time or place.

We may sidestep here the problems involved in the proposed trait measurement of groups of people, or the personality theory to be used in the interpretation of its data, in order to point out how far removed it is from the original purpose and definition of social character or basic personality. For the old character theorist it is coherence, style, the intrinsic similarity of parts that mattered, not a demonstration of trait frequency. He looked for the counterpart of particular traits in institutions (family, religion, economy) and in symbolic forms (art, ceremonials); in short, he sought the embodiment of personality traits everywhere but in the person—in the "whole culture."

Current multi-causal theories and pluralist conceptions of society do not mix well with such a simplified and unitary conception of individual and social cosmos. Thus, major objections have been raised as to the appropriateness of regarding every society as a harmonious whole, the parts of which interrelate and mutually express some underlying pattern or unity or character. This grandiose aim, it has been argued, removes us from our more routine but realistic task of building an empirical and disciplined science. Insistence upon general harmony or functional interrelationship or ethos leads us from exploring the complicated connections that actually exist in favor of some general statement about them (Gerth & Mills, 1953, p. 343).

In the past when social scientists concerned themselves with the problem of "character" or "style," they usually viewed it in association with specific groups or strata.[2] Congruities between personality and the social system depended on explaining the selective breeding of certain personality types, but far from relating this explanation to a psycho-cultural theory, it was derived from a theory of social leadership

[2] For example: "Those who speak of a 'national' way of thought are, in fact, thinking of the thought of a particular period of national life, and within that period only the thought of a particular social stratum which happens to have a decisive influence." K. Mannheim, *Essays in Sociology and Social Psychology*, f.n., p. 122.

and dominance. The search was not at all for standard psychological types, but for social historical models—Fouillé's élite of "representative men" or Bagehot's "objects of imitation," emphasizing the style-setting role of national élites, or an individual historical model like Weber's Puritan of the Protestant Ethic. These were the bearers of particular values and were often treated as representatives of particular institutions. They were by no means regarded as the exclusive embodiment of the "whole culture," but exemplified a particular training, mentality and outlook. Emphasis on universally distributed traits or a flat statement of psychic homogeneity, however, simply takes for granted what was, in this doctrine, problematic: a tendency (even if not automatic or universal) toward a downward diffusion of the style, outlook and habit of leading strata. Here, for example, the British gentleman represents a historic case very different from the Samurai, for the Bushido code embodied a general ideal but conduct was too specifically prescribed according to social stratum to permit close imitation. To be sure, there may be found today the counterpart of the older theory of a national élite in constructs like the "new Soviet man," along with often dramatic and highly presumptive statements of contrast with "traditional Russian character" (Kluckhohn, 1961).

Finally, it should be observed that in the field of social psychology, where the linkage of personality to social process has concentrated on such key problems as leadership, social movements, and the problem of social change, there may be seen in the work of Erich Fromm a remarkable coalescence of these many trends and perspectives. "Different societies or classes within a society have a specific social character and on its basis different ideas develop and become powerful." (Fromm, 1941, p. 279). This idea, which lies at the heart of *Escape from Freedom,* became not only the inspiration for research on the authoritarian personality but for new formulations of the general relationship between personality and social and political movements. Here the focus shifted from analysis of leadership to analysis of the needs, aspirations and anxieties of followers—and hence to their political choices and identifications.

From a theoretical point of view, perhaps the most interesting aspect of Fromm's formulation is the way in which he combines, in the character principle, new and old doctrines as to its working. Its heroic aspect is gone, but not its inherent power to engender change. It is not the power of individuals to control events but the power of events— to evoke needs and tensions in individuals who must then seek new solutions, ideologies and leaders—that constitutes the problem of social change. In contrasting individual and social character, therefore, a new application of the character principle emerges: it involves both psychological and social determinism, but also a measure of individual choice and option.

PARSONS' PERSONALITY SYSTEM AND SOCIAL SYSTEM

Few sociologists have sought to define personality; few engage in the labor of prescribing where the psychology of personality ends and sociology begins. The view that personality and social system represent "discrete systems" but that an important task of the sociologist is to discover and analyze their points of interaction is identified with the work of Talcott Parsons.

At first glance, it might seem that in order to sustain a thorough and consistent differentiation between personality and social system, Parsons is forced to depend on an archaic and rigid schematizing: person vs. environment, individual vs. society, psychology vs. sociology. This allegation of "isomorphism" (Baldwin, 1961) misses the repeated emphasis on "interaction" and "interpenetration" of the two systems; but the fact remains that the theory begins not with the principle of interaction (which comes later) but with separate and autonomous spheres of interest. In practice, these distinctions, often hopelessly difficult to maintain, often also simply do not matter.

The Parsonian view of personality is singular in its rigid and narrow definition in psychobiological terms. "Role-taking" and the "internalization of social values" are defined in this scheme as social, not psychological processes. Therefore, the area left to the personality system (and its practitioners) is a narrowly prescribed domain of "need dispositions." The personality psychologist—very often, in the past, overly ambitious to describe the "whole person"—perhaps justly feels that he has been robbed of his real interests and concerns. The idea of personality when bereft of "social person" does indeed represent an extreme impoverishment and restriction of the self.

Parsons has, at different times, defined personality as (1) the behavioral system of an organism (Parsons, 1951a, p. 69); (2) the relational system of a living organism interacting with a situation (Parsons, 1951b, p. 17); and (3) an interdependent set of need dispositions organized about internalized social objects (roles, values) (Parsons,

1955, p. 139, p. 146). Moreover, unlike most sociologists, he has presented a theory of personality structure (Parsons, 1955, Ch. 3). Here, in contrast to strict social behaviorism, and following the psychoanalytic model, personality is viewed in depth and its stratified aspects again brought into focus. Besides a general "qualitative differentiation" of the personality (in terms of established lines of motivation), Parsons points to its "hierarchical organization." He believes that this needs to be defined so that we may account for the "relative strength" of different motives. Personal history again becomes important because it describes how the relative strength of motivation has come about— namely, as a "balance" established between different needs in the course of development (e.g., dependency and autonomy or instrumental and expressive "need components"). Finally, there are cross-ties that bind different motivations into role expectations. These cross-ties are, simply, internalized social values. It is at this point that personality structure becomes bound to role-taking, the personality to the social system.

Like Allport (1955), but unlike more thorough-going role theorists, Parsons does not equate personality with role-taking. "Role involvements do not exhaust the orientation or interest system of any personality. . . . He has internal or narcissistic or non-social aspects. For all of these reasons . . . it is not possible to infer directly back and forth from personality structure to role behavior" (Parsons, 1951b, p. 45).

According to Parsons' theory of social action, the social act itself is the center about which both personality system and social system are built. On the one side are given the need dispositions of the personality; on the other, the claims and values of the social system. Essentially, the two systems are pulled together by combining psychoanalytic and role theory. This constitutes Parsons' analysis of the socialization process and the mechanics are fundamentally social. We are given the needs of the personality and the social objects that satisfy them; these objects, through the process of loving identification, become internalized. They are internalized through role-taking, and with their internalization, we get the social values they represent. The allocation of roles in the social system and the socialization processes of the individual, then, are the same thing viewed in different perspectives (Parsons, 1951b, p. 207). Only the "mechanisms of personality functioning" (Parsons, 1955, Ch. 4) remain narrowly psychological; here we are given the application of learning theory to the discrimination and cognition of social objects.

Parsons' theory has been criticized on many grounds: its lack of clarity, the disproportionate effort devoted to establishing parallelism and symmetry between personality and social system, its overlapping presentation from different perspectives (Black, 1961). A more telling, though not unrelated, criticism of the theory refers to its propensity for systematizing what still remain factional views in sociology and psychology, with social psychology as a battle-ground.

In this theory of systems and social action are incorporated personality as dispositional-set (the personality system), mechanisms of peronality functioning (learning theory), the socialization process (based on psychoanalytic and role theory), as well as the idea of basic personality structure. Since virtually everything is incorporated at some point into the system, it is scant wonder that interpretations of it vary. Some see in it a rigid parallelism of personality and social system (and it is true that Parsons has often repeated that the same principles of organization apply to both); others view it as a Herculean labor to spell out in detail the interpenetration of personality and social system. Few would quarrel with the principled statement of interaction between personality and social system; this has, in fact, become a common assumption and working premise for both sociologists and psychologists. But, inevitably, controversy enters any discussion of "discrete systems," for it is difficult to draw boundaries that do not belittle one sphere while enlarging the other.

It is not the absence of psychological constructs (they abound) but their relocation in the whole system that is likely to disturb the psychologist. They are removed from the territorial base he has chosen as his point of departure and viewed as social process or social function. Only the behaviorally determined and determinable aspects of personality functioning, as these interlock with the social system, become significant. Enormous emphasis is placed on the concepts of identification, internalization, role-taking—all processes which bind the system together.

The older conception of personality as the realm of the individual and the unique is quite lost in this view. Another aspect of its insignificance may be seen in the schematic analysis of disparities between the individual and the social. Ordinarily, there is a dove-tailing of subjective need disposition and the fulfillment of role expectation. (This comes about originally through identification and internalization of social objects like the mother.) But Parsons superimposes upon this, in analyzing the personality structure of the individual, an "alienation-conformity" dimension which, as the name suggests, indicates a general disposition to conform or not to conform with the expectations of others. This conformity-alienation balance in the individual, he tells us, becomes a central focus of the "articulation of the motivational system of the personality with the structure of the social system" (Parsons, 1951b, p. 32). Actually, what it provides is a ready bridge to the analysis of social deviation—i.e., of failures of "articulation." Whereas traditionally the personality principle has implied sovereignty of the individual and allowed individual differences to be viewed problematically, here sources of uniqueness, peculiarity, or deviance are described in terms of systemic balance or imbalance and a near-mechanical "articulation" of personal motivation and social structure. It is not a view calculated to please the psychologist; moreover, it is likely to confirm his suspicion that, in the perspective of sociology, neither personality nor the problem of individual differences is intrinsically important at all.

Within the field of sociology, old and borrowed theories of personality have been eclipsed by a rigorous social behaviorism and the functionalist or interaction theory of Talcott Parsons. To the extent that a redefinition of self and personality in strictly empirical terms has come to dominate social psychology, a sociological perspective on the determinants of person and personality has become correspondingly influential. How, then, can we account for the regular resurgence of the quite different view that there is more to man than what he does, more than his appearance and surface presentation—chance elements, possibly nameless and inexpressible, that lend uniqueness and vitality to his behavior?

This *"je ne sais quoi"* aspect of self and personality theory, which has always been spoken in the language of idealism, has also had its representatives in social theory. It is a principle that has come down to us in a variety of forms as "choice," "voluntarism," "self-realization," "spontaneity"; its function has been to accentuate dynamic and unpredictable factors and to counter the dead weight of a social world viewed in deterministic terms with the self-engendered principle of change and movement in life.

Today such views have come to rest within the field of psychology. There they are usually accompanied by a re-affirmation of the principle of individuality as against all overriding determinisms, past and present, from instinct theory to behaviorism; and there, too, will be found dedication to the idea of the "whole person" or "whole personality." In relation to social behaviorism, specifically, its argument has cus-

tomarily been that role-taking neither completes nor exhausts our knowledge of person *qua* person. This is, for example, Allport's view when
he writes (Allport, 1955, pp. 77-8):

> We are all forced to play roles that we regard as alien to us;
> we know they are not propriate but merely personate.
> Yet, in spite of all such conflicts, we develop our personal style
> of living. Some characteristics of this style lie on the surface and serve
> to mask our natures. But at the same time . . . our style proceeds from
> the proprium outward and cannot help but reveal our schemata of values.
> A task for psychology in the future is to find methods for relating
> style to its fundaments in personality.

Allport has, in fact, simply repeated the traditional concerns and
interests of character and personality study. Stated in this way, the
problem is not one that either psychology or social psychology can
as yet begin to answer. But it does suggest that a philosophic conviction
underlying the very idea of "character," "personality," or "self" is much
subtler than any of the specific problems of defining or measuring
traits and more complex than the difficulties of tracing uniformities of
character or personality. There remains a stubborn insistence that a
person cannot be defined solely in terms of his behavior; there is a
recurrent notion that if we define the self in behavioristic terms we
are missing part of the person. That indefinable part was, in the past,
called soul; it may now be variously labeled "style of life" or "character" or "inner self." Its elusiveness is linked to the fact that it is indeed
hard to know another person completely; but it is also linked to our
ideas of privacy and our implicit assumption of a kind of absolute
solitariness of the other that we cannot really bridge.

Many would view the breakdown of our unifying conceptions of
the self as a reflection of larger and more general social processes. The
"fractured" or "segmentalized" self is, from this standpoint, an apt
image of the social existence of modern man who has lost his sense of
structure and of relatedness to social organization as a whole. He no
longer views life in its totality—nor himself; he takes part in limited
scenes; he is a congeries of roles whose congruence or harmony becomes
a highly relative matter. We may recall, in this connection, that when
Harry S. Sullivan called the view that there exists a unique individual
self the "delusion of unique individuality," Erich Fromm noted that just
as Freud had taken the competitiveness characteristic of the beginning
of the century as a "natural phenomenon," so Sullivan takes the fact

of the alienated person lacking selfhood and experiencing himself as a response to the expectation of others as "part of human nature" (Fromm, 1955, p. 193).

The idea of the whole character or personality stands in strained and discordant relationship to the idea of the empirical self, not because we do not experience others in this way but because we have no adequate terms in which to summarize that experience and still keep our feet on the ground. The dominant questions today are: Why not focus on the action itself instead of on the character or personality we infer behind it? Why the preoccupation with inner and hidden propensities? We may see these as understandable reactions to a long-standing theoretical impasse. Character and personality theory, old and new, from old characterology to psychoanalysis, has, in its show of devotion to "wholeness," retained an obscure attachment to the mystery of the person. The sociologist has, for his part, contributed to the unveiling of this mystery by detailing the social processes and the social setting which both define and limit the workings of this abstract personality.

REFERENCES

ALLPORT, G. W. *Becoming.* New Haven: Yale Univer. Press, 1955.

BALDWIN, A. L. Parsonian theory of personality. In M. Black (Ed.), *The social theories of Talcott Parsons.* Englewood Cliffs, N. J.: Prentice-Hall, 1961.

BECKER, E. Socialization, command of performance and mental illness. *Amer. J. Sociol.,* 1962, *67,* pp. 494-501.

BENDIX, R. Compliant behavior and individual personality. *Amer. J. of Sociol.,* 1952, *58,* pp. 292-303.

BLACK, M. (Ed.) *The social theories of Talcott Parsons.* Englewood Cliffs, N. J.: Prentice-Hall, 1961.

BORGATTA, E. F., COUCH, A., & BALES, R. Some findings relevant to the great man theory of leadership. In A. P. Hare, E. Borgatta, & R. F. Bales (Eds.), *Small groups, studies in social interaction.* New York: Alfred A. Knopf. 1955.

DUIJKER, H. J. & FRIJDA, N. H. *National character and national stereotypes.* Vol. I. *Confluence.* Amsterdam: N. Holland Publishing Co., 1960.

FROMM, E. *Escape from freedom.* New York: Farrar & Rinehart, 1941.

FROMM, E. *The sane society.* New York: Rinehart Co., 1955.

Frondizi, R. *The nature of the self.* New Haven: Yale Univer. Press, 1953.

Gerth, H., & Mills, C. W. *Character and social structure.* New York: Harcourt Brace, 1953.

Ginsberg, M. *Reason and unreason in society.* Cambridge: Harvard Univer. Press, 1948.

Ginsberg, M. Problems of national characteristics and attitudes. *Int. soc. sci. bull.,* 1951, *3,* pp. 214-18.

Goffman, E. *The presentation of self in everyday life.* New York: Doubleday Anchor, 1959.

Golembiewski, R. *The small group.* Chicago: Univer. of Chicago Press, 1962.

Gorer, G. & Rickman, J. *The people of great Russia.* London: Cresset Press, 1949.

Halmos, P. *Solitude and privacy.* London: Routledge & Kegan Paul, 1952.

Hare, A. P. *Handbook of small group research.* New York: Free Press of Glencoe, 1962.

Hare, A. P., Borgatta, E., & Bales, R. F. (Eds.) *Small groups, studies in social interaction.* New York: Alfred A. Knopf, 1955.

Hartmann, H., Kris, E., & Loewenstein, R. Some psychoanalytic comments on "culture and personality." In Wilbur & Muensterburger. (Eds.), *Psychoanalysis and culture.* New York: Int. Universities Press, 1951.

Haythorn, W. Influence of individual members on the characteristics of small groups. In A. P. Hare, E. Borgatta, & R. F. Bales (Eds.) *Small groups, studies in social interaction.* New York: Alfred A. Knopf, 1955.

Inkeles, A. National character and modern political systems. In F. L. K. Hsu (Ed.) *Psychological anthropology.* Homewood: Dorsey Press, 1961.

Inkeles, A., & Levinson, D. National character: the study of modal personality and sociocultural systems. In G. Lindzey (Ed.) *Handbook of social psychology,* Vol. 2. Cambridge: Addison Wesley, 1954.

Kaplan, B. Cross cultural use of projective techniques. In F. L. K. Hsu (Ed.) *Psychological anthropology.* Homewood: Dorsey Press, 1961.

Kardiner, A. *Psychological frontiers of society.* New York: Columbia Univer. Press, 1945.

Klineberg, O. A science of national character. *J. of soc. Psychol.,* 1944, *19,* pp. 147-62.

Kluckhohn, C. Studies of Russian national character. In Inkeles, A., & Geiger, K. (Eds.) *Soviet society.* Boston: Houghton Mifflin, 1961.

Kornhauser, A. Analysis of "class" structure of contemporary American society: psychological bases of class divisions. In Berelson, B., & Janowitz, M. (Eds.) *Reader in public opinion and communication.* Glencoe: Free Press, 1953.

LINDESMITH, A. R., & STRAUSS, A. A critique of culture-personality writings. *Amer. Sociol. Rev.,* 1958, 36, pp. 297-303.

MANNHEIM, K. *Essays on sociology and social psychology.* New York: Oxford Univer. Press, 1953.

MEAD, G. H. *Mind, self and society.* Chicago: Univer. of Chicago Press, 1940.

MEAD, M., & METREAUX, R. *Study of culture at a distance.* Chicago: Univer. of Chicago Press, 1953.

MERTON, R., BROOM, L., & COTTRELL, L. *Sociology today.* New York: Basic Books, 1959.

NETT, E. Evaluation of the national character concept in sociological theory. *Social Forces,* 1958, 36, pp. 297-303.

PARSONS, T. Personality and Social Structure. In Stanton, A., & Perry, S. (Eds.) *Personality and political crisis.* Glencoe: Free Press, 1951. (a)

PARSONS, T. *The social system.* Glencoe: Free Press, 1951. (b)

PARSONS, T., & BALES, R. *Family, socialization and interaction process.* Glencoe: Free Press, 1955.

RIECKEN, H., & HOMANS, G. Psychological Aspects of Social Structure. In G. Lindzey (Ed.), *Handbook of social psychology,* Vol. 1. Cambridge: Addison Wesley, 1954.

SLATER, P. Parental Role Differentiation. *Amer. J. of Sociol.,* 1961, 67, pp. 296-308.

SPINLEY, B. *The deprived and the privileged.* London: Routledge & Kegan Paul, 1953.

VERBA, S. *Small groups and political behavior.* Princeton: Princeton Univer. Press, 1961.

IV

Methods of Personality Assessment

15

Concepts of Personality Growing from Multivariate Experiment

Raymond B. Cattell

I. THE MEANING OF MULTIVARIATE EXPERIMENT

The topic of the present chapter is the multivariate experimental approach to personality. Perhaps the word "theory" should be added, but this can be determined later, for theories are all things to all men.

On seeing the title it might be natural to ask what is a multivariate experimental design? What distinguishes it from classical designs? A proper indication of the equal and supplementary roles of bivariate, classical and multivariate experimental designs is often neglected in the educational process. It should be appropriate therefore to devote a few words to an explanation of how the multivariate emphasis may be important. The physical sciences developed a type of experiment in which it was traditional to speak of a *dependent* variable and an *independent* variable; they would manipulate the independent variable and see what happened to the dependent, while piously hoping they were keeping everything else under control. If one reads the life of Wundt, it can be seen that he was tremendously impressed by the physical sciences, particularly by their professional status. Indeed, Wundt, Titchener and other early psychological experimenters showed an almost indecent haste in their meticulous imitation of the physical sciences. On the other hand, one sees in Galton, and a few more truly original minds, the development of methods perhaps better adapted to

413

the behavioral sciences in the long run—methods that might be called multivariate because they handle many variables at once in a global way.

Since this topic in itself deserves a series of lectures, this chapter is necessarily limited to sketching rather than elucidating precisely the fundamental distinctions of these designs. Essentially however, it may be said that multivariate methods are distinguished from the bivariate methods first, as stated above, by treating many variables at once, and taking care to look at the totality of manifestations simultaneously and holistically. Secondly, they differ by not requiring manipulative control, but allowing things to happen in nature as they normally happen. Thirdly, they develop refined statistics, to tease out by analysis what they cannot separate by brute physical control. There are, of course, advantages and disadvantages to both approaches. The Wundt-Pavlov approach, which exemplifies the traditional experiment of the physical sciences, is direct and positive. (Those two psychologists may be thought of together since though different in many ways, they are essentially in the same biophysical science tradition in psychology.) However, the possibility of positive manipulation—so attractive in some situations— leaves the bivariate experimentalist quite at a loss when he cannot manipulate. Since humans are most disinclined to permit manipulation of anything of vital emotional significance, applications of the bivariate experimental approach are necessarily limited. Indeed, as most of us who work with human personality realize all too well, one has to forego experimental control long before one gets to the matters that are of real importance in psychology.

As a result, it is easy to see that historically there has been a tendency for those who adhere rigidly to the bivariate, classical, experimental approach to veer off from vital psychological issues in one of two directions. They retreat either into doing their experiments on animals—studying something they believe to be the emotional life of animals, and the personality development of animals—or into finding out more and more about what is less and less important in the human being, from an emotional and dynamic point of view. This does not mean that it need be less and less important from a cognitive point of view. For example, one may experiment with humans on visual perception, or on hearing, and do highly important work, from that point of view. But even then there is a tendency to slide from psychology to physiology. These two escapes from the real problem of studying total human behavior, though honored by tradition, have constituted the inevitable Nemesis of slavishly restricting one's thinking to the notion of manipulative, bivariate experimentation. Yet this "ideal" of method has been urged upon generations of students by the classical brass instrumentalists. Actually there is yet another defect in the concept of experiment as manipulation; namely, that when one manipulates, one does not always change only what one wants to change. If one wishes to investigate the effect on a dog of loss of the adrenal glands, and one operates on the dog, something more occurs than simple removal of the adrenal glands. Minimally, there is shock together with many other secondary effects. In contrast, using multivariate design, it is possible to obtain highly useful knowledge about the function of the adrenals without insult to the integrity of the organism. That is, it would be possible to isolate factor-analytically the naturally varying influence of *adrenaline,* manifested through, say, twenty variables, and observe how that factor changes naturally in strength over time, and what varies with it.

I. RELATIONS OF CONCEPT DEVELOPMENT FROM MULTIVARIATE, BIVARIATE AND CLINICAL APPROACHES

Beyond the experiment itself, there resides in the narrow bivariate design yet one more serious difficulty and this lies in the development of concepts. This can be illustrated by using a concrete example, namely the measurement of anxiety, and experiments on anxiety and its role in clinical situations. A widespread human tendency has been to believe that *because there is one word there must be one thing,* and the bivariate experimeter has, typically, blindly made this assumption. He believes he is being sufficiently sophisticated when he states, "I define anxiety operationally as tremor (or some other single variable)" and he then goes on to try relating anxiety so defined to some thing, such as rate of learning, or onset of neurosis, or whatever it might be. But he has already begged one of the fundamental questions, namely, whether anxiety is one thing or several.

To pursue this, let us suppose we have a set of variables, a, b, c, d, and e, as represented by the points in Diagram 1, that are recognized behavior manifestations, in what is believed to be the general area of anxiety. The classical bivariate experimenter described above has chosen one of these—let us say 'b'—to stand for his concept of anxiety. He now investigates the relation between b and the outside thing he is interested in relating to anxiety, say, x, representing "rate of learning" in Diagram 1. If his experiment yields a significant relationship the outcome has limited utility; he has discovered *some* structure . . . but if he obtains a negative result, i.e., no relationship, he really does not know which has failed, his postulate that b is anxiety (and x representative of rate of learning) or his hypothesis. The line between a postulate and a hypothesis can be discussed ad lib by philosophers, and we have

DIAGRAM 1

DANGERS IN THE USE OF OPERATIONAL DEFINITIONS
NOT FACTOR ANALYTICALLY CHECKED

CONCEPT 1   CONCEPT 2
Anxiety   *Rate of Learning*

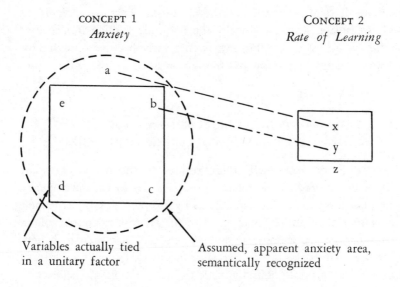

Variables actually tied   Assumed, apparent anxiety area,
in a unitary factor   semantically recognized

no need to get into that side track here. Using the sense in which we normally distinguish between them, we may now ask what he should do, now that he doesn't know whether his *hypothesis,* that anxiety affects learning, has failed—or whether his *postulate* (that this is the operation by which anxiety is measured) has failed. With such a negative result, he either gives up the whole subject as unrewarding or chooses new variable to represent anxiety, and starts again. And so he "shops around" over many variables in the hope of getting a firm and positive relation somewhere.

On the other hand, the multivariate experimentalist proceeds very differently, and by two steps. First he asks a question that the other has never asked. "Is there such a thing as a unitary factor in this area or are there two or three factors?" Perhaps he finds that certain of the variables in the original block of "possibles" (the square block b, c, d, e in Diagram 1) are affected by, and united in, a factor-analytically discovered unitary function, and others are not. He avoids the failure of the conclusion which arises in the first case because one cannot know whether the variable—like b—happened to lie in the pattern, or whether—like a—it was never in the real factor pattern of anxiety.

By this means, one escapes a potentially long period of trial and error aimed at hitting on the variable that is a good measure of the anxiety concept. One may raise, of course, the semantic question, "Why is the unitary thing behind b, c, d and e to be called anxiety?" Whether the b, c, d, e block is to be "called" anxiety is surely just a semantic question. If there is something unitary in this area which the dictionary has already agreed roughly to designate anxiety, that is just as good a label for it as any. It doesn't really matter—one may call it U.I.24, as we do in our universal index of factors, and refer all findings to that index symbol just as well.

With this glimpse of the multivariate experimenter's procedure, let us now return to the bivariate experimenter and suppose that the second possible alternative has occurred; namely, that he does find a relation of his variable (we assume he happened to choose b, c, d, or e) to a learning measure. Still, he doesn't know *how much* of the correlation of that measure with learning is due to the factor common to all four variables and how much is due to what the factor analysis would call specific, i.e., something present in b alone, and not in c, d or e. After all, it is quite usual for at least half the variances in a measure of that kind to be a measure of something other than the common factor. The experimenter does not know whether he got the obtained experimental connection through, so to speak, the *something else* or the *something,* i.e., the general concept concerned in a, b, c, and d. Here the multivariate researcher may have a very solid advantage in the relating of his concept to experimental data, for there exist formulae whereby he can estimate this factor. Once he has the loadings of these variables in the factor, he can estimate that factor itself—the concept—with a known degree of validity from the measures of several individual variables. Generally he can improve the estimate by successive factor analytic experiments until the greater part of the variance on these measures *is* the factor. But in any one variable said "operationally to define the concept," one may never get—as pointed out above—more than a fraction of the measurement to represent the concept.

So far, we have been examining efficient ways to pursue and check a hypothesis, but where do our hypotheses in personality come from in the first place? Some people, like impressive conjurors, prefer to give the impression that they drew them out of a hat—implying that a good head was in the hat! But, though no statistics are available to support the statement, it is the writer's belief that the great majority of those discussed in a book such as this would be found to be abstracted from clinical and sociological observation. Although some would deny to psychoanalysts the origins of their concepts, most of them would in fact be expressed in that watered down form of psychoanalysis which has arisen since Freud. Many a psychologist seems to have sought claims to originality by restating Freud's hypotheses with a new name, or by disagreeing with the master over some matter of dotting i's and crossing t's!

This has certainly been the main story of experiments on projection, defense mechanisms, therapy, etc., until quite recently. However, in the last decade, a faint light has appeared on the horizon which may prove to be the dawn of a totally new scientific day. This springs from a source entirely distinct from clinical and sociological general observation, in fact it springs from multivariate and metric experimental observation on personality of a kind which has never before existed. These dawning hypotheses—they are scarcely yet integrated enough for theories—are different in kind from anything which preceded them and have no more need to lean on past clinical theories than a modern physicist's caesium clock needs to be checked for its evaluation of time against a medieval water clock. These concepts have already proven so fruitful that it is high time for the pack of graduate student researchers, and all the old hue and cry of the psychoanalytic school, to be called to the scent of new theories deriving from the factor analytic structural findings on personality that have matured in the last few years.

Although, as will be demonstrated, this new approach is rich with precise, radical and fruitful theories, precisely experimentally investigable, it would be an act of intellectual snobbery to deny that its concepts have ancestry of a kind in the ideas and approaches prevalent in the first half of the century. That ancestry lies in the spirit of clinical investigation, though not in its often undisciplined and impotent methods. The common basis in clinical and multivariate—especially factor analytic—approaches is far wider than either of these two specialties is apt to recognize. The clinician, in contrast to the old style brass instrument "experimentalist," has habitually looked at things holistically. He has been concerned with the whole person, and also with the totality of situational variables. Frequently he has literally been trying to perform factor analysis in his head. For example, when he developed the idea that something exists called the ego, and that a dynamic unity exists that may be called the super ego, or that certain particular defense mechanisms are operative, he has inferred these entities from observations of many things which co-vary. He has begun with patient observation, but of a multivariate kind, and then he has let his memory operate selectively upon the series of patients he has seen to ask what "goes together." In fact, he has done really just what the multivariate experimentalist is doing; but he has done it without recording measurements at the time, and above all without benefit of a fully thought out mathematical model and the help of an electronic computer.

Although there can be little doubt that if one strips down the method of the clinician, this is what it becomes, yet we shall be disappointed if we expect the clinician to admit this and accept at once the mathematical models and computing procedures of the multivariate experimentalist. His training has usually been as remote as possible from mathematics. Indeed, one must be prepared to find that when the clinician gets an urge to be really experimental, he naively does a classical, bivariate, brass instrument experiment that denies his whole birthright. There are striking exceptions to this as in the work of Ackerman (1942), Baggaley (1958), Barratt (1962), Berg (1955), Burt (1940), Butler (1954), Cartwright (1957), Campbell (1950), Coan (1959), Damarin (1963), Digman (1963), Dingman (1958), Eysenck (1952), Fiske (1949), Geertsma (1959), Holzman (1963), Horn (1961), Howard (1961), Karson (1958, 1959, 1961), Lorr (1953, 1955), McQuitty (1954), Meehl (1954), Moran (1959), Norman (1960), Peterson (1959), Schaie (1958), Sells (1957, 1962), Sweney (1962, 1963), Taylor (1950), Thorndike (1961), Watson (1959), Wittenborn (1951) and some others. But these are an unusual kind of clinical psychologist, though, let us hope, a vanguard.

III. THE DIFFERENCE OF THEORY FROM CLINICAL AND EXPERIMENTAL PHASES OF RESEARCH

In spite of this common approach, refined by the above mentioned leaders into explicit multivariate experimental designs, we must recognize a clear gap—indeed, some people think a chasm—between the older set of theories deriving from clinical psychology and those proposed here, which derive from multivariate experiment. Parenthetically, the term "multivariate experiment" is used here rather than simply "experiment" because bivariate experiment has had mainly a hypothesis-testing role, compared to the hypothesis-generating function of multivariate experiment. Bivariate experiment has tested mostly theories from the clinical field. That which is really new in the area of personality theory deriving from experiment, is generally the offspring of the bolder multivariate experimental designs.

The main difference between the clinical inheritance of theory and that now growing from multivariate experiment is seen obviously at first in the introduction of precise measurement and complex calculation into the latter. But this brings with it a still more striking difference in terms of exactness with regard to *the stage of observation at which it is considered profitable to develop theories.* In the experimenter's view, the clinician has developed elaborate theories all too soon, and they have plagued and misled him. The issue of when to introduce a theory is an old one, which spreads out psychologists into many camps, extending say from B. F. Skinner (1953) at one pole, who considers theories unnecessary, all the way to theory lovers who say they are really less interested in science than in its clothing of theories. Except in so far as the latter are sometimes philosophers rather than scientists, the experimenter has no radical disagreement with them; of course there must be theorizing, but it is a question of *when.*

Let us go to an older science, for greater clarity, and ask whether chemistry benefited most from great theory lovers like Stahl, or empiricists like Cavendish and Dalton? Should the chemist sit in an armchair and generate theories, or play around in the laboratory and see what happens when you mix this and that, or weight now and weight then?

Theory lovers think they have a final answer to this when they say "People only investigate when they have a theory to test." They overlook the fact that the investigator may have several dozen theories, or that his theories may be so broad as to amount virtually to a profound sense of curiosity. The latter simply requires the investigator to play around with data and look for the jewels of lawful relation which turn up. This approach has unquestionably been more fruitful than that of those who loved elaborating theories rather than testing them. Applying this observation to psychology, it can be argued that personality theories should be generated from dependable observations of correlational, quantitative, lawful relationships *when* they become visible in multivariate experimental data—rather than on the basis of casual everyday observation and consulting room hunches.

Just as Galileo's telescope brought new astronomical theories, Leewenhoek's microscope new biological concepts, and Dalton and Lavoisier's use of the chemical balance brought the modern atomic theory, so we in psychology stand in this decade at the beginning of radical new theoretical developments based on the growth of multivariate experimental methods. The waste of putting new wine in old bottles is here to be avoided only if we recognize that new instruments require new theory, no longer confused with and tied down to the old. It may be in order for the factor analyst to describe a certain factor as "ego strength" out of respect for certain scientific continuity of ideas. Nevertheless, theorists should recognize that a number of altogether new, more precise, and testable features have developed in the new concept. Actually, in so far as there are irrational rigidities in distinguishing the old and the new, they come more from the adherents of the old. Just as Galileo complained that philosophers refused to look through his telescope, so we find some clinicians unwilling to try out their theories by using the personality factor batteries that have been provided for them with such great expenditure of technical skill.

Before looking in more detail at personality theory from experiment, and while speaking of the problem of getting a proper perspective on the relation of the older and newer sources of theory, two other difficulties may be mentioned. First, the factor analyst is now accustomed to recognize the influence of many functionally unitary structures—typically a score or so—in any behavioral act, whereas the clinician has been used to three or four as his stock in trade. Meehl (1954) even argues that the clinician's mind is unable to extend beyond half a dozen factors and that feeding him information on more fails to improve his predictions. The recent definition of twenty-one factors in objective behavioral measurements (Hundleby, Pawlik & Cattell, 1964) is a number which has apparently appalled some clinical reviewers, though chemists and physicists seem able to handle a larger number, respectively, of elements and fundamental particles. Instead of running from these expanding lists, the clinician would do better to accept them as a new intellectual challenge and an opportunity to develop theory more closely in touch with reality.

A second difficulty in bringing the new theories properly into relation with the old springs from a difference of subjects. Multivariate experimental research has spread across the whole normal population range, which includes the abnormal clinical sub-set as the tails of the distribution. The experimenter has looked for the patterns of normal personality structures to inform the abnormal, whereas the clinician has seen normality through the inverted telescope of abnormality. Now, the statistician is normally very allergic to one's choice of sample, and if anyone in ordinary experimental work had gone on doing for fifty years what clinicians have habitually done, simply taking abnormal samples and generalizing from them about the normal personality, the statistician would long since have denied him scientific status. Perhaps the clinician's data bias is not as serious as it might appear, but surely there is some distortion for which the clinical theories have not yet been corrected. It would be more, or at least equally, instructive to approach personality in the opposite way, namely by determining structure in the normal and then seeing what happens to concepts so formed when they are seen afresh in the abnormal minority. Fortunately, among psychologists, if not psychiatrists, these points are now more widely accepted.

IV. PERSONALITY STRUCTURE CONCEPTS AS DEVELOPED FROM MULTIVARIATE EXPERIMENT

The independence of the factor analytic concepts of personality structure from earlier, pre-metric theories starts from the very beginning—namely, in the choice of behavior to be observed. If a lover of clinical theory asks where can one begin observing if one does not have a theory, the answer is that one can begin, as did the *personality sphere concept,* with the notion of a stratified, representative sample of daily behavior from our culture. Our first analysis began with the trait sampling study of Allport and Odbert (1936), on a theory of *representative design* which since has become more familiar to psychologists through the writings of Brunswick (1947). The personality researcher starts by casting as wide a net as possible, representing every area of behavior, and then looks for the total structure in that domain. However, as soon as structure begins to emerge, the researcher begins forming theories about what these structures are. With new variables suggested by these theories he re-enters the *cycle of the hypothetico-deductive experimental procedure.* He now has a testable hypothesis, expecting some new variable to correlate with the factor that he has reason to interpret as of such and such a kind. Initially it is not only legitimate, but highly desirable, by this design, to start without a hypothesis—at least, anything beyond the personality sphere concept. (As to this multidimensional sphere on the surface of which lies all behavior, there is needed a whole technical discussion, but it suffices to indicate the concept at this point). As an illustration of what happens when one starts this broad approach, it should be pointed out that, when aiming in the questionnaire area at factoring all possible questionnaire items, we found that most questionnaires surveyed, covering work up to 1945, were heavily weighted in the clinical area. If we had not added questions dealing with dimensions we had seen in the ratings of normal people, at least half a dozen of the present questionnaire factors in the 16 P.F. test would never have been found. The clinical data was yielding something around seven, eight, nine factors—much as the MMPI tends to give to this day. But we had found twenty factors in the rating field and it would seem reasonable that we should also find, as we eventually did, twenty in the questionnaire field. (In the 16 P.F. test as finally produced for general use, we threw away four of low variance— as a fisherman throws away something that's too small to take home!) However, the main point of this research history is that representative design led to wider concepts of personality structure than had been reached clinically, though the clinical concepts were well brought out in our first half dozen factors.

With this indispensable perspective on reasons for preferring certain methods, we can turn, henceforth in this chapter, more to substantive psychological theory than method, though a word must be said even here on a difference of factor analytic method between the present writer and his colleagues on the one hand such as Baggaley (1958), Coan (1958, 1959), Pawlik (with Hundleby et al, 1964; with Cattell, 1962) and Sweney (1962, 1963), and on the other hand such writers as Eysenck (1952), Guilford and Zimmerman (1947). For psychologists not technically in the field are sometimes confused by differences of opinion between the latter, who rotate for orthogonal factors, or who take out only a few factors; and Cattell and his coworkers who take out as many factors as Tucker's (or some other non-arbitrary test) indicates, and then rotate for *maximum simple structure with oblique factors*. The latter position to which general opinion has moved over the last decade, is that the true, unique, simple-structure solution is not attainable if factors are artificially restricted to orthogonality, and that factors, as influences interacting in a common universe, are in any case bound to be somewhat correlated. Orthogonal factors are only a very rough approximation to the unique oblique factors, and can be gravely misleading.

Another difference that has characterized the systematic attack on the structural problem over the last twenty years by this writer and his colleagues has been a deliberate interrelating of structures extending beyond any single factor experiment and matrix. These extensions and cross-comparisons have been systematically made:

1. across the three possible media of observation,
    (i) L-data (life record, *in situ* behavior, sometimes obtained by ratings and often called criterion data).
    (ii) Q-data, self evaluation, questionnaire response, introspective, consulting room evidence.
    (iii) T-data, actual behavioral responses in controlled situations evoking temperamental and dynamic responses.
2. across ages. The personality structure has been factored and compared by cross sections at 4-5, 7-8, 10-13, and adult levels.
3. across techniques. Factors have been compared from R—, Incremental R, Q, and P-techniques to check on the degree of efficacy of the functional utilities (Cattell, 1946).
4. across cultures. The Q-data factors from the 16 P.F. have in particular been compared and found reasonably constant across American, Australian, British, French, Italian and Japanese culture samples.
5. across measurement modalities—ability, temperament and motivation. It has happened in the past that a factor found in abilities has been assumed to be an ability factor, where later inclusion of personality variables shows that it was actually a personality factor perceived in its outcrop only in ability manifestations. All factors must be ultimately considered together. For this reason, the new dynamic factors have been factored with the older temperament factors, to check that they are indeed new dimensions.

Since this organization of research is well known from previous presentations in books (Cattell, 1946, 1957, 1958, 1959, 1961b; Cattell and Scheier, 1961) only a few points need to be emphasized here. A conspective test is one with a perfect conspect reliability coefficient (Cattell, 1957), i.e., any two psychologists will obtain the same value in scoring it. Both Q- and T-data are commonly in the form of conspective tests, i.e., objective in scoring, but T-data is objective in a more fundamental psychological use of the term. The latter, by definition and operation is not self-evaluative and the individual does not know on what he is actually being scored. The main concern of our laboratory over twenty years has been to produce personality factor measures as *objective* tests. But due to the higher technical standards and time demands of T-data, many psychologists continue to apply questionnaires despite the availability of the Objective-Analytic (O-A) Personality Battery (Cattell, 1946; 1959).

A second point to note is that behavior ratings are a rather poor form of L-data (life record data), being substantially biased by instrument factors (Cattell, 1961; Fiske, 1949). Better L-data would be obtained by numerical counts, through time sampling, of how many times a person helps someone, how many car accidents he has, etc. Although the nature of some twenty L-data factors (see descriptions below) parallels very closely that of some twenty Q-data, or "mental interior" factors, the correlation between corresponding factors, as everyone knows, is far from perfect. Indeed, the presence of large instrument factors in both, but particularly in ratings, needs to be partialled out before the identity of these exterior and interior views of the same behavior can be demonstrated.

However, the *meaning* of the L- and Q-data factors is more immediately apparent than that of T-data factors, for behavior embedded in everyday life terms and expressed in introspection is more familiar to us and closer to the clinical theories than are the new objective test variables. Consequently, it was first in the former that the largest factor, indexed as A in the alphabetic list index of the 16 PF was recognized in normals to be the same as that largest dichotomy that Bleuler and Kretschmer (1929) had recognized in the abnormal—namely, the cyclothyme-schizothyme factor. People high on A are easygoing, good natured, naturally expressive of their emotions, while those low on A are withdrawn, critical and insistent on dependability.

Beyond A there are some twenty factors, some of which are well known for other reasons while others have not been recognized before the days of factor analytic research and require more investigation if we are fully to understand them. Factor B is our old friend, "general intelligence"—Spearman's g. Factor C is ego strength; D is a temperamental excitability, and E is dominance-submissiveness. F is surgency; G is super-ego strength, though only part of what is covered in psychoanalytic discussions; and H is apparently a second, genetic component in the cyclothyme-schizothyme area, and so on. A very considerable criterion prediction power has accumulated for these factors, in a series of published researches (Cattell, 1957; Cattell et al, 1961; Cattell & Scheier, 1961), mostly summarized in the Handbooks for the 16 P.F., the High School Personality Questionnaire (Cattell et al, 1961, Cattell & Scheier, 1961) and the Child Personality Questionnaire (Porter & Cattell, 1961). The criteria available range from school achievement, through clinical syndromes and prognoses, to accident proneness, delinquency, leadership, research creativity, etc.

The question of how these factors interact in the total personality must be left until objective test and motivation factors have been discussed.

V. THE NATURE OF OBJECTIVE TEST (T-DATA) FACTORS

Few psychologists outside two or three laboratories are yet acquainted with the immense variety of behavioral tests on which T-data personality structure is based. Professor F. W. Warburton, of Manchester University, has recently undertaken (since the structural researchers themselves seemed too busy!) to make available some 500 of these devices and their rationales in a Compendium (Cattell & Warburton, 1961), so we shall make no attempt to describe them here. However, out of their inter-correlations, pursued over more than fifteen large and different human population samples, have arisen some twenty-one factors, to date (Hundleby, Pawlik & Cattell, 1964). These are numbered in the Universal Index (Cattell, 1957), U.I. 16 through 36, since ability factors as reviewed by French (1951) were already 15 in number when this index was started and any separation from abilities would have been arbitrary.

After much research, and the discovery of a substantial number of criterion relations, we are more ready to give names to these. For example, Eysenck has called U.I. 23 the neuroticism factor, and although the studies of Scheier (1961) show that no fewer than six of the twenty-one factors actually distinguish neurotics from normals at the 1 per cent level of confidence, yet it is to the credit of the Maudsley group that they first demonstrated the powerful connection of this U.I. 23 factor (since interpreted as *ergic regression* by Cattell and Scheier) with neuroticism. The U.I. 23 loading pattern is shown in Table 1.

TABLE 1

PERFORMANCES AND TEST RESPONSES AFFECTED BY THE
REGRESSION FACTOR, U.I. 23
(Eysenck's "Neuroticism")

Performance	Factor Loading
Relative inability to do simple addition and subtraction mentally	.57
More stuttering and upset of speech with delayed auditory feedback	.57
Slower and more erratic recognition of upside-down forms	.57
Aspiration level high relative to performance (in coding)	.55
Poor ability to coordinate simultaneous spatial cues	.55
Low metabolic rate change in response to stimuli	.50
Less readiness to tackle unpleasant activities	
More numerous "indecisive" responses in questionnaires	.44
More errors in reciting alphabet with prescribed skipping	.42
More rapid increase of errors when made to hurry	.31
Higher motor-perceptual rigidity	.29
Affected more by color than form in artistic preferences	.25
Higher body sway in suggestibility sway test	.20

These twelve measures, each corresponding to a precisely defined, replicable behavioral situation, illustrate the variety of performances affected by the "inability to mobilize" which strongly distinguishes neurotics from normals.

Another factor which has readily been recognized is U.I. 24. This has provided a unique determination of batteries for *anxiety* measurement, such as were not previously possible. It reveals anxiety as only *one* component among several in neurosis. It also shows that it is probably the influence responsible for low social desirability scores in the questionnaire work of Edwards (1957). This factor is an apt one for illustrating in the course of the present chapter, the relations of *traits*, found by R-technique, to *states* found by P-technique, and *trait-states*, i.e., fluctuation states in a trait level, found by incremental R- and P-techniques (Cattell, 1957; Holtzman, 1963). The loading pattern of anxiety as a state is essentially the same as, yet in particulars different from, the form of anxiety as a characterological trait. For example, systolic blood pressure loads the former more than the latter (see Table 2).

TABLE 2

PATTERN OF THE ANXIETY FACTOR OBTAINED IN TERMS OF
INDIVIDUAL DIFFERENCES

A. AS A TRAIT

Title and Direction of Behavioral Variable	Loading (Correlation with the Factor)
More susceptibility to annoyance	56
More willingness to confess common frailties	47
More tendency to agree	38
Higher heart rate	30
Slow reaction time (irregularly warned)	28
Low writing pressure	28
Low total physical strength	27
High critical severity	25
Faster rate of autonomic type of conditioning (Electrical skin resistance reflex)	25
Low hand steadiness	22
High emotionality of comment	20
High self-criticism/self-approval ratio	19
High (pH) saliva (alkaline)	19
Slow speed of perceptual judgment (Letter comparison)	18

B. AS A STATE

Objective tests:

Raised cholinesterase in serum	.78
Higher hippuric acid (in urine)	.74
Higher willingness to admit common faults	.58
High susceptibility to annoyance	.46
Faster rate of respiration	.45
High plasma 17-OH in blood	.43
Faster heart rate	.30
High systolic pulse pressure	.29
Lower pH saliva (acid)	.23
Faster reversible perspective	.19
Greater volume of saliva secreted	.13

Questionnaire Primaries:

C—, Low Ego Strength	—.77
Q_3—, Low Will control	—.51
Q_4+, More Ergic Tension	—.48
Q+, More Guilt Proneness	.37
M+, More Autia, Non-Conformity	.31

The use of factor analysis with change scores to discover the dimensions of state change has revealed some seven to nine states (Cattell, 1957; Cattell & Nesselroade, 1961), e.g., excitement, fatigue, etc., and in doing so has made an important distinction between anxiety and stress response (Cattell & Scheier, 1961). These state concepts and scores are necessary to the complete description of personality at a given moment.

The pattern called U.I. 28 is an intriguing one which combines high moral standards with general asthenia, acceptance of authority values but conflict with authority, together with difficulties over perception of time. It has been called *apnicia*, an acronym from "asthenia through premature introjection of control" and represents something approached by certain psychoanalytic concepts of the super ego (Cattell, 1962).

A far more familiar pattern is represented by U.I. 32, which from its correspondence with ratings, we know to be the core of covariation at the heart of the extraversion-introversion concept. In this connection we may point out that the relationship between the L- and Q-data factors on the one hand, and the T-data on the other, is that second order factors in the first seem to align with first order factors in the T-data. A large, second-order factor in the 16 P.F., which is clearly extraversion, loads factors A, cyclothymia, F, surgency, Q_2, lack of self-sufficiency, and so on. As Table 3 shows, these also load the objective test factor U.I. 32 which is independently recognized as extraversion.

Among the primary personality factors a second-order structure has now been independently obtained with high congruence by Knapp, Scheier, Pawlik and others (Cattell et al, 1961; Pawlik & Cattell, 1962). The nature of the seven second-order factors can only be discussed here in a brief general way, in connection with organization concepts below. Also, the reader must be referred to texts (Cattell, 1946; Cattell & Scheier, 1961; Hundleby et al, 1964) for study of the twenty-one hypotheses connected with the intriguing patterns presented by the twenty-one primary factors. Whatever hypothesis about a personality dimension has been generated in the mind of a personality theorist, it is highly probable that in so far as it is real it will be expressed in one of these patterns. Being derived from a very wide array —over 1,000 kinds—of behavioral measures, the U.I. factor series are likely to constitute most of the major personality concepts one could think of. If we are correct in urging the young psychologist to abandon wooly, pre-metric, clinical concepts and to seek his theories in patterns

TABLE 3

U.I. 32 EXVIA-INVIA

MI Number	Title and Direction of Variable	Factor Loading
282	Greater number of objects perceived in unstructured drawings	+.34
316	Higher fluency on own relative to other people's personal characteristics	+.26
763	Higher total fluency on own *and* other peoples' personal characteristics	+.26
24d	Lower ratio of final (speeded) to initial (slow) total score: CMS	—.33
5	Higher ratio of regularly to irregularly warned reaction time	+.25
108	More confident assumption of skill in untried performance	+.22
146a	Lower absolute accuracy in perceptual Gestalt completion	—.26
152	Less tendency to agree	—.25
273	Higher proportion of fluency on self	+.25
219	Fewer common frailties admitted	—.24

of a more precise nature derived from more searching instrumentality, it is here that he may best find them. Here also the bivariate experimentalist can most profitably turn when he wants a battery to represent a single concept, operationally, in some manipulative study, e.g., anxiety, dominance, genital inhibition, exvia, in relation to biochemistry, learning, etc.

Indeed, the sensible division of labor among specialists today is that the factor analyst should provide from his complex art the measures which "classical" (bivariate) experimenters and clinicians can employ in experiments directed to finding out more about the natural history, growth curves, physiology and learning reactivity of factors.[1]

---

[1] This amounts to saying that the factor analysts are in a sense instrument makers and others are instrument users. Many psychologists are not yet mentally prepared for such specialization, yet it surely needs to be done. There is far too much of a tendency for someone in some remote clinic or university to say "I would like to measure the effect of extroversion upon this, or anxiety upon that," and then just go into the next office and make himself a measure for it! It reminds one of the medical man of fifty years ago, who had a little pharmacy in the garage and went back and mixed his own pharmaceuticals. But nowadays this is regarded as a highly specialized activity, which large drug houses look after, with many skilled chemists engaged for the purpose. So here, in the mental measurement field it seems, at least as regards

VI. THE DOMAIN OF DYNAMIC TRAITS

By dynamic traits we mean those connected with interest and motivation, the measures of which have the quality of changing most in response to changes in situational incentives (Cattell, 1957). The first reaction of clinicians to multivariate experimental study of this domain was that it would prove too subtle and evanescent to be caught by factor analytic procedures. But in the end it proved one of the most successful applications of all, for the structure was unusually clear, and checked well from R-technique to P-technique. As those familiar with these developments of the past decade will recognize, the new concepts which have appeared are:

(1) The measurement of interest strength no longer by self-rating, opinionnaires, as in the Strong and Edwards tests, but by objective devices. Some seventy physiological, defense-mechanism and learning theory manifestations of motive strength have been shown, as objective variables, to factor first into seven primary *motivation component* factors, and secondly, into two second order motivation components. The latter are called the *integrated* (I) and *unintegrated* (U) component in any interest. Motivation strength can thus be determinately, non-arbitrarily measured in respect to interest in any course of action.

(2) The factoring of large numbers of interests and attitudes has shown that most dynamic structures reduce to nine or ten primary ergs, e.g., sex, fear, gregariousness, assertion, curiosity, that are presumably innate and a number of sentiments, e.g., to home, career, wife, and the self-concept (the self-sentiment) that are presumably acquired aggregates of attitudes learned in relation to social institutions.

An attitude is now no longer defined as "for or against an object" but as a vector showing the strength of a response (in a stimulus-response definition) in terms of the amount of satisfaction given to a number of ergs and sentiments, by that mode of response, as shown in Diagram 2.

---

personality factor measurements, that this is a highly technical endeavor, best done by a number of laboratories concentrating on it and getting all the necessary skills and apparatus and computer programs to do it. But at the same time it is extremely important that the external criterion relationships of these factors be investigated by others; consequently it is surely important to have a good understanding on this exchange among specialists—between the clinician, the factor analyst and the controlled experimenter.

DIAGRAM 2

REPRESENTATION OF ATTITUDE INTEREST I_j VECTOR ON ERGIC COORDINATES

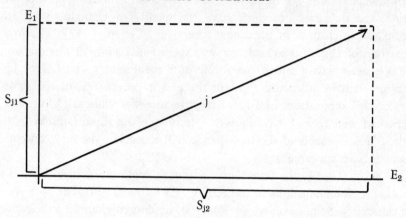

Along with these findings that have come to be referred to as the study of the dynamic calculus, have developed the concept of the *dynamic lattice* (Cattell, 1959) and certain concepts of conflict. It is asserted that the ergic unitary traits found by factor analysis are actually, at any given moment, *ergic tension levels*, resolvable as follows:

$$(1) \quad E = (S + k) [C + H + (P - aG)] - bG$$

where, E = ergic tension
S = strength of stimulus situation (k is a constant to avoid zero values)
C = constitutional component in drive strength
H = history of stimulation of drive, notably of imprinting
P = internal physiological transitory state
G = degree of current gratification of drive
a and b are constants representing respectively the effect of gratification directly on physiological appetite and on psychological drive responsiveness

$$(2) \quad I_{ji} = s_{j1} E_{1i} \cdots + s_{jn} E_{n1} + s_{j1m} M_{1i} \cdots + s_{jnm} M_n + \text{a specific}$$

where E are ergs, as in (1) above, and the M's are sentiment strengths. (The s's are the values for fixing the vector projections in Diagram 2 above.)

Now the conflict in any given attitude or other interest can be defined as:

$$(3) \quad C = \frac{\overset{n}{\Sigma s}}{n - \Sigma s}$$

where Σs is the sum of loadings in (2) without regard to sign and Σ is the algebraic sum, sign considered. This quotient has been compared with conflict ratings by psychiatrists and other criteria of conflict and found to work out very well. Essentially, it compares the amount of drive which "gets through" to actual expression with initial amount of activated drive need.

A second approach which has been found to give values corresponding to clinical concepts of degree of conflict is the contrast of the degree of integrated and unintegrated expression. This may be written:

$$(4) \quad C_j = \frac{U_j}{U_j + I_j}$$

where U_j and I_j are measures on the above second-order motivation components for the given interest j. For example, in our culture it is found that this value is higher for most sex interests than for curiosity, gregariousness, etc.

For practical work in the clinic, industry and school, two dynamic test batteries have now been set up: The Motivation Analysis Test, MAT for adults (Cattell and Horn, 1963), and the School Motivation Analysis Test, SMAT, for children (Sweney, 1962). Each measures, by the four best known objective motivation devices, ten factors which constitute the main ergs and sentiments. The I and U measures on these have yielded valuable checks on conflict, while the totals have been shown to predict criteria, e.g., school achievement, with validity over and above what is attainable from tests covering ability and personality variance. This reminds us that in the complete prediction of a response, R_j, it is necessary to include factors (source traits) of all three modalities, as summarized in equation (5), which may be called the "total personality prediction."

$$(5) \quad R_j = s_{A1j} A_1 \cdots s_{Anj} A_n + s_{P1} P_1 \cdots + s_{Pnj} P_n + s_{D1} D_1 \cdots + s_{Dn} D_n$$

Here D is a dynamic source trait (covering both E's, ergs and M's, engrams (sentiments and complexes). (To avoid complication of writing, the i subscripts, indicating a particular individual, have been omitted.)

VII.   PERSONALITY AND LEARNING

Learning is of four kinds:

(1) Simple conditioning

(2) Means-end learning (where a goal exists and the organism is rewarded to the extent that it approaches it).

(3) Integration learning

(4) Ergic goal sublimation

The third and fourth have been missed by most learning theorists though they are very important for personality learning. Integration learning arises where there are several independent dynamic goals and the organism has to learn to maximize its total satisfaction by inhibiting (suppressing or repressing) some satisfactions in favor of others.

The types of situation which the organism can encounter, in terms of personality learning, have been summarized in a series of choice points or "dynamic crossroads" as set out in the Adjustment Process Analysis chart in Cattell and Scheier (1961, Diagrams 12-1 and 12-2, pp. 306-307, 318-319), to which reference can be made.

If we now define personality learning as a *multi-dimensional change in response to experience of a multi-dimensional situation*, it becomes desirable to express this relation of personality, situational experience and learning in matrix terms. If certain values are set in the above APA chart (from experiment) for the modification of certain personality source traits by a single experience of each kind of path, we have what may be called a personality-path-transformation matrix, or PPT matrix, as in Diagram 3.

If next we know the frequencies for any given individual with which he is exposed to experiences along these various paths, we can

DIAGRAM 3

THE PERSONALITY-PATH TRANSFORMATION MATRIX

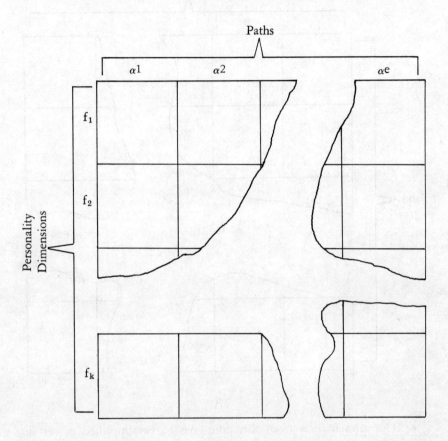

construct a Path Experience Matrix for him, as in Diagram 4 (Note: it will be a single vector for any one individual, as in Diagram 5 on page 437):

DIAGRAM 4

THE INDIVIDUAL PERSON-PATH
EXPERIENCE RECORD MATRIX

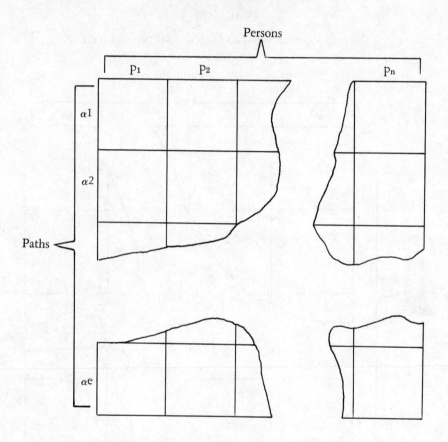

Our presentation from this point has to be simplified in certain ways. First, the experience of frustration, repression, etc., in the APA chart will differ in its effect upon personality according to the magnitude and nature of the dynamic tendency that is frustrated. We shall ignore this for the first presentation. Secondly, the relation of experience to learning could be one of several mathematical expressions, e.g., additive or multiplicative. We shall assume as most probable that the gain can be expressed as the product of the number of experiences by the magnitude and nature of the learning experience at each.

DIAGRAM 5

1. *Calculation of Expected Personality Profiles from Record of Path Frequencies (Experience)*

   Formula (i) C = AB, which can be set out in detail as follows:

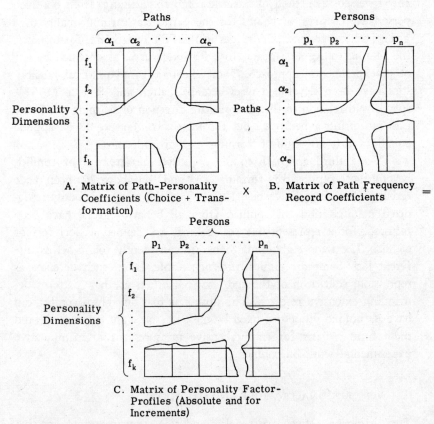

A. **Matrix of Path-Personality Coefficients (Choice + Transformation)** X B. **Matrix of Path Frequency Record Coefficients** =

C. **Matrix of Personality Factor-Profiles (Absolute and for Increments)**

2. *Calculation of Path Frequency Experience from Personality Profile*

   Formula (ii) $B = A^{-1}D^{-1}C$, where $D = AA^1$

3. *Calculation of General Path-Personality Coefficients from Experimental Data*

   Formula (iii) $A = CB^1D^{-1}$, where $D = BB^1$

Reproduced from Raymond B. Cattell and Ivan H. Scheier, *The Meaning and Measurement of Neuroticism and Anxiety* (New York: The Ronald Press Company, 1961), Diagram 13-2, p. 341, by permission of the publisher.

In that case, knowing the individual's experience in the multi-dimensional situation, and the teaching character of each situation or path, a learning calculation can be made by the following matrix multiplication (Diagram 5).

The above matrix treatment, which may be called the Personality Learning Calculus, is not only a method of applied prediction, but suitably reversed, a method of basic research for arriving, from observed personality changes, at values for the particular learning quality of a given path experience. The values in the PPT matrix are, for instance, the familiar tangents (mean) to a learning curve, as obtained by any other experimental approach. These theoretical and practical possibilities have been developed elsewhere by Cattell and Scheier (1961), specially in relation to that unfortunate direction of learning which we call "acquiring a neurosis" but the matrix concepts could be applied equally well to any kind of learning, e.g., of leadership.

Yet a third approach to the objective measurement of conflict, beyond those expressed in formulas (3) and (4) above, has been made recently (Cattell and Sweeney, 1964). Therein, many commonly recognized manifestations of conflict, from all behavior areas, have been factored, for a representative set of what are defined as loci foci of conflict. The same eight dimensions are consistently found across different loci. Some are clinically recognizeable, being such defenses as repression, restriction of the ego, etc., but others are new patterns demanding extensive research. The upshot is that any given conflict can have its unique properties fixed by measures on eight dimensions, and these form a basis for comprehensive measurement in manipulative experimental work on conflict.

VIII.   PERSONALITY, ROLE AND SITUATION

The distinction between personality and role is an important one that will also be entered upon here in connection with some other important definitions, namely that of the situation. The general factor specification equation, set out as equation (5), page 434, above, it should be remembered, defines both the stimulus situation j and the personality i. (The subscripts for i were omitted for simplicity from that particular equation.) For the s's, which are obtained experimentally as factor loadings, have been so symbolized because they are in fact *situational indices*. Thus we may take out from the specification equation, the situational indices and write them as the dimensions of a particular stimulus situation, s_j as follows:

$$(6) \quad s_j = [s_{j1}, s_{j2} \cdots \cdots s_{jn}]$$

These S's are a statement of the average meaning of the situation within the given group. They define the extent to which it evokes this drive and that drive, or this ability and that ability. They are statements of the psychological dimensions of the situation, and, like the factors themselves, they are independent but oblique dimensions. Thus, with this device, it is possible objectively to classify situations taxonomically by the resemblances of their profiles. Thus psychology can handle situations just as it has handled individuals in regard to their individuality and their classifiable properties. Actually there are always two quantitative contributions to the meaning of any situation (the meaning being defined by the response that is made to it) from two different sources. These two contributions are first the average meaning, as given by the S's above, and secondly, the personal meaning, as given by the individual's particular endowment of those personality factors which are involved in the perception and response.

The puzzle for psychology in regard to role has been the question whether the change in perception which generates a change in action when a person steps into a role, is due to a change in the situational indices, or a change in the personality. That is to say, does the individual *see* the situation differently, or is he a *changed individual* in the role situation? It has been shown elsewhere that we have the resources in our formulae (Cattell, 1957; Cattell, 1962a; Cattell, 1963) to handle the problem either way, and it is a matter of experiment to decide which will be more convenient. For example, if we regard the personality as remaining unchanged, then we may find that for all role situations we must clip a different series of constants as shown by the k's in (7) below, to the s's when the given situation of equation (5) above is encountered afresh in a role situation.

$$(7) \quad \text{Out of Role } R_j = s_{j1} t_{1i} + s_{j2} t_{2i} \cdots \cdots + s_{jn} t_{ni}$$
$$\text{In Role k } R_{jk} = s_{j1} k_1 t_{1i} + s_{j2} k_2 t_{2i} \cdots s_{jn} k_n t_{ni}$$

The alternative is to suppose that the situational indices remain the same, but that the individual's endowment in the personality dimensions changes when he steps into a role situation.

$$(8) \quad (Sjn \ Kjn) \ Tni = Sjn \ (KjnTni)$$

In this case we can calculate the k's first by comparing the factor loadings for a given focal situation in and outside of a role situation, and then shift these to modify the personality instead of modifying the situational indices as shown in (8) above. Both these treatments utilize the notion of a focal stimulus and a global situation around it, which modifies the focal stimulus j, in the total situation of stepping into a role K.

Elsewhere we have argued that the best procedure at present, pending further investigation, is the first one (the left side in (8)) in which we recognize that a global situation changes the loadings of the personality factors. However, we further recognize that it especially does so on *one particular dynamic structure,* a sentiment, which we call the role factor. This is a set of habits and attitudes acquired by an individual who is used to stepping into the role. The main difference in his behavior and that of another person who is unaccustomed to the role is that produced by the large loading on this factor in the role situation. Since the person unendowed with the role will have only a small trait score, the large s_j will have nothing to multiply and there will be no major change of behavior. The ambient situation around the focal situation which converts it to a global role situation is then called *a modulator* (Cattell, 1963). Modulators may be divided into exmodulators, which operate as situations, and inmodulators which operate as moods and physiological conditions modifying a whole class of responses (Cattell, 1963).

Although we have chosen the first alternative, it may well be, when further investigation is made, that it will prove most economical, in terms of general theory and computation, to consider that something of *both* kinds of modification occurs. Thus, it may be that although stepping into a role does not modify the strength of abilities and temperament traits, yet it *could* modify the operative level of certain dynamic traits, normally treated as independent, fixed E's and M's in the specific equation. The stepping into a role would then be represented by a loading on a role factor, of a kind which does not enter into the reactions of the focal stimulus, together with a *modulation of other* dynamic factors, by a set of k's as suggested above—(8) right. Certainly it seems desirable to represent certain temporary changes in personality by clipping a set of k's to the standard personality and trait levels. Indeed, this is unavoidable in the case of the inmodulators or states, which, as we have shown in the introduction, are already psychologically recognizable factors. For example, if a person in a state of anxiety reacts differently toward a whole lot of specific situations, then when we know that Situation A causes an individual to become anxious, we must introduce a modulator set of k's, when Situation A occurs, such that all subsequent reactions to stimuli take cognizance of these changes in the levels of the state factors which enter into the usual specification equation. In short, when we wish to predict in particular circumstances it may prove theoretically most economical to write a general specification equation and then write statements for the inmodulators and exmodulators which temporarily change the individual's reactivities. It may be noted, that this treatment could also be handled by matrix multiplication methods.

It will be noted that if we allow the ambient situation, which causes an individual to step into a role, to be represented by a grid of k values attached to his dynamic factors (particularly), then we are allowing one factor, namely the role factor, to act in a multiplicative instead of an additive fashion to other factors. This instance creates an opportunity to discuss the general additive model used here. It is sometimes said that an additive and linear model for the operation of personality influences upon behavior is too simple. This may prove to be so, but there is absolutely no proof at present that it is! Science always begins with the simplest assumption and stays with it until, as sometimes happens, complicating modifications are forced upon it. The fact is that the additive model is an approximation to a multiplicative model and it would not, if the real relation *happened* to be multiplicative, fail to discover the existence of personality structures, providing that the measurements are made over relatively small ranges. Consequently, the best procedure in research has been to use the simple model, to locate the factors thereby, and then, if a more complex relationship really exists, to iterate again on this basis using some modified model.

Actually, if we really believe that in a certain psychological area the factor endowments multiply each other instead of add to one another, it is possible to investigate this directly by *transforming all test scores* to logarithms and then factoring these logarithmic values. One will then get on the right hand side of the equation the logarithms of the factor endowments, and will need to make a corresponding change in estimating the factors. One will also have altered the model in that the s's will have become powers to which the factors are to be raised. So far, however, the instances where a multiplicative relationship appears definitely indicated as a possibility are very few, namely those occurring between one or two "cooperative" (Cattell, 1957) factors. At the present stage of research we have every reason to be satisfied with the factor model, compared to any other model that has been suggested or used in personality research. Its special value is that it grows, i.e., that it is capable of giving a first approximation to the structure, from which the existence of more complex structure can be checked by further kinds of experiment.

IX. SUMMARY

(1) The multivariate experimental method is one that proceeds as in clinical method but with greater precision of measurement and analysis. It has a major and indispensable role to play, compared with the bivariate method, in most phases of personality research.

(2) The use of such methods interactively and systematically, notably using R- and P-technique factor analysis in combination, and operating upon L-, Q-, and T-data, representatively sampled from the total personality sphere, has led to very consistent results in regard to the discovery of twenty or so, distinct, but oblique personality factors.

(3) Some of these personality factors represent with greater clarity concepts already reached by the clinician, but others add totally new dimensionality and powers of prediction to personality study.

(4) Higher order factor structures are also found meaningfully among these factors. Some of them have turned out to be the concepts needed for relating mental interiors, as seen in questionnaires, to behavioral exteriors, as determined by rating and objective testing. However, it is also necessary to set aside instrument factors in proceeding from any one of the three media to any other.

(5) In the dynamic field we must distinguish motivational component factors and dynamic structure factors. The latter turn out to be either ergs or sentiments (engrams). Some effective formulations, agreeing well with clinical and other criteria, are possible in this area in terms of resolving the ergic tension levels into components, expressing conflict as the difference between total and expressed drive, and expressing conflict as the difference between integrated and unintegrated component strength in a particular direction of interest. These equa-

tions also permit attitude change to be formulated as a vector change in regard to meaningful ergic components.

(6) There are four types of change which enter into personality learning. The most important of these, integration learning, has been seriously neglected. Personality learning, as a multidimensional change in relation to experience of a multidimensional situation, can be handled in terms of matrix algebra, utilizing the Adjustment Process Analysis Chart, and the Path Experience Matrix, to operate on the personality factors of the individual concerned.

(7) The distinction of personality and role can be handled either as a change of general perception, or as a change in personality, when the individual steps into a role situation. A theory of modulators is proposed to handle this, and it is suggested that further research will be necessary before one can decide whether the standard specification equation, utilizing one large role factor,' suffices. Alternatively, it may be necessary to introduce multiplicative relationships, in which the stimulation of the role factor produces simultaneously certain changes in other factors, notably in dynamic source traits.

(8) The model for the interaction of personality and situation used here, gives dimensions to situations as well as dimensions to personality. In so doing, it recognizes, incidentally, that the measurement of the dimensions of a personality is intimately tied to the situations in a culture, and that the meaningful dimensions of a situation are, reciprocally, tied to the type of organism which is introduced into that situation. The factor specification equation that is customarily used to bring these two kinds of dimension together, in what is really a development of the old stimulus-response formula, is at present restricted to additive action of factors and linear relations of factors to each other and to variables. However, this restriction would not prevent the method being effective in discovering the real factors, providing the range of variation of variables is small, in any given experiment. Consequently, it has the capacity, by iterative procedures and by the building of special experiment upon factor analytic experiment, to proceed to more complex formulations if they are found to be necessary. In particular, if a multiplicative action of factors rather than an additive one is believed to be present, it can be handled by logarithmic factor analysis.

The definition of personality developed by workers in the field cannot be made more precise in words than it has already been made in mathematical formulae. However, one can expand upon and re-express the notions involved in these formulae. In this way, one might verbally characterize the definition as a multidimensional interactional theory of personality, or, with one particular emphasis, as *the theory of personality as a point of intersection*. For if we define the situation by a set of dimensions, and then proceed further (as is not done here, but elsewhere (Cattell, 1957; Cattell, 1962a; Cattell, 1963), to recognize the syntality and synergy of groups (similarly as structures having their dimensionality related to that of individuals), then it will be seen that the point or node at which these various dimensions most frequently intersect is the reference point constituted by the single individual. In other words, for the purpose of defining dimensions, and for the purpose of prediction, the individual personality is definable as that which is more important than any other entity in this universe of measurements. Expressed in looser terms, we may say that the task of the individual in his development is to adjust both to a set of given dimensions —mainly abilities and temperamental traits—in himself, and to certain dimensions of a situation, and that in doing so he develops the new dimensions that we recognize as dynamic engram (not erg) factors. The particular kinds of adjustment that he brings about will show themselves most in the higher order factor analysis of the dynamic factor realm, and it is possible, as suggested elsewhere (Cattell, 1957), that the ego, or self, will appear in the total personality as the highest order factor regulating the hierarchy of factors.

·

REFERENCES

ACKERSON, L. *Children's behavior problems*. Chicago: Univer. of Chicago Press, 1942.

ALLPORT, G. W. & ODBERT, H. S. Traitnames; a psycholexical study. *Psychol. Mon.*, 1936, 47, 171, 63.

BARRATT, E. On impulsivity. Personal communication to R. B. Cattell, 1962.

BERG, I. A., & RAPAPORT, G. M. Response sets in a multiple-choice test. *Educ. psychol Measmt.*, 1955, 15, 58-62.

BRUNSWICK, E. *Systematic and representative design of psychological experiments.* Berkeley: Univer. of California Press, 1947.

BURT, C. L. *The Factors of the Mind.* London: Univer. of London Press, 1940.

BUTLER, J. The use of a psychological model in personality testing. *Educ. psycho. Measmt.*, 1953, 15, 77-89.

CAMPBELL, D. T. The indirect assessment of social attitudes. *Psychol. Bull.*, 1950, 47, 15-38.

CARTWRIGHT, D. S. & ROTH, I. Success and satisfaction in psychotherapy. *J. Clin. Psychol.*, 1957, 13, 20-26.

CATTELL, R. B. The description of personality: I. Foundations of trait measurement. *Psychol. Rev.*, 1943, 50 559-594.

CATTELL, R. B. The measurement of interest. *Char. & Per.*, 1945, 4, 147-169.

CATTELL, R. B. *The description and measurement of personality.* Cleveland: World Book Co., 1946.

CATTELL, R. B. *Personality and motivation structure and measurement.* New York: Harcourt, Brace & World, 1957.

CATTELL, R. B. The dynamic calculus: a system of concepts derived from the objective motivation measurement. In G. Lindzey (Ed.), *Assessment of Human Motives.* New York: Rinehart, 1958.

CATTELL, R. B. The dynamic calculus: concepts and crucial experiments. In M. R. Jones, (Ed.), *The Nebraska Symposium on Motivation.* Lincoln, Neb.: Univer. of Nebraska Press, 1959. (a)

CATTELL, R. B. Personality theory growing from multivariate quantitative research. In S. Koch (Ed.) *Psychology: A Study of A Science.* New York: McGaw-Hill, 1959. (b)

CATTELL, R. B. Theory of situational, instrument, second order and refraction factors in personality structure research, *Psychol. Bull.*, 1961, 58 160-174. (a)

CATTELL, R. B. (chapter) In Uhr & Miller (Eds.), *Drugs and Behavior.* New York: Wiley & Co., 1961. (b)

CATTELL, R. B. Group theory, personality and role: a model for experimental researches. In F. A. Geldard, (Ed.), *Defence Psychology.*, Pergamon Press, 1962. (a)

CATTELL, R. B. The parental early repressiveness hypothesis for the 'authoritarian' personality factor, U.I.28., *J. genet. Psychol.* 1962. (b)

CATTELL, R. B. Personality, role, mood, and situation-perception: A unifying theory of modulators. *Psychol. Rev.*, 1963, 70, 1-18.

CATTELL, R. B. & BAGGALEY, A R. A confirmation of ergic and engram structures in attitudes objectively measured. *Australian J. Psychol.*, 1958, 10, 287-318.

CATTELL, R. B. & COAN, R. W. Objective-test assessment of the primary personality dimensions in middle childhood. *Brit. J. Psychol.*, 1959, 50, 235-252.

CATTELL, R. B., COAN, R. W. & BELOFF, H. A re-examination of personality structure in late childhood, and development of the High School Personality Questionnaire. *J. exp. Educ.*, 1958, 27, 73-88.

CATTELL, R. B., & HORN, J. *The Motivation Analysis Test.* Champaign, Ill.: I.P.A.T., 1963.

CATTELL, R. B., & HORN, J. Experimental evidence on the structure of the self. (in preparation).

CATTELL, R. B., HORN, J., & BUTCHER, H. J. The dynamic structure of attitudes in adults: a description of some established factors and of their measurement by the Motivational Analysis Test. *Brit. J. Psychol.,* 1962, 53, 1, 57-69.

CATTELL, R. B., KNAPP, R. R. & SCHEIER, I. H. Second-order personality factor structure in the objective test realm. *J. consult Psychol.,* 1961, 25, 345-352.

CATTELL, R. B., & NESSELROADE, J. *The IPAT Psychological State Battery.* Champaign, Ill.: I.P.A.T., 1961.

CATTELL, R. B., & PETERSON, D. R. Personality structure in four and five year olds in terms of objective tests. *J. clin. Psychol.,* 1959, 15, 355-369.

CATTELL, R. B., PICHOT, P., & RENNES, P. Constance interculturelle des facteurs de personalité mésures par le test 16 P.F. 11. Comparaison Franco-Américaine. *Rev. de Psychologie appliquée,* 1961, 11, 165-196.

CATTELL, R. B., RADCLIFFE, J. A., & SWEENEY, A. B. The objective measurement of motivation structure in children. *J. clin. Psychol.,* 1960, 16, 227-232.

CATTELL, R. B., & SCHEIER, J. H. *The meaning and measurement of neuroticism and anxiety.* New York: Ronald Press, 1961.

CATTELL, R. B., & STICE, G. J. *The 16 P.F. Questionnare.* Champaign, Ill.: I.P.A.T., 1955.

CATTELL, R. B., & SWENEY, A. B. Components measurable in manifestations of mental conflict. *J. abnorm. N soc. Psychol.,* 1964.

CATTELL, R. B. & WARBURTON, F. W. Cross-cultural comparison of patterns of extraversion and anxiety. *Brit. J. Psychol.,* 1961, 52, 3-16.

DAMARIN, F. L., & CATTELL, R. B. The methodology of process investigation. In R. B. Cattell (Ed.), *Handbook of multivariate experimental psychology.* New York: Rand-McNally, in press.

DIGMAN, J. M. The principal dimensions of child personality as inferred from teacher's judgments. *J. ed. Res.,* in press.

DINGMAN, H. F. The relation between coefficients of correlation and difficulty factors. *Brit. J. statis. Psychol.,* 1958, 9, 13-18.

EDWARDS, A. L. *The social desirability variable in personality assessment and research.* New York: Dryden, 1957.

EYSENCK, H. J. *The scientific study of personality.* London: Routledge & Kegan Paul, 1952.

FISKE, D. W. Consistency of the factorial structures of personality ratings from different sources. *J. abnorm. soc. Psychol.,* 1949, 44, 329-344.

FRENCH, J. W. The description of aptitude and achievement tests in terms of rotated factors. *Psychol. Monogr.,* No. 5, 1951.

GEERTSMA, R. H., McANDREW, C., & STOLLER, R. J. Medical student orientations towards the emotionally ill. *AMA Arch. neurol. Psychiat.,* 1959, 81.

GUILFORD, J. P. *Personality.* New York: McGraw-Hill, 1959.

GUILFORD, J. P. & ZIMMERMAN, W. S. Some A.A.F. findings concerning aptitude factors. *Occupations,* 1947, *26,* 154-159.

HOLTZMAN, W. Some methodological issues in P-technique. In C. C. Harris (Ed.), *The Measurement of Change.* Madison, Wisc.: Univ. of Wisconsin Press, in press.

HORN, JOHN. Structure in measures of self sentiment, ego and superego concepts. M.A. thesis, Univer. of Illinois, 1961.

HOWARD, K. Objective personality and motivational correlates of delinquency adaptations. Symposium, APA, 1961.

HUNDLEBY, J., PAWLIK, K., & CATTELL, R. B. The first 21 personality source traits in objective behavioral tests. In preparation.

KARSON, S. The Sixteen Personality Factor test in clinical practice. *J. clin. Psychol.,* 1959, *15,* 174-176.

KARSON, S. & POOL, K. B. Second order factors in personality measurement. *J. consult. Psychol.,* 1958, *22,* 299-303.

KARSON, S., & WIEDERSHINE, L. J. An objective evaluation of dynamically oriented group psychotherapy. *Int. J. group Psychother.,* 1961, *11,* 166-174.

KRETSCHMER, E. *Korperbau und charakter.* 7th and 8th improved and enlarged edition. Berlin: Springer, 1929.

LEVANTHAL, D. B., McGAUGHRAN, L. S., & MORAN, L. J. Multivariate analysis of the conceptual behavior of schizophrenic and brain-damaged patients. *J. Abnorm. Soc. Psychol.,* 1959, *58,* 84-90.

LORR, M., JENKINS, R. L., & O'CONNOR, J. P. Factors descriptive of psychopathology and behavior of hospitalized psychotics. *J. abnorm. soc. Psychol.,* 1955, *50,* 7-86.

LORR, M., RUBENSTEIN, E., & JENKINS R. L. A factor analysis of personality ratings of out-patients in psychotherapy. *J. abnorm. soc. Psychol.,* 1953, *48,* 511-514.

McQUITTY, L. L. Pattern analysis illustrated in classifying patients and normals. *Educ. psychol. Measmt.,* 1954, *14,* 598-604.

MEEHL, P. *Clinical vs. actuarial prediction.* Minneapolis: Univer. of Minnesota Press, 1954.

MORAN L. J., & MEFFERD, R. B. Jr. Repetitive psychometric measures. *Phychol. Rep.,* 1959, *5,* 269-275.

NORMAN, W. T. A spatial analysis of an interest domain. *Educ. psychol. Measmt.,* 1960, *20,* 347-361.

PAWLICK, K., & CATTELL, R. B. Third order factors in objective personality tests. *Brit. J. Psychol.,* 1964.

PORTER, R., & CATTELL, R. B. *The Child Personality Questionnaire.* Champaign, Ill.: I.P.A.T., 1961.

SCHAIE, K. W. Differences in some personal characteristics of "rigid" and "flexible" individuals. *J. clin. Psychol.*, 1958, *14*, 11-14.

SELLS, S. B. *Essentials of psychology.* New York: Ronald Press, 1962.

SELLS, S. B., TRITES, D. K., & PARISH, H. S. Correlates of manifest anxiety in beginning pilot trainees. *J. aviat. Med.*, 1957, *28*, 583-588.

SKINNER, B. F. *Science and human behavior.* New York: Macmillan, 1953.

SWENEY, A. B. Ein klares bild der furcht anfgrund von objektiven motivation tests. *Arch f.d. ges. Psychol.*, 1962, *113*, in press.

SWENEY, A. B., & CATTELL, R. B. Relationships between integrated and unintegrated motivation structure examined by objective tests. *J. soc. Psychol.*, 1962, *57* (*1*), 217-226. (a)

SWENEY, A. B. & CATTELL, R. B. *The School Motivation Analysis Test.* Champaign, Ill.: IPAT, 1962. (b)

TAYLOR, C. W. Maximizing predictive efficiency for a fixed total testing time. *Psychometrika* 1950, *15*, 391-406.

THORNDIKE, R. L., & HAGEN, E. *Measurement and evaluation in psychology and education.* (2nd ed.) New York: Wiley, 1961.

WATSON, R. I. The search for objectivity. In B. M. Bass and I. A. Berg (Ed.), *Objective approaches to personality assessment.* Princeton, N. J.: D Van Nostrand, 1959.

WITTENBORN, J. R. Symptom patterns in a group of mental hospital patients. *J. consult. Psychol.*, 1951, *15*, 290-302.

16

Problems in Measuring Personality

Donald W. Fiske

In appraising the degree of advancement of a scientific field, one of the criteria that has been proposed is the level of mensuration (Wolfle, Marquis & Sears, 1949). Against this absolute standard, the science of personality does not fare well. But in comparison with many other parts of psychology and with other social sciences, its standing is not so poor: although personality has some serious problems of measurement that are peculiar to its subject-matter, it also shares many of its difficulties with other sciences of behavior. Whatever its relative standing, its measurement problems call for intensive analysis and for efforts toward their solution.

A critical weakness in the scientific study of personality is the relative lack of adequate measurement operations. While many tests, instruments, and assessment devices are available, each has its basic limitations. It is often held that the more penetrating techniques are not objective while the so-called objective instruments are superficial. The importance of improving the operations for measuring personality cannot be overemphasized, for it has been said with justification that the history of science could be written in terms of advances in instrumentation. In the personality area, tests and other measurement devices are the instruments by which systematic data are collected.

This chapter will not catalogue and evaluate the numerous specific procedures available for assessing personality. That task has already been carried out in various ways (Buros, 1959; Vernon, 1953). Nor will this paper attempt to present test theory in general, since several excellent sources can be consulted for this material (e.g., in increasing order of technical difficulty, Cronbach, 1960; Guilford, 1954, Ch. 13-16; Gulliksen, 1950). The focus of this chapter will be on some problems peculiar to personality measurement and some difficulties in psychological measurement that are especially serious for the area of personality. Even within this topic, it will be impossible to consider all relevant questions. The serious student seeking a full introduction to personality measurement should be acquainted with the social desirability problem (which is discussed, together with other relevant material, in Bass and Berg, 1959), with the extensive literature on response sets (Jackson & Messick, 1958), and with the contributions of such people as Loevinger (1955, 1957) and Cronbach (1954). The critical analysis of the methodology for appraising self-acceptance published by Crowne and Stephens (1961) provides specific illustrations of several problems to be examined below.

It is axiomatic that measurement is necessary in the scientific study of personality. Both placing a person in a diagnostic category and preparing a case study are measurement operations, broadly construed. Of more general significance is the role of measurement in testing the theoretical propositions embedded in a given systematic view of personality. Such statements as "frustration leads to aggression" or "anxiety arouses the affiliative tendency" cannot be subjected to empirical appraisal until appropriate operations can be identified for measuring frustration, aggression, anxiety and affiliation.

Measurement operations can also serve the important function of providing data permitting the refinement or revision of concepts. If the indices for two concepts covary highly among people, the investigator must consider the possibility that one new concept should replace the pair. In a more common situation, two or more indices believed to represent the same concept are found to be uncorrelated; here one or more of the indices may be failing to reflect the concept, or the postulated characteristic may manifest itself differently in different people, so that no single index can be taken as the operational definition of the characteristic.

Measurement requires no theory. When a person sets out to measure things, he need have in mind only a variable or a classification scheme. Measurement is atheoretical but should not be anti-theoretical. The view of measurement presented in this chapter seems congruent with diverse conceptual positions. The few assumptions on which it is based should be acceptable to most personality theorists. (a) Science in general, and personality in particular, is a theoretical construction that exists in the minds of people, both scientists and laymen. (b) There is some consistency over time in the manner or mode of each person's interaction with his environment. (c) There is sufficient regularity and similarity in the overt behavior of different individuals to permit the fruitful description of these individuals in terms of a common set of variables.

THE EVALUATION OF A MEASUREMENT OPERATION

The evaluation of a test or of any other measurement operation is based ultimately on just one criterion: the degree of correspondence between the measurement operation and the concept which the technique is designed to measure. This property is, of course, commonly referred to as *validity*. It should be noted that validity applies to all measurement operations; it is crucial not only for tests but also for diagnoses, ratings, measures of therapeutic outcome, indices of learning, indices of socio-economic class, measures of performance, etc. While this criterion is obvious, it is frequently overlooked because the experimenter restricts his measurement operations to a single procedure for a given concept and comes to accept the test score or the reading of the dial as the equivalent of the concept, i.e., as the complete and unquestioned operational definition of the concept.

In classical test theory, validity is the correlation between a test and a criterion. The criterion may be an actual, empirically accessible variable. This usage is currently conceptualized as *concurrent* or *predictive* validity ("Technical recommendations for psychological tests, etc.", 1954). This view of the criterion is unsatisfactory because, in most basic research, there is rarely an experimentally available variable which can serve as the complete and adequate representation of the concept. Again, the criterion may be a hypothetical true score. This approach is undesirable because it ignores the matter of congruence with the independently formulated construct in which one is interested.

The approach of this chapter will be very close to that identified as *construct validity* (Cronbach & Meehl, 1955; Loevinger, 1957). In this orientation, the basic question can be stated in simple terms: do the scores or indices produced by a given operation for measurement behave as measures of the relevant concept should behave? Do they show the pattern of intercorrelation with other variables, the differences between groups and between conditions that have been predicted in the prior development of the concept in its theoretical framework?

A logical analysis of validity indicates that it has two aspects: What proportion of the total domain of the concept is covered by the test instrument? What proportion of the variance of the test scores is associated with the concept? A vocabulary test covers only a portion of what is defined as intelligence. On the other hand, a test of general information may include variance not only from intelligence but also from motivation and socio-economic level. In the area of personality, an attitude measure such as the F Scale may cover only part of authoritarianism but may also be affected by the disposition to acquiesce or respond positively, or by a disposition to select socially desirable response alternatives, tendencies which may or may not be included within one's definition of authoritarianism. Each of these types of departure from congruence between test and concept is found in one or another of the problems in measuring personality that will be discussed below.

All efforts in the construction and refinement of tests and measuring instruments have the ultimate objective of improving validity. Even reliability, the other key concept in test theory, is a property in the service of validity. The most common type of reliability index is that indicating homogeneity or internal consistency, i.e., the degree to which the several items or parts of a test are measuring the same thing. Of course, it is not desirable to have each item measure exactly the same thing at the same level because all items but the first would then be redundant. Different items are required to differentiate people with different amounts of the characteristic being assessed and to sample different aspects of the variable. Most traits and attributes associated with personality are not narrow and specific (such as degree of liking for the way in which one's father eats his soup) but are relatively broad and many-faceted (such as the degree to which one modifies one's perception or response as external conditions are altered). Hence the optimal level of correlation between parts of a test is a function of the postulated homogeneity of the concept at which it is aimed.

Similar considerations apply to the other common form of reliability—stability, the extent to which a test orders people in the same way on two separate occasions. Ideal measures of feeling of well-being or of alertness should obviously have lower stability values than scores reflecting attitudes toward familiar objects. Finally, there is the type of reliability which is of particular importance in the study of personality: agreement between observers, judges, or raters. Ordinarily, maximal values for inter-judge agreement are sought when the problem is that of assigning a score to an individual on the basis of a given protocol. On the other hand, the same person may be validly rated on friendliness in different ways by judges representing separate roles, such as a superior, a peer, and a subordinate. In short, a reliability figure for a given measuring instrument must be evaluated not in terms of some abstract, absolute standard but rather against the presumed characteristics of the underlying concept. To promote validity, the reliability of the test should conform to the reliability of the variable as construed.

THE NATURE OF THE PERSONALITY CONSTRUCT

A personality theory involves a set of constructs and their interrelationships. Each theoretical term is embedded in a "nomological net" (Cronbach & Meehl, 1955), a set of propositions which in large part conveys the meaning of the concept. Broadly speaking, such concepts are of two kinds, those referring to processes and those referring to traits. This distinction is, however, primarily determined by the interests and objectives of the theorist. The two kinds of constructs are different ways of conceptualizing the same basic observations.

The student of personality is ultimately concerned with processes that go on within the individual. Since the processes cannot ordinarily be directly observed, the investigator uses as his datum the response emitted by the individual. Thus the basic observation is the response of a person to a stimulus situation at a particular moment.

Some investigators are more concerned with the processes than with the individuals in whom they occur. Such experimenters may study the projections in subjects' interpretations of inkblots or other ambiguous stimuli. They may investigate inhibitory mechanisms inferred from the observation that males verbalize fewer sexual associations when a female experimenter is present. In such research, a typical design may call for a comparison between the means of two groups of subjects identified on some independent basis or between the means for the same group of subjects under two different conditions. In either instance, the experimenter is not interested in the individual subject as an individual.

Other investigators are interested in whether or not the process takes place in a particular individual. They wish to determine the prevalence of the process in the individual: does it occur more frequently in this individual than in that one? These investigators conceptualize in terms of traits, i.e., dispositions which have varying strengths in different people. They see these traits as characteristics of persons which exist over a period of time. More specific designations falling under this general term are needs, motives, cognitive tendencies, attitudes, and interests.

To measure the strengths of a trait in different individuals, the investigator presents the same conditions to each person and observes the frequency of the response used to identify the trait or disposition. He keeps the conditions constant so that the variation in observations can be attributed to the separate subjects. In contrast, his colleague who is interested in the process typically keeps the persons constant so that he can study the effects associated with different conditions.

Both kinds of students of personality can, in principle, use the same observations, the responses of persons under specified conditions. However, one set of researchers ordinarily observes many individuals under each condition while the other observes each person when confronted with each of a large number of stimulus situations. The former increase the dependability of their results by pooling subjects while the latter seek dependable scores by pooling responses to different stimuli. Th former set treats individual differences as error variance while the latter treats stimulus differences as error variance. (Compare Cronbach's [1957] discussion of "The Two Disciplines of Scientific Psychology.")

All investigators of personality are concerned with dependability because the fundamental object of study is a process, something that occurs or does not occur at a particular moment, something that is latent or potential. Under a given set of conditions, a process may occur in most people of a given type, but rarely if ever will it occur in all persons at all points in time. Conversely, the tendency for the process to occur in any one person is only a tendency: it has a relative frequency of occurrence for that person in each of a class of situations. It may be a tendency that occurs fairly often, as in a disposition to be interested in other persons, or it may occur rarely, as in a specific phobia.

The above discussion has been presented in very general terms. A full exposition would include an explicit statement of the components of the situation or the conditions to which a person is responding. It would discriminate between the focal stimulus and the background stimuli, the latter including the physical situation, the experimenter, the instructions, the effects from preceding stimuli, etc. However, the main point remains: persons studying processes and persons concerned with traits must work with the same basic data, the observations of the responses of persons in particular settings. Furthermore, all students of personality are confronted with problems of measurement, the only difference being that some problems may be more critical for one type of research than for the other. The experimenter is measuring when he studies a process and must be concerned with matters of generalizability (or reliability) and validity.

The main body of this chapter will be devoted to the consideration of several problems in personality measurement. While each problem may be stated in abstract terms, it will usually have concrete significance for most, if not all, situations in which personality is being measured. The problems have arisen out of empirical work rather than from an armchair critique.

PROBLEM 1: THE INADEQUACY OF DEFINITIONS

Most of the variables in personality theories have definitions that are insufficient from the viewpoint of measurement. The limitations stem primarily from the nature of personality: its variables are not as intuitively obvious as some of the basic dimensions of physics nor as tied to specific operations as other dimensions in the natural sciences. Moreover, the observations generating personality concepts are made in the clinic or in the unsystematic world of everyday experience, places in which it is difficult to specify the antecedent conditions with any precision.

With a few exceptions which will be considered later, personality variables tend to be of two kinds: intuitive or informal generalizations and systematic constructs. Variables of the first kind are labeled by a word from lay language, such as dominance or anxiety. They may have no verbal definition, leaving their meaning to be conveyed by the materials used in their measurement, or they may be defined in everyday, non-technical terms and illustrated by references to common observations outside the clinic. Occasionally, some effort is made to restrict the label by ruling out some common usages or connotations.

As usually presented, variables identified in this general way are really impossible to measure precisely. In spite of any efforts to delimit the notion, such traits are typically too broad and vague; the theorist hopes that the particular flavor the dimension has for him will emerge from its context, from the more or less loosely structured framework in which it is discussed. Even variables that have been as carefully described as Murray's (1937) needs cover a considerable range of behaviors, stimuli, and settings. For example, the need for Achievement may have any of a number of foci, according to such considerations as a person's interests. It may take a variety of forms, including not only accomplishing but also manipulating, organizing, aspiring, competing, and persevering.

An indirect consequence of the breadth of the conceptualization of the typical personality variable is that its definition is not sufficiently explicit and specific. The delineation usually fails to indicate the stimulus conditions in conjunction with which the dimension may be assessed. While this unfortunate omission may stem from an assumption that these conditions are self-evident, it tends to suggest that the appearance of the behavior coded by the variable is spontaneous or internally generated regardless of the external setting. In addition, it unfortunately permits the experimenter to use any of a wide variety of conditions for his assessment, and thus greatly decreases the possibility of comparability of measurements in different research studies.

The usual definition also provides no rules for differentiating the given variable from others. The same response may have several interpretations. For example, active participation in an intellectual discussion might seem to demonstrate one or more of several needs: achievement, defendence, dominance, exposition, exhibition, order, recognition, or understanding. Where one response, taken by itself, is an insufficient basis for classifying and estimating the strength of a disposition, the formulation of the variable should contain specifications of the minimum unit of behavior from which it is possible to make such differential and quantitative judgments.

A second kind of personality variable is that which is identified by a technical term not defined in the abridged dictionary, a word coined for a special purpose. Examples are "anality," "incongruence," or "endocathection." Variables designated in this way have one important advantage over those of the first kind: while they are less readily comprehended, they have less surplus meaning derived from literary and loose common parlance. In other respects, they typically suffer the same difficulties as the other sort of dimension.

Why are personality variables so inadequately defined? One source of the difficulty resides in the peculiar nature of the subject matter of personality. Our everyday existence requires us to develop a series of first-order principles to guide our interactions with other people. Hence the personality theorist not only must determine the accuracy of these primitive propositions and conceptualizations but must also go beyond these in his scientific work and deal with problems at a higher level of abstraction than those first encountered by scientists in other fields, such as geology, geography, and astronomy (Scriven, 1956).

What consequences for measurement stem from this state of affairs? First, it is extremely unlikely that any personality variable possessing the usual broad label and definition can be comprehensively appraised by any single technique. The very diversity of potential forms and loci of manifested behavior falling within the territory embraced by the term renders this possibility most improbable. Second, these conditions prevent the investigator from being able to determine in any systematic manner the degree to which his measurement operations comprehend the variable. A related obstacle is encountered when he seeks to learn whether his measurements contain variance from extraneous, irrelevant sources (a matter which will be discussed shortly).

How can this problem be met by the investigator whose research interests require him to measure a variable defined in one of these ways? From what has been said above, it would follow that his first step must be to prepare a complete statement of the variable. Such an explication may well include a word or phrase for economical identification of the variable (rather than some abstract symbol such as a Greek letter). It should then go on to specify the responses subsumed under the variable and the one or more sets of conditions under which these responses may be observed for purposes of measurement.

These specifications should include not only the environmental setting but also the internal state of the person. The description should also bring out the basis for estimating the strength of the disposition. The basis may be any of several: frequency of a single common response (e.g., talkativeness may be determined by the proportion of time a person talks when in the presence of another), frequency of an unusual response, perhaps as presence or absence (e.g., paranoid tendency might be indicated by a single, clear-cut manifestation of a complete misinterpretation of another's behavior), or quality, in instances where greater strength of the disposition is defined by a different response than that indicating a lower level of the variable.

In delineating a personality variable, the investigator must make explicit both the high and the low end of his continuum. Many traits, especially those referring to neurotic or other pathological dispositions, are identified solely by the more overt and noticeable pole. For example, what is the opposite of rigidity? Is it inconsistency, conformity, stimulus-bound behavior, flexibility, or adaptability? Furthermore, some continua should run from one form of maladaptation through adaptive responses to an opposite type of maladjustment. A continuum having compulsive concern with minutiae at one end should extend through appropriate emphasis on both details and overall considerations to preoccupation with wholes at the other. (Compare the scales described in Cartwright, Kirtner, and Fiske, 1963.)

This conceptual problem should be differentiated from the operational aspect. Many scales are designed to measure the extent of a person's tendency to show a particular kind of behavior which in the extreme is maladaptive. On some of these scales, it may be that the optimal point is at a low score but not a zero score; a complete or almost complete absence of such dispositions may be indicative of an inclination toward an opposed pole which is also maladaptive.

When an investigator has such a delineation of his variable, he will be able to judge the degree of congruence between his concept and any actual or planned set of operations for measuring the variable. He can determine not only the extent to which a single test or instrument embraces the domain of the concept but also the probability that the procedure will produce measurements with variance from irrelevant sources. Investigators working in this way will tend to emphasize relatively narrow concepts, a tendency that is clearly desirable as long as such concepts can be shown to have significant relationships with other meaningful variables.

There are some personality variables that do not fall into either of the two classes discussed above. These are variables defined in terms of specific operations: for example, movement as noted in Rorschach responses, manifest anxiety as measured by the Taylor scale, and leveling tendency as determined by the Squares Test. From the measurement view, these are ideal variables: the congruence between each concept and its operations is perfect. The investigator using such variables can immediately turn to two types of questions: What are the psychometric properties of the variable? What is the theoretical significance of the concept? The first question can be answered in the usual ways, for example by determining the intercorrelations of the part scores (which may be the responses summed to obtain the final index) and by determining the stability of the index over time. The second question can be studied by empirical investigations of the relationships between this variable and others with which it has apparent similarity or postulated theoretical connections. The problem of inadequacy of definition could be completely avoided by restricting experimental work to promising variables of this kind. Such an approach to the scientific study of personality may well advance the field more than persistent efforts to subject to empirical test theoretical propositions about concepts so broadly defined that any one set of measurement operations can reflect only a tiny portion of their domains.

PROBLEM 2: THE PROBABILISTIC NATURE OF RESPONSE TENDENCIES

Personality is concerned with tendencies, with dispositions, rather than with such all-or-none, present-or-absent matters as: "Does this person own a car?" "Does he speak English?" or "Can he define 'mantis'?" More exactly, the strength of a personality variable in a given person is indexed by the proportion of times that he makes a particular response in a specified situation. In any situation, a person can be observed to make different responses at different times; he has many potential responses available to him. To give but one example, Weinar, Brown, and Kaplan (1956) have shown that, when so instructed, a person can continue to give new responses to the Rorschach ink-blots when the set of cards is presented to him several times in succession. The reponses observed on any one occasion are only a sample of potential responses.

This problem has qualitative and quantitative aspects. In a relatively unstructured situation, responses indicative of discrete variables compete. Faced with a Rorschach card, a person may give a response determined by color or one determined by shading. The emission of one interpretation may inhibit the elicitation of the other (Fiske, 1959). Hence the proportions of observed responses falling into different categories are not independent of each other but, rather, show the relative strengths of the several dispositions. In principle, two persons may have the same strength of one tendency but have different proportions of responses manifesting the disposition because of differences in the strengths of one or more other variables. Hence relatively unstructured techniques yield basic data of the form; "tendency A is stronger than tendency B in this individual today."

For more fruitful comparisons of persons with respect to a single variable, the situation must be structured so that the observed responses can be scored to provide an estimate of that variable. Even under such a condition, much variability of responses over time is common. On tests commonly used to assess personality, the proportions of responses repeated on a second testing after an interval of one or more weeks vary from .16 to .80. There is the additional complication that, for each separate procedure, reliable individual differences are usually found in the extent of variability in responses over time. Such differences appear to be associated with the specific instrument, or at least with a type of instrument, rather than themselves indicating a general characteristic of the individual. Previous papers have discussed these matters at considerable length and have presented the findings of many research studies on this topic (see Fiske, 1961, and sources cited there). Instead of repeating such material, this section will examine the implications of the problem for the measurement of personality.

Measurements based on observed responses in unstructured situations have low general utility. They can be used to determine whether a variable is predominant over other variables in one sort of subject but not in another. They can also be used to isolate types of subjects, each type being identified by a relative order of strengths for a set of variables. On the other hand, they cannot be used with any confidence for ordering individuals on a single continuum taken without regard for possible competing variables. Conditions which do not constrain responses are a striking instance of incongruence between concept and measure resulting from the intrusion of irrelevant sources of variance.

Probably even more serious is the question of the extent to which the index obtained in such conditions embraces the total domain of the concept. If the definition of the variable specifies particular antecedent conditions, an index based on a setting where the determinants of the responses cannot be made explicit is clearly questionable, if not inadequate. The more completely an investigator has defined a variable, the less likely it is that he will be satisfied with measurements in unstructured settings.

In both unstructured and structured testing situations, the rare response is less stable than the common one. Idiosyncratic responses are less likely to be repeated than popular ones. The occurrence of an unusual response can be used as evidence for the presence of a disposition, although the absence of that response does not necessarily indicate a low strength for that tendency. Note, however, that an unusual response can occur in individuals varying widely in strength of disposition, the observation only indicating that the strength is above some minimal level.

In structured procedures presenting the appropriate setting for assessing a given variable, the variability problem takes the form of instability of obtained measurements. The scores for any one day may have high homogeneity but have an unsatisfactorily low correlation with scores obtained on another day. The set of responses given by a subject on one day is influenced by factors affecting that set of responses while other factors affect the set given on the second testing. Here the extraneous variance, while systematic, is not readily attributed to other personality variables; rather, it is due to the lack of experimental control over the subjects' experiences prior to the testing. Such factors obviously reduce the correspondence between the measurements and the concept.

How can an investigator cope with the problem of the probabilistic nature of response tendencies as it affects measurements? Two possibilities are available. The preferred approach is to look for sets of stimuli (items) and for testing conditions that will yield scores of appropriate stability. Of course, the investigator must estimate the degree of stability that the actual variable possesses. Everyday observation indicates that personality variables should not be construed as highly stable dispositions, unvarying over time. While a case could be made for maximizing the stability of the measurements pertinent to a variable so that test stability was considerably higher than the postulated stability of the variable, such an effort would seem certain to reduce the congruence of test and variable, especially for fluctuating variables such as mood.

A second mode of coping with the problem is expensive and therefore less practical: one could administer a test on each of several occasions, to minimize the contribution of bias associated with any single day. In the abstract, this is the ideal approach, however its drawbacks are several. To gain access to subjects on several occasions not only is costly and difficult but also the effects on responses of repeated exposures to the test materials must be considered. This orientation therefore deserves the expenditure of considerable time and effort to determine its potential value.

Studies of repeated testing have recently been made by Kenneth Howard whose unpublished results are cited here by his permission. He has administered some standard personality inventories to several groups three or four times with intervals of several days to a week between each successive pair of trials. First, as one might expect, he found increasing stability with more trials: the third trial correlates more highly with the second trial than the second does with the first. Apparently experience with a test is associated with higher stability of responses. (Previous studies of changes in responses have shown greater change between the first and second trials than between any subsequent pair.) Second, there is a slight tendency toward greater differentiation of individuals on later trials. The average correlation between individuals tends to be lower on the third trial than on the first, especially on tests with a high level of intercorrelation on the first testing. These findings support the possibility of increasing the stability of personality measurements, and perhaps also the differentiation between individuals, by giving the subjects an opportunity to become acquainted with a test and a chance to develop a consistent mode of reacting to it. It remains to be determined whether these objectives can be accomplished in a single session with repeated testing or by some other method of familiarizing subjects with the test.

PROBLEM 3: THE SPECIFICITY OF PERSONALITY MEASUREMENTS

In the opening part of this chapter it was pointed out that a personality variable is a disposition to respond in a given way to particular stimuli in a designated setting. The section on the inadequacy of definitions stressed the breadth of typical conceptions of traits, together with a failure to specify stimuli and conditions. In contrast to the generality of most trait concepts, there is an extensive body of empirical studies demonstrating marked specificity in personality variables as commonly measured. One can search the literature in vain for clear evidence of the generality of personality traits as ordinarily construed.

Let us look first at the degree of association between separate operations. At the item level, within a single test, it is apparently possible to find moderate levels of intercorrelation. By appropriate methods of test construction, one can obtain reasonably high indices of internal consistency or homogeneity of items. While the reliability of the typical personality inventory is certainly below that of the usual test of aptitude or achievement, it is adequate for research purposes although ordinarily not high enough for dependable classification of the individual. Therefore some generality exists over items within the framework of a single instrument.

The agreement between tests purporting to assess the same personality variable is much less satisfactory. While there are instances in which two instruments of the same type (e.g., two inventories) show intercorrelations in the order of .50, the usual value is below that level. More generally, the more dissimilar the two methods of assessing a variable, the lower the correlation between them (cf. Campbell & Fiske, 1959, for examples from personality and other areas of psychology).

Most if not all procedures for measuring personality yield scores containing a high proportion of method variance. Analytically, this variance can have several sources. An obvious and not unexpected source is the person providing the data. A subject's description of himself will understandably depart from his description as provided by other people. In addition, persons in different relationships to the subject may see him differently (for an example of such effects on evaluations of pre-therapy status and of changes during therapy, see Cartwright, Kirtner & Fiske, 1963). Method factors may also be associated with type of item content, with format of items, and with test instructions. Finally, there is variance associated with the total setting, with the meaning of the situation for the subject. The same subjects taking a test anonymously for research purposes may have a quite different distribution of scores than would be obtained if the test were part of the requirements for admission to a school or for employment.

Because factors associated with method introduce extraneous sources of variance, they markedly attenuate the correspondence between test and concept. In addition, they make it certain that no one instrument can be expected to provide adequate assessments of a variable unless that variable is defined essentially by the operations involved in the procedure or unless the variable is otherwise defined very narrowly.

The significance of this specificity associated with individual tests is probably underestimated by most researchers in the personality field. Yet anyone surveying the literature on any given variable—leadership, rigidity, anxiety, or any other—cannot fail to be impressed by the fact that independent methods of measurement show little if any association. It may well be that the typical personality variable as ordinarily construed will turn out to refer to a broad class of traits. Each current concept may embrace a series of dispositions serving perhaps the same function in the personality structure but appearing in different forms and patterns in different people so that there is no communality among the several discrete tendencies.

For the investigator wishing to measure a given variable, the implication of this discussion should be obvious. He should make every possible effort to determine the kinds and extent of method factors in his measuring instruments. He should also avoid the economical but dangerous practice of restricting himself to a single instrument, but rather should employ a minimum of two procedures as dissimilar in method as possible. Only when he can demonstrate comparable findings from different ways of measuring his variable can he begin to hope that he is getting at the core of his concept and is not misinterpreting systematic method variance as trait variance.

PROBLEM 4: THE DISTORTION RESULTING FROM INDIVIDUALITY

Measurements of different individuals cannot meaningfully be compared unless the conditions have been identical for the several applications of the procedure (Fiske & Butler, 1963). Two balloons containing the same amount of gas will have different sizes if one is in the sun and one is in the shade. Two persons with the same strength of a behavioral tendency may obtain different scores if the test for that disposition is given under different conditions. In measuring personality, it is usually assumed that the stimuli (items) and the situation have the same meaning for all subjects, so that any differences in scores are functions of real differences on the trait being measured. This assumption is questionable.

Consider first the interpretations of the words used in rating scales or inventories. Loehlin (1961) has provided evidence for individual differences in ascribing meanings to descriptive adjectives. Similar differences in the interpretation of inventory items have been reported by Eisenberg (1941).

At present, there is no standard method for determining the extent to which the items possess communality of meaning. Work on this problem is currently in progress by the author. He is developing a rationale for assessing the homogeneity of persons over items, the dual or transpose of the usual homogeneity of items over persons. Preliminary data suggest that these two types of homogeneity are empirically independent of each other; i.e., one may be low when the other is high.

Individual differences in the meaning of the test situation are another source of possible distortion of measurements. Schachtel (1945) discussed "subjective definitions of the Rorschach test situation and their effect upon performance." Among the many factors affecting Rorschach responses as outlined by Miller (1953) are the subject's reaction to the examiner and to the test setting. An extensive discussion of these and related problems has been published by Sarason (1954). While these writers have emphasized one test, the problem exists not only for other projective tests but also for interviews, inventories, and other methods of assessing personality.

Finally, there is the theoretical problem of individuality in the manifestation of a trait within different persons and in the role played by that trait within diverse personality structures. The nomothetic approach assumes that there is sufficient communality among individuals with respect to various traits to permit meaningful comparisons. This fundamental postulate is more an article of faith than a demonstrated empirical fact. Even if there is a reasonable basis for accepting this basic axiom in the scientific study of personality, it is unlikely that a given trait has the same position in the personality structures of all persons. For example, the need for achievement will have a more important place and more significant interrelationships with other variables in a person for whom this need is of much greater than average strength. The investigator studying this variable must consider not only whether differences in its importance can distort observed measurements but also the possibility that the need will show qualitative differences at different levels of strength.

Two exceptions may be noted for the problem of distortion due to individuality. In the first place, techniques involving relatively unstructured situations and ambiguous stimuli capitalize on the subject's idiosyncratic interpretations and perceptions. They obviously require a highly skilled and perceptive examiner who can infer the subject's view of the test situation and can also detect specific influences unique to the given conditions, such as the effects of his own feelings toward the subject.

In the second place, the problem of individual interpretation of test items is not present in tests developed by empirical keying. In such an approach, the meaning of the item is not assumed a priori, but rather resides in obtained correlations with independent criteria (cf. Meehl, 1945). An item answered differently by paranoids and the general population can be included in a scale of paranoid tendency regardless of the apparent content of the item or of any bizarre interpretations that may occur to the paranoids. Furthermore, it makes no difference whether paranoids have different interpretations of the standard conditions for administering the scale, provided that these conditions are objectively the same for the original group and any subsequently tested group.

The investigator must face this problem of individuality in his development of the stimuli and the setting for measuring a personality variable. In most instances, he should seek manifest evidence that the situation has the same significance for all subjects and that the subjects are homogeneous in responding to the items. If a student of personality wishes to meet this latter criterion, it may be necessary for him to modify the prescriptions usually offered as guides for the construction of aptitude tests (for example, with respect to the range of endorsement values of items).

PROBLEM 5: THE PECULIAR SITUATION IN WHICH PERSONALITY IS MEASURED

Although many of the problems to be considered in this section have been mentioned earlier, their significance is so great that they deserve special attention and separate emphasis. This section concerns the unique set of conditions employed in personality testing. Since a more complete examination is being published elsewhere (Fiske & Butler, 1963), only the major outline of the issue will be presented here.

It has already been pointed out that, strictly speaking, measurements of different objects can be compared only if the same procedures were employed in making the observations so that the measurements are determined solely by the different degrees of the measured quality possessed by the various objects. Such conditions are ordinarily met in tests of ability. The instructions to the subject as well as the nature of the items make clear that ability is being assessed. Especially in our culture, subjects are familiar with such tests. They know what is meant by the notion of a "right answer," and they try to give as many as they can. The examiner attempts to structure the situation so that motivation will be optimal: he makes sure that the subjects are trying and discards the papers of those who are not; he also seeks to prevent the mobilization of anxiety, emotion, and excessive drive that could impair performance. Furthermore, it is apparent to the subject that the examiner is working with him to maximize his score. As a consequence, in ability testing there is sufficient consensus among subjects on the meaning of items, the task, and the situation so that comparisons between scores can be made with reasonable confidence.

Personality testing differs from ability testing in almost every one of these respects. The instructions do not specify that personality is being measured but rather use some innocuous phrase such as "what you are like." The subjects are told that there are no right answers, but that they should indicate what is true for them; the criteria for determining what response they should make are certainly vague. An exhortation to do one's best is not pertinent here. Even more important, the examiner and the subject are no longer working together. The examiner wants to find out something of which the subject is probably unaware, a condition that understandably generates anxiety and possibly antagonism in the subject. The whole situation is one with which the subject is not familiar; his past experience gives him little help in his attempts to cope with the task before him. These differences between the conditions for testing ability and personality undoubtedly contribute a great deal to the lower stability, lower internal consistency, and lower correlations with other variables that are generally found for measures of personality.

One way to meet this problem is to make the most of the lack of structure by determining what motivations emerge when subjects confront an ambiguous situation, classifying subjects according to the needs manifested, and building a science around the resulting typology. A better way to cope with the difficulty would seem to be to develop procedures that will elicit homogeneous interpretations by subjects but will still provide indices of the strengths of dispositions. Such procedures may set a reasonable task that the subject can willingly undertake, a task which, however, will involve responses that differentiate persons on relevant variables. Some tests of temperament and cognitive style meet these requirements. Following the instructions, the subject makes a series of perceptual judgments of apparent size, movement, etc.; examples are the color-form tests of Hess and of Thurstone, and tests indicating field dependence, equivalence range, and leveling vs. sharpening tendencies (Gardner, Holzman, Klein, Linton & Spence, 1959). Such procedures must, of course, be checked for psychometric adequacy, i.e., for homogeneity and appropriate degree of stability. One other consideration must also be raised. Even though the test and the setting are designed to avoid the problems discussed earlier in this section, the procedure may be of little or no value: it may yield scores that are unrelated to the presumed correlates of the variable under study. As our earlier consideration of specificity may have implied, some procedures may elicit stable response tendencies that are specific to a particular set of unique conditions not resembling any situation in everyday life. This problem is the topic of the next section.

PROBLEM 6: THE QUESTION OF REPRESENTATIVENESS

The preceding material implies that it may be very difficult to obtain indices that relate to the way a person manifests his dispositions in his life outside the testing room. The objective of personality measurement can be stated as the description of the subject as he usually behaves, not as he can be expected to respond in the artificial and temporary conditions of the assessment situation. In contrast, the purpose of testing ability is not such an appraisal of normal functioning, but rather the estimation of potential ability, of maximum capacity under optimal conditions. No one expects a person to use all of his intelligence in everything he says or does. Here is another possible strategy for personality measurement: perhaps one should attempt to assess a person's maximum tendency toward a particular kind of behavior under conditions designed to provoke it or to facilitate its appearance. This approach could be feasible for socially desirable traits such as cooperativeness, and possibly also for leadership or initiative. In principle, undesirable characteristics might be measured in meaningful, seemingly naturalistic situations that imposed stress on the subjects. Just as an ability test determines the upper limit of competence, so it might be possible to ascertain the upper limit of the capacities or coping mechanisms that are classified as personality traits.

In addition to the atypicality of the laboratory or testing situation, the subject is generally unfamiliar with the instructions, the stimuli, and the responses. When, in everyday life, is one asked to report how he usually feels about something, or what he usually does, or what he thinks an ink blot looks like? Perhaps of greatest importance is the limitation placed on the subject's responses. In ordinary situations, a person has considerable or complete freedom with respect to the form or structure of his behavior, and much freedom as to its content. In tests, the subject is typically restricted to choosing one response from among a limited set of alternatives, all of which may seem to be categorical, inappropriate, or unnatural for him. Thus it may be not only the unrepresentativeness of the situation and stimuli but also the atypicality of the permitted responses that reduce the possible generalization from personality measurements.

A testing instrument in which each separate item is keyed for only one variable is unrepresentative in still another respect. In most everyday situations, one tendency is more or less in competition with other tendencies, one motive may be in conflict with another—but we tend to measure only one variable at a time. This approach is probably a sound initial procedure. Eventually, however, we shall have to deal with the problem of the relative strengths of various incompatible tendencies that cannot be manifested simultaneously.

Granted that a testing situation is not representative of the situations to which an investigator wishes to generalize (Brunswik, 1956; Hammond, 1954), how serious is this potential handicap? This answer can be obtained not by armchair speculation but by empirical study. In quality control and other areas of engineering, samples of a batch of material are assessed in the laboratory to determine whether they meet certain specifications. These observations are then used as a basis for generalizations about the performance of the whole batch under conditions in the field which are quite different in many respects but which make specified demands on the material. By analogy it is suggested that, in principle, it should be possible to make measurements in a testing room that can be generalized to everyday behavior. The empirical evidence for the specificity of personality measurements, however, provides little basis for optimism about success in this endeavor. On the other hand, personality variables with narrow definitions specifying the conditions under which the tendencies may be observed may well prove amenable to such generalizations from the laboratory or testing room.

Closer scrutiny of the problem suggests that, in operational terms, it is meaningless to talk of the way a person usually behaves. It is impossible to find a single measure or a composite score that represents with complete adequacy the behavioral tendencies subsumed under one of the current trait-concepts. The best that can be done is to have an expert judge process a large and representative body of observations and protocols concerning a subject and reduce them to a single index of central tendency through an implicit weighting of the diverse data. Alternatively, a series of separate measures can be objectively combined to produce a composite score, as Vernon (1953) has proposed. Both of these approaches have clear limitations: the first is influenced by characteristics of the particular judge and the second may be biased by the nature of the specific techniques selected to contribute part-scores.

To advance the scientific study of personality, the most promising program would seem to involve a coordinated attack on the problem from both the conceptual and the measurement sides. The concepts to be used in experimental work should be delimited by explicit specification of the conditions under which the dispositions can be observed. The procedures for assessment should be designed to cover these conditions through two or more sets of operations. In this orientation, overlap between concept and operations would be maximized by restricting the statement of pertinent conditions to a set which could feasibly be built into the measurement operations. Careful design of the tests could reduce the amount of extraneous variance associated with method. The adequacy of the final battery would, of course, have to be checked empirically. The homogeneity of the battery would be evident in the intercorrelations between the scores obtained by the separate sets of operations. The possible presence of method variance could be determined by correlating the score from each set of operations with that from similar methods intended to get at other, unrelated personality concepts. Finally, the construct validity of the composite score could be tested by finding the degree to which its pattern of intercorrelations with other variables approached that postulated from the theoretical framework in which the particular concept was embedded.

PERSONALITY MEASUREMENT IN RETROSPECT AND PROSPECT

It is unfortunate that the personality theorist usually has a temperament and a set of interests and values quite different from those of the psychometrician. There has been a lack of understanding and only a minimum of interaction between the people interested in measurement and those interested in studying personalities and in conceptualizing the personality domain. Rarely is a theorist competent in measurement or a psychometrician sympathetic to the efforts of the conceptualizer. In the past, when a theorist wished to test his hypotheses, he all too often confined his techniques to subjective observations or crude and unreliable procedures.

On the other side, the psychometricians have usually sought objective, dependable criteria, often at the expense of theoretical significance. They have used available external criteria, such as clinical diagnosis or vocational membership. Sometimes they begin by emphasizing crude content validity and then rely on the bootstrap operation of item-test correlation.

Progress in the science of personality requires the rapprochement

·of theory and measurement. The theorist must define his constructs in explicit and complete form so that experimental situations can be designed to assess them. The definitional statement must include specification of the responses subsumed under the disposition, criteria for differentiating these responses from those associated with the other variables, delimitation of the conditions under which these responses may be observed, and some indication of the presumed stability of the behavioral tendency. The methodologist designing the measurement operations must use all his knowledge and ingenuity to develop a procedure that will be perceived in the same way by different subjects and will minimize the contaminating contributions of method factors, effects associated with reactions to features of the testing situation that are outside the concept as delineated. His evaluation of the adequacy of his product should employ criteria determined by the distinctive features of the domain of personality. Only by close collaboration between the theorist and the methodologist can we determine to what extent it is possible to measure personality as it is construed today.

REFERENCES

BASS, B. M., & BERG, I. A. (Eds.) *Objective approaches to personality assessment.* Princeton, N. J.: Van Nostrand, 1959.

BRUNSWIK, E. *Perception and the representative design of psychological experiments.* Berkeley: Univer. of California Press, 1956.

BUROS, O. K. (Ed.) *The fifth mental measurements yearbook.* Highland Park, N. J.: Gryphon Press, 1959.

CAMPBELL, D. T., & FISKE, D. W. Convergent and discriminant validation by the multitrait-multimethod matrix. *Psychol. Bull.,* 1959, *56,* 81-105.

CARTWRIGHT, D. S., KIRTNER, W. L., & FISKE, D. W. Method factors in changes associated with psychotherapy. *J. abnorm. soc. Psychol.,* 1963, *66,* 164-175.

CRONBACH, L. J. Report on a psychometric mission to clinicia. *Psychometrika,* 1954, *19,* 263-270.

CRONBACH, L. J. The two disciplines of scientific psychology. *Amer. Psychologist,* 1957, *12,* 671-684.

CRONBACH, L. J. *Essentials of psychological testing.* (2nd ed.) New York: Harper, 1960.

CRONBACH, L. J., & MEEHL, P. E. Construct validity in psychological tests. *Psychol. Bull.*, 1955, *52*, 281-302.

CROWNE, D. P., & STEPHENS, M. W. Self-acceptance and self-evaluative behavior. *Psychol. Bull.*, 1961, *58*, 104-121.

EISENBERG, P. Individual interpretation of psychoneurotic inventory items. *J. gen. Psychol.*, 1941, *25*, 19-40.

FISKE, D. W. Variability of responses and the stability of scores and interpretations of projective protocols. *J. proj. Tech.*, 1959, *23*, 263-267.

FISKE, D. W. The inherent variability of behavior. In D. Fiske & S. Maddi, *Functions of varied experience.* Homewood, Ill.: Dorsey, 1961. Pp. 326-354.

FISKE, D. W., & BUTLER, J. M. The experimental conditions for measuring individual differences. *Educ. psychol. Measmt.*, 1963, in press.

GARDNER, R., HOLZMAN, P. S., KLEIN, G. S., LINTON, HARRIET, & SPENCE, D. P. Cognitive control, a study of individual consistencies in cognitive behavior. *Psychol. Issues*, 1959, *1*, Whole No. 4.

GULLIKSEN, H. *Theory of mental tests.* New York: Wiley, 1950.

GUILFORD, J. P. *Psychometric methods.* (2nd ed.) New York: McGraw-Hill, 1954.

HAMMOND, K. R. Representative vs. systematic design in clinical psychology. *Psychol. Bull.*, 1954, *51*, 150-159.

JACKSON, D. N., & MESSICK, S. Content and style in personality assessment. *Psychol. Bull.*, 1958, *55*, 243-252.

LOEHLIN, J. C. Word meanings and self-descriptions. *J. abnorm. soc. Psychol.*, 1961, *62*, 28-34.

LOEVINGER, JANE. Some principles of personality measurement. *Educ. psychol. Measmt.*, 1955, *15*, 3-17.

LOEVINGER, JANE. Objective tests as instruments of psychological theory. *Psychol. Rep.*, 1957, *3*, 635-698. (Monogr. Supplement 9.)

MEEHL, P. E. The dynamics of "structured" personality tests. *J. clin. Psychol.*, 1945, *1*, 296-303.

MILLER, D. Prediction of behavior by means of the Rorschach test. *J. abnorm. soc. Psychol.*, 1953, *48*, 367-75.

MURRAY, H. A., et al. *Explorations in personality.* New York: Oxford, 1938.

SARASON, S. B. *The clinical interaction: with special reference to the Rorschach.* New York: Harper, 1954.

SCHACHTEL, E. G. Subjective definitions of the Rorschach test situation and their effect upon performance. Contributions to an understanding of Rorschach's test, III. *Psychiat.*, 1945, *8*, 419-448.

SCRIVEN, M. A possible distinction between traditional scientific disciplines and the study of human behavior. In H. Feigl and M. Scriven (Eds.), *The foundations of science and the concepts of psychology and psychoanalysis.* Minneapolis: Univer. of Minnesota Press, 1956. PP. 330-339.

Technical recommendations for psychological tests and diagnostic techniques. *Psychol. Bull. Suppl.,* 1954, *51,* 201-238. (Part 2 of No. 2.)

VERNON, PHILIP E. *Personality tests and assessments.* London: Methuen, 1953.

WEINER, L., BROWN, E., & KAPLAN, B. A comparison of the ability of normal and brain injured subjects to produce additional responses on a second administration of the Rorschach test. *J. clin. Psychol.,* 1956, *12,* 89-91.

WOLFLE, D., LIKERT, R., MARQUIS, D., & SEARS, R. Standards for appraising psychological research. *Amer. Psychologist,* 1949, *4,* 320-328.

17

The Clinical Method
in Personality Assessment

Sol L. Garfield

Clinical observations of behavior have resulted in speculations and formulations of primary importance in the development of the study of personality as a major area in psychology. Although a number of psychologists out of scientific zeal have at times been critical of the contributions of clinicians, many if not most of the ideas, concepts, and theoretical formulations in the area of personality have come from clinicians (Hall & Lindzey, 1957). The emphasis in contemporary psychology on objectivity, quantitative methodology, and operational definitions, however, has without doubt led many psychologists to be highly skeptical of the contributions of the clinician to the behavioral sciences (Eysenck, 1961; Sarbin, Taft & Bailey, 1960). Such value judgments have contributed to the relatively low scientific status of clinical methods despite wide acceptance of their practical utility.

While it is true that there are currently many competing personality theories derived from clinical work with emotionally disturbed individuals, the mere variety of views alone cannot explain the negative orientation toward the clinical method. A number of contrasting or conflicting views also exist in other areas of psychology such as the field of learning, but in this area, competition of ideas is viewed in a very different light. The critical difference may be in the type of concepts used, the methods employed, and the types of formulations or predictions offered in clinical appraisals.

Clinicians are characteristically attracted to theories which postulate internal personality processes and structures only indirectly open to observation. Working as he does with individuals about whom he must ordinarily make a variety of predictions and recommendations, the clinician is reluctant to depend exclusively upon his observations of his client's behavior during the brief diagnostic encounter. Rather, he prefers to assume that from the sample of behavior he has observed he can draw inferences regarding the client's future behavior.

Critical non-clinicians generally contest this approach to the study of behavior and the assumptions which underlie it. Behaviorists object to the postulation of internal structures and processes on the ground that these cannot be translated into operational terms. Specialists in measurement decry the absence of adequate predictive or concurrent validity data to support inferences the clinician makes from tests, from nosological categories or from personality theories. Experimentalists find little support for such convictions as clinicians advance regarding the factors which determine a subject's response to a test stimulus.

Thus the battle is joined. The clinicians note the discomfort of the non-clinician when he is faced with idiographic data and the task of making a decision about an individual. The non-clinicians observe the lack of cogency of the clinician's formal defence of his inferential judgments. Yet beneath the apparent acrimony with which the debate is carried out in the professional literature, a large measure of mutual respect exists. The psychologist-clinician may lack the cachet of full scientific support of his operations but he demonstrates the security necessary to act decisively in the face of human crises with such tools as he possesses. The psychologist-scientist may have little comfort to offer his fellow man at present, but he represents the aspirations for a future in which the contributions of psychology to human welfare are dependably based on sound empirical evidence.

In terms of what has been said, it is pertinent first of all to attempt a detailed description of how the clinical process appears to function when used in the study of personality. From this we can proceed to a discussion in greater depth of the features which characterize the clinical method or approach—how it differs from other methods, the strengths and weaknesses of this approach, and its place in the contemporary scene. Attention will be focused on general features or aspects of the clinical method rather than on specific techniques. From this point of view, the clinical approach includes psychotherapeutic interactions as well as those which are more traditionally labeled as diagnostic.

CLINICAL TECHNIQUES AND THE CLINICAL METHOD

The contemporary clinical psychologist uses a somewhat limited variety of techniques, a practice which reflects on the one hand greater sophistication with respect to standardization of tests and on the other a growing recognition that it is the clinician who contributes the vital ingredient to an evaluation rather than the test itself. Hence, in the formal evaluation of intellectual functioning, only two or three extensively studied tests are in wide usage, while in projective testing there is growing conviction that adding techniques in personality studies does not necessarily open additional parameters of personality for investigation. In addition to standardized tests and the at least semi-standardized projective techniques, the clinical psychologist uses more frankly subjective techniques, many of which are common to other clinical disciplines. They include the observation of behavior, the accumulation of data concerning the client's personal and social history and various kinds of verbal interactions in the framework of the interview. Since most of these methods are relatively well-known (Garfield, 1957; Watson, 1951) detailed descriptions of them will not be presented here. Rather, the emphasis will be on how such methods are used in the clinical situation and on those features which appear to be most characteristic of the clinical approach to personality.

Before proceeding further, it may be worthwhile to attempt some differentiation between techniques used by the clinician and the clinical method or approach. Many of the studies of the efficiency of clinical prediction and of the validity of clinical procedures have focused on specific techniques. For example, studies of diagnostic interpretations made from specific test data or scores have been viewed as data indicating limitations in the clinical method (Grant, Ives & Ranzoni, 1952; Holtzman & Sells, 1954; Little & Shneidman, 1959; Meehl, 1954, 1960). It should be made clear however, that many of these studies are not really evaluations of the clinical method as it will be described here, but evaluations of a specific test or technique. As will be demonstrated later, the clinical method is not synonymous with a particular test or technique which clinicians may employ. In drawing this distinction, the intention is not to dismiss the results of studies which are critical of the predictive efficiency of the clinician utilizing specific techniques, although one finds positive as well as negative findings in the literature (Chambers & Hamlin, 1957; Garfield, 1957; Silverman, 1959). It is important however, to differentiate the validation of specific techniques from the validation or appraisal of a clinician using clinical methods and procedures in a clinical situation. The two are not identical. A Rorschach protocol by itself may show relatively little indication of severe personality disturbance but the way in which the patient handles the card or inspects it, or interacts with the examiner while responding may provide significant clues.

DESCRIPTION OF THE CLINICAL METHOD

A given test or technique, whether it be the Wechsler Adult Intelligence Scale or the Rorschach, can be used as a more or less straightforward psychometric tool, or it can be used in a clinical manner. What are the attributes of the clinical process which can be delineated and which appear to differentiate it from the psychometric method? An example may help to clarify our discussion. Therefore, let us examine how a clinician may employ a standard intelligence test in the evaluation of a given patient. While he will be interested in the level of performance as reflected in the IQ, this aspect alone can be viewed as being within the traditional psychometric approach. Computing a score and interpreting it in the light of a table of norms requires little clinical judgment, for as Holt (1961) has observed, clinical judgment is exclusive of the combination of quantitative data or scores. The test becomes a clinical tool or method when the clinician becomes a part of the analytical and interpretive process. It is this combining of psychologist and test that leads one to consider the process as uniquely clinical in approach. The focus shifts from the test to the psychologist (clinician) and here we have what is really the essence of the clinical method, regardless of the techniques used. Lest this seem somewhat vague, let us analyze what the psychologist does in this process and what he contributes to the study of personality.

First, the clinician observes the subject from the time he meets him until the examination is over. To the psychometrically oriented psychologist, this may seem to have little to do with the formal testing of intelligence. Nevertheless, the clinician is constantly observing the individual and instead of remaining detached and objective so as not to be influenced by what he sees, he attempts to utilize his observations to the fullest extent possible. How the patient responds to his greeting, what kind of an interaction takes place before the examination begins, and all of the other behaviors evident in response to the examiner and to the test stimuli are all potential data for analysis and interpretation by the clinician. These all become part of the testing situation as seen by the clinician and consequently are integral parts of the clinical method. Some of the behaviors which can be observed in a standard testing situation are rather commonplace and need only be listed here. These include such obvious aspects as how the subject responds to the examiner. Does he appear anxious, deferential, self-critical or antagonistic? Does he tend to seek praise or reinforcement from the examiner when he is able to give an appropriate response? Does he appear to be fearful in response to items which seem difficult? Does he become easily irritated or frustrated? These are some of the observations which the clinician may routinely make. The significance which the clinician assigns to these behaviors will, of course, be influenced by his own theoretical framework and experience.

In addition to making note of the relatively overt behavior of the patient, the clinician may interpret this by drawing inferences from what is manifest about underlying bases for and motivations of the patient's behavior. He may interpret the pedantic verbalization of a patient as being an indication of the need to impress the examiner, or as a use of intellectual ability to alleviate anxiety. In a similar manner, the clinician may view certain types of delayed or incorrect responses as symptoms of anxiety and inefficiency in relation to stress. A client's misperceptions of certain types of stimuli may constitute the basis for inferences about conflicts within the individual. These are just a few examples of how the clinician utilizes his knowledge of theory to make inferences about the personality of the examinee.

Thus, the theoretical framework which the clinician uses as a guide to his observations and formulations about the case at hand is a variable of importance. It is basic to the "cognitive activity of the clinician"—the ingredient which truly distinguishes the clinical method from other methods of studying personality. What the clinician is sensitive to, what he looks for and how he evaluates the various aspects of observable behavior are heavily influenced by his theoretical views. It should also be clear, however, that two individuals with the same orientation may differ in minor or occasionally in significant respects in how they actually evaluate the client and in the final conclusions they reach.

The clinician also relies on his own experience with techniques and with personality difficulties. This includes both formal types of experience such as knowledge of research literature on techniques and psychopathology as well as the clinician's own first hand professional experience. In the past, clinicians were perhaps more inclined to rely on their own experience than on research reports of others. Emphasis on one's own experience is indeed a most interesting aspect of the clinical decision making process. In essence, the observation of Patient A seems to resemble in some ways the clinician's previous observation of Patient B. In some instances the clinician can list precisely why this is so. In other instances there may be some awareness but the conscious cues may be limited or vague. In any event, the clinician may be strongly influenced in his own judgment by his own previous experience and success with what he believes are similar types of cases—regardless of the experience of others. If he has had experience with a number of similar cases then obviously he may have a high degree of confidence in his interpretations and their validity. Regardless of his level of confidence, however, it should be underlined that the clinician brings to bear in his analysis of any case all of his previous clinical experience with similar as well as with other types of cases. If he has been particularly impressed with certain behaviors in a given class or type of patient, any perception of similar behaviors in a patient will play an important role in his diagnostic and therapeutic decisions.

On the basis of his experience with various groups of patients, therefore, the clinician will be sensitive to certain types of test responses and behaviors in the clinical situation. Erratic performance, discrepancies in quality, particular patterns of response, and unusual types of responses will be cues for diagnostic inferences about the patient. Although certain general patterns derived from previous research or personal experience may be used as guidelines, the clinician does not necessarily operate as an actuary or computer. A schizophrenic patient for example, may show either disorganization in his thought processes or a comparative lack of disorganization. He may do poorly on some tests of concentration or he may do well. One peculiar response in one test record may be given heavy weight in the clinician's judgment about a particular patient whereas a virtually identical response may be played down in analyzing the record of another patient. In a similar way, some patients with brain damage may show markedly poor performance on a test of immediate memory, whereas others may score well on this particular type of test. Some records may present a congruent pattern in terms of the patient's personality and behavior, whereas another may reveal many types of inconsistencies and contradictory findings. In the latter instance, it is the clinician's task to attempt to give meaning to these apparent inconsistencies and to advance formulations to explain them. In this type of task we have an example of one of the important and unique aspects of the clinical method—the use of the clinician in evaluating and integrating diverse types of data.

The clinician's role and objectives in the evaluation of a patient, then, are quite different from those of the psychometrician or measurement expert. He is not interested solely in the performance of the subject, as measured by a quantitative score. In fact his orientation is quite critical of what at times appears to be an overly narrow emphasis by others on operational definitions of performance. The clinician would not necessarily agree with those who would equate the intellectual ability and functioning of several individuals simply because they gained identical scores on a standardized test. He is much more interested in evaluating patterns of performance, qualitative differences, and generally in attempting to explain or interpret the total performance. For example, let us consider three individuals who have each secured IQ's of 70 on the WAIS. From one point of view their performances are the same. Each of these individuals functions poorly and each would be considered as mentally defective by some psychometricians. However, in spite of what may be considered as operationally equivalent levels of intellectual performance, the clinically oriented psychologist would probably describe these three clients in discriminably different ways. In case A, he might be impressed by the sincere desire of the patient to cooperate, his apparent difficulty at times in verbalizing the word he is seeking, his slowness and difficulty on certain types of visual-motor tasks, a trend toward perseveration of response, and an average performance on two verbal and untimed tests. Because of the particular pattern and degree of variability in subtest performance, Case A obtained an IQ of 70. However, the clinician's diagnostic impression could be that of a possible organic brain syndrome.

In Case B there is also evident a pattern of marked variability among the subtest scores; among other things, the subject obtains an above average score on Vocabulary and an extremely low score on Comprehension. Some of his language is stilted; he uses words inappropriately; he fails simple items and occasionally succeeds on more difficult items. His attention is variable but generally poor; he combines unrelated and extraneous material; he exhibits stereotyped mannerisms and some of his responses are judged to be peculiar. In this case, the clinician might decide that he is dealing with a seriously disturbed individual of above average intellectual ability who, in terms of current diagnostic convention, would be classified among the schizophrenias.

Finally, in case C we encounter still a different pattern. All of the subtest scores are below average, the variability is modest, the language used is relatively simple, the subject does better on non-verbal items, he responds well to praise from the examiner, and there do not appear to be any unusually deviant or pathological responses. In this instance, the clinician would be inclined to diagnose the individual as mentally retarded. Thus, in our three hypothetical cases with identical IQ's, the clinical evaluation would lead to three different diagnostic conclusions—and what is of great importance, three different plans for future care.

As indicated in our preceding illustration, the clinician is interested in understanding what is responsible for a given response, and not merely in the score assigned to the response. Two responses which receive identical scores may reflect quite different styles of response or in other ways provide clues about the individual's personality. As Schafer (1948, pp. 17-18) has pointed out, responses to test items are "verbalized end-products of thought processes" initiated by the test stimuli:

"A test response is not a score; scores, where applicable, are abstractions designed to facilitate intra-individual and inter-individual comparisons, and as such they are extremely useful in clinical testing. However, to reason—or do research—only in terms of scores and score-patterns is to do violence to the nature of the raw material. The scores do not communicate the responses in full. . . . The subject communicates more than he willingly intends; he also communicates more than can be scored. Test responses, because they represent the subject's style of thinking, allowed for inferences concerning predominant features of character make-up."

Hence, the clinician, when he uses a particular test, is also using more than the test alone. He himself, as an observing, hypothesis formulating and organizing mechanism, is an important part of the evaluation process. While he will be influenced by quantitative and statistical findings pertinent to the test itself, he generally will not feel obligated to apply such information in a routine manner. Generally, he will "work in terms of contexts of responses, checking the implications of any one response pattern against the implications of all other responses and patterns. When enough patterns can be found having one or two major implications in common, an interpretation becomes possible" (Schafer, 1948, p. 20). Usually the clinician will look for an emerging and congruent pattern of response which he can interpret on the basis of his experience and theoretical knowledge.

While the clinical psychologist generally seeks patterns of response which appear to fit together, he is not bound by rigid rules or procedures. This may be either a positive or negative attribute, depending upon how one views the situation. In some instances, as has been indicated, one particular finding may be considered important enough to over-ride several other findings. However, in another instance, the clinician may decide to give more weight to the several findings and to undervalue the significance of what appears to be a highly deviant or pathological response. While this behavior thus appears to differ from a rigorous statistical weighting of various types of response, it should not be viewed as merely capricious behavior on the part of the clinician. He is bringing his experience and sensitivity to bear on the problem of evaluating the diverse cues provided by means of his interaction and examination of the patient. In the one case, he is moved to give greater weight to a particular response than he apparently does in a second and comparable case. In trying to analyze this seeming contradiction, or inconsistency, we are obliged to face some complex and difficult features of the clinical process of inference. Why does the clinician respond in the particular way that he does? In most instances, regardless of whether he ultimately proves to be correct or incorrect in his final formulation, the clinician can give a fairly adequate account of his reasoning. In other circumstances, his account is vague and unconvincing. He may allude to the particular way a response was verbalized or to the unusual way it was presented. In other instances, it is more difficult to verbalize clearly or communicate what is set off in the clinician or what it is which makes him "feel" that a particular response is really the key to the problem at hand. In the latter instances what the clinician experiences appears to be something akin to empathy, resonance or dimly perceived insight. One is led to agree with Meehl (1954) that this delicate process cannot be considered as being akin to subliminal perception. The clinician *is* responding to certain cues and he *is* aware of something that influences his perception and judgment about the case at hand. However, difficulty is encountered in putting his marginal perceptions into words that communicate adequately to others just what cues he is responding to and why. In this connection, the writer recalls a clinical staff meeting at which a patient was presented. In the discussion which followed, everyone but the clinical director agreed that the patient showed little severe psychopathology and could be best described as an "inadequate personality." The clinical director stated that there was something about the patient which made him feel that he was a catatonic schizophrenic and that he would expect him at some point in his life, to show florid catatonic symptoms. When asked why he felt this way, he exhibited some hesitation, but finally made some reference to the posture, facial stare and faintly perceived lack of feeling or warmth on the part of the patient—all of which impressed the staff very little. The patient was then released from the hospital but was returned in three weeks in a catatonic stupor. This case by itself proves nothing, of course. The clinical director was not always right, and we kept no account of his particular pattern of "hits" or "misses." However, it does illustrate how the clinician responds to cues and his difficulty in verbalizing and communicating the cues to which he responds. The process here is quite likely similar to what may occur in the early stages of the creative process of hypothesis formation and in related creative operations. In some instances, there may occur a sudden flash of insight, the "eureka" phenomenon. In others, however, it appears to be a more groping and dimly perceived process.

The preceding paragraphs perhaps may strike some non-clinical readers as mostly a statement of faith. It must be acknowledged that detailed inquiries into the clinical process are relatively few and what has been attempted here is a necessarily brief description of what appears to occur in the process of making a clinical judgment.

A thoughtful appraisal of clinical judgment as a type of disciplined inquiry dealing mainly with verbal meanings has recently been presented by Holt (1961), and several carefully reasoned descriptions of clinician's operations have been published by Meehl (1954, 1959, 1960). Meehl, incidentally, although critical of some aspects of clinical methodology, has been incorrectly identified as opposed to clinical methods.

BASIC FEATURES OF THE CLINICAL PROCESS

From our preceding discussion, that has attempted to illustrate how the clinical process operates and to distinguish between a psychometric and a clinical approach, we can also gain a few insights concerning the more basic and unique aspects of the clinical method. First, the clinical method relies heavily on the observations of the clinician. Whatever the clinician sees constitutes potential data and conceivably may influence his final judgment about the case. Underlined here is the "sensitivity" of the clinician in his role as a participant-observer. "Listening with the third ear" (Reik, 1948) and "seeing with the third eye" (Meehl, 1960) are phrases that have been used to describe this observational and reactive sensitivity of the clinician. Observation, guided by experience, research and theory is an unequivocally important component of the clinical method.

Second, and basic to the entire undertaking, is the clinician's own personality—his abilities, skills, sensitivity to others, his past experience, motivational structure and defenses. While we give a certain amount of lip service to this as a variable in clinical work, relatively little research has been done on the clinician as a variable. Yet, we are beginning to accumulate some data which suggests that clinicians differ in therapeutic efficiency with certain types of patients and that they differ also in diagnostic acumen (Chambers & Hamlin, 1957; Truax, 1962; Whitehorn & Betz, 1954, 1960). This should come as no surprise to psychologists who have long been aware of individual differences. Nevertheless, most discussions of clinical methods have tended to focus on the techniques used—Rorschach, MMPI, psychoanalysis—rather than how they are actually used by a specific clinician (Garfield, 1957; Watson, 1951; Meehl, 1960).

A third aspect of the clinical method is its flexibility. The clinician in his contacts with the patient will commonly use some form of verbal interchange in addition to his observations of behavior. Generally, this takes place in an interview situation but is not necessarily limited to this context. The flexibility is manifested in that the clinician, in trying to secure information and understanding about the patient, proceeds in any direction he chooses and follows whatever line of inquiry seems appropriate. Thus, with one patient he may assume a passive role and let the client freely present his story. With another individual he may ask specific questions and even offer confrontations as a means of structuring and guiding the interaction. If necessary a number of interviews or tests can be used to secure additional information. Areas which do not appear to be of great consequence may be granted little attention, while significant issues can be pursued intensively. In contrast to some of the techniques utilized in the study of personality, the clinician can adapt his approach to that of a particular individual. In this connection it is important to point out that the adaptation of the clinician to the particular individual at hand is also important in the securing of information. If a given patient is extremely tense, the clinician must utilize approaches to the patient which will put him at ease and encourage his confiding in the clinician. In a similar vein, if the clinician feels that a given individual is deliberately distorting information, he may convey this feeling to the patient in the hope of thereby securing more adequate data. Flexibility operates both in terms of the modes of relating to the patient and in terms of what and how information is sought. It should be reiterated that here again the therapist's theoretical views and his experience will guide his clinical interactions.

A fourth distinguishing feature of the clinical method is its emphasis on the individual case (Murray, 1938). In many other areas of psychology and in research investigations generally, there is an emphasis on group trends and on the importance of securing adequate samples as a basis for inference. However, the primary emphasis in clinical work and with the clinical method is the emphasis on trying to understand and to work with a specific individual. The aim of the clinical method is to understand the individual person in relation to some desired goal, usually treatment or some other form of disposition. The clinician is interested in a particular person at a particular time, and only secondarily in persons or personalities in general. This point of view is necessarily accompanied by an emphasis on the uniqueness of the individual personality. While John Jones may have certain features that are shared by other individuals, only John Jones has this particular constellation and organization of personality. One may compare John Jones in certain ways with other individuals with whom some similarities and differences can be noted, but the point of reference is still that John Jones can be differentiated from these others, and is seen as a unique personality. Thus, what has come to be known as the idiographic point of view is a basic orientation with regard to the clinical method (Allport, 1937, 1961; Burton & Harris, 1955).

Closely related to the concern with the individual case and the uniqueness of the individual are certain other value systems which are revered by the clinician and criticized by the more rigorous non-clinical worker in the area of personality. This includes operations or conceptions that are sometimes referred to as global or "holistic," in which the emphasis is placed on seeing the total individual. By this emphasis the clinician implies that it is only by understanding the totality of the individual's personality that one gains an adequate or comprehensive understanding of the person. A related emphasis is that each aspect of the individual's personality is truly meaningful only when it is seen in relation to other aspects. Only from a holistic point of view, from seeing the individual as a totality, can one fully understand his behavior, his motivation and his conflicts. Worthwhile predictions for the individual can ensue only when one attains this understanding.

This point of view has been emphasized by Allport (1937, 1961) who, although primarily an academician rather than a clinician, has been perhaps the most persistent supporter of the idiographic "personalistic" point of view in psychology. From this position, one is primarily concerned with the understanding and prediction of the individual case and not with norms or statistics based on groups. Allport (1961, p. 20) has expressed this view as follows:

"To say that 85 in 100 boys having such and such a background will become delinquent is not to say that Jimmy, who has this background, has 85 in 100 chances of being delinquent. Not at all. Jimmy, as an individual, either will or will not become delinquent. There is no 85 percent chance about him. Only a complete knowledge of Jimmy will enable us to predict for sure."

The preceding discussion has attempted to highlight the clinical emphasis on understanding the "total individual." Such an emphasis has been criticized by other psychologists who believe that some actuarial basis is required for reliable understanding and prediction (Meehl, 1954; Sarbin, Taft & Bailey, 1960). If each individual is truly unique, how can one utilize past experience to understand a particular client? This, obviously, is a difficult question to answer and seems to highlight a basic difference in viewpoint between those valuing an idiographic approach and those supporting a nomothetic approach. It should be made clear, however, that the clinician's insistence on an individual frame of reference does not mean that they do not utilize general principles of behavior and personality. Rather, the implication is that general principles are utilized in a somewhat different manner and with somewhat different goals in mind. Here again an illustration may serve to clarify the issue at hand. Allport (1937) in discussing the lack of agreement among the various methods used in the Hartshorne and May studies of character, points out that a seeming inconsistency in behavior can be viewed as understandable and predictable if one focuses on the individual case. In one situation a boy (when handling money) will be honest, but in another (changing answers on an examination) he will display what appears to be dishonest behavior. However, when one investigates this case and reaches an understanding of it, the apparent inconsistency is seen in a different light. In this hypothetical case, the individual's dishonest behavior in one situation can be viewed as a manifestation of the boy's need to impress the teacher and have her regard him positively. Thus, when fully understood, the boy's behavior is meaningful and (hopefully) predictable. The frame of reference and the general traits and dimensions used in the particular study, therefore, were not appropriate ones for understanding the individual case.

Most clinical orientations, regardless of theoretical allegiance, do place primary emphasis on understanding the individual case. Even though various kinds of categorizations or generalizations pertaining to personality may be utilized in the study of the individual case, the basic orientation is an idiographic one. A profile of test scores or behavior ratings also do not suffice in this regard. They indicate how a given individual performs or is judged on various traits or attributes as compared with some norm, but they fail to give an adequate or integrated picture of the individual. From the viewpoint of the clinician, the matter of organization and integration of the components of personality are lacking in such descriptions, and it is these aspects that are crucial to understanding and describing the individual *qua* individual. It is not enough to say that an individual is intelligent, retiring and anxious. These must be unified or related as parts of a more comprehensive view of the person. There may be two individuals who are intelligent, retiring and anxious and yet they appear and behave differently.

Closely related to the preceding points is another theoretical position which receives greater emphasis in the clinical method than in most other approaches to personality, referred to usually as an emphasis on "dynamics," or the motivational structure of the person. In their desire to understand the person, clinical psychologists are interested in looking beyond the overt behavior of the individual. Why does the individual behave in ways contrary to those dictated by reality? Why does he engage persistently in what appear to be self-defeating patterns of behavior? Following the leads contributed by Freud and a host of others since his time, clinicians have sought to understand the "why's" or the "dynamics" of the individual's behavior (Munroe, 1955). At times it has appeared to some, including clinicians, that there has been an over-emphasis on "underlying" motivations and on speculations concerning the hidden causes of the patient's behavior. Nevertheless, one of the great contributions to the study of personality from the clinical field has been the exploration of motivations existing outside of awareness. The concept of unconscious motivational forces—urges, wishes, or conflicts that cannot be consciously described by the individual client—has given us a powerful conceptual tool for understanding "irrational" behavior. Clinical workers have been particularly responsive to such concepts because they have helped to provide a more comprehensive understanding of the individual case. Previous to the development of such concepts, clinicians working with disturbed individuals were prone to rely on organic explanations of disturbed behavior or to reject any attempt at understanding in favor of a descriptive frame of reference. The utilization of dynamic motivational concepts has provided what continues to be regarded by most clinicians as a fruitful, enlightening avenue to the understanding of the individual and as a highly useful set of concepts for explaining an individual's particular constellation of symptoms and behaviors. It provided a means by which the clinician could more readily integrate various divergent aspects of behavior into some meaningful totality.

The emphasis on the dynamics of behavior not only provided an important theoretical framework for appraising, interpreting and understanding personality but several clinical techniques were also products of this development. Such techniques as the interpretation of dreams, the analysis of symbols, free association, word association and others were products of the psychoanalytic movement and related theoretical developments. These developments also contributed directly or indirectly to the subsequent development of projective techniques. These, while differing among themselves in terms of the specific stimuli and rationale used, had as their major objective the securing of data about underlying motivations, conflicts and defenses. It was hypothesized that an individual subject's response to the projective stimuli may be indicative of aspects of personality of which the subject himself in unaware. Projective techniques were also considered to be methods which allowed for an integrative rather than an additive approach to personality assessment.

THE CLINICAL METHOD AND THE METHODS OF SCIENCE

The clinical method or approach has been compared with other approaches to the study of personality (Hall & Lindzey, 1957; Meehl, 1954; Sarbin, et al, 1960). As contrasted with psychometric or experimental methods, the clinical method is certainly less objective and less rigorous. Each approach has both its strengths and its limitations, and later we shall look at some of the limitations of the clinical approach. In the following paragraphs, however, the emphasis will be on some of the similarities of the clinical process to the procedures followed in scientific inquiry.

As we know, a scientific investigation begins with the formulation of a hypothesis, and with the development of procedures to secure data which will be adequate to confirm or reject the hypothesis. After the data are collected, preferably in an atmosphere of objectivity, and with the aim of reliable quantification, they are appropriately analyzed and some conclusions drawn with regard to the hypothesis tested. If the investigator's propositions appear to be supported or confirmed by his data, the investigator can place some confidence in his hypothesis, can relate it to other findings and plan additional experiments. If the findings seem not to support the hypothesis, it can be discarded or modified, depending upon other cues or information available to the investigator. Support for a hypothesis does not make it true, but plausible. Subsequent hypotheses may also "explain" the data but in a more parsimonious or comprehensive way. The results of scientific inquiry, therefore, in Dewey's terms, lead to "warranted assertions" (1938).

Something similar to this process appears to be operative in the clinical process, although it has not yet been systematically studied. The clinician appears to operate in somewhat the following manner: a client is referred because of some particular problem. On the basis of his previous experience with comparable types of problems, the clinician may begin to formulate, explicitly or otherwise, tentative hypotheses about the new patient even before he has seen him. These will to a degree guide his interview with the patient, the selection of specific tests, and his observations of the individual's behavior. As he continues in his interactions with the patient he may secure data which lead him to modify his previous hypotheses and to set up new ones. Some hypotheses may be adequate for explaining parts of the data, but may fail to provide a satisfactory explanation for all of the data availble. The clinician thus goes through a process of hypothetico-deductive reasoning until he comes up with a set of propositions which appear adequate to explain all or most of the data at hand. These "warranted assertions" are in due course integrated into a formulation about the patient. If all information appears to fit together in some meaningful manner and to explain plausibly the subject's behavior, the clinician permits himself a feeling of closure—of having successfully synthesized the various parts of the puzzle into a meaningful, comprehensive "picture" which he can communicate to others.

While the clinical process of inference thus may resemble in some respects the procedure used in scientific research, it is of course not identical with it. Much of what the clinician does may not be explicitly stated nor does he always proceed in a systematic or rigorous manner. He may be too ready to accept certain hypotheses and to disregard data that are inconsistent with these hypotheses. If he looks only for confirmation of pre-existing hypotheses and glosses over material that challenges these hypotheses, he is obviously not behaving in a scientific manner. The clinician's personality may also make him more sensitive to certain kinds of data and less so to others. Other differences of consequence, about which more will be said shortly, concern the type of constructs used and the external validation of the clinician's inferences and pronouncements. Some of the inferences made by clinicians are practically untestable as stated by them, and this aspect of the clinical process is what appears to irritate so many experimentally oriented psychologists. However, not all of the clinicians' statements fall into this category, and they can be validated by other types of available information. While there have been numerous reports on the validation of specific clinical techniques (Ainsworth, 1954; Garfield, 1957; Watson, 1951) clinicians generally do not make serious efforts to validate their work. We will deal more specifically with this and related problems later in the chapter.

Before concluding this section, it may be useful to comment briefly on one aspect of the clinical process which is quite analogous to an important part of the scientific process. This has reference to the process of hypothesis creation and to what has been called the "context of discovery" (Reichenbach, 1951). The scientific enterprise can be viewed as consisting of two main aspects—the creation of ideas and hypotheses, and the systematic testing or verification of these ideas.

These two related aspects are manifested in the field of physics where individuals are frequently designated as theoreticians or experimentalists. Psychology, for reasons which need not concern us here, has appeared to lay heavy stress on the one aspect, namely the aspect of "justification" or verification. Admittedly, the clinical method has displayed glaring weaknesses in this regard. However, in the other context of scientific investigation, in the observation of potential problems for research and in the creation of significant ideas, hypotheses and theories, the clinical approach to personality has contributed greatly to our understanding of the field (Dollard & Miller, 1950; Hilgard, 1952; Hall & Lindzey, 1957; McClelland, 1955; Meehl, 1954). In fact, more intensive study of the process by which important hunches, ideas and hypotheses are created by gifted clinicians and researchers alike might contribute significantly to a deeper understanding of the creative process in science.

THE CLINICAL METHOD IN PSYCHOLOGY

The preceding pages have been devoted to a portrayal of essential aspects and features of the clinical approach to personality. The objective has been mainly that of exposition rather than of evaluation. Before proceeding to an appraisal of clinical methods, however, it may be worthwhile to discuss briefly, from a historical perspective, the impact which such methods and their attendant value systems have had on the field of psychology.

While psychology can fairly lay claim to a long history of participation in clinical work, dating at least to the founding of the first psychological clinic by Witmer in 1896, the association with clinical methods and tradition was not especially strong. As most individuals familiar with the history of psychology know, psychology has striven to be primarily a laboratory science and has attempted to pattern its development after some of the well-established scientific fields. Most of the well known psychologists worked in academic settings and were concerned with academic or laboratory pursuits. The development of a usable test of intelligence by Binet and Simon gave some impetus to the applications of psychology to clinical settings. Psychologists, although in relatively few numbers, began to utilize such techniques in hospitals, clinics, and institutions for the retarded. The scope of such clinical work, however, was limited and emphasized the administration of individual tests of intellectual ability. As the testing movement developed within psychology, there was also an accompanying emphasis on objective approaches to the study of human behavior. Psychologists were interested in the measurement and quantification of psychological functions. In the emphasis on rigor and objectivity there was a tendency to decry and avoid any approaches which had a subjective flavor. Clinical psychologists were first accepted in clinical settings because they brought objective procedures that were seen as a contribution to the study of the client. The values, therefore, which seemed to be held by most psychologists were opposite to those which have been described previously as constituting basic features of the clinical method.

Nevertheless, other movements were afoot that were developing from other sources and that laid stress on other approaches to the understanding of human behavior and personality. Psychoanalysis and its derivatives were clearly of major importance. In addition, the rise of the mental hygiene movement, the development of projective techniques, and the developing interest in the field of personality also had significant impact. With the advent of World War II, a number of other developments took place that eventually led to the creation of a somewhat new model for clinical psychology. Without specifying these developments here, it can be said that the post-war developments in the field of psychology led to striking changes in the roles, activities and orientations of those engaged in clinical psychology (Garfield, 1957). Relatively ready acceptance of dynamic theories of personality, the utilization of projective techniques and the involvement with psychotherapy eventually led to a more dynamic and "clinical" view. Although the clinical psychologist utilized some of the same techniques which had been used in the previous era, the techniques, as we have seen earlier, were used in a quite different way and with different objectives. Greater emphasis was placed on the judgmental role of the clinician, and in essence, there was a shift from an emphasis on psychometrics and objectivity to an emphasis on subjective clinical judgment.

These developments also have had impact on American psychology in general. While at times the increased expansion of clinical psychology has appeared to create some rift between experimental and clinical psychologists, the viewpoints and theories coming from the clinical field have also influenced theoreticians and researchers in the traditional fields of psychology (Hall & Lindzey, 1957; Hilgard, 1952; McClelland, 1955). Many of the concepts derived from clinical work with patients eventually have become part of the vocabulary of psychology and have stimulated much in the way of experimental investigation. Let us now turn to the relationship of clinical methods to the development of theories of personality.

THE CLINICAL METHOD AND PERSONALITY THEORY

In addition to the use of clinical methods in the diagnosis and treatment of individuals with personality problems, clinical methods and clinicians have played a most important role in the development of personality theories. Certainly, theories developed by individuals who were primarily clinicians are among the most important and influential of existing theories in the field of personality. The theoretical contributions of Freud, Adler, Jung, Horney, Sullivan, Murray and Rogers are well known. Each of these clinicians, most of them outside the official boundaries of psychology, has made significant contributions to the field of personality. Whether the contributions forthcoming from the clinical method are more significant or less than those produced by statistical or experimental approaches is a question not easily answered at present. Such a question clearly involves value judgments and consequently is not a particularly good question to be posed to scientists or clinicians. A more meaningful question, perhaps, is whether the clinical approach to personality has contributed something of substance to our knowledge and research in this field. The writer has already indicated that he believes the answer is unquestionably in the affirmative. While this view is not shared by all psychologists, there is enough consensus to indicate that it is not just a partisan opinion (Dollard & Miller, 1950; Hall & Lindzey, 1957; Hilgard, 1952).

It is important, however, to look more closely at what the nature of the contributions of the clinical approach to personality are. Several of these can be mentioned briefly, although some reference to them has been made previously. First, it can be said that clinical workers helped to focus scientific attention on the field of personality. When the early psychologists were primarily concerned with other types of problems in the laboratory, clinicians were studying disturbed personalities and developing hypotheses and theories about human personality. Second, clinicians have emphasized the complexity of personality and the need to take what has been variously termed a holistic, organismic or molar view of the person. This emphasis has had a decisive influence on the whole field of personality. As Hall & Lindzey (1957, pp. 543-544) stated it: "One of the features that distinguished personality theory historically from other varieties of psychological theory was an emphasis upon holism. Consistent with this observation is the fact that most contemporary personality theorists may be accurately classed as organismic. . . . It is evident, then, that the usual contemporary personality theory places heavy emphasis upon the importance of studying behavior 'organically' without attempting to isolate small segments of behavior for microscopic study."

A third important contribution which clinical approaches have made to personality theory pertains to the emphasis on previous life experiences as a determinant of the individual's behavior. While clinical theories vary as to the particular type of early experience they regard as being of greatest importance, most of them do attach considerable significance to earlier periods of development as factors in personality formation. To fully understand personality, one generally must look beyond the current situation.

Reference has already been made to other factors emphasized in clinical approaches to personality that can also be seen as contributions to personality theory. The emphases on dynamics and motivation are now more generally accepted as of basic importance for the field of personality and for other areas of psychology as well (Hilgard, 1952; McClelland, 1955). According to Hilgard (1952, p. 24), "The topics of psychodynamics are not side issues for psychology. They lie at the very heart of psychological subject matter, for we cannot understand motivation, learning and forgetting, perceiving, personality development, or social behavior until we understand the issues of psychodynamics." The matter of "unconscious" motivating forces also appears to be less of a controversial issue today than it was some years ago. In general, the emphasis on psychodynamics has tended to enlarge the scope of personality theory and of psychology in general.

Another feature of clinical approaches to personality is the coming to grips with significant human problems of personality adjustment. The theories and speculations of clinicians, fanciful as some may seem, have been derived from problems which are significant to both the individual and society. Although one cannot evaluate in any adequate fashion what impact this has had on other approaches within psychology, a quick perusal of various introductory and other standard texts in psychology indicates the significant impact this trend has come to have. Psychology has decidedly moved outside the university laboratory and has become concerned with a wide range of problems of human adjustment.

Finally, as indicated by Hall and Lindzey (1957) one means of appraising personality theories is in terms of how well a theory stimulates research. Admittedly this is a complicated question. However, it is evident that several clinical theories, or theories derived from clinical approaches, have led to extensive research investigation. The psychoanalytic theories of personality in particular have not only generated a vast amount of research (Hall & Lindzey, 1957; Hilgard, 1952), but in addition have influenced other kinds of theoretical formulations. The theoretical approach of Dollard and Miller (1950) is one outstanding example. Even such a staunch experimentalist as Eysenck (1961) has based a moderate amount of his work on theories developed by Jung. Further, a number of important concepts which are in wide use today in psychology—e.g., anxiety, displacement, repression, projection, etc.—are largely derived from clinical investigations and formulations about personality. What would many graduate students today do about finding dissertation problems if such clinically derived concepts were suddenly to disappear?

It is defendable, therefore, to say that clinical approaches to personality have contributed greatly to the development of important theories of personality. The clinical approach has been particularly fruitful in providing a rich source of hypotheses and concepts for research investigation and has enlarged greatly our view of personality.

LIMITATIONS IN THE CLINICAL APPROACH TO PERSONALITY

In the preceding pages, the writer has presented what are to him some of the main features, strengths and contributions of the clinical approach to personality. The presentation would not be complete however, without some appraisal of the limitations also apparent in this approach. Like other approaches, the clinical method has both strengths and deficiencies and the latter have not gone unnoticed (Garfield, 1957; Meehl, 1954, 1960; Sarbin et al, 1960; Thorne, 1961). Further, as we shall see, aspects of the clinical process which are viewed as virtues from one vantage point, can also be seen as deficits when viewed from another.

One of the strengths of the clinical method is its reliance on the sensitivity, perceptiveness and cognitive ability of the clinician. This is at the same time one of its great weaknesses. In the final analysis, the method is no better than the individual clinician who is utilizing it at a particular time. To state that clinicians differ seems obvious and even trite. Nevertheless, this obvious fact has received little recognition in serious discussions about the clinical method. Although this method generally has been viewed in an abstract manner, yet in practice we deal with individual clinicians. A few are highly perceptive and creative and contribute greatly to our understanding of personality. They highlight the contribution which the clinical method can make to the advancement of man's understanding of himself. However, there are also others. This means inevitably that the hypotheses and pronouncements of individual clinicians have to stand the test of verification, and that clinicians should strive to validate their procedures and conclusions. The results of several recent studies are most pertinent here. One was a study by Holtzman and Sells (1954) of the ability of clinical psychologists, utilizing certain kinds of test data, to make predictions about a sample of aviation cadets. As a group, the clinician's predictions were no better than chance, and this finding has been viewed as a critical one for the clinical approach. However, in terms of our present discussion, there was another finding of importance. This was that considerable variability existed among the clinicians, the number of successful judgments ranging from four to fourteen out of a possible twenty. One clinician performed significantly worse than chance, while the predictions of two others were significantly better than chance when ratings of the clinician's confidence were considered. Another study of clinical judgment, based on Rorschach protocols, showed somewhat comparable findings (Chambers & Hamlin, 1957). On a task involving five judgments, five of the twenty clinicians in this study had complete success while two made no correct judgments at all!

Two other studies concerned with psychotherapy also have secured results pertaining to the variable effectiveness of clinicians. In one group of studies it was demonstrated that certain clinicians were more effective in therapeutic work with schizophrenic patients than was another group of clinicians (Whitehorn & Betz, 1954, 1960). In another study, it was found that patients improved with certain kinds of therapists and showed signs of increased disturbance with others (Truax, 1962). These findings, it seems to me, highlight the importance of the clinician as a basic variable in the clinical process, and the need for greater specificity when discussing the effectiveness of clinical procedures. If one compares the effectiveness of the *average* performance of a group of clinicians with that of an actuarial procedure on certain types of tasks, it is not surprising that the former do not shine by comparison. We might anticipate that some clinicians will do poorly on some types of problems and others will do well. Future research requires greater specification of the types of problem which specific clinicians can handle best. Furthermore, studies of mediocrity in the clinical field do not promise much in the way of advancing our knowledge of the clinical process. A study of a few gifted and highly creative clinicians may contribute much more than a study of thousands of relatively unskilled and inept clinicians. As one of my friends has put it, we can learn much more about violin playing from studying a Heifetz than we can from studying 1,000 ordinary violinists—even though the latter N is considerably larger.

Unless we study our clinicians adequately, there will always be some uncertainty about the efficacy of the clinical process. As some have suggested, we must evaluate or "calibrate" the clinician. As stated by Hammond (1955, p. 257), "it is suggested that we consider the clinician not as a *reader* of instruments, as tradition has it, but as an instrument to be analyzed and understood in terms of a probability model."

Another important criticism which can be made of clinical methods pertains to the general area of the communication of clinical findings (Garfield, Heine, & Leventhal, 1954; Thorne, 1961). One aspect concerns the concepts and the language used by clinicians. Although one may be sympathetic with formulations which emphasize dynamic concepts or hypothetical constructs, one must also point out the difficulties inherent in trying to verify the clinicians' formulations when stated in such terms. If a patient is viewed as having "castration anxiety" or "at the deepest level has repressed infantile rage," what do these designations really mean and how do we go about verifying these inferential judgments? Unless these statements are translated into some types of behaviorial statements or unless some specific predictions are offered, no opportunity for verification is possible.

The clinician in his descriptions of clients is also guilty of some other sins. One of these concerns the use of descriptive statements which are almost universally applicable to any person—e.g., "this client is not functioning at maximum efficiency at the present time." Many clinical descriptions also contain statements which are exceedingly vague (purposely?) and at times these personality descriptions may include statements which appear to be inconsistent with each other. The clinician must modify these habits and communicate his findings in such a manner that they are clearly related to possible behaviors of the individual and, consequently, are testable.

Somewhat related to the preceding criticism is a tendency for clinicians to intermingle descriptive terms which refer to different levels of personality without specifying their point of reference. Not only should the behavioral level be distinguished from aspects of personality outside the client's awareness, but whenever possible the implications for behavior of such inferences as "repressed hostility" or "latent homosexuality" should be stated. In a somewhat similar way, the clinician should indicate aspects of personality which appear clearly observable, features which he infers with a fair degree of confidence, and other aspects which he speculates about on the basis of very limited cues. This would allow for a better appraisal of the clinician and eventually for the improvement of the clinical process of inference.

Another criticism which has been made of clinical approaches to personality is that they have tended to emphasize pathology. Since clinicians have worked mainly with disturbed individuals, this criticism seems to be merited. When clinicians are asked to appraise "normal" individuals they are more prone to see maladaptive and pathological features of personality than positive ones (Cox & Sargent, 1950; Garfield, 1957; Little & Shneidman, 1959). Although clinicians have stated that much can be learned about normal personality attributes and mechanisms from the study of disturbed individuals who exhibit extreme instances of these attributes, the fact remains that relatively few "normal" individuals have been studied as intensively as pathological ones. This, however, would appear to be a limitation which can be overcome. (Murray, 1938).

In evaluating the clinical process, one should also attempt to appraise the usefulness and validity of what is forthcoming from the clinical interaction in the day to day activities of clinicians as a group— a matter that we have mentioned only indirectly thus far. Apart from hypothesis creation and theory construction, how does the clinical approach fare on a practical level or in comparisons with other approaches? How valid or useful are the judgments or predictions which the clinician makes? This is an extremely complex issue, and to treat it adequately would involve an evaluation of a tremendous variety of therapeutic and diagnostic endeavors, for much of which adequate data are lacking (Garfield, 1957). Nevertheless, it is too important an issue to bypass without comment. Although truly adequate data for making such an evaluation are lacking, this fact alone should make clinicians sensitive to the responsibility that they have for verifying their operations and for attempting to secure such data. A number of studies of diagnostic judgment in clinical psychology have produced results that are distinctly embarrassing to the clinician (Cox & Sargent, 1950; Grant, Ives & Ranzoni, 1952; Little & Shneidman, 1959; Meehl, 1960; Thorne, 1961). Attempts to compare clinical predictions with actuarial predictions have also brought forth findings that have been viewed as detrimental to the clinician's professional self-esteem (Meehl, 1954; Sarbin et al, 1960). While many of the studies referred to in these appraisals may not be really adequate tests of the clinical approach as described previously, and thus are not necessarily devastating to the clinical point of view, they do pose a definite challenge to clinicians. Critical self-appraisal and research programs adequate to the problem are called for, even though the problems posed are difficult ones.

From our brief survey of the problem it appears that the clinician, or the clinical process, has fared well when viewed from within the context of discovery. However, when viewed from the context of justification, the clinical approach has tended to fare poorly. While some of the research investigations in this latter category are frequently seen by clinicians as not appropriate for the adequate evaluation of clinical propositions and procedures, in the long run it is up to the clinicians to devise more adequate tests for demonstrating the utility and validity of their approaches. Needless to say, such research will require all the ingenuity the clinicians can muster.

Finally, something should be said about the relation of clinical methods to other methods. As we have noted, clinical methods, like other methods, have their virtues as well as their limitations. Clinical approaches are particularly well suited to the development of hypotheses and concepts resulting from the observation of individuals in a variety of situations in which the perceptiveness, sensitivity and empathy of the clinician play a major role. The clinician as a flexible "instrument" is free to follow unknown leads and unpredictable paths. In the words of Reichenbach (1951, p. 231), "The act of discovery escapes logical analysis: there are no logical rules in terms of which a discovery machine could be constructed that would take over the creative function of the genius." On the other hand, once hypotheses are clearly stated, other procedures may be more efficient in testing out their validity or in extending their usefulness. For a particular phase of the scientific enterprise one method may be better than others. In a similar way, of the various approaches to personality, some may be superior to others for specific purposes. Some viewpoints and methods offer greater precision and rigor than others, while at the same time, their scope may be considerably less than that of others. Rather than limiting ourselves to only one approach that we may consider *the* approach to personality, we would do better to select what appears to be the most fruitful approach in terms of the problem at hand. Insights gained from the clinical approach, for example, may not be obtained from other approaches. However, such insights may be refined by the use of experimental or statistical techniques. In some instances, aspects of different methods may be combined. "When the special advantages of both the clinical and the actuarial approach are combined, one can formulate explicit criteria which function better than either method can by itself" (Meehl, 1959, p. 108). To state categorically that one approach is superior to another is essentially meaningless and engenders controversy without resolution. We need to explore which approaches are best for what kind of problems.

In the long run, as Zubin (1955, p. 109) has pointed out, the goal "is the verifiable understanding and prediction of human behavior and to achieve this goal, the observations of the clinicians and his hunches as well as the verification of these hunches by the actuary are essential." Some individuals, because of their own personal makeup, will show a preference for one approach over another. Those who prefer methodological rigor and precision cannot dwell happily in the intuitive, mysterious and free-wheeling domain of the clinician. There are others, however, for whom the richness of personality and the dynamics of behavior can be grasped best by the sensitive and inquiring human observer, unhampered by artificial restrictions. Luckily or unluckily, there is still enough unknown in the area of personality to challenge us all.

REFERENCES

AINSWORTH, MARY D. Problems of validation. In B. Klopfer, Mary D. Ainsworth, W. G. Klopfer, & R. R. Holt (Eds.) *Developments in the Rorschach Technique.* Vol. I. Yonkers: World Book Co., 1954, Pp. 405-500.

ALLPORT, G. W. *Personality: A psychological interpretation.* New York: Holt, 1937.

ALLPORT, G. W. *Pattern and growth in personality.* New York: Holt, Rinehart & Winston, 1961.

BURTON, A., & HARRIS, R. E. *Clinical studies of personality.* New York: Harper & Bros., 1955.

CHAMBERS, GUINEVERE S., & HAMLIN, R. The validity of judgments based on "blind" Rorschach records. *J. consult. Psychol.,* 1957, *21,* 105-109.

COX, BEVERLY, & SARGENT, HELEN. TAT responses of emotionally disturbed and emotionally stable children: Clinical judgment versus normative data. *J. proj. Tech.,* 1950, *14,* 61-73.

DEWEY, J. *Logic. The theory of inquiry.* New York: Holt, 1938.

DOLLARD, J., & MILLER, N. E. *Personality and psychotherapy.* New York: McGraw-Hill, 1950.

EYSENCK, H. J. (Ed.) *Handbook of abnormal psychology.* New York: Basic Books, 1961.

GARFIELD, S. L. *Introductory clinical psychology.* New York: Macmillan, 1957.

GARFIELD, S. L. HEINE, R. W., & LEVENTHAL, M. An evaluation of psychological reports in a clinical setting. *J. consult. Psychol.,* 1943, *18,* 281-286.

GRANT, MARGUERITE Q., IVES, VIRGINIA, and RANZONI, JANE H. Reliability and validity of judges' ratings of adjustment on the Rorschach. *Psychol. Monogr.,* 1952, *66,* No. 2 Whole No. 334).

HALL, C., & LINDZEY, G. *Theories of personality.* New York: Wiley, 1957.

HAMMOND, K. R. Probabilistic functioning and the clinical method. *Psychol. Rev.* 1955, *63,* 255-263.

HILGARD, E. R. Experimental approaches to psychoanalysis. In E. Pumpian-Mindlin (Ed.) *Psychoanalysis as a science,* Stanford, Calif.: Stanford Univer. Press, 1952.

HOLT, R. R. Clinical judgment as a disciplined inquiry. *J. nerv. ment. Dis.* 1961, *133,* 369-382.

HOLTZMAN, W. H., & SELLS, S. B. Prediction of flying success by clinical analysis of test protocols. *J. abnorm. soc. Psychol.,* 1954, *49,* 485-490.

LITTLE, K. B., & SHNEIDMAN, E. S. Congruencies among interpretations of psychological test and anamnestic data. *Psychol. Monogr.* 1959, *73,* No. 6 (Whole No. 476).

McCLELLAND, D. C. *Studies in Motivation.* New York, Appleton-Century-Crofts, 1955.

MEEHL, P. E. *Clinical versus statistical prediction.* Minneapolis: Univer. Minnesota Press, 1954.

MEEHL, P. E. A comparison of clinicians with five statistical methods of identifying psychotic MMPI profiles. *J. counsel. Psychol.,* 1959, *6,* 102-109.

MEEHL, P. E. The cognitive activity of the clinician. *Amer. Psychologist,* 1960, *15,* 19-27.

MUNROE, RUTH. *Schools of psychoanalytic thought.* New York: Dryden Press, 1955.

MURRAY, H. A. *Explorations in personality.* New York: Oxford Univer. Press, 1938.

REICHENBACH, H. *The rise of scientific philosophy.* Berkeley: Univer. of California Press, 1951.

REIK, T. *Listening with the third ear.* New York: Farrar, Straus, 1948.

SARBIN, T. R., TAFT, R., & BAILEY, D. E. *Clinical inference and cognitive theory.* New York: Holt, 1960.

SCHAFER, R. *The clinical application of psychological tests.* New York: International Univer. Press, 1948.

SILVERMAN, L. H. A Q-sort study of the validity of evaluations made from projective techniques. *Psychol. Monogr.,* 1959, 73, No. 7 (Whole No. 477).

THORNE, F. C. *Clinical judgment.* Brandon, Vermont: Journal of Clinical Psychology, 1961.

TRUAX, C. B. Effective ingredients in psychotherapy: An approach to unraveling the patient-therapist interaction. Presented at Amer. Psychol. Ass., St. Louis, 1962.

WATSON, R. I. *The clinical method in psychology.* New York: Harper & Bros., 1951.

WHITEHORN, J. C., & BETZ, BARBARA J. A study of psychotherapeutic relationships between physicians and schizophrenic patients. *Amer. J. Psychiat.,* 1954, *111,* 321-331.

WHITEHORN, J. C., & BETZ, BARBARA J. Further studies of the doctor as a crucial variable in the outcome of treatment with schizophrenic patients. *Amer. J. Psychiat.,* 1960, *117,* 215-223.

ZUBIN, J. Clinical vs. actuarial prediction: A pseudo-problem. *Invitational conference on testing problems.* Princeton-Los Angeles: Educational Testing Service, 1955, Pp. 107-128.

Index

A

Ackerson, L., 419, 444
Ader, R., 273, 288
Adey, W R., 106
Adience, 87, 96; behavior, 99-101; motivation, 99, 102, 105
Adler, A., 234-56
Adler, D. L., 146, 160
Adlerian point of view, 234-56; Theory, 230, 234-56
Activation level, acute, 89, 94, 99-100; chronic, 85-6, 89-92; two types of, 88
Actones, 187
Adorno, A. A., 379, 384
Aggression, 33, 68-9
Ainsworth, Mary D., 490, 500
Ajimone-Masson, C., 108
Allee, W. C., 68, 77
Allen, G., 74, 77
Allport, G. W. 162-204, 293, 302, 322, 325, 385, 403, 406-7, 422, 444, 485-6, 500
Allport F. H., 204, 302
Allport-Vernon Study of Values, 36
Alpert, M., 70, 78
Alternativism, constructive, 207
Altrocchi, J., 49-50, 57-8
Amerongen, F. K., 107
Analysand, 116, 120
Analyst, 120, 121

Anderson, C., 154, 155, 160
Anderson, H. H., 156, 160
Ansbocher, H., 31, 58, 236, 240, 242, 244, 247, 256
Ansbocher, Rowena, 236, 240, 242, 244, 247, 256
Anthony, A. A., 379, 384
Anthropology, 376, 381; and behaviorism, 362; field work in, 363; functionalism in, 362; and psychoanalystic theory, 353
Antonovsky, M. F., 384
Apricia, 429
Approach avoidance, conflict, 14-15, 18, 20; graduates of, 16; tendencies toward, 15, 17
Archetypes, 75
Arenberg, D., 35, 60
Aronson, E., 357, 359
Asch, S. E., 325
Ashby, C., 311, 325
Aspiration, level of, 156
Atkinson, J. W., 26, 29, 34-5, 58, 60, 155, 160, 336, 342, 360·
Austin, G. A., 319, 326
Autonomy, 99; functional, 201
Aversive conditioning: avoidance, 272; escape, 272; punishment, 273
Avoidance conditioning, 376
Ayllon, A., 281, 288
Ayres, B. C., 384
Azrin, N. H., 282, 289